Introducing Linguistics

Introducing Linguistics brings together the work of scholars working at the cutting-edge of the field of linguistics, creating an accessible and wide-ranging introductory level textbook for newcomers to this area of study. The textbook:

- Provides broad coverage of the field, comprising five key areas: language structures, mind and society, applications, methods, and issues;
- Presents the latest research in an accessible way;
- Incorporates examples from a wide variety of languages – from isiZulu to Washo – throughout;
- Treats sign language in numerous chapters as yet another language, rather than a 'special case' confined to its own chapter;
- Includes recommended readings and resource materials, and is supplemented by a companion website.

This textbook goes beyond description and theory, giving weight to application and methodology. It is authored by a team of leading scholars from the world-renowned Lancaster University department, who have drawn on both their research and extensive classroom experience. Aimed at undergraduate students of linguistics, *Introducing Linguistics* is the ideal textbook to introduce students to the field of linguistics.

Jonathan Culpeper is Professor of English Language and Linguistics in the Department of Linguistics and English Language at Lancaster University, UK.

Beth Malory is Lecturer in English Linguistics at University College London, UK, and Visiting Research Fellow in the Department of Linguistics and English Language at Lancaster University, UK.

Claire Nance is Senior Lecturer in Phonetics and Phonology in the Department of Linguistics and English Language at Lancaster University, UK.

Daniel Van Olmen is Senior Lecturer in Linguistic Typology and Language Change in the Department of Linguistics and English Language at Lancaster University, UK.

Dimitrinka Atanasova is Lecturer in Intercultural Communication in the Department of Linguistics and English Language at Lancaster University, UK.

Sam Kirkham is Senior Lecturer in Phonetics in the Department of Linguistics and English Language at Lancaster University, UK.

Aina Casaponsa is Lecturer in Language, Cognition and Neuroscience in the Department of Linguistics and English Language at Lancaster University, UK.

LEARNING ABOUT LANGUAGE

Series Editors:
Brian Walker, Huddersfield University, UK; **Willem B. Hollmann**, Lancaster University, UK; and the late **Geoffrey Leech**, Lancaster University, UK

Series Consultant:
Mick Short, Lancaster University, UK

Learning about Language is an exciting and ambitious series of introductions to fundamental topics in language, linguistics and related areas. The books are designed for students of linguistics and those who are studying language as part of a wider course.

Also in this series:

For more information about this series please visit: www.routledge.com/series/PEALAL

Introducing Linguistics

EDITED BY JONATHAN CULPEPER,
BETH MALORY, CLAIRE NANCE,
DANIEL VAN OLMEN, DIMITRINKA ATANASOVA,
SAM KIRKHAM, and AINA CASAPONSA

Routledge
Taylor & Francis Group
LONDON AND NEW YORK

Linguistics &
English Language

Lancaster
University

Designed cover image: Beth Malory

First published 2023
by Routledge
4 Park Square, Milton Park, Abingdon, Oxon OX14 4RN

and by Routledge
605 Third Avenue, New York, NY 10158

Routledge is an imprint of the Taylor & Francis Group, an informa business

British Library Cataloguing-in-Publication Data
A catalogue record for this book is available from the British Library

Library of Congress Cataloging-in-Publication Data
Names: Culpeper, Jonathan, 1966– editor.
Title: Introducing linguistics / edited by Jonathan Culpeper [and 6 others].
Description: Abingdon, Oxon ; New York, NY : Routledge, 2023. | Series: Learning about language | Includes
  bibliographical references and index. | Summary: "Introducing Linguistics brings together the work of scholars
  working at the cutting-edge of the field of Linguistics, creating an accessible and wide-ranging introductory level
  textbook for newcomers to Linguistics"—Provided by publisher.
Identifiers: LCCN 2022032840 (print) | LCCN 2022032841 (ebook)
Subjects: LCSH: Linguistics. | LCGFT: Essays.
Classification: LCC P121 .I56 2023 (print) | LCC P121 (ebook) | DDC 410—dc23/eng/20220804
LC record available at https://lccn.loc.gov/2022032840
LC ebook record available at https://lccn.loc.gov/2022032841

ISBN: 978-0-367-49302-8 (hbk)
ISBN: 978-0-367-49301-1 (pbk)
ISBN: 978-1-003-04557-1 (ebk)

DOI: 10.4324/9781003045571

Typeset in Sabon
by Apex CoVantage, LLC

Access the companion website: www.routledge.com/cw/culpeper

Contents

v

Preface

Linguistics, in essence, is the study of how a language or languages work. Crucially, it has nothing to do with being able to speak a lot of languages. In this book, you will learn something about how a range of different languages work. But why would you want to bother with this? In fact, why bother with linguistics as a field of study? Here are some brief reasons why we should study language:

1 Language is a distinctive human characteristic, and part of our biology. It is not only reflected in our speech organs, but has a profound and complex relationship with our thinking.
2 Language is inextricably involved with the development of other cognitive faculties, as well as with cognitive disorders.
3 Language is the primary means by which human history is preserved. It is the prism through which we can understand the past, and thus build a better future.
4 Language is central to all human endeavours. It enables people to develop, shape and sustain ideas and artefacts, communities, ideologies and cultures, games and aesthetic pleasures.
5 Language is central to the creation, maintenance and negotiation of identities and relationships. It can be used in a variety of ways to influence what others think and do.
6 Language is neither simple nor transparent. It is infinitely creative, and largely produced with little conscious awareness.

Of course, everybody 'knows' about language. The problem is that we don't have the complete set of tools to talk about the detail, nor do we know exactly where to apply the tools. When we talk about language, often it is in terms of limited language myths, sets of evaluative beliefs – ideologies held within particular communities – about how language is. For example, for many languages speakers believe that there was a past linguistic golden age when language was wonderful. They even set up academies, such as the Académie Française in France or the Accademia della Crusca in Italy, whose job it is to preserve the supposed wonderfulness of the past from the pollution of new developments. The problem here is articulated in point 6 earlier: it's not that simple and much language works with little conscious awareness. For instance, British people often condemn new developments in British English, attributing them to 'pollution' from American English. The problem here is that they are unable to accurately identify what really is American English. One of the editors of this book has repeatedly tested a set of words on British people, asking whether they are British or American English. Nobody has ever got them all right. The word *kissogram*, for instance, is typically attributed to American English even though, if its roots are traced, it is in fact a British English creation. The ideological thinking here is probably along the lines of: if it sounds new and culturally dodgy, it must be American English. Of course, linguists aren't free from these ideologies either and those ideologies are important, deserving study in their own right, but the linguistics enterprise is chiefly founded on data, on evidence derived from observation and experimentation.

What should a linguistics book cover? We took into account two factors: what we wanted to teach in our first-year linguistics course, and what others taught or wanted to teach in their first-year linguistics courses (as indicated by a survey conducted by Routledge in 2018). The result is a broad view of what constitutes linguistics. We have five groups, each containing six chapters (though not all of equal length):

- Language structures;
- Mind and society;
- Applications;
- Methods;
- Issues.

We do not think, though they are important, that linguistics is just about structural matters (this group comprises a little over a fifth of the book); or that structures can be discussed without consideration of humans (their mental faculties mediating language and their societies constructed by and in language); or that linguistics is an abstract endeavour (it can be and is applied to 'real' world issues); or that knowledge about linguistics is worth much without an understanding of how, methodologically, that knowledge might have been derived; or that philosophical issues and 'hot' debates – and some with which the public might be familiar – should be downgraded or excluded. This comprises our take on linguistics. Consistent with this, no one single theory or approach dominates this book. For instance, Noam Chomsky, one of the most famous linguists, holds sway in various textbooks, especially with respect to how grammar is approached. We deliver basic grammatical concepts without a strong commitment to a single grammatical approach, but then we also devote an Chapter 26 to discussing different grammatical approaches.

British readers, and possibly others, may wonder what makes this book distinct from English language textbooks. There are three factors. One is that the majority of the chapters will contain examples from and discussions of a variety of languages, including sign languages. A side point to note here is that sign languages are not given one specific chapter as if they are special languages, but are treated in various chapters as just another language variety. English examples will not be excluded, not least because they represent what many readers will be familiar with and so represent a good starting point, but they will not hold sway. Another factor is that the contents of the book will not be constrained by topics that have a special bearing on English. Topics such as language acquisition, forensic linguistics, data visualisation and linguistic relativity – to name but a few – are simply not the bread and butter of the majority of English language textbooks. The final factor is that there will be slightly more emphasis on theory than is typically the case in English language textbooks.

Except for the Issues section, each chapter will typically have the following characteristics:

- It will be pitched at a level appropriate to first-year undergraduates;
- It will contain an introductory overview of the area, including explanation and illustration of all necessary concepts and frameworks, and more focused discussion or case studies, often including research undertaken by the author;
- Each chapter will have copious illustration, including, for example, textual examples, diagrams, graphics and images;
- The use of real data will be a feature throughout the chapters; and
- Each chapter will have web-based recommended follow-up readings and resource materials.

The fact that the chapters will vary in length according to the section they are in is a reflection of how much space we think they will need. Further, we recognise that a very limited number of individual chapters may need more space, particularly, chapters dealing with subject areas that readers might find difficult. Regarding the web-based supporting materials, the website will mirror the structure of the book. Each chapter will typically have (the Issues chapters being exceptions):

For students

- A list of any relevant web resources, and brief description of them;
- Five multiple choice questions designed for the students to check their understanding.

For teachers

- Two short exam questions;
- One seminar exercise (or collection of tasks) designed to last one hour.

As you may have gathered, our target readership is first-year undergraduates. Having said that, we would expect extension upwards and downwards. For example, we can imagine uptake in many countries at postgraduate level, where students wish to acquire a grounding in linguistics (for example, students who sidestep from cognate subjects), or even scholars who simply want to reinforce their background in linguistics, possibly by plugging holes or finding out about the latest thinking. As for the readership's study area, we expect, rather obviously, interest from students undertaking linguistics, language science or language-related studies. The fact that we have defined linguistics broadly, and taken account of what current tutors of linguistics want to teach via a survey, should guarantee broad appeal. We would also assume some uptake in modern foreign languages, communication studies, psychology and education.

One of the unique features of the book is that at the time of writing the authors and the editors are all members of staff of the Department of Linguistics and English Language at Lancaster University (with the welcome exception of one co-author!). The Department is probably the largest linguistics department in England, and perhaps Britain, and one of the very best. This book constitutes our view of what linguistics, as a subject, is. Our particular motivation for producing this book is to address problems that may well be shared by other linguistics departments. Since its foundation in 1974, the Department has had a linguistics course for its first-year undergraduates. However, it has never had a satisfactory textbook for the course. Many textbooks had limited coverage or 'pushed' a particular theory or approach. Some had little consideration of best pedagogical practice. Over the years we have tried using suites of textbooks and even 'work-packs'; nothing was entirely successful. An additional problem that arose from 1990 onwards is that we launched our English Language undergraduate degree, which had its own first-year undergraduate course. We want to make sure that our linguistics course is sufficiently distinct. We hope that this book will solve these problems.

Jonathan Culpeper and the Editorial Team

Lancaster, 2022

Section one

Language structures

1 Phonetics

Sam Kirkham and Claire Nance

1.1 Introduction

Phonetics is the study of speech sounds produced by humans. This includes how we use our vocal tract to produce speech, as well as how these sounds are transmitted through the air. Phonetics aims to develop a comprehensive understanding of the sounds of speech. This makes it a rather diverse area, spanning the biology of the vocal tract, the physics of sound and the sensation of hearing. In this chapter, we give a basic overview of some fundamental aspects of phonetics, with a focus on understanding the vocal tract and how to describe speech sounds. While phonetics has historically mainly considered spoken languages, sign language researchers also analyse the details of how particular signs are produced. It is, therefore, possible to describe the phonetics of sign languages, which we will do later in this chapter.

Phonetics fundamentally involves describing how speech sounds (or signs) are produced. This differs from **phonology**, which involves classifying the sounds/signs of a language into a system (see Chapter 2). This distinction is not always entirely straightforward, because there can be considerable degrees of overlap between phonetics and phonology. We can consider a more extreme example to illustrate the difference. Imagine that you have a recording of a speaker. A phonological analysis would involve establishing which sounds are important units for distinguishing between the words of that language and how they work together as a system. In this case, a phonologist would want to know whether a particular sound distinguishes one word from one another (e.g. the 'p' and 'b' in 'pit' vs. 'bit') or whether a particular sound may vary but does not distinguish one word from another

What's the deal with brackets?

One thing that is very helpful to learn early on in your studies in linguistics is how notation conventions are used.

One of the most important conventions is the use of brackets to show what kind of example we are referring to. When referring to sounds on a phonetic level (i.e. talking about the physical production of sounds in actual speech), we use square brackets – like [ðɪs]. When referring to phonemes as part of a sound system, as in Chapter 2, we use slashes – like /ðɪs/. You might also see angle brackets like <this> used. These are used to refer to graphemes, or how something is written.

DOI: 10.4324/9781003045571-2

(e.g. the use of a glottal stop instead of /t/ in English words such as 'butter', which does not change the meaning of the word). Crucially, this means we need to know something about the language that is being spoken. A phonetic analysis would involve describing the details of how those sounds are produced. In principle, this would not require us to know the language being spoken, because we can still hear or analyse the sounds and relate them to the existing inventory of human speech sounds.

In this chapter, we introduce some fundamental aspects of phonetics. We begin by explaining the production of speech, including breathing and the anatomy of the vocal tract (Section 1.2). We then cover the production of consonants and vowels, including how to describe these sounds (Section 1.3), followed by a more detailed section on phonetic transcription (Section 1.4). Finally, we discuss phonetics in sign languages (Section 1.5).

1.2 The production of speech

Speech fundamentally involves movement. One kind of movement concerns the muscles and organs of the vocal tract, which must be carefully moved and positioned in order to produce speech sounds. Another kind of movement involves the movement of air, with most speech sounds moving air out of the lungs, through the vocal tract, and out through the nose and mouth. A third kind of movement is the nature of sound itself. Sound is the result of air particles moving and vibrating. These vibrations are caused by movements of the vocal tract, after which they continue to spread through the air until they lose energy and the sound dies out. The movement of air particles causes the human ear drum to vibrate in response. The brain then processes these vibrations, which allows us to perceive them as sounds.

In this section, we provide an outline of how speech is produced. We describe the anatomy of the vocal tract and how the vocal tract organs are used to make speech sounds. For a much more detailed treatment of speech anatomy for linguists see Gick et al. (2013).

1.2.1 Breathing

Perhaps the most simple and regular way in which humans move and manipulate air is breathing. Simply put: if we cannot breathe then we will find speech – and, indeed, life – very challenging! We begin this section with an overview of the anatomical structures used for breathing and a simple overview of how these structures work.

Inside the chest are two lungs. Each lung is made up of light tissue, containing small pockets that fill with air. The lungs are then connected to the **trachea**, which is connected to the **larynx** in our neck, which then leads to the mouth and nose. See Figure 1.1 for a diagram showing the lungs, trachea and larynx.

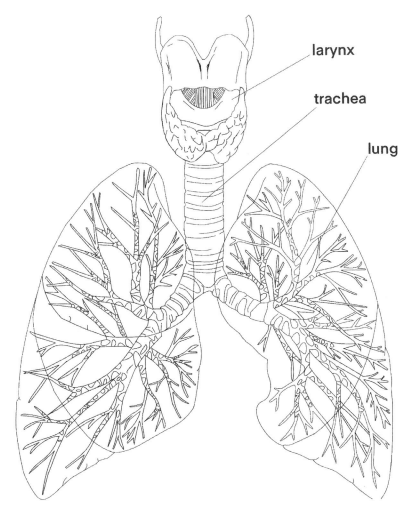

Figure 1.1 A diagram of the human larynx, trachea and lungs.

Source: Adapted from Patrick J. Lynch. https://en.wikipedia.org/wiki/File:Lungs_diagram_detailed. svg available under a Creative Commons Attribution 2.5 Generic License.

Breathing involves expansion and contraction of the lungs, which corresponds to filling up the lungs with air (expansion) and pushing air out of the lungs (contraction). We breathe differently when we speak compared with normal breathing at rest. Relaxed breathing (often called **tidal breathing**) is very regular, with consistent expansion and contraction of the lungs. At rest, we spend roughly similar amounts of time breathing in and breathing out. In contrast, speech breathing involves much smaller and quicker adjustments, as we are often trying to stop all of the air rushing out at once, so that we can release it gradually depending on how much air each speech sound requires.

Now that we have briefly covered how humans breathe, let's think about the types of breath used for speech. Most sounds in the world's languages involve air travelling from the lungs and out through the mouth. This is what is often called a **pulmonic egressive** breath source, with *pulmonic* meaning 'lungs' and *egressive* meaning 'outwards'. Not all sounds in all languages are produced in this way, and we will return to cases where sounds are *not* pulmonic egressive in Section 1.3.1.5.

1.2.2 The larynx and voicing

The larynx is an organ found in the neck; specifically, it is located at the end of the **trachea** or windpipe (see Figure 1.1). When air enters or exits the lungs, it must travel through the larynx. This is of incredible importance, because movements of the larynx can help to shape the air that travels through it, allowing us to create a greater variety of sounds.

The larynx is a structure made up of a series of cartilages and muscles, all of which serve to move and protect the larynx in various ways. The larynx contains the **vocal folds**, which can open and close in order to modify the size of the opening between them. The vocal folds are two folds of tissue that sit on top of other muscles in the larynx. The air flows through the vocal folds during speech and the gap between them can be adjusted, spanning a range of positions from wide open to completely closed. When the vocal folds are held open, air can freely travel through them, and when the vocal folds are closed shut, air stops at the blockage. A schematic diagram of the closed and open vocal folds is shown in Figure 1.2. It is worth noting that the gap between the vocal folds is often called the **glottis**. This is not a physical structure, but instead represents the space between the vocal folds. The opening and closing of the vocal folds allows us to control when air

Scan the QR code to see vocal folds in action.

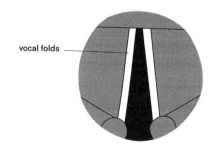

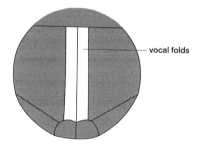

Open vocal folds　　**Closed vocal folds**

Figure 1.2 A schematic diagram of the open and closed vocal folds.

does and does not flow from the lungs into our mouth. Most of the interesting action, however, occurs in-between these two states of completely open and completely closed.

When the vocal folds are held close together and air is pushed through them, they start to vibrate against one another. You can feel this phenomenon if you sustain a 's' sound and then transition into a 'z' sound, like 'sssssssszzzzzzzz'. Now do this again and softly place your fingers of the front of your neck. During the 'zzzzzzzz' you should feel a vibrating or buzzing feeling in your neck: this is the vocal folds vibrating against each other. This vibration of the vocal folds is called **voicing**. As we will see in Section 1.3, voicing is a key dimension of speech and it involves the vocal folds rapidly vibrating against each other.

In focus: vocal folds or vocal cords?

The vocal folds are made up of **mucus membrane**, which means they are a membrane that is laid on top of another muscle. This membrane is covered in mucus, which is a slippery protective substance produced by the body and keeps the membrane moist. You may sometimes hear the term 'vocal cords' (or its misspelling, 'vocal chords') instead of vocal folds, but vocal folds is now the commonly accepted term. This change in terminology is because 'cord' implies a band or a string, whereas we now know that the vocal folds are more like folds of tissue that wrap around the 'vocalis' muscle, which is contained within the larynx.

The mucus that covers the vocal folds is very important, as it keeps them moist and stops them from drying out. Drier vocal folds tend to become stiffer and more inflamed. As a consequence, it requires greater effort to vibrate the vocal folds, thus increasing stress and fatigue on the muscles of the larynx. This is one reason why breathing in smoke, such as smoking cigarettes, is so bad for your voice, because it dries out the mucus (alongside a range of other negative consequences).

1.2.3 The oral cavity

The oral cavity is the area above the larynx, containing the tongue, teeth and other relevant structures, shown in Figure 1.3. The **tongue** is a highly complex organ, made up of some highly flexible muscles. We typically segment the tongue into different regions, which conveniently help us to describe which part of the tongue is used in producing a particular sound. The **tongue tip** is the very tip of the tongue. The **tongue blade** is the front part of the tongue just behind the tongue tip. The **tongue dorsum** is the mid part of the tongue, while the **tongue root** is the lower and backer part of the tongue.

We now move to the outer structures of the oral cavity. The **upper lip** and **lower lip** are terms we use to describe the complex set of muscles around the outside of the mouth. The **upper teeth** and **lower teeth** are located just behind the lips. These are parts of the vocal tract that are easily visible to other people.

Inside the mouth, we can describe a range of points on the vocal tract, which we often refer to when describing the production of speech. These are all labelled

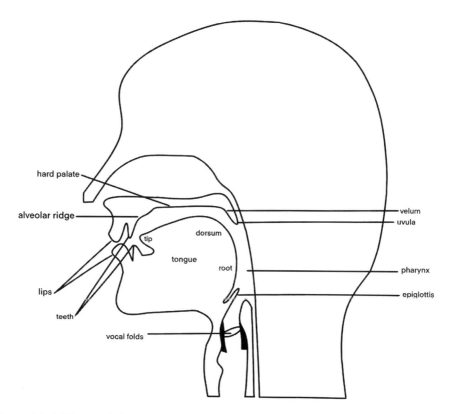

Figure 1.3 Midsagittal diagram of the vocal tract.

Source: Adapted from https://commons.wikimedia.org/wiki/File:VocalTract.svg available under a Creative Commons Attribution 3.0 Unported License.

in Figure 1.3 – we would also encourage you to move your tongue inside your mouth in order to identify these parts of your own vocal tract. The **alveolar ridge** is a bump located just behind the upper teeth. You can feel it if you place your tongue just behind your teeth and then slowly move it backwards. Just after this begins the **hard palate** (or just 'palate'), which is the bony roof of the mouth. It is distinguished from the **velum** or **soft palate**, which is further back from the hard palate. You can feel the difference between the two as the velum is made of a soft fleshy tissue, in contrast to the bone that makes up the hard palate. A key function of the **velum** is that it is moveable: it can be lowered or raised, which affects how air flows through the vocal tract. The **uvula** is a small grape-like tissue that hangs off the end of the velum. The surface opposite the tongue root, right at the back of the vocal tract, is the **pharyngeal wall**. We often describe the space between the pharyngeal wall and the tongue root as the **pharynx**, which is roughly the back of the throat. Finally, the **epiglottis** is a flap of tissue located at the base of the tongue root. It stays open during speech but can fold over the top of the larynx to prevent food from going into the lungs.

1.2.4 The nasal cavity

The nasal cavity is the space above the hard palate and behind the nose in Figure 1.3. When the velum is lowered or open, air can travel through the space between the back of the throat and the velum. When air bounces around the nasal cavity, it imparts a different quality to the sound than if the air only bounces around the oral cavity. If you sustain a vowel followed by 'n' then you can feel this tickling sensation in the back of your throat and behind your nose (e.g. 'aaaaaaaannnnnnnn'). As we noted, the velum controls the opening and closing of the entry to the nasal cavity.

1.3 Articulatory description of speech sounds

This section covers basic description of sounds, using what we often call 'articulatory descriptions'. Essentially, this involves describing sounds in terms of how the different parts of the vocal tract are used. We covered the parts of the vocal tract already, so this section will demonstrate how these terms can be used to form descriptions of speech sounds. Here, we will cover the production of vowels and consonants. These aren't the only aspects of speech and, indeed, the majority of the world's languages use tone, as well as things like stress and intonation, to make meaning in words. We cover these aspects of speech in Chapter 2. In this section, we will give examples of words from English, but we want to stress that phonetics is the study of speech sounds in general. The use of English here is simply a convenience; we anticipate that you already understand English, given that you are reading this chapter, but you may not understand all of the other languages to which we refer.

1.3.1 Consonants

1.3.1.1 What is a consonant?

Consonants are sounds that involve a significant obstruction of the air as it flows through the vocal tract. To understand what we mean by this, let your vocal tract come to rest and breathe in a relaxed fashion. Your lips should be parted and your tongue will be in a rest position, with air flowing up over the tongue and out through the lips. This is an **unobstructed** vocal tract, as there is nothing impeding or restricting the passage of air. By contrast, now raise your tongue tip up to your alveolar ridge. This should stop the air flowing out of your mouth, because the vocal tract is now **obstructed** by the tongue tip against the alveolar ridge. Consonants involve obstruction or narrowing of the vocal tract in various ways, which we will learn about soon. Consonants can be described using what is typically called the 'voice-place-manner' system. As we mentioned earlier, not all consonants are produced as pulmonic egressive sounds, so we may also describe the **airstream mechanism** in consonants, which describes the direction and source of air in the vocal tract. We will now discuss all these ways of describing consonant production.

1.3.1.2 Voicing

'Voice' describes whether a sound is **voiceless** or **voiced**. As we saw in Section 1.2.2, a voiced sound involves the vocal folds vibrating against one another, which creates a buzzing sound. By contrast, when the vocal folds are held open, we describe the sound as voiceless.

1.3.1.3 Place of articulation

'Place' describes the **place of articulation** of the sound. Consonant sounds typically involve two main articulators. The articulator that moves is called the active articulator and the articulator that it moves towards is called the passive articulator. For example, the sound [t] at the beginning of the word *tap* involves the tongue tip in contact with the alveolar ridge. The tongue tip is the active articulator, because it moves up to the alveolar ridge. The alveolar ridge cannot move and is, therefore, the passive articulator. Another example is the [b] at the beginning of the word *bat*. While this sound involves both the upper and lower lip, it is the lower lip that moves up to meet the upper lip. As a result, the lower lip is the active articulator and the upper lip is the passive articulator. We describe a consonant's **place of articulation** after the passive articulator, which we will now cover in greater detail. Table 1.1 lists the different places of articulation, and the active/passive articulators in each case.

Table 1.1 A list of different places of articulation and the active/passive articulators involved in each.

Place of articulation	Active articulator	Passive articulator
Bilabial	Lower lip	Upper lip
Labiodental	Lower lip	Upper teeth
Dental	Tongue tip	Upper teeth
Alveolar	Tongue tip/blade	Alveolar ridge
Postalveolar	Tongue tip/blade	Postalveolar
Retroflex	Tongue tip/blade	Hard palate
Palatal	Tongue dorsum	Hard palate
Velar	Tongue dorsum	Velum
Uvular	Tongue dorsum	Uvular
Pharyngeal	Tongue root	Pharyngeal wall
Glottal	Vocal folds	Vocal folds

Table 1.2 will help to explain each place of articulation in a little more detail. Where possible, we try to give an example of a common English sound, which we would encourage you to say aloud and try to feel the active and passive articulators involved in the production of that sound. Symbols inside square brackets represent International Phonetic Alphabet (IPA) symbols, which we will explain in more detail in Section 1.4.

Table 1.2 Description of consonant places of articulation.

Place of articulation	Description of sound production
Bilabial	sounds are made using both lips. The term 'bilabial' essentially means 'two lips' (bi + labial). In such cases, the lower lip is usually the active articulator, as it is raised to meet the upper lip. Examples from English include the [b] in 'ban' and the [m] in 'man'.
Labiodental	sounds are made using the lower lip (labio) and upper teeth (dental). In principle, it is possible to produce a sound using the upper lip and lower teeth, but this does not commonly occur as a sound in the world's languages, so labiodental typically means lower lip and upper teeth. Examples from English include the [f] in 'fine' and the [v] in 'vine'.
Dental	sounds involve the front of the tongue against the upper teeth. Examples from English include [ð], which is the first sound in 'this'.
Alveolar	sounds are made at the alveolar ridge, with the tongue tip making contact with – or coming close – to the alveolar ridge. Examples from English include the [t] in 'tip' and the [d] in 'dip'.
Postalveolar	sounds are made behind the alveolar ridge. You can feel this by producing a sound at the alveolar ridge, such as the [s] in 'sip', and then slowly moving back the [s] until it sounds more like the sound in 'ship'. The 'sh' is articulated at the postalveolar region.
Retroflex	sounds are made with the tongue curled back and articulated against the hard palate. Note that this is one case where a place of articulation is named according to the shape of the active articulator (the tongue) rather than the passive articulator (the palate). Retroflex sounds are particularly common in many Indian languages, such as Hindi.
Palatal	sounds are producing using the tongue body against the hard palate. Examples from English include [j], which is the first sound in 'yellow'.
Velar	sounds are produced using the tongue dorsum raised towards the velum or soft palate. Examples from English include the [g] in 'gate'.
Uvular	sounds are produced using the uvula, which vibrates or trills against the rear of the oral cavity. These do not occur in English but you might be familiar with the 'r' sound in French, which is uvular [ʁ].
Pharyngeal	sounds that involve constricting the muscles surrounding the pharynx. In some cases, a sound may also be described as 'pharyngeal' if it involves the tongue root retracted far back into the pharynx. These sounds do not occur in English, but are common in Arabic. For example, the [q] sound in the Syrian city 'Raqqa'.
Glottal	sounds are made at the **glottis**, which is the space between the vocal folds inside the larynx.

◼ 1.3.1.4 Manner of articulation

Consonants involve some obstruction in the vocal tract. A consonant's **manner of articulation** describes how much obstruction is involved in the production of a sound. This can be grouped into three broad types: (1) complete closure, where there is a full obstruction of airflow; (2) close approximation, where there is partial narrowing of the vocal tract; (3) open approximation, where there is only very minimal narrowing of the vocal tract. These are described in Table 1.3.

Table 1.3 Description of consonant manners of articulation.

Manner of articulation	Description of sound production
Plosive	sound produced with complete closure of the vocal tract. The term 'plosive' refers to the release of the constriction in the vocal tract, which results in an 'explosion'. Plosives are often grouped under the term stop consonants, because they also involve stopping of the airflow. Examples from English include the [p] in 'pen' or the [t] in 'tip'.
Fricative	sounds where the vocal tract is not completely blocked, but there is a narrow opening through which sound travels, making it a case of close approximation. Air is pushed through this small opening, which has the effect of producing a turbulent or 'hissing' noise. Examples from English include the [s] in 'sing' or the [v] in 'vine'.
Approximant	sounds produced with only minimal narrowing of the vocal tract, making it a case of open approximation. This contrasts with fricatives, which involve greater narrowing of the vocal tract. Fricatives involve turbulent noise whereas approximants do not, meaning that approximants bear some similarities with vowel sounds. Examples from English include [j], which is the first sound in 'yes' and [ɹ], which is the first sound in 'red'.

The fricative and approximant manners reviewed in Table 1.3 are assumed to involve air flowing along the top of the tongue. In contrast, a **lateral fricative** or **lateral approximant** involves a similar of manner articulation to fricatives and approximants, but air flows around the sides of the tongue instead of along the top or midline of the tongue. Alongside this, we also have a further three manners of articulation in Table 1.4.

A final manner of articulation that is not described in the IPA chart is an **affricate**. This is because it's actually a combination of two other manners: **plosive** and **fricative**. Essentially, an affricate is the combination of a stop plus a fricative, which are produced as a simultaneous sound, such as the 'ch' at the beginning and end of the word *church*.

Table 1.4 More manners of articulation.

Manner of articulation	Description of sound production
Nasal	sound involves an open or lowered velum, allowing air to travel into the nasal cavity and escape through the nose. Examples from English include the [n] in 'nice' and [m] in 'mice'.
Trill	involves the tongue tip hitting the alveolar ridge a number of times in a rapid fashion (typically three or four times). This is the 'rolled r' sound that occurs in languages such as Spanish and is represented using the symbol [r].
Tap or flap	involves a single very quick tap of the tongue tip against the alveolar ridge.

1.3.1.5 Airstream mechanisms

Most sounds in most of the world's languages are produced when air comes out of the lungs (pulmonic egressive). However, this is not always the case. Sometimes, sounds are instead produced by sucking air *into* the vocal tract. A very common non-linguistic sound that is pulmonic ingressive would be a 'snort' sound, where air is sucked up into the nose and travels down into the lungs. The different ways in which air can move are referred to as **airstream mechanisms**. Airstream mechanisms can be divided into whether air is going out of the vocal tract (egressive), or coming into the vocal tract (ingressive).

Egressive sounds include all the consonants we have described so far; for example, the [t] in 'tap' and the rolled 'r' trill sound. Ingressive sounds involve air being sucked inwards. This can occur in click consonants in languages spoken in southern and eastern Africa such as isiZulu.

When a speaker produces a click, air is sucked inwards towards the velum. The tongue tip can be placed in different positions to form different clicks; for example, on the back of the teeth, or behind the alveolar ridge.

Because clicks are produced with air being sucked inwards towards the velum, they are known as **velaric ingressive** sounds. There are other kinds of consonants which are not produced with a pulmonic egressive airstream. If you would like more information on these, see Ladefoged and Johnson (2015, Chapter 6).

Scan the QR code to watch a video of the vocal tract movements involved when producing a click sound inside an MRI scanner.

If you would like to hear different clicks in isiZulu and understand how they are produced in words, you can scan this code to watch a video.

1.3.1.6 Putting it all together

We can now put our consonant descriptions together. Table 1.5 shows how some selected consonants could be described using the voice, place, manner and

Table 1.5 Example consonant descriptions.

Consonant	Voice	Place	Manner	Airstream
't' as in 'tap'	voiceless	alveolar	plosive	pulmonic egressive
'f' as in 'fit'	voiceless	labiodental	fricative	pulmonic egressive
rolled 'r'	voiced	alveolar	trill	pulmonic egressive
dental click	voiceless	dental	click	velaric ingressive

airstream mechanisms we have just discussed. We can describe every consonant using a unique three-part voice-place-manner label, which is very useful when describing and comparing consonant sounds.

 ### 1.3.2 Vowels

Earlier, we defined consonants as sounds that involve an obstruction or narrowing of the vocal tract. In contrast, vowels are sounds that do not involve obstruction or significant narrowing. In practice, what counts as a vowel or consonant also interacts with its role in the **phonology** of a language and, therefore, defining vowels and consonants is not an entirely phonetic matter – it is also partly to do with how a language's sound system is structured.

The voice-place-manner system is less typically used for vowels. Vowels typically tend to be voiced, so we can adopt the default assumption that vowels are voiced unless stated otherwise. All vowels also tend to have a similar manner of articulation, with a relatively unobstructed vocal tract. When describing vowels, we instead usually use a system that assumes we are looking at a side view of the head, and then a vowel is described by (1) the highest point of the tongue; (2) how far forwards the highest point of the tongue is; and (3) whether or not the lips are rounded.

For example, in Figure 1.4 we show two vocal tracts producing vowel sounds: a long 'eeeeee' sound (as in 'bee'), and a long 'oooooo' sound (as in 'boo'). In the first sound, the middle part of the tongue is high in the oral cavity and forwards towards the teeth. In the second sound, the middle part of the tongue is high in the oral cavity and pulled backwards. If you look closely at the lips, you can see that in the second vowel sound the lips are protruded. We can therefore describe these sounds as follows: for 'eeeeee' we can say it is high, front, with unrounded lips. For 'oooooo' we can say it is high, back, with rounded lips.

1.4 Transcribing speech sounds

In the previous sections, we explained how to describe speech sounds using articulatory descriptions, such as 'voiceless alveolar plosive' or 'high front rounded vowel'. While this system is very useful, it is not particularly concise. Imagine we want to transcribe all the sounds in the production of a given word or sentence. It would be quite a mouthful to list the voice-place-manner and vowel descriptors for each individual sound! Instead, we can use a specially designed alphabet for

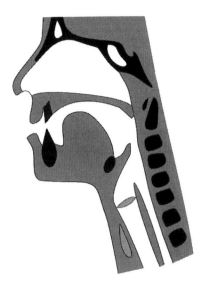 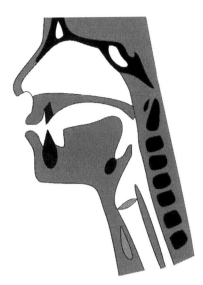

Figure 1.4 Midsagittal diagram of tongue position during the production of vowels /i/ (left) and /u/ (right).

transcribing and notating the sounds of the world's languages: the International Phonetic Alphabet.

The International Phonetic Alphabetic (or IPA for short) is a comprehensive system for transcribing the sounds of the world's languages. This system aims to provide a way of transcribing linguistically relevant detail for all languages. The guiding principle of the IPA is that a single symbol represents a single sound.

Because the IPA chart aims to comprehensively represent the huge diversity in sounds used across the world's languages, there will be quite a lot of sounds shown on the chart that are not familiar to you yet. It typically takes an extended university course in phonetics to become familiar with all the symbols, and then a lot of practice to learn how to produce and use all of them. We aren't able to do this in this chapter, but in this section, we will explain how the chart works and where you can find each piece of information. This way, you'll be able to navigate the chart and begin to learn more about the symbols. Don't worry if you don't know all the phonetic terminology yet; learning the chart is a process. If you'd like to hear sound clips of any speech sounds shown here, we have included a list of websites at the end of the chapter.

1.4.1 Pulmonic consonant table

The pulmonic consonant table from the IPA chart is shown in Figure 1.5. The table is set out according to all the places and manners of articulation we already introduced in Section 1.3.1. As you can see from the text at the bottom of the table, symbols are usually shown in pairs and the symbol on the left is voiceless, while the one on the right is voiced. For example, if we look at the symbol [x], the chart shows this as a voiceless velar fricative. This is the sound at the end of the Scottish Gaelic word *loch*, which is also used in Scottish English, to mean 'lake'.

CONSONANTS (PULMONIC) © 2015 IPA

	Bilabial	Labiodental	Dental	Alveolar	Postalveolar	Retroflex	Palatal	Velar	Uvular	Pharyngeal	Glottal
Plosive	p b			t d		ʈ ɖ	c ɟ	k ɡ	q ɢ		ʔ
Nasal	m	ɱ		n		ɳ	ɲ	ŋ	ɴ		
Trill	ʙ			r					ʀ		
Tap or Flap		ⱱ		ɾ		ɽ					
Fricative	ɸ β	f v	θ ð	s z	ʃ ʒ	ʂ ʐ	ç ʝ	x ɣ	χ ʁ	ħ ʕ	h ɦ
Lateral fricative				ɬ ɮ							
Approximant		ʋ		ɹ		ɻ	j	ɰ			
Lateral approximant				l		ɭ	ʎ	ʟ			

Symbols to the right in a cell are voiced, to the left are voiceless. Shaded areas denote articulations judged impossible.

Figure 1.5 Pulmonic consonants. IPA Chart.

Source: http://www.internationalphoneticassociation.org/content/ipa-chart, available under a Creative Commons Attribution-Sharealike 3.0 Unported License. Copyright © 2015 International Phonetic Association.

1.4.2 Non-pulmonic consonant table

In Section 1.3.1.5, we discussed click sounds in isiZulu, which are produced with a velaric ingressive airstream. You can see the IPA symbols for clicks and other non-pulmonic consonants under the pulmonic consonant table on the IPA. This is shown in Figure 1.6.

CONSONANTS (NON-PULMONIC)

Clicks	Voiced implosives	Ejectives
ʘ Bilabial	ɓ Bilabial	ʼ Examples:
ǀ Dental	ɗ Dental/alveolar	pʼ Bilabial
ǃ (Post)alveolar	ʄ Palatal	tʼ Dental/alveolar
ǂ Palatoalveolar	ɠ Velar	kʼ Velar
ǁ Alveolar lateral	ʛ Uvular	sʼ Alveolar fricative

Figure 1.6 Non-pulmonic consonants. IPA Chart.

Source: http://www.internationalphoneticassociation.org/content/ipa-chart, available under a Creative Commons Attribution-Sharealike 3.0 Unported License. Copyright © 2015 International Phonetic Association.

1.4.3 Vowel quadrilateral

The IPA vowel symbols are organised in terms of the descriptive labels we earlier learned for vowels. The vowels are organised around a four-sided shape, referred

16

to as the 'vowel quadrilateral'. This shape aims to correspond to the position of the tongue in sideways view of the vocal tract (see Figure 1.7). For example, high vowel sounds, like the sound 'eeeeee' we looked at earlier, are represented at the top of the quadrilateral. This sound is represented by the symbol [i]. Front vowels are to the left, back vowels to the right. The text at the bottom of the quadrilateral explains that when vowel symbols are in pairs, the one to the right represents a vowel produced with rounded lips, whereas the one to the left is assumed to be unrounded (see Section 1.3.2). There are quite a lot of vowel symbols here, to cover the diversity of human languages. You will learn more about all these sounds as you continue your journey in phonetics. If you'd like to hear how all these different symbols sound, we've included a list of clickable IPA charts with sound files at the end of this chapter.

VOWELS

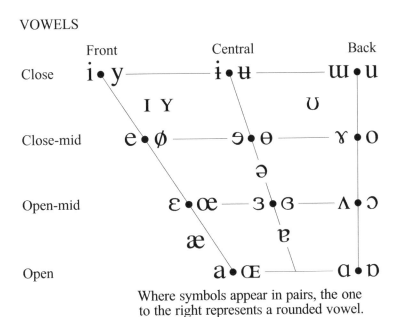

Where symbols appear in pairs, the one to the right represents a rounded vowel.

Figure 1.7 Vowel quadrilateral. IPA Chart.

Source: http://www.internationalphoneticassociation.org/content/ipa-chart, available under a Creative Commons Attribution-Sharealike 3.0 Unported License. Copyright © 2015 International Phonetic Association.

In focus: describing vowel articulation

It has long been known that the now established model of describing vowels in terms of the highest point of the tongue is not always faithful to actual tongue position in real speech. For example, X-ray studies of the tongue in the early 1900s showed that a vowel such as [e] sometimes involves a higher tongue position than [ɪ], despite the IPA quadrilateral in Figure 1.7 showing [ɪ] as having a higher tongue position. This has led other phoneticians to describe vowel production in a different manner. For example, Wood (1982) uses terms like 'palatal', 'velar', 'upper pharyngeal' and 'lower pharyngeal' to describe broad regions of vowel articulation. We find evidence of a similar system of description dating back to Indian scholarship in the fifth century BCE, which made a three-way distinction between palatal, pharyngeal and labio-velar vowels. Despite this, the vertical/horizontal description of tongue position remains widely used today, because it is still relatively accurate and permits a slightly more specific way of describing vowel quality.

1.4.4 Diacritics

If we need more detail, beyond the basic vowel and consonant symbols described previously, we can use diacritics to add to the transcription. This is helpful when we maybe want to describe a production that seems to be 'in-between' two sounds on the IPA chart, but does not have a symbol of its own to show this. The diacritics are shown at the bottom of the IPA chart, and we present them here in Figure 1.8. For example, in Icelandic *n ýta* means 'to use' and *hn ýta* means 'to knot'. In

DIACRITICS Some diacritics may be placed above a symbol with a descender, e.g. ŋ̊

̥ Voiceless	n̥ d̥	̤ Breathy voiced	b̤ a̤	̪ Dental	t̪ d̪	
̬ Voiced	s̬ t̬	̰ Creaky voiced	b̰ a̰	̺ Apical	t̺ d̺	
ʰ Aspirated	tʰ dʰ	̼ Linguolabial	t̼ d̼	̻ Laminal	t̻ d̻	
̹ More rounded	ɔ̹	ʷ Labialised	tʷ dʷ	̃ Nasalised	ẽ	
̜ Less rounded	ɔ̜	ʲ Palatised	tʲ dʲ	ⁿ Nasal release	dⁿ	
̟ Advanced	u̟	ˠ Velarised	tˠ dˠ	ˡ Lateral release	dˡ	
̠ Retracted	e̠	ˤ Pharyngealised	tˤ dˤ	̚ No audible release	d̚	
̈ Centralised	ë	̃ Velarised or pharyngealised	ɫ			
̽ Mid-centralised	e̽	̝ Raised	e̝ (ɹ̝ = voiced alveolar fricative)			
̩ Syllabic	n̩	̞ Lowered	e̞ (β̞ = voiced bilabial approximant)			
̯ Non-syllabic	e̯	̘ Advanced tongue root	e̘			
˞ Rhoticity	ɚ a˞	̙ Retracted tongue root	e̙			

Figure 1.8 Diacritics symbols. IPA Chart.

terms of pronunciation, these two phrases are produced with the same vowels and consonants, except the nasal consonant in *hn ýta* is voiceless. It sounds like it is whispered as there is no vocal fold vibration during the sound. We can show these words using the IPA as follows: *n ýta* 'to use' [niːta]; *hn ýta* 'to knot' [n̥iːta]. The tiny circle under [n̥] in the second phrase means it is voiceless. The symbol after the first vowel [iː], which looks similar to a colon, means the vowel is long. As speech varies considerably across languages, there are of course a lot of diacritics! You will learn more about these in context as you progress in learning about phonetics.

1.4.5 Prosody

As we mentioned in Section 1.3, describing speech sounds involves much more than just vowels and consonants! The IPA can be used to transcribe the 'prosodic' aspects of speech, which are things beyond the level of the segment, such as tone and intonation. These prosodic aspects are also sometimes referred to as 'suprasegmental'. We cover these in more detail in Chapter 2, but for now you can look at the symbols on the IPA chart used for describing prosodic characteristics of speech (Figure 1.9). You might already know about some of these concepts. For example, you might be aware that many languages use variation in pitch, otherwise known as **tone**, to contrast between words. In Burmese, the words for 'hard' and 'towering' use the same vowels and consonants but are produced with low and high tones respectively. We could show this using the suprasegmental or prosodic diacritics below as: 'hard' [maː˩] and 'towering' [maː˦]. We are just giving one example here to explain how prosodic features can be expressed using the IPA. There are lots of different prosodic aspects to speech and the extensive symbols in Figure 1.9 allow phoneticians to describe these. Typically, you won't be required to learn all of these at the start of your studies in linguistics! But our aim here is to show you where to find them.

1.5 Sign language phonetics

So far, we have discussed phonetics of spoken languages. It is also possible to discuss phonetics of sign languages in a parallel manner, such as lower-level details of how different signs are produced. In Chapter 2, we discuss the structural differences between how different signs are produced more fully (sign language phonology). If you are interested in this topic, you will want to read Chapter 2 as well. In this section, we will discuss an example study which has considered the detail in how signs are produced (phonetics).

Rimor et al. (1984) wished to investigate how signs are produced when signers are asked to speed up their delivery. The idea behind this was that they could investigate hypotheses about change over time in American Sign Language. The authors hypothesised that many processes of historical change in language originate in how language users change their delivery when speaking/signing

SUPRASEGMENTALS

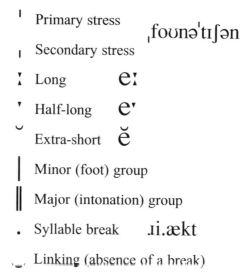

ˈ Primary stress   ˌfoʊnəˈtɪʃən

ˌ Secondary stress

ː Long   eː

ˑ Half-long   eˑ

˘ Extra-short   ĕ

| Minor (foot) group

‖ Major (intonation) group

. Syllable break   ɹiˈækt

‿ Linking (absence of a break)

TONES AND WORD ACCENTS

LEVEL			CONTOUR		
e̋	or ˥	Extra high	ě	or ˄	Rising
é	˦	High	ê	˅	Falling
ē	˧	Mid	e᷄	˧˦	High rising
è	˨	Low	e᷅	˨˩	Low rising
ȅ	˩	Extra low	e᷈	˦˥˩	Rising-falling
↓	Downstep		↗	Global rise	
↑	Upstep		↘	Global fall	

Figure 1.9 Suprasegmental symbols. IPA Chart.

Source: http://www.internationalphoneticassociation.org/content/ipa-chart, available under a Creative Commons Attribution-Sharealike 3.0 Unported License. Copyright © 2015 International Phonetic Association.

quickly. Language users might take 'shortcuts' in pronunciation to get their meaning across quickly, for example saying *gonna* instead of *going to*. Over time, such 'shortcuts' can become part of a language's structure (see Chapter 8 for more information). To investigate this hypothesis in American Sign Language, Rimor et al. asked signers to produce five signs in clear, slow signing, and in speeded up versions. When speeded up, the signs often underwent changes in how they were produced (their phonetic form). For example, two handed signs tended to be produced with one hand, larger movements became smaller, and movements were repeated fewer times. These differences in how sign structure (phonology) is implemented (phonetics) are an indication of phonetic differences in sign production.

1.6 Conclusions

This chapter has explained some of the fundamentals of phonetics. We took a brief tour of the vocal tract, learned how to describe the main parts of the vocal tract used for speech, and how we can describe speech sounds according to the articulators used to produce them. We also examined the distinction between vowels and consonants, and saw how phonetic transcription is a flexible method for writing down details about speech that we can hear. Finally, we discussed how spoken language phonetics also has parallels in sign languages.

References

Gick, B., Wilson, I. and Derrick, D. 2013. *Articulatory Phonetics*. Chichester: Wiley-Blackwell.

Ladefoged, P. and Johnson, K. 2015. *Course in Phonetics*. 7th ed. Stamford, CT: Cengage Learning.

Rimor, M., Kegl, J., Lane, H. and Schermer, T. 1984. Natural phonetic processes underlie historical change and register variation in American Sign Language. *Sign Language Studies*, 43: 97–199.

Wood, S. 1982. X-ray and model studies of vowel articulation. *Lund University Department of Linguistics Working Papers*, 23: 1–192.

2 Phonology

Claire Nance and Sam Kirkham

2.1 Introduction

In this chapter we consider phonology, that is, how small elements of language are put together to form meaningful utterances in speech or sign languages. Phonology concerns sound/sign structure and systems. For example, we look at how vowels in a particular language combine as part of a system, or how tone contrasts are distributed across a language family. When we listen to speech in a language we don't understand, it can be hard to know where each word begins and ends, and where each individual sound begins and ends. Sometimes, it is even hard to know where each sentence starts and ends, especially if someone is speaking quickly. The same is true for a string of signing in sign languages. Human children are faced with the same challenge when they begin acquiring language: how to chop up a continuous stream of speech/signs into meaningful chunks which can be understood as language. A child, or adult acquiring a new language, has to decode bits of the stream of speech/signs and work out what is useful for understanding the meaning and what is not. For example, a difference in the vowel in the Scottish Gaelic words *mac* 'son' /maʰk/ and *muc* 'pig' /muʰk/ is important for distinguishing these two words. But it is not important for their meaning whether they are spoken with a low-pitched voice or a high-pitched voice. Phonologists work out what is important for meaning-making in each language and compare patterns across languages in order to understand the fundamental nature of how humans communicate effectively with one another.

There is clearly a lot of overlap between phonetics (see Chapter 1) and phonology: both areas of linguistics consider speech sounds or the smallest units in sign languages. Typically, phonetic or phonological analysis of speech will make use of the International Phonetic Alphabet. But the emphasis is slightly different in a phonetic study compared to a phonological one. For example, a phonetic study might consider the precise acoustic nature of a particular consonant, but a phonological study would examine how that consonant forms part of a system in a particular language or across languages.

In the rest of the chapter, we first consider how different sounds combine to make the meaningful difference between words such as Scottish Gaelic *mac* 'son' /maʰk/ and *muc* 'pig' /muʰk/ (Section 2.2). We then consider examples of different spoken phonological structures: vowels and consonants in Section 2.3, and then

DOI: 10.4324/9781003045571-3

prosody in Section 2.4. The final section discusses phonological structure in sign languages (Section 2.5).

2.2 Phonemes

In the Introduction, we discussed the example of two very similar Scottish Gaelic words, *mac* 'son' /maʰk/ and *muc* 'pig' /muʰk/, and said that the quality of the vowel is what distinguishes these two words and means that they have different semantic values (i.e. one string of sounds means 'son' and one means 'pig'). This is an example of a minimal pair: a pair of words differing in only one sound. We can use minimal pairs to work out which sounds are important for meaning in which languages. For example, the *mac* and *muc* pair demonstrates that the difference between /a/ and /u/ is important in understanding Scottish Gaelic words. To put this into phonological terminology, we can say that /a/ and /u/ are phonemes in Scottish Gaelic. /a/ and /u/ are phonemes in many languages. We could also find a minimal pair for these vowels in French (e.g. in the words *ballet* /bale/ 'ballet' and *boulet* /bule/ 'idiot').

In order for a sound to count as a phoneme in a particular language, it needs to contrast with something else in a phonetically identical environment. What we mean by this is that the surrounding sounds must be the same in both members of a minimal pair. For example, the words *bit* /bɪt/ and *bat* /bat/ are a minimal pair in English, demonstrating the phonemes /ɪ/ and /a/. In this example, the surrounding context of the phonemes in question is the same, that is, each phoneme is preceded by /b/ and followed by /t/. However, the words *bin* and *bat* would not be a minimal pair because one word ends in /n/ and one in /t/, so we can't technically use these words to tell us anything about phonemes. We could do the same with word-initial or word-final phonemes too. For example, the French words *vu* /vy/ 'saw' (verb) and *bu* /by/ 'drank' are a minimal pair demonstrating the phonemes /v/ and /b/. The environment is identical because each consonant is preceded by a word boundary and followed by a /y/ vowel. Another way of phrasing this is to say that the sounds /v/ and /b/ are in contrastive distribution in French. This means that the sounds contrast with one another when they occur in the language, and they are therefore phonemes.

So far, we have focused on examples of common vowels and consonants which are phonemes in many languages. But not all languages have the same phonemic inventory, and not all dialects of each language have the same phonemic inventory. For example, the sound [ð] is a phoneme in English. We can prove this with the existence of a minimal pair such as *load* /ləʊd/ and *loathe* /ləʊð/. However, in Spanish, the sound [ð] occurs, but it is not a phoneme. For example, the word *duda* 'doubt' is pronounced [duða], but when the initial consonant is preceded by a vowel, as in *mi duda* 'my doubt' this would be pronounced [mi ðuða] with a voiced fricative instead of the voiced plosive. What we can see from this short Spanish example is that instead of minimal pairs, we have predictable variation in the production of the phoneme /d/. There are no words in Spanish where the difference between [d] and [ð] makes a difference in meaning. From this, it is not possible to say that [ð] is a phoneme in Spanish.

 ## 2.2.1 Allophonic variation

The previous example demonstrates that different languages have different phonemes. We also saw that the variation in Spanish /d/ is predictable from its environment: where a vowel precedes /d/, it becomes [ð]. This is an example of allophonic variation (i.e. variation in the production of a particular phoneme based on its phonetic environment). The different variants are known as allophones. In this example, we can say that the Spanish phoneme /d/ has two allophones: [ð] occurs in when surrounded by vowels, and [d] occurs elsewhere.

Let's consider another example. In Table 2.1 there are some Japanese words and phonetic transcriptions containing the vowels [i], [u], [i̥] and [u̥]. The little circles underneath [i̥] and [u̥] mean that these vowels are voiceless (produced with no vocal fold vibration, see also p. 6). They sound like someone is whispering them.

Table 2.1 Examples of Japanese vowel voicing allophony.

Japanese transcription (IPA)	English meaning
[ika]	squid
[ʃi̥karu]	scold
[kidesu̥ka]	is it a tree?
[ki̥tal]	north
[tsuda]	(person's name)
[tʃi̥kai]	near
[ku̥sai]	smelly
[kie̥N]	mood
[ʃizuka]	quiet
[ki̥seN]	steamship
[kaɡitai]	I want to sniff
[totʃida]	it's land

Source: From Tsujimura (2014: 41).

Looking through Table 2.1, it is possible to begin to predict where we will see [i] and where we will see [i̥] depending on the surrounding consonants. The same is true of [u] and [u̥]. The vowels [i] and [u] are produced as voiceless [i̥] and [u̥] when they are surrounded by voiceless consonants. For example, in the similar words [kiɡeN] 'mood' (voiceless [k] and voiced [ɡ]) and [ki̥seN] 'steamship' (voiceless [k] and voiceless [s]). From this example, we can say that in Japanese the phonemes /i/ and /u/ have voiceless allophones when surrounded by voiceless consonants. You might ask why /i/ is the phoneme and [i̥] the allophone rather than the other way around. Usually, the allophone which occurs in the 'elsewhere' condition is considered to be the phonemic representation. In this context, [i̥] occurs in the very specific context of being surrounded by voiceless consonants and [i] occurs everywhere else. So we can say that /i/ has the allophone [i̥] in voiceless environments, and [i] elsewhere. The same is true for the Spanish example earlier: [ð] occurs in certain contexts and is an allophone of the phoneme /d/.

You will notice that we have been using brackets around the transcriptions slightly differently throughout this discussion. When writing about phonemes, we use slanted brackets // to go around our broad phonetic transcription. When doing a more detailed, narrow phonetic transcription which includes detail about allophones, we use square brackets [ ] to go around the transcription. If you're not sure whether a sound is a phoneme or not, for example in a language you don't know, you can use the square brackets to show you haven't made assumptions about phonological structure. This means that we aren't yet sure if something should be shown as a phoneme. In the next section we will look at some example inventories of vowels and consonants across languages to examine how languages differ in the phonemes used.

In focus: the International Phonetic Alphabet as phonological analysis

When we transcribe speech using the International Phonetic Alphabet, we usually show representations of vowels and consonants, and other aspects of speech such as length and tones which we will cover in the next section. For example, if we transcribed the Thai words for 'galangal' and 'leg' we would have /kʰàː/ and /kʰǎː/. These transcriptions show some detail: aspiration /ʰ/ (a puff of air after the 'k'), the different tones on the vowel (i.e. /à/ and /ǎ/), and that the vowel is lengthened, shown by the /ː/ symbol. (See Section 2.4 for more information about vowel length and tone.)

However, this transcription doesn't show us whether the words are spoken by, for example, a female voice. When we use the IPA, there are some decisions about speech which are built in for us. In this case, the IPA doesn't show the gender of the speaker because the people who designed the IPA didn't think that this would be phonologically meaningful. Examples such as this demonstrate that it is important to remember that the IPA is a tool designed by phoneticians. It is not a faithful replication of all elements of a spoken utterance but picks and chooses to some extent to show phonologically important units.

The first IPA chart was published in 1888 and included symbols based on the sounds phoneticians encountered in mainly widely spoken western European languages such as English, French, German and Spanish. Since then, the chart has been revised to describe variation across the phonologies of the world's languages. However, it is important to remember the foundations of the IPA are based in western Europe and may be biased to best describe languages from this region. Scan the QR code to see the development of the IPA chart over the years.

SCAN ME

2.3 Vowels and consonants

This section considers how segments are used as phonological units in different languages. In spoken phonetics and phonology, the term 'segment' refers to any individual sound. These can be divided into vowels and consonant sounds and used contrastively as phonemes. Some sounds are a bit tricky to strictly classify as either vowels or consonants and we will come back to these later.

2.3.1 Vowels

Vowels are sounds produced with little or no constriction in the vocal tract. For example, the vowel /i/ is the eeee sound in a word like English *bee* /biː/ or Scottish Gaelic chì /çiː/ 'will see'. It is produced with the tongue body raised towards the hard palate, but air still flows smoothly over the tongue and out through the mouth. The vowel /ɔ/ in English *thought* /θɔːt/ or Scottish Gaelic *boc* /pɔʰk/ 'male goat' is produced with the tongue body lower and further back in the mouth, and rounded lips. In Chapter 1, we saw the main ways to describe vowels and their corresponding IPA symbols. Here, we will consider how vowels are used as part of a system across different languages. We will compare a small vowel system (Abkhaz, a north Caucasian language), with a more complex and larger vowel system (Scottish Gaelic).

Abkhaz only has two contrastive vowel sounds: /a/ and /ə/, but these vowels vary allophonically depending on the surrounding consonants (see Figure 2.1).

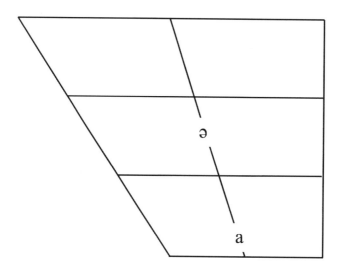

Figure 2.1 Abkhaz vowel system. Based on Andersson et al. (2021).

Scottish Gaelic has a larger vowel system, contrasting short and long vowels as well as many diphthongs. Diphthongs are two vowel sounds mashed together, for example the sound in English 'buy' [bai]. This word is considered to have two segments: a consonant [b] and a diphthong [ai]. The Gaelic diphthongs are shown in the schematised plots in Figure 2.2. Diphthongs are represented by arrows from their starting segment to the second segment. As we can see from comparing just these two languages, there is considerable variation across the world's languages as to which vowels are used in phonology, and the number of vowels. Abkhaz has an unusually small system, and Scottish Gaelic has a fairly large system.

If you would like to look at more examples for comparison, you can compare the world's languages by scanning the QR code.

2.3.2 Consonants

Consonants, on the other hand, are sounds produced with total or partial constriction in the vocal tract. For example, the plosive sound /p/ is produced with

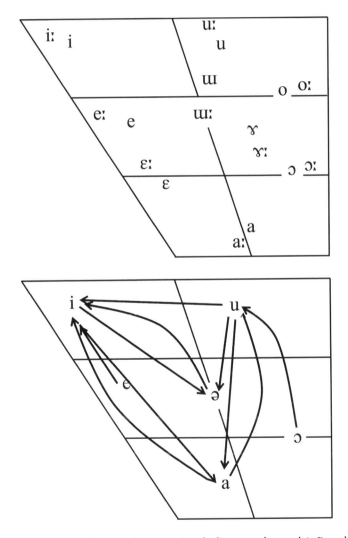

Figure 2.2a, b Scottish Gaelic vowel system (excluding nasal vowels). Based on Nance and Ó Maolalaigh (2021).

a closure at the lips, which is then released. The fricative sound /x/ is produced when the tongue body is raised towards the velum and a small opening is left for air to escape through (i.e. a partial constriction). This opening is so narrow that the air molecules don't flow smoothly and turbulence is created leading to a hissing noise we refer to as frication. Chapter 1 outlined the main ways of describing consonants in terms of voicing, place, manner and airstream mechanism. Again, here we will instead work through some examples of different consonant systems from the world's languages to exemplify the extremes of a smaller system (Hawaiian) and an extremely large system (N|uu).

Hawaiian, a Polynesian language, has one of the smallest consonant inventories, contrasting only eight consonants. These are shown in Table 2.2. For context, the average number of consonants in a language is around 22 (scan the QR code for more information).

N|uu, on the other hand, has one of the largest documented consonant systems. This Khoisan language is very endangered and spoken in South Africa and possibly Botswana. The consonants of N|uu are shown in Table 2.3. If you consult the International Phonetic Alphabet, you can see that this table has been divided up according to airstream mechanism. On the IPA, there are only five symbols for click consonants, but N|uu has a huge number of clicks: 45 of them! When clicks are contrasted in languages that use them, typically they are combined with other elements, either other consonants (usually velar or uvular consonants) and/or other kinds of vocal fold vibration represented by IPA diacritics. N|uu uses both of these strategies to form its enormous click inventory. You will also note the new term, affricate. This refers to when two consonant sounds are put together in one segment, for example in the English word *church*, which contains the affricate /tʃ/ at the start and at the end. Sometimes affricates are shown with a tied symbol to show that they are one segment (i.e. [t͡ʃ]).

When looking at Table 2.3, you might see some IPA symbols which you haven't come across before. You can refer back to Chapter 1 if you would like more explanation of consonant symbols. For now, though, you don't need to know exactly what all of them mean; you will learn more about phonetics as you continue studying linguistics. To listen to sound files of different click sounds and see videos of how they are produced, you can scan the QR code and click on the click symbols of the IPA chart, or you can search for videos on YouTube of click languages such as N|uu or Zulu.

Table 2.2 Hawaiian consonants.

	Bilabial	Labiodental	Alveolar	Velar	Glottal
Nasal	m		n		
Plosive	p			k	ʔ
Fricative		v			h
Lateral			l		

Source: Based on Parker Jones (2017).

Table 2.3 Consonants in N|uu.

Pulmonic consonants

	Bilabial	Alveolar	Palatal	Velar	Uvular	Glottal
Stop	p b	t d	c cʰ ɟ	k kʰ g q		ʔ
Affricate		ts	cχ			
Nasal	m	n	ɲ		ŋ	
Fricative	f	s	z		χ	ɦ
Approximant		ɾ				
Lateral		l				

Ejectives

	Bilabial	Alveolar	Palatal	Velar	Uvular	Glottal
Affricate		ts'		kχ'	qχ'	

Clicks

	Labial-uvular	Dental-uvular	Alveolar-uvular		Palatal-uvular
			Central	Lateral	
Stop	ʘ ʘq	ǀ ǀʰ ǀq ǀqʰ	ᵑǀ ! !ʰ !q !qʰ	ᵑǃ ‖ ‖ʰ ‖q ‖qʰ	ᵑ‖ ǂ ǂʰ ǂq ǂqʰ ᵑǂ
Nasal	ᵑʘˀ ᵑʘ	ᵑǀ ᵑǀˀ ᵑǀ	ᵑǀʰ ᵑǀˀ ᵑǀ	ᵑ‖ʰ ᵑ‖ˀ ᵑ‖	ᵑǂʰ ᵑǂˀ ᵑǂ
Affricate	ʘχ	ǀχ	!χ	‖χ	ǂχ
Ejective affricate		ǀχ'	!χ'	‖χ'	ǂχ'

Source: Adapted from Miller et al. (2009).

2.3.3 Neither vowel nor consonant?

Some sounds are quite tricky to classify as either vowels or consonants. For example, a group of sounds are referred to as 'semi-vowels' or 'glides' and include /j/, /w/ and /ɥ/. We can find these sounds in the French words *sien* /sjɛ̃/ 'his/hers/ theirs', *soin* /swɛ̃/ 'care', and *suint* /sɥɛ̃/ 'grease on sheep's wool', or in English *yes* /jɛs/ and *went* /wɛnt/. Semi-vowels are dynamic, in that they move through one tongue configuration to another, and they also contain many elements of a vowel. For example, in the palatal glide /j/, the sound starts something like the vowel /i/ with a high tongue body but no frication in the vocal tract. The lips are then rounded and the second part of the glide is something like the vowel /ø/. However, in terms of their phonology, semi-vowels often act similarly to consonants. In the French examples earlier, the semi-vowel combines with an /s/ sound to form the opening part of a syllable, a position typically occupied by consonants. In the English examples, the semi-vowel *is* the opening part of the syllable. In these syllable contexts, a semi-vowel behaves similarly to a consonant, and a 'full' vowel is required to form the rest of the syllable. For this reason, these segments are referred to as semi-vowels as they don't quite fit the description for either vowels or consonants.

Another group of sounds in this position are referred to as 'syllabic consonants'. This phrase describes a group of consonants which occupy positions in the syllable usually reserved for vowels. Czech has many syllabic consonants. For example, the word for 'wolf' in Czech is *krk* /krk/. This word is produced with no vowel, but an *rrrr* sound can act similarly to a vowel to fill in the middle of this word. Syllabic consonants are sort of the opposite of semi-vowels: their production is similar to a consonant with obstruction in the vocal tract, but their phonology is similar to vowels in that they occupy the middle of a syllable.

2.4 Prosody

Prosody (also known as 'suprasegmentals') refers to everything which is not segments, that is, not vowels and consonants. Here, we will consider several aspects of prosody: duration, tone, stress, intonation and syllable structure.

2.4.1 Duration

We have already touched upon one aspect of prosody: earlier, we used the length diacritic [ː] to show that some vowels are longer than others. Manipulating duration is one way in which languages vary prosodically. Many languages have long and short vowels which indicate the difference between words as part of a phonological contrast. For example, the Scottish Gaelic word *teth* /tʃʰe/ 'hot' has a short vowel. The word *tè* 'woman' is pronounced with exactly the same vowels and consonants, but the vowel is longer /tʃʰeː/. Helpfully, Scottish Gaelic spelling shows this long vowel with an accent in the orthography. In Thai /fǎn/ means 'to dream', but /fǎːn/ means 'to slice'. Both words have the same vowels, consonants and rising tone, but a longer vowel makes the contrast in meaning.

2.4.2 Tone, stress and intonation

We will now consider tone in a bit more detail. Tone can be described as the use of prosodic features, especially variation in pitch, at the word level to contrast in meaning. Around 70% of the world's languages use tonal contrasts, so this is a very common linguistic feature although it is not used in English. We've already seen some examples of tones from Thai, and the full set of five tones from Standard Thai can be seen in Table 2.4. Thai has three tones which are level in pitch (mid, low and high), and two tones which change in pitch during the vowel (falling and rising). Languages which have tones which change in pitch are referred to as contour tone languages, and are very common in East Asia. Other example languages would include Mandarin Chinese, Cantonese and Vietnamese.

Table 2.4 Tones in Standard Thai.

IPA	Meaning	Tone
kʰāː	to get stuck	mid
kʰàː	galangal	low
kʰâː	I	falling
kʰáː	leg	high
kʰǎː	to engage in trade	rising

Source: From Tingsabadh and Abramson (1993).

Not all tone languages have such large systems with tones that change in pitch. Languages with smaller tone systems which are consistent in pitch are referred to as register tone languages. These systems are typical of African tone languages though they are found in many areas of the world. Some example words and corresponding tones from Ega (spoken in Côte d'Ivoire) are in Table 2.5. Ega has three level tones, which is typical of West African tone languages. These are often shown in the orthography of the language.

Table 2.5 Tones in Ega.

IPA	Meaning	Tone
ní tá	I speak	high
ní tā	I spoke	mid
ní tà	I chew	low

Source: From Connell et al. (2002).

Tone is the use of prosodic features for contrastive meaning between words. There is another word-level prosodic pattern referred to as stress. Stress is also the use of prosodic features at the word level, especially pitch, but unlike tone, stress doesn't usually make a contrast between two different words. For example, in the English word *lever*, the first syllable is usually stressed. We could show this in the IPA as [ˈliːvə]. The superscript oblong before the [l] indicates that this syllable has primary stress. If someone pronounced *lever* as [liˈvə] with stress on the second syllable, it might sound a bit unusual, but we would still understand it as the same word. Typically, stressed syllables are produced with higher pitch, longer duration and louder than unstressed syllables.

Some languages have predictable stress which always falls on the same syllable of each word. For example, in northern dialects of Breton stress falls predictably on the penultimate syllable in a word. The word for the language, 'Breton', is *Brezhoneg*, pronounced [bʁeˈzɔ̃nɛk] in northern dialects. The southern Breton dialect, Vannetais, also has predictable stress, but it falls on the final syllable in the word such that *Brezhoneg* is pronounced [bʁezɔ̃ˈnɛk]. As stress is predictable in Breton dialects, Breton is known as a language with fixed stress. In other languages, stress is less predictable, such as Modern Greek. Greek has variable stress (i.e. stress can occur on any syllable) and helpfully this is marked in the orthography with an accent. For example, εννιά [εˈɲa] 'nine' has stress on the final syllable, but δέκα 'ten' [ˈðɛka] has stress on the first syllable.

In focus: is English a tone language?

In English there is a small set of identical words which differ in stress. These are known as diatones and developed a sound change over the past 400 years. In each case, the vowels and consonants are the same, but the stress pattern is different between the noun and verb forms of the word. Some examples can be seen in Table 2.6.

Table 2.6 Some examples of diatone pairs in English. Stress is shown with an acute accent.

Noun	Verb
Récord	Recórd
Résearch	Reséarch
Pérmit	Permít
Ímport	Impórt
Éxport	Expórt
Prótest	Protést

Here, we have examples of where prosody is used to make a contrast between two different words. This is the definition of tone! Not stress. So is English a tone language? Although we can see tone-like characteristics in this small set of words, phonologists generally say that English is not a tone language. This is because these are a limited set of words which are closely related in meaning anyway (the difference between a noun and a verb), rather than two unrelated lexical items. The tone-like contrast is not widespread across the language, so we instead think of the diatones as an exception to the rule rather than a fundamental property of English phonology.

So far, we have concentrated on prosodies which affect individual syllables or individual words. A larger structure which affects the prosody of a whole utterance is known as intonation. This is the use of prosodic features, especially pitch, across a longer stretch of speech. Intonation is the broad overarching melody to a particular utterance and varies widely across different languages and dialects. It is common to find falling pitch at the end of statements. This is because of an aerodynamic effect by which speakers are using up the air in their lungs towards the end of an utterances, which lowers the tension on the vocal folds and lowers pitch. An example dialect which does this would be Connemara Irish. However, not all languages and dialects conform to this pattern. The next-door dialect to Connemara, Donegal Irish, instead has phrase-final rising intonation in statements. This is cross-linguistically quite unusual, but is found in Donegal Irish, and in the intonation of several UK English dialects such as

Liverpool, Belfast, Glasgow and Birmingham. A comparison of declarative statements in Connemara Irish and Donegal Irish is in Figure 2.3. In Connemara we find a series of falls associated with each stressed syllable. In Donegal on the other hand, each stressed syllable is associated with a rising pitch.

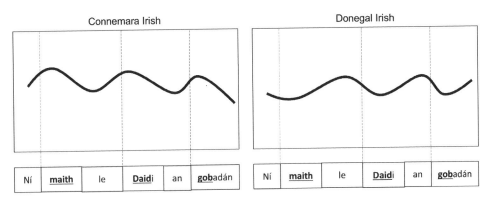

Connemara Irish						Donegal Irish					
Ní	**maith**	le	**Daid**i	an	**gob**adán	Ní	**maith**	le	**Daid**i	an	**gob**adán

Figure 2.3 Comparison of statements in Connemara and Donegal Irish. Stressed syllables are shown in underlined and bold. The sentence means 'Daddy doesn't like the sandpiper'. Schematic representation of pitch contours based on Dalton and Ní Chasaide (2007).

While many languages and dialects have falling intonation in statements, intonation is often varied to show different kinds of question. For example, yes-no questions are often realised with rising intonation, but information questions (e.g. *Why did you go?*) can vary. In UK English, these are often produced with a falling intonation.

In focus: Swedish word accents

Several languages have a sort of half tone system, that is, tonal contrasts across a limited set of words. These are usually referred to as 'word accents' or 'lexical pitch accents'. Example languages which follow this pattern are Swedish, Japanese, Serbo-Croat, Ancient Greek, Luxembourgish and Scottish Gaelic. Here, we will look at some examples from Stockholm Swedish.

In Stockholm Swedish, every stressed word has one of two accents. There are around 350 pairs of words distinguished by their tonal pitch pattern alone (i.e. whether a word is produced with Accent 1 or Accent 2). Accent 1 is a single falling pitch, but Accent 2 has two pitch peaks. A representation of the accents can be seen in Figure 2.4, with the example words *anden* 'the duck' and *anden* 'the ghost'. Some other example pairs of words in Stockholm Swedish are in Table 2.7.

Not all dialects of Swedish have word accents! In Finland, around 6% of the population speak Swedish as their first language. The dialect of Swedish spoken in Finland is spoken without word accents. You can scan the QR code to watch a video about Swedish word accents.

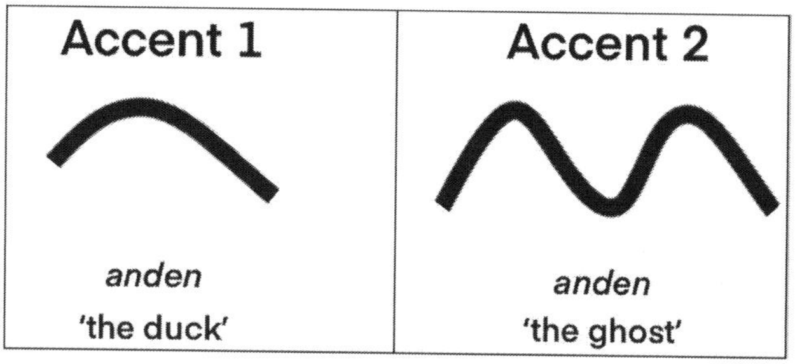

Figure 2.4 Example representations of Stockholm Swedish word accents.

Table 2.7 Example words with different Stockholm Swedish word accents.

Accent 1	Meaning	Accent 2	Meaning
anden	the duck	anden	the ghost
tomten	the yard	tomten	Father Christmas
slutet	the end	slutet	closed
buren	the cage	buren	carried
vaken	ice hole	vaken	awake
tummen	the inch	tummen	the thumb
värden	the host	värden	the values

2.4.3 Syllables

When discussing the role of tone, stress and intonation we discussed these features in relation to syllable structure. Syllables are to some extent an intuitive concept: in many language contexts speakers are able to talk about the 'beats' in a word, or sections of a word. In societies where early education and literacy is common, it can be difficult to separate whether syllables are an intuitive concept, or whether we are taught about them at a very early age when learning to read. There is, however, some evidence from early writing systems which suggests that syllables are indeed an important unit for processing language as well as reading and writing. One of the earliest written records we have is from Mycenaean Greece in the form of the Linear B alphabet. This alphabet was used in Crete and the surrounding Greek mainland around 1450–1200 BCE. In this society, literacy would not be widespread, but the alphabet developed to represent syllables rather than individual sounds. For example, 𐀛 represents [ni] and 𐀗 represents [mo]. This suggests that to some extent syllables must be an important linguistic unit if they were chosen to represent speech in an early alphabetic system.

Linguistically, syllables can be quite tricky to precisely define. For now, we will say that they represent a unit of speech/signing which is somewhere in between a segment and a word. Of course, some words are only made of up one segment and one syllable (e.g. *eye* [ai]), but many words can be made up of multiple segments and multiple syllables. So we can say that every syllable has at least one segment in it, and every word has at least one syllable. While some words are easy to divide into syllables, for example *important* could be divided up as im.por.tant, other words are less straightforward. Consider the word *family*. This could be pronounced as [fam.li] with two syllables, or [fa.mɪ.li] with three syllables. We might use the first pronunciation in fast or informal speech, and the second pronunciation if we wanted to emphasise the word. Similarly, the word *film* is often produced as [fɪ.ləm] with two syllables in Irish and Scottish English, and some areas of northern England.

As we can now see, in some contexts syllable structure can vary according to formal/informal context, speech rate, and dialect or idiolect. Syllables are also subject to language-specific rules, or to put it another way, each language syllabifies a stream of speech slightly differently. For example, if an English speaker encountered this stream of segments [rasta], they might syllabify it as [ra.sta]. However, in Spanish there are no syllables which begin [st], so a Spanish speaker might syllabify the same sequence as [ras.ta] by applying the rules of Spanish to this new string of segments. This is known as a phonotactic rule: a rule about how segments can occur within syllables.

When we describe syllables, it can be helpful to talk about the different constituent parts and how they operate in relation to phonotactic rules. For example, earlier on we discussed syllabic consonants in Czech and how the 'r' in *krk* 'wolf' operates as the middle bit of a syllable. More precisely, we can now call this part of the syllable the nucleus. Every syllable has a nucleus and it is almost always a vowel. We have to say 'almost always' due to exceptions like the example from Czech. The other parts of a syllable are shown in Table 2.8.

Table 2.8 Parts of a syllable.

Name	Description	Present in every syllable?
Onset	The opening segment of a syllable. If present, always a consonant.	No
Rhyme	The rest of the syllable after the onset. Comprised of the nucleus (always present) and the coda (if present).	Yes
Nucleus	The central part of the syllable. Almost always a vowel.	Yes
Coda	The closing segment of a syllable. If present, always a consonant.	No

To exemplify these terms further, we will draw the syllable structure for four different English words with different kinds of syllables: *walk, buy, egg, eye* (Figure 2.5). Each syllable (often represented by the Greek letter σ) always has a rhyme. Within each rhyme there is always a nucleus. In English, the other parts are optional: sometimes there is an onset (in *walk* and *buy* but not *egg* and *eye*), and sometimes there is a coda within the rhyme (in *walk* and *egg*, but not *buy* and *eye*).

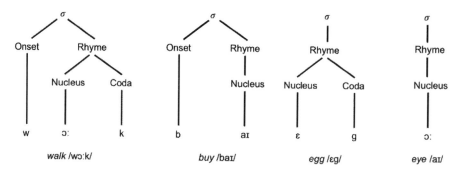

Figure 2.5 Variety of syllable structures in English words.

Other languages have more constrained syllable structures and less optionality. For example, in Mandarin Chinese, the only segment which can form a coda is a nasal consonant. Otherwise, there are no codas. Other languages have larger, complex, syllable structures. For example, Georgian is known for having very long consonant sequences. The word for 'trainer' is /mts'vrtnɛli/ beginning with six consonants (the /ts'/ sequence is considered as two consonants in one segment – i.e. an affricate). Discussions about exactly how sequences like this should be syllabified in Georgian are ongoing, but currently it seems as though syllabic consonants are not a feature of the language and therefore this really does represent an onset with six consonants!

In focus: syllables in Arrernte

Arrernte is a language spoken in central Australia. Research into this language caused some of the widely held beliefs about syllable structure to be re-examined. Previously, it was thought that the default way of syllabifying any sequence in any language would be consonant and then vowel. For example, if a speaker encountered the sequence [atatatata], its default syllabification would always be [a.ta.ta.ta.ta]. This was due to linguists examining a variety of languages and observing that this general pattern holds. However, data from Arrernte challenge this notion and show that some languages will default to a pattern where syllables begin with a vowel instead [at.at.at.at.a]. The list of words in Table 2.9 is from Breen and Pensalfini (1999) and describes a word game called 'Rabbit talk' in Arrernte.

In order to form the Rabbit talk version of each word, the initial syllable is added to the end of the word (e.g. *itirem* becomes *iremit*). The final two words show what happens with monosyllabic words: the syllable [ey] is added to the start of the word. These rules only make sense if the syllable structure of Arrernte is analysed as Vowel and then Consonant (i.e. [em.eŋ] rather than [e.meŋ]). Arrernte shows that previous preconceptions about features considered 'universal' in language may be challenged when the diversity of the world's languages are taken into account. Other languages with underlying Vowel Consonant syllable structures include Irish and Scottish Gaelic.

Table 2.9 Arrernte words and Rabbit talk forms.

Arrernte word	Rabbit talk form	Meaning
emeṉ	eŋem	plant food
eṉtem	emeṉt	giving
ekʷeŋetʼek	eŋetʼekekʷ	to put in
itirem	iremit	thinking
ulkeṯ	eṯulk	monitor lizard
alpetʼek	etʼekalp	to go back
aṯʷ	eyaṯʷ	initiated man
ik	eyik	foot

Source: From Breen and Pensalfini (1999).

2.5 Phonology in sign languages

Most of the discussion in this chapter so far has been about individual units of sound used in combination to form speech. Sign languages also make use of minimal units combined together into longer stretches of signing. And prosodic structures such as intonation and syllables are also applicable to sign languages.

In the definition of phonology discussed in Section 2.1, we talked about how small units can be combined to form the meaning of different words. These units can be individual segments, or can be parts of signs. Previously, it was wrongly thought that sign languages were a series of picture representations made with the hands. For example, it was wrongly thought that a signer would create a picture of, for instance, a tree and then a picture of the next item they wanted to discuss. Pioneering work by Stokoe (1960) demonstrated that signs in American Sign Language are made up of three abstract parameters, which can be substituted to build up different meanings. Stokoe demonstrated that signs vary according to (1) hand configuration, (2) hand location and (3) the hand movement used. We could think of these configurations as similar to consonant voice, place and manner, or to vowel height, frontness and rounding. Each specific hand gesture can then be combined to form something parallel to the concept of a phoneme.

We can find minimal pairs distinguished by hand configuration, location and movement. The example in Figure 2.6 shows some minimal pairs from Israeli Sign Language. In Panel a, one hand is raised towards the mouth and moves from one side to the other. The difference between the signs for *mother* and *noon* is in the hand configuration: in *mother* the index finger is extended, but in *noon* the fingertips are all touching. Everything about these signs is identical apart from the hand configuration so we can say that these signs form a minimal pair contrasting in hand configuration. In Panel b, the signer uses one hand which starts as a clenched fist and then opens. The movement is away from the body. There is a difference between *send* and *tattle* in that the *send* sign starts at the shoulder, and the *tattle* sign starts at the mouth. These signs are therefore a minimal pair contrasting in sign location. Finally, in Panel c, there is a minimal pair according to sign movement. In the sign for *escape*, the movement is in a straight line. In the sign for *betray*, everything is identical apart from the movement which is rising. This difference means that the signs are a minimal pair contrasting in movement.

The examples show that sign languages have phonological structure and minimal units comparable to segments and phonemes in spoken languages. Prosody is also used in sign languages to give structure to longer stretches of signing and enable the person watching to chunk up stretches of signs. In sign language phonology, each movement is usually considered to represent a syllable. It is thought that people watching the signs use movements as a way of chunking and linking up different signs. In spoken language, if the speaker wanted to emphasise elements of what they were saying, they could manipulate the prosodic markers such as duration and loudness to do so. In sign languages, this can be achieved with prosodic markers such as the magnitude of a movement. Movement magnitude can be increased to show emphasis. Similarly, signers can also use their eyebrows to show emphasis. Sign languages have multiple ways of showing utterance-level prosody (i.e. intonation). Intonation is usually achieved with a variety of prosodic markers such as

(a)

Figure 2.6 Example minimal pairs in Israeli Sign Language from Sandler (2017).

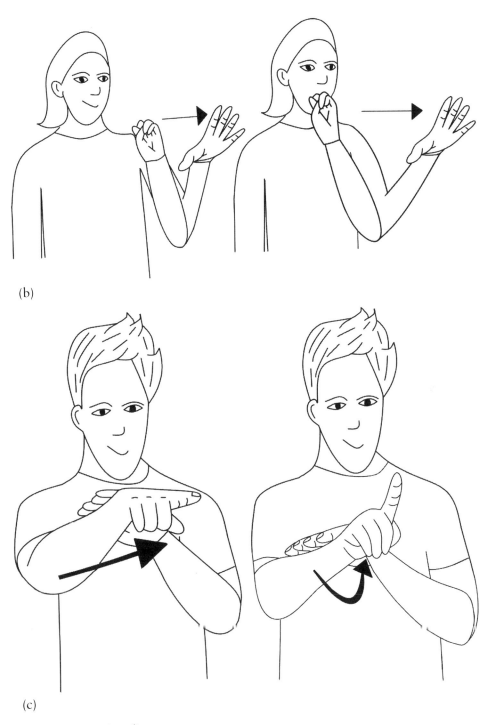

(b)

(c)

Figure 2.6 (Continued)

tilting the head at the end of an utterance, lowering the eyebrows and shoulders, or a large intake of breath. In this way, the signer can visibly demonstrate that an utterance is finished and can give structure to a long stretch of signs.

As sign languages usually develop in contexts where large numbers of deaf people come together to communicate, this can also lead to differences developing between communities. In countries such as the UK, France and the US, the opportunity for large numbers of deaf people to communicate in the 1800–1900s was often provided in residential schools (see also p. 148). In contemporary contexts, deaf students are often integrated into mainstream schooling and many residential schools have now closed. However, phonological and lexical variation according to the location of residential schools still exists in British Sign Language and in American Sign Language. For example, a study by Bayley et al. (2002) looked at phonological variation in the sign for *one* in American Sign Language. They found considerable variation in hand configuration: some signers use an open palm, and some signers use a sign with only the index finger and thumb extended. This variation was linked to sociolinguistic factors such as age, location and ethnicity.

American Sign Language (ASL) varies considerably due to ethnicity. This is because when residential schools were first set up, white and black students were separated due to segregation. Black signers refer to their variety as Black American Sign Language (BASL). BASL typically differs from ASL along several phonological and phonetic dimensions. For example, BASL signs are generally made in a larger signing space (different movement space), BASL makes greater use of two-handed signs rather than one-handed signs (hand configuration) and BASL signs can be made at a different location such as lowering the location from the forehead to the cheek. You can read more about BASL in McCaskill et al. (2011), search on YouTube/TikTok or scan the QR code to see watch a video demonstrating some of the signs.

www.youtube.com/watch?v=3HDm3k x3rhY

To summarise this section, sign languages demonstrate many of the phonological properties of spoken languages. They use combinations of minimal contrastive units to form longer elements (different signs), and we can find minimal pairs to demonstrate phonological contrast. Prosodic variation is used to structure sections of signing allowing the person watching to divide up a stream of signs into meaningful units and utterances. Like spoken languages, sign languages vary phonologically according to contextual and sociolinguistic factors.

2.6 Conclusion

This chapter has shown that all languages combine small, meaningless units in order to build up different bits of speech or signing. We initially discussed vowels and consonants as minimal units and showed how they can form a minimal pair test to examine the phonological structure of a particular language. Vowels and consonants used in minimal pairs are referred to as phonemes and are special sounds which are used contrastively in a language-specific way. Section 3.4 considered how languages use prosodic variation to make meaning. In particular, we considered duration, tone, stress and intonation, and then syllable structure. Like different vowels and consonants, different tones can be used to form minimal pairs and do so in around 70% of the world's languages. Finally, Section 3.5 applied these concepts to sign languages in order to demonstrate that sign languages also use minimal contrastive units to form meaningful utterances.

References

Andersson, S., Vaux, B. and Pysipa, Z. (Şener). 2021. Cwyzhy Abkhaz. *Journal of the International Phonetic Association*. Online first.

Bayley, R., Lucas, C. and Rose, M. 2002. Phonological variation in American Sign Language: The case of 1 handshape. *Language Variation and Change*, 14(1): 19–53.

Breen, G. and Pensalfini, R. 1999. Arrernte: A language with no syllable onsets. *Linguistic Inquiry*, 30(1): 1–25.

Connell, B., Ahoua, F. and Gibbon, D. 2002. Ega. *Journal of the International Phonetic Association*, 32(1): 99–104.

Dalton, M. and Chasaide, A. N. 2007. Nuclear accents in four Irish (Gaelic) dialects. In *Proceedings of the XVIth International Congress of the Phonetic Sciences*. Saabrücken: University of Saarbrücken.

McCaskill, C., Lucas, C., Bayley, R. and Hill, J. 2011. *The Hidden Treasure of Black ASL: Its History and Structure*. Washington, DC: Gallaudet University Press.

Miller, A. L., Brugman, J., Sands, B., Namaseb, L., Exter, M. and Collins, C. 2009. Differences in airstream and posterior place of articulation among Nǀuu clicks. *Journal of the International Phonetic Association*, 39(2): 129–161.

Nance, C. and Maolalaigh, R. Ó. 2021. Scottish Gaelic. *Journal of the International Phonetic Association*, 51(2): 261–275.

Parker Jones. 2017. Ōiwi. *Journal of the International Phonetic Association*, 48(1): 103–115.

Sandler, W. 2017. The challenge of sign language phonology. *Annual Review of Linguistics*, 3: 43–63.

Stokoe, W. C. 1960. Sign language structure: An outline of the visual communication systems of the American deaf. In *Studies in Linguistics: Occasional Papers (No. 8)*. Buffalo: Dept. of Anthropology and Linguistics, University of Buffalo.

Tingsabadh, M. R. K. and Abramson, A. 1993. Thai. *Journal of the International Phonetic Association*, 23(1): 24–26.

Tsujimura, N. 2014. *An Introduction to Japanese Linguistics*. Oxford: Wiley.

3 Morphology
Daniel Van Olmen

3.1 Introduction

Words are, in essence, sound strings. For the word *unmanageable*, for example, we can transcribe that string as [ʌnˈmanɪdʒəbəl]. There is, however, more to this word than these sounds. It is made up of three smaller parts, each with their own meaning:

* *un-* 'not'
* *-manage-* 'control'
* *-able* 'able to be . . . ed'

Together, these parts produce the meaning 'not able to be controlled'. The study of the structure of words like *unmanageable* is what **morphology**, this chapter's topic, is concerned with. It examines how words are formed in a language and how their forms differ from or resemble those of other words. Morphology's ultimate aim is to uncover the entire system behind the ways that a language builds its words. Maybe somewhat confusingly, though, the term 'morphology' is used not only for the STUDY of that system but also for the system itself. So when a linguist writes 'the morphology of English nouns', they are usually referring to the system behind forming nouns in English or the formal characteristics of English nouns, rather than the academic study of the phenomenon.

Words are, evidently, central to morphology. But what is a word really? When confronted with a sentence such as example (1), speakers of English are no different from those of other languages: they have clear, shared intuitions about the words that it contains. What motivates those intuitions about *my*, *bills*, *are* and *unmanageable* is harder to determine.

(1) My bills are unmanageable.

It is sometimes suggested that words are the things between spaces. This orthography-based idea appears to work well for (1), and is what word processors use to produce word counts, but fails in many other regards. Spoken language, for one, does not separate words with spaces. Neither does, say, the Thai script, as in (2) – where the words สุนีย์ 'Sunee', ย้าย 'moved' and โต๊ะ 'table' are all written together.

DOI: 10.4324/9781003045571-4

(2) Thai (Iwasaki and Ingkaphirom 2005: xvii)

สุนีย์ย้ายโต๊ะ

'Sunee moved the table.'

Another definition that we often find goes as follows:

Words are the smallest meaningful forms of language that have a certain autonomy/independence from other forms.

There are various ways that this notion of autonomy has been formulated. A form can be argued to be independent from other forms if, for instance, we can pause between them or put yet other forms between them. In this view, *bills* in (1) counts as independent from *my* and *are*, because we can say *my* UHM *bills are unmanageable* or *my bills* TRULY *are unmanageable*. This evidence is, however, not sufficient to establish that *bills* constitutes a word. We also need to show that it is the SMALLEST form with such autonomy. Put differently, we should not be able and are in effect not able to pause or insert anything between any parts of *bills*. Take the *-s* ending. It IS a meaningful part, conveying plurality, but has no independence from *bill*. Pausing before it is not possible – *bill-uhm-s*?!

If we now look at the numerous words in a language, we can identify similarities between certain words in the smaller parts that they can combine with, as well as differences with other words in such combinations. *Letter*, for instance, resembles *bill*: it too can combine with *-s*, as in (3), to express plurality. But we cannot attach this ending to *unmanageable* or *friendly* to convey the plurality of a quality. These words in turn can easily appear with or without *un-*, as *manageable* or *unfriendly*, while adding *un-* to *are* or *seem* results in the non-existent words *unare* and *unseem*.

(3) His letters seem friendly.

Words with the same (im)possible combinations can be said to form a **word class**. Such classes receive perhaps familiar-sounding labels like 'adjective' for *unmanageable* and *friendly* or 'noun' for *bills* and *letters*. The words in a class also tend to occur in the same positions in sentences or phrases. Take the 'verbs' *are* and *seem* in (1) and (3). They both occupy the same place between noun and adjective.

Word classes are discussed in more detail at the end of this chapter, in Section 3.5. We first need to get to grips with the ways that words are constructed. Section 3.2 focuses on the smallest building blocks, also known as morphemes. In Section 3.3, we make a distinction between two main types of forming words, inflection and derivation, and Section 3.4 considers efforts to classify the world's languages based on their morphology.

3.2 Morphemes

3.2.1 What are they?

The three parts of *un-manage-able* are the smallest units of language with meanings of their own. The technical term for such units is **morphemes**. To clarify this concept, we can contrast it to phonemes and words:

- Unlike morphemes, a phoneme does not mean anything in itself: /m/ sets *moral* apart from *coral* but does not make a separate contribution to *moral*'s overall meaning. The morpheme *a-*, by contrast, does make such a contribution in *amoral* 'lacking moral judgement'.
- Unlike words, morphemes are not necessarily independent from other forms. *-Able* and *a-* can serve as examples.

The way to spot the morphemes in a word is comparing the word to other words. At first glance, we might think, for instance, that the Māori word for 'teach' in (4), *whakaako*, is made up of only one morpheme or, put differently, that it is a **simplex word**.

(4) Māori
    ako 'learn'   *whaka-ako* 'teach' (i.e. 'cause to learn')
    kite 'see'   *whaka-kite* 'reveal' (i.e. 'cause to see')

However, when considering the word for 'learn', *ako*, it should become clear that *whakaako* consists of *whaka-* and *-ako*. The second part of this **complex word**, we already know. The first one can be assumed to mean something like 'cause to . . .'. After all, teaching is causing someone to learn. Confirmation for our assumption comes from *kite* 'see' and *whakakite* 'reveal'. The morpheme *whaka-* combines with *kite* to produce the literal meaning 'cause to see'. And making someone see something is of course equivalent to revealing it to them.

Identifying morphemes is not without its difficulties, though (Table 3.1).

Table 3.1 Challenges that we may face when analysing morphemes.

Problem	Discussion
What looks like a morpheme in one word may not be a morpheme in another.	The word *reader* can be split into *read-* and *-er*. The second morpheme has the meaning 'someone who . . .' and occurs in, say, *learner* and *hiker* too. In *daughter*, by contrast, *-er* is not a morpheme. A daughter is obviously not a person that 'daughts' and we cannot assign any other independent meaning to *-er* in this simplex word.

Problem	Discussion
Different morphemes may just happen to have identical forms.	The -er that we find in *tougher* is not the same as the -er in *reader*. It adds to *tough* the meaning not of 'someone who . . .' but of 'more'.
What is a simplex word in one language may be a complex one in another.	The English word *teach* contains just one morpheme but its Māori equivalent in (4) has two. In a sense, 'teach' is presented as a singular concept in English but as a combination of 'cause' and 'learn' in Māori. Similarly, Dutch *oksel* 'armpit' is a simplex word but its English counterpart a complex one, combining *arm* and *pit* to refer to the body part.
Should we analyse *perspire* as *per-spire* or not?	Comparing *perspire* to PERCeive and ASPIRE appears to suggest that there are two parts. They go back to Latin: *per* 'through' and *spirare* 'breathe'. But it is unclear and perhaps doubtful whether speakers of English still 'actively' recognise them. It would be hard anyway to describe the separate meaning contributions that *per-* and *-spire* make to *perspire*. So it seems reasonable to consider *perspire* a simplex word.

Making decisions when faced with such problems is not always easy. Would you analyse *nat-* in *native* and *nation* as a morpheme alongside *-ive* and *-ion*, also found in *active* and *action*?

In focus: do sign languages have morphemes too?

We already know from Chapter 2 that signs are made up of specific hand locations, movements, etc. that, if altered, can bring about a difference in meaning. These components roughly amount to phonemes, in other words. A morpheme would then be the smallest combination of particular components with a meaning of its own. In the Sign Language of the Netherlands (NGT), for instance, pointing one's index finger to the floor – a sign involving a specific movement and configuration of the hand – stands for 'deep'. Like many words, it cannot be broken down further and must be regarded as simplex, consisting of a single morpheme. Signs can be complex too, however, and sometimes in peculiar ways. One possible sign for 'shallow' in NGT is putting one's index finger on the nose and then pointing that finger to the floor, as in Figure 3.1.

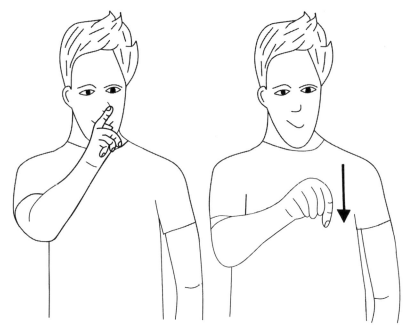

Figure 3.1 'Un-' and 'shallow' in the Sign Language of the Netherlands. Credit: Beth
Malory.

3.2.2 One morpheme but different forms?

A closer look at a morpheme may reveal that its actual form varies depending on
context. The plural morpheme in English is a case in point. It sounds like [s] in
cats but [z] in *dogs* and [əz] in *sizes*. It may even take the form of [n] or a vowel
change (or more), as in *oxen* and *feet* [fiːt] versus *foot* [fʊt]. Such variants of a
single unit of meaning are called its **allomorphs**.

Variation of this kind is usually not random. We cannot simply replace [s] in
cats by [z] or [əz]. The results, [kætz] and [kætəz], are unacceptable words in
English. What determines the 'choice' here is the final sound of the word that we
wish to pluralise:

- If that word ends in a sibilant consonant like [z] in *size* and [ʃ] in *wish*, we
  always get [əz], like in *sizes* and *wishes*.
- If its last sound is a non-sibilant voiced consonant or a vowel, the allomorph
  [z] is used, as in *dogs* and *avocados*.
- If the word ends in a non-sibilant voiceless consonant, we find [s], like in *cats*
  and *cups*.

In short, the variation between [s], [z] and [əz] exhibits a clear pattern and we
can describe this pattern in terms of the sound environments in which the plural

morpheme occurs. Technically, we would state that these allomorphs are **phonologically conditioned**. We could also add that they are in **complementary distribution**, which means that they are used in mutually exclusive contexts. As the previous list shows, each allomorph appears in a sound environment where the other ones can never appear.

Let us now try to apply these phonological conditions to *ox*. Since the word's final sound is the sibilant [s], we would expect it to take the [əz] ending in plural *oxes*. We find [n] instead, though, which raises the question whether we missed something in the description of our phonological conditions. Does a word ending in [ks] or [ɒks] perhaps always get [n]? The answer to both questions is no. The behaviour of *box*, for one, is completely regular. Its plural is *boxes*, not *boxen*. So we can conclude just one thing: it is the word *ox* itself that determines the plural morpheme's form. In technical terms, we say that [n] is **lexically conditioned**: in a sense, we explicitly need to add, to the entry for *ox* in our mental lexicon/vocabulary, that it takes this plural ending. Another case of this type of conditioning is the vowel change in *foot* and *feet*, as it is specific to this word.

3.2.3 Types of morpheme

The morphemes in words like *oxen* and *unmanageable* are not all the same. We can distinguish different types based on independence and function. The criterion of independence allows us to make a distinction between free and bound morphemes:

- **Free morphemes** can, in principle, occur on their own. In *oxen* and *unmanageable*, *ox* and *manage* are part of a longer word. But they can be used independently, without -*en*, *un*- or -*able*. Evidence for this claim comes from phrases like *the year of the ox* and *I can manage*. So we regard the morphemes *ox* and *manage* as free.
- **Bound morphemes** exhibit no such independence. Examples of this type of morpheme are -*en*, *un*- and -*able*. They can never appear on their own as words (note that -*able* [əbl] 'able to be . . . ed' is different from the free morpheme *able* [eɪbl] 'having the ability to'!).

Morphemes like -*en*, *un*- and -*able* are also often called **affixes** and the form that they attach to is called a **base**. A base can be a single morpheme: -*able* attaches to *manage* to produce *manageable*. A base may also consist of multiple morphemes, however. In the word *managers*, for instance, -*s* attaches to *manager*, which is made up of the free morpheme *manage* and the affix -*er*.

Affixes come in different types too (Table 3.2).

Table 3.2 Types of affix that we can distinguish.

Type of affix	Definition	Examples
prefix	precedes the base	*un-* in *un-manageable* Māori *whaka-* 'cause' in *whaka-ako* 'teach' See example (4) in Section 3.2.1 for more information.
suffix	follows the base	*-en* in *ox-en* Kurdish *-ik* in *hirç-ik* 'teddy bear' This suffix conveys the smallness of what is referred to. *Hirç* without *-ik* means 'bear'.
circumfix	surrounds the base	Dutch *ge-* . . . *-d* '-ed' in *ge-noem-d* 'named' *Genoemd* is the counterpart of *named* in *they have named their baby Gary*, the so-called 'past participle'. We might be tempted to analyse *ge* as a prefix and *-d* as a suffix. But this analysis ignores the fact that *ge-* and *-d* are both needed to form the past participle of *noem* 'name'. The one cannot appear without the other: *genoem* and *noemd* do not exist. So *ge-* . . . *-d* is, in fact, a single unit that surrounds its base.
infix	occurs inside the base	Eastern Newari *mo* 'not' in *ni-mo-pul* 'not return' This language from Nepal does not use a free morpheme like *not* to negate words like *return*. Instead, to negate *nipul* 'return', it puts the affix before the final syllable of the word and breaks it up this way.

Fun fact!

It is sometimes assumed that forms such as *abso-bloody-lutely* and *fan-fucking-tastic* in English are infixes. However, since *bloody* and *fucking* are words rather than morphemes, these examples are not created through infixing but via **tmesis**. This is the process of inserting a word between two parts of another.

Note that English does not really have any infixes. At first sight, *-er-* in *managers* may look like one but it does not actually split up its base. What we have here is two suffixes. The base *manage* acquires the suffix *-er* to become *manager*. This word then forms the base to which the suffix *-s* attaches itself to produce *managers*.

The distinctions made in the earlier examples are based on independence, as well as position with respect to a base. The second criterion, of function, distinguishes lexical morphemes from grammatical ones. To appreciate this difference, consider (5).

(5) We watched the Queen's speech yesterday and a nice movie about shopaholics.

The **lexical morphemes** here are, from start to finish: *watch, Queen, speech, yesterday, nice, movie, shop* and *-aholic*. They have these traits:

1   They have relatively concrete meanings,
    • referring to specific actions, people, things, qualities and points in time
    • and expressing together the main content of the sentence.

2   They are generally easily replaceable by other morphemes because:
    • many other 'contentful' morphemes exist;
    • new ones are developed all the time;
    • and there is little in a sentence like (5) stopping us from swapping, say, *movie* for *documentary* or *speech* for *webinar*.

3   They can be free or bound morphemes, with *-aholic* as an example of the latter – it has the concrete meaning 'addicted to' and turns *shop* into a new contentful word.

The **grammatical morphemes** in (5) are, from left to right: *we, -ed, the, 's, and, a, about* and *-s*. They have the following characteristics:

1   They have more abstract meanings.
    • They can convey how a sentence's content fits into the situation in which it is uttered (e.g. *we* in (5) informs us that the act of watching was performed by the speaker and at least one other individual).
    • They can express how various pieces of content relate to each other in a sentence (e.g. *'s* in *the Queen's speech* indicates that the Queen has some sort of ownership over the speech, as its writer or deliverer).

2   They are much less easily replaceable than lexical ones because:
    • there are fewer of them;
    • languages do not regularly create new ones – for example, we can substitute the word *a* in *a nice movie* for only a handful of alternatives, such as *some*;
    • and their presence is often required – for example it is impossible to leave out *-ed* in *watched* in (5) because the event is set in the past (*we watch the Queen's speech yesterday* in an unacceptable sentence in English).

3   They can be free morphemes, like *we* and *a*, or bound ones, like *'s* and *-ed*.

The distinction between lexical and grammatical morphemes is closely linked to that between inflection and derivation, the two main types of forming words with which the next section is concerned.

49

3.3 Inflection and derivation

3.3.1 What are they?

Inflection is the process of changing a word's form to make it fit into a sentence grammatically. Take *eat* and *sandwich* in (6).

(6) The professor always eats two sandwiches.

We have to add the grammatical morphemes *-s* and *-es* to these words or, put differently, inflect them to get a well-formed sentence. Without those suffixes or inflections, we would have the unacceptable sentence *the professor always eat two sandwich*. The *-s* on *eat* is needed because a single person who is not the speaker or addressee is doing the eating (no suffix appears in both *professors always eat* or *I/you always eat*!). Technically, we would say that the verb here agrees with its 'third person singular subject' (see Section 3.5.3 for third person and Chapter 4 for subject). The *-es* on *sandwich* is required because *two* indicates that there is more than one of them.

An important characteristic of inflection is that it does not really modify a word's lexical meaning: *-s/-es* adds grammatical information but does not change the activity/thing that *eat/sandwich* refers to. Inflection does not alter the class to which a word belongs either. *Eats* is still a verb in (6) and *sandwiches* a noun. Inflection can also generally be described as regular and productive. By **regular**, we mean that an inflectional change has the same predictable effect whenever it is implemented. Whether *-s* attaches to *eat*, *read* or *write*, it always expresses that a single third party is doing the activity. **Productive** means that the same inflectional change can applied to many, if not most, words of a similar type. *-Es*, and its allomorphs, can be added not just to *sandwich* but also to *bill*, *letter*, *shopaholic* and so on.

Derivation, then, is the process of making NEW lexical words and has very different traits. It does modify a word's meaning, for one thing. If we combine *manageable* with the bound lexical morpheme *un-*, for instance, we get a novel word with the opposite meaning. Derivation often alters a word's class at the same time. *Alphabet* counts as a noun but *-ise* turns it into the verb *alphabetise*. Derivation is typically also less regular than inflection. A derivational affix often has a 'standard' meaning but may have unexpected meanings with particular words. From what we know about *-er* in words such as *manager* and *worker*, for example, we would assume – but wrongly so – that *cooker* signifies 'someone who cooks', instead of 'hob'. Finally, derivation is less productive too. We cannot blindly add the same derivational affix to all words of a similar class. There tend to be numerous exceptions and strange incompatibilities. Take French, which uses *-eur* '-ness' to turn *grand* 'great' and *froid* 'cold' into *grandeur* 'greatness' and *froideur* 'coldness'. However, this suffix cannot serve to express 'smallness' or 'shyness'. The derivations for those words are not *petiteur* and *timideur* but *petitesse* and *timidité*.

3.3.2 Inflection in detail

Both examples of inflection in Section 3.3.1, *-s* and *-es* in *eats* and *sandwiches*, are suffixes. This is not surprising, since inflection frequently takes the form of affixes in the world's languages. Still, other ways to inflect words exist. To illustrate the possibilities, let us look at how plurality is conveyed across the globe:

> For more about plurality in the world's languages, check out the World Atlas of Language Structures online!

- **Internal modification of the base.** Vowel changes, like in Kashmiri, are a case in point. In this language from India and Pakistan, the plural of *mōl* 'father' is *māl'* 'fathers' and that of *gagar* 'mouse' *gagur* 'mice'. Base modification may also involve a change in tone. In Ngiti, a language from the Democratic Republic of the Congo, for instance, the word for 'chief' is *kamà*. Its first syllable has mid tone and its second low tone. To pluralise it, we can turn both into high tones, as in *kámá* 'chiefs'.
- **Reduplication**, which is the morphological phenomenon whereby a base or part of a base gets repeated (think *night* and the expression *night-night* 'sleep tight'!). One language that sometimes uses this process to convey plurality is Indonesian: *kuda* means 'horse', *kudakuda* 'horses'. We also find it in Washo, a Native American language. Its plural reduplication is just partial, though. To pluralise *gewe* 'coyote', we repeat only the final syllable: *gewewe* 'coyotes'.
- **Suppletion**, which is when entirely unrelated morphemes are used. Ket, a language from Russia, can serve as an example. It has a few words of which the plural looks completely different: *oˑks'* 'tree' versus *aˀq* 'trees', *diˑl'* 'child' versus *kʌˀt* 'children'. There is no 'rule' whatsoever linking the two.

Inflection can convey various types of information in the world's languages – too many, in fact, to cover in this chapter. A few widespread types will have to suffice (Table 3.3).

Table 3.3 Types of information that inflection can express.

Category	Discussion
number	informing us how many there are of something, for example, plural *sandwich-es* versus singular *sandwich*
	Nama, spoken in Southern Africa, distinguishes singular *piri-s* 'goat', dual *piri-ra* 'two goats' and plural *piri-di* 'three goats or more'.

(Continued)

Table 3.3 (Continued)

Category	Discussion
tense	informing us when something is happening, for example, past tense *we watch-ed* versus present tense *we watch*

> The Nigerian language of Ijo in (7) uses *-ɲɪmɪ* to express future tense.
> (7) Ijo (Williamson 1965: 74)
>
> | *a* | *bó-ɲɪmɪ* |
> | --- | --- |
> | she | come-FUT |
>
> 'She is going to come.'

case	informing us how words in a sentence relate to the verb

> In Latin in (8a), the suffix *-a* on *agricola* tells us that the farmer is doing the carrying and *-am* on *puellam* that the girl is being carried. They signal, more precisely, that the farmer and the girl are the respective 'subject' and 'object' (see Chapter 4) of *portat* 'carries'.
> (8) Latin
>
> a.
> | *agricol-a* | *puell-am* | *portat* |
> | --- | --- | --- |
> | farmer-SBJ | girl-OBJ | carries |
>
> 'The farmer carries the girl.'
>
> b.
> | *agricol-am* | *puell-a* | *portat* |
> | --- | --- | --- |
> | farmer-OBJ | girl-SBJ | carries |
>
> 'The girl carries the farmer.'
>
> When we switch the suffixes around, like in (8b), with *-a* on *puella* and *-am* on *agricolam*, the girl becomes the doer and the farmer the undergoer.

In focus: how to represent languages other than English?

Linguists often write about languages that their reader does not know. To make sure that they understand the structure of what is discussed, linguists can use the three-line system in (7) and (8). The first line presents the original language in such a way that all words are separated by spaces and all morphemes within words by hyphens. The third line gives a proper English translation of the first one. The middle line, lastly, features a 'gloss' for every single original morpheme. The gloss for lexical morphemes, like *bó* in (7) and *puell* in (8), is their closest English equivalent, so *come* and *girl* here. For grammatical morphemes, like *-ɲɪmɪ* in (7) and *-a* in (8), capitalised abbreviations are used, like FUT (future) and SBJ (subject).

> Check out the Leipzig Glossing Rules for all principles of the system and a list of abbreviations!

SCAN ME

3.3.3 Beyond derivation

The new words mentioned in Section 3.3.1, like *alphabet-ise* and *cook-er*, are all built through affixes. The term 'derivation' is actually often reserved for this way of creating words. Languages have other means at their disposal, however, to make novel words:

- **Reduplication**, repeating (part of) a base, is used for inflection but can also serve to construct new free lexical morphemes. Compare these two words from Tausug, spoken in Malaysia and the Philippines: *magbichara* 'speak' versus *magbichara-bichara* 'gossip'.
- In **conversion**, we simply use a word belonging to one class as one of another class, with no extra affixes. *Drink*, for instance, is originally a verb, as in *I drink too much*. But in *I need a drink*, it acts as a noun.
- **Blends** merge two words into one, phonetically and meaning-wise. *Motorway* and *hotel* blend into *motel* and *breakfast* and *lunch* into *brunch*.
- **Clippings** cut long words short. In Dutch, for example, it is very common to clip *alstublieft* 'please' and *asociaal* 'antisocial' to *alstu* and *aso*.
- In an **acronym**, we pronounce the first letters of a complex phrase as one new word. *Laser* or *Light Amplification by stimulated Emission of Radiation* is a case in point.
- In an **initialism** we utter the first letters of a complex expression as separate syllables: *BBC*, short for British Broadcasting Corporation, sounds like [biːbiːsiː], not [bəbs].

One way of creating new words that may need a few more words of explanation is **backformation**. To explain it, let us consider English *curator*. This word has been in the language since the Middle Ages. English got it from Latin, via French. Probably around 1900, speakers of English started to see (subconsciously) a similarity between *-or* in *curator* and *-er* in *worker* and *reader*. In those words, they could easily remove the suffix to get *work* and *read*. So they assumed that they should be able to do the same with *curator*. The result was *curate*, as in *a Monet expert shouldn't curate a Manet exhibition*. Importantly, this word is the innovation! It is not the base from which *curator* is derived. Another example of backformation is *emote* from *emotion*.

The last phenomenon to be discussed here is **compounding**. It is the process of combining free lexical morphemes to make a new word. Mandarin Chinese, for instance, puts *hū* 'exhale' together with *xī* 'inhale' to create *hūxī* 'breathe'. Compounding occurs in English too, as *bookstore* and *Facebook* show. We can also use these two words to illustrate a distinction often made.

- The meaning of an **endocentric** compound like *bookstore* is directly inferable from its parts: the word refers to a store selling books. Other cases include *razor-sharp* and *south-east*.
- The meaning of an **exocentric** one like *Facebook* cannot be deduced from the parts *face* and *book*. Other examples are *egghead* 'intellectual' and Dutch *feestvarken* 'birthday boy/girl', literally 'party-pig'.

3.4 Morphological types

In Sections 3.1 to 3.3, we have introduced the basic notions of morphology. This knowledge allows us to now have a look at the long-standing tradition in linguistics of classifying languages based on the way that they form words and words into sentences.

The first criterion that the classification relies on is **synthesis**. We can paraphrase it as the extent to which a language uses bound morphemes and separate words. To understand its relevance, compare English in (9) to Chukchi, spoken in Russia, in (10). (Note that 1PL stands for first person plural 'we/us' and IMP for imperative, even if these abbreviations' meanings are not especially important.)

(9) Let us whet our knives!
(10) Chukchi (Skorik 1948: 73)
     mə-wala-mna-rkən
     1PL.IMP-knife-whet-1PL.SBJ
     'Let us whet our knives!'

Both sentences convey the same meaning. But they differ greatly in the number of bound morphemes and words present. Example (9) has hardly any bound morphemes (one exception is *-s* in *knives*) and neither does English in general. A language like English, with no/few bound morphemes and numerous distinct words in a sentence, is considered **analytic** (or isolating). In contrast, (10) contains one word consisting of various bound morphemes. The term for languages with such an extraordinary number of bound morphemes is **polysynthetic**. This type of language often has single words that equate to entire sentences – with several separate words – in other languages, like in (10) versus (9).

English and Chukchi are extremes in a sense (though Mandarin Chinese is probably even more analytic than English). Many languages would employ a moderate number of bound morphemes and fewer distinct words than English but more than Chukchi. As (11) and (12) show, for instance, the Latin equivalent of (9) and (10) has three words, the Turkish equivalent two words. (The examples contain many new abbreviations: M means masculine, PL plural, POSS possessive, SBJV subjunctive, PRS present, ACT active and OPT optative. Certain readers may be familiar with some of these notions but probably not all of them. This is not something to worry about too much! The crucial thing to bear in mind here is that each abbreviation stands for a separate grammatical meaning.)

To learn more about notions such as subjunctive (mood) and active (voice), check out the Summer Institute of Linguistics' glossary of linguistic terms!

(11) Latin
cultr-os   *nostr-os*   *exacu-a-mus*
knife-OBJ.M.PL   1PL.POSS-OBJ.M.PL   whet-SBJV.PRS-1PL.ACT
'Let us whet our knives!'

(12) Turkish
bıçak-lar-ımız-ı   *bile-ye-lim*
knife-PL-1PL.POSS-OBJ   whet-OPT-1PL
'Let us whet our knives!'

Both these languages are therefore (standardly) **synthetic** (instead of polysynthetic).

We can still make a distinction between them, though. The classification's second criterion, of **fusion**, comes into play. Fusion concerns the number of meanings that a morpheme expresses. A fused morpheme is one that has more than one meaning. An example of this type of morpheme is *-os* in *cultros* 'knives' in (11). It tells us:

- that the knives are undergoing the whetting or, more precisely, that they are the object of the sentence – hence OBJ in the gloss;
- at the same time, that 'knife' is masculine in Latin (see *In focus*!) – hence OBJ.M;
- and, also simultaneously, that there is more than one knife – hence OBJ.M.PL.

In short, *-os* expresses three different meanings. Now, when synthetic languages have many fused morphemes like *-os*, like Latin, we call them **fusional**. It is also possible, however, for synthetic languages to possess few fused morphemes. Turkish is a case in point and is classified accordingly as **agglutinating**. The difference may become clear when we compare how 'plural' and 'object' are articulated in (11) and (12). In Latin, we have one morpheme that conveys both meanings. In Turkish, we can see one morpheme for each meaning: *-lar* expresses 'plural' (and just that) and *-ı* 'object' (and only that).

The classification, summarised in Figure 3.2, is handy. We can use the terms to give someone a quick idea of a language's morphology.

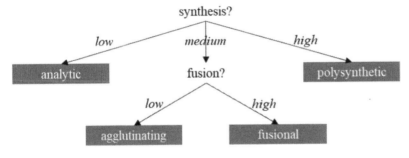

Figure 3.2 Morphological types.

However, it is essential to keep in mind that the boundaries between types are vague. Analytic languages may have some bound morphemes nevertheless (recall -s in *knives*!), or synthetic languages could possess similar amounts of fused and non-fused morphemes.

In focus: what does it mean for Latin 'knife' to be masculine?

In many languages, nouns (see Section 3.5.2) referring to males behave slightly differently from nouns referring to females. If we want to say 'a man/stallion' in French, for instance, we have to use *un* 'a', as in *un homme/étalon* 'a man/stallion'. For 'woman' or 'mare', however, *une* 'a' has to be used: *une femme/jument* 'a woman/mare'. We therefore set the first group apart, as having masculine **gender**, from the second one, with feminine gender.

This difference in behaviour is not limited to clearly male and female nouns, though. Every noun in French requires either *un* or *une*. It is *un verre* 'a glass' and *une cuillère* 'a spoon' (never *une verre* or *un cuillère*), although there is nothing male about a glass or female about a spoon. The randomness of gender with such nouns becomes evident when we look at other languages. In German, for example, *Löffel* 'spoon' requires the masculine form of 'the', that is, *der* (versus *die* for feminine nouns and *das* for a third group of so-called neuter nouns). So, when we say that the Latin word for 'knife' is masculine, we mean that it exhibits the same distinct behaviour as words like *puer* 'boy' and *socer* 'father-in-law'.

With our knowledge of morphemes (Section 3.2), inflection and derivation (Section 3.2) in the world's languages (Section 3.4), we can now comfortably turn to the various classes of word that all of this morphology allows us to distinguish.

3.5 Word classes

3.5.1 What are they?

We already know, from Section 3.1, that different classes of words can be distinguished in a language and that '**word class**' here means a group of words which are:

1   exhibiting similar morphological behaviour – of the types discussed in this chapter;
2   able to appear in the same positions in sentences.

For English, for instance, we can establish a class of words that can take the suffixes -er and -est – like in *smaller, smallest* – or, alternatively, appear with *more* and *most* – like in *more/most difficult*. These words also occur in similar positions: before words like *job*, as in *a small/simple job*, and after words like *is*, as in *the job is simple/hard*. Words like *believe* and *follow* are clearly unable to behave this way. They form another class with their own characteristics. They can, for example, take the suffix *-ed*, like in *he believed/followed me*. They also have the ability to occur after words like *must*, as in *she must believe/follow you*.

The typical term for this first word class is 'adjectives', that for the second one 'verbs'. Traditionally, such classes have been defined mainly in terms of meaning. Verbs, for instance, would be words denoting actions. This definition works well for, say, *drive*. But does *know* in *I know Bulgarian* really refer to an action? Moreover, words that are not verbs can express actions too, like *destruction* in *the destruction of Troy*. So basing our description of word classes solely on meaning is probably not the best approach.

Yet, even definitions relying on morphology and position must take into account that not every member of a class necessarily displays all its features. Compare *alone* and *solitary*, for example. Both can appear with *more* and after *is*, as in (13), and should be considered adjectives.

(13) The man is more alone/solitary than ever.

Like a 'proper' adjective, *solitary* may also occur in a context like *a solitary man*. *Alone*, however, does not share this feature: *an alone man* is not acceptable in English. So, even when not defined in terms of meaning, word classes are fairly fuzzy concepts.

Things get more complicated still when we examine word classes across languages. We know from Section 3.4 that morphology varies greatly between languages. As a consequence, word classes can only truly be defined for individual languages. Take the ability of English verbs to take *-s* (in the present tense). *Work* stays the same in *I/you/we/they work* but requires *-s* with the so-called 'third person singular': *he/she/it works*. This feature is specific to English. We should not put it forward as a universal property of verbs. The Afrikaans for *work*, for one, is always the same: *ek/jy/ons/julle/hulle werk* 'I/you/we/y'all/they work' but also *hy/sy/dit werk* 'he/she/it works'.

We cannot even assume that all languages distinguish the same word classes. To illustrate this, let us consider *uluyaa* 'red' in Mednyj Aleut, a now extinct language from Russia, in (14) (3SG means third person singular).

(14) Mednyj Aleut (Sekerina 1994: 24, 27)
    a. *ulaa*   *uluyaa-it*
      his.house   red-3SG.PRS
      'His house is red.'
    b. *acignax̂* *igax̂taa-it*
      teacher   fly-3SG.PRS
      'The teacher flies.'

Sentence (14a) means 'his house is red'. Our first instinct may therefore be to analyse the word as an adjective, like its English counterpart. We need to look at (14b) too, though. We can see there that the verb *igax̂taa* 'fly' takes the present tense suffix *-it*, which closely resembles *-s* in *flies*. A closer look at (14a) reveals that *uluyaa* also has this suffix! A more literal translation of this sentence would be 'his house reds'. So *igax̂taa* and *uluyaa* actually behave the same way morphologically and there is generally nothing setting words like *uluyaa* apart from other word classes in Mednyj Aleut. In short, the language has no separate class of adjectives.

In the remainder of this chapter, we discuss the word classes that we find most commonly around the world. A basic distinction (see also Section 3.2.3) is made between:

- **major/lexical** classes, which tend to have many members and recruit new ones all the time – for example, verbs, nouns, adjectives and adverbs;
- **minor/grammatical** classes, which normally have fewer members and do not acquire new ones easily – for example, auxiliaries, pronouns, adpositions, conjunctions and determiners.

3.5.2 Major classes

Verbs have the following characteristics:

- <u>Meaning</u>: They typically express the event that an entire sentence centres around. The type of event is varied: in *I know Bulgarian*, it is a state; in *they fell asleep*, a change of state; in *you're reading a textbook*, an activity.
- <u>Morphology</u>: They frequently inflect for tense in the world's languages. *Believed* with *-ed* is a case in point. Verbs also often signal what their doer/subject or undergoer/object is. In Tawala in (15), from Papua New Guinea, the prefixes on the verb inform us what its subject is and the suffixes what its object is. The prefix *i-* says third person SINGULAR, which means that the single dog is doing the killing here. The suffix *-hi* reads third person PLURAL and makes clear that the multiple chickens are undergoing the action.

(15) Tawala (Ezard 1997: 99)
   kedewa   kamkam   i-uni-hi
   dog   chicken   3SG-kill-3PL
   'A dog killed the chickens.'

- <u>Position</u>: They often occupy fixed positions in sentences. In Tawala, verbs always occur at the end. In English, they can only follow (and not precede) auxiliaries. It is *she must believe*, not *she believe must*.

The features of **nouns** are:

- <u>Meaning</u>: They normally denote entities, like *textbook* and *rhinoceros*, or concepts, like *truth* and *love*.

- Morphology: They regularly inflect for number in the world's languages. *Cats* with *-s* is a case in point. They also frequently inflect for case. We can just refer to (11) for an illustration: *-os* on the Latin noun *cultros* 'knives' signals that it is the undergoer/object of the sentence.
- Position: They tend to occupy a predetermined position compared to words relating to them. For instance, if we wanted to qualify the noun *textbooks* with the adjective *incomprehensible*, we would have to say *incomprehensible textbooks* and not *textbooks incomprehensible*.

Adjectives exhibit these traits:

- Meaning: They specify properties or qualities of nouns.
- Morphology: In many languages, they can take so-called 'comparative' marking, as in *small-er*, and 'superlative' marking, as in *small-est*. Adjectives also regularly inflect for the number, gender and/or case of the noun that they accompany, showing that they belong together. Take the French for 'an intelligent boy/girl'. The adjective appears as such with the masculine singular noun 'boy': *le garçon intelligent*. But it takes *-e* when the noun is feminine and singular: *la fille intelligente*.
- Position: Their position often varies depending on the way that they specify a property or quality of a noun: *the job is difficult* versus *the difficult job*. In the first one, we are explicitly stating with the sentence that 'the job' has the property 'difficult'. This use of adjectives is call **predicative** (and is, in English, when they occur after verbs like *be*). In the second way, we just present 'the job' as having the property 'difficult'. This use of adjectives is termed **attributive** (and is, in English, when they precede nouns).

The characteristics of **adverbs**, finally, are the following:

- Meaning: They can modify verbs, like *gradually* in (16a), where it describes the manner of the increase. They are also able to modify adjectives, as in (16b), where the adverb *too* specifies the degree of expensiveness. And they can modify sentences too, like *fortunately* in (16c), which conveys the speaker's attitude toward the sentence's content. It is paraphrasable as 'it is fortunate in my view that'.

(16) a. Prices have increased gradually.
     b. Petrol is too expensive.
     c. Fortunately, we own an EV.

- Morphology: They tend to be simplex and unchangeable words. In English, this is the case for adverbs like *too*, *here* and *now*. But it is not true for all adverbs in the language. Many adverbs of manner and attitude can be analysed as a combination of an adjective and the suffix *-ly*: *gradual-ly* and *fortunate-ly*.
- Position: They can occupy various positions in sentences, as (16) shows.

3.5.3 Minor classes

The first class to be discussed here is **auxiliaries**. In English, they comprise words like *may* in *you may enter*, *will* in *temperatures will rise* and *do* in *they do not exist*. These look a lot like verbs. *Do*, for one, can inflect for tense: *they did not exist*. Auxiliaries are nevertheless different from (lexical) verbs in a number of respects.

1. They usually occur together with a regular verb, in a fixed order. In English, they precede the verb; in other languages, they may have to follow it.
2. They offer grammatical information about the event expressed by the verb. Some situate the event in time, like future tense *are going to*, in *temperatures are going to rise*. Other auxiliaries place it in the so-called 'modal' realm of possibility and necessity. In *you may enter*, for instance, the speaker employs *may* to create the possibility for the hearer to enter. Yet other auxiliaries may not have much meaning at all. They are just required by the grammar of the language. In English, we cannot simply put *not* in something like *they exist*. We do not say *they exist not* but insert *do* to say *they do not exist*.
3. Languages typically have only a limited number of auxiliaries, which often exhibit slightly peculiar behaviour. *Should*, for instance, does not take the expected *-s* with *he/she/it*. It is *he/she/it should work*, not *he/she/it shoulds work*.

Pronouns are words like *they* and *something* in English. Their main characteristic is that they occupy, on their own, the same position in a sentence as a noun and any words accompanying that noun. *They* in (17b) is in the same slot as *our excellent agents in Rome* in (17a) and, in a sense, replaces it. The same holds for *something* in (17b) and *a conspiracy* in (17a).

(17) a. Our excellent agents in Rome uncovered a conspiracy.
     b. They uncovered something.

A widespread feature of pronouns is their ability to inflect. *They* can again serve as an example, with its case inflection. Its subject/doer form is *they*, as in (17b); its object/undergoer form is *them*, as in *he carried them*. Languages also frequently have different sets of pronouns for more specific purposes (Table 3.4).

Table 3.4 Types of pronoun that we can distinguish.

Type of pronoun	Used to
personal	refer to the different parties in a conversation
	– first person includes the speaker (e.g. *I* and *we*); – second person includes the hearer but not the speaker (e.g. *you*); – third person only involves other parties (e.g. *she*, *it* and *they*).

Type of pronoun	Used to
interrogative	ask questions
	WHO uncovered a conspiracy? *WHAT did they uncover?*
reflexive	refer to the same referent as the subject
	The professor cited HERSELF. *Sam Smith believes in THEMSELF.*
possessive	express ownership
	The book is HERS. *I am yours.*
indefinite	refer to unspecific people, things, etc.
	They uncovered SOMETHING. *EVERYONE needs time to relax.*

Note that not all languages make the same distinctions in their personal pronouns. German, for one, distinguishes a singular second person *du* 'you person' from a plural one *ihr* 'you people'.

Examples of our next word class, **adpositions**, are *of* and *with*, in (18). They relate a noun (and its associated words) to the rest of the sentence. The types of relations that they can express are quite varied. *Of* in (18a) connects its noun *France* to *President* as something that they have some sort of ownership over. *With* in (18b) links *a fork* to the event of eating soup as its method. Adpositions also often convey temporal relations (*during dinner*) and spatial ones (*in Paris*).

(18) a. The President of France is arriving tomorrow.
     b. Can you eat soup with a fork?

What adpositions across languages have in common is that they tend not to exhibit any inflection. Languages do differ in the order of adposition and noun:

- In English, adpositions precede their nouns, like in (18). We call this kind of adposition a **preposition**.
- In Nepali, adpositions come after their nouns. This language's equivalent of *from Pokhara* (a Nepalese city) is *Pokhara dekhi*. The term for adpositions such as *dekhi* 'from' is **postposition**.

Conjunctions are invariable words that join a word or a group of words with another one of the same type. In (19a), for instance, *and* connects the noun phrase *his boyfriend* to the noun *Tariq*, as an addition. In (19b), *but* links the sentences *the sorcerer sighed* and *his eyes . . . on them*, and expresses some contrast between them. Here, *when* also joins two sentences: *his eyes glistened* and *he put a deadly curse on them*. The relation between them is one of time.

(19) a. Tariq and his boyfriend want to go on holiday.
    b. The sorcerer sighed but his eyes glistened when he put a deadly curse on them.

Conjunctions can join sentences in further ways. A sentence can be linked to another one as a condition ('if'), a reason ('because') and a concession ('although'), among other things.

    Our last word class is **determiners**. It is, however, more of a cover term for sets of words that may behave similarly in a language but often have very different morphological and positional characteristics in languages. What they share is the following: they occur with nouns and specify which entity/concept that a noun is referring to, or how many entities/concepts that it is referring to (Table 3.5).

Table 3.5 Types of determiner that we can distinguish.

Type of determiner	Used to
demonstrative	point to the referent of a noun
	In English, THIS *apple* is one close to the speaker while THAT *apple* is one further away.
article	signal whether or not the speaker assumes the addressee can identify the referent
	If they presume that this is not the case, they would say AN *apple* in English. In their view, the apple is thus far unknown to the addressee. Otherwise, the speaker would say THE *apple*.
quantifier	indicate the number of referents
	For example, EACH *apple* and *enough apples* in English.

3.6 Conclusion

In this chapter, we have discussed the various ways that languages build words. We have also seen how these words form different classes. Language is obviously more than separate words, though. Words combine to make bigger units and such units combine to create sentences. The ways in which they do that is the topic of the next chapter.

References

Ezard, B. 1997. *A Grammar of Tawala*. Canberra: Pacific Linguistics.

Iwasaki, S. and Ingkaphirom, P. 2005. *A Reference Grammar of Thai*. Cambridge: Cambridge University Press.

Sekerina, I. A. 1994. Copper Island (Mednyj) Aleut (CIA): A mixed language. *Languages of the World*, 8: 14–31.

Skorik, P. 1948. *Ocerk po syntaksisu cukotskogojazyka: Inkorporatsija* [Outline of Chukchee Syntax: Incorporation]. Leningrad: Ucpedgiz.

Williamson, K. 1965. *A Grammar of the Kolokuma Dialect of Ijo*. Cambridge: Cambridge University Press.

4 Syntax
Daniel Van Olmen

4.1 Introduction

Sentences are, in essence, strings of words. But just like there is more to the word *unmanageable* than the sound string [ʌnˈmanɪdʒəbəl] (see Chapter 3), a sentence like (1) exhibits considerable internal structure.

(1) She opened her lecturer's letter without delay.

Intuitively, some words are more closely linked to each other than to other words. For example, *letter* seems to have a tighter bond with *lecturer's* than with *without*. In fact, the entire sequence of words *her lecturer's letter* appears to form one unit in the sentence. The same holds for the string *without delay*, while *she* looks like a unit on its own. Moreover, there clearly exists order within and across these units. We cannot put the words of the units in (1) in just any order, as the unacceptable sentence in (2a) shows. This is true of the units themselves too, as evidenced by (2b).

(2) a. *[She] opened [letter lecturer's her] [delay without].
    b. *[Her lecturer's letter] opened [without delay] [she].

Our instinct also suggests that some units are tied to the verb more strongly than other units. *Opened* in (1) seems to require the presence of both *she* and *her lecturer's letter*, the person opening and the thing opened. If we omit *she*, for instance, we get the ill-formed sentence in (3a). *Without delay*, by contrast, offers supplementary information about the action conveyed by the verb. *Opened* does not actually need this expression of speediness to be there: (1) is perfectly acceptable without it, as (3b) shows.

(3) a. *Opened her lecturer's letter without delay.
    b. She opened her lecturer's letter.

In focus: what does * mean?

Linguists employ the asterisk in at least two ways. In (2), * indicates that the sentence is ill-formed: it does not adhere to the system that the language

---

DOI: 10.4324/9781003045571-5

has to combine words into larger units and sentences. The symbol can serve a similar purpose for morphologically or phonologically ill-formed words. Yet, it is also used by linguists who reconstruct unattested ancestors of languages. They would write the word for 'five' in Proto-Indo-European – the ancestor of languages like English, Greek and Hindi – as *pénk^{w}e, to signal not that it is ill-formed but that it is the form hypothesised for this unattested language.

The way that a language combines words – like *without* and *delay* – into units – like *without delay* – and such units then into entire sentences – like (1) – is called its **syntax**. It enables us to relate the meanings of separate words to one another and thus to express a limitless number of complex ideas. This incredible system is the topic of the present chapter! It starts, in Section 4.2, with a discussion of the units that words can form, also known as phrases (or constituents). In Section 4.3, we look at how phrases are combined to make clauses, a higher-level structure consisting of one verb (phrase) and the (non-verbal) phrases that relate to it. Section 4.4, finally, focuses on the even higher-level structure of the sentence, which may contain more than one clause.

To get a sense of the difference between sentences and clauses, consider *she opened the letter as soon as she got it.* There are two verbs here, each coming with related phrases that make up a clause: *she opened the letter* and *she got it.* These clauses are linked by *as soon as* to form a (complex) sentence.

4.2 Phrases

4.2.1 How to detect phrases

4.2.1.1 Tests

Our initial analysis of the phrases in (1) was purely intuitive. Linguists, like all scientists, prefer more objective evidence, however. That is why they have developed a number of tests that we can apply to see whether something is a **phrase** (Table 4.1). The answer to this question is yes if, after application of the test, the clause is still well-formed. Let us now use (4) to illustrate these tests.

(4) The neighbours planted the new trees in the garden yesterday.

Table **4.1** Tests that we can apply to see whether something is a phrase.

Test	Question to ask	Examples
Movement	can we 'front' the candidate phrase or move it to another position in the clause?	• is *the neighbours* a phrase in (4)? YES, because we can front it or, put differently, move it to a position between *it is* and *that* and put the rest of the clause after *that*: IT IS **the neighbours** THAT *planted the new trees in the garden yesterday.* • is *yesterday* a phrase in (4)? YES, because we can move it to another position in the clause: **Yesterday**, *the neighbours planted the new trees in the garden.* • is *new trees* (without *the*!) a phrase in (4)? NO, because fronting or moving produces ill-formed sentences if we keep *the* in its original place: *It is **new trees** that the neighbours planted the in the garden yesterday.* *The neighbours planted the in the garden **new trees** yesterday.*
Substitution	can we replace the candidate phrase by a single word – typically a pronoun, an adverb or a question word?	• is *the new trees* (with *the*!) a phrase in (4)? YES, because we can replace it by the pronoun *them*: *The neighbours planted **them** in the garden yesterday.* • is *in the garden* a phrase in (4)? YES, because we can replace it by the adverb *there*: *The neighbours planted the new trees **there** yesterday.* • is *the neighbours planted* a phrase in (4)? NO, because no single word exists that can replace it: ***Who** the new trees in the garden yesterday.* *Who* can be a substitute for just *the neighbours*, of course, but not for *the neighbours* plus *planted*!

Test	Question to ask	Examples
coordination	can we add – with *and* – something of the same class or structure to the candidate phrase?	• is *new* a phrase in (4)? YES, because we can add another adjective to it with *and*: *The neighbours planted the new **and special** trees in the garden yesterday.* • is *the garden* a phrase in (4)? YES, because we can add another structure of article plus noun to it with *and*: *The neighbours planted the new trees in the garden **and the greenhouse** yesterday.* • is *in the* a phrase in (4)? NO, because adding another structure of preposition plus article to it produces an ill-formed clause: **The neighbours planted the new trees in the and **around the** garden yesterday.*

The rationale behind these tests is varied.

- **Movement** is based on the following strong tendency in the world's languages: the different components of a phrase need to be next to one another. When we try moving just part of a phrase, as we did for *new trees* without *the*, this requirement is violated. Only full phrases can be moved.
- **Substitution** is directly motivated by the fact that the various components of a phrase make up one entity. If we can replace a string of words by a single one that somehow fills in for all of them, we demonstrate that they are indeed one unit.
- **Coordination**, lastly, works because, across languages, only phrases can normally be linked by 'and'. This restriction makes intuitive sense: how can you join one thing up with a second thing if the first thing is not even really a thing/unit, like *in the* in (4)?

It is important to stress, though, that none of the tests is bullet proof. Attempting to front *new*, for instance, produces the ill-formed sentence in (5). Fortunately, we know from our earlier coordination test that *new* is nevertheless a phrase.

(5) *It is new that the neighbours planted the trees in the garden yesterday.

Similarly, if we apply substitution to *their own business* in (6a), we get (6b) – a fairly awkward stand-in for the original clause. We may therefore be inclined to reject it as a phrase. Fronting, however, yields much better results, as in (6c), especially if we add some emphasis to *own*. So *their own business* appears to be a phrase after all.

(6) a.   People should mind their own business.
    b.   ?People should mind it.
    c.   It is their OWN business that people should mind.

In short, if something fails a test, we should always try the other ones before making a decision. It is, essentially, enough for a word or string of words to pass one of the tests to be considered a phrase.

4.2.1.2 Embedding

The attentive reader may have spotted something exciting in Table 4.1 (for linguists at least!). According to our tests, both *the garden* and *in the garden* count as phrases in (4) and so do both *new* and *the new trees*. What these facts show is that phrases can occur inside of or, put differently, be **embedded** within other phrases. One way of representing the structures of *in the garden* and *the new trees* is given in (7).

(7) a.   [in [the garden]]
    b.   [the [new] trees]

We could offer many other, even more complex examples of embeddings. Those in (8) are just the tip of the iceberg.

(8) a.   Time travel is [[extremely] dangerous].
    b.   I am [bored [by [this chapter]]].
    c.   He always goes to [cities [with [skyscrapers]]].

The possibilities are endless, actually. We can use *cities with skyscrapers* in (8c) to demonstrate why.

• The first level – [*cities* [*with skyscrapers*]] – reveals that phrases starting with nouns, like *cities*, can contain phrases beginning with adpositions (a term defined in Chapter 3 as covering prepositions and postpositions), like *with*.
• The second level – [*with* [*skyscrapers*]] – shows that these phrases with initial adpositions, in turn, include phrases starting with nouns, like *skyscrapers*.

Of such a phrase beginning with a noun, we already know that it can contain a phrase with an initial adposition. So why not add one, like *near parks* in (9a)? Crucially, we can, in principle, do this process of embedding over and over again. It may get a little ridiculous after a while, like in (9b), but it proves at the same time that syntax indeed allows us to express an infinite number of ideas.

(9) a.   He always goes to [cities [with [skyscrapers [near [parks]]]]].
    b.   He always goes to cities with skyscrapers near parks without space for playgrounds with equipment for . . .

Implicit in our discussion of *cities with skyscrapers* is that there are different kinds of phrases. It is not just phrases with nouns and phrases with adpositions, though, as the following section makes clear.

4.2.2 Types of phrase

Let us consider *the new trees* in (4) and *extremely dangerous* in (8a) again. In both cases, there is one word that is more central to the phrase: the noun, *trees*, in the first one and the adjective, *dangerous*, in the second one. For instance, if we try and leave out *trees* in (4), we get the ill-formed clause in (10a). By contrast, removing the adjective *new* from the phrase, like in (10b), causes no problems whatsoever.

(10) a.   *The neighbours planted the new in the garden yesterday.
     b.   The neighbours planted the trees in the garden yesterday.

Likewise, if we wanted to substitute *extremely dangerous* in (8a) with a single word, we would have to use another adjective. *Unsafe* in (11a) would be a possibility. Replacing the phrase by another adverb, however, is impossible, as (11b) shows.

(11) a.   Time travel is unsafe.
     b.   *Time travel is very.

The word that a phrase is centred around is called its **head**. Any other words in a phrase are the **modifiers** of the head. So in *extremely dangerous*, for example, the adjective *dangerous* is the head and the adverb *extremely* its modifier.

Phrases whose head is an adjective behave differently from phrases whose head is a noun. *Extremely dangerous* can, for instance, occur inside of *the new trees*: *the extremely dangerous new trees*. Embedding the other way around does not work, though: **extremely the new trees dangerous*. We therefore need to distinguish different types of phrase, based on the word class that the head belongs to. Recurrent types in the world's languages are noun phrase, verb phrase, adpositional phrase, adjectival phrase and adverbial phrase. But they do not all exist in every individual language. A language without adjectives (see Chapter 3) has no adjectival phrases, of course.

4.2.2.1 Noun phrase

A **noun phrase** or **NP** is a phrase whose head is a noun, like *assistants* or *shop* in (12a), or a pronoun, like *some* or *it* in (12b). Its potential modifiers include adjectives and adpositional phrases, such as *new* and *in this shop* modifying the head *assistants* in (12a).

(12) a. [The new assistants in [this shop]] are helpful.
    b. [Some] like [it] hot.

Whether determiners like *the* and *this* count as modifiers is a matter of much debate, which we cannot go into in this introductory chapter. Let it suffice to say that:

- proper modifiers are optional – the adjective and the adpositional phrase in the NP *the new assistants in this shop* can easily be left out, as *the assistants are helpful* shows;
- nouns typically require SOME determiner to be present, in English at least – the NP *this shop* may feature other determiners, like in *the shop* or *any shop*, but would be ill-formed without one, as **the new assistants in shop* shows.

For more about the order of adjectives and nouns in the world's languages, check out the World Atlas of Language Structures online!

An important trait of NPs is that the various words within them tend to occur in a fixed order. In English, for instance, demonstratives always precede adjectives, which in turn always come before nouns. We can see this order in the translation of (13) and any other arrangement is clearly impossible (e.g. **big deep that river*). The order of words within NPs may differ from language to language, though. Ewe, spoken in Ghana and Togo, in (13) is a case in point: demonstratives like *má* 'that' always follow adjectives like *gã̌* 'big' and *goglŏ* 'deep', which in turn always come after nouns like *tɔ* 'river'.

(13) Ewe (Ameka 1991: 77)

tɔ	gã̌	goglŏ	má
river	big	deep	that

'that big deep river'

As discussed in Chapter 3, in many languages, modifiers also inflect for certain properties of their head noun.

- In Dutch, for one, *jongen* 'boy' belongs to a group of similarly behaving nouns that we call masculine and *huis* 'house' to one called neuter. When the adjective *klein* 'small' modifies an indefinite neuter noun, it does not change: *een klein huis* 'a small house'. But when modifying an indefinite masculine noun, it takes the ending *-e*: *een kleine jongen* 'a small boy'.
- Likewise, the English demonstrative *this* with singular nouns, like in *this dialect*, changes to *these* with plural nouns, like in *these dialects*.

The technical term for this phenomenon – a word changing form because of a word that it relates to – is **agreement**.

4.2.2.2 Verb phrase

A **verb phrase** or **VP** is a phrase whose head is a verb. Some examples of VPs are given in (14). The auxiliaries, which always precede the verb in English, can be considered modifiers (although this is, again, not uncontroversial).

(14) a.   They [eat] snails.
      b.   They [must eat] snails.
      c.   They [are going to be eating] snails.

They have a variety of meanings.

- *Must* conveys obligation, which is part of the domain of **modality** – covering expressions of how necessary, possible, desirable or real an event is.
- *Are going to* marks the (future) time of the event or, put differently, (future) **tense**.
- *Be*, plus *-ing*, presents the event as a continuous activity. This meaning belongs to the domain of **aspect**, which conveys not when something happens but how it extends over time.

In other languages, such meanings are expressed by elements bound to the verb in a particular order. Take Nyankore, spoken in Uganda, for instance. If we want to say that some event will take place in the DISTANT FUTURE in this language, we need to attach *rya-* to the verb as in (15). It always precedes the verb and follows the marker referring to the doer (or rather, subject – see Section 4.3), 'he' here. (The ending *-a* is modal. Its INDicative meaning signals that the event is in the realm of reality – instead of, say, the desirable, conveying something like 'may he hit!'.)

(15) Nyankore (Morris and Kirwan 1972: 83)
      a-rya-teer-a
      he-DIST.FUT-hit-IND
      'he will hit'

In focus: is *snails* part of the VP in *they eat snails*?

It is often maintained that VPs are not limited to the verb and its auxiliaries. The VP in (i)a would also include the embedded phrases *snails*, *in Paris* and *yesterday* as modifiers of the head *ate*. One argument in favour of this position, for English, comes from substitution. In the answer in (i)b, a single verb *did* stands in for *ate* and all phrases following it.

(i) a. My parents [ate snails in Paris yesterday].
    b. Who ate snails in Paris yesterday? – My parents did.

In many other languages, the evidence from the tests for an English-like 'extended' VP is less convincing. The structure of VPs may thus not be the same in all languages. In the rest of this chapter, we will therefore work with a 'narrow' analysis of the VP, which does not include any other phrases, even for English.

4.2.2.3 Adpositional phrase

An **adpositional phrase** or **PP** is a phrase that has an adposition as its head and contains an NP (the first P in the traditional abbreviation PP stands for PREposition or POSTposition). Some examples are given in (16): the postposition *aside* heads a PP that includes the NP *a number of exceptions* and the preposition *in* a PP containing the NP *English*.

(16) [A number [of exceptions] aside], postpositions do not occur [in English].

At first sight, it may seem somewhat counterintuitive to analyse adpositions as heads. Is *English* not more central to *in English* than *in*? We should not underestimate the importance of *in*, though. Without it, *English* would be unconnected: **postpositions do not occur English*. The adposition tells us HOW the NP is related to the rest of the clause. More proof that adpositions are the heads is provided by Latin in (17).

(17) Latin
    a. *ad*   *puellam/*puellā*
        toward   girl
        'toward the girl'
    b. *cum*   *puellā/*puellam*
        with   girl
        'with the girl'

After *ad* 'toward', in (17a), the singular noun for 'girl' can only look like *puellam*; after *cum* 'with', in (17b), only like *puellā*. The adpositions determine the noun's form, in other words. We have seen this sort of behaviour before, of course – within NPs, where the noun determines the adjective's form in Dutch or the demonstrative's form in English. So adpositions clearly have the same function in PPs as nouns in NPs, that of head!

4.2.2.4 Adjectival and adverbial phrases

The final two types are **adjectival phrases** or **AdjPs** and **adverbial phrases** or **AdvPs**. Some examples of AdjPs are presented in (18). Their heads are the adjectives *afraid* and *bad*, which are further modified here by the PP *of the dark* and the adverb *really*.

(18) a. I'm [afraid of the dark].
     b. We watched a [really bad] movie.

In (19), we see some instances of AdvPs. Their heads are the adverbs *well* and *yesterday*. The first one features yet another adverb, *very*, which modifies *well*.

(19) Tyrion slept [very well] [yesterday].

With this knowledge of phrases, we can now display the structure of entire clauses.

4.2.3 How to represent phrases

If we applied our tests to (20), we would find the following phrases: the NPs *we* and *the rest of the ship*, the VP *will paint* and the AdjP *black*. The tests would also reveal that the second NP contains the PP *of the ship*, which in turn has the embedded NP *the ship*.

(20) We will paint the rest of the ship black.

A common way of representing the structure of a clause like (20) is through so-called **syntactic trees**. They come in various shapes and forms, depending on the theoretical approach of the linguist drawing the tree. In the version in Figure 4.1:

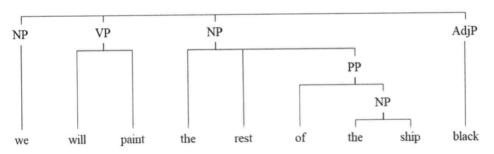

Figure 4.1 Syntactic tree for *we will paint the rest of the ship black*.

- all non-embedded phrases (i.e. *we*, *will paint*, *the rest of the ship* and *black*) occur as separate 'nodes' at the top of the tree;
- we link them to one another with the upper horizontal line because, together, they make up a clause (in that sense, they ARE embedded in the clause);

- each phrase receives a label describing its type (e.g. NP for *we*);
- if a phrase has no embedded phrases, we use vertical lines to join its label directly to the word(s) that it contains (e.g. VP to *will* and *paint*);
- if a phrase does include an embedded phrase, we create a new node in the tree at a lower level and assign it a label (e.g. *of the ship* gets the label PP, which appears under the label NP used for the entire phrase *the rest of the ship*).

Another way of capturing the structure of (20) involves brackets around every phrase, like in (21a). Embedded phrases are represented by brackets within brackets. For such instances, we need to take care that every [is closed by a corresponding]. So *ship* in (21a), for example, is followed by three closing brackets: the first one signals the end of the NP [*the ship*], the middle one that of the PP [*of* [*the ship*]] and the last one that of the NP [*the rest* [*of* [*the ship*]]]. To specify the type of each phrase, we can add the right label after its opening bracket and before its closing bracket, as in (21b).

(21) a. [We] [will paint] [the rest [of [the ship]]] [black].
     b. [NP We NP] [VP will paint VP] [NP the rest [PP of [NP the ship NP] PP]NP] [AdjP black AdjP].

These systems of displaying structure are useful because they can, for instance, help us spell out ambiguity. Consider (22a). This clause has two potential interpretations: 'she photographed the boy who had a phone' and 'she used a phone to photograph the boy'.

(22) a. She photographed the boy with a phone.
     b. It is the boy with a phone that she photographed.
     c. It is with a phone that she photographed the boy.

They have different structures, though, as fronting shows.

- If we front *the boy with a phone*, as in (22b), only the first interpretation is possible. The test reveals that, when (22a) means 'she photographed the boy who had a phone', *the boy with a phone* forms a single NP with an embedded PP *with a phone*. So the structure of the first interpretation looks as follows in Figure 4.2.

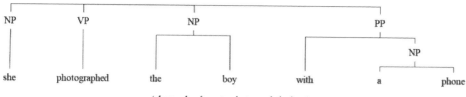

'she used a phone to photograph the boy'

Figure 4.2 Syntactic tree for *she photographed [the boy with a phone]*.

- If we just front *with a phone*, as in (22c), only the second interpretation is possible. This test reveals that, when (22a) means 'she used a phone to photograph the boy', *with a phone* is a non-embedded phrase on par with *she, photographed* and *the boy*. So the structure of the second interpretation is (Figure 4.3):

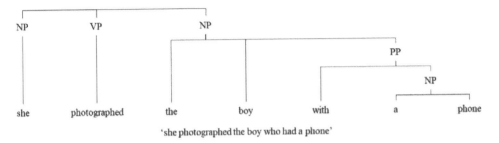

'she photographed the boy who had a phone'

Figure 4.3 Syntactic tree for *she photographed [the boy] [with a phone]*.

Determining the phrase structure of a clause is the first step in its analysis. The next one is answering the question that Section 4.3 is about: what is each phrase actually doing in the clause?

4.3 Clauses

We know from Sections 4.1 and 4.2 that a **clause** is a unit consisting of one VP and other types of phrase that are somehow linked to that VP. These relations can be analysed in different ways. In Section 4.3.1, we look at them from the point of view of meaning and introduce the notion of semantic role and the distinction between arguments and adjuncts. Section 4.3.2 studies the relations from a grammatical perspective and discusses concepts such as subject and object. In Section 4.3.3, finally, we distinguish different types of clause.

4.3.1 Meaning relations

4.3.1.1 Semantic roles

A first way to approach the question what each phrase is actually doing in a clause is, as mentioned earlier, to focus on meaning. In (23), for instance, there are three non-embedded phrases – besides the VP *are blowing up*: the NPs *they* and *the mine* and the PP *with a few sticks of TNT*.

(23) [They] are blowing up [the mine] [with a few sticks of TNT].

Meaning-wise, these phrases all relate to the VP in a different manner. *They* is the doer of the action while *the mine* is undergoing it. *With a few sticks of TNT* conveys the means by which the action is carried out. The technical term for the part that a phrase plays with regard to the verb in a clause's meaning is **semantic role**. The list of semantic roles includes (see Table 4.2):

Table 4.2 Semantic roles that a phrase can have in a clause.

Semantic role	Definition	Examples
agent	the doer or wilful initiator of an event	*They are blowing up the mine.* *I was bitten **by a dog**.*
patient	the undergoer of an event, typically going through a change because of it	*I was bitten by a dog.* *The lecturer sent **a letter** to her student.* *I goes through a very clear change, from unscathed to injured. The change that a letter undergoes is more abstract: it is one of location or ownership.*
recipient	the receiver of some patient in an event	*The lecturer sent a letter **to her student**.* *Tom gave **Jerry** a cake.*
beneficiary	the entity profiting from an event	*Tom baked **Jerry** a cake.* *Dawn poured a glass of wine **for Jennifer**.* Note the difference between *Tom gave Jerry a cake* and *Tom baked Jerry a cake*! In the first clause, Jerry actually got a cake. In the second one, this is not guaranteed. Tom may have baked a cake for Jerry but could have dropped it on the floor before being able to give it to him.
experiencer	the entity in some physical, cognitive or emotional state	***She** saw the mouse.* ***He** is afraid.* *She* is not an agent here. Since agents are wilful, we can always add *on purpose* to a clause with an agent. This works for *she looked at the mouse on purpose* but is weird for **she saw the mouse on purpose*. The reason is that you CAN be in control of looking at something but not of seeing something.
possessor	the more or less abstract owner of another entity	***Jack** has got blue eyes.* ***Captain Sally** has a lover in every port.*

Semantic role	Definition	Examples
location	the place at which an event takes place	*Captain Sally has a lover **in every port**.* ***Berlin** will be very warm tomorrow.*
time	the time at which an event takes place	*Berlin will be very warm **tomorrow**.* ***These days**, money does buy happiness.*
instrument	the means by which an event is performed	*These days, **money** does buy happiness.* *They are blowing up the mine **with a few sticks of TNT**.*

Other distinctions are possible. In the realm of location, for example, we could distinguish the source of movement (e.g. *going from Spain*) from its goal (e.g. *going to Italy*). The semantic roles in the table are the most prominent ones, however. We should also emphasise that these meaning relations are independent from form:

- the same semantic role can be expressed by different types of phrase – the NP *they* in *they are blowing up the mine* is an agent and so is the PP *by a dog* in *I was bitten by a dog*;
- different semantic roles can be conveyed by the same phrase type in the same position – the clause-initial NP in *she saw a mouse* is an experiencer, that in *Jack has got blue eyes* a possessor and that in *money does buy happiness* an instrument.

For two final comments, we can look at (24). First, phrases embedded within other phrases do not have a semantic role at the level of the clause. Consider the NP *the queen's* in (24a). It is part of the NP *the queen's necklace*, which functions as the patient of the clause. But we cannot link *the queen's* itself straight to the verb *stole*. (Within the NP *the queen's necklace*, we could nonetheless say that it serves as the possessor of *necklace*.)

(24) a. He stole [[the queen's] necklace].
     b. He is [a thief].

Second, not every phrase has a semantic role. Consider the NP *a thief* in (24b) and the roles' definitions in the table. None really appears to fit. *A thief* plays no distinct meaningful part in the 'event of being'. It just completes the description of *he*.

4.3.1.2 Arguments and adjuncts

The phrases in a clause can be differentiated in terms of semantic roles. But we can also make a binary distinction in phrases – which, in a sense, bridges meaning and form – between arguments and adjuncts.

- **Arguments** are phrases whose presence in the clause is generally necessary. They contain the entities directly involved in the event or, put differently, are required by the meaning of the verb.
- **Adjuncts** are phrases that provide extra information about the event. They are not immediately evoked by the verb and can typically be left out.

To appreciate the difference, let us examine (25a). The verb in this clause, *lit*, seems to entail two entities: an agent, the one lighting something, and a patient, the one being lit. The phrases with those semantic roles, *the detective* and *her cigarette*, are compulsory in the clause. If we leave them out, we get the ill-formed examples in (25b) and (25c). They are the arguments, in other words. The AdvP *eagerly*, by contrast, does not need to be expressed, as (25d) shows. It offers additional information about the way that the cigarette was lit. So it is an adjunct.

(25) a. [The detective] lit [her cigarette] [eagerly].
b. *Lit her cigarette eagerly.
c. *The detective lit eagerly.
d. The detective lit her cigarette.

Some more examples are given in (26). The phrases in bold are arguments while those in italics are adjuncts. (Try taking each one out and see whether the clause is still well-formed!)

(26) a. **[Nicholas]** put **[the pizza]** **[in the oven]** [*two hours ago*].
b. **[He]** is sleeping [*quite soundly*] [*on the sofa*] [*now*].

Occasionally, though, arguments may be left implicit nevertheless. We will all agree, for example, that the event of eating normally requires an agent – the eater – and a patient – whatever (or whoever . . .) is eaten. Yet, in the clause *I am eating* in (27), only one argument is present, the agent *I*. We obviously understand that something is being eaten. But its exact nature is not relevant in the situation in (27), which is why it is absent from the clause.

(27) Don't bother me! [I] am eating.

The distinction between arguments and adjuncts is rooted in the verb's meaning. It is also reflected in syntax, however: languages tend to treat arguments differently from adjuncts. The attentive reader may, for instance, have noticed that, in the English examples given earlier, the argument phrases occur closer to the verb than the adjunct ones. It is such grammatical rather than meaning-based relations that the next section is concerned with.

4.3.2 Grammatical relations

4.3.2.1 Subject

A first way that an argument can be related to the verb grammatically is as its **subject**. Some examples are given in (28), between square brackets. What they immediately show is that we cannot describe the notion of subject in terms of meaning. *Penguins* in (28a) has the semantic role of agent, *my house* in (28b) that of patient and *Sansa* in (28c) that of experiencer.

(28) a.   [Penguins] rarely attack polar bears.
     b.   Last week, [my house] burned down.
     c.   [Sansa] doesn't like Daenerys.

Subject is a grammatical notion, with particular syntactic and morphological features. In English, these features include the following (Table 4.3):

Table 4.3 How to identify a subject in English.

Feature	Discussion
The subject is an NP that normally comes directly before the VP in statements.	In (28a), the VP *attack* is preceded by the phrases *rarely* and *penguins*. Since *rarely* is an AdvP and not an NP, *penguins* is the subject. In the same vein, *burned down* in (28b) is preceded by the phrases *last week* and *my house*. Both are NPs but *my house* is the subject because it occurs right before the VP.
	Some exceptions exist, though! In *here comes Johnny*, for instance, the subject *Johnny* actually follows the verb.
When the subject is a singular third party, the verb takes the ending -*s* in the present tense.	The NPs in (28a), *penguins* and *polar bears* are both plural third parties (they do not include the speaker or the addressee). If we make *polar bears* singular, the verb stays the same: *penguins rarely attack a polar bear*. However, if we turn *penguins* singular, the verb changes: *a penguin rarely attacks polar bears*. The fact that *attack* takes -*s* when *penguins* is made singular shows that it, rather than *polar bears*, is the subject here.
	The verb does not change with first or second person singular versus plural subjects: *I/we/you/y'all rarely attack polar bears* (barring a few exceptions, e.g. *I am* but *we are*). There are also no changes in the past tense: *penguins/a penguin rarely attacked polar bears*.

(Continued)

Table 4.3 (Continued)

Feature	Discussion
When the subject is a personal pronoun, it takes the form of *I*, *he*, *she*, *we* or *they* rather than *me*, *him*, *her*, *us* or *them*.	In (28c), we have two NPs, *Sansa* and *Daenerys*. If we replace *Daenerys* by a personal pronoun, we have to use *her*. *She* would result in an ill-formed sentence: **Sansa doesn't like she*. So *Daenerys* is not the subject. But if we substitute *Sansa* by a personal pronoun, only *she* is an option. **Her does not like Daenerys* is not an acceptable clause. So *Sansa* is the subject here.

> Not all personal pronouns have a form specific to the subject. The second person looks like *you* both as a subject, as in *you don't like Daenerys*, and not as a subject, as in *Sansa doesn't like you*.

We can use these features to identify the subject of an English clause. Applying them blindly to other languages would not work, though. Languages differ in the properties that the subject has. In Irish, for one, its position is not before but immediately after the verb, which starts the clause. *Na sagairt* 'the priests' in (29) is a case in point.

(29) Irish (Dillon and Ó Cróinín 1961: 166)

léann	[*na*	*sagairt*]	*na*	*leabhair*
read	the	priests	the	books

'The priests are reading the books.'

Moreover, in French, the verb does not only change or, put differently, **agree** with third person singular subjects in the present tense. In the simple past, the verb ends in: *-ais* with a first person singular subject, like in (30a); *-ions* with a first person plural one, as in (30b); and *-iez* with a second person plural one, like in (30c). (And, in Afrikaans, the subject has no effect on a verb's form at all!)

(30) French
    a. *j'attaqu-ais*
       'I was attacking'
    b. *nous attaqu-ions*
       'we were attacking'
    c. *vous attaqu-iez*
       'you all were attacking'

Likewise, in Latin, it is not just pronouns that possess a form specific to the subject. The (feminine singular) nouns in (31) take a form ending in *-a* when they are the subject of the clause. This noun is *puella* 'girl' in (31a), whose meaning is therefore 'the girl loves the queen', and *regina* 'queen' in (31b), meaning 'the queen loves the girl'.

(31) Latin
  a. *puell-a*   *regin-am*   *amat*
      girl-NOM   queen-ACC   loves
      'The girl loves the queen.'
  b. *puell-am*   *regin-a*   *amat*
      girl-ACC   queen-NOM   loves
      'The queen loves the girl.'

This phenomenon, of words changing form to signal their grammatical relation, is called **case** (see also Chapter 3) and the term for the form/case of subjects is NOMinative. So we can describe *I, he, she, we* and *they* in English as nominative personal pronouns. (Note, though, that, in many languages, all pronouns are like *you* in that they do not change form at all. Mandarin Chinese is such a language.)

4.3.2.2 Direct object

When a verb has two arguments, they may be linked to it grammatically not only as its subject but also as its **direct object**. In (32), we provide some examples. It is evident that this grammatical relation too is undefinable in terms of semantic roles. *Roads* in (32a) is a patient, *the gods* in (32b) an experiencer and *the lands of Mordor* in (32c) a location.

(32) a. They built [roads] last week.
     b. Your sacrifice pleases [the gods].
     c. Orcs inhabit [the lands of Mordor].

The grammatical features of the direct object in English, which we can use to identify one in a clause, are the following (Table 4.4):

Table 4.4 How to identify a direct object in English.

Feature	Discussion
The direct object is an NP.	All bracketed phrases in (32) are NPs. In a clause like *she laughed at me*, by contrast, the phrase *at me* is an argument but also a PP. So it is typically not analysed as a direct object, even if it shares other features with this grammatical relation (see the following examples!).
The direct object comes immediately after the VP in statements with two arguments.	In (32a), two NPs follow the VP, *roads* and *last week*. The one that needs to come directly after *built* is the direct object (consider the ill-formed clause *they built last week roads*). Similarly, *the gods* in (32b) and *the lands of Mordor* in (32c) immediately follow rather than precede the VP and are therefore direct objects rather than subjects.
	There are exceptions. Consider *Marlowe* in *I have never read Shakespeare but Marlowe, I adore*. The 'normal' order of *I adore Marlowe* shows that it is the direct object. Its current special position, before *I adore*, highlights the contrast with *Shakespeare*.

(Continued)

Table 4.4 (Continued)

Feature	Discussion
The direct object can become the subject of a corresponding passive clause.	The **passive** is a way of shuffling grammatical relations around in a clause. In the so-called **active** clause in (32c), *orcs* is the subject. In the corresponding passive *the lands of Mordor are inhabited by orcs*, the original subject turns into a *by*-phrase and, most importantly here, the direct object becomes the subject. How do we know that *the lands of Mordor* is the subject now? Because, when we make it singular, the verb changes: *the land of Mordor is inhabited by orcs*.

> We can use this feature to rule something out as a direct object. For instance, *a nurse* in *he was a nurse* is not a direct object because it cannot be the subject of a corresponding passive: **a nurse was been by him*. But we should not use this test as definitive proof that something is a direct object. We can, for example, turn *me* in *she laughed at me* into the subject of *I was laughed at by her*. But it is part of the PP *at me* and therefore not a direct object.

The direct object's properties – just like the subject's – vary between languages. Its clause position, for one, may be different. In Irish, the direct object normally comes after verb and subject, like *na leabhair* 'the books' in (29). In German Sign Language, it typically occurs between subject and verb, like the sign BEER in (33).

(33) German Sign Language (Bross 2020: 82)
marjolaine beer buy
'Marjolaine bought a beer.'

Words may also change form or, more technically, case to indicate that they are the direct object of a clause. In Latin, for instance, (feminine singular) nouns take the ending *-am* when they are the direct object, like *reginam* 'queen' in (34) – versus the ending *-a* when they are the subject, like *puella* 'girl' here. The term for the case of direct objects is ACCusative.

(34) Latin
puell-a   *regin-am*   *amat*
girl-NOM   queen-ACC   loves
'The girl loves the queen.'

In focus: so English is an SVO language?

The basic order of subject (S), direct object (O) and verb (V) is a good way to characterise a language's syntax. In English, it is ordinarily S before V before O, which is why we call the language SVO. Irish, by contrast, is a VSO language, like in (29), and German Sign Language an SOV one, as in (33). Crucially, the order of S, O and V is not an isolated fact, which is why

For more about the order of S, O and V in the world's languages, check out the World Atlas of Language Structures online!

it is often a good shorthand for a language's syntax. For example, SVO/VSO languages tend to have prepositions and SOV ones postpositions. SOV languages are also likelier to mark S and O by cases than SVO/VSO languages. What is remarkable too is that more than 80% of the world's languages have one of the three orders already mentioned. The other possible orders of S, O and V – VOS, OVS and OSV – have all been attested but are very rare. What they share is that S comes after O. In the three frequent orders, we find the opposite situation. So we could say that languages generally prefer the subject to precede the direct object!

4.3.2.3 Indirect object

An argument may also be grammatically linked to a verb as its **indirect object**. This grammatical relation is, however, only found in clauses that already possess a direct object. In (35a), for example, the indirect object *Bill* appears alongside the direct object *ten pounds*. Without this second phrase, the clause would not make much sense: *Gaius lent Bill*. The indirect object's typical semantic roles are recipient, as in (35b), and beneficiary, as in (35c).

(35) a. Gaius lent [Bill] ten pounds.
b. Laura gave [Sharon] a kiss.
c. Felix poured [Tom] a drink.

Further characteristics of the indirect object in English are (Table 4.5):

Table 4.5 How to identify an indirect object in English.

Feature	Discussion
The indirect object is an NP.	All bracketed phrases in (35) are NPs. We can rephrase them as PPs, like in (35a) as *Gaius lent ten pounds to Bill* and in (35c) as *Felix poured a drink for Tom*. As PPs, they are typically not analysed as indirect objects, however, but as obliques (see the following examples!).
The indirect object comes before the direct object.	The verb *gave* in (35b) is followed by two NPs. The first one is the indirect object and the next one the direct object. If we switch them around, we get the ill-formed clause *Laura gave a kiss Sharon*.

(Continued)

Table 4.5 (Continued)

Feature	Discussion
The indirect object can become the subject of a corresponding passive clause.	We already know that direct objects can become the subject of a corresponding passive clause. This fact is confirmed for *ten pounds* in (35a) by *ten pounds were lent to Bill by Gaius*. Indirect objects have the same property, as the clause *Bill was lent ten pounds by Gaius* shows.

In many languages, words may again possess a form/case specific to the indirect object. Latin (feminine singular) nouns, for instance, end in *-ae* when they function as an indirect object. In (36), *regina* 'queen' has the nominative ending *-a* and is the subject, *puellam* 'girl' takes the accusative ending *-am* and is the direct object while *gemmae* 'jewel' has the so-called DATive ending *-ae* and is the indirect object. So the clause means 'the queen gives the girl a jewel'.

(36) Latin
    regin-a puell-am   gemm-ae   donat
    queen-NOM   girl-ACC   jewel-DAT   gives
    'The queen gives the girl a jewel.'

4.3.2.3 An aside about transitivity

We can now differentiate clauses, based on whether they have a subject, direct object and/or indirect object. Clauses with a subject only, like (37a), are called **intransitive**. Clauses that just have a subject and a direct object, such as (37b), are considered **transitive** and, finally, clauses with a subject, a direct object as well as an indirect object, such as (37c), are called **ditransitive**.

(37) a. [My house] burned down.
     b. [They] built [roads] last week.
     c. [Laura] gave [Sharon] [a kiss].

It is important to realise, though, that a clause's (in/di)transitivity is not the same as the number of arguments it has. Consider (38a). This clause has three arguments: leaving *he*, *the pizza* or *in the oven* out produces the ill-formed examples in (38b).

(38) a. He put the pizza in the oven.
     b. *Put the pizza in the oven./*He put the pizza./*He put in the oven.
     c. The pizza was put in the oven by him.
     d. *The oven was put the pizza in by him.

Yet, it is not ditransitive! *He*, as a nominative pronoun, is obviously the subject. And *the pizza* is the direct object, as it can become the subject of the corresponding passive in (38c). But *in the oven* is not an indirect object. It cannot, for one, be the subject of a corresponding passive, as (38d) makes clear. In short, (38a) is a transitive clause with three arguments.

4.3.2.4 Subject and object complements

To conclude Section 4.3.2, we need to discuss three more grammatical relations. The first one is **subject complement**, an example of which is offered in (39a). The NP *leader of the Green Party* follows the VP, like a direct object, but is not actually a direct object. This fact is evident from the ill-formed clause in (39b): *leader of the Green Party* cannot become the subject of a corresponding passive.

(39) a. She became [leader of the Green Party].
     b. *Leader of the Green Party was become by her.

What the NP actually does is complement information about the subject, by describing it further or identifying it. Subject complements appear with so-called linking or **copular** verbs – like *be, become, feel* or *smell* in English. They also do not need to be NPs, as (40) shows.

(40) a. Ahmed is [in Norway] right now.
     b. This fish smells [bad].

The second, related grammatical relation is **object complement**. At face value, the NP *leader of the Green Party* in (41a) may again look like a direct object but this analysis is contradicted by the ill-formed passive (41b). What the NP really does is complement information about the actual direct object *her*: she is now leader of the Green Party. Like subject complements, object complements need not be NPs. The AdjP *crazy* in (41c) is a case in point.

(41) a. They have made her [leader of the Green Party].
     b. *Leader of the Green Party has been made her by them.
     c. The children drove me [crazy].

4.3.2.5 Oblique

Our final grammatical relation is **oblique**. This term refers to any phrase that relates to the verb but has not received 'special' grammatical treatment as its subject, direct or indirect object and is not a subject or object complement. Some examples are given in (42).

(42) a. They built roads [last week].
     b. He is sleeping [quite soundly] [on the sofa].
     c. He put the pizza [in the oven].

Obliques are typically adjuncts: the NP *last week* in (42a) and the AdvP *quite soundly* and the PP *on the sofa* in (42b) all offer additional and optional information. Argument obliques exist as well, however. *In the oven* in (42c) is one of them.

In focus: do all languages have the same grammatical relations?

The answer to this question is negative. Let us, for instance, have a look at the first person singular (1SG) in Kewa, spoken in Papua New Guinea. Clause (i)a suggests that its 'direct object' form, corresponding to English *me*, is *ní* and example (i)b that its 'subject' form, corresponding to English *I*, is *némé*. But this analysis runs into problems in (i)c. The equivalent of *I* here is not *némé*, as we would expect, but *ní*.

(i) Kewa (Franklin 1971: 63, 71, 70)

    a. *áápímí*   *ní*   *táa*   c.*ní*   *pírawa*
       who   1SG   hit   1SG   sat.down
       'Who hit me?'   'I sat down.'
    b. *némé*   *irikai*   *táwa*
       1SG   dog   hit
       'I hit the dog.'

To describe what is going on, linguists typically distinguish:

- S, the sole argument of an intransitive clause ('I' in 'I sat down');
- A, the first argument of a transitive clause ('I' in 'I hit the dog');
- P, the second argument of a transitive clause ('me' in 'who hit me?').

In English, the S in (ic) is identical in form/case to the A in (ib), both appearing as *I*. And the P in (ic) looks different, like *me*. These forms are the (nominative) subject and the (accusative) direct object as we know them. In Kewa, however, the S in (ic) has the same form/case as the P in (ic): *ní*. And the A in (ib) is different: *némé*. Calling either of these forms the (nominative) subject or the (accusative) direct object would not do justice to the facts. Clearly, the grammatical relations in Kewa diverge from those in English. Kewa is, moreover, just the tip of the iceberg! (By the way, a form like *ní* – used for both S and P – is usually said to exhibit **absolute** case. The case term for a form like *némé* – used just for A – is **ergative**).

4.3.3 Subordinate versus (types of) main clauses

Most of our linguistic examples until now have been instances of the same 'declarative main' clause type. A **main clause** is a clause that is not embedded within another clause. To clarify this notion, we can contrast it to the structures bracketed in (43).

(43) a. You should never have told him [that we skipped the meeting].
     b. Her girlfriend was preparing dinner [when Aiko got home].

Both *we skipped the meeting* in (43a) and *Aiko got home* in (43b) are obviously clauses, each with a verb and phrases related to it. They also act as a phrase within another clause, though, as the substitution test in (44a) and the movement test in (44b) demonstrate. Such clauses – embedded within another clause through, for example, conjunctions like *that* and *when* – are called **subordinate**. We discuss them in more detail in Section 4.4.

(44) a. You should never have told him [this].
     b. It is [when Aiko got home] that her girlfriend was preparing dinner.

A main clause, like the entire structure from *you* to *this* in (44a), is not part of another clause. This does not mean, to be clear, that a main clause cannot itself contain subordinate clauses! In (43b), for instance, the main clause runs from *her girlfriend* to *home* but also includes the subordinate clause *when Aiko got home*, as the brackets in (45) show.

(45) [Her girlfriend was preparing dinner [when Aiko got home]].

In most languages, main clauses come in different types too. The most frequently recurring ones across the world are these (Table 4.6):

Table 4.6 The types of main clause that we can distinguish.

Clause type	Examples	Discussion
declarative	*He went to the market.* *She is lying about it.*	**Declaratives** are clauses whose typical function is to state how things are. In English, they are characterised by the order of first subject and then VP: *he went* and *she is lying*.
interrogative	*Did he go to the market?* *How is she lying about it?*	**Interrogatives** are clauses that normally serve to ask questions. A distinction is usually made between **polar** ones, to which the answer is 'yes' or 'no' (e.g. *did he go to the market?*), and **content** ones, which request further information (e.g. *how is she lying about it?*). English interrogatives are largely characterised by the inverted order of first auxiliary and then subject: *did he* and *is she*.
imperative	*Go to the market!* *Let's lie about it!*	**Imperatives** are clauses whose standard function is to urge someone to do something. What sets them apart from other clause types in English is the typical absence of the subject *you* in second person imperatives ((*you*) *go to the market!*) and the auxiliary *let* at the start of the clause in other imperatives (*let's lie about it!*).

(Continued)

Table 4.6 (Continued)

Clause type	Examples	Discussion
exclamative	*What a market he went to!* *How dishonest she is!*	**Exclamatives** are clauses that generally serve to express surprise or admiration. What distinguishes them from other clause types in English is the use of a question word (*what/how*) but – compared to interrogatives – the lack of inversion of the subject. *How dishonest she is!* is an exclamative, *how dishonest is she?* an interrogative.

SCAN ME

For more about how polar interrogatives are formed in the world's languages, check out the World Atlas of Language Structures online!

Languages vary greatly in the way that they differentiate clause types. In English, for instance, the main contrast between polar interrogatives and declaratives is inversion: *are they going?* and *they are going*. But this kind of distinction is actually extremely rare in the world's languages. Most languages are like Maybrat, spoken in Indonesia. The polar interrogative (46a) differs from the declarative (46b) only in the presence of a QUESTION word *a*.

(46) Maybrat (Dol 1999: 220, 271)
    a. *ana* *mamo* *Kumurkek*   *a*
       they   go   Kumurkek   Q
       'Are they going to Kumurkek?'
    b. *ana* *mamo* *Kumurkek*
       they   go   Kumurkek
       'They are going to Kumurkek.'

Furthermore, not every language distinguishes all clause types. For example, the sole way of urging a person to eat in Onge, spoken in India, is to say (47).

(47) Onge (Dasgupta and Sharma 1982: 34)
    n-ilokowale-nene
    you-eat-FUT
    'You will eat.' or 'Eat!'

The standard interpretation of this clause is a statement about the future: 'you will eat'. So it is, in fact, declarative. Only in particular contexts (and probably with a particular intonation) does (47) get the reading 'eat!'. It would therefore be wrong to regard it as a distinct imperative clause type. (English would resemble Onge if *eat!* did not exist in the language and we were only able to say – with a specific intonation – *you will eat!* to get someone to eat.)

With our knowledge of how phrases can relate to one another in terms of meaning (Section 4.3.1) and grammar (Section 4.3.2) to form different types of clause (Section 4.3.3), we can now comfortably turn to the issue of clauses forming sentences.

4.4 Sentences

A sentence is a syntactic unit that consists of one or more clauses. When it contains just one clause, like (48a), we talk of a **simplex sentence**. In a sense, the clause *she smiled* coincides with the sentence *she smiled* here. Such cases are what we have mainly focused on thus far in this chapter. When a sentence contains more than one clause, like (48b) and (48c), we talk of a **complex sentence**.

(48) a. [She smiled].
  b. [She smiled] but [she was unhappy].
  c. [She said [that she was unhappy]].

Clauses in a complex sentence can be connected in different ways:

- In (48b), the two clauses *she smiled* and *she was unhappy* are syntactically independent from one another or, put differently, neither is embedded within the other. This kind of connection – where multiple main clauses are linked through conjunctions such as *and*, *but* and *or* – is called **coordination**. The phenomenon is not restricted to clauses, of course, as the coordinated NPs and AdjPs in (49) show (see also Section 4.2.1).

(49) [John] **and** [Mary] are wanted [dead], [alive] **or** [undead].

- In (48c), the clause *that she was unhappy* is embedded within another clause. We can use the substitution test to show this: in *she said it*, the pronoun *it* stands in for the clause within the other clause. Such a connection – where one clause is a syntactic part of another – is called **subordination** (see also Section 4.3.3).

  This distinction between main and subordinate clauses manifests itself in the syntax of many languages. Take Dutch, for example. As a main clause, in (50a), 'she was unhappy' has the order of first the subject *ze* 'she', then the verb *was* 'was' and, lastly, the adjective *ongelukkig* 'unhappy'.

(50) Dutch
  a. Ze   glimlachte   maar   ze   was   ongelukkig.
     she   smiled   but   she   was   unhappy
     'She smiled but she was unhappy.'
  b. Ze   zei   dat   ze   ongelukkig   was.
     she   said   that   she   unhappy   was.
     'She said that she was unhappy.'

However, as a subordinate clause, in (50b), 'she was unhappy' literally translates as 'she unhappy was'. The reason is that, unlike in any other clause type, Dutch requires the entire VP to be in final position in subordinate clauses.

Subordination itself is not a uniform domain either. We can divide it further in (at least) two cross-cutting ways. A first one is based on the form of the verb. The pair of subordinate clauses in (51) can illustrate it.

(51) a. The study showed [that the vaccine was effective].
     b. The study showed [the vaccine to be effective].

- In a **finite** subordinate clause, like (51a), the verb adopts a finite form or, in other words, one able to inflect for, say, agreement and tense. This is the case with *was*: it becomes *were* when we pluralise *vaccine* (*that the vaccines were effective*) and we can change it to *is* to express present tense (*that the vaccine is effective*).
- In a **non-finite** subordinate clause, like (51b), the verb form is non-finite and does not allow such inflection. *Be* – the so-called **infinitive** form, which is found after *to* and auxiliaries like *can* and *must* – fits this bill. We cannot alter it in any way to convey the tense difference that *was* versus *is* conveys. *Be* also does not change if we pluralise *vaccine* (*the study showed the vaccines to be effective*).

Other non-finite verb forms that can appear in an English subordinate clause are the *-ing* form (e.g. *swimming*) and the so-called **past participle**, the form that we normally use after *I have . . .* (e.g. *swum*).

A second way that we can divide subordination – and the last leg of this chapter! – has to do with the role that the subordinate clause plays in the main clause (Table 4.7):

Table 4.7 The types of subordinate clause that we can distinguish.

Type	Examples	Discussion
complement	non-finite *She told him [to leave the city].* *I don't like [you climbing trees].* finite *Ask yourself [whether it was right]!* *He said [that he was unhappy].*	**Complement clauses** are subordinate clauses that function as an argument of the main clause verb. Non-finite *to leave the city* is a case in point because, without it, the main clause is incomplete. The same holds for finite *whether it was right*: the main clause *ask yourself* is ill-formed if we do not add what actually needs to be asked.

Type	Examples	Discussion
adverbial	non-finite [*When baking cakes,*] *you need flour.* *They went out* [*to buy wine*]. finite [*If I leave*], *will you join me?* *She remarried* [*after he was gone*].	**Adverbial clauses** are subordinate clauses that serve as an adjunct of the main clause verb. Non-finite *when baking cakes*, for instance, can easily be left out. The main clause *you need flour* is perfectly well-formed without it. The same is true of finite *if I leave*. Adverbial clauses can express a range of meanings including purpose, condition, time and reason. In English, they are often introduced by conjunctions like *in order to*, *if*, *when* and *because*. The traditional term 'adverbial' is perhaps not especially transparent. But it is not entirely arbitrary! If a clause contains an adverb/AdvP, it is almost always an adjunct, just like the subordinate clause type named after it.
relative	non-finite *She skipped the event* [*held in Rio*]. *The man* [*coming over*] *is my uncle.* finite *The dog* [*that bit me*] *was a beagle.* *My TV,* [*which I bought yesterday,*] *is broken.*	**Relative clauses** are subordinate clauses that are embedded within an NP and modify the noun by providing more information about it. Non-finite *held in Rio*, for instance, is part of the NP *the event held in Rio*. Movement tests can show that this is case. We cannot front *held in Rio* (**it is held in Rio that she skipped the event*) without also fronting *the event* (*it is the event held in Rio that she skipped*). The same holds for finite *that bit me* in *the dog that bit me*.

4.5 Conclusion

In this chapter, we have examined how words can form phrases of different kinds – like AdjPs and NPs. We have also seen how such phrases can create clauses, establishing various meaning relations – like agents and experiencers – and various grammatical relations – like subjects and indirect objects – with the VP. Among the clauses constructed this way, we have furthermore identified distinct types – like declaratives and interrogatives. And, finally, we have discussed how such clauses can be combined – through coordination and subordination – to form complex sentences. This whole 'building process' is what syntax is all about. How we actually use the sentences that we build in conversations, texts and the like is the domain of other fields of linguistics.

References

Ameka, F. K. 1991. *Ewe: Its Grammatical Constructions and Illocutionary Devices*. Canberra: Australian National University.

Bross, F. 2020. *The Clausal Syntax of German Sign Language: A Cartographic Approach*. Berlin: Language Science Press.

Dasgupta, D. and Sharma, S. R. 1982. *A Hand Book of Onge Language*. Calcutta: Anthropological Survey of India.

Dillon, M. and Cróinin, D. Ó. 1961. *Teach Yourself Irish*. London: English Universities Press.

Dol, P. H. 1999. *A Grammar of Maybrat: A Language of the Bird's Head, Irian Jaya, Indonesia*. Leiden: Leiden University.

Franklin, K. J. 1971. *A Grammar of Kewa, New Guinea*. Canberra: Pacific Linguistics.

Morris, H. F. and Kirwan, B. E. R. 1972. *A Runyankore Grammar*. Nairobi: East African Literature Bureau.

5 Semantics
Christopher Hart and Vittorio Tantucci

5.1 Introduction

Semantics is the branch of linguistics that studies meaning as a property of words and sentences. Principally, this involves describing what it is that speakers know when they know the meaning of a word or sentence belonging to their language. This is in contrast to morphology and syntax, which are concerned with the structural properties of words and sentences. It is also in contrast with pragmatics, which is concerned with the meaning of utterances in specific contexts of use. Semantics itself can be divided into lexical semantics, which is focused on the meanings of words, and phrasal or sentential semantics, which is focused on larger structures.

Traditional approaches to semantics have viewed meaning in terms of direct correspondences between words and the world. From this perspective, the meaning of a word equates to the real-world entities that it refers to, so that the meaning of *cat* lies in the set of feline entities it identifies. This approach is therefore sometimes described as a referential theory of meaning. It is associated more with philosophy than with linguistics, having its roots in the writings of the philosopher John Stuart Mill (1867). Though reference is no doubt an important aspect of meaning, there are obvious inadequacies to such an approach (e.g. what would be the referent of *ugly* or *unicorn?*) and exclusively referential theories do not form part of modern linguistic semantics.

Modern linguistic approaches to semantics do not see meaning as residing in the external world but rather in the system of a given language and the knowledge that speakers have of it. Modern-day lexical semantics can be broadly divided into two camps: **componential** approaches, which have their roots in the so-called 'structuralist' ideas of Ferdinand de Saussure, and **cognitive** approaches, which have been developed within the field of cognitive linguistics and are associated with scholars including George Lakoff and Charles Fillmore.

In this chapter, we focus primarily on lexical semantics from these two perspectives. In Section 5.2, we introduce some basic notions and distinctions that are fundamental to the study of meaning. In Section 5.3, we introduce componential approaches to word-meaning before, in Section 5.4, introducing cognitive approaches. In Section 5.5, we turn briefly to sentential semantics, before concluding the chapter in Section 5.6.

DOI: 10.4324/9781003045571-6

5.2. Some basic ideas

5.2.1 Aspects of meaning

A first important distinction is between what Frege (1892) called **sense** and **reference**. Sense and reference capture two different ways in which a word can have meaning. Words can mean something in terms of the general idea they express, in which case we talk about their sense, or they can mean something in terms of the real-world entities they pick out, in which case we talk about their reference. Most words have both a sense and can be used referentially. For example, the word *dog* in (1) conjures the idea of DOG while in (2) the word refers to a particular real-world dog.

(1) *A dog* makes a good companion.
(2) She brought *a dog*.

Sense is in some way primary in so far as it is our sense of a word that enables us to use it in reference to particular entities in the world. The speaker of (2), for instance, would not be able to use the word *dog* to refer to a specific creature if they didn't have an idea of what the word meant. Some words, however, such as proper names, possess only reference. Since in reference the meaning of a word is wedded to the context in which it occurs, it is normally treated as a matter of pragmatics rather than semantics.

Another important distinction when addressing the sense of a word is between its **denotation** and its **connotation**. The denotation of a word represents its 'core' literal meaning, as might be defined in a dictionary. Thus, *dog* may be said to denote all domesticated canine animals. The connotation of a word lies in the psychological associations it evokes. For example, many people will associate dogs with being loyal, friendly and affectionate while others may associate them with being aggressive. The connotations of a word are thus dependent on experience and may vary more from one speaker to another. There is some debate in linguistics as to whether such connotative aspects of meaning are the proper business of semantics. Componential approaches argue that connotative meanings are part of world knowledge rather than linguistic knowledge and therefore lie outside the scope of semantics. Cognitive semantics, by contrast, argues that linguistic knowledge and world knowledge cannot truly be separated and that semantic analysis should attend to the full extent of a word's meaning.

A third fundamental distinction that is traditionally made is between **literal** and **non-literal** or **figurative** meaning. In both (1) and (2), *dog* is used literally. However, *dog* may also be used figuratively in expressions like *It's a dog-eat-dog world* and *He's like a dog with a bone*. Figurative forms of language include **metaphor**, **simile**, **irony** and **hyperbole**. In many textbooks, figurative language is analysed within pragmatics as a feature of context-specific speaker meaning. However, it turns out that much more of language is figurative than people think and some figurative forms of language like metaphor are in fact highly conventional – so much so that they're not necessarily recognised by speakers as figurative. As an example, an expression like *I've run out of time* is metaphorical because it speaks about time in terms of a finite resource like money. Observations such as these have led researchers in cognitive semantics to claim that there is no principled distinction that can be drawn between literal and metaphorical uses and that metaphor is a fundamental aspect of meaning in language and thought (Lakoff and Johnson 1980).

5.2.2 The lexicon

Word forms (phonological and graphic) and their meanings are said to be stored in the **lexicon** – a repository of semantic knowledge. In traditional theories of language, the lexicon is separate from syntax – the set of rules that govern how words may be combined in sentences. From this perspective, the language system is made up of distinct sub-systems with vocabulary and grammar representing different components. Entries in the lexicon are called **lexemes** and include the uninflected forms of a word and the various inflected forms of it, such as its plural or past tense form.

The nature and organisation of the lexicon is subject to considerable debate. Does it, for example, include connotative meanings or are these not part of linguistic knowledge per se? Does it include metaphorical meanings or are these formed only temporarily on the basis of pragmatics? The lexicon is often described as a kind of mental dictionary. However, the lexicon is likely to differ from a dictionary in at least two important respects. First, dictionaries are organised alphabetically whereas the lexicon is organised thematically with words grouped together into **lexical fields** (Trier 1931) by virtue of their meaning rather than their form. Second, dictionaries take the form of lists whereas the lexicon is more like a network with lexemes belonging to the same lexical field being interconnected by means of various lexical or **sense relations** (see Section 5.3.2).

5.2.3 The linguistic sign

Saussure developed the notion of the **linguistic sign** in his (1916) *Cours de Linguistique Générale*. For Saussure, the study of meaning in linguistics belongs to the more general study of signs known as semiotics. Language is seen as a system of signs in which each sign is made up of two integral components: the concept or idea **signified** and its **signifier** in the form of a sound pattern. This relationship is represented by the ovals in the diagram reproduced as Figure 5.1. Crucially, the relationship between signifier and signified is arbitrary. That is, with the exception of rare cases, such as **onomatopoeia**, there is nothing about the sound form of a word that predicts its meaning. Or put the other way, there is nothing about the meaning of a word that explains its form. This is what allows the same concept to be signified by different forms across the world's languages.

Figure 5.1 Saussurian sign system.

Source: Based on Saussure (1974: 115).

Hence, the words for dog in French (*chien*), Spanish (*perro*) and German (*hund*) are very different to one another. People are often surprised to learn that even onomatopoeic words actually vary considerably across languages where words representing the sound of a dog's bark, for example, include *woof* (English), *gav* (Russian) and *wang* (Mandarin). More recently, however, the assumption of arbitrariness has been challenged with some research suggesting that iconicity – whereby there is some kind of resemblance between the form of a word and its meaning – is much more extensive in language than just onomatopoeia and is in fact a general property of language (see Focus Box 1).

At this point, we face the problem of exactly how to pin down the sense or meaning of a word. To say that the meaning of the word *dog* is the concept of DOG that it signifies is circular and uninformative. What is needed is a way of capturing or modelling the concepts that words signify. The major contribution of Saussure was to see the meaning of a word as given by its place within a system where it stands in relations of contrast with other words that are part of the same system. Hence, part of the meaning of *dog* is determined by the existence of other words like *cat*, *kitten*, *puppy* and the like. This relationship is represented in Figure 5.1 where each word is linked to other words in the language.

5.3 Componential approach

5.3.1 Semantic features

For a large-scale lexical database of English words and sense-relations check out **WordNet**.

Componential approaches share the view that meaning is atomistic, which is to say comprised of multiple elements. Componential analysis therefore involves decomposing the sense of a word into its constituent semantic elements or **features**. The meaning of a word is then a function of contrasts in semantic features that define it in relation to other words. Of course, words are not immediately related to all other words in the lexicon but rather are defined relative to other words within the same lexical field. Let's take a well-trodden example to illustrate. The words *boy*, *girl*, *man* and *woman* belong to the same lexical field in so far as they all denote human beings. However, they differ according to other semantic

Table 5.1 Semantic features of *man, woman, boy* and *girl*.

	HUMAN	ADULT	FEMALE
Man	+	+	-
Woman	+	+	+
Boy	+	-	-
Girl	+	-	+

Source: Lyons (1995: 108).

Table 5.2 Semantic features of *chair*.

Semantic features: *chair*

• OBJECT	• PORTABLE
• PHYSICAL	• SOMETHING WITH LEGS
• NON-LIVING	• SOMETHING WITH BACK
• ARTEFACT	• SOMETHING WITH SEAT
• FURNITURE	• SEAT FOR ONE

Source: Katz (1972).

features. *Man* contrasts with *woman* and *boy* contrasts with *girl* in the feature MALE/FEMALE while *man* contrasts with *boy* and *woman* contrasts with *girl* in the feature ADULT/CHILD. The sense of each of these four words can thus be captured in terms of the common and contrasting semantic features set out in Table 5.1.

Let's consider another well-known example in the word *chair*, which can be seen to contrast with words like *stool* and *table*. Katz (1972) suggested that the concept denoted by the word *chair* can be decomposed into the semantic features listed in Table 5.2.

5.3.2 Sense relations

An important contribution of Saussure has been to view entries in the lexicon as connected to one another by means of different sense relations. Various such relations are identified, including **synonymy, antonymy** and **hyponymy** (see Section 5.4.4 on polysemy). Synonymy is a relation whereby two words have the same meaning which, from a componential perspective, is to say that they share the same set of semantic features. Examples include *dog/hound, boy/lad* and *chair/seat*. Antonymy is a relation of opposition or exclusion whereby words share all but one semantic feature. Thus, *girl* and *boy* are antonyms of one another because they differ only in the value [+/- FEMALE]. Various types of antonymy exist. In **binary antonyms** (*dead/alive*) the negative of one guarantees the positive of the other – except in zombie movies, one is either dead or alive. By contrast, in **gradable antonyms** (*hot/cold*) the negative of one does not necessitate the positive of the other. If you say it is not hot, it does not necessarily mean that it is cold. Other types of antonymy include **reverse antonymy** (*climb/fall*) and **converse antonymy** (*buy/sell*). Hyponymy is a relation of inclusion such that the hyponym includes all the features of a more general hypernym plus at least one more. Thus, *spinster* is a hyponym of *woman* because it has the semantic features [+ HUMAN], [+ADULT], [+FEMALE] plus the additional feature [-MARRIED]. Some componential approaches attempt to identify a set of basic features that exist for all of the world's languages (e.g. Wierzbicka 1996).

5.3.4 Problems with componential approaches

Componential or decompositional analysis was the most prominent approach to lexical semantics throughout the twentieth century. Part of its appeal is that it chimes with traditional views of sentence meaning as resulting from combinations of smaller units in the form of words and phrases. Its 'algorithmic' nature also makes it attractive to computational linguists (see Chapter 18). However, componential analysis suffers from a number of problems and is no longer as widely supported as it once was, especially in the light of credible alternatives. To illustrate some of these problems, let's begin with the issue of synonymy. A feature-based analysis, focused exclusively on denotation, fails to account for intuitively felt differences in meaning as well as empirically verified differences in usage between alleged synonyms. A componential analysis predicts that two words will mean the same thing – will be synonymous with one another – when they share the same set of semantic features. For example, *boy/lad* both denote young male human. However, *boy* and *lad* do not seem to mean quite the same thing, since *lad* carries additional meanings connected to societal expectations and stereotypes. It is this additional meaning of *lad* that allows us to say *He's a bit of a lad* but not *He's a bit of a boy*. Once we move beyond denotation, rarely, if ever, do we find true synonymy.

Similarly, let's take another well-rehearsed example. The denotation of the word *bachelor* is captured by the semantic features [+HUMAN] [+ADULT] [-FEMALE] [-MARRIED]. Such an analysis predicts that any individual who meets these criteria is necessarily a bachelor. However, on such a definition, the Pope would qualify as a bachelor and the Apostolic Palace in Vatican City would be a *bachelor pad*. Most people agree that, though it may be technically true, the Pope is not a bachelor as they understand the term.

It is not just words denoting social categories that encounter such problems. Think again about *chair*. A feature-based analysis suggests that all things to which the label *chair* may be applied are equal in their 'chairness'. However, the world of chairs is very diverse and most speakers agree that some chairs are more chair-like than others. That is, they correspond more closely with their central idea or image of a chair. For example, for most people, an office chair is a better example of a chair than a high chair. Neither is it just things that are subject to these effects, but actions and properties too. For example, the word *swim* is likely to bring to mind one style of swimming over others (i.e. front crawl or breast stroke but not butterfly).

All of this suggests that there is more to the meaning of a word than its denotation and that this forms an integral part of speakers' linguistic knowledge. Componential approaches have therefore been criticised for being psychologically inadequate and unrealistic, as well as lacking in experimental evidence (Fodor et al. 1975). In fact, the available evidence suggests that words are represented as wholes and are not parsed in terms of smaller units. An alternative, more contemporary approach, which claims to be psychologically plausible and which does receive experimental support, is cognitive semantics.

5.4 Cognitive semantics

In this section, we introduce cognitive semantics by looking at some of the key theoretical constructs it proposes to account for word meaning. These are: symbolic assemblies (5.4.1), prototypes (5.4.2), frames (5.4.3), image schemas (5.4.4) and conceptual metaphors (5.4.5).

5.4.1 Symbolic assemblies

Reminiscent of the Saussurian sign, cognitive semantics argues that language is made up of a system of **symbolic assemblies** in which forms are paired with concepts. Crucially, however, the concepts in such symbolic assemblies are not characterised by sets of semantic features but rather take the form of abstract, holistic mental images. Thus, the word *cat* represents a symbolic assembly in which the phonological form /kæt/ 'points to' our mental image of a cat, as in Figure 5.2. (While philosophers of language favour dogs in their examples, linguists tend to be cat people!)

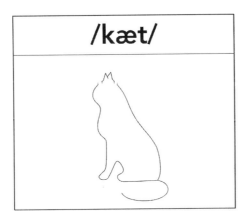

Figure 5.2 Symbolic assembly or form-meaning pairing.

Figure 5.3 Milo the cat (Chris' cat immortalised in a textbook!)

It is important to note that the image of a cat in Figure 5.2 is not intended to represent any particular cat, as in Figure 5.3. The images in a symbolic assembly are abstract or **schematic**, serving to capture the 'essence' of their instantiations in the world.

In focus: iconicity in sign and spoken language

Recall from Section 5.2 that the relationship between form and meaning in language is normally assumed to be arbitrary with only a few exceptions, such as onomatopoeia, exhibiting any degree of iconicity. One form of language in which we might expect to find greater levels of iconicity is **sign language**. And indeed, sign languages display iconicity in a variety of different ways. For example, the American Sign Language (ASL) signs for CHAIR and SIT shown in Figure 5.4 resemble human legs making contact with the seat of a chair (the motion is signed once for the verb and twice for the noun). Across languages, concepts that are inherently 'plural' such as KISS or ARGUE, which involve two participants, tend to be represented by two-handed signs, which reflects that plurality.

Chair   **Sit**

Figure 5.4 Iconicity in signs for CHAIR and SIT.

Iconicity is found in other aspects of sign language besides signs for objects and actions. For example, to express the intensifier *very* (as in *very bad*) in ASL the sign it is modifying is held before being rapidly released. The rapid release marking the intensification resembles our experience of intensity as the build-up and sudden release of pressure, as when opening a can of fizzy drink that has been shaken.

For a dictionary of sign entries, including videos, across more than 30 languages check out Spreadthesign.

It is now widely accepted that iconicity is a feature of sign languages, whereas previously, people had sought to deny that signed languages involved iconicity as this would make them fundamentally different from spoken language. However, recent research suggests that iconicity is also prevalent in spoken language. One way that iconicity is manifested in spoken language is in **sound symbolism**. For example, in a well-known experiment, dubbed the **kiki-bouba** experiment, subjects across languages given the words *kiki* and *bouba* and the shapes in Figure 5.5 overwhelmingly (95%) associated the shape on the left with the word *kiki* and the shape on the right with the word *bouba*. This is interpreted as evidence of sound symbolism where the roundness of the 'bouba' shape corresponds with the rounded shape of the mouth when pronouncing *bouba* while the spikiness of the 'kiki' shape

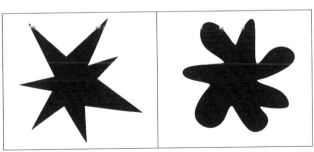

Figure 5.5 Shapes used in kiki-bouba experiment.

corresponds with the tauter more angular configuration of the articulators when pronouncing *kiki*.

Kiki and *bouba* are, of course, nonsense words. However, sound symbolism is also found in real words. For example, in English adjectives of size, words expressing SMALL, such as *little* or *tiny*, are associated with high front vowels /ɪ/ and /i/, which result in a smaller opening of the mouth. Conversely, words expressing LARGE, such as *large* or *gargantuan*, are associated with the low back vowel /ɑ/, which results in a larger opening of the mouth.

Sources: Lepic et al. (2016); Ramachandran and Hubbard (2001); Wilcox (2004); Winter and Perlman (2021).

In focus: images in context

An interesting finding from experimental studies in cognitive semantics is that, in language processing, the basic mental image evoked by a word varies slightly depending on the context in which it is used. For example, subjects given sentences like (3) and (4) and then asked to say whether objects in pictures like Figure 5.6 had featured in those sentences responded faster when the image matched the implied orientation of the object. The explanation for this effect is that in processing sentences like (3) and (4) people activate a mental image that contains contextually determined details such as orientation, which is then compared with the actual image presented in the task.

(3)   The man hammered the nail into the wall.
(4)   The man hammered the nail into the floor.

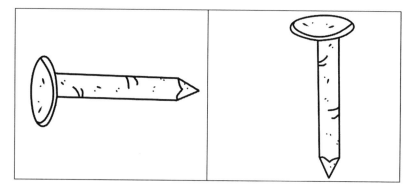

Figure 5.6 Horizontal vs. vertical orientation.

Source: Stanfield and Zwaan (2001).

Recall from Section 5.3.4 the problems encountered by a componential approach. Two types of conceptual structure proposed in cognitive semantics help to address these problems: **prototypes** and **frames**.

5.4.2 Prototypes

Concepts organise our world into **categories** (Lakoff 1987). On a componential analysis, such categories have clear boundaries which an entity either falls within or outside of and all entities that fall within it are equal in their membership. There are some categories for which this works, such as ODD NUMBER, where every number either falls within the category or not and no odd number is any more odd than another. But there are many cases for which it works less well. Consider the category of objects denoted by *ball*. Now consider the extent to which a rugby ball falls into this category. And now consider the extent to which a football falls into this category. Most readers will feel that a football is definitely a ball but may have had some difficulty deciding whether a rugby ball really counts as a ball or not. After all, it is not even round. Cognitive semantics accommodates this by arguing that categories are organised radially around a central example or **prototype** and that their boundaries are blurred or **fuzzy** so that an object can potentially belong to more than one category (think of a tomato!). Hence, for most people, a football represents a prototypical ball while a rugby ball is less prototypical and a disco ball is less prototypical still and may not be considered an example of a ball at all. Evidence that concepts are organised this way comes from **goodness of exemplar** experiments conducted by Eleanor Rosch in cognitive psychology and on whose work Lakoff's (1987) theory of categories and prototypes is based. Note that prototypes and radial

In focus: goodness of exemplar experiments

Rosch (1975) conducted a series of experiments in which subjects were given categories and a list of potential members and then had to rate members on a scale of 1–7 according to how good an example of the category they are. Provided that subjects were drawn from the same speech community, results tended to converge on particular orders. This suggests that for speakers of a given language, not all members of a category are equal. Some members are more central members than others. Table 5.3 shows the highest and lowest ranking members of three categories.

Table 5.3 Selection of goodness-of-exemplar ratings.

Rank	Bird	Fruit	Furniture
Top five (from more to less representative)			
1	Robin	Orange	Chair
2	Sparrow	Apple	Sofa
3	Bluejay	Banana	Couch
4	Bluebird	Peach	Table
5	Canary	Pear	Easy chair

(Continued)

Table 5.3 (Continued)

Rank	Bird	Fruit	Furniture
Bottom five (from more to less representative)			
5	Turkey	Nut	Closet
4	Ostrich	Gourd	Vase
3	Emu	Olive	Ashtray
2	Penguin	Pickle	Fan
1	Bat	Squash	Telephone

Source: Rosch (1975: Appendix).

structures are subject to individual and cultural variation, depending on experience. For example, Rosch found that for Jordanians the category denoted by *fruit* includes DATE as a central member, which is not the case for most UK speakers.

5.4.3 Frames

On a componential analysis, the meaning of a word extends only as far as its denotation, which represents something like a dictionary definition. Cognitive semantics argues that the lexicon is more like an encyclopaedia than it is a dictionary and that the meaning of a word lies in the vast amounts of background knowledge it connects with. Let's consider again the word *bachelor*. Fillmore (1982) argues that in order to understand the meaning of the word *bachelor* one has to know more than its denotation. One has to know something about the institution of marriage, including typical marriageable age. That is, one has to recognise the **frame** against which the word means something. As another example, the word *vegetarian* can mean what it means only against the backdrop of a predominantly meat-eating society. For Fillmore, then, a frame is the encyclopaedic knowledge that a word accesses and which is necessary in order to appreciate its meaning. Such bodies of knowledge are not specific but are generalisations over experience. So, for example, one common type of experience is a commercial transaction. Fillmore argues that words like *buy*, *sell*, *pay*, *spend*, *cost*, *charge*, etc. are related by, and make sense in terms of, an underlying COMMERCIAL TRANSACTION frame, which is minimally made up of four **frame elements**: BUYER, SELLER, GOODS and MONEY (see Figure 5.7).

Elements like BUYER, SELLER, GOODS and MONEY represent **participant roles** within the frame for commercial transactions. The meaning of verbs like *buy* and *pay* includes information as to how many and which of such participant roles are required when used in a sentence. This is referred to as the **valence** or **argument structure** of a verb (see also Chapter 4 on arguments versus adjuncts). For example, *buy* is typically **divalent** requiring the roles of BUYER and GOODS to be fulfilled leaving SELLER as optional as in (5a). *Pay*, by contrast, is typically **trivalent** requiring the roles of BUYER, GOODS and MONEY to be specified as in (5b).

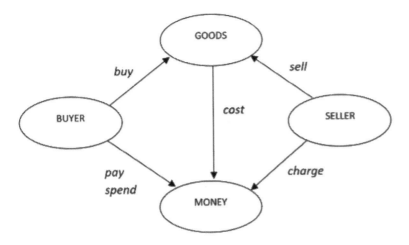

Figure 5.7 COMMERCIAL TRANSACTION frame.

5a. Jane bought a new car (from the garage).
5b. Jane paid £500 for a new car.

While participant roles are particular to a given frame, a more generic set of **semantic** or **thematic roles** such as AGENT and PATIENT are identified which characterise the meaning of verbs at a more schematic level (see Chapter 4).

5.4.4 Image schemas

If frames represent distillations over aspects of cultural experience (e.g. commercial transactions are conducted in different ways in different cultures), another type of conceptual structure, which represents universal aspects of experience, is **image schemas**. Image schemas represent recurring patterns of experience that we have of our bodies and of interactions in the physical environment – that is, **embodied** experience. They emerge in basic domains like ACTION, FORCE, SPACE and MOTION and come to form the meaningful basis of certain words as well as grammatical constructions (see Chapter 26). One image schema is the CONTAINER schema, which arises from our early experiences of observing containment, of being contained and of our bodies themselves being containers. The CONTAINER schema consists of three structural elements: an inside and an outside defined by a boundary. This schema forms the conceptual basis of prepositions *in* and *out* as well as the verb *enter*. For example, the meaning of *in* as in (6) is modelled in Figure 5.8, where the **trajector** (TR) is situated inside a container which provides the **landmark** (LM). (It is conventional in cognitive semantics to refer to located entities in a spatial expression as 'trajectors' and reference entities as 'landmarks').

For a lexical database of English words linked to over 1,200 semantic frames, check out **FrameNet**.

SCAN ME

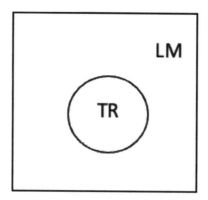

Figure 5.8 CONTAINMENT schema.

In focus: embodiment as simulation

If one sense of the term embodiment is that certain concepts are derived from physical experience, another is that understanding language involves **simulations** of physical experience. So, for example, understanding a word like *kick* involves mentally simulating the action of kicking. One source of evidence that language involves such simulations comes from **Functional Magnetic Resonance Imaging** (FMRI), which shows brain activity during language processing. For example, it has been shown that when subjects read verbs relating to the leg, mouth or hand as in *kick*, *chew* and *grab*, areas of the brain responsible for executing leg, mouth and hand movements are activated, as can be seen in Figure 5.9.

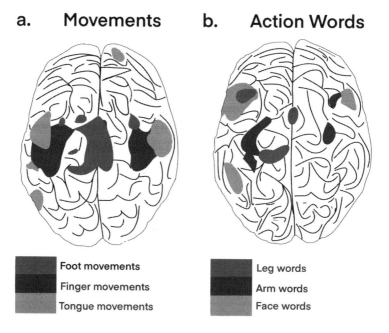

Figure 5.9 FMRI scans of brain activity in action words compared to movements.

Interestingly, it is not only literal senses of words that activate associated brain areas but metaphorical senses too. For example, metaphorical expressions drawing on the source domain of TEXTURE, such as *a rough day,* activate the region of the brain responsible for our sense of touch.

Sources: Hauk et al. (2004); Lacey et al. (2012).

(6) The toys are in the box.

As with other concepts, such as CAT in Figure 5.2, the image diagrammed in Figure 5.8 is not of any specific type of container and content, such as a cup of tea or a box of toys, but is rather a generalisation over scenes involving containment. Image schemas thus represent the common skeletal structures and relations that multiple situations can be 'boiled down' to. Other image schemas include UP-DOWN, FRONT-BACK, CONTACT, SUPPORT and many more.

The meanings of prepositions like *in, on, over, above, below, under, through* and *around* are not, it turns out, as simple as a single image schema. Prepositions are highly **polysemous**, which is to say they have multiple senses or that they code for a variety of relational situations. Such alternate meanings are represented conceptually in variations or **transformations** of the central schema. For example, in their study of *over,* Brugman and Lakoff (1988) identified several spatial senses where the nature of the landmark and/or the relation between the trajector and the landmark is subtly different. A few of these are exemplified in Figure 5.10 with the core sense in the middle.

Image schemas provide structure and organisation to our experience of basic domains like SPACE and ACTION but they also come to structure whole other domains of experience via metaphorical projection. Many non-spatial senses of prepositions are derived via processes of metaphoric extension.

5.4.5 Metaphor

The concepts expressed by language are connected to one another in many ways in vast networks of knowledge. One way that concepts are connected is through **metaphor**. Many people think of metaphor as an aesthetic device which is found primarily in literary works like novels and poems. A major insight of cognitive semantics is that metaphor in fact pervades ordinary language and does so in systematic ways. Thus, while some metaphors certainly are novel, many are highly conventionalised. This leads cognitive semanticists to treat metaphorical expressions in language as evidence of more general or abstract metaphorical modes of thought in which concepts or sets of concepts are connected to one another across a system of **conceptual metaphors** (Lakoff and Johnson 1980). As a result of this system, much of the way we think turns out to be metaphorical.

A conceptual metaphor consists of a mapping from a **source domain** onto a **target domain** such that the target domain is understood, at least partially,

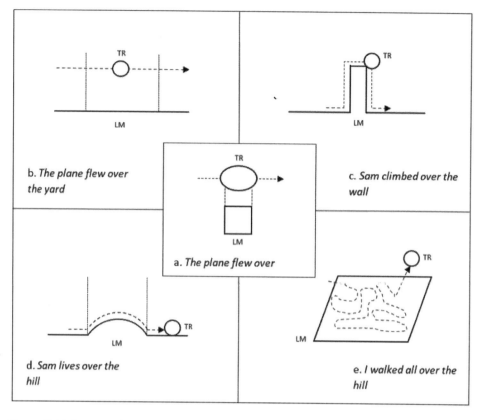

Figure 5.10 Image-schematic representations for various senses of *over*.

Source: Based on Brugman and Lakoff (1988).

in terms of the source domain. Thus, when we say *I've spent my time wisely*, this reflects a conceptual metaphor in which the source domain of MONEY is mapped onto the target domain of TIME. Source domains are typically concrete or familiar aspects of cultural or embodied experience (represented in frames and image schemas) while target domains are more abstract, less tangible areas of experience like time, relationships or emotions. For example, mental states and emotions are often conceptualised as containers resulting in metaphorical senses of *in* and *out* such as (7a–c):

(7a) She was in a state of shock.
(7b) She fell in love.
(7c) She came out of a coma.

Conceptual metaphors give rise to metaphoric **entailments**. Entailments are implications within the target domain that arise as a consequence of the 'logic' carried over from the source domain. So, for example, just as one can literally be trapped inside a container so one can feel trapped by their emotions.

Lakoff (1987) argues that expressions like those in (8) point to a rich and complex conceptual metaphor ANGER IS HOT FLUID INSIDE A CONTAINER in which the image is of heat being applied to a container of liquid so that the liquid rises, resulting in increased pressure within the container which must be released. In this metaphor, the body corresponds to a container and anger corresponds to hot fluid within the container. When sufficient heat is applied, the anger rises and causes one to lose control, which corresponds to an explosion of the container. Figure 5.11 contains a list of some of the other conceptual metaphors identified in cognitive semantics.

(8a) That makes my blood boil.
(8b) I felt the anger rise inside me.
(8c) I had reached boiling point.
(8d) I was simmering with rage.
(8e) I was fuming.
(8f) I needed to let off some steam.
(8g) I blew my top.
(8h) I flipped my lid.

5.5. Above the word

When it comes to meaning in units larger than the word (i.e. phrases and sentences), a similar division can be seen between philosophical and linguistic approaches. Within philosophy, Davidson (1967) argues that to know the meaning of a sentence is to know the circumstances under which the **proposition** expressed by it would be true. That is, to recognise its **truth conditions**. Thus, the meaning of a sentence like (9) is reducible to the set of facts that we would need to know in order to determine whether or not it is true.

Some conceptual metaphors:

- ANGER IS HEAT
- ARGUMENT IS WAR
- CHANGE IS MOTION
- CONTROL IS UP
- DESIRE IS HUNGER
- EMOTIONAL STABILITY IS BALANCE
- HAPPY IS UP
- IDEAS ARE FOOD
- IDEAS ARE OBJECTS
- INTIMACY IS PROXIMITY
- OBLIGATIONS ARE FORCES
- RELATIONSHIPS ARE JOURNEYS
- SIMILARITY IS PROXIMITY
- TIME IS MONEY
- TIME IS MOTION THROUGH SPACE
- THEORIES ARE BUILDINGS
- QUANTITY IS SIZE
- UNDERSTANDING IS GRASPING
- UNDERSTANDING IS SEEING
- WORDS ARE CONTAINERS

Figure 5.11 Partial list of conceptual metaphors.

(9) Scafell Pike is the tallest mountain in the Lake District

Like a referential theory of word meaning, such an approach quickly encounters problems. For example, it can only apply to declarative sentences. Other sentence types (e.g. interrogatives and imperative) do not express propositions and therefore cannot be true or false.

Within modern linguistics, approaches to phrasal or sentential semantics fall into a similar division as approaches to lexical semantics. **Compositional** approaches see meaning as deriving from the smaller units of which a sentence is composed (i.e. words) and the particular way in which those units are combined (i.e. grammar). However, compositional approaches also run into problems. For example, **idioms** present a problem for compositional approaches where

---

In focus: metaphor across cultures

Some metaphors, which are called **primary metaphors**, appear to be universal, grounded in embodied experiences that connect source and target domains. For example, ANGER IS HOT FLUID INSIDE A CONTAINER is motivated by the fact that increased body heat is a genuine physiological effect of anger. However, metaphors vary considerably across cultures and even primary metaphors are elaborated in slightly different ways. For example, in Japanese, the container in the conceptual metaphor ANGER IS HOT FLUID IN A CONTAINER is not the whole body as it is in English but specifically the stomach/bowel area (*hara*):

(10a) Harawata ga neikurikaeru
       One's intestines are boiled
(10b) Ikari ga hara no soko wo guragura saseru
       Anger boils the bottom of one's stomach

And in Chinese, the container can be various body parts while the fluid is based on the culturally salient notion of *qi* ('vital energy'):

(11a) Xin zhong de nuqi shizhong wei neng pingxi
       The anger qi in one's heart
(11b) Bie yi duzi qi
       To hold back a stomach full of qi
(11c) Bu shi pi qi fa zuo
       To keep in one's spleen qi
(11d) Yuji zai xiong de nuqi zhongyu baofa le
       The pent-up anger qi in one's breast finally explodes

Source: Kövecses (2003: 152).

---

the meaning expressed by an idiom does not arise from the meanings of its constituent parts. For example, nothing about the combination of *kicked* and *the bucket* in (10) gives you the meaning DIED. Rather, it seems that idioms are represented in the lexicon as whole 'chunks'.

(10) She kicked the bucket

Idioms are usually treated as rare or irregular features of language. However, in **cognitive approaches**, it has been shown that idiomatic expressions are actually very common in language and that much more of language might be idiom-like than is normally thought.

The key claim is that grammar and semantics form part of a continuum. Another way of putting this is that, like words, *grammatical structures are themselves meaningful* and stored in long-term memory alongside words and other smaller constructions as whole units. To understand this claim, it is useful to start by looking further at idioms.

Idioms are a central issue in the componential vs. cognitive debate within semantics. The reason is that idioms are incompatible with the assumption of a strict separation between grammar and the lexicon, as in many componential approaches. In fact, idioms are not just fixed combinations of words like [*kick the bucket*] but can often be modified both lexically and syntactically. For example, [*the X-er, the Y-er*] may occur as [*the more the merrier*] or [*the bigger they come the harder they fall*]. Idioms with this kind of flexibility are said to be **partially schematic** (Fillmore et al. 1988), as they are made of both fixed/specific (*the*, -*er*) and schematic/abstract (X, Y) components. This is important because, rather than just being conceptualised as strings of words, they simultaneously feature semantic and morphosyntactic properties. If we think again of the idiom [*the X-er, the Y-er*], no matter which words fill the X and the Y slots, the idiom will always mean that to an increase of the element X corresponds an equal increase of the element Y. Similarly, the very structure of [*PULL* Obj's *leg*] (cf. Bybee 2010) means *teasing*, no matter what is the tense or the aspect of the verb, or the identity of the animate object. And again, the idiom [*HAVE a* NP] (Wierzbicka 1988) will always express that some agent engages in some 'pleasurable and somewhat brief activity', as in [*having a walk*], [*yesterday she had a stroll*], [*let's have lunch*] and so on. These are semantic meanings that are conveyed by the very grammatical structure of those expressions, rather than via the composition of lexical and morphosyntactic components.

Now, once we accept that idiomatic meaning is present in grammatical structure, it then becomes challenging to find linguistic constructs that are not – to varying degrees – idiomatic and, therefore, semantically meaningful. Bluntly put, **grammatical structure is meaningful**.

This is one of the strongest arguments that has been made in favour of the existence of **constructions** (Fillmore et al. 1988; Goldberg 1995; Tomasello

2003), which are considered by cognitive linguists as the fundamental building blocks of human language. Constructions are pairings of form and meaning which just like words or morphemes make up 'symbolic assemblies'. Consequently, no strict division between grammar and lexicon is really possible.

Grammar is learned via a repeated process of exposure to linguistic constructions of various length and complexity, all involving the simultaneous categorisation of structure and meaning. The language knowledge of an adult can be thought of as a so-called **constructicon** (Fillmore et al. 2003), which is as a huge, constantly updated network of constructions that share some features with one another, vary in degree of abstraction, and – most importantly – are semantically meaningful.

5.6 Conclusion

In this chapter, we have introduced you to the field of semantics with a focus on two different approaches to word meaning: componential analysis and cognitive semantics. In doing so, we have explored meaning as it resides in the language system. Along the way we have also highlighted some contemporary issues and methodological advances in the field of semantics. In the next chapter, you will explore how meaning is made when the language system is put to use in interactional settings.

References

Brugman, C. and Lakoff, G. 1988. Cognitive topology in lexical networks. In S. Small, G. Cottrell and M. Tanenhaus (Eds.), *Lexical Ambiguity Resolution: Perspectives from Psycholinguistics, Neuropsychology, and Artificial Intelligence*. San Mateo, CA: Morgan Kaufmann, pp. 477–508.

Bybee, J. 2010. *Language, Usage and Cognition*. Cambridge: Cambridge University Press.

Davidson, D. 1967. Truth and meaning. *Synthese*, 17: 304–323.

Fillmore, C. 1982. Frame semantics. In Linguistics Society of Korea (Ed.), *Linguistics in the Morning Calm*. Seoul: Hanshin Publishing, pp. 111–137.

Fillmore, C. J., Johnson, C. R. and Petruck, M. R. 2003. Background to framenet. *International Journal of Lexicography*, 16(3): 235–250.

Fillmore, C. J., Kay, P. and O'Connor, M. C. 1988. Regularity and idiomaticity in grammatical constructions: The case of let alone. *Language*, 64(3): 501–538.

Fodor, J., Fodor, J. A. and Garrett, M. F. 1975. The psychological unreality of semantic representations. *Linguistic Inquiry*, 6: 515–532.

Frege, G. 1892. Über sinn und bedeutung [On sense and reference]. *Zeitschrift für Philosophie und Philosophische Kritik*, 100: 25–50.

Goldberg, A. E. 1995. *Constructions: A Construction Grammar Approach to Argument Structure*. Chicago: University of Chicago Press.

Hauk, O., Johnsrude, I. and Pulvermüller, F. 2004. Somatotopic representation of action words in human motor and premotor cortex. *Neuron*, 41(2): 301–307.

Katz, J. J. 1972. *Semantic Theory*. New York: Harper & Row.

Kövecses, Z. 2003. *Metaphor and Emotion: Language, Culture, and Body in Human Feeling*. Cambridge: Cambridge University Press.

Lacey, S., Stilla, R. and Sathian, K. 2012. Metaphorically feeling: Comprehending textural metaphors activates somatosensory cortex. *Brain and Language*, 120(3): 416–421.

Lakoff, G. 1987. *Women, Fire and Dangerous Things: What Categories Reveal About the Mind*. Chicago: University of Chicago Press.

Lakoff, G. and Johnson, M. 1980. *Metaphors We Live By*. Chicago: University of Chicago Press.

Lepic, R., Börstell, C., Belsitzman, G. and Sandler, W. 2016. Taking meaning in hand: Iconic motivations in two-handed signs. *Sign Language Linguistics*, 19: 37–81.

Lyons, J. 1995. *Linguistic Semantics: An Introduction*. Cambridge: Cambridge University Press.

Mill, J. S. 1867. *A System of Logic*. London: Longmans.

Ramachandran, V. S. and Hubbard, E. M. 2001. Synaesthesia: A window into perception, thought and language. *Journal of Consciousness Studies*, 8: 3–34.

Rosch, E. 1975. Cognitive representations of semantic categories. *Journal of Experimental of Psychology*, 104(3): 192–233.

Saussure, F. de. 1916. *Cours de Linguistique Générale [Course in General Linguistics]*. Translated by R. Harris, 1983. London: Duckworth.

Saussure, F. de. 1974. *Course in General Linguistics*. Edited by C. Bally and A. Sechehaye, translated by W. Baskin. Glasgow: Fontana/Collins.

Stanfield, R. A. and Zwaan, R. A. 2001. The effect of implied orientation derived from verbal context on picture recognition. *Psychological Science*, 12: 153–155.

Tomasello, M. 2003. *Constructing a Language*. Cambridge, MA. Harvard University Press.

Trier, J. 1931. *Der deutsche Wortschatz im Sinnbezirk des Verstandes*. Heidelberg: C. Winter.

Wierzbicka, A. 1988. *The Semantics of Grammar*. Amsterdam: John Benjamins.

Wierzbicka, A. 1996. *Semantics: Primes and Universals*. Oxford: Oxford University Press.

Wilcox, S. 2004. Cognitive iconicity: Conceptual spaces, meaning, and gesture in signed languages. *Cognitive Linguistics*, 15(2): 119–147.

Winter, B. and Perlman, M. 2021. Size sound symbolism in the English lexicon. *Glossa: A Journal of General Linguistics*, 6(1): 79, 1–13.

6 Pragmatics
Jonathan Culpeper and Claire Hardaker

6.1 Le chiffre indéchiffrable – what is pragmatics?

In one of the earliest books on the subject, entitled *Pragmatics*, Stephen Levinson offers a brief definition of pragmatics:

> pragmatics is the study of language usage.
>
> (Levinson 1983: 5)

But he then posits *several* other definitions (1983: 5–35), and in turn dissects each one, demonstrating repeatedly that none is adequately capable of capturing the scope and depth of the field. Fast-forward 25 years, and matters had not improved. The very first sentence of Ariel's (2008) *Pragmatics and Grammar* monograph simply states that,

> Pragmatics has been notoriously hard to define.
>
> (Ariel 2008: 1)

Some attempt to define it by contrasting it with other areas of study. Pragmaticians can spend as much time explaining what pragmatics *isn't* as what it is, and the two most typical exemplars of what it is *not* are syntax and semantics.

At its simplest, syntax might describe itself as the study of how we create larger linguistic units from smaller ones. It considers, maps and describes the *monadic relationship between word and word*, ranging from parts of speech like the links between nouns and determiners, to the way these units might combine into phrases, clauses, sentences and so forth (see Chapters 3 and 4).

At a similarly elementary level, semantics might define itself as a field that looks at the meaning conveyed by individual or clusters of words. As we saw in the previous chapter, semantics is broadly interested in the *dyadic relationship between the words and the world*, and semanticists might study anything from synonymy and metaphor through to predication, entailment and more.

At a glance, it might seem that after this, there is little left worth studying: one field has annexed the structures of language, and the other has annexed its meanings. What is left for pragmatics? Again, at an introductory level,

DOI: 10.4324/9781003045571-7

pragmatics is interested in the ***triadic relationship between the words, the world, and the users of those words*** (the idea of a triadic relationship can be found in Morris 1938: 6–7). Pragmaticians are not just concerned with how each word relates to others, or with what a dictionary can tell us about those words. We want to know what they mean to users at that precise moment in that particular context.

Such definitional attempts as these are not entirely without merit. Most would agree that the *necessary* ingredients of pragmatics are such things as *language use*, *meaning* and *context*. But these elements are not sufficient to distinguish pragmatics from other areas, such as sociolinguistics (see Chapter 7) or even usage-based approaches to grammar (see Chapters 25 and 26).

What we really need is a more pragmatic approach to defining pragmatics! Rather than considering a list of necessary and sufficient conditions that sharply define pragmatics, we can simply note what pragmatics typically focuses on. Culpeper et al. (2018: 3) suggest:

> the focus of pragmatics research is meanings that arise from the use of communicative resources in context, and in particular, the meanings implied by speakers, inferred by hearers, and negotiated between them in interaction.

None of this will make much sense in the abstract, so let's look at pragmatics in action.

6.2 Meal deals, meanings and misfires

In 2019, *Emmerdale* and *Dr Who* actress Jenna Coleman was interviewed by *The Guardian*, a UK newspaper. The interviewer, Greenstreet, asked her, 'What was your most embarrassing moment?' and Coleman responded thus:

> Buying a sandwich at Leeds train station. The man said to me: 'Do you want to go for a drink?' I said, 'I am so sorry, I've got a boyfriend.' And he replied, 'No, it's a meal deal: if you take a sandwich, you can get a drink as well.'
> (Greenstreet 2019)

It's a merely seconds-long, three-turn conversation on an extremely trivial topic, and yet one can understand why this might rank as Coleman's most embarrassing memory. For what probably felt like a short eternity until she could pay for her sandwich and escape, Jenna had to endure that most unenviable of social calamities – the **pragmatic misfire**, a term proposed in Austin (1962: 16), a seminal work in pragmatics. Intuitively, despite being grammatically and semantically perfectly formed, many of us will recognise how catastrophically wrong this conversation has gone. It has gone *pragmatically* wrong, through the *unsaid* meanings, and we can explain this in detail.

The whole scene is precipitated by the question, 'Do you want to *go for* a drink?' Deliberately or otherwise, the man formulated his question rather as someone perusing a menu might say, 'I think I'll *go for* the pasta'. In both Coleman's scenario and this little pasta fiction, 'go for' could be replaced with 'choose', and the overall meaning would not be materially altered. However, the question, 'Do you want to go for a drink?' has a second and entirely separate meaning. Through repeated use, it has become (semi-)**conventionalised**, imbued with a **non-literal meaning** that roughly translates to 'Would you like to go on a date?'. Conventionalised pragmatic meanings will be discussed in Section 6.5. Note that these two meanings also involve at least two different understandings of what the words 'Do you want to *go for* a drink?' are doing. Is it acting as an enquiry, and thus requesting or eliciting information? Or is it acting as an offer to go on a date? Requests, offers, warnings, threats, apologies and so forth are **speech acts**, something that will be the topic of Section 6.3.

The problem for Coleman is that, as in most conversations, to avoid seeming unduly ignorant, she has a split second to infer the most probable meaning and then make a meaningful response. And her answer, 'I've got a boyfriend' tells us – people's responses are often a good source of evidence of how they understood (or have 'taken') something – that in that instant, she has interpreted this not as a transactional enquiry for information, but as a romantic overture; an offer to go on a date.

Note that Coleman's answer is not direct, straightforward and efficient. For strict efficiency, she might have simply replied, 'No', and the misfire might never have come to light. But we are also generally socialised into handling sensitive topics like rejection (and the criticism usually implied therein) more gently. One classic way to achieve this is via a range of **pragmatic strategies**, including **politeness**, which we will discuss further in Section 6.5. Accordingly, rather than a blunt rejection, Coleman references her boyfriend. But even this, in a strictly logical light, doesn't make immediate sense unless (1) one assumes that a deeper meaning is being **implied** by what she said (and takes the trouble to work that meaning out, i.e. to infer it), and (2) one draws on assumed **background knowledge**, or more specifically **common ground** (knowledge the participants assume that the other participants are also assuming to be involved) to work it out. On background knowledge, note the importance of cultural knowledge shaping meaning – if you come from a culture where 'meal deals' do not exist, you will probably miss the meaning 'do you want the free drink which is part of the deal?' and assume the meaning 'do you want to pay for an additional free drink?'. (1) and (2) allow us to infer the implied (unsaid) elements of her answer roughly as follows: 'I am so sorry, I've got a boyfriend *and our pre-existing relationship precludes each of us from going on dates with others*'.[1] How we generate implications through conversation is the focus of Section 6.4. Note that terminology such as *imply* or *implication* refer to meanings generated by the speaker.

We would add here that pragmatic misfires are not always excruciating. Frequently they're minor bumps on the conversational road that we often just as quickly recognise, repair and forget moments later. The problem in this particular case is that Coleman's mistake allows a further **pragmatic inference** to be drawn about her character and beliefs. Her error enables others to conjecture that she is so extraordinarily vain that she can even mistake a shop assistant's routine query for infatuated admiration.

This inference is unlike the **conversational implicature** of monogamy in (1) earlier. It does not rely on a seemingly non-logical answer to trigger attempts to infer the speaker's deeper meaning. Instead, it relies on an **associative inference**. This is the shared world knowledge as described in (b), and involves the way that we draw connections. In this particular case, we might have specific ideas about the kinds of people who would so readily assume that they are being showered with romantic attention, their egotism, how (un)pleasant they might be to know, and so forth.

As this short example demonstrates, nebulous, intangible understandings can diverge widely from the literal, fully conventional meanings of the actual words used.

To bring this section to a close, we could describe syntax as the meaning *in* the lines that one can recover by parsing the structural principles of the language, and we could say that semantics is the meaning *behind* the lines that can be recovered from sources such as other users of that language. By contrast, we can think of many areas of pragmatics as the meaning *between* the lines, rather like linguistic ghosts whose insubstantial forms might be successfully negotiated into being, or challenged, or plausibly denied or even entirely exorcised from the conversation.

The various types of meaning discussed in this section, and their relationships with language and context, are displayed in Table 6.1.

6.3 The word is the deed: speech act theory

The basic insight of speech act theory, a mainstay of pragmatics, is simply that language does not just convey information from one person to another.[2] In particular, the traditional way of thinking about the meanings of sentences in semantics is to talk of **propositions** and whether they are true or false (see also Chapter 5). The sentence 'Jonathan and Claire are writing this chapter' contains a true proposition about what Jonathan and Claire are doing – at least it was true at the time of writing!

However, the modern founder of speech act theory, and arguably of pragmatics, J.L. Austin (who was born and spent his youth in Lancaster, UK, where all the authors in this book teach and do research) argued that there was more to it. Austin started by pointing to a special class of verbs whose purpose is to 'do things', as illustrated by the following, slightly adapted examples (Austin 1962: 5):

• I (hereby) **name** this ship the QE2. (Said whilst smashing a bottle against a ship)

Table 6.1 Types of pragmatic meaning.

Relationship	Meaning type	Basis	Example
Language ↑ ⏐ ↓ *Context*	**Non-pragmatic meaning**	Conventional meanings of particular forms of language derived from knowledge of the language (i.e. their semantics and grammar)	'I've got a boyfriend', a declarative sentence with the literal meaning that a certain state of affairs in the world pertains (i.e. that the 'I' 'has' a 'boyfriend', a male partner)
	Conventionalised pragmatic meaning	Meanings of particular forms of language derived from assumptions about their typical implied meanings in context (i.e. their conventionalised associations with pragmatic meanings)	'Do you want to go for a drink?', not an enquiry about wanting to quench one's thirst or wanting a meal deal option, but, non-literally, generating the potential meaning of an offer to go on a date
	Conversational pragmatic meaning	Meanings of particular language interactions derived from assumptions about how the exchange of information works	'I've got a boyfriend', in context (following an offer to go on a date, and assuming that normal conversational assumptions apply), generating the meaning 'no'
	Associative pragmatic meaning	Meanings of any aspect of language derived from assumptions about what it usually co-occurs with	'I've got a boyfriend', in context (i.e. following an ambiguous/indeterminate offer to go on a date, and assuming that vain people too readily assume that others are in love with them), generating the potential meaning that the speaker is vain

- I (hereby) **pronounce** you husband and wife. (Said in the course of a marriage ceremony)
- I (hereby) **bequeath** my watch to my brother. (Said in a will)

A key feature of the **performative verb** is that it names the action being performed in the sentence. It is not a matter of whether the action is true or false, but whether it comfortably fits the context. If so, it is 'felicitous' – that is, it successfully performs the action. A dock worker who is not officially appointed to perform the ceremony of naming a ship could say the words, 'I name this ship the QE2', and even smash a bottle of champagne against the vessel, but they would not successfully perform the act, because they are not felicitous in that context.

The adverb 'hereby' is considered one possible test that helps to identify these performative verbs (though it is not entirely reliable). For example, 'I hereby feel good today' is somewhat awkward, and therefore this test would lead us to determine that 'feel' is not a performative verb.

In focus: speech acts shaped by cultures

Theorists such as Austin were influenced by the world around them, by their cultural milieu. Examples such as the ones containing performative verbs given earlier, not to mention references to cricket and the like, reflect the traditional British middle-class Oxford Don of 50+ years ago. Performative or speech act verbs are formal linguistic traces of speech acts, and speech acts encapsulate the actions that are done in a particular culture. Rosaldo (1982: 228) notes that John R. Searle, a pupil of Austin's, 'uses English performative verbs as guides to something like a universal law'. Performative verbs used by the Ilongots, who inhabit an area of the Philippines, illustrate that such verbs are not at all universal. For example, in most Western cultures, the performative verb of promising (in English 'I *promise* (to) X') is taken to mean that the speaker is personally committed to doing something in the future. But the Ilongots have no ready equivalent, as Rosaldo (1982: 219) elaborates. The nearest they have to a promise is *sigem*, which performs a formulaic oath by salt. So, promising for them means not a personal commitment but a commitment to deep beliefs in the natural world. If somebody doesn't keep their promise, it dissolves like salt.

Towards the end of his work, Austin (1962) concluded that all utterances involved action of some kind, not just sentences with performative verbs. They are all 'speech acts' (e.g. assertions, requests, commands, apologies, threats, compliments, warnings, advice), or what Austin (1962: 99) called **illocutionary acts**. To illustrate the point, consider these two sentences:

1 I promise to give you the money back tomorrow
2 I'll give you the money tomorrow

The first is an explicit speech act of promising, deploying the performative verb 'promise' which names the act being performed (note also that 'hereby' could be inserted before 'promise'). The second is an implicit speech act. From it, we can *infer* that those words in that context constitute the speech act of a promise (though it is plausibly deniable). Both capture what the speaker does in saying something: that is, a promise is performed.

Austin's mantle was picked up and carried by John R. Searle, who made a number of contributions, of which we shall mention two: **felicity conditions** and **directness**. We have already mentioned that the success of the speech act depends on **felicity conditions** – the presence of appropriate contextual factors. Searle (e.g. 1969) attempted to formalise those conditions into **constitutive rules** (i.e. rules that create the activity itself, like a game of chess or football), and as an exemplar, Table 6.2 displays Searle's felicity conditions for the speech act of promising. The rightmost column is based on Searle (1969: 57–60).

Table 6.2 Felicity conditions and promising.

Felicity condition	Clarification	Exemplification: promising
Propositional content	What the utterance is about	Future A (act) of S (the speaker)
Preparatory	Contextual pre-requisites	1 H (the hearer) wants S to perform A 2 It is not obvious that S will do A in the normal course of events
Sincerity	The beliefs, feelings and intentions of the speaker	S intends to do A
Essential	What is needed for the act to be performed (i.e. the mutual recognition that the speaker intends an utterance to count as a certain act)	Counts as an undertaking by S of an obligation to do A

The idea is that such rules can distinguish one speech act from another, thereby creating a comprehensive and precise descriptive scheme cataloguing all possible speech acts. For instance, if we want to change a promise into a threat, all we need to do is change the first preparatory condition to 'H does not want S to perform A'.

However, though pioneering and valuable, Searle's classification has problems. First, such neat categorisations do not capture the fuzzy-edged reality of speech acts. For instance, the boundaries between suggestions, advice, warnings and threats heavily blur into each other. Additionally, sometimes one utterance can evoke several speech acts, and it may not be immediately (or ever!) apparent quite which one was meant. As the example in Section 6.2 demonstrates, 'Do you want to go for a drink?' could have been a simple question or an offer to go on a date. It is, in fact, plausible that the speaker intended this precise indeterminacy. Via this tactic, the shop assistant could ask for a date, but swiftly pretend another meaning if faced with rejection. Alternatively, it may even have been an unpleasant prank played on a stream of unsuspecting customers to while away the day.

Second, Searle, unlike Austin, aligned speech acts with particular internal properties of the speaker, their beliefs, feelings and especially intentions (see Sbisà 2002). Note, for example, the sincerity condition. In effect, a speech act is what you intend to do in saying something. The problem here is that working out the speaker's intentions is far from straightforward, since we can't reach into other people's minds. The intentions that hearers may attribute to speakers may not be the ones that they actually have. Sometimes even speakers themselves may not know the intentions that they have until they emerge in a conversation, if indeed they ever do.

The notion of directness in speech act theory captures the fact that there is no necessary correspondence between a grammatical clause type and a speech act. Table 6.3 captures conventional or **direct** correspondences.

Table 6.3 Conventional sentence type-speech act correspondences.

Utterance (said by parent to child)	Clause type	Speech act
Finish your homework	Imperative	Command
Have you finished your homework?	Interrogative	Question/enquiry
Your homework is finished	Declarative	Assertion

As Table 6.4 shows, sometimes there is a conventional match between sentence type and speech act; however pragmaticians tend to be much more interested in the many cases where this does *not* occur.

Table 6.4 Conventional sentence type-speech act correspondences and directness.

Utterance (said whilst trying to lift something heavy)	Sentence type	Speech act	Directness
Give me a hand	Imperative	Request	Direct
Can you give me a hand?	Interrogative	Request/(Question)	(Conventionally) indirect
You've got strong arms and big hands	Declarative	Request/Assertion	(Non-conventionally) indirect

What makes 'Give me a hand' direct is that the sentence type and the speech act match. The other utterances are indirect; there is no match, or, in Searle's terms, 'cases in which one illocutionary act is performed indirectly by way of performing another' (1975: 60). 'You've got strong arms and big hands' looks like an assertion about aspects of the person's physique. However, in an appropriate context, like somebody trying to lift a heavy object, it is easy to see that it might be an implied request, a hint that help is requested. 'Can you give me a hand?' is ambiguous between being a literal question about the *ability* to give a hand and a request to actually assist. However, not only can a context push it towards being a request, but the particular form of the question does. *Can you [X]* is conventionally associated with requests to some degree – when we see or hear it, we know a request is likely.[3] It can be seen as conventionalised in two different ways.

Searle (1975) argues that conventionally indirect speech acts are constructed around a key part of the speech act they are trying to do. So, a preparatory condition of a request is that the person you are asking has the ability to do it. This is why utterances such as 'Please make it rain tomorrow' don't work as normal requests in most belief systems. A question about one's ability to do something orientates to a preparatory condition of a request. Incidentally, remember that speech acts are culturally sensitive; indirect speech acts, outside English-speaking cultures, may focus on other key parts of the speech act. The structures realising requests, or indeed any other speech act, are not universal – there is no equivalent to *Can you [X]* in Japanese, for example.

An alternative perspective on conventionalisation is that formulae like *Can you [X]* simply become associated over time with doing requests. The requestive meaning is the (semi)-conventionalised pragmatic meaning associated with the form (see Table 6.1). In the same way, the 'Do you want to go for a drink?' from our example earlier can be seen as a (semi)-conventionalised indirect offer to go on a date.

One feature to note of the indirect requests of Table 6.4 is that their requestive meaning can be denied. Thus, if the person you asked was busy and reacted irritably to your request, you could deny you had asked for help . . . at least to some extent! And as noted, this is particularly handy for risky requests like asking someone on a date. **Deniability** is one of the reasons such requests are often discussed in relation to **politeness**.

In focus: variation in how speech acts are realised across cultures and languages

One might ask the question: what degree of indirectness is required in a particular situation in a particular culture? A whole sub-field of pragmatics – cross-cultural pragmatics – has evolved around differences (and similarities) in the way pragmatics works across cultures. For example, one cultural stereotype is that the British tend to prefer indirect ways of doing things in their interactions. Is this empirically true? The Cross Cultural Speech Act Realisation Patterns project (Blum-Kulka et al. 1989), perhaps the biggest project of its kind, examined requests and apologies in British English, American English, Australian English, Hebrew, Danish, German, Russian, Canadian French and Argentinian Spanish, deploying between 94 and 227 informants per language. They found that all cultures use more conventional requests (e.g. 'could you pass me the salt?') than other types; direct requests are least frequently used by the English; but no culture uses hints with any great frequency. So, there is partial support for the stereotype: it's not the case that the British opt for the most indirect strategy (it would be absurd to communicate all the time in hints!), but they avoid the most direct way of doing things.

Such studies are not without their problems. For example, equating whole nations with just one culture does not capture the cultural variation within them (see also Chapter 12). Also, these studies tended to focus on words and grammar, and ignore the role of prosody (the sound, the melody with which something is said), to say nothing of gesture, all of which could make an act more or less direct.

6.4 Between the lines: conversational implicature and the unsaid

Meaning in interaction is so much more than the mere words. Consider this messaging thread in Figure 6.1.

This interaction illustrates a conversational pragmatic meaning misfire. Meanings of particular language interactions are derived from assumptions about how the exchange of information works. Here the addressee (on the right)

Figure 6.1 A conversational pragmatic misfire.

assumes that 'I am here for you' refers to the 'tough time' they are 'going through', and so they infer a meaning approximating to 'I support you'. In reality, the speaker presumably intended to convey, 'I'm present at your location in the taxi that you ordered, ready to collect you and take you somewhere'.

Grice's (1975) **Cooperative Principle** (CP) was designed to capture how meanings are derived through a certain logic in the way information is exchanged. The CP is formulated thus:

> Make your contribution such as is required, at the stage at which it occurs, by the accepted purpose or direction of the talk exchange in which you are engaged.
>
> (1975: 45)

The first thing to note here is that cooperation in this context is an instrumental, linguistic concept, not a social or even philanthropic one. It refers to the **exchange of information** (giving enough to meet the needs of the talk exchange), *not* to friendly, harmonious, benevolent or otherwise altruistic behaviours (doing what the other person wants). Table 6.5 illustrates this point and also how semantic meaning is distinct from pragmatic meaning.

Table 6.5 Cooperation and conversational implicature.

Exchange		Cooperation		Speaker B meaning	
A (seeing B make a cup of tea) says . . .	Speaker B replies . . .	Informational cooperation	Social cooperation	Semantic (literal) meaning	Pragmatic meaning (implicature)
Will you make me a cup of tea?	Okay.	Yes	Yes	Yes [I will make you a cup of tea]	-
Will you make me a cup of tea?	No.	Yes	No	No [I won't make you a cup of tea]	-
Will you make me a cup of tea?	I've got to leave in a minute.	No	No	I must leave in a minute	No [I won't make you a cup of tea]

The yes-no question 'Will you make me a cup of tea?' is most straightforwardly answered by 'yes' (or 'sure', 'okay', etc.) or 'no'. The third option, 'I've got to leave in a minute' does not immediately answer the question. But if we assume that the CP applies, it is relevant at a deeper level: we can infer A's intended meaning or **implicature**, namely, 'no, I won't make you a cup of tea, because I lack the sufficient time to do so'.

Relevance is just one way in which the CP operates. Grice (1975) proposed that the CP consists of the four **maxims** governing the way the conversational contribution is made. These are summarised in Table 6.6.

Table 6.6 The maxims of the Cooperative Principle.

Maxim	Informational focus
Quality	Truth of information
Quantity	Amount of information
Relation	Relevance of information
Manner	Clarity of the expression of the information

Table 6.5 demonstrates an example in which relevance is the issue – A answers with 'I've got to leave in a minute' which **flouts** the maxim of relation and generates an implicature.

Let's illustrate the full set of maxims. Imagine that an individual named Hamlet is having family problems. He's reading a book when he's asked by Polonius (who is often annoying) 'What do you read, my Lord?' Hamlet could respond in various ways, as illustrated in Table 6.7.

Table 6.7 Illustrating the maxims of the Cooperative Principle.

Hamlet responds	Maxim flouted	Notes
Your face, where men may read strange matters.	Quality	This is obviously untrue; we can't read faces in the literal, linguistic sense.
Words.	Quantity	This is obvious; it doesn't provide sufficient information to answer the question.
Hark! Is that the savage clamour of a bear?	Relation	This response has no relationship to the question.
A tome of the greatest of dreams, yet the worst of nightmares.	Manner	*Tome* is an unnecessarily obscure word for a book, and this answer is long without providing any meaningful detail.

In fact, if you haven't recognised it already, our examples are developments of an exchange in Shakespeare's play, *Hamlet*. Here is the original version:

Polonius: What do you read, my Lord?
Hamlet: Words, words, words.

(Act 2, Scene 2)

In *Hamlet* proper, both the maxims of quantity and manner are flouted. *Words, words, words* does not provide sufficient information, and it is unnecessarily repetitious. Here, it would seem that Hamlet views the question as an unwelcome intrusion, that he cannot or will not convey a more informative answer, and would like to be left alone. Our other three examples in Table 6.7 trigger similar implicatures. However, note that because implicatures are inferred from what is said in the specific context, they tend to have an intangible, nebulous quality. As a result, if Hamlet were challenged, he could quite easily deny these meanings. It is not surprising that politicians often enjoy conveying meanings via implicatures!

It is worth noting that Grice outlined other possibilities besides merely **flouting** maxims. Perhaps the most obvious additional case to mention is **violation**. This is surreptitious non-adherence to one or more maxims, or in ordinary everyday terms, the speaker lies with the intention of not being caught.

Finally, Grice intended, perhaps somewhat controversially, to place his Cooperative Principle within **general pragmatics**. That is to say, it was not intended to be specific to any particular language or social context, but a general mechanism for capturing the ways that we generate meanings.

6.5 From pragmalinguistics to sociopragmatics

Grice's Cooperative Principle is assumed to be of general application – it applies to any conversation or interaction involving an exchange of information. However, as noted by Leech (1983), sometimes instead of general pragmatics, we have pragmatics that is anchored by the specifics of the language, that is to say, **pragmalinguistics**, and sometimes we have pragmatics that is anchored by the specifics of the social context, that is to say, **sociopragmatics**.

We have, in fact, already met pragmalinguistics. Table 6.1, displaying types of pragmatic meaning, noted conventionalised pragmatic meaning, which on a scale from more linguistic meaning to more contextual, leans towards the more linguistic end. Such meanings are linked to particular forms of language which have typical implied meanings acquired from their regular use in particular contexts; in other words, the forms have (semi-)conventionalised associations with their pragmatic meanings. We gave the example of 'Do you want to go for a drink?' not being an enquiry about wanting to quench one's thirst or wanting a meal deal option, but, non-literally, implying the meaning of an offer to go on a date. But there are many other types of conventionalised or semi-conventionalised pragmatic meaning, some of which are displayed in Table 6.8.

Table 6.8 Types of conventionalised pragmatic meaning.

Technical label for category	Examples	Brief definition
Performative verb	*Promise, apologise, warn, bet, invite, declare, request, offer, name, advise,* etc.	Verbs that name the action they perform (cf. Austin 1962).
Speech act formulae	*Could you* and *please* are both associated with requests; *sorry* is associated with apologies; rising intonation is associated with speech acts that question or enquire; etc.	Particular words or expressions that signal a particular speech act (what Searle 1969: 30 referred to as illocutionary force indicating devices).

(Continued)

(Continued)

Technical label for category	Examples	Brief definition
Conventional implicatures	*But, even, yet*, etc.	Particular words or expressions that generate implicatures (contrasting with conversational implicatures which work in relation to the exchange of information) (cf. Grice [1975] 1989: 25). For example, in 'It's sunny but cold', *but* implies that an expectation before the word is contradicted by what comes after.
Presuppositions	Definite noun phrases (e.g. 'My car is red' presupposes the existence of my car), WH-questions (e.g. 'When do we begin?' presupposes that there is a point at which we begin); counterfactual conditionals (e.g. 'If I had carried all that, I would have been exhausted' presupposes that I hadn't carried all that'); change-of-state verbs (e.g. 'Stop doing that' presupposes that the person had started); etc.	Particular words or expressions that imply information that is old, noncontroversial, taken for granted, in the background.
Discourse markers	*Anyway, okay, well, however, so, on the other hand*, etc.	Particular words or expressions that indicate how one should understand one bit of discourse in relation to another.

Needless to say, pragmalinguistic resources vary across languages. Figure 6.2, a caption on a packet of English biscuits, illustrates this point.

The slogan, *C'est Anglais, mais c'est bon!* ('It's English, but it's good!') depends on a conventional implicature triggered by *mais* 'but'. The implicature is that what precedes is contrary to what follows: the stereotype of English food in France is that it is bad, but despite this, these English biscuits are good.

Figure 6.2 McVitie's biscuits and conventional implicature in French.

Sociopragmatics is

> positioned on the more social side of pragmatics, standing in contrast to the more linguistic side. It is focussed on the construction and understanding of meanings arising from interactions between language (or other semiotic resources) and socio-cultural phenomena. . . . It often considers norms emerging in such contexts, how they are exploited by participants, and how they lead to evaluations of (in)appropriateness.
>
> (Culpeper 2021)

In everyday social contexts, pragmatic phenomena allow us to subtly, and sometimes not so subtly, convey our attitudes, perspectives, and thoughts about our relationships, what we think of ourselves, how we feel about matters, and what we believe about others. They allow us enormous linguistic elasticity in how we approach the diplomacy of breaking difficult news, the creativity of telling novel jokes, the sociality of conveying office gossip, and far more besides. Further, this room for manoeuvre can be, and routinely is, exploited. Imagine, for instance, a manager suggesting to an assistant that, 'It would be good if this office was tidied before the CEO visits'. The underpaid assistant might find it highly inconvenient to recognise the implicit command and decide not to bother tidying. Indeed, precepts of *malicious compliance*, *working to contract*, and *letter of the law* are rooted in ignoring pragmatic, schematic, and conventionalised meanings in favour of near- and absolutely literal interpretations. Unfortunately, for our office assistant, the consequences of playing pragmatics games may be disciplinary action or even unemployment. All this, and more, falls under the heading of sociopragmatics.

If there is one topic that is central to sociopragmatics, it is **politeness**, and more recently **impoliteness**. Linguistic (im)politeness is connected with the final statement in the previous quotation. It is much to do with what is evaluated as accepted and expected, given the norms of a particular situation and culture. For example, in British culture, asking for a coffee in a coffee shop might involve the words, *A coffee please*, or *Could I have a coffee?* Such expressions are considered polite: they are accepted and expected. In Italy, this might instead involve *Mi dai un caffè* ('Give me a coffee') or *Un caffè* ('A coffee'). From a British perspective, all other things being equal, such relatively direct expressions are far less accepted and will generally be unexpected, and they might result in evaluations of rudeness. In fact, in the Italian context, the norms are different, and so such expressions are actually accepted and expected, with the result that an evaluation of rudeness is extremely unlikely.

The most famous approach to politeness is that of Brown and Levinson (1987). In their vision, linguistic politeness involves communicative strategies designed to (1) counterbalance the negative effects on the hearer that might arise as a result of your intended actions, and (2) make it more likely that you will achieve your goal. For example, let's compare: 'Make me a coffee' with 'Would you mind making me a coffee?' The first is a direct request (made with an imperative verb), but the second as an indirect request (it is literally formulated as question). Note the connection with our discussion of speech act directness. In British culture, the indirect request is likely to be evaluated as more polite, and be associated with situations in which more politeness is required.

According to Brown and Levinson (1987), how much politeness is required in a situation is determined by three variables:

- **Power** (more relative power → less politeness), for example, borrowing from a student vs. borrowing from a tutor;
- **Social distance** (more familiar → less politeness), for example, borrowing from your best friend vs. borrowing from a stranger;
- **Size of imposition** (more imposing → more politeness), for example, borrowing the only pen someone has vs. borrowing one of their many pens.

Brown and Levinson (1987) provided an impressive amount of detail regarding the possible linguistic substance of politeness. They formed a number of categories broadly spanning a scale of directness. Where very little politeness is required, one can be direct, or in their terms 'bald on record'. Where a huge amount of politeness is required, they point out that one can simply opt out, and just not do the thing that would require all that politeness. In between, there are three other possibilities representing the core of politeness work. Imagine asking someone to help lift a heavy object. The following examples illustrate the three categories available. Note that the labels are Brown and Levinson's (1987); the descriptions and examples are ours:

(1) **Off-record hints,** for example, 'Good grief this is so heavy!'

(2) **Negative politeness**, that is, soften the utterance so that it displays a reluctance to impose. This can include strategies such as:

  a. being conventionally indirect: 'Can you lend a hand?'
  b. pessimism: 'I don't suppose you could lend a hand?'
  c. hedging: 'Actually I wondered if you might have a moment to help?'
  d. apologising: 'I'm sorry, I don't want to trouble you but could you help?'
  e. politeness markers: 'please'.
  f. specific lexical and grammatical features such as questions, negatives, and conditionals.

(3) **Positive politeness**, that is, sweeten the utterance to display a positive opinion of, an interest in, or solidarity with the hearer, before moving onto the face-threatening act. This can include strategies like:

  a. paying attention to the hearer: 'Hi! It's so lovely to see you!'
  b. expressing interest, approval or sympathy: 'You're in amazing shape!'
  c. using in-group identity markers: 'Darling', 'Mate'.
  d. seeking agreement: 'This has been such a warm day'.
  e. assuming common ground: 'I know how you feel', and so on.

Ultimately, (im)politeness is a sociopragmatic matter because it involves evaluations of utterances in their contexts. But (im)politeness has a more pragmalinguistic side too. Utterances that are regularly used to perform politeness, like *please* and *thank you*, acquire the associations of politeness, even when they are not doing that kind of work. This becomes vividly apparent when we consider the many thousands of tweets sent during the COVID-19 pandemic that contain the phrase, 'Thanks covid!' Unsurprisingly, the vast majority of these are not sincere. Instead, they are expressing sarcasm, anger and frustration about bereavements, missed loved ones, awful symptoms, lost pay, cancelled events, loneliness and far more besides. The sarcasm only works in these cases because we understand that thanks are normally associated with politeness, yet here they are doing the opposite.

In focus: pragmatics, politeness and sign language

We have referred to 'utterances' doing politeness, and indeed much pragmatics talks about 'utterances', not to mention 'speakers' and 'hearers'. In fact, politeness, impoliteness or indeed any kind of pragmatic phenomenon are not limited to spoken language. And it is not just writing either; non-verbal material can achieve pragmatic meanings, including (im)politeness. Let's briefly consider the case of **sign languages**. Mapson (2014) showed that in British Sign Language (research suggests that American Sign Language is similar) tight lips are used when only a small amount of politeness work is needed, whereas 'polite grimace' (a tight smile, with lips either open or lightly closed) is used when somewhat more politeness work is needed. These are illustrated in Figure 6.3.

(a)   (b)

Figure 6.3 Polite expressions: 'tight lips' on the left and 'polite grimace' on the right.

Source: Mapson (2014: 170). By kind permission of Rachel Mapson and the signer Frankie McLean.

Mapson (2014) drew attention to the fact that a much wider array of features, beyond the lips and the face, are used in sign languages to achieve politeness evaluations. To that she noted a 'side tilt' (tilting the head alone or head and upper body combined) and 'polite duck' (lowering the head and slightly raising or hunching the shoulders), as illustrated in Figure 6.4.

All this is to say nothing of what can be achieved through manual (hand) gestures, such as finger-pointing.

It is not, of course, the case that what happens in one medium is totally separate from what happens in another, but there can be overlaps and parallels. This is the case when one considers politeness expressed in verbal speech and politeness expressed in sign languages. For example, Brown and Levinson (1987) point out that there is an association between raised pitch and politeness, and subsequent researchers have confirmed this. But this could be, and indeed regularly is, combined with raised eyebrows, which Mapson (2014) notes as a possible politeness feature in British Sign Language.

(a)   (b)

Figure 6.4 Polite expressions: 'side tilt' on the left and 'polite duck' on the right.

Source: Mapson (2014: 174). By kind permission of Rachel Mapson and the signer Frankie McLean.

6.6 Pragmatics in practice

From our examples on meal-deal misfires, uncomplimentary biscuits, awkward texts and moody Shakespearian protagonists, it may seem that pragmatics ranges from the interesting to the fun, but that it isn't really critical to real-life communication. This final section is a more sober counterbalance. In contexts like frontline response and critical infrastructure, the very woolliness and indeterminacy of pragmatics presents a serious issue. In a range of high-stakes contexts, efforts are routinely made to standardise language use, usually through pre-agreed terminology and scripts that have explicit, codified, non-negotiable meanings. To put it differently, a lot of time is spent on reducing or even removing the potential for pragmatic inferencing specifically to prevent individuals from arriving at their own subjective, imprecise and potentially incorrect interpretations.

Imagine that an army general in an active warzone radios ground troops to say, 'We are retaking the township by midnight'. Is this an update on the situation, or a command to attack? Once again, misinterpretation could cause untold harm to both civilians and soldiers. And yet, even the consequences of warzone miscommunications can be readily eclipsed by another altogether more commonplace arena that exists around us, in nearly every town and city worldwide. On a daily basis, massive transportation networks like airlines, trains, and ferries are responsible for millions of lives, and the individuals in charge of these vessels and vehicles must routinely produce unambiguous communication with passengers, control centres and each other, despite the fact that everyone involved may speak different first languages.

Pragmatic miscommunications are certainly not always the result of different first languages. Even speakers of the same first language can make egregious communicative errors. In just one real-life case, an air traffic control tower told a pilot that they were cleared to land on Runway 24, but then as the plane approached, added, 'Can you make Runway 15L?' The pilot agreed that they could, inferring that they were now required to land on Runway 15L. In reality, the tower still intended the plane to land on Runway 24, but wanted them to then turn left onto Runway 15L as soon as possible after touchdown (NASA 2003). Whilst this case resolved itself without incident, one can easily imagine a much less favourable conclusion, especially if the situation had been compounded by poor visibility, tiredness or extreme stress. Research from both airlines and independent bodies suggest that around 70% of aviation safety incidents and accidents are a result of problems with communication and information transfer (Lautman et al., cited in Orasanu 1993: 137; Connell 1996: 20; Tajima 2004: 453–454).

Huge efforts over many decades have been made by all participants to eradicate misfires, ambiguity and confusion, and yet these problems still arise. By itself, this comprehensively demonstrates the ubiquity of pragmatics, and its centrality to our communicative repertoires, irrespective of the languages we may speak. To return to our opening arguments, then, it may be extraordinarily difficult to define pragmatics, but everyone who uses language is immersed in it. Sometimes our lives even hang in the balance because of it, and yet, research in this field is still in its relative infancy.

Notes

1 In practice, of course, her relationship dynamic might be very different, but the point here is that she is utilising a shared stereotype about relationships which may or may not reflect her lived reality to produce an indirect, softened rejection of an assumed advance.
2 The fact that it is called *speech* act theory does not mean it is only applicable to speech. Thinking in terms of 'pragmatic acts' might be a more accurate term.
3 In practice, there is a difference between seeing and hearing. Spoken requests tend to be less ambiguous because the prosody (melody) of the request can give additional clues that it is indeed a request.

References

Ariel, M. 2008. *Pragmatics and Grammar*. Cambridge: Cambridge University Press.

Austin, J. L. 1962. *How to Do Things with Words*. Oxford: Oxford University Press.

Blum-Kulka, S., House, J. and Kasper, G. (Eds.). 1989. *Cross-Cultural Pragmatics: Requests and Apologies*. Vol. XXXI. Advances in Discourse Processes. Norwood, NJ: Ablex.

Brown, P. and Levinson, S. C. 1987. *Politeness: Some Universals In Language Use*. Cambridge: Cambridge University Press.

Connell, L. 1996. Pilot and controller communication issues. In B. G. Kanki and V. O. Prinzo (Eds.), *Methods and Metrics of Voice Communication*. Washington, DC: US Federal Aviation Administration, pp. 19–27.

Culpeper, J. 2021. Sociopragmatics: Roots and definition. In M. Haugh, D. Kádár and M. Terkourafi (Eds.), *The Cambridge Handbook of Sociopragmatics*. Vol. Cambridge Handbooks in Language and Linguistics. Cambridge: Cambridge University Press, pp. 15–29.

Culpeper, J., Mackey, A. and Taguchi, N. 2018. *Second Language Pragmatics: From Theory to Research*. New York and London: Routledge.

Greenstreet, R. 2019. Jenna Coleman: 'I didn't get into drama school. I felt like Billy Elliot'. *The Guardian*, 16 February.

Grice, H. P. 1975. Logic and conversation. In P. Cole and J. L. Morgan (Eds.), *Syntax and Semantics, Vol. 3: Speech Acts*. London and New York: Academic Press, pp. 41–58.

Grice, H. P. 1989. *Studies in the Way of Words*. Cambridge, MA: Harvard University Press.

Leech, G. N. 1983. *Principles of Pragmatics*. London: Longman.

Levinson, S. C. 1983. *Pragmatics*. Cambridge: Cambridge University Press.

Mapson, R. P. 2014. Polite appearances: How non-manual features convey politeness in British Sign Language. *Journal of Politeness Research*, 10(2): 157–184. http://doi.org/10.1515/pr-2014-0008

Morris, C. W. 1938. Foundations of the theory of signs. In O. Neurath (Ed.), *International Encyclopedia of Unified Science*. Vol. 1. Chicago: University of Chicago Press.

NASA. 2003. Runway confusion   by request *Callback*, October, 289.

Orasanu, J. M. 1993. Decision-making in the cockpit. In E. L. Wiener, B. G. Kanki and R. L. Helmreich (Eds.), *Cockpit Resource Management*. San Diego, CA: Academic Press, pp. 137–172.

Rosaldo, M. Z. 1982. The things we do with words: Ilongot speech acts and speech act theory in philosophy. *Language in Society*, 11(2): 203–236. http://doi.org/10.1017/S0047404500009209

Sbisà, M. 2002. Cognition and narrativity in speech act sequences. In A. Fetzer and C. Meierkord (Eds.), *Rethinking Sequentiality: Linguistics Meets*

Conversational Interaction. Amsterdam and Philadelphia: John Benjamins, pp. 71–97.

Searle, J. R. 1969. *Speech Acts: An Essay in the Philosophy of Language*. Cambridge: Cambridge University Press.

Searle, J. R. 1975. A taxonomy of illocutionary acts. In K. Gunderson (Ed.), *Language, Mind, and Knowledge*. Minneapolis: University of Minnesota Press, pp. 344–369.

Tajima, A. 2004. Fatal miscommunication: English in aviation safety. *World Englishes*, 23(3): 451–470. http://doi.org/10.1111/j.0883-2919.2004.00368.x

Section two

Mind and society

7 Sociolinguistics

Beth Malory and Karin Tusting

7.1 What is sociolinguistics?

Sociolinguistics studies the relations between language and society, and how language relates to social structures. Every act of language transmits social information. Every time we communicate, our language operates **indexically** to situate us as social beings. Perhaps our speech/signing reveals us to be from a certain part of the country, from a particular socio-economic background, or from a certain generation. This is **indexicality**, the process of association between linguistic forms and social meaning. Indexicality works as a heuristic, or shortcut, which helps us to pigeonhole other users of the language according to our internalised stereotypes. We do this, even when we try not to. All language use can therefore be seen as a 'series of **acts of identity**' in which people reveal both their personal identity and their . . . social roles' (Le Page and Tabouret-Keller 1985: 14). Sometimes, these acts of identity are conscious choices, as in the following 'in focus' box.

> **What does saying 'loo' say about you?**
>
> In the 2000s, a television advertising campaign for toilet cleaner in the UK asked the audience, 'what does your loo say about you?', showing footage of a horrified guest recoiling at a badly maintained toilet. Without casting aspersions on the state of anyone's loo, we can just as fruitfully ask, 'what does *saying* 'loo' say about you?'.
>
> The indexical relationship between linguistic forms and social meaning means that *loo* and many of the variants that could replace it transmit information about the social identity of the language user. What assumptions and judgements might you make if someone used *lavatory, bog, restroom, crapper, shitter* or *khazi* instead?

In focus: *pain au chocolat, chocolatine* or something else . . . ?

For centuries, France has been divided over what to call chocolate-filled pastries. The debate has spawned memes, jokes like the one in Figure 7.1, and even, in 2018, a debate in the French Parliament! Dialect mapping of regional variation, see Figure 7.2, reveals that it isn't quite as straightforward as Figure 7.1 might have us believe.

DOI: 10.4324/9781003045571-9

Figure 7.1 More expensive pastries for sale under the name *pain au chocolat*.

Figure 7.2 Dialectal variation map showing where different terms are used.

In addition to the dominant variant, *pain au chocolat*, and the variant dominant in the South West, *chocolatine*, other variants such as *petit pain au chocolat*, *petit pain* and *croissant au chocolat* also occur. There is even a website where French speakers can vote for their preferred variant!

https://chocolatineoupainauchocolat.fr/
Scan the QR code to visit the 'Chocolatine ou Pain au Chocolat' website!

SCAN ME

Our social identities are also revealed through acts which are below the level of consciousness. We may attune our linguistic behaviours to those of our interlocutors, without even realising what we are doing. Equally, we might **accommodate** by consciously or unconsciously altering our language to be more like that used by a particular group, if we want to 'fit in'.

Some languages have standard varieties used for formal or educational purposes. In less formal settings, people might use a more vernacular variety. Standard varieties are often regarded as more **prestigious** than vernacular varieties. This is known as the **standard language ideology**. There is no linguistic basis for this hierarchical conception of language prestige, but it is important that linguists understand how users of the language think and feel about it (known as 'folk linguistic' beliefs). Figure 7.3 shows how languages are often conceived as a hierarchy.

The standard variety is not selected for linguistic reasons, but arises based on a range of social, political, geographical and other factors. For instance, when Greece became independent in the nineteenth century, a form of Greek called Katharevousa, (meaning 'purified') and based on Ancient Greek, was selected as the official language, because of its high prestige and its use in ancient literature. This was a powerful way to connect the new modern Greek nation with its Classical roots. However, the way people actually spoke was quite different. In 1976, the official language was changed to a completely different form of Greek, Demotic (meaning 'of the people'), based on spoken language. This is a good illustration of how decisions about standard languages are driven by broader political, social and cultural values.

Lippi-Green (1997) describes the hierarchical thinking which places vernacular variants below standard norms as a process of 'language subordination'. She proposes that certain languages or language varieties (and by extension those who speak them) are commonly associated with negative traits such as ugliness, illogicality or incoherence (p. 68). Cameron coined the phrase 'verbal hygiene' to describe **prescriptive** attempts to make language 'conform more closely to . . . ideals', whether of 'beauty, truth, efficiency, logic, correctness [or] civility' ([1995] 2012: vii). Verbal hygiene, Cameron argues, is a universal of humanity; although '[o]ur norms and values differ', she writes, 'what remains constant is that we have norms and values' (p. 9).

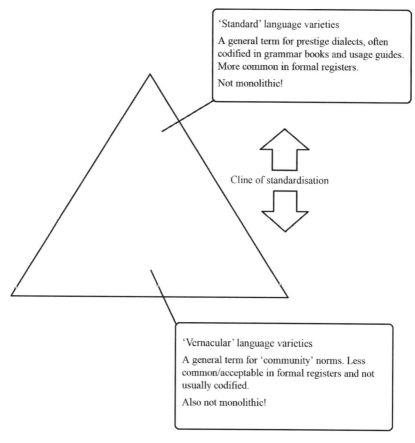

Figure 7.3 The standard language hierarchy.

It should, by now, be clear that the study of language in its social context is inseparable from language attitudes and ideologies. How, then, do language attitudes impact the way language is used? How can we study language in use without letting our own attitudes get in the way? We will start our consideration of these questions with a look at where sociolinguistics started.

7.2 Key concepts in sociolinguistics

Sociolinguistics as an independent discipline began with variationist research in the 1960s, which demonstrated structured variation in language for the first time. Sociophonetic research conducted by Labov on the island of Martha's Vineyard in Massachusetts

This early work developed the tool of the linguistic variable, a linguistic unit with two or more variants which could be correlated with other social and/or linguistic variation.

(1963) and later in New York City (1966) showed that there was a relationship between linguistic and social patterns. Labov had noticed that there was a difference between how residents of different areas of Martha's Vineyard pronounced the diphthongs /au/ and /ai/, as in *mouth* and *price*.

> The first wave of quantitative sociolinguistics used broad surveys and looked for correlations between linguistic variation and global (preconceived) social categories, such as sex and socio-economic class.

He showed that these diphthongs were an index of speakers' feelings about the island community and their place within it, as well as attitudes to the growing tourist industry. This confirmed his initial hypothesis that there was a distinction between those who lived in areas with a traditional economy based on fishing and those who lived in areas dependent on tourism.

In focus: all in a day's shopping for Labov!

Labov's early work is regarded as the foundation stone of what is called 'variationist' sociolinguistics. One of its most famous studies was completed in a single day. Labov selected a socially sensitive feature of pronunciation, **postvocalic** [r], and studied its use in three very different department stores on the Lower East Side of NYC. By asking questions intended to elicit the answer 'fourth floor' from 274 sales assistants, Labov demonstrated that use of [r] was socially stratified. **Rhoticity** (pronunciation of the [r]) was most common in Saks Fifth Avenue, the shop with the highest social ranking, lowest in Klein's, the shop with the lowest social ranking, and middling in Macy's, which was somewhere in between in social status. Basically, he found that the fancier the shop, the more postvocalic [r] was pronounced.

In some contexts, like that described in the box, it is easy to identify the variant with higher social status. Postvocalic [r] was pronounced more in fancier shops, because in this context, it was being evaluated in accordance with mainstream norms. This is **overt prestige**, where a variant's social value is linked to a widely accepted set of norms. In terms of the standard language hierarchy depicted in Figure 7.3, such norms sit at the top.

Prestige is not always this straightforward however, since variants can also be evaluated in accordance with local norms and values. This is called **covert prestige**. For example, Danish language ideology organises varieties of language into a hierarchy like that in Figure 7.3, with so-called 'high' Copenhagen dialect, *rigsdansk*, at the top and so-called 'low' Copenhagen dialect, *withkøbenhavnsk*, at the bottom. At one time, *withkøbenhavnsk* was seen as a working-class variety and severely stigmatised, whilst *rigsdansk* was considered more formal, and appropriate in public situations. It seems, however, that young Danes no longer associate *withkøbenhavnsk* with working-class speech, but rather with dyna-mism and informality. It is often used in the context of modern mass media, whilst *rigsdansk* is still considered more appropriate for school and business. Kristiansen (2003) argues that young Danes operate with two standards: 'one for the school, where excellence is perceived in terms of "superiority"' and assessed in relation to traditional notions of overt prestige, and 'one for the media, where excellence is perceived in terms of "dynamism"' and assessed in relation to newer notions of covert prestige (p. 67).

Complex conceptualisations of prestige like this prompted a movement away from research using hierarchically ordered social groups. Early socio-linguistic studies of urban areas had generally used large speaker samples and the Labovian framework of the 'speech community', in which socio-economic class, age and sex were axes of social variation. The 1980s and 1990s, how-ever, witnessed a growing tendency for research to focus on smaller communi-ties or single neighbourhoods instead, often involving groups of economically similar speakers. From this work, the important concept of **social networks** emerged.

L. and J. Milroy (Milroy 1987; Milroy and Milroy 1992) were piv-otal in replacing the traditional speech community framework, and its focus on economic and other demographic differences, with a **social network model** that focused on interactive ties at a local level. Dense and multi-plex social networks, represented in Figure 7.4, were found to reinforce linguistic norms, operating to maintain the linguistic status quo.

> The second wave of quantitative sociolinguistics paid more attention to the local context and social meaning of linguistic variables. Key concepts here are the **social network** (Milroy 1987; Milroy 1992) and **community of prac-tice** (Eckert and McConnell-Ginet 1992).

The social network framework has been used to explain patterns of language maintenance and change. For instance, Spanish remains dominant in some areas of the US state of New Mexico, such as the village of Córdova – why is this? According to Gonzales Velásquez (1995), because of the size of the village, its history and the role of the church within it, it is characterised by dense, multi-plex networks which support transmission of language and culture between generations. Looser, less multiplex networks might well have led to language shift to English, the dominant national language. Where people's networks within the village were weaker, with more contacts outside it with English speakers, they were more likely to be bilingual.

Framing understandings of language variation in relation to local contexts and social values was a huge step. It moved sociolinguistic research away from its traditional focus on large-scale, quantitative, correlational methods towards ethnographic approaches, which explore local social identities. We will now dis-cuss the methods used in different approaches to sociolinguistics.

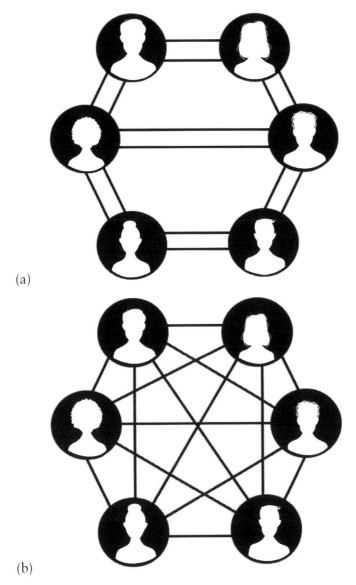

(a)

(b)

Figure 7.4 Dense (a) and multiplex (b) social networks.

7.3 Different approaches to sociolinguistics

7.3.1 Variationist sociolinguistics

The goals of variationist sociolinguistics are to identify parts of the language which are variable, to track changes and to understand which factors correlate with variation. Languages, of course, vary at many levels, and variables can be identified in terms of the 'levels' of language outlined in Section two of this volume. We might focus on phonological, morphosyntactic or discourse-pragmatic variables. Variationist sociolinguistics relates linguistic variation and change to social groupings such as class, gender and geographical location. For example, Bayley et al.'s (2002) study of variation in American Sign Language signs for the number '1' shows geographical variation associated with the location of former residential schools for deaf children, and also ethnic variation, as previously black deaf children and white deaf children were educated separately due to segregation.

As we have already seen, such research tended historically to use quantitative methodological approaches. Quantitative analyses use numerical data, such as calculating the frequency of a certain vowel or grammatical structure among different groups of people. This kind of research focuses on statistical patterns created when groups of language users are categorised together. It therefore belongs squarely to the **empiricist** research tradition, and aims to observe language in use in an unbiased manner. This means minimising observer effect as far as is practicable, and attempting to analyse data through replicable quantitative procedures. Minimising observer effects means trying to escape the **observer's paradox**, which was identified by Labov (1972) as the tension which results when trying to observe language used by subjects who do not feel self-conscious.

Observation remains the cornerstone of variationist linguistics, and methodologies used in variationist studies are often geared towards limiting the impact of the researcher's presence on the practices which are observed. Methods include surveys of linguistic variation, attitude surveys, sociolinguistic interviews which elicit a range of different speech types, real-time studies (sampling language data at different points in time to study change) and apparent time studies (collecting data from people of different generations, as a proxy for change over time). These research techniques are often used together. Milroy and Milroy (1985) combined in-depth interviews with surveys. Eckert (2000) combined experiments on language attitudes with interviews about usage. One reason for this kind of methodological pluralism in variationist sociolinguistics has been an increasing focus on the study of how people perceive language, researching *language beliefs, language attitudes, language ideologies* or *language regard*.

7.3.2 Interactional sociolinguistics

In the 1960s, the dominant 'generative' approach in linguistics aimed to understand language as a system reflecting deep structures of the brain. It distinguished between **linguistic performance** – actual speech produced by speakers, with all its errors and inconsistencies – and **linguistic competence**, knowledge of the underlying grammatical systems of the language. Early generative approaches argued that the 'proper' focus of linguistics was the underlying competence, rather than the imperfect performance (Chomsky 1965; see Chapter 25).

Interactional sociolinguistics challenged this position. The central argument of this field was that the most important thing to understand is not abstract knowledge of grammatical norms, but the rules and norms around how to communicate in a social context: what it is appropriate to say, when, how and to whom. Hymes states (1974: 75) that 'A child from whom any and all of the grammatical sentences of a language might come with equal likelihood would be of course a social monster'. In contrast to the idea of linguistic competence, Hymes labelled this **communicative competence**. He developed the mnemonic SPEAKING to indicate the different factors to consider in any communicative situation, illustrated in Figure 7.5. Why not apply these questions to a situation you have witnessed recently?

The methods used in interactional sociolinguistics are rooted in the principle of observing language as it is used in naturally occurring interactions. They usually combine participant-observation, recorded using fieldnotes, and analysis of video and audio-recorded interactions (Rampton 2020; see Chapter 22 on Field Methods for more on these methods in data collection).

Interactional sociolinguistics has always been closely connected with social critique, emerging as it did during a period of struggle for civil rights, and developing as a means of understanding the connections between language and significant social

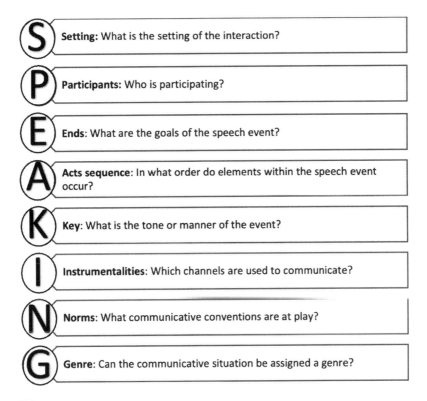

Figure 7.5 SPEAKING acronym.

Source: Based on Hymes (1974).

issues. It has continued to address social issues such as the role of language in the construction of identity, language in conditions of globalisation and superdiversity, and the dynamics of talk, hierarchy, power and inequality in institutions.

Case study: sociolinguistics and signed languages

In 2021, the status of British Sign Language (BSL) in the UK was significantly enhanced when actor Rose Ayling-Ellis won the popular ballroom dancing competition *Strictly Come Dancing*. Rose was born deaf, and BSL is her first language. Her popularity gave a huge boost to public interest in BSL. Enrolments in one firm offering BSL courses went up by more than 2000% (www.bbc.co.uk/news/newsbeat-59474819).

Although BSL was recognised as a minority language of the UK in 2003, it had no 'official' legal status, meaning there was no requirement for public bodies to promote the language or to provide resources such as BSL interpreters for public services. However, a bill to give BSL this legal status is, at the time of writing (early 2022), currently going through Parliament. Partly as a result of this increased public support for BSL, it is likely to become law.

The fact that up till now legal recognition and support for BSL as a language has been missing illustrates the importance of defining and recognising sign languages *as* languages. Sociolinguists of sign language are interested, among other things, in attitudes and ideologies towards sign language, which have important consequences in enabling or preventing access to resources and in supporting the language.

Sign languages are languages of people who have frequently been disempowered by ableist and oralist ideologies, which assume that the ideal for deaf people is for them to approximate to hearing people as much as possible. From this perspective, sign language is seen as a lesser means of communication than speech. At times, it has even been discouraged in favour of attempting to maximise deaf people's use of spoken language. In contrast, a culture- and language-oriented non-deficit view values sign languages as central to deaf history and culture, indeed to the very existence of the deaf community. The sociolinguistic study of sign language is important for giving signed languages status. Kusters and Lucas (2022) argue that to resist medical and oralist perspectives on deafness, sociolinguists must defend the notion that sign languages are real languages, with arbitrary sign-meaning relationships and grammatical systems, rather than elaborate forms of gesture.

Relationships between sign languages can be complex. As will be outlined in Chapter 8, sign languages have emerged in different contexts and at very different scales. Residential schools for the deaf, which brought together deaf children and young people from widely dispersed areas, have been particularly important to the historical development of national sign languages such as British and American Sign Language (ASL); but sign languages do not always sit neatly within national borders. Local sign languages have developed in areas with large numbers of deaf people, for instance where hereditary deafness is particularly prevalent, and these local sign languages may have little in common with the national sign language of that country. Hierarchies between sign languages reflect social hierarchies. Village/rural sign languages may be seen as less sophisticated than national sign languages. In the US, Black ASL is frequently positioned as being of lesser quality than standard ASL, reflecting patterns of racial inequality (Hill and Tamene 2022).

Decisions about how to name and classify sign languages have consequences for the support and recognition available for that language (Hou and de Vos 2022). Tensions exist between recognising multiple local varieties, and prioritising the national sign language to maximise support. Political and ideological factors may be the deciding influences here. Palfreyman and Schembri (2022) explain that pairs such as 'Indian Sign Language' and 'Pakistani Sign Language' may be very similar in purely linguistic terms, but are named as distinct for reasons to do with national and regional identity.

Language contact has also shaped the development of sign languages, and is also tied up with broader ideologies and power relationships. Colonisation, missionary activity and educational development have spread dominant national Western sign languages, particularly ASL, around the world. While this has resulted in many national sign languages being strongly influenced by ASL in their lexis and grammar, their speakers nevertheless may resist classifications of these as variants of ASL to highlight their local nature (Palfreyman and Schembri 2022). Contact between spoken and signed languages also affects many sign languages. Features such as mouthing and finger-spelling may be heavily ideologically loaded, reflecting the dominant oralist tradition and the historical marginalisation of the deaf community (Adam and Braithwaite 2022).

Kusters and Lucas (2022) argue that studying sign languages provides additional perspectives to develop many key areas of sociolinguistics including multilingualism, language variation and language ideologies. This is because of the deficit perspectives and hierarchical ideologies historically associated with sign languages, and the complex multimodal nature of contact between different sign languages, and between signed and spoken languages. In the past, the field of sign language sociolinguistics was made up primarily of hearing researchers. As the field develops, it is increasingly deaf sociolinguists who are leading the way. The dialogue articles drawn on in this discussion box were all produced by one deaf and one hearing researcher working together. Sociolinguistic characterisations of sign languages have important material consequences. It is the people who are positioned within these social and language ideologies who should be the ones making decisions about language classifications, significant areas of research and, ultimately, how we conceptualise sign language within sociolinguistics.

7.4 Some key areas of interest in sociolinguistics

7.4.1 Language and identity

Many sociolinguists are interested in language use and the construction of identity. As we have seen, using particular sociolinguistic variables can index belonging to a particular social class or grouping. One key way of thinking about this connection is to use the idea of style. Eckert (2012) writes of three 'waves' of sociolinguistics. The quantitative study of the correlations between social categories and sociolinguistic variables was the 'first wave', and ethnographic studies which explain local variation by local categories were the 'second wave'. Eckert identifies a 'third wave' which draws on the concepts of style and identity to, in effect, reverse the focus of the discipline. Rather than starting from social categories and using these to explain linguistic variation, third wave sociolinguistics explores how speakers use sociolinguistic variation in dynamic, creative and changing ways to construct their identities by 'stylistic practice'. This means using sociolinguistic variables as part of a broader semiotic repertoire which might include clothing choices, ways of moving, even displays of particular kinds of emotion to construct recognisable identities or 'personae'.

Eckert's own ethnographic research in an American high school is part of this third wave. She showed how different social groupings in the school – from the sporty, success-oriented 'Jocks' to the anti-authority 'Burnouts' – used different sociolinguistic variants. These correlated with other elements of personal style, like clothes and music. Eckert argues that patterns of language use are acquired through belonging to particular communities of practice. More recent studies of youth identities show similar patterns. Ethnographic study of the language of Latina girls involved with gangs in Northern California (Mendoza-Denton 2008) showed how their sociophonetic patterns in both English and Spanish correlate with other symbols of identity such as make-up and clothes to index the groups girls belong to. Communities of practice offer spaces for young people to develop their identities using linguistic and other stylistic indices. Hernández and Ramírez (2021) describe the importance of sports teams as safe spaces for Basque-speaking adolescents to practise their use of the language in informal contexts and develop their identities as Basque speakers.

Case study: language and gender

The observation that women and men use language differently, and that their roles in driving language change differs, was a linchpin of early variationist sociolinguistics. Labov, for example, noted in his New York City study (1966) that women's pronunciation varied a great deal between formal and informal speech, whilst men's did so to a lesser degree. Female speakers were also using innovative forms in casual speech, thus initiating change. By contrast, on Martha's Vineyard, Labov had found that men were initiating the change by which the diphthongs /au/ and /ai/ were becoming raised and centralised. His explanation for this distinguished between conscious and unconscious change, or 'change from above' and 'change from below'. He concluded that women lead changes that come from above the level of social awareness and involve new variants with overt prestige, whereas men initiate changes that spread from below and move away from mainstream norms. Labov referred to this as the **gender paradox** (2001: 293).

The work described in this box so far falls into the 'survey era' of sociolinguistics; being mainly concerned with urban dialectology like that of Labov and Trudgill, and typified by a focus on social hierarchies and distinctions. During this phase, 'sex' was conceptualised as a fixed, universal variable which determined use of language variables alongside other key categories such as class, age and ethnicity. Seminal studies (e.g. Labov 1966; Trudgill 1974) found that within every social class, women used more standard forms than men. This was explained with reference to women's perceived status-consciousness, and men's association of vernacular forms with traditional notions of masculinity. Feminist critiques, however, pointed out that the traditional sociolinguistic framework tended not just to describe differences but to invoke and reinforce sex stereotypes, characterising gendered difference as a function of biological sex binaries.

The social network approach inaugurated in the 1980s identified and explained difference at the much more manageable level of the individual or small group, rather than the larger 'speech community'. This 'zoomed in' approach allowed questions to be asked about the local context of language variation at the precise time when research was being conducted. This approach typified what Eckert labelled 'second wave' sociolinguistic research. This paradigm shift allowed sociolinguists like the Milroys to study gendered difference not as indexically linked to a speaker's identity, but as culturally constructed in a particular social milieu. As outlined earlier, Milroy and Milroy explained women's leading role in the process of innovation in their Belfast study with reference to women's less dense and multiplex ties within social networks. The concept of the community of practice was also introduced in a ground-breaking paper by Eckert and McConnell-Ginet (1992), which likewise examined the construction of gender norms in specific social contexts. A community of practice is defined as 'an aggregate of people who come together around mutual engagement in an endeavour' (1992: 464). Like the Milroys' social network theory, this concept moved sociolinguistics away from approaches which had focused on hierarchical and comparative models of social identity in general, and in particular the simplistic gender normative and heteronormative research model of earlier decades. By the mid-1990s, what Cameron calls 'a paradigm organized around the concept of binary gender difference' (2005: 482) had shifted to a research perspective 'concerned with the diversity of gender identities and gendered practices' (p. 490).

Developments in our understanding of the relationship between gender and language have reflected enormous developments in gender theory over the past 50 years. It is increasingly accepted in academic circles that gender and gender identities are socially constructed – including through language use – and are variable, dynamic and culturally constituted; that gender is something we actively do. Reflecting ideas like this, gradually, language and gender studies moved away from conceptions of gender as acquired through socialisation and towards an understanding of gender as something that is actively performed. This has been accompanied by an increased emphasis on diversity and intersectionality. Women are no longer seen as a homogenous group; similarities and differences amongst groups of all gender identities are regarded as equally important. This has implications for understanding power dynamics, since it replaces an understanding of 'the patriarchy' as a homogenous group of oppressors with a notion of power as fluid and discursively enacted and resisted.

It is important, however, that we recognise the systematic differences which structural inequalities have produced. For example, it is accepted that gender variation in Irish Sign Language (ISL) is a relic of historical segregation of the sexes in Irish Deaf schools, leading linguists to question whether this variation has 'become an integral part of the grammar of ISL' (Leeson and Grehan 2004: 68). Likewise, research into gender-linked perceptions of pitch amongst speakers of Japanese has led researchers to conclude that being a woman with a higher pitched voice may be advantageous in Japanese society. Indeed, Ohara (2001) found that Japanese native speakers employed high voice pitch levels in Japanese but not when speaking in English, reflecting 'awareness of the difference between social meanings attached to voice pitch in the two cultures' (234).

A significant finding arising from early variationist sociolinguistics was that systematic differences between men's and women's speech could be observed empirically. Much sociolinguistic research in the intervening decades has been devoted to trying to pinpoint why this was the case, and to drawing up theories to explain these differences. These theories have evolved over time. Early theories developed to explain the relationship between gender and language presupposed gender polarisation and biological sex difference. Nowadays, there is recognition that gender is culturally constituted and context-dependent, as well as that there are other social parameters and relations which we must also take account of. It might be tempting to regard earlier theories of language and gender as primitive, but they were an important means of advancing the conversation around language, difference and oppression.

7.4.2 The sociolinguistics of multilingualism

Our discussion has focused mostly on contexts where only one language is being used. However, a great deal of communication around the world takes place in settings where people are using multiple languages. In many contexts, choices about language are not just about which sociolinguistic variables are used, but also about which language to use, and/or how to draw on and mix resources from multiple different varieties (see Chapter 11). Different languages or varieties may be used for formal and for informal settings, a phenomenon known as **diglossia** (Ferguson 1959; Fishman 1967). For instance, in Arabic-speaking countries the local vernacular variety of Arabic may be habitually used for everyday interactions, and Standard Arabic for more 'official' contexts like education or the law. Language choice may be connected to prestige and status and/or to economic advantage, and across a society this can lead to a shift from the use of one language to another. This can eventually lead to a language dying out completely. Some sociolinguists have argued strongly for the importance of defending such threatened languages (e.g. Skutnabb-Kangas 2000; see Chapter 28 on maintaining linguistic diversity).

In everyday speech and interaction in multilingual contexts, mixing languages is very common. This is often called **code-switching**, and sociolinguists try to identify grammatical, conversational and social patterns in how it occurs. Recently, however, some sociolinguists have begun to ask whether it is even appropriate to talk about speakers switching between different 'codes' at all. Garcia and Li Wei (2014) argue that it makes more sense to think of bilingual and multilingual speakers drawing on their complete set of linguistic resources as a single system in a fluid and flexible manner, using the term **translanguaging**. Makalela (2015) analyses self-recordings of the language used by young people in five superdiverse townships in Johannesburg, South Africa, to show how they developed a new variety – *kasi-taal* – which mixes resources from several local languages, blurring boundaries between them in a multi-layered way. Translanguaging is particularly a feature of language use in superdiverse contexts characterised by flows of migration, and recent work in sociolinguistics has focused on language in these kinds of contexts.

7.4.3 The sociolinguistics of globalisation

We live in a world characterised by extensive flows of migration and tightly networked relationships of people and companies. Vast numbers of people live in superdiverse cities with populations from all over the world who bring very different linguistic repertoires, and have enormously unequal access to economic and social resources. Sociolinguistics has an important role to play in understanding the part played by language in such patterns of social injustice.

Blommaert (2010) argues that we need urgently to develop a 'critical sociolinguistics of globalization'. This must, he says, address the inequalities in access to power and resources – including linguistic resources – between people from the disadvantaged 'periphery' and the more advantaged 'centre'. Blommaert's work draws extensively on empirical descriptions from ethnographic fieldwork to show how language-related patterns of power and inequality play out on the ground, with very significant personal and social consequences. For instance, he shows how a man he calls Joseph, seeking asylum in the UK, is rejected because his complex repertoire of linguistic resources – acquired over the course of a life disrupted by conflict and violence from his earliest childhood – did not match the expectations held by the Home Office that Rwandan refugees would unproblematically speak Kinyarwanda as their first language. Similarly, Piller (2016) argues that we need an applied sociolinguistics that addresses how language mediates social inequality in contemporary societies, where linguistic diversity is the norm, but where support for people with multilingual language resources is not. Her case studies show the social injustices faced by people with diverse linguistic resources, for instance children being unable to access monolingual education in schools, or migrants facing linguistic discrimination in job interviews.

Globalisation describes not just migration and flows of people, but also the tightly networked global capitalist economy within which these flows take place. Sociolinguists have studied how language plays a part in, and is affected by, this economic system. Heller and Duchêne (2012) argue we need to understand how our late capitalist globalised economy treats language increasingly as an economic commodity, tied up in discourses of profit, to add to the more well-established understanding of language as a symbol of nationhood or identity. An employee working in a market economy may have 'added value' if they have access to a wider linguistic repertoire, for example in an off-shore call centre in Pakistan (Rahman 2009) where the ability to produce a 'native-like' English or standard American accent can guarantee job security. The nature and effects of the commodification of languages in late capitalism are important focuses of the sociolinguistics of globalisation.

Case study: the sociolinguistics of youth language

Young people, particularly adolescents, are often the innovators who bring in new language forms and lead language change (Kerswill 1996). Studying the language of teenagers and adolescents has helped sociolinguists to understand how language changes and develops, influenced by connections between language and identity. Cheshire (1982) showed how nine non-standard syntactical forms were used in the everyday, informal communication of a group of 26 working-class adolescents in Reading, a medium-sized town in Berkshire in the UK. She showed that their use of these variants correlated with the extent to which they belonged to a 'vernacular subculture' in which activities like fighting and engaging in small criminal acts were valued. This was an important precursor to the research on language variation, style and identity described earlier. Rampton ([1999] 2017) demonstrated adolescents in London flexibly and creatively mixing the various different languages that were used in their community, particularly Panjabi, African-Caribbean Creole and stylised Asian English, for purposes like humour, building peer relationships and gaining status, a process he called 'crossing'. This work challenged fixed ideas about group identities, and informed later research on translanguaging and on language use in superdiverse settings.

More recent sociolinguistic research has identified language varieties used especially by young people that mix features associated with different languages and ethnic heritages. In the UK, this includes particularly Jamaican and Caribbean creoles, but also South Asian and West African languages, as well as features from Indian and African Englishes, initially called 'Multicultural London English' (MLE, Cheshire et al. 2011). Similar patterns of youth language have been identified widely across Britain, first in urban areas and now more generally. A less London-centric term such as 'Multicultural British English' is now preferred, to indicate how young people in many different settings around the country are incorporating features of MLE into their local language varieties, but also seeing this as just a standard teenage way of speaking (Drummond 2018). Similar youth urban vernaculars associated with multiethnic, often economically disadvantaged groups, have been found across the world, for instance Rinkeby Swedish (Milani and Jonsson 2012), Kiezdeutsch in Germany (Wiese 2015) or Sheng in Kenya (Githiora 2018). While public discourses and language ideologies often evaluate these practices very negatively, this can be seen as an example of translanguaging – young people creatively mixing a wide range of linguistic resources, and potentially changing some of the patterns of the language as they do so.

7.5 Conclusion

This chapter has introduced sociolinguistics, a diverse field which addresses the connections between language and society from a range of different perspectives. While early variationist sociolinguistics sought to explain patterns of language variation in relation to social characteristics like age, gender and, especially, class, more recent work focuses on language and the construction of social identities, and how people use language variation in creative ways to index social identities that are meaningful to them. We have addressed the methods that are used in sociolinguistics, from large-scale surveys down to fine-grained analysis of video-recordings of interaction. And we have seen how the focus of the field has broadened to incorporate attention to language in a changing society, looking at globalisation and inequalities of power. Despite the diversity of the field, some aims remain constant: making the connection between language and society, and understanding how local meaning-making interactions relate to social features and trends. Language is always used in social contexts, and conveys social meanings; adopting a sociolinguist's view on the world opens up fascinating questions to explore every day.

References

Adam, R. and Braithwaite, B. 2022. Geographies and circulations: Sign language contact at the peripheries. *Journal of Sociolinguistics*, 26(1): 99–104. https://doi.org/10.1111/josl.12521

Bayley, R., Lucas, C. and Rose, M. 2002. Phonological variation in American Sign Language: The case of 1 handshape. *Language Variation and Change*, 14: 19–53.

Blommaert, J. 2010. *The Sociolinguistics of Globalization*. Cambridge: Cambridge University Press.

Cameron, D. 2005. Language, gender, and sexuality: Current issues and new directions. *Applied Linguistics*, 26(4): 482–502.

Cameron, D. [1995] 2012. *Verbal Hygiene*. London: Routledge.

Cheshire, J. 1982. *Variation in an English Dialect*. Cambridge: Cambridge University Press.

Cheshire, J., Kerswill, P., Fox, S. and Torgersen, E. 2011. Contact, the feature pool and the speech community: The emergence of Multicultural London English. *Journal of Sociolinguistics*, 15(2): 151–196.

Chomsky, N. 1965. *Aspects of the Theory of Syntax*. Cambridge, MA: MIT Press.

Drummond, R. 2018. Maybe it's a grime [t]ing: Th-stopping among urban British youth. *Language in Society*, 47(2): 171–196.

Eckert, P. 2000. *Language Variation as Social Practice: The Linguistic Construction of Identity in Belten High*. Oxford: Blackwell.

Eckert, P. 2012. Three waves of variation study: The emergence of meaning in the study of sociolinguistic variation. *Annual Review of Anthropology*, 41(1): 87–100. https://doi.org/10.1146/annurev-anthro-092611-145828

Eckert, P. and Mcconnell-Ginet, S. 1992. Think practically and look locally: Language and gender as community-based practice. *Annual Review of Anthropology*, 21: 461–490.

Ferguson, C. A. 1959 Diglossia. *Word*, 15: 325–340.

Fishman, J. 1967. Bilingualism with and without diglossia. Diglossia with and without bilingualism. *Journal of Social Issues*, 23(2): 29–37.

Garcia, O. and Wei, L. 2014. *Translanguaging: Language, Bilingualism and Education*. London: Palgrave Macmillan.

Githiora, C. 2018. Sheng: The expanding domains of an urban youth vernacular.

Journal of African Cultural Studies, 30(2): 105–120. http://doi.org/10.1080/13 696815.2015.1117962

Gonzales Velásquez, M. D. 1995. Sometimes Spanish, sometimes English: Language use among rural New Mexican Chicanas. In K. Hall and M. Bucholtz (Eds.), *Gender Articulated: Language and the Socially Constructed Self*. London and New York: Routledge, pp. 421–446.

Heller, M. and Duchêne, A. 2012. Pride and profit: changing discourses of language, capital and nation-state. In A. Duchêne and M. Heller (Eds.), *Language in Late Capitalism*. London: Taylor and Francis, pp. 1–21.

Hernández, J. M. and Ramírez, J. A. 2022. Communities of practice and adolescent speakers in the Basque Country. Research and transformation face-to-face. *Journal of Multilingual and Multicultural Development*, 43(1): 32–42. http://doi.org/10.1080/01434632.2021.1998078

Hill, J. and Tamene, E. H. 2022. Hierarchies and constellations: Language attitudes and ideologies of signed languages. *Journal of Sociolinguistics*, 26(1): 113–117. https://doi.org/10.1111/josl.12525

Hou, L. and de Vos, C. 2022. Classifications and typologies: Labeling sign languages and signing communities. *Journal of Sociolinguistics*, 26(1): 118–125. https://doi.org/10.1111/josl.12490

Hymes, D. 1974. *Foundations in Sociolinguistics: An Ethnographic Approach*. Philadelphia: University of Pennsylvania Press.

Kerswill, P. 1996. Children, adolescents, and language change. *Language Variation and Change*, 8(2): 177–202. http://doi.org/10.1017/S0954394500001137

Kristiansen, T. 2003. Language attitudes and language politics in Denmark. *International Journal of the Sociology of Language*, 159: 57–71.

Kusters, A. and Lucas, C. 2022. Emergence and evolutions: Introducing sign language sociolinguistics. *Journal of Sociolinguistics*, 26(1): 84–97. https://doi.org/10.1111/josl.12522

Labov, W. 1963. The social motivation of a sound change. *Word*, 19(3): 273–309.

Labov, W. 1966. *The Social Stratification of English in New York City*. Washington, DC: Center for Applied Linguistics.

Labov, W. 1972. *Sociolinguistic Patterns*. Philadelphia: University of Pennsylvania Press.

Labov, W. 2001. *Principles of Linguistic Change, Vol. 2: Social Factors*. Malden, MA: Blackwell Publishers Inc.

Leeson, L. and Grehan, C. 2004. To the lexicon and beyond: The effect of gender on variation in Irish Sign Language. In M. Van Herreweghe and M. Vermeerbergen (Eds.), *To the Lexicon and Beyond: Sociolinguistics in European Deaf Communities*. Washington, DC: Gallaudet University Press, pp. 39–73.

Le Page, R. B. and Tabouret-Keller, A. E. 1985. *Acts of Identity: Creole-based Approaches to Language and Ethnicity*. Cambridge: Cambridge University Press.

Lippi-Green, R. 1997. *English with an Accent: Language, Ideology, and Discrimination in the United States*. London: Routledge.

Makalela, L. 2015. Translanguaging practices in complex multilingual spaces: A discontinuous continuity in post-independent South Africa. *International Journal of the Sociology of Language*, 234: 115–132. https://doi.org/10.1515/ijsl-2015-0007

Mendoza-Denton, N. 2008. *Homegirls: Language and Cultural Practices among Latina Youth Gangs*. Oxford: Blackwell.

Milani, T. M. and Jonsson, R. 2012. Who's afraid of Rinkeby Swedish? Stylization, complicity, resistance. *Journal of Linguistic Anthropology*, 22: 44–63. https://doi.org/10.1111/j.1548-1395.2012.01133.x

Milroy, J. and Milroy, L. 1985. Linguistic change, social network and speaker innovation. *Journal of Linguistics*, 21: 339–384.

Milroy, L. 1987. *Language and Social Networks*. 2nd ed. Oxford: Blackwell.

Milroy, L. and Milroy, J. 1992. Social network and social class: Toward an integrated sociolinguistic model. *Language in Society*, 21(1): 1–26.

Ohara, Y. 2001. Finding one's voice in Japanese: A study of the pitch levels of L2 users. In A. Pavlenko, A. Blackledge, I. Piller and M. Teutsch-Dwyer (Eds.), *Multilingualism, Second Language Learning, and Gender*. Berlin and New York: Mouton De Gruyter, pp. 231–256.

Palfreyman, N. and Schembri, A. 2022. Lumping and splitting: Sign language delineation and ideologies of linguistic differentiation. *Journal of Sociolinguistics*, 26(1): 105–112. https://doi.org/10.1111/josl.12524

Piller, I. 2016. *Linguistic Diversity and Social Justice: An Introduction to Applied Sociolinguistics*. Oxford: Oxford University Press.

Rahman, T. 2009. Language ideology, identity and the commodification of language in the call centers of Pakistan. *Language in Society*, 38(2): 233–257. https://doi.org/10.1017/S0047404509090344

Rampton, B. [1999] 2017. *Crossing: Language and Ethnicity among Adolescents*. London: Routledge.

Rampton, B. 2020. Interactional sociolinguistics. In K. Tusting (Ed.), *The Routledge Handbook of Linguistic Ethnography*. London: Routledge, pp. 13–27.

Skutnabb-Kangas, T. 2000. *Linguistic Genocide in Education, or Worldwide Diversity and Human Rights?* Mahwah, NJ: L. Erlbaum Associates.

Trudgill, P. 1974. *The Social Differentiation of English in Norwich*. Cambridge: Cambridge University Press.

Wiese, H. 2015. 'This migrants' babble is not a German dialect!': The interaction of standard language ideology and 'us'/'them' dichotomies in the public discourse on a multiethnolect. *Language in Society*, 44(3): 341–367. http://doi.org/10.1017/S0047404515000226

8 Historical linguistics
Beth Malory

8.1 Introduction

This chapter outlines the aims and techniques of historical linguistics, the study of how languages change and develop over time. We will begin, in Section 8.2, with a brief description of the background and development of historical linguistics as a field of study. In Section 8.3, we will then examine why languages change over time, how these changes come about and how they spread. Following this, we will consider the types of change observed in languages, highlighting notable theories to explain these changes. Examples will be given of how changes manifest at the various 'levels' of language introduced in Section One of this volume; including phonology, grammar, lexis and semantics. Section 8.4 then outlines the main techniques that historical linguists use to study language change. Having read this chapter, you should have a working knowledge of the ways in which languages change, as well as an understanding of the reasons for these changes, and the ways in which linguists can identify and study them.

8.2 What is historical linguistics?

The languages of the past have been a source of fascination throughout history, but never have we had so much insight into the history and **prehistory** of languages as we do now. The Romans, for example, noticed similarities between their language, Latin, and Greek, and assumed that Latin was descended from Greek. We now know that they in fact shared a common ancestor: **Proto-Indo-European** (PIE). They were, as Figure 8.1 shows, different branches on the same family tree.

Later, during the Middle Ages, attempts were made to prove that Hebrew was a common ancestor for

> **A chip off the old block . . . ?**
>
> A lot of the language we use to talk about language uses the metaphor of family. We talk about 'parent' languages, 'daughter' languages and 'ancestor' languages. We even, as in Figures 8.1 and 8.6, use 'family' trees to show how languages are 'related'.

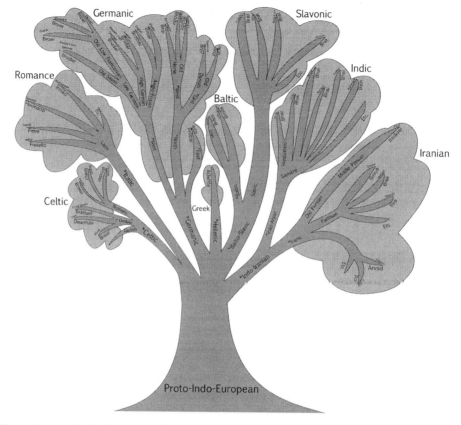

Figure 8.1 An Indo-European 'family' tree.

all languages. The focus here was on European languages, and attempts to prove that these were descended from Hebrew were confounded by the simple fact that they are not!

It was only when colonial activity began in India in the seventeenth century that the theory of a common ancestor language *no longer in existence* emerged. Commonalities between Sanskrit, the ancient literary language of India, contemporary European languages, and Classical Latin and Greek was a stunning discovery. How could a language used 5000 miles from Rome have shared features with the language of the Romans? From this question, the theory of a common ancestor arose. Today, we know that Sanskrit, Ancient Greek and Latin, as well as such disparate languages as Bengali, Persian, Russian, Greek, Spanish, Dutch and English, are all descended from Proto-Indo-European.

Historical linguistics is therefore not only of the study of language history, but also of how languages change over time and how they are related. The goals of historical linguists can therefore be regarded as threefold:

1	To describe changes in a given language/set of languages.
2	To theorise about how and why language changes.
3	To identify language families by reconstructing linguistic prehistory.

The ways in which these three goals are pursued are governed by three fundamentals of the field:

1	**All living languages change**. Languages in use cannot remain static; they are in a constant state of flux.
2	**Language change is not random**, even if we cannot always pinpoint what exactly has motivated a change.
3	**Language cannot change without contact**. Language change can only spread if humans interact in some way.

It's important to bear in mind that language change gets a lot of bad press, even nowadays. We can probably all think of something about language that we (or someone we know) do not like. It can be tricky to put this aside, but the academic discipline of linguistics aims to approach language change dispassionately, and to *observe* rather than *judge* what happens.

8.3 Why and how do languages change?

Language change begins with **innovation**, but without contact, changes cannot spread. The technical terms for these processes are **Actuation, Adoption** and **Propagation**. You may also see them referred to as **Innovation, Selection** and **Diffusion**. The following sections will set out what we know (and, just as importantly, what we don't!) about these processes (Figure 8.2).

Figure 8.2 Processes of language change.

8.3.1 Actuation

Weinreich, Labov and Herzog provided a basis for all subsequent research on actuation in a seminal article of 1968, proposing that the actuation of **diachronic** change is always **synchronic** variation. That is, language simply cannot change over time without an innovation occurring.

Having established this, the next obvious step is to ask *why* actuation occurs, and this is where things get trickier. As Figure 8.3 shows, explanations for actuation fall into two camps, broadly speaking. **Teleological** explanations treat language as an abstract system, in line with structuralist approaches to language. According to this school of thought, language 'change is cumulative and [is] directed towards some goal' (McMahon 1994: 327). By contrast, non-teleological explanations assume no end goal to changes, and as Figure 8.3 shows, we can think of these, broadly, as unintentional changes.

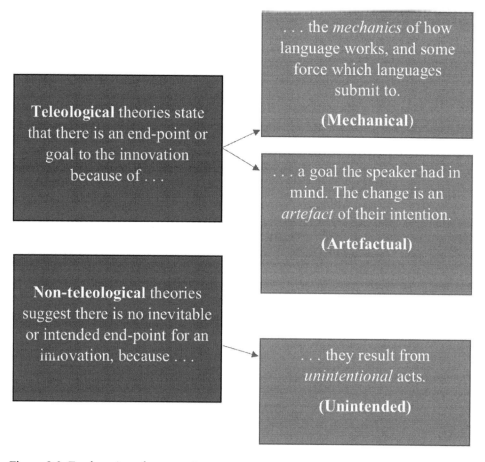

Figure 8.3 Explanations for actuation.

The reasons why these sorts of changes may come about are summarised in Table 8.1. Here, the first column details **mechanical** theories of teleological change, which seek to make generalisations about language change – often leaving us with more questions than answers.

Table 8.1 Theories of language change.

Teleological		Non-teleological
Teleological (mechanical)	Intended (artefactual)	Unintended
Preservation of distinctions to avoid ambiguity The theory that languages 'try' to preserve one-to-one mapping between a linguistic form and its conventional meaning or function, for example by avoiding homonymy.	Expressiveness Speakers innovate in order to say something that their existing linguistic repertoire cannot express. Commonly attested in poetic contexts – for example, Roald Dahl's invention of *churgle* ('laugh').	Hypercorrection Hypercorrection occurs when someone overextends or misapplies a linguistic convention, for example using *campi* instead of *campuses* in English.
Preservation of uniformity through analogical changes Theory that some force drives languages towards uniformity (e.g. learners using the plural forms *fishes* and *sheeps*).	Clarity Speakers innovate in order to avoid being misunderstood.	Hypocorrection Hypocorrection occurs when someone tries to conform to a standard norm, but falls short and produces a hybrid form which is neither conventional in their dialect or the standard variety.
Preservation of symmetry The theory that holes in the 'pattern' of language need to be filled, for instance in phonological chain shifts.	Economy Speakers innovate to save energy or time (e.g. **lenition**).	Errors The theory that hearers misperceive sounds and then reproduce those sounds.

We are on firmer ground with the **artefactual** explanations for teleological change in the central column of Table 8.1, simply because we have more evidence to work with. Whereas mechanical explanations for innovation attempt to make generalisations, artefactual explanations are narrower in scope. These identify contexts where innovations occur at an individual level, fulfilling specific communicative needs.

In focus: linguistic data in the digital age

It seems likely that language change driven by error and replication may be growing more frequent in this era of informal computer-mediated communication. The spelling *yay or nay* for the phrase conventionally spelled *yea or nay* is becoming increasingly frequent in internet discourse. For example, data from the NOW monitor corpus of internet news language in English (scan the QR code to register and try this corpus for yourself!) shows that the phrase with the *yay* spelling occurs almost twice as often as the *yea* spelling.

It seems plausible that, with huge repositories of internet language data becoming available to researchers, future research may even be able to attempt to trace the actuation of written changes such as this.

SCAN ME

As Table 8.1 shows, attempts to shape an overarching mechanical theory around actuation are problematic, but it is certainly possible to identify factors involved in individual changes and types of change. What we can know with certainty is that 'languages don't change; people change language through their actions' (Croft 2000: 4). It's important to bear in mind that these changes are not always intentional, however. The third category of explanation for actuation, given in the third column in Table 8.1, relates to innovation which comes about accidentally.

Actuation is therefore a complex and intractable issue, and one for which more has been theorised than proven. Happily, more is known about how changes spread after innovation has occurred, as we will explore in Section 8.3.2.

In focus: analogy at work

What is the past tense of *to screenshot*? *Screenshot, screenshotted, screenshat* are attested as past tense forms of *to screenshot*, as users of the language attempt, by analogy, to make this unusual new verb conform to regular rules of English verb conjugation.

Shot is the past tense form usually used for *to shoot*, whilst adding the *-ed* suffix is the most common method of signalling the past tense in English, so both of these would appear to be valid ways of signalling that the action of screenshotting happened in the past.

Screenshat would only really make sense if the infinitival form was *to screenshit*. (Hopefully not a verb that is much called for . . . in any tense.)

8.3.2 Adoption

In 8.3.1, we explored how language changes arise. Next, we consider how such changes become established features of a language. This process is referred to as **adoption** or **selection**. Adoption occurs when alternative variants are selected, instead of the status quo being maintained through **normal replication** of existing linguistic variants. Like the processes of actuation which we discussed

Table 8.2 Forces which promote normal replication or adoption of alternative variants.

	Intended	Unintended
Normal replication	**Conformity to convention** (clarity) Normal replication occurs more often than not, because we have a vested interest in conforming to convention. This maximises our chance of being understood!	**Entrenchment** (habit) Normal replication also results from the **entrenchment** of norms, when users of the language are so accustomed to doing things in a certain way that they rarely deviate from convention.
Adoption	**Acts of identity** As we saw in Chapter 7, linguistic practice can be seen as a 'series of acts of identity in which people reveal both their personal identity and their . . . social roles' (Le Page and Tabouret-Keller 1985: 14). Acts of identity include: • Accommodation; The adaptation of the speaker's language or language style to those they interact with. • Prestige (overt or covert); How prestigious a variant is considered to be, either according to codified standards at a societal level, or implicit norms at a community level. • Prescriptive forces. The imposition of norms perceived as prestigious, virtuous or desirable in some other way, by those who consider themselves authorities in this regard.	**Change in entrenchment** Entrenchment can decline if a variant is not used. Changes in entrenchment can thus pave the way for the adoption of a competing variant.

in Section 8.3.2, this can be intentional or unintentional. Table 8.2 lists the forces which promote the normal replication of existing variants, or the selection of newer ones.

As Table 8.2 shows, normal replication occurs because people want to be understood, and due to habit. Adoption

Did you know?

If you have ever noticed your own or someone else's pronunciation change, depending on who else is present, then you have first-hand experience of accommodation!

occurs for a number of reasons; mostly related to the impressions people want their language to give to others. If we regard language as a series of acts of identity, then speakers continually perform their identities, and an important aspect of this performance is likely to relate to how prestigious a linguistic variant is regarded to be.

As we saw in Chapter 7, Labov (1966) and Trudgill (1972) suggest that both **overt** and **covert prestige** can influence usage. Overt prestige is the kind associated with speaking 'correctly'; whereas covert prestige is the hidden positive evaluation which is ascribed to non-standard variants. It has been suggested, for instance, that the **glottalisation** of word-final [t] is undergoing a change driven by covert prestige in England at present, since glottal stops are no longer the stigmatised reserve of the urban working classes, but frequently also a feature of higher prestige accents, such as those of younger British royal family.

Why not find a YouTube clip of the UK monarch's Christmas Message and see if you can detect any glottalisation?

Think prescriptivism is a thing of the past? Think again!

How different are the spelling and grammar checkers in word processing and email programmes from grammar books and usage guides?

Prestige can also be determined by **prescriptive** forces in a society, whereby certain variants are promoted, whilst others are **proscribed**. Some countries have official institutions established for the sole purpose of regulating a language. These are known as language **academies**, and perhaps the most famous ones are those found in France (L'Académie française), Italy (l'Accademia della Crusca) and Spain (La Real Academia Española). Academies for national languages can be found in all parts of the world, however; for example, in Bangladesh (the Bangla Academy), Japan (the National Institute for Japanese Language and Linguistics) and Russia (the V.V. Vinogradov Russian Language Institute). Academies intended to regulate minority languages also exist, for example in South Africa (Nasionale Taalliggaam vir Afrikaans) and Basque Country (Euskaltzaindia), whilst more than a dozen academies intended to regulate dialects of Arabic exist across the Middle East and northern Africa.

8.3.3 Propagation

Propagation, the diffusion of a variant through a linguistic community, requires social contact. Many factors can impact a change at this point, as it becomes entrenched. Some of these factors, like patterns of migration, settlement and population density, are broadly anthropological and even geographical. Others, such as power dynamics and prestige, are political.

Before the advent of technologies which bypass distance, geographical features played an important role in determining how language varieties developed. For instance, the remoteness caused by the less inhabited mountainous areas of Mid Wales caused significant dialectal divergence between northern and southern dialects of Welsh. The isogloss on the map in Figure 8.4 shows the major dialect break between the Welsh of North and South Wales.

Figure 8.4 Map of Wales with isogloss.

In this era of mass media and efficient communication technologies, geography plays less of a role in maintaining distinctions between dialects. It is this kind of context that we would expect **dialect levelling**. In Wales, for example, centralised government and broadcasting are mechanisms which promote levelling; no matter where you are in the country, it is the northern variant *allan* ('out') that you will see on roads and road signs, and the Welsh-language broadcaster S4C is based in South Wales, with South-Walian dialects most frequently heard on air.

In focus: Americanisms in British English

The impact of broadcast media can be seen in other languages, too, of course. Have you ever heard someone moan about 'Americanisms' in British English? A common bugbear in this regard is the past participle *gotten*. This variant is accused of infringing on the *got* of British Standard English in sentences such as *she has gotten/got taller*.

In fact, *gotten* was pretty common in England during the Early Modern period, but then went into decline. Since the Second World War, it has experienced a resurgence in the United States, and it seems to be growing increasingly frequent in the UK too, perhaps due to the ubiquity of American TV and films.

Cocoliche: a hybrid dialect

This Spanish-Italian dialect is a contact variety with roots in the Spanish and Italian dialects spoken by immigrants to Argentina in the nineteenth and twentieth centuries. Structural similarities between Spanish and Italian contributed to hybridisation, and Cocoliche has been described as 'an unstable linguistic continuum' (Maiden 2014: 179) where usage can vary in closeness to either Spanish or Italian, depending on the linguistic background of a speaker. The label 'Cocoliche' was pejorative, and the dialect is now considered historic.

The physical movement of people, whether by migration, travel or exploration, is another means of diffusing linguistic variants. Patterns of settlement and population density are key here, as tight-knit or multi-cultural communities result in more rapidly spreading language change than occurs in sparsely populated or insular ones.

The propagation of linguistic variants can also be determined by political forces such as power and prestige. Linguistic imperialism, whereby a conquering people overpowers and oppresses an Indigenous population and imposes its linguistic norms (whether purposefully or incidentally), is one way that this can happen. A language that spreads in this way is called a **hegemonic** language. The history of French, for example, can be seen as a series of conquests and subjugations, as Table 8.3 shows.

The linguistic influence in colonial contact situations can go both ways. Scan the QR code to see a list of common words in English which are loanwords from Indigenous American languages.

Whilst the languages of oppressed peoples have had much less influence on those of conquering peoples than vice versa, it is common to find influence of an Indigenous language at a local level. In Irish English, we find the so-called 'after perfect', where the word *after* is used to express **perfect aspect** and indicate that the completed action occurred in the recent past, for example *he is after scoring a goal*. This construction results from the contact situation between the language of the occupying English and the occupied Irish over several centuries, and reflects perfect marking in Irish.

SCAN ME

Table 8.3 A (very brief) history of French.

Historical period	Significant events	Language period	Language evolution
First century BCE	Roman Invasion brings Latin to what is now France.	Vulgar Latin	Before this, France was primarily populated by Celtic-speaking peoples, whom the Romans called the Gauls. Celtic languages, Gaulish among them, and Latin co-existed for centuries, but Gaulish was ultimately supplanted by Vulgar Latin from around the fifth century onwards.
Fifth century CE	Germanic tribes invade, bringing Germanic languages such as Frankish.	Old French	Frankish influence is considered responsible for causing such divergence from Latin that the separate language of 'Old French' can be identified. Prior to this, the different dialects of Latin remained mutually intelligible.
Ninth–fourteenth centuries CE	In the tenth century, French royalty make their court in Paris. As royal dominion increases, so too does the prestige of *francien*, the dialect spoken by royalty.	Middle French	By the tenth century, the dialects of the north were heavily influenced by Frankish, whereas southern dialects remained closer to Latin.
Fourteenth–sixteenth centuries CE	Use of French continues to expand. A royal edict of 1539 bans Latin in legal contexts, and the advent of printing brings moves to standardise.	Classical French	**Did you know?** The Germanic influence of Frankish shapes French to this day, and has given it a very distinct flavour compared to other Romance languages. The French word for French, *français*, is itself derived from the Franks!
Seventeenth–eighteenth centuries CE	In 1635, the French Academy is founded to regulate the language. During this period, France gains prestige abroad and becomes the international language of diplomacy.		

(*Continued*)

169

Table 8.3 (Continued)

Historical period	Significant events	Language period	Language evolution
Eighteenth century CE	By the time of the Revolution in 1789, French was spoken by the majority of the urban middle classes, but a 1790 survey found that outside of Paris, 45% of the population were unable to speak French. The Revolutionaries believed that a single national language would promote unity and associated regional dialects with conservatism, royalism and opposition to the new French Republic.	Modern French	The Modern period is defined by efforts to eradicate the native regional languages of these speakers, and impose French as a national language, through legislation, education and mass media . . . and by the spread of French internationally, through colonialism.
Nineteenth century CE onwards	During this period, France amassed an enormous Empire across the globe, with the result that French is now the official language of 29 countries and many more overseas territories.		

Did you know?

Since 1994, it has been illegal in France to use Anglicisms in official government publications. In a 2019 statement, L'Académie française (see Section 8.3.2) warned of an existential threat to French from an 'invasion of Anglo-Saxon terms'. Despite this, the eminent French Dictionary *La Petit Larousse* announced plans to add *cluster, click-and-collect, batch cooking* and *mocktail,* to name just a few, to its 2022 edition.

Such local influence is, of course, dwarfed by the impact which the languages of colonial powers, such as French and English, have had on the languages of oppressed populations. The key, then, to linguistic dominance as changes propagate, would seem to be political power and prestige.

8.4 Types of language change

8.4.1 Phonological change

Phonological, or sound, change, has been more rigorously studied than any other type of linguistic change, with the result that we know a great deal about how the phonology of a language changes. The first thing to note is that sound changes rarely happen in isolation. In 8.3.1, the concept of phonological **chain shift**, whereby movements of neighbouring sounds are coordinated in order to preserve contrasts within the system (Foulkes et al. 2001), was introduced. This means that when one vowel or consonant in the 'chain' of a language moves, the others do too.

In 1822, Jacob Grimm (yes, he of fairy tale fame!) documented the regular sound changes whereby certain sounds in the **parent** language, Proto-Indo-European, became other sounds in the **daughter** language, Germanic.

Grimm's Law explains the systematic divergences that we can observe in present-day Germanic and Romance languages. The PIE voiceless plosive [p], for example, became [f] in Germanic daughter languages English and German, but remained [p] in Romance daughter languages French and Italian. Hence, we find systematic differences between these present-day language families, as shown in Table 8.4.

Table 8.4 Systematic differences in present-day Germanic and Romance languages.

PIE	Germanic	Germanic		Romance	
p	f	English	German	French	Italian
		Foot	Fuß	Pied	Piede
		Father	Vater	Père	Padre
		Feather	Feder	Plume	Piuma
		Fish	Fisch	Poisson	Pesce

Other apparent language mysteries can also be solved by researching historical sound change. English spelling is notorious for its inconsistency, and the absence of a systematic set of relationships between spelling and pronunciation. This is, in part, due to changes in pronunciation in the fifteenth and sixteenth centuries, particularly in the vowel system. The main series of changes, known to English historical linguists as the Great Vowel Shift, changed the quality of all the long vowels. This began in the early fifteenth century and was complete by the late seventeenth century. Table 8.5 shows how the pronunciation of some common English words has changed since the Middle English period.

Table 8.5 Pronunciation changes between Middle English and the present day.

Word	Middle English (c.1100–1450)	Early Modern English (c.1450–1650)	Present-day English
name	[aː]	[ɛː]	[eɪ]
clean	[ɛː]	[eː]	[iː]
sweet	[eː]	[iː]	[iː]
blind	[iː]	[əɪ]	[aɪ]
robe	[ɔː]	[oː]	[əʊ]
goose	[oː]	[uː]	[uː]
cow	[uː]	[aʊ]	[aʊ]

Figure 8.5 shows the fundamental changes which took place during the Great Vowel Shift, with the dark grey arrows showing the direction of change. It is thought that all of the vowels became closer (see Chapter 1), except for those which were already as close as they could be. These became diphthongised, with the lighter grey arrows showing their probable trajectory.

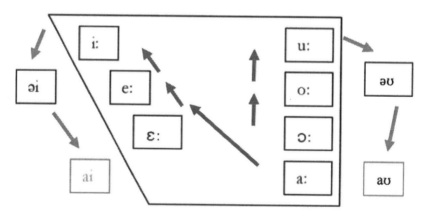

Figure 8.5 Major changes to the English vowel system during the 'Great Vowel Shift'.

8.4.2 Grammatical change

As we saw in Chapter 3, languages are categorised as either **synthetic** or **analytic**. Analytic languages have more or less fixed word orders, using extra words and context to convey meaning. In English, an analytic language, the meaning of the sentences *the girl loves the sailor* and *the sailor loves the girl* is dictated by the word order. In Latin, however, as a synthetic language, this is not the case. As we saw in Chapter 4, however, synthetic languages like Latin use word endings to signal which element of a sentence plays which role. Bearing this in mind, as well as the facts that *nauta* means 'sailor', *amat* means 'loves' and *puella* means 'girl', what do you think the following Latin sentences mean?

Nautam puella amat
Puella nautam amat
Puella amat nautam

In fact, all three of the Latin sentences mean the same thing: 'the girl loves the sailor'. This is because the role that each word plays in the sentence is signalled not by word order, but by word endings. Thus, no matter where *puella* occurs, it remains the subject of the sentence because the *-a* affix signals this, and wherever *nautam* occurs, it remains the direct object because the *-am* affix signals that. To change the meaning to 'the sailor loves the girl', we would have to swap these inflections to make *puellam amat nauta*, or an alternative sentence containing these elements.

This movement from reliance on synthetic constructions to analytic means of expressing meaning is known as analyticisation, and is by no means simply a historical trend. It would, for instance, appear that German is moving from a synthetic genitive construction to a new prepositional genitive, with von dem Haus ('of the house') now increasingly replacing des Hauses ('the house's').

There seems to be a diachronic trend for synthetic patterns to be replaced by analytic ones. Present-day English has a fixed word order; this is why *the girl loves the sailor* and *the sailor loves the girl* mean different things. The grammar of English has become increasingly analytical over the course of its history, with the number of inflected word endings decreasing dramatically, and grammatical meanings coming to be expressed instead by word order and function words such as prepositions. This was not the case in Old English, a synthetic language, where differences in word order did not affect the meaning of the sentence.

Analyticisation is far from the whole story in terms of grammatical change, though. **Grammaticalisation**, another major focus for historical linguists interested in grammar, is 'the process whereby lexical items and constructions come in certain linguistic contexts to serve grammatical functions, and, once grammaticalized, continue to develop new grammatical functions' (Hopper and Traugott 2003: xv). Hopper and Traugott (2003: 7) propose that grammaticalisation follows a particular trajectory, or cline, which is shown in Figure 8.6, along with an example from English.

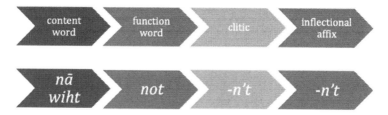

Figure 8.6 The cline of grammaticalisation, with an English example.

Figure 8.6 illustrates how the Old English lexical phrase *nā wiht* ('nothing') was eroded to the adverb *not*, then **cliticised** to *n't*. In Present-Day English, *-n't* has been reanalysed as an inflectional feature of modal or auxiliary verbs. As Figure 8.6 also shows, each step in this development is consistent with the cline of grammaticalisation.

8.3.3 Lexical change

Just as the phonology and grammar of languages change over time, so too does vocabulary. Perhaps the most salient process by which this change occurs is **borrowing**, when new words are acquired from another language, becoming **loanwords**.

In focus: French-English borrowing, a (very long) two-way street

We touched earlier upon attempts to limit the influence of English on French, and next time you are in France for *le weekend*, perhaps doing a spot of *le camping*, you could head to *le pub* for *un cocktail* or *un gin*, and judge for yourself how successful the endeavours of linguistic purists have been!

Of course, French has still contributed many times more loanwords to English, than English has to French. Following the Norman invasion of 1066, around *10,000* loanwords entered English! The big difference is that time makes these loans less obvious. If you are offered some *mutton, lettuce* or *bacon* in English, you are unlikely to recognise that these were French loanwords into Middle English; whereas if you are offered *un scotch, un sandwich, ou le chewing gum* in French, the **etymology** would still be quite transparent.

Of course, borrowing is by no means the only process by which new words can appear. Common processes of word formation are detailed in Chapter 3.

Lexicalisation is also an important phenomenon in terms of lexical change. Just as grammaticalisation turns lexical items into content words, lexicalisation is the process by which grammatical constructions which carry meaning are reduced to single words or morphemes. For example, the Irish Gaelic greeting *Dia duit* and its customary response, *Dia is Muire duit*, have been lexicalised. Literally, they mean 'God be with you', and 'God and Mary be with you', respectively. In practical terms, however, they are used to mean 'hello' and 'hello to you, too'.

The process of lexicalisation can also be observed in sign languages, where it has been noted that the practice of **fingerspelling** can result in new signs being added to a language:

> There is a difference between full, formal fingerspelling and lexicalized fingerspelling, but it is easy to see how quickly the process of lexicalization begins. Just think about how you would fingerspell someone's name if you were introducing them for the first time and then how the form of that fingerspelling would change if you used the name over and over again in a conversation. The changes that you observe are examples of lexicalization.
>
> (Valli and Lucas 2000: 68)

Lexicalisation in sign languages can be considered complete when a sign conforms to the conventions of its language. For example, Battison noted that in American Sign Language (ASL), no single sign utilised more than two **handshapes** (1978). Hence, some signs may be deleted from ASL fingerspellings, as they undergo lexicalisation. For example, in the fingerspelling of *yes*, there is only a sign *y* and a sign *s*.

Likewise, the English word *garlic* was originally a noun phrase (Old English *gār* 'spear' + *lēac* 'leek'), which became lexicalised through compounding and **coalescence**, becoming *gārlēac*. Present-day **multi-word units** in English, such as *going to* and *don't know* are also arguably undergoing lexicalisation. We can hypothesise that the derivation of *gonna* and *dunno* may one day be as unclear to users of future varieties of English as that of *garlic* is to us.

That the derivation of some lexicalised items remains obvious, whilst that of others is lost, ties the issue of lexical change inextricably to semantic change, to which we now turn.

> In the lexicon of Modern Mandarin, disyllabic words are most common. In the lexicon of Old Chinese, however, monosyllabic words were dominant. Many originally monosyllabic words were replaced over time with disyllabic ones; a process known as **disyllabification**. Some of these disyllabic words were formed through **compounding**, but most were derived from syntactic constructions or syntactically unrelated word strings; in other words, through **lexicalisation** (Dong 2012: 237).
>
> The Mandarin construction 干嘛 *gànma* 'do-what', for example, underwent lexicalisation historically, shifting away from its original literal meaning and coming to mean 'why' (Tantucci 2021: 56–58).

8.3.4 Semantic change

Semantic change is change in meaning over time. This type of change can occur in many different ways, as is outlined in Table 8.6.

> If you have institutional access, the *Oxford English Dictionary* can be an invaluable resource for investigating meaning change:

175

Table 8.6 Types of semantic change.

Process	Explanation	Example
Broadening	The process by which a word's meaning extends or broadens.	In Mandarin, the verb 过 *guo* ('to pass-through') has come to also be used as an aspectual particle, meaning 'to have experienced something'.
Semantic bleaching	The process, common in English with intensifying adverbs, by which a word's meaning reduces in intensity.	*I'm literally starving.* *He's awfully kind.* *That's pretty stupid.* *Bloody good job.*
Narrowing	The process by which the meaning of a word becomes less inclusive or less general.	*Yakuza* (Japanese 'gangster'), once had much less serious connotations, meaning something closer to English 'ruffian' or 'vagabond'.
Pejoration	The process by which words become associated with less pleasant things than before.	The Old English verb *stincan* meant 'smell', without negative connotation. Tenth-century writer Ælfric of Eynsham wrote, "Ic stince swote" ('I smell sweet').
Amelioration	The process by which words become associated with more pleasant things than before. This is less common than pejoration.	*Sustainable* is quite a fashionable word nowadays, referring to 'activity which does not degrade the environment or deplete finite resources'. In Early Modern English, however, it merely meant 'capable of being endured'.

Idiot and *knackered* once had much more specific meanings. Can you find out what they were?

Common in present-day language with brand names, e.g. Hoover, Google.

Going down in the world

Going up in the world

How about *awesome*?

Interestingly, the same root in a parent language can undergo different processes in different daughter languages:

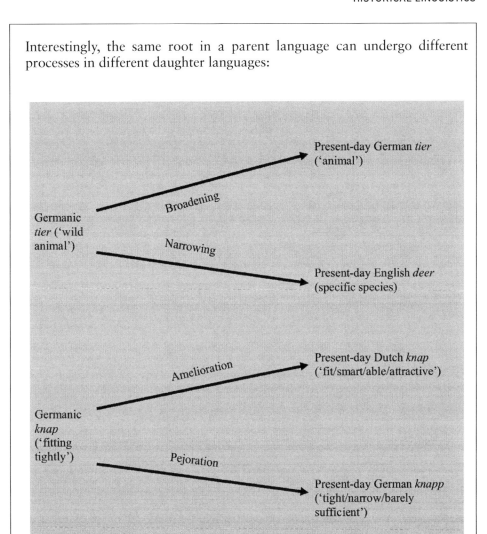

When we trace the journey of a word through its history, often we will be able to see it undergo one or more of the processes outlined in Table 8.6. Consider the orthographic form <anon> in English, and how its meaning shifted over time (Table 8.7).

Table 8.7 Changing meanings of the orthographic form <anon>, Old English to present-day English.

Date	Periodisation	Process	Orthographic form	Meaning	Example
c.450	Old English (c.450–c.1100)		on ān(e)	Literally 'in/into one'	'Heo me on an sagað þaet heo mæglufan minre ne gyme, freondrædenne' (Cynewulf, c.800)
c.1100		Lexicalisation	onān		'She says that she cares not for husbanclove or conjugal love'
c.1175	Middle English (c.1100–c.1450)	Narrowing	anon	Used by the fourteenth century to mean 'at once, straightaway'	'Gief he felde were, me sceolden anon eter gate [hine] gemete' (An Bisþal, c.1200)
c.1380					'A-non vndo þe gates!' (Piers Plowman, c.1360)
c.1450	Early Modern English (c.1450–c.1650)	Semantic bleaching	anon(e)	By 1450, was being bleached of this sense of immediacy	'Thenne anone Balan dyed but Balyn dyed not tyl the mydnyghte after. And anone as they had stablysshed theyr londes' (Le Morte d'Arthur, 1485)
c.1530		Broadening	anon	Comes to mean 'soon, shortly'	'The seconde woo is past, and beholde, the thyrd woo wyll come anon' (Tyndale's Bible, c.1530)

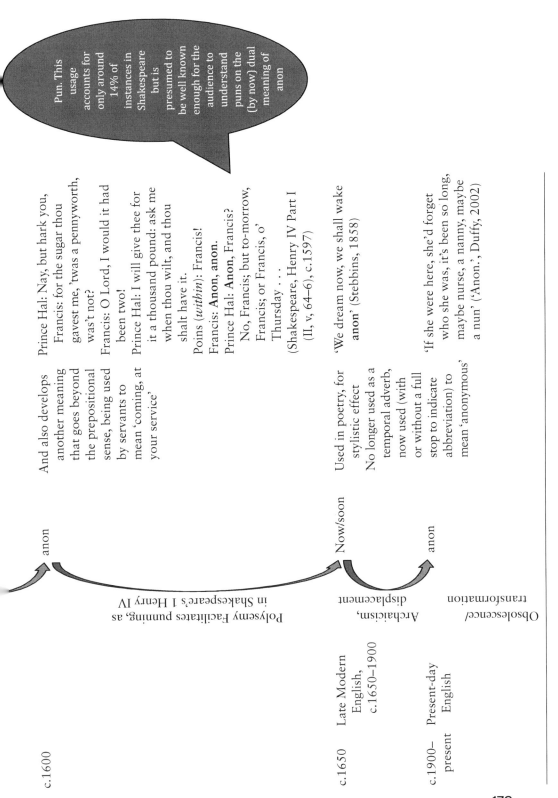

Do you think there might be something about temporal adverbs (and the human condition) which predisposes them to semantic bleaching? Can you think of any others that may be undergoing a similar process in present-day usage?

8.4 How do we know?

While reading this chapter so far, you might reasonably have been thinking: how can we possibly *know* all this? How can we know how languages sounded centuries, or even millennia, ago? The answer, of course, is that we simply do not know *all* of what has been laid out. Some is known; some is theorised. In this section, we will address the *how*.

There are three main ways that historical language change is investigated.

1   Primary data: records of how language was actually used.
2   Secondary data: metalinguistic commentaries.
3   Linguistic reconstruction: reconstruction of the prehistory of a language or language family.

Using primary data to study language history is arguably the most straightforward methodological approach. A researcher studying changes in vocabulary during a recent century will probably have a great deal of data to use. There are exceptions, however. Languages and dialects which are under-represented in textual data cannot be explored effectively in this way. Indigenous and marginalised or minority languages, pidgins, creoles and spoken dialects will be among these. For the twentieth century, recordings and transcriptions of spoken language may be available, but again these will over-represent prestige varieties, as will representations of speech from earlier periods, for instance transcripts of court or parliamentary proceedings and dramatic texts. We must be aware of historical data gaps which preserve and perpetuate social hierarchies by excluding marginalised language varieties and speakers from the available dataset.

Even where **extant** linguistic data are available for research, we must therefore regard results with some caution. This is also true because much of the language data which have been preserved will be printed, and there will have been significant scope for interference with the author's language. In Late Modern England, for example, it was customary for authors to rely upon printers to emend texts to adhere to norms of correctness. Likewise, some texts will have been reprinted many times throughout their history, obscuring their true age. There is also inherent variability in more oral registers, such as medieval poetry, which would have been transmitted orally, and only occasionally recorded in writing.

Many historical linguists use **corpus**-based methods (see Chapter 21); building and using **corpora** of texts to investigate how language was used during a particular period, or over time. Scan the QR code to see a list of historical corpora available for use in this kind of research.

Look back at Table 8.7: can you see how searching for the orthographic form 'anon' in a corpus of Old and/or Middle English texts might be misleading?

Using computers to process very large quantities of primary data allows generalisations to be made about the way that language was used historically. In addition to those general challenges associated with using historical data outlined earlier, however, we must add specific challenges associated with using a computer to retrieve results. Orthographical and typographical variation over time can, for instance, pose problems.

Secondary data include texts such as dictionaries and grammar books. Often, these will not be unbiased commentaries on language usage, but will be **prescriptive** in tone. We must therefore regard their evidence with caution; someone writing about a linguistic bugbear may overstate its frequency, whilst someone who wants to promote a variant may exaggerate its prestige.

We are quite often on shaky ground, then, when relying on secondary data, and it is always desirable to try to triangulate our findings with primary data. But what if this is impossible, because there are *no* primary data to rely upon? Table 8.8 considers how the history of sign languages can be explored, when for much of their evolution, we only have secondary data to rely upon.

Our reliance on secondary data means that our understanding of sign language history is patchy. We know from Plato that deaf Athenians were communicating with signs at around 385 BCE, and there are other references in Ancient Greek which reveal that this was not a society with a strong understanding of sensory impairment. Children born deaf seem to have been considered incapable of learning, which tells us about societal attitudes, but nothing about the actual gestures used by deaf people to communicate.

Consider this timeline of what we know about signed language history up to 1800. How does it compare to the timeline in Table 8.7, for the single English word, *anon*?

This timeline shows how little is known about how deaf people communicated historically. Table 8.8 shows, the roots of the predominant sign languages used today can be traced back only to the 1700s. British, Australian and New Zealand Sign Language (BANZSL), of which the British, Australian and New Zealand sign languages are considered dialects, evolved from Braidwood's (see Table 8.8) sign language, known as 'Old British Sign Language'. Swedish, Maritime and Northern Irish sign languages evolved from this system, too. On the other hand, the French, American, Dutch, German, Russian, Brazilian and Irish sign languages evolved from the 'Old French Sign Language' codified by Épée and his successors. This means that, unlike spoken language, British (BSL) and American (ASL) sign languages are almost completely mutually unintelligible, whilst ASL

Table 8.8 A selective timeline of known information about sign language development

Period	Surviving information	Century	Description
Ancient Greece	No surviving information about specific signs or sign languages.	Fifth century BCE	Plato describes deaf people expressing themselves through gesture. Aristotle: 'those who are born deaf all become senseless and incapable of reason'.
Middle Ages	No surviving information about specific signs or sign languages.	Sixth century CE	Different categories of deaf citizens recognised in the Roman Empire.
		Seventh century CE	Bishop of Hagulstad (England) said to have taught a young deaf man to read, write, and speak verbally.
Renaissance	No surviving information about specific signs or sign languages.	Fifteenth century CE	Dutch author Rudolph Agricola describes a deaf-mute who learned to read and write.
		Sixteenth century CE	Italian physician Dr. Girolamo Cardano (1501–1576) states that deaf individuals can be taught to 'hear' by reading and to 'speak' by writing, a revolutionary recognition that hearing is not necessary for comprehension.
The Enlightenment	Some surviving information about specific signs and sign languages.	Seventeenth century CE	*The Simplification of Letters and the Art of Teaching the Mute to Speak* is published in Spain in 1620, based on the author's observations of a system of teaching based on the written alphabet, **manual alphabet**, and lipreading. This method is thought to be based on those used by Benedictine monks to circumvent their vow of silence and its manual alphabet is the basis for present-day American Sign Language (ASL). *Chirlogia*, a manual of **fingerspelling**, published in 1644. The **handshapes** in the book are still used in British Sign Language (BSL) today. 1644 also sees the publication of *Treatise on the Nature of Bodies* in England; said to popularise the idea that deaf people could learn.

Elements of Speech with an Appendix Concerning People, Deaf & Dumb is published in England in 1669, outlining a two-handed manual alphabet.

Didascalocophus is published in England in 1680, detailing a version of the fingerspelling alphabet said to be the first developed specifically for deaf people. The placement of vowels in this alphabet is still recognisable by users of BSL and other signed languages that have developed from BSL.

Surdus Loquens is published in Holland in 1698. It advocated **oralism**, and outlined procedures for teaching lipreading.

First written record of deafness on Martha's Vineyard is produced in 1714. Due to heredity and intermarriage, up to 25% of the population was deaf between 1700–1900. As a result, Martha's Vineyard Sign Language (MVSL) was used by deaf and hearing residents alike.

Institut National de Jeunes Sourds de Paris founded by Charles-Michel de l'Épée in 1760. Épée assimilated the signed language of his pupils from across France, and from these created Old French Sign Language, which ultimately spread across France. Also in 1760, the fee-paying Braidwood Academy for the Deaf and Dumb is established in Edinburgh.

Épée publishes *Instruction of the Deaf and Dumb by Means of Methodical Signs* in 1776, followed by a second edition entitled *The True Way of Instructing the Deaf and Dumb, Confirmed by Long Practice*, in 1784.

Observations on the Deaf and Dumb, by Samuel Heinicke, published in Saxony in 1778. Heinicke also established a school for deaf children, which advocated purely oral methods.

Épée dies in 1789, leaving his dictionary of sign language unfinished. His work is continued by his successor, Roch-Amboise Cucurron Sicard, who published his *Course of Instruction for the Teaching of Deaf-Mutes* in 1800.

shares around 60% of its signs with present-day French Sign Language (LSF). To frame this in terms of the family tree analogy introduced with Figure 8.1, the Indo-European family tree, BSL has a completely separate family tree than the one for ASL and LSF.

In the absence of either primary or secondary data to facilitate research on historical languages, **linguistic reconstruction** is used. Reconstruction aims to recover as much as possible of a prehistoric ancestor language. This is how pre-historic ancestor languages like Proto-Indo-European and Proto-Germanic have been identified and partially reconstructed. The **workflow** of the comparative method is summarised in Figure 8.7.

This kind of calculated guesswork allows language family trees like the one in Figure 8.1 to be drawn up.

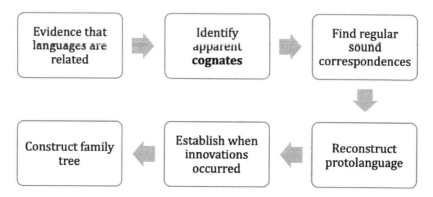

Figure 8.7 A workflow of the comparative method for linguistic reconstruction.

Source: Adapted from Durie and Ross 1996).

8.5 Conclusion

This chapter has introduced some of the different ways languages change, outlined why these changes might occur and provided insight into how historical linguists study diachronic language change. It will have been clear throughout this chapter that there is a significant degree of overlap between historical linguistics and other areas of linguistic research, such as the 'levels' of language discussed in Section one of this volume, other sub-fields such as sociolinguistics (see Chapter 7), and methodological approaches such as corpus linguistics (see Chapter 21). It may also have been clear that there is significant crossover with other research disciplines, such as archaeology and anthropology, and this will become even clearer if you go on to read Chapter 29 of this volume, on the evolution of languages.

To study historical linguistics, then, is not only to study how languages change in a formal sense; it can also provide us with an understanding of the past that we could otherwise never have. That we know that Proto-Indo-European had words for birch, beech, oak and willow trees; for bear, fox and wolf; but not fig, grape or olive; elephant, monkey or tiger, is hugely significant in terms of reconstructing the prehistory of human civilisation. The language used by a society, whether millennia ago or in the last century, is a window into that society, and an opportunity to make discoveries that no other medium could allow.

References

Battison, R. 1978. *Lexical Borrowing in American Sign Language*. Silver Spring, MD: Linstok Press.

Croft, W. 2000. *Explaining Language Change: An Evolutionary Approach*. London: Longman.

Dong, X. 2012. Lexicalization in the history of the Chinese language. In Janet Zhiqun Xing (Ed.), *Newest Trends in the Study of Grammaticalization and Lexicalization in Chinese*. Berlin: Mouton de Gruyter, pp. 235–274.

Durie, M. and Ross, M. (Eds.). 1996. *The Comparative Method Reviewed: Regularity and Irregularity in Language Change*. Oxford: Oxford University Press.

Foulkes, P., Docherty, G. and Watt, D. 2001. The Emergence of Structured Variation. *University of Pennsylvania Working Papers in Linguistics*, 7(3).

Hopper, P. and Traugott, E. 2003. *Grammaticalization*. Cambridge: Cambridge University Press.

Labov, W. 1966. *The Social Stratification of English in New York City*. Washington, DC: Center for Applied Linguistics.

Le Page, R. and Tabouret-Keller, A. 1985. *Acts of Identity: Creole-Based Approaches to Language and Ethnicity*. Cambridge: Cambridge University Press.

Maiden, M. 2014. *A Linguistic History of Italian*. London: Routledge.

McMahon, A. 1994. *Understanding Language Change*. Cambridge: Cambridge University Press.

Tantucci, V. 2021. *Language and Social Minds: The Semantics and Pragmatics of Intersubjectivity*. Cambridge: Cambridge University Press.

Trudgill, P. 1972. Sex, covert prestige and linguistic change in the urban British English of Norwich. *Language in Society*, 1: 179–184.

Valli, C. and Lucas, C. 2000. *Linguistics of American Sign Language: An Introduction*. Washington, DC: Gallaudet University Press.

9 Language acquisition
Silke Brandt and Patrick Rebuschat

9.1 Introduction

This chapter provides a brief introduction to language acquisition research. Our survey focuses on child and adult language learning, so we cover both the acquisition of native languages (L1) and of additional languages (L2, L3, etc.). In doing so, we will first describe the methods typically used to investigate language learning (Section 9.2) before introducing a range of topics that have been widely studied over the past 50 years. We describe the mechanisms by which language is acquired, explaining these in terms of the age-old debate about the role of 'nature' and 'nurture' (Section 9.3). In the following two sections we then review factors that affect the course of language development. We begin by focusing on factors that are generally associated with the nurture side of language acquisition (Section 9.4). Here, we are going to look at different properties of the linguistic input that infants and children receive from their caregivers and peers and how they process this input to learn the phonology, lexicon and grammar of the target language. We will also look at the role of interaction and instruction in language acquisition. Next, we will explore factors that are associated with the nature side of the debate (Section 9.5). We discuss how learning is affected by our genetic endowment, our age, the languages we have acquired previously, and by cognitive and socio-cognitive variables. We have decided to keep this survey broad, going for breadth of coverage rather than depth, in the hope that you will find a topic that sparks your interest. You can then further explore this exciting research by consulting helpful textbooks such as Brooks and Kempe (2012), Clark (2016), De Houwer (2021) or Ortega (2009).

9.2 Methods

The scientific study of language acquisition draws on a range of methods, which we here can only touch upon very briefly.[1] Theoretical reflection on how languages are learned has a rich and long-standing tradition in philosophy, but it is only in the twentieth century that empirical studies started to systematically explore the many facets underlying the process of language learning. Broadly speaking, we can pursue two basic strategies for answering research questions.

DOI: 10.4324/9781003045571-11

We can either observe what happens in the world without interfering. This is the case in studies referred to as '**observational**' or '**correlational**', where the researchers observe behaviour and try to see links between different factors. Or, we can design an experiment to alter some aspect of the environment in controlled conditions and observe the effect this has on behaviour. This is the case of experimental research (see Chapter 20). Both strategies are empirical and essential for the development of science.

In observational research, phenomena of interest are observed and systematically described. For example, many researchers have meticulously transcribed the interaction of children with their interlocutors in naturalistic settings, and then shared these transcripts via the Child Language Data Exchange System (CHILDES, scan the QR code to visit the website), an important, free repository for data of first language acquisition. Over 4000 studies have analysed corpora in CHILDES (MacWhinney 2000), primarily to describe the language development of young children and the characteristics of child-directed speech of adults. In adult second language acquisition, many researchers have systematically described the activities and interactions that take place in classrooms, either by relying on coding schemes (a grid with categories that are considered important in language teaching, which can be completed by the researcher as they observe the class) or by recording and transcribing the classroom discourse (see also Chapter 22 on field methods). Classroom-based studies such as these have provided us with a better understanding of how adults learn languages in formal educational settings.

https://childes.talkbank.org/

In correlational research, we try to establish if there is a link between two or more things that tend to co-occur. For example, in a series of studies on infant word learning, Smith, Yu and colleagues used head-mounted cameras to record gaze data from both infants and parents while they were playing (e.g. Yu et al. 2019). They observed which objects 9-month-old infants paid attention to whilst playing, and how frequently their parents named these objects. They found that generally, the more the parents named objects when they and their children were focusing on the same object, the larger the vocabulary size of the infants at 12 and 15 months of age.

An early summary of this line of research can be found in Linda Smith's keynote, which she gave in 2016 during a conference at Lancaster University. You can access the video via YouTube: www.youtube.com/watch?v=h6O0yIVCkAI&t=1995s

Another example of correlational research is Slevc and Miyake's (2006) investigation of the relationship between musical ability and second language proficiency. Native Japanese speakers who had learned English as a second language completed a series of tests that measured, among other things, their proficiency in English (phonology, vocabulary, grammar) and their musical ability (e.g. tonal memory, pitch detection). Slevc and Miyake found that participants' scores on the tests of musical ability were correlated with their scores on the subset of English proficiency tests that measured receptive and productive phonology. That is, the Japanese participants who scored high in musical ability also tended to score high in the English pronunciation and comprehension tasks. These correlational studies provide evidence that certain aspects of language acquisition are connected, but they cannot tell us anything about whether one causes the other.

In experimental research, by comparison, we try to discover causal relationships between variables. That is, we want to establish whether our manipulation of one variable has an effect on another variable. For example, the artificial language learning paradigm is a widely used technique to study how infants, children and adults acquire language in the lab (see the case study to follow). Here, researchers first create a miniature language that contains different linguistic features of interest (e.g. different types of word order). They then expose participants to the artificial language under different exposure conditions. One group might be asked to simply listen to artificial language sentences, while the other might be asked to discover the rules that determine word order. The groups are then tested to see what aspects of the artificial language they have learned and to see what effect, if any, the exposure condition had on learning. Many studies investigating the effectiveness of different educational treatments in adult language learning follow a similar design. Participants might receive the same task (e.g. describe a sequence of pictures using the second language) but under different treatment conditions. For example, one group might receive no feedback when they make a mistake in their descriptions, while two other groups receive feedback, but of different types. At the end, all groups are tested to see if the different treatment manipulations affected learning.

Case Study 1: Artificial language learning

Psychologists and linguists have used artificial languages to study the cognitive processes underlying language acquisition and processing for close to a century now. A recent paper by Rebuschat et al. (2021) illustrates the fundamental ideas behind this widely used experimental paradigm.

Research aims: We investigated whether statistical learning (see Section 9.3) was powerful enough to enable learners to simultaneously learn the vocabulary and grammar of a novel language. This is an important question as in real life we learn many things at the same time and not necessarily in succession.

Artificial language: We developed an artificial language that contained 16 pseudowords (words that followed English phonotactics but that do not exist in English, e.g. rakken, nellby, jeelow, fisslin). These were divided into nouns, verbs, adjectives and grammatical markers that served to indicate the agent and the patient of each sentence. The grammar of the artificial language was based on Japanese. Sentences could either be SOV or OSV (i.e. the verb phrase (VP) had to be placed in final position but the order of subject and object noun phrases (NP) was free).

Experimental task: Adult native speakers of English were exposed by a cross-situational learning task (see Figure 9.1). In the task, participants saw two dynamic scenes on the screen, each depicting alien characters performing different actions, and heard an artificial language sentence (e.g. 'Haagle chelad tha goorshell sumbark noo fisslin'). Their task was to decide which scene the sentence described. They received no feedback, so the only way to learn the new vocabulary and grammar was by keeping track of information across many learning trials, hence 'cross-situational learning'.

Main findings: We found that cross-situational statistical learning was sufficiently powerful to facilitate acquisition of both vocabulary and grammar from complex sentence-to-scene correspondences. Impressively, learners rapidly acquired information about the new language without intending to and by simply keeping track (unconsciously) of the statistical information in the input.

Figure 9.1 Screenshot of an experimental trial used to investigate the statistical learning of an artificial language. In the task, adult learners were presented with two dynamic scenes, each depicting aliens performing different actions (jumping, hiding, lifting or pushing), and played an artificial language sentence describing just one of the scenes. The participants' task was to indicate the scene the sentence referred to. See Case Study 1 for further information.

Source: Materials adapted from Rebuschat et al. (2021).

Language acquisition is a complex, multifaceted phenomenon. A thorough understanding of how languages are learned, of the factors that affect our ability to learn new languages, and of optimal ways of teaching language requires an increasing range of empirical methods and approaches, each of which can provide another piece to the puzzle of language acquisition. Now that we have a better understanding of some of the approaches used in the study of language learning, let's look at some of the key topics that have been investigated and debated over the years.

9.3 Learning mechanisms

One of the key questions in language acquisition is *how* humans learn language. This question can be broken down into two broad sub-questions of nature and nurture:

1 Nature: What type of innate knowledge and skills do children and language learners need in order to learn language?
2 Nurture: How much of language can be learned from the linguistic input that children and language learners are exposed to?

The answers to both questions depend on the linguistic theory you are adopting (see Chapter 25). According to the generative-nativist theory (e.g. Chomsky 1965), the linguistic input, or nurture, only plays a minor role in language acquisition, especially when it comes to the acquisition of syntax. In particular, according to the **poverty of the stimulus** argument, it is impossible to derive syntactic rules from the input because this often contains utterances that break the rules of grammar. In addition, syntactic rules are structure-dependent, but this structure is not evident on the surface of the input. For example, if you only paid attention to the surface of utterances (i.e. the order in which words occur), you could hypothesise that, in English, yes-no questions, such as (2), are formed by moving the first copula 'is' of the corresponding declarative (1) to the beginning of the sentence:

(1) The man is an actor.
(2) Is the man _ an actor?

Applying this surface-based rule to more complex sentences would yield ungrammatical questions, such as (3):

(3) Is the man who _ standing at the bar is an actor?

Apparently, children do not produce such errors, and this is taken as evidence that they apply a structure-dependent rule, which could be formulated as: if you want to turn a complex sentence into a yes-no question, you need to move the copula of the main clause, not the embedded clause, to the beginning of the sentence, as illustrated next:

(4) Is the man [who is standing at the bar] _ my uncle?

It is assumed that the hierarchical structure of a main clause with an embedded clause and the structure-dependent rule cannot be derived from the input. Instead, the solution to the poverty of the stimulus problem is to propose that humans are born with an innate knowledge of linguistic categories, structures and structure-dependent rules, often referred to as Universal Grammar.

In contrast, the usage-based theory (e.g. Tomasello 2003) suggests that linguistic categories, structures and rules can be derived from the input, and that it is domain-general mechanisms and skills, rather than domain-specific knowledge, that allow humans to learn language. Instead of assuming that humans are born with a Universal Grammar, it is suggested that they apply more general skills, such as pattern finding, analogy and intention reading, to derive linguistic regularities from the environment. Over the past 30 years, a substantial amount of research has explored the role of statistical learning in language acquisition. Statistical learning refers to the (unconscious) ability to detect which linguistic elements tend to appear together in the input and to make use of this information to learn language. For example, when hearing 'myprettybabyhasaprettysmile', the syllables 'pre' and 'ty' co-occur more often than other syllables (e.g. 'ty' and 'ba'). In a seminal study, Saffran et al. (1996) have shown that 8-month-olds are sensitive to these co-occurrences and can use this information to extract words from a continuous speech stream. Since these early empirical demonstrations of statistical learning in infants, many studies have shed further light on this important process, and it is now well-established that statistical learning can be used by child and adult learners to acquire a range of linguistic features, from sounds and words to morphology and syntax (see Case Study 1). Importantly, statistical learning is not limited to language. For example, infants also detect co-occurrences of shapes in visual patterns and of tone sequences, which means that this innate skill is not only applied to the learning of language but also to other domains. Neither is statistical learning limited to humans, as studies clearly indicate that other animals can do so, too (Boros et al. 2021)!

9.4 Factors from 'nurture'

9.4.1 Exposure to language

Even though the generative-nativist and the usage-based approaches disagree on how *much* of language can be derived from the input and what kind of innate skills children and learners have to bring to the task, all theoretical approaches would agree that language acquisition would be impossible *without* any linguistic input. In some extreme cases, so-called 'feral' children grow up without any linguistic input. The most famous case is probably Genie, who had been locked away for 11 years with very little exposure to language or any other form of human interaction. At the age of 14 she was rescued by social services. However, despite being exposed to language from then on, she struggled to fully acquire syntactic rules (e.g. Curtiss 2014).

While cases such as Genie's are thankfully rare, the importance of input can also be seen in the development of language in deaf children. About 95% of deaf children are born to hearing parents, which means that they are likely to grow up without much exposure to a sign language early in development. Unfortunately, not being exposed to a sign language early on has negative consequences for their later acquisition not just of sign, but also spoken and written language (Mayberry 2007). In contrast, deaf children growing up with deaf parents and an early exposure to sign language often become fluent bilinguals in both a sign and a spoken language. Overall, data from 'feral' children and studies with deaf children suggest that learning any type of language requires early exposure to a language system, which is accessible to the learner.

Another question is whether the quality and the quantity of the input matter. In order to answer these questions, researchers have investigated cross-linguistic differences in how and how much caregivers talk to their children and whether these potential differences might affect the learning outcome. Across a variety of language communities (e.g. English, Hebrew, Japanese, Russian), caregivers tend to adopt a specific genre when talking to infants and younger children. This child-directed speech, occasionally referred to as 'Motherese', can differ from adult-directed speech in various ways. For example, compared to adult-directed speech, child-directed speech tends to show higher pitch and exaggerated intonation contours. When talking to children, caregivers also tend to use shorter utterances and fewer embedded clauses. Most of these features of child-directed speech are supposed to support language acquisition, and it could be assumed that children who are exposed to a lot of child-directed speech also show better or faster language acquisition. However, child-directed speech is not evident in all cultures, and in some cultures, such as Walpiri in Australia, caregivers tend to not address pre-verbal children at all. In general, these cross-linguistic differences seem to have no or very little effect on the language-learning outcome. In addition, even in cultures that use child-directed speech, it is estimated that only 15% of children's linguistic input is directly addressed to them. The other 85% is language that children just overhear.

What seems to have a bigger impact than cross-linguistic differences in child-directed speech are differences within cultures that can be associated with caregivers' socio-economic statuses, based on their education degrees and income. In general, caregivers from higher socio-economic backgrounds tend to talk more, but they also use a greater variety of words and syntactic structures. For example, mothers with university degrees talk twice as much as mothers without degrees. And these differences in quantity and quality do have an impact on the learning rate and outcome. At the age of 18 months, children from higher socio-economic backgrounds know almost twice as many words than their peers from lower socio-economic backgrounds, and this gap widens even further as children grow older (Fernald et al. 2013). Finally, children from higher socio-economic backgrounds tend to use more complex sentences than children from lower socio-economic backgrounds.

9.4.2 Interaction

In the previous section, we discussed how the quantity and quality of the linguistic input can affect the learning rate and outcome. We also briefly mentioned the fact that most of the language children hear is not directly addressed to them and that they must learn a lot from overhearing, too. However, simply overhearing speech does not seem to provide an ideal learning condition. For example, Kuhl et al. (2003) were interested to see whether English-learning infants would be able to (re)learn Mandarin tones. Typically, infants growing up in English-speaking environments will have lost the ability to distinguish between different Mandarin tones, and other non-native sound contrasts, by the age of 12 months. Kuhl and colleagues exposed 9-months old infants who were growing up with English as an ambient language to three different learning conditions in which they were exposed to Mandarin. One group of infants interacted with native speakers of Mandarin with book reading and free play. The other two groups were only exposed to Mandarin via audio or audio and video, without any inter-action. At the end, only the group who interacted with the Mandarin-speaking adults showed an ability to distinguish between Mandarin tones. The other two groups performed as poorly as a group of infants who had only interacted with native speakers of English.

Interaction also seems to be crucial for children's vocabulary development. For example, studies such as the one conducted by Yu et al. (2019) have shown that children can learn the meaning of new words and labels by following their caregivers' gaze to the object or event that they are labelling. Word learning can also be supported by children's understanding of the interlocutor's communicative intention or their understanding of what is new to the interlocutor when they utter a new word. For example, when a child and an adult have played with two out of three objects already and then the adult comes back into the room with excitement and produces a new word, the child will (rightly) associate that new word with the object that the child and adult had not jointly played with before.

Finally, interaction can also support children's acquisition of syntactic rules. Whereas the generative-nativist account has often stressed that children do not get any or enough corrective feedback from their caregivers when they produce ungrammatical sentences such as 'nobody don't like me', some studies have shown that caregivers often provide feedback in a more indirect way and that children can learn from this so-called indirect negative evidence. One way that adults can provide indirect negative evidence is by providing so-called **recasts** to correct the ungrammatical utterance, as illustrated in this example (5) by Brooks and Kempe (2012):

(5) Erica: I want fish fingers over my dinner.
Erica's mother: Yes, let's have fish fingers for dinner.

After these recasts, children often tend to start producing these sentences in the right format, too. Similarly, children can retreat from so-called overgeneralisation errors (i.e. an over-creative use of syntactic rules) by paying attention to the way that their caregivers phrase a sentence with the same intended meaning they had in mind. If the child, for example, said 'he disappeared the rabbit' and heard an adult say 'he made the rabbit disappear', they can recover from their overgeneralisation and adapt the conventional and grammatical way of expressing their intended meaning.

9.4.3 Instruction

We do not require instruction to learn language. By the time we begin primary school, much of our native languages are in place, and in principle we could continue our linguistic development without ever attending school. Remember that compulsory school education is a relatively recent phenomenon in the history of humanity and obviously we learned languages before that!

Even in the case of second language acquisition, many learners acquire the new language to high levels of proficiency in naturalistic settings (i.e. by residing in the target language country and without taking foreign language classes). But while we might be able to learn language without making use of language classes, apps or other educational tools, there is substantial empirical evidence that instruction makes a difference. For example, in the case of child language development, we know that attending school will significantly benefit linguistic development in several ways. At the most basic level, school provides additional exposure to language and opportunities for interaction, which is particularly important for bilingual children whose home language is different from the one used in school. Importantly, school plays a central role in the development of literacy. Learning to read and write is essential for many, if not most, aspects of daily life, from simply using the internet or reading printed materials such as newspapers, books or medicine labels to filling out job applications and completing ballot papers in elections and referenda. Instruction and guided practice, as provided in primary and secondary schools, significantly supports the development of basic and advanced literacy skills in children and adolescents, thus contributing to social mobility and a fairer society.

Instruction is also particularly important in the context of second language acquisition, and a significant amount of research over the past 40 years has investigated, in great detail, what type of instruction works best for different aspects of language. Hundreds of studies have investigated the effectiveness of instructional manipulations on second language learning in adults. Taken together, these studies show that all domains of language (e.g. phonology, vocabulary, grammar, pragmatics) are amenable to teaching, that educational interventions can increase how fast we learn, and that instruction might even be necessary for some features of language (e.g. inflectional morphology, as described below).

But what type of instruction works best? The answer to this question can be found in several meta-analyses that have been published since 2000 (e.g. Spada and Tomita 2010). Instruction type is generally divided into two broad categories. 'Explicit instruction' is any type of pedagogical intervention that leads learners to pay attention to language forms (e.g. to notice the English past tense -ed) or to become aware of metalinguistic rules (e.g. 'the English past tense is formed by adding an -ed to the verb stem'). When teachers discuss grammar rules in the foreign language classroom or provide metalinguistic corrective feedback, they are relying on explicit instructional techniques. In contrast, 'implicit instruction' is any type of intervention in which learners focus on the meaning of what is being said and are not led to consciously notice particular forms that are part of the treatment. For example, when teachers intentionally select texts in which the learning target (say, German plurals) is particularly frequent for use in classroom tasks, or when they provide corrective feedback in the form of recasts, they are using implicit instructional techniques. Meta-analyses show that both implicit and explicit instruction are beneficial (i.e. they both promote learning) but that explicit types tend to show a greater learning effect. However, they also reveal that there is much we still don't know yet. It is now evident that the effectiveness of different types of instruction (implicit vs. explicit) is mediated by the learning target (what is being learned, e.g. simple or complex features of language) and by the profile of the individual learner (e.g. their age, previously acquired languages, motivation, working memory capacity, personality and so forth). Current empirical research is addressing the complex interplay of instruction type, learning target and individual learner profile, an essential step towards the development of intelligent computational tools that permit the provision of optimised instruction for individual learners.

9.5 Factors from 'nature'

9.5.1 Genetics

After having discussed the 'nurture' side of language acquisition, let's return to the 'nature' side. The question focuses on which innate skills humans bring to the language acquisition task. Whereas most language acquisition researchers agree that humans must be born with some special innate skills that set us apart from other species and make us the only species that has developed language, there is disagreement over whether these mechanisms are domain-specific only used to learn language, or whether they are domain-general, used to support the learning of different types of information other than language (see also Chapter 11, p. 238; Chapter 29, p. 485).

In the past, one group of children has served as the perfect example to support the generative-nativist idea that children are born with Universal Grammar, that is, domain-specific knowledge of syntactic categories, structures and rules which does not depend on developments in other cognitive domains. In the UK and other parts of the world, more than 7% of children are diagnosed with Developmental Language Disorder, previously also referred to as Specific Language Impairment (SLI). Early studies suggested that the only thing that these children struggle with is language acquisition – despite having normal hearing and typical IQs, for example. However, more recent research has shown that they often tend to also struggle with working-memory tasks, auditory processing or sequence learning. In addition, Developmental Language Disorder often co-occurs with other developmental disorders such as autism or ADHD. These later findings provide more support for usage-based and constructivist theories of language acquisition, according to which language acquisition builds on domain-general skills such as statistical learning and intention reading. For example, early difficulties in auditory processing can cascade into problems in language processing and learning later in life.

At the same time, there is evidence that Developmental Language Disorder has a genetic cause. Bishop (2006) looked at Developmental Language Disorder in mono- and dizygotic twins. Monozygotic twins are genetically identical, whereas dizygotic twins share less genetic material. She found that monozygotic twins were much more likely to have the same language profiles than dizygotic twins. In other words, when one monozygotic twin is diagnosed with Developmental Language Disorder, it is very likely that the other twin receives the same diagnosis. This supports the idea that language has a genetic basis. However, as mentioned before it is not clear whether this genetic basis is a domain-specific Universal Grammar or whether it consists of domain-general skills, such as auditory processing and working memory.

9.5.2 Age effects

As we have seen, it is clear that severely depriving infants and children from exposure to language and from interaction with other speakers will result in significant linguistic and cognitive deficits, which cannot be fully compensated later in life. What is subject to considerable debate, however, is the role of age effects in additional language learning (Hartshorne 2021). We know that children can become native speakers of two or more languages if they are exposed to them early in life, but the picture seems far more complex when it comes to language learning after puberty. We can learn to communicate in another language throughout our lifespan and even achieve high levels of proficiency. But is it ever possible to develop native-like proficiency in another language later in life? Or is there a 'critical period' (Lenneberg 1967) after which this becomes impossible due to maturational constraints? The answer depends, in part, on the aspect of language we are considering and on the sensitivity of the tests we use to measure linguistic ability.

In the case of vocabulary, there is relatively little evidence for age effects in learning. Our ability to rapidly learn novel words in both our native and non-native languages appears to be largely preserved throughout much of our lives. In contrast, in the case of pronunciation, age effects are frequently reported in the research literature. Many studies show that we are very unlikely to avoid a 'foreign accent' if we begin learning our second language after the age of 8–10. This could be for several reasons, including a decline in our ability to perceive or to produce subtle phonetic differences that exist in the second language but not in our native language(s). Remember, for example, that English-learning infants quickly lose the ability to distinguish between Mandarin tones when they do not interact with native speakers of Mandarin. Finally, in the case of grammar, the evidence is mixed. Many studies, including a recent one with over 1 million participants, report age effects for the acquisition of morphology and syntax (Chen and Hartshorne 2021). As with pronunciation, there appears to be a window of opportunity beyond which our ability to develop the second language to native-like levels declines, though with grammar learning this window appears to close later (as late as age 17, depending on grammatical feature). Having said that, many of these studies relied on grammaticality judgement tasks to measure proficiency in the second language, an offline task that is more likely to tap into explicit knowledge than implicit knowledge of language. Psycholinguistic studies using online tasks, including eye-movement recordings and electroencephalography (a method that records neural activity via electrodes placed on the scalp), have failed to provide evidence of age effects in the processing of second language morphosyntax by highly proficient learners.

9.5.3 Cross-linguistic influence

Another widely studied topic is the effect of previously acquired languages on subsequent language learning. For example, do the languages we acquired during childhood affect our ability to learn a new language later in life? The assumption in the 1950s and 1960s was that our native language(s) are the most important factor determining success in second language learning. Lado (1957) proposed that similarities and differences between the two languages could account for ease and difficulty of learning. If our native language is similar to the second language (e.g. Dutch and German), the new language should be easier to learn because structures that are similar between languages will be 'transferred' from one language to the other. But if the two languages are very different (e.g. Portuguese and Mandarin) the learner would face greater challenges. This proposal led to a substantial amount of cross-linguistic research, including the systematic comparison of languages (referred to as 'contrastive analyses'), to aid the development of teaching materials uniquely adapted to learners with specific language backgrounds. However, research in the late 1960s and 1970s that analysed the errors made by second language learners pointed towards a significant problem with Lado's Contrastive Analysis Hypothesis: not all errors that occurred were predicted, and not all predicted errors occurred. Contrary to what was expected, errors due to differences between the first and second languages were much less frequent than originally assumed. (In some studies, as little as 3% of errors seemed to be due to cross-linguistic interference.) In the 1970s, these findings, together with the discovery of developmental sequences in child language development and the popularity of generative-nativist accounts of language acquisition, led to the view that our first language(s) might only play a very minor role in second language learning. But further research since the 1980s has confirmed that this might substantially underestimate the role of our native languages in subsequent language learning.

So, where do we stand today? Many studies, including large-scale computational analyses with thousands of learners, confirm that our native languages are important predictors of success in the acquisition of novel languages. For example, the languages we have previously acquired might affect our learning rate (how fast we learn the new language) and our ultimate attainment (how proficient we become eventually). However, they also show that the impact is mediated by a number of other important variables. For example, older learners appear more subject to cross-linguistic influence than younger children, and transfer is more likely to occur at low levels of proficiency and less likely at high levels of proficiency. That is, we are more likely to feel the impact of our previously acquired languages in the early stages of learning a new language. Likewise, transfer is more frequent for some domains of language (e.g. phonology, vocabulary and discourse) than others (grammar). Finally, while early research emphasised the effect of the first language on the acquisition of a second language, more recent research has revealed that all previously learned languages (L1, L2, L3, etc.) affect the acquisition of subsequent languages. For example, **typological** distance between the different languages mediates the amount of cross-linguistic influence and the learnability of novel languages. Importantly, it is also clear that transfer can go in multiple directions, not just from the first to the second language but also from the second to the first language, from the third to the second, and so forth.

9.5.4 Cognitive variables: the case of attention

If we intend to learn a new language, we need exposure to this language and, ideally, plenty of opportunity to interact with other speakers. However, exposure and interaction are clearly not enough. Evidence for this comes from published case studies with adult learners who fail to acquire certain morphosyntactic features despite decades' worth of input to the second language and substantial contact with other speakers (see, e.g. the case of Patty, as described in Lardiere 2007). It is true that, in the case of these learners, the native and target languages are often very typologically distant (say, Mandarin and English), but this alone doesn't explain why input and interaction do not suffice for acquisition to take place. One explanation is that we don't just need to be exposed to the new language, we also have to process the information in a manner that is conducive to learning. In this context, a significant amount of research has explored the role of cognitive variables (such as attention, awareness, executive function, working memory, declarative and procedural memory) in language learning. For example, there is substantial evidence that attention plays an important, if not essential, role when we learn a new language. As previously mentioned, many studies with infants and young children show that 'joint attention' (essentially when a child and adult are focused on the same object or event while interacting with each other) helps children discover the meanings of novel words. The recent studies by Smith, Yu and colleagues, mentioned earlier, in which the authors used sophisticated head-mounted cameras to record gaze data from both infants and parents while they were playing, are particularly illuminating in this regard (e.g. Yu et al. 2019).

In the case of adult language learning, the role of attention has also been extensively explored. Schmidt (1990) proposed the **Noticing Hypothesis**, according to which a linguistic stimulus in the new language can only be acquired if the adult learner has directed their attention to it. If the learner does not consciously 'notice' the item-to-be-acquired (e.g. inflectional morphemes), then the item is not available for further cognitive processing and it cannot be stored in long-term memory. This would explain why adult learners often fail to acquire specific aspects of the second language despite many years of exposure to these items while residing in the target language countries. Schmidt would argue that, in these cases, the learners simply did not attend to the items in the input. This could be due, for example, to differences in the way the native and the target languages function.

To illustrate, let's consider the well-studied case of English tense acquisition by native speakers of Mandarin. English uses inflectional morphemes to mark tense relations on the verb (e.g. the regular past tense is formed by adding an *ed* to the verb stem). In contrast, Mandarin expresses tense using other words (e.g. time expressions, *zuotian*, yesterday), or through contextual inference. As a result, native speakers of these languages are likely to pay attention to different cues to draw inferences about event time. In the case of English, the most reliable cue about tense can be found at the end of the verb, but in Mandarin, the most reliable cue will be the temporal adverb. So, when native Mandarin speakers begin learning English, they need to learn to direct their attention to the inflectional morphemes at the end of verb as these carry important grammatical information. The problem is that occasionally this is not the only source of temporal information in English. Often, though not always, English speakers add a temporal adverb to the sentence (e.g. 'Yesterday, I walked to the beach.'). In these cases, the learner can easily infer that the event took place in the past simply by paying attention to the adverb, just like they would in their native language, and the English verb ending can be safely ignored without affecting the correct interpretation of tense. There is thus less pressure on the learner to re-learn how to deploy their attention to process second language sentences more accurately. The inflectional morpheme is also low in salience, that is, it is very difficult to detect in the speech stream; this is because affixes are generally monosyllabic, unstressed and often not overtly realised (meaning, they are not pronounced, as in the earlier example sentence). So, even if the learner tried to pay attention to verb endings, this could be challenging as the affix is unlikely to stand out in the speech stream. Failure to consistently 'notice' the learning target could thus partially explain why learners fail to acquire some but not other aspects of the second language despite substantial exposure and interaction.

Debates about the role of attention in language learning continue. There is still theoretical and empirical discussion about whether attention is necessary and sufficient for learning to occur, as Schmidt (1990) argued. Some researchers argue that we can learn without attention; others agree with Schmidt that attention is necessary, but disagree with him that it is sufficient. They point to the fact that attention just makes stimuli available for subsequent cognitive processing, and that working memory plays a key role in storage and retrieval of items from long-term memory stores. There is also debate about the type of attention that is required. For example, recent research challenged the long-standing notion that joint attention is essential for infant word learning, arguing that infant sustained attention is the better predictor of success in word learning. But none of these debates seriously challenge the notion that attention plays an important role when we learn a new language.

9.5.5 Socio-cognitive variables

In addition to purely cognitive mechanisms, language development has also been shown to interact with socio-cognitive skills. While the generative-nativist approach advocates a modular view of the brain, where there is little interaction and inter-dependency between language and other socio-cognitive skills, the usage-based approach suggests that there is a high degree of interaction and inter-dependency. As mentioned previously, skills like statistical learning, auditory processing, attention, and intention reading play a fundamental part in language acquisition.

Interestingly, there is also some evidence that language supports some socio-cognitive skills. For example, a good number of studies have shown that children's linguistic skills predict their ability to understand others' perspectives.

In particular, children who have learned mental verbs such as 'know' and 'think' and complement-clause constructions such as 'he thinks that it's raining' tend to also be able to understand that others can have false beliefs (i.e. beliefs that differ from reality). And it can be suggested that the linguistic tools allow children to represent others' beliefs and knowledge states (e.g. de Villiers 2007). This is the focus of Case Study 2.

Case Study 2: Language and understanding false beliefs

Many studies suggest that language acquisition supports children's understanding of false belief (the understanding that someone can have a belief that differs from reality). However, it is unclear which aspects of language children need to acquire in order to be able to represent and understand false belief.

Research aims: In a longitudinal study, de Villiers and Pyers (2002) investigated temporal relationships between children's understanding of false belief and complement clauses (as illustrated in the following). At the beginning of the study, children were aged 3–5 years and did not show a stable understanding of false belief yet. Over the period of one year, they were repeatedly tested on their understanding of false belief and complement clauses.

False belief task: One of the tasks to test children's understanding of false belief is the Sally Ann task. Children are told and shown a story where one character (Sally) hides an object in location A. In Sally's absence, another character (Ann) moves the object to location B. Then Sally returns and children are asked to predict where she would look for the object. The correct answer is location A because Sally does not know that the object has been moved to location B. However, children only start to give this correct answer around the age of 4.

Complement-clause task: One way to test children's understanding of complement clauses is to tell them a short story, such as 'Tina said that she found a monster, but it was really the neighbour's dog'. And then ask them 'What did she say', with the correct answer being 'that she found a monster'. Children who do not understand these sentences yet, however, would respond with 'dog'.

Main findings: The researchers found that children's understanding of complement clauses was a good predictor of their understanding of false belief. For example, children who started to show an understanding of complement clauses in a test session when they were 4 years old tended to then also show an understanding of false belief when they were tested again a couple of months later (e.g. at the age of 4.5). False belief, on the other hand, did not predict children's understanding of complement clauses. These results suggest that complement clauses allow children to represent and acquire false belief.

9.6 Conclusion

In this chapter, we have briefly surveyed methods and topics covered in language acquisition research. Research on how we learn language can be found across many disciplines, from linguistics and developmental psychology to philosophy and neuroscience, and naturally this chapter could only touch very lightly on many fascinating topics. We hope this survey becomes a starting point for further exploration of the topics you find of particular interest, for example in the context of an undergraduate dissertation, and we encourage you to consult our recommendations for further readings in the accompanying web resources, if you are wondering what to read next.

Note

1 The chapters in Hoff (2011) and Mackey and Gass (2012) introduce different methods used in (first and second) language acquisition research and provide helpful guidance on how to use them.

References

Bishop, D. V. 2006. What causes specific language impairment in children? *Current Directions in Psychological Science*, 15(5): 217–221. https://doi.org/10.1111/j.1467-8721.2006.00439.x

Boros, M., Magyari, L., Török, D., Bozsik, A., Deme, A. and Andics, A. 2021. Neural processes underlying statistical learning for speech segmentation in dogs. *Current Biology*, 31(24): 5512–5521.e5.

Brooks, P. J. and Kempe, V. 2012. *Language Development*. Chichester, UK: Wiley.

Chen, T. and Hartshorne, J. K. 2021. More evidence from over 1.1 million subjects that the critical period for syntax closes in late adolescence. *Cognition*, 214: 104706.

Chomsky, N. 1965. *Aspects of the Theory of Syntax*. Cambridge, MA: The MIT Press.

Clark, E. 2016. *First Language Acquisition*. Cambridge: Cambridge University Press.

Curtiss, S. 2014. *Genie: A Psycholinguistic Study of a Modern-day Wild Child*. London: Academic Press.

De Houwer, A. 2021. *Bilingual Development in Childhood*. Cambridge: Cambridge University Press.

de Villiers, J. 2007. The interface of language and theory of mind. *Lingua*, 117(11): 1858–1878. https://doi.org/10.1016/j.lingua.2006.11.006

Fernald, A., Marchman, V. A. and Weisleder, A. 2013. SES differences in language processing skill and vocabulary are evident at 18 months. *Developmental Science*, 16(2): 234–248. https://doi.org/10.1111/desc.12019

Hartshorne, J. K. 2021. When do children lose the language instinct? A critical review of the critical periods literature. *Annual Review of Linguistics*, 8: 143–151.

Hoff, E. (Ed.). 2011. *Research Methods in Child Language: A Practical Guide*. Chichester, UK: Wiley.

Kuhl, P. K., Tsao, F. M. and Liu, H. M. 2003. Foreign-language experience in infancy: Effects of short-term exposure and social interaction on phonetic learning. *Proceedings of the National Academy of Sciences of the United States of America*, 100(15): 9096–9101.

Lado, R. 1957. *Linguistics Across Cultures: Applied Linguistics for Language Teachers*. Ann Arbor, MI: University of Michigan Press.

Lardiere, D. 2007. *Ultimate Attainment in Second Language Acquisition: A Case Study*. London: Routledge.

Lenneberg, E. H. 1967. *Biological Foundations of Language*. Chichester, UK: Wiley.

Mackey, A. and Gass, S. M. (Eds.). 2012. *Research Methods in Second Language Acquisition: A Practical Guide*. Chichester, UK: Wiley.

MacWhinney, B. 2000. *The CHILDES Project: Tools for Analyzing Talk*. 3rd ed. Mahwah, NJ: Lawrence Erlbaum Associates.

Mayberry, R. 2007. When timing is everything: Age of first-language acquisition effects on second-language learning. *Applied Psycholinguistics*, 28(3): 537–549. http://doi.org/10.1017/S0142716407070294

Ortega, L. 2009. *Understanding Second Language Acquisition*. London: Routledge.

Rebuschat, P., Monaghan, P. and Schoetensack, C. 2021. Learning vocabulary and grammar from cross-situational statistics. *Cognition*, 206, Article 104475.

Saffran, J. R., Aslin, R. N. and Newport, E. L. 1996. Statistical learning by 8-month-old infants. *Science*, 274(5294): 1926–1928.

Schmidt, R. W. 1990. The role of consciousness in second language learning. *Applied Linguistics*, 11(2): 129–158.

Slevc, L. R. and Miyake, A. 2006. Individual differences in second-language proficiency: Does musical ability matter? *Psychological Science*, 17(8): 675–681.

Spada, N. and Tomita, Y. 2010, Interactions between type of instruction and type of language feature: A meta-analysis. *Language Learning*, 60: 263–308.

Tomasello, M. 2003. *Constructing a Language: A Usage-Based Theory of Language Acquisition*. Cambridge, MA: Harvard University Press.

Villiers, J. D. and Pyers, J. E. 2002. Complements to cognition: A longitudinal study of the relationship between complex syntax and false-belief-understanding. *Cognitive Development*, 17: 1037–1060.

Yu, C., Suanda, S. H., and Smith, L. B. 2019. Infant sustained attention but not joint attention to objects at 9 months predicts vocabulary at 12 and 15 months. *Developmental Science*, 22(1): e12735.

10 Studying discourse
Beth Malory

10.1 What is *discourse*, anyway?

Before we consider any subject, it is important for us to define what that subject is. Generally speaking, this is a fairly straightforward endeavour. In Section one, we saw that phonetics can be simply defined as the 'study of speech sounds produced by humans', for example (Chapter 1, p. 3) and that morphology is the 'study of the structure of words' (Chapter 3, p. 42). The study of discourse cannot be summed up in such simple terms, and neither can the concept of 'discourse' itself. Indeed, everything about the study of discourse is in some way contested. From what *discourse* is, to what the goals and remits of 'discourse studies' or 'discourse analysis' are, to whether we should say we are doing 'discourse studies' or 'discourse analysis', this is a topic fraught with questions and challenges. The purpose of this chapter is to lay out these questions and challenges in straightforward terms which will allow you to read the other chapters in this volume which discuss discourse with confidence (see Chapter 12 on communication and culture, Chapter 16 on Critical Discourse Analysis, and Chapter 17 on workplace communication).

Part of the problem we face when approaching the much more nebulous concept of *discourse*, by contrast with *phonetics* or *morphology*, is that it means different things in different contexts. Of course, this is true of all linguistic items to some degree, but for a simple comparison, let's consider the word *language*. Whether you say this word in a bar or café, on the television news, in a sociology or psychology seminar, or in the presence only of other linguists, it will be understood in more or less the same way (providing your interlocutors speak the same language as you do and understand the word you use). Somewhat confusingly, the same cannot be said about *discourse*. If you say *this* word in a bar or café, or on the television news, it is likely to be understood in a very general sense; something along the lines, perhaps, of the *Concise Oxford English Dictionary*'s (*COD*) definitions:

a   written or spoken communication or debate
b   a formal written or spoken discussion of a topic
c   (linguistics) a text or conversation

This entry informs us that *discourse* has very general meanings, along the lines of 'communication or debate', or a 'formal . . . discussion', but also exists as a

DOI: 10.4324/9781003045571-12

technical term (an incredibly vague one, apparently!) within the discipline of linguistics. As you are currently reading a chapter on discourse in a linguistics textbook, this will probably not be breaking news. The complicating factor is that *discourse* is not only used in such contexts as bars, cafés and TV news, where definitions (a) and (b) might suffice, and in linguistic contexts, where (c), despite its vagueness, might. So, what of the sociology or psychology seminar? Will any of the *COD* definitions be used there? Probably not, because as Mills (1997) notes, the word *discourse* 'has become common currency in a variety of disciplines: critical theory, sociology, linguistics, philosophy, social psychology and many other fields, so much so that it is frequently left undefined, as if its usage were simply common knowledge' (p. 1). As Mills also, wryly, points out, *discourse* is a word 'often employed to signal a certain theoretical sophistication in ways which are vague and sometimes obfuscatory' (1997: 1). In other words, it's one of those words that's sometimes used vaguely in order to sound a bit cleverer, which is no help in trying to pin down its meaning(s).

What we have, then, is a word used in a wide range of contexts, with a range of meanings which are often vague and imprecise. This can make it pretty frustrating and confusing to try to understand what *discourse* is, how it's studied, and why that's important and interesting; and this chapter is here to try to straighten those things out. To that end, in Section 10.2, we will look at the different definitions/approaches which tend to be taken within linguistics and closely related disciplines. In Section 10.3, we will consider how discourse analysts approach sign languages, and why it's important not to over-privilege spoken and written language and overlook the insights sign discourse offers us. In Section 10.4, we will consider the importance of multimodality to the study of discourse, and in Section 10.5, we will consider some of the challenges of studying discourse in a linguistic context. By the end of this chapter, you should feel confident in your ability to define *discourse* in a number of ways, to identify different approaches to discourse study and to conduct your own basic discourse study.

10.2 How do we approach discourse?

We saw in Section 10.1 that attempts to define *discourse* can be fraught with difficulty. This can make approaching the study of discourse a little daunting, but the good news is that within linguistics, there are three main definitions that tend to be used. These form the basis for the majority of approaches to the study of discourse, and will therefore be our focus in this section. These definitions, which don't need to mean much to you at this stage, and which we will unpack as we go, are as follows:

1   *Discourse* is language 'above the clause or above the sentence'.
2   *Discourse* is language 'in use'.
3   *Discourse* is a form of social practice in which language plays a key role.

To these, we must add a fourth definition of *discourse*, as it is often used in linguistic studies. This is, perhaps, the most straightforward of all. According to this fourth definition:

4   *Discourse* is a means of identifying a number of texts as a cohesive aggregate.

According to this last definition, *discourse* is a way of lumping together disparate language data that has something in common (cf. Baker 2006: 4). This could be a particular focus, **genre** or **register**. Thus, we may find references to 'environmental discourse' or 'antiracist discourse', which appears in a variety of sources but shares a broad subject focus. Likewise, we may find references to 'digital discourse', referring to language data from the internet. At the level of register, we may even find references to very broad categories such as 'written discourse'. As we explore approaches to discourse which ascribe to definitions (1–3), it is useful to bear the general definition in (4) in mind, and to consider how it interacts with (1–3), as well as with the dictionary definitions given in 10.1. One final thing to note, before we get into the different approaches, is that you will probably notice that 'discourse analysis' and 'discourse studies' both appear in linguistic literature on discourse. These used to be used interchangeably, but in recent years the word *analysis* has been more associated with research that is more language-focused (the approaches tending to align with definitions (1) and (2)) and *studies* has tended to be more associated with discourse research which is more broadly oriented (aligning more with definition (3)).

10.2.1 Language above the clause or sentence

Definition (1) approaches discourse as 'language above the level of the sentence or above the level of the clause' (Stubbs 1983: 1). To understand what this means, it is useful to look back to Section one of this volume, Language structures, and note, as do Cameron and Panović (2014), that 'the traditional aim of linguistics is to describe and explain the way language works as a system: what its basic units are and what the rules are for combining them' (4). The different kinds of language structures introduced in Section one are often conceptualised as levels of language. Thus, the smaller units of language which exist on one level can combine with one another to form larger units on a higher level. This metaphor is shown in Figure 10.1.

From Figure 10.1, it should be clear what the definition of *discourse* as 'above the level of the sentence/clause' means. As Cameron and Panović (2014) *explain*:

[a]s your units get larger (e.g. words are larger than sounds and sentences are larger than words), you metaphorically move 'up' from one level to the next. If discourse analysis deals with 'language *above* the sentence', that means it looks for structural patterns in units which are larger, more extended, than one sentence.

(p. 4)

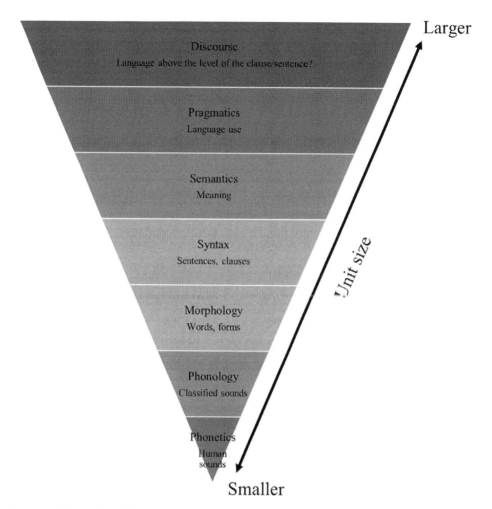

Figure 10.1 Levels of language.

Approaches focused on the interactions between grammar and discourse, sometimes referred to as the **grammar-discourse** interface, tend to take this approach. According to this view, to quote Haselow and Hancil (2021),

> grammar and discourse complement each other: discourse can only be based on grammar, since the units it comprises must be based on a selective use of grammar, and grammar is integrated in emergent discourse, since no grammatical unit is produced in a communicative vacuum, but serving specific discourse goals.

(p. 9)

We can also place **systemic functional linguistics** (SFL), developed by Halliday, into this category. According to Martin, this framework seeks to 'move beyond the structural resources of grammar and consider discourse relations that transcend grammatical structure' (1994: 62). An important feature of SFL, however, is its focus on the 'rank scale' or organisation of the linguistic 'constituents' which comprise language. Halliday describes grammar not as a set of formal rules but a 'network of systems, or interrelated sets of options for making meaning' (1994: 15) through paradigmatic substitution. This sounds complicated, but really just means that when you create the sentence 'I'm going to the [room with the toilet in it]', you have a choice about which word you want to slot into that **paradigm** (see p. 139 for a fairly exhaustive list of English options, if you are so inclined). In this context, a paradigm refers to a set of units that can be substituted for one another, to mean more or less the same thing. It is important to note that this is not the same as the research paradigms explored later. Halliday conceptualises the constituents at different ranks as all interrelated, and each constituent consisting of one or more units from the rank below, as Figure 10.2 shows.

According to this kind of definition, discourse should probably have had its own chapter in Section one of this book. But would that have made sense? A number of criticisms have been levelled at approaches which conceptualise discourse in this way. First, although as Mithun notes, it was once the case that 'mainstream theories of grammar viewed language as a set of hierarchical structures whose components should be studied as autonomous systems', it has

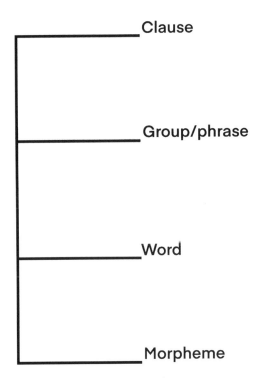

Figure 10.2 The evolution of Halliday's 'rank scale' over time.

now become clear that 'none of these components can be understood fully in isolation' (2015: 39). If, as Mithun concludes, '[a] language is much more than a set of structural parameters' (2015: 39), then can we really approach discourse in this way? Of course, for ease of teaching or study, we need to separate different topics as we learn the fundamentals, but whether discourse fits into this model is a whole other question.

Second, we must ask whether it is even possible to distinguish cohesive collections of language, using only structural or formal criteria. Stubbs gives the example of a radio announcer saying, 'later, an item on vasectomy, and the results of the do-it-yourself competition' (1983: 93). We can assume (and, indeed, hope!) that these two statements are entirely unrelated, but if we consider only the structural properties of the available text, then do we have any evidence for that? Or are we relying on something *beyond* language structure? As Cameron and Panović note, 'once we get "above the sentence", our ability to make sense of sequences and decide whether/how they are connected involves more than applying a set of quasi-grammatical rules' (2014: 5). This point relates to the concept of cohesion, or the establishment of local links and relationships within communication; whereby one element of text is interpreted in relation to another. These relationships are very often formally marked by things like conjunctions (as with 'and' in the vasectomy example), adverbs and anaphora. Though some regard cohesion as linkage which is structural (cf. Stubbs 1983), then, it seems that we need more than formal evidence to identify cohesion.

Finally, it has also been argued that discourse does not need an entire sentence, or even clause, in order to exist. Widdowson (1995) gives the examples of signs which read 'LADIES', or 'P' to indicate a car park. In the years since Widdowson provided the former example, it has arguably become even more appropriate. In the context of public debates about public toilets and transgender rights, 'LADIES' might say more than ever before, without transcending the clause or the sentence at all. Likewise, in the context of a language that has

> **In focus: cohesion and coherence?**
>
> It's important to note that the concept of **cohesion** is different from the concept of **coherence** when we're talking about discourse. As with all things discourse-related, what these terms mean is somewhat contested, but it might be easiest to think of it in terms of **cohesion** as local linkage between the vasectomy and the DIY competition in Stubbs' example (1983: 93) and **coherence** as the global linkage which allows us to use our broader contextual understanding to interpret communication. So, cohesion tells us that the vasectomy and the DIY competition aren't linked directly, despite the *and*, because that wouldn't make sense. But our contextual understanding of the radio announcer's role allows coherence to tell us that they are both to be featured in the radio programme concurrently. Thus, Brown and Yule (1983), for example, argue that 'human beings do not require formal textual markers before they are prepared to interpret a text. They naturally assume coherence, and interpret the text in light of that assumption' (66).

been subject to oppression and subsequent revitalisation attempts (more on this in Chapter 28), such as Irish, the presence of 'LADIES' alongside 'MNÁ' ('women') is a discursive choice. So too would be the choice to use English 'WOMEN' rather than 'LADIES'.

Having identified problems with approach (1) then, which conceptualises discourse in structural terms, we will move on to approach (2), whereby discourse is considered to be 'language in use'.

10.2.2 Language in use

Definition (2) of discourse, given earlier, refers to the study of discourse as being concerned with 'language in use' (Brown and Yule 1983). At the core of this approach is the idea that a language system cannot be understood fully, without considering how it functions by looking at concrete examples of the language in the context in which they are used. To the twenty-first century student of language, this may seem confusingly self-evident. How else, you might ask, would we study how language works, than by observing how language is used . . . ?

The thing to bear in mind, though, is that traditionally, the study of linguistics was mostly theoretical, and based on the analysis of unnatural language rather than empirical observations of natural language data (cf. Saussure [1922] 1966; Chomsky 1965). This 'unnatural' language usually consisted of invented examples, and for obvious reasons this approach has generally fallen out of favour. As Chafe notes, it was 'as if one tried to study birds by building airplanes that were rather like birds in certain ways, and then studied the airplanes, because they were easier to control than the birds themselves' (1994: 17), concluding, unsurprisingly, that '[t]here is much to be gained from examining language as it really is' (1994: 17). Against this backdrop, the definition of discourse as 'language in use' seems slightly less vague and nebulous, but there is still more to it than merely considering real and concrete, rather than invented and abstract, linguistic examples.

In the context of the classroom, for example, Sinclair and Coulthard (1975) inaugurated a method of discourse analysis which can be placed into this category, and which can be considered a litmus test for whether or not a lesson is communicative. Sinclair and Coulthard's approach identified five units of discourse, which they numbered with roman numerals as follows. (I) lesson, (II) transaction, (III) exchange, (IV) move and (V) act. These are arranged in a hierarchy, as shown in Figure 10.3.

As in the hierarchical approaches to discourse outlined in 10.2.1, all of the units in this hierarchy (apart from act, at the bottom) are formed of units from the ranks below. Unlike in the hierarchy shown in Figure 10.1, however, this hierarchy does not relate directly to language structures. Instead, as Figure 10.3 shows, they are units of discourse. The most influential element of this model is the notion that there are three types of move (IV) which make up an exchange

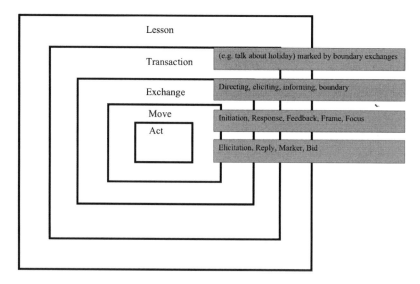

Figure 10.3 Sinclair and Coulthard's hierarchy of discourse units.

(III). These are initiation (I), response (R) and feedback (F). This is known as the **IRF structure** and is a common sequence of utterances in classroom interactions. The 'feedback' element of this structure is what differentiates much interaction in educational settings from everyday conversation. We might, for example, find that the following interaction occurs in everyday conversation:

A. How do you spell necessary?
B. N-E-C-E-S-S-A-R-Y
A. Thanks.

Here, (A) asks a question, receives a satisfactory answer, and expresses their appreciation. By contrast, we might find that a classroom interaction which begins in the same way ends with feedback instead of gratitude:

A. How do you spell necessary?
B. N-E-C-E-S-S-A-R-Y
A. Very good.

We can expect this provision of feedback because, in a classroom setting, we know that the teacher is probably not struggling to remember something, but is eliciting information from a learner to test their knowledge. You can read more on how language is studied in classroom settings in Chapter 15 on language in the curriculum and Chapter 23 on linguistic fieldwork, but for our purposes here, the most important thing we can take from the work of Sinclair and Coulthard is that this kind of approach to discourse focuses on the structural relationships between concrete examples in context. When we discussed cohesion in 10.2.1, we noted the difficulty of accounting for coherence grammatically (I'm sure you will recall Stubbs' vasectomy example!). Brown and Yule quote Labov (1970) in this regard, as saying that:

> it is on the basis of . . . social, but not linguistic, rules that we interpret some conversational sequences as coherent and others as non-coherent.
>
> (quoted in Brown and Yule 1983: 226)

This view of discourse situates language use squarely in the social realm, placing emphasis on the 'language-user's ability to make . . . connections "outside" the text' (Gough and Talbot 1996: 221). This approach to discourse is closely associated with the work of Brown and Yule, who famously stated that

> the analysis of discourse is, necessarily, the analysis of language in use. As such, it cannot be restricted to the description of forms independent of the purposes or functions which these forms are designed to serve in human affairs.
>
> (1983: 1)

Key to this approach is its emphasis on communicative function in context. Indeed, Brown and Yule (1983) suggest that language has two functions: the interactional function, and the transactional function. Interactional communication, they argue, is important for maintaining social relations, but does little else. The focus of this kind of information is listener-oriented, and it relies upon implicit understanding. Take, for example, the following exchange in informal French:

(1) a. Salut, ça va?
         Hi, how are things?

     b. Ça va.
         Everything is fine.

> **In focus: a field in its own right?**
>
> If you have already read Chapter 6 and/or Chapter 7, you may well be thinking that some of the ideas from the present chapter are rather familiar. Indeed, there is a lot of overlap between research on discourse and other linguistic sub-disciplines like pragmatics (Chapter 6) and sociolinguistics (Chapter 7). There are no sharp dividing lines between linguistic sub-disciplines, which is why you will find the chapters of this volume peppered with references to other chapters in this volume. The boundaries of sub-disciplines are fuzzy and porous, and as a newer field than many, this is perhaps truer of discourse analysis.

The function of this exchange is purely interactional, it serves only as an acknowledgment of the relationship between (1a) and (1b) and is therefore an example of **phatic** communication. It stands to reason that B's response would not impart sufficient information about their health and wellbeing for (1a) to go ahead and perform a medical procedure on them. In a transactional exchange, the goal would instead be to communicate something specific. As an example, consider the following exchange in French:

(2) a. Où sont les toilettes?
         Where are the toilets?

    b.   Ils sont au sous-sol, à côté des vestiaires.
        They are in the basement, next to the changing rooms.

Here, the meaning is purely transactional. (2a) requires information about the location of the toilets and (2b) provides it. Of course, most language is neither purely interactional nor purely transactional, but rather a mixture of the two. We could, for example, introduce some interactional elements into the last example, like so:

(3) a. **Excusez-moi, est-ce que je peux utiliser** vos toilettes **s'il vous plaît?**
        Excuse me, could I please use your toilets?

     b. **Bien sûr.** Ils sont au sous-sol, à côté des vestiaires.
        Of course. They are in the basement, next to the changing rooms.

     c. **Merci beaucoup. Au revoir, monsieur.**
        Thank you. Goodbye, sir.

     d. **Au revoir, madame.**
        Goodbye, madame.

This exchange contains both interactional and transactional elements. (3a) still asks, obliquely, the location of the toilet by asking permission to use them, and is given information about their whereabouts. Thus the same transactional functions are fulfilled as in the previous example. But there is also the language in bold, which fulfils interactional functions. In line 1, (3a) says both 'excuse me' and 'please' and in line 3, 'thank you' and 'goodbye', whilst in line 2, (3b) says 'of course', and in line 4, 'goodbye'. Both also use appropriate forms of address to show respect. This tendency of language to be both interactional and transactional to some degree leads Brown and Yule to categorise language as either 'primarily interactional' or 'primarily transactional' (1983: 23).

Brown and Yule also write extensively on the importance of other aspects of the context in which discourse is produced (1983: 60–69). They differentiate between 'discourse-external context', which relates to variation in terms of who is speaking, who is listening, where they are, what the time is, what topic is being discussed, etc., and 'discourse-internal context'. This latter type of context relates to common background knowledge and shared conventions. By its nature, then, this kind of approach to discourse places emphasis on the social context in which discourse is produced. Schiffrin, indeed, goes as far as to argue that in order

> [t]o understand the language of discourse, we need to understand the world in which it resides; and to understand the world in which language resides, we need to go outside of linguistics. When we return to a linguistic analysis of discourse – to an analysis of utterances as social interaction – I believe

that we will find that the benefits of our journey have far outweighed its costs.

(1994: 419)

The social context of discourse is therefore a crucial element of approaches to discourse research which align with definition (2) of discourse, as 'language in use'. But, you might be wondering, isn't that the approach based on the third definition, (3)? If we're now saying that 'language in use' is all about social practice, then how is that different from definition (3)? The answer is that it's all about degrees and focus. Schiffrin, as quoted earlier, places emphasis on 'return[ing] to a linguistic analysis' after 'go[ing] outside of linguistics' to consider the social world (1994: 419). The focus here is clearly on the language, and how the social can shed light on language. To return to the differentiation between discourse analysis as language-focused and discourse studies as more broadly focused, this is discourse analysis. Approaches which align with definition (3), regarding discourse as social practice, tend to fall more into the category of discourse studies, and it is to these approaches that we now turn.

In focus: Discourse Communities

In Chapter 7, the concept of the *community of practice* (CofP) was introduced. A related but distinct concept is that of the *Discourse Community* (DC). This is a term first introduced by Nystrand (1982), and taken up by Swales (1990: 24–27), who suggests that DCs have six defining characteristics:

1   A broadly agreed set of common public goals.
2   Mechanisms for intercommunication.
3   Participatory mechanisms for information and feedback.
4   Utilisation of one or more genres in the furtherance of its aims.
5   Specific lexis used by members in order to fulfil its goals.
6   A threshold level of members with a suitable degree of expertise.

If you have read Chapter 7 already, you may be thinking that this really does sound an awful lot like a CofP. And, indeed, a grouping can be characterised as both a CofP *and* a DC. In Malory (2021), for example, I show that Late Modern literary reviewers from different publications were *both* a CofP and a DC, despite feuding constantly for almost a century, because they shared the common public goal of imposing conservative linguistic norms on their readers and reviewed authors (192).

There are a few factors which distinguish these two concepts from one another, however. First, the members of a DC may not be aware that they are tied together by 'sharing discourse practices', and these 'may only become "visible" through the course of time' (Watts 1999: 43). The threshold for determining whether a CofP exists is arguably higher, too. A CofP, according to Eckert and McConnell-Ginet (see also Chapter 7) 'is defined simultaneously by its membership and by the practice in which that membership engages' (1992: 464). This definition places much stronger emphasis on membership ties than Swales' DC definition, and indeed Eckert and McConnell-Ginet give examples of a choir, a family and a friendship group. Ideological and commercial rivals, as in my (Malory 2021) example, do not fit as straightforwardly into this paradigm as they do into that of the DC. Here, the focus is not so much on the *community* element as its output: discourse! According to Swales, a DC does not require 'assimilation of world view' or 'a threshold level of personal involvement' (1990: 31). The production of discourse, rather than the situational context in which language is produced, is the focus. This mirrors the difference in focus between definitions (2) and (3) in Section 10.1, and the approaches to discourse research with which they align.

10.2.3 Discourse as social practice

The final definition of *discourse* provided sees it as 'as a form of social practice in which language plays a key role'. This is discourse in its broadest linguistic sense, and approaches based on this definition move the emphasis of the relationship between language and context much further towards context. It follows that this moves the focus of discourse research away from a purely linguistic focus, and indeed this final approach that we will consider *is* the least narrowly linguistic in focus. This approach arguably originates with Foucault (1969), who argues that discourses 'systematically form the objects of which they speak . . . what they do is *more* than use signs to designate things' (p. 54; emphasis added). For Foucault, it is this 'more' which is crucial, and this approach thus pays more attention to the social and historical context in which the discourse is situated; in other words, seeing language as a social act.

This is a contextual focus distinct from the focus on context of approaches such as Brown and Yule (1983), discussed in 10.2.2. That is a more immediate, situational context, which is less explicitly focused on the social and political. By comparison, discourse researchers in this tradition, who view discourse as social practice, consider:

> the relationship between texts, processes, and their social conditions, both the immediate conditions of situational context *and* more remote conditions of institutional and social structures.
>
> (Fairclough 2001: 26; emphasis added)

This 'relationship' between text and context is often described as **dialectal**, or two-way, since discourse is considered to be 'shaped by situations, institutions and social structures, but it also shapes them' (Fairclough and Wodak 1997: 258). This approach has given rise to the kinds of **critical** approach discussed in Chapter 12, on culture and communication, and Chapter 16, on **Critical Discourse Analysis (CDA)**, which is an umbrella term used to describe critical research on discourse. In this context, 'critical' means social critique, or a focus on 'the way social-power abuse and inequality are enacted, reproduced, legitimated, and resisted by text and talk in the social and political context' (van Dijk 2015: 467). In its focus on social problems and political issues, rather than just discourse structures, this approach is inherently multidisciplinary. Whilst retaining some degree of focus on the discourse structures which had primacy in the approaches outlined in 10.2.1 and 10.2.2, this approach seeks not just to describe such structures, but to explain them as artefacts of the social world, and especially of social hierarchy and power dynamics. **Hegemony,** or the consolidation of power and influence, is a crucial concept here, since critical approaches focus on the ways discourse structures enact and reinforce dominance in society. The element of critique is foregrounded to such an extent in some critical approaches to discourse research that CDA has been characterised as 'a social movement of politically committed discourse analysts' (van Dijk 2015: 466).

This may be a surprising thing to read. Social movements are more associated with campaign groups, than academic research, surely? And haven't we been drumming into you from day one of your linguistic studies the need for linguists to observe, dispassionately and without prejudice, language as it happens? As Critical Discourse Analysis has its own chapter in this volume (Chapter 16), there is no need for us to consider these approaches in great detail here. One thing it is important to address briefly, though, is the way in which different **research paradigms** (or approaches) determine research methods. For our purposes, there are three research paradigms of particular relevance: **positivism**, critical orientation and **poststructuralism**. Positivism is essentially an **empiricist** research paradigm, which aims to observe empirical phenomena, use **quantitative** methods to measure these and draw **objective**, reliable and often generalisable conclusions. By contrast, critical researchers argue that there is no such thing as an objective research approach, and moreover that the goal of research activity should be to bring about social change. **Poststructuralism** likewise focuses on social relations and the interaction of discourse and power, but with greater focus on the construction of the self through language and the **deconstruction** of prevailing ideologies and norms (Macdonald et al. 2002). Critical and poststructuralist research has tended to be qualitative, and less focused on attempts to scale research to reach generalisability, and has challenged the idea that more evidence means more robust conclusions.

We can think of these research paradigms as existing on a continuum, where belief in an objective truth, which can be reached through research, lies at one end, and belief that there is no objective truth that can be reached through research lies at the other end. You will encounter linguistic research at various points on this continuum throughout your linguistic studies, and most will probably occupy a sort of middle ground. Here, as in the words of Baker (2010), there is awareness that 'linguistics is not like *Star Trek*: we do not say "Computer, tell me about modal verbs over the past hundred years" and receive an immediate answer. Instead, human decision-making is normally involved at almost every stage' of linguistic research (p. 11). We must also, of course, be aware that there will be social forces acting upon us which condition us to *want* to look at modal verb use within this time frame. Of course, as Baker says elsewhere, there is a balance to be struck here: 'we need to be aware that our research *is* constructed, but we shouldn't deconstruct it out of existence' (2006: 11). In other words, we need to be aware that forces are acting upon us, but that doesn't mean we shouldn't carry on our research, or not consider our results meaningful.

This quick introduction to the concept of research paradigms should help in Section 10.5.3, where we will consider some of the challenges of different approaches to researching discourse.

10.3 Discourse analysis and sign languages

In many ways, research on discourse in sign language is exactly the same as every other kind of discourse research that we have addressed in this chapter up to this point. However, there are a few distinctions that need to be made. For example, by its nature, the study of sign language demands that attention must be paid to factors such as facial expression and body shifting. In the context of spoken language (and, as outlined in the 'in focus' box on pp. 131–133 in Chapter 6, it is from a spoken-language centric position that much communication has been studied until lately, to the exclusion of sign language), such factors are considered to be **paralinguistic** or **extralinguistic** factors. Paralinguistic elements include things like pitch, volume and speed, whilst extralinguistic components are non-verbal means of communicating, such as expressions, gesture and movement. Whilst these extralinguistic elements are fairly distinct from spoken language, the boundary between them and sign language is necessarily much less clear. For example, as we will see, the severity of a blow to the head could be signalled by more extreme facial expressions as the sign is produced (see Figure 10.4). Partly for this reason, Winston and Roy distinguish between **discourse-focused** and **discourse-based** studies in sign language. Discourse-focused approaches, they suggest, 'consider the broader text and context and intentions of interactants, exploring how the parts build the meaning of the whole' (2015: 95–96), whereas discourse-based methods 'focus on discrete elements taken from discourse' (96). Such focus on individual units of discourse meaning, argue Winston and Roy, 'provide windows into the structures and functions of discourse as a whole' (2015: 96), in the context of signing.

To take an example, let's consider the concept of **referential spatial mapping** (Winston 1991). This means gesture, for example towards objects and entities within the immediate signing area, for the purpose of referring to something. Winston argues that spatial maps are an important device for structuring signed communication (1991) and demarcating cohesive segments of discourse (Winston and Roy 2015: 103). According to Winston, spatial mapping is used in comparison, performance (i.e. constructing actions and dialogue) and the mapping of events in temporal terms (i.e. 'looking forward' to an event). In Winston and Roy (2015), the authors argue that spatial mapping helps to form so-called 'discourse frames', which is a means of creating the kind of cohesion we discussed in Section 10.2. For example, Winston (1992) reports that in a poetry lecture in American Sign Language (ASL), the signer establishes one side of the signing space to characterise poetry as an art, and the other side to characterise poetry as a science.

Elsewhere, Winston found that a signer could refer back to such a spatial map, even when it had been established much earlier in an interaction (1995: 96). Such use of space for cohesive purposes is almost unique to sign languages, and provides a useful demonstration of the ways in which sign language discourses require their own conceptual framework in some ways.

Other features of sign language discourse are not unique to sign language, however, but also prevalent in spoken language. For example, **depiction** is the representation of a physical scene that is in some way analogous to the real-world event or phenomenon being described. Consider, for example, the following English sentence:

1   She slammed straight into the beam with her head.

Here, the strength of the collision between the head and the beam is signalled by 'slammed', but in the following sentence, the **onomatopoeic** form 'THWACK' and an **iconic** (see also p. 101) gesture increase this sense that the collision was violent:

2   She slammed, THWACK, straight into the beam with her head [gesture in which the hand slaps the forehead].

Likewise, in British Sign Language (BSL), the sign for a bump on the head displays iconicity (see also Chapter 5). This is shown in Figure 10.4.

In this instance, the signer can likewise signal the severity of the blow to the head by tapping their head harder, as well as by exaggerating the accompanying

Figure 10.4 'Bump on the head' in BSL.

facial expression of pain. In both spoken language and sign language, then, language users often combine multiple communicative devices, such as words or signs, gesture and enactment, to produce **multimodal** 'composite utterances' (Enfield 2009), which use more than one semiotic **mode**. We can, then, learn a lot from considering how researchers approach the discourses of sign language, and take into consideration the **paralinguistic** or **extralinguistic** factors involved in all forms of communication. Interest in this kind of multimodal analysis was once very rare, but it has grown considerably since the 1990s, partly as a result of the advent of new and highly multimodal digital media. It is to this area of focus to which we now turn.

10.4 Studying multimodal discourse

Consider a typical Twitter feed. It will almost certainly contain writing and images (if only profile thumbnails). It may also contain other types of graphics, such as drawings, memes and emojis. There may be moving images, such as GIFs and embedded video clips. Depending on your settings, these clips may play music or speech at you as you scroll. How all these modes interact is the focus of multimodality.

Discourse can be considered multimodal if 'its meaning is realized through more than one semiotic code' (Kress and van Leeuwen 1996: 183), such as written language *and* an image, in the case of a meme, or a speaker *and* a sign language translator on a TV programme. As I mentioned in concluding the previous section, growing interest in multimodality has come about partly as a result of the kind of assault on the senses we receive when we venture into a digital world like Twitter and encounter complex semiotic combinations. As we saw in the previous section, however, multimodality is actually a normal feature of all human communication. It is just that the kind of extralinguistic and paralinguistic features of interaction have been neglected, outside of sign language studies.

If we accept that all human communication is multimodal, then we can never approach discourse as purely written, spoken or signed. Even a piece of paper with writing on it will communicate something visual, above and beyond the semiotic power of the written words. The appearance, spacing and even quantity of the writing also carries meaning. It is for this reason that the back of a used envelope may not, for example, be the appropriate medium for a Valentine's Day card. For this reason, van Leeuwen (2004) suggests that we don't distinguish discourses as 'written' or 'spoken', giving the linguistic mode primacy, but instead distinguish between communicative acts which are 'performed' and 'inscribed' (8). The notion of 'performance' is intended to foreground the kinetic and gestural elements of speech, whilst 'inscription' highlights the semiotic importance of visual and graphic aspects of written language. Importantly, therefore, van Leeuwen's distinction emphasises the spatial dimension of communication in a way that will be familiar from 10.3. This distinction is made with the apparent intention of challenging the way in which language has traditionally been over-privileged in communication research. For our purposes, in exploring how discourse can be approached, this is the crucial point, but if you would like to learn more about multimodality in a critical context, then you can read Chapter 16 (see, in particular, p. 321).

10.5 Challenges in analysing discourse

Having outlined what discourse is and how it can be (and has been) approached, we must now consider some of the challenges of actually studying discourse. These can be placed into three categories: the logistical, the ethical and the analytical, and we will now consider them briefly in turn. Many of these challenges are not exclusive to discourse research, and this will therefore consist largely of referring to other chapters in the book where more detail may be found.

10.5.1 Logistical challenges

Having spent many pages describing differing approaches to the study of discourse earlier on in this chapter, it might now be helpful to consider what all definitions of *discourse* and all approaches to studying it have in common. The main commonality is that they all require natural data for analysis. Whether a discourse researcher seeks to study signed or spoken classroom language, multimodal digital environments, academic writing or something else entirely, they will need first to gather data. Sometimes, as is discussed in Chapter 21, appropriate data for a study is already available. In that case, you can simply access your corpus, and away you go. Often, however, this will not be the case. You may need to construct your own corpus (see p. 384), or to conduct fieldwork (see Chapter 22). If you are gathering spoken language, you will need to get it into some kind of written format (see Chapter 23).

10.5.2 Ethical challenges

As is discussed in detail in Chapter 19, most universities have ethical guidance on research using 'human subjects'. Nowadays, this usually includes the use of social media data, which is an increasingly popular way for students to conduct research projects. Before you conduct your first study in discourse research, it would be a good idea to read Chapter 19, and ensure that you have considered all the potential ethical ramifications and harm of your proposal, as well as gone through any formal processes for procuring permission from your institution.

10.5.3 Analytical challenges

As we saw in our discussion of research paradigms in Section 10.2.3, there are long-standing debates within the field of linguistics about the strengths and weaknesses of different methodological approaches to studying communication. In particular, as we saw in the distinction between positivism, often associated with quantitative research, and poststructuralism, often associated with qualitative research, there have been discussions about scientific validity and a general tendency to regard studies of discourse as 'subjective' and 'deficient' (Ancarno 2020: p. 175), because it is considered to be 'rel[iant] on introspection'. The perceived 'decreased partiality and increased representativeness' of language studies using quantitative and computational methodologies, according to Ancarno, is often used to justify the use of corpus approaches in discourse studies. According to this view, such methodologies are 'often presented as discourse analysis whose validity is boosted by the use of **corpus methods** (see Chapter 21) of analysis perceived as more "scientific" or "empirical"'. The 'in focus' box considers how approaches to discourse research which use corpus methods can benefit from this methodological synergy.

In focus: using linguistic corpora to study discourse

The use of corpora (see Chapter 21) to study discourse has been known by various terms since corpus-based linguistic analysis really took off in the 1990s and 2000s. These include 'corpus-discourse analysis' and 'discourse-oriented discourse analysis', but the term **corpus-assisted discourse studies** (**CADS**) is now increasingly prevalent. In line with the different definitions of *discourse* identified in Section 10.1 and the relatedly different approaches to studying discourse explored in Section 10.2, researchers using corpus methods to study discourse have used different approaches and defined their approaches differently. Partington, for example, stresses the methodological aspect of the endeavour, referring to CADS as the 'investigation and comparison of features of particular discourse types, integrating into the analysis, where appropriate, techniques and tools developed within corpus linguistics' (2010: 88). Taylor and Marchi (2018) instead focus their definition on the discourse-as-social-act approach outlined in Section 10.2.3:

> CADS . . . seeks to capture the recurring traces left by social routines . . . by discursively producing and reproducing habitual patterns of understanding and acting. From this point of view, the starting point of the analysis is not linguistic but social (Biber 1993: 244): what CADS seeks to characterise is not a particular language or linguistic variety but rather a particular situation, purpose or function repeatedly enacted within a speech community.
>
> (p. 61)

The fact is, however, that any form of CADS is a **mixed methods** approach, which combines discourse research and corpus methods. Combining these approaches usually means mixing qualitative and quantitative methods of analysis, and this in itself can have enormous benefits. As Ivankova and Cresswell note, such '[m]ixed methods research, with its focus on the meaningful integration of both quantitative and qualitative data, can provide a depth and breadth that a single approach may lack by itself' (2009: 135). The quantitative component of CADS is sometimes regarded as providing a 'boost', whereby 'corpora are seen to reduce subjectivity . . . or increase objectivity' (Ancarno 2020: p. 174), but it is probably more helpful to think in terms of combined benefits of different approaches than subscribe to what Ancarno calls these 'discourse-analysis-as-deficient-views of CADS' (2020: p. 175).

10.6 Conclusion

As we saw in Section 10.1, defining *discourse* and differentiating and understanding the various approaches taken by discourse researchers can be tricky. The purpose of this chapter has been to lay out *why* it can be tricky, *how* discourse is defined in linguistics *and* how it's studied. In 10.1, we defined *discourse*, both in terms of general use, with reference to a number of dictionary definitions, and in linguistics specifically. In Section 10.2, we then explored the different approaches which align with the three main definitions used in linguistics. In 10.3, we considered the differences and similarities between the study of sign language discourse and other forms of discourse, and we followed up on this in Section 10.4 with a consideration of the importance of paying attention to *all* the potential ways that humans make meaning; of which language is only one! In Section 10.5, we considered briefly some of the challenges that we might face in designing our own study for researching discourse, with signposts to other chapters which will be helpful. By now, you should be able to define *discourse* in a number of ways, identify different approaches to researching discourse, and even feel confident in beginning to think about how to conduct your own basic study. If you would like to learn more about discourse, you can read Chapter 12 on communication and culture, Chapter 16 on Critical Discourse Analysis and Chapter 17 on language in the workplace.

References

Ancarno, C. 2020. Corpus-assisted discourse studies. In A. de Fina and A. Georgakopoulou (Eds.), *The Cambridge Handbook of Discourse Studies*. Cambridge: Cambridge University Press, pp. 165–185.

Baker, P. 2006. *Using Corpora in Discourse Analysis*. London: Continuum.

Baker, P. 2010. *Sociolinguistics and Corpus Linguistics*. Edinburgh: Edinburgh University Press.

Biber, D. 1993. Representativeness in corpus design. *Literary and Linguistic Computing*, 8(4): 243–257.

Brown, G. and Yule, G. 1983. *Discourse Analysis*. Cambridge: Cambridge University Press.

Cameron, D. and Panović, I. 2014. *Working with Written Discourse*. London: Sage.

Chafe, W. 1994. *Discourse, Consciousness, and Time*. Chicago: University of Chicago Press.

Chomsky, N. 1965. *Aspects of the Theory of Syntax*. Cambridge, MA: The MIT Press.

Eckert, P. and McConnell-Ginet, S. 1992. Think practically and look locally: Language and gender as community-based practice. *Annual Review of Anthropology*, 21: 461–490.

Enfield, N. 2009. *The Anatomy of Meaning: Speech, Gesture, and Composite Utterances*. Cambridge: Cambridge University Press.

Fairclough, N. 2001. *Language and Power*. 2nd ed. London: Pearson.

Fairclough, N. and Wodak, R. 1997. Critical discourse analysis. In T. van Dijk (Ed.), *Discourse as Social Interaction*. London: Sage.

Foucault, M. 1969. *The Archaeology of Knowledge*. Oxon: Routledge.

Gough, V. and Talbot, M. 1996. 'Guilt over games boys play': Coherence as a focus for examining the constitution of heterosexual subjectivity on a problem page. In Carmen Caldas-Coulthard and Malcolm Coulthard (Eds.), *Texts and Practices: Readings in Critical Discourse Analysis*. Oxon: Routledge, pp. 215–230.

Halliday, M. 1994. *An Introduction to Functional Grammar*. 4th ed. London: Edward Arnold.

Haselow, A. and Hancil, S. 2021. *Studies at the Grammar-Discourse Interface: Discourse Markers and Discourse-related Grammatical Phenomena*. Amsterdam: John Benjamins.

Ivankova, N. and Cresswell, J. 2009. Mixed methods. In J. Heigham and R. Croker (Eds.), *Qualitative Research in Applied Linguistics: A Practical Introduction*. London: Palgrave Macmillan.

Kress, G. and van Leeuwen, T. 1996. *Reading Images: The Grammar of Visual Design*. Routledge.

Labov, W. 1970. The study of language in its social context. *Studium Generale*, 23: 30–87.

Macdonald, D., Kirk, D., Metzler, M., Nilges, L. M., Schmepp, P. and Wright, J. 2002. It's all very well, in theory: Theoretical perspectives and their applications in contemporary pedagogical research. *Quest*, 54: 133–156.

Malory, B. 2021. *Prescriptivism in Action: Evaluating the Production and Reception of Reviewer Prescriptivism in Late Modern English*. Unpublished PhD thesis. Lancaster University.

Mills, S. 1997. *Discourse*. Oxon: Routledge.

Mithun, M. 2015. Discourse and grammar. In Deborah Tannen, Heidi E. Hamilton and Deborah Schriffin (Eds.), *The Handbook of Discourse Analysis*. 2nd ed. Oxford: Wiley Blackwell, pp. 9–41.

Nystrand, M. 1982. Rhetoric's audience and linguistics speech community: Implications for understanding writing, reading, and text. In Martin Nystrand (Ed.), *What Writers Know: The Language, Process, and Structure of Written Discourse*. New York: New York Academic Press, pp. 1–28.

Saussure, F. [1922] 1966. *Course in General Linguistics*. New York: McGraw-Hill.

Schiffrin, D. 1994. *Approaches to Discourse*. New York: Wiley.

Sinclair, J. and Coulthard, M. 1975. *Towards an Analysis of Discourse: The English Used by Teachers and Pupils*. Oxford: Oxford University Press.

Stubbs, M. 1983. *Discourse Analysis: The Sociolinguistic Analysis of Natural Language*. Chicago: University of Chicago Press.

Swales, J. 1990. *Genre Analysis: English in Academic and Research Settings*. Cambridge: Cambridge University Press.

Taylor, C. and Marchi, A. (Eds.). 2018. *Corpus Approaches to Discourse: A Critical Review*. Routledge.

van Dijk, T. 2015. Critical discourse analysis. In Deborah Tannen, Heidi Hamilton and Deborah Schiffrin (Eds.), *The Handbook of Discourse Analysis*. 2nd ed. Oxford: Wiley Blackwell.

van Leeuwen, T. 2004. *Discourse and Technology: Multimodal Discourse Analysis*. Washington, DC: Georgetown University Press.

Watts, R. 1999. The social construction of standard English: Grammar writers as a 'Discourse Community'. In Tony Bex and Richard Watts (Eds.), *Standard English: The Widening Debate*. Routledge: London.

Widdowson, H. 1995. Discourse analysis: A critical view. *Language and Literature*, 4(3).

Winston, B. 1995. Spatial mapping in comparative discourse frames. In K. Emmorey and J. Reilly (Eds.), *Language, Gesture, and Space*. Mahwah, NJ: Lawrence Erlbaum Associates, pp. 87–114.

Winston, E. A. 1991. Spatial referencing and cohesion in an American Sign Language text. *Sign Language Studies*, 73(1): 397–410.

Winston, E. A. 1992. Space and involvement in an American sign Language lecture. In *Expanding Horizons: Proceedings of the Twelfth National Convention of the Registry of Interpreters for the Deaf*. Silver Spring, MD: RID Publications.

Winston, E. A. and Roy, C. 2015. Discourse analysis and sign languages. In Adam Schembri and Ceil Lucas (Eds.), *Sociolinguistics and Deaf Communities*. Cambridge: Cambridge University Press.

11 Bilingualism and multilingualism

Claire Nance and Aina Casaponsa

11.1 Introduction

Across the world, it is extremely common for people to speak more than one language. It is difficult to know exactly how common the phenomenon is, but it has been estimated that over half of the world's population use more than one language in their daily lives. Whatever the exact figure, multilingualism is a phenomenon shared by several billion people and therefore it is an important concept in the study of human communication. As it is such a fundamental aspect of language use, we might expect there to be a clear and straightforward definition of what a bilingual or multilingual person might be! Unfortunately, this is not the case and different academics use a variety of different definitions. These definitions might focus on age of acquisition, frequency and domains of use, proficiency and self-identification. Each study in the context of bilingualism or multilingualism will have its own focus, where any of these factors might be the most important. Here, we will adopt the broad working definition from Grosjean (2010: 4) such that 'Bilinguals are those who use two or more languages (or dialects) in their daily lives'.

Although this definition is broad and might clarify some things, it also throws up more questions. Namely, 'Why *bilinguals*, and not *multilinguals*?' and second, 'What is a language or a dialect anyway?'. Again, practice varies across different academic studies so if you are reading about this topic you might want to see which definitions the author uses. Generally speaking, the term 'bilingualism' is extended to refer to 'two *or more* languages' such that a 'bilingual' might actually speak four languages. Here, we will use the term 'bilingual' to discuss people who speak two or more languages, and use the term 'multilingualism' to highlight contexts or individuals where it is significant that more than two languages are used. It is also difficult to draw a firm distinction between a 'language' and a 'dialect'. For example, we could refer to two very linguistically similar varieties such as Lancashire English and Yorkshire English as different dialects. But this word could also refer to mutually unintelligible, linguistically very different 'dialects' such as Cantonese and Shanghainese. Here, we have chosen Grosjean's broad definition as it encompasses situations such as Cantonese and Shanghainese. Also, many of the linguistic and social phenomena we will discuss in this chapter

DOI: 10.4324/9781003045571-13

are also relevant to individuals who master two closely related dialects such as Lancashire and Yorkshire English.

In the rest of this chapter, we will first discuss the social implications of bilingual and multilingual societies: how should nations plan for the linguistic needs and rights of a bilingual population? (Section 11.2). Second, we focus on linguistic aspects of bilingualism: how children acquire more than one language, how adults acquire more than one language and how language users might deploy more than one language in a stretch of communication (Section 11.3). Finally, we turn to the psycholinguistic aspects of bilingualism and examine how multiple languages are stored, accessed and deployed by users (Section 11.4).

11.2 Social implications of multilingualism

At an individual level, speakers in a multilingual setting have the option (in theory) to choose which language they speak. Practically, this doesn't seem to be a random choice, but is shaped by many factors such as which language(s) the interlocutor is most likely to understand, but also sociolinguistic and economic conditions. Here we look at what factors might feed into this choice, and some examples of how a state might plan to meet the language rights and needs of a multilingual population and ultimately influence language use.

An influential model for describing the contexts in which a language is used is Ferguson's (1959) model of diglossia (see also Chapter 7). Ferguson uses this concept to describe the language choice in many societies where languages function in so-called 'High' and 'Low' domains. By this, Ferguson means that one language is reserved for formal or 'High' settings such as speeches in Parliament, religious services, education, new broadcasting, formal literature. Another language is used in 'Low' settings such as the family, informal conversation, soap operas, cartoons and folk literature. One of Ferguson's examples is the use of Swiss German and Standard German in Switzerland. These varieties are at times mutually unintelligible, yet most speakers in (German-speaking) Switzerland are able to use both. Typically, Standard German is used in formal contexts and Swiss German in family and conversational contexts. Clearly, Ferguson's model was published a long time ago and recent social changes such as greater use of informal language from social media in public life might be blurring these boundaries, as we saw with Danish dialects in Chapter 7 (see 143–144).

Some societies might plan explicitly to change the nature of what is considered a 'High' variety and what is considered a 'Low' variety in an attempt to shift the balance of which language speakers choose, and are able to, use. They might do this in order to protect the linguistic rights of a minority group, or maintain something unique about their nation. Conversely, language planning can also take place to promote a state language at the expense of others. Such decisions and choices are ultimately influenced by historical context and political conditions. Here, we will look at two examples of language planning for different political goals. The examples are from the same nation, Scotland, but at two different points in time: 1872 and 2005. We have chosen these dates to give an indication of how different language planning efforts can have very large implications for the multilingual context of a place, and its inhabitants. Our focus here is on how language policy in education can impact the use of a minority Scottish language, Scottish Gaelic, and the language choices of its speakers. Gaelic is a Celtic language historically associated with the Highlands of Scotland.

The year 1872 is significant in Scotland as this is the year that compulsory universal education was introduced for all children aged 5–13. Before 1872, education across Scotland was provided by a variety of associations and in the Highlands, these were mainly religious organisations. The new state schools aimed to prepare pupils practically for work life, and it was assumed that this meant acquisition of English for those who spoke Gaelic at home. Due to limited economic resources in Highland areas, this often meant very little support for Gaelic and a promotion of English as the 'useful', 'practical' language in education (this is by no means a purely historical phenomenon, as is explored in Chapter 15). There are reports of corporal punishment being used in some places when children spoke Gaelic to one another. Over time, such policies coupled with lack of economic opportunity led to greater numbers of families choosing to use English. To put this into Ferguson's model, planning to explicitly situate English as a 'High' language used in education eventually led to English mainly displacing Gaelic in 'Low' contexts such as the family.

The second timepoint we have chosen to exemplify language policy implications for bilingualism is 2005 in Scotland. This is the year that the Gaelic Language Act was implemented, which affords the same legal status to Gaelic and English in Scotland. Quite a change from 1872 policy! Now, political opinion surrounding minority languages and bilingualism has considerably changed and state support for such languages across the world has mainly increased. In Scotland, this change has in particular led to the development of an immersion schooling system where children can receive their entire education in Gaelic (i.e. using Gaelic in a 'High' context in Ferguson's model). This education is available to those who speak Gaelic at home, and those who do not, thus providing bilingual opportunities for children across Scotland. The change in policy has huge implications for speakers and bilingualism! For example, there are now three Gaelic-immersion primary schools in Glasgow, a city where Gaelic has not been spoken as a community language for many centuries. In the 2011 UK Census, it was reported that the number of Gaelic-speaking children across Scotland had risen slightly. This is a big achievement for a minority language which has been endangered for some time. It is thought that this increase is due to expanded education provision stemming from new language policies. For more information on Gaelic language policies and their implications for bilingualism see McLeod (2020).

228

In focus: multilingual Ghana

The example of language policy in Scotland focused on only two languages: English and Scottish Gaelic. Many societies around the world plan for a huge diversity of languages and negotiate how to write policies which safeguard the rights of minorities, but are also practical and reflect prevailing public opinion. In Ghana, a republic in West Africa, around 80 different languages are used, including at least three sign languages. Due to this huge diversity, the Ghanaian government has chosen one language to be the official language, English, as well as 11 government-sponsored languages (Akuapem Twi, Asante Twi, Dagaare, Dagbani, Dangme, Ewe, Ga, Gonja, Kasem, Mfantse, Nzema). There are also plans to make French the second official language in order to improve links to surrounding Francophone countries.

In practice, the status of official and government-sponsored languages mean that Ghanaians typically receive their primary education in a government-sponsored language and English, with secondary education conducted mainly in English; a situation discussed in detail in Chapter 15. As adults, most Ghanaians are highly multilingual and it is not uncommon for Ghanaians to use four or five languages. English has now been used in Ghana

If you would like to read and hear Nigerian and Ghanaian Pidgin being used, have a look at the BBC Pidgin news site: www .bbc.com/pidgin.

for hundreds of years and due to the multilingualism of its users, Ghanaian English has evolved as a distinct variety where phonology, grammar and lexis will be influenced by the other languages used by its speakers. Alongside Ghanaian English, a variety known as 'Ghanaian Pidgin English' has developed from the creoles spoken during the transatlantic slave trade in West Africa.

In this section we have considered some of the society-wide implications of bilingualism and multilingualism, and we have considered the choices states need to make in order to plan for the linguistic rights of their population. These policy and planning decisions can have big impacts on the nature of bilingualism in a population, as can be demonstrated by comparing different time points in Scottish history. In the next section, we consider the detail of language use in bilingual and multilingual speakers themselves.

11.3 Linguistic aspects of multilingualism

Many people who use more than one language often have different levels of proficiency in their different languages. It is important to know that this doesn't make someone a 'bad' speaker of a particular language, just that their circumstances mean they develop different skills in different contexts. This is completely natural! For each constellation of factors contributing to a bilingual's linguistic development, we can expect different outcomes on their language production, and how the two or more languages are stored in the brain (see more in Section 11.4). Here, we will explore three common kinds of bilingual individual, and discuss the implications of each on language production in the two languages. It is important to note that there any many, many labels for how to describe different kinds of bilingualism. If you would like to learn more about these, have a look at Li (2007: 6–7). We end the section with a discussion on code-switching (i.e. using more than one language in a short stretch of language).

11.3.1 Simultaneous bilingual children

We will first discuss the experience and language production of simultaneous bilingual children, (i.e. children who learn two or more languages from birth or very early childhood). Research into bilingualism has now comprehensively demonstrated that it does not disadvantage a child's linguistic development to acquire more than one language at once. When a child is acquiring more than one language, it is typical that they will learn the word for a particular concept in one language before the other. This might mean that some areas of vocabulary are acquired later than others. For example, a child hearing French and Yoruba might learn the words for 'cat' and 'dog' in Yoruba, if they hear them first in this language, and the words for 'digger' and 'tricycle' in French. Overall, if we include ability in both languages, this child would show typical language development, but the child would need exposure to words in both languages in order to learn the vocabulary of each language comprehensively.

For bilingual speakers, it is natural that the two languages interact and influence one another to some extent, as we will see in the rest of this section. For simultaneous bilinguals, it is expected that this interaction between languages is lesser than, for example, an adult learning a new language for the first time. However, as Grosjean puts it, bilingual children are 'not two monolinguals in one person' (Grosjean 1989). What he means by this is that the context of simultaneous bilingual children is special and specific, as are their language productions. It is now thought that the languages of a bilingual are separate, but interacting. We will discuss this more in Section 11.4, but here we will look at the outcome of this interaction for language production. We will focus our examples on the context of phonetics and phonology in bilinguals, but if you would like an example about grammar in simultaneous bilingual children, see Döpke (1998).

We will consider an example of simultaneous bilingual production in French-English bilinguals in Canada. In Paradis (2001), the study considers 2-year-old children acquiring French and English at home. Paradis played a game with the children where they had to repeat multisyllabic made-up words. The idea was to study how the children repeated and shortened the words. For example, when children first learn multisyllabic words such as 'banana', this is often shortened to 'nana'. Paradis wanted to see whether children shortened words according to the phonology of one language or another. The results showed that where the made-up words were similar to English phonological structure, the children shortened them according to English phonological rules. Similarly, when the words were similar to French phonological structure, the children shortened them according to French phonological rules. This demonstrates that children are acquiring the phonology of two languages separately. The really interesting result from Paradis' work concerns words which were ambiguous (i.e. they could be interpreted as conforming to either French or English phonology). In an English play setting, the bilingual children performed differently to the monolingual English-speaking children for the ambiguous words, and showed some influence of French patterns. This final result suggests that the two language systems of bilingual children interact, and that we can see evidence of this in their speech.

11.3.2 Sequential bilingual adults

While children who acquire two (or more) languages more or less simultaneously are known as 'simultaneous bilinguals', people who acquire one (or more) languages one after another are known as 'sequential bilinguals'. This scenario is very common in younger children who learn a second language on entering the school system. Here, we will focus on adult sequential bilinguals, for example (young) adults who learn a second language in a classroom, or learn a new language when emigrating to a new country. As with simultaneous bilinguals, some interaction between languages is natural and expected. This interaction is often the influence of the first learned language on subsequent languages as anyone who has learned a new language will well be aware! Such an influence often persists even in very advanced second language users. The research also demonstrates that the L2 (second language) influences back on the L1 (first language). As we saw with simultaneous bilinguals, this is part of the special configuration when two or more languages are present in an individual's language system.

Such interaction between languages can be very long term, or much shorter term. For example, Mennen (2004) considers the intonation of Dutch L1 speakers who have learned Greek to degree-level and are very proficient Greek speakers. Mennen measured the timing of when these Dutch L1 speakers produced maximum pitch in Greek and Dutch sentences, comparing them to monolingual speakers. She showed that the Dutch L1 bilinguals were not quite the same as Greek monolinguals in their Greek intonation, but they were also different from Dutch L1 monolinguals in their Dutch intonation. Mennen uses these results as evidence for long-term bidirectional influence between languages in bilingual speakers.

While the work we discussed previously shows long-term effects of sequential bilingualism on speech, there are also demonstrated short-term effects. For example, Sancier and Fowler (1997) recorded a Brazilian Portuguese L1, American English L2 speaker as she travelled back and forth between the US and Brazil. They measured aspects of her consonant production and noted that her English consonants were more Portuguese-like when she had just spent time in Brazil. This result shows that short-term language exposure can lead to a dynamic interaction between languages in bilingual language users.

11.3.3 Heritage bilinguals

As we said earlier, different bilinguals will have different levels of ability in different languages, and might be more comfortable using one than the other. This can also depend on context. For example, a Gaelic-English child who attends a Gaelic medium primary school might feel more comfortable discussing mental arithmetic in Gaelic than in English. This doesn't mean that they are incapable of discussing maths in English! It just means that they haven't used English for this reason yet. They could acquire this skill very quickly if needed. For large numbers of bilingual speakers, the language they feel most comfortable using changes over time. This change in what is referred to as 'language dominance' depends on the role each language plays in that speaker's social circle, and the wider societal uses of the language.

The term 'heritage bilingual' has become widely used in the twenty-first century to describe the experiences of many immigrant families in particular. The term is widely used to describe families in the United States where the parents immigrated from, for example, Korea or Mexico, and who speak, for example, Korean or Spanish to their children. The children learn Korean or Spanish as their L1 in the home. On entering the school system and engaging with more activities in US society, the children become bilingual in English and sometimes English-dominant bilinguals. However, they retain some abilities in their first language, Korean or Spanish in this example. This context where language dominance changes is especially relevant to immigrant settings and is known as heritage bilingualism. We can describe such speakers as a heritage speaker of Korean or Spanish, for example. You might think that heritage bilingualism sounds a lot like a kind of sequential bilingualism, and this is indeed the case. However, this term is increasingly being used to describe the experiences of large numbers of children from immigrant contexts who have a certain experience of minority to majority language sequential bilingualism, and changing language dominance over time.

Sometimes heritage speakers are highly proficient in the heritage language, other heritage speakers are not easily able to produce sentences, but often retain excellent understanding skills. A common feature of heritage speakers' language ability is that they usually retain excellent perceptual skills in the heritage language, despite changing language dominance. For example, Chang (2016) considered heritage speakers of Korean and how they could discriminate consonants found in Korean but not found in American English, their dominant language. Chang's participants learned Korean as their first language in the home, but when recorded as young adults, they described their Korean proficiency as low to medium. Chang demonstrates that although such speakers' language production skills in Korean might not be the same as a Korean-dominant speaker, the heritage speakers' perception skills were excellent and extremely similar to the Korean-dominant bilinguals who were raised in South Korea.

11.3.4 Code-switching

As well as specific effects on an individual's speech, signing or grammar, a very common feature of bilingual language use is 'code-switching'. Similar to the term 'bilingualism', there are a lot of different definitions about precisely what 'code-switching' refers to! Here, we have again adopted a broad definition: the use of two or more languages in a short stretch of speech/signing. In the mid-twentieth century it was wrongly assumed that code-switching implied some kind of language deficit. In some cases, people who are learning a new language may resort to using phrases from their dominant language, for example if a Spanish-speaking secondary school pupil is learning German for the first time, they might insert Spanish words into a German sentence. In this specific educational setting of a foreign-language classroom, a teacher might want to encourage sentences entirely in German.

However, it has now been demonstrated that code-switching is a natural behaviour of fully competent bilinguals and should not be stigmatised. When bilinguals communicate with one another in languages that they both understand, then they will draw on their shared resources for greatest communicative effect. The example interaction in Table 11.1 is adapted from Smith-Christmas (2012: 99), where two older female Scottish Gaelic-English bilinguals (Isabel and Nana) are speaking informally with each other on the phone. In this extract we can see several examples of code-switching. For example, Isabel uses the English

Table 11.1 Interaction between two fluent Scottish Gaelic-English bilinguals illustrating code-switching.

Line	Speaker	Utterance	Gloss
1	Isabel	bha mi ag ràdh ri Fiona	I was saying to Fiona
2		's dòcha gun deach thu	perhaps you went
3		an ra- rathad ceàrr timcheall air *you know*	the wrong way about it
4		biodh aca 's dòcha	let them be perhaps
5		nam biodh tu air a ràdh riutha air an toiseach	if you [Nana] had said to them at the start
6		faodaidh tu a' chlann a thoirt leat	you can take the children with you
7	Nana	Oh aye aye	Oh aye aye
8	Isabel	*they're so ver- they are so childish*	they're so childish
9	Nana	aye	aye
10	Isabel	*they're so too they're still t- too child-like themselves*	they're still too child-like themselves
11	Nana	aye 's dòcha	aye perhaps

Source: Adapted from Smith-Christmas (2012: 99).

233

tag 'you know' in line 3 at the end of an otherwise Gaelic utterance. Switching tags is a very common form of code-switching. Similarly, Nana says 'Oh aye aye' in line 7. It is difficult to say whether this utterance is in Gaelic or English. These languages have been in contact for hundreds of years in Scotland and the words 'Oh' and 'aye' are now considered Gaelic as well as English. Perhaps the most striking code-switches are in lines 8 and 10 where Isabel produces whole utterances in English during an otherwise Gaelic conversation. Smith-Christmas argues that Isabel is doing this to demonstrate that she is making a negative judgement about Nana's actions, and uses the code-switch to underline her negative stance. Examples such as these indicate that fluent bilinguals use code-switching as a resource for extra effect when speaking to one another.

An influential model of code-switching is Myers-Scotton's (2002) Matrix Language Frame model, which explains how switches are usually embedded into the frame of a matrix language. For example, we could say that in line 3 of Table 11.1, Isabel embeds an English tag 'you know' into a Gaelic matrix sentence. This model goes some way to explaining the nature of bilingual utterances containing elements of more than one language. Some researchers have noted, however, that in highly multilingual language productions, it is sometimes not possible to tell what is the 'matrix' language and what is the 'embedded' language. In these contexts, as was outlined in Chapter 7, some researchers prefer to use the term 'translanguaging', rather than code-switching, as a term to describe constant use of more than one language within a short section of speech/signing. This term also better highlights the agency of the language user who is producing the utterance and using multiple language resources.

For example, Li (2018) presents examples of translanguaged words from 'New Chinglish', a variety used by Chinese-English bilinguals combining elements of English and Chinese. The example words in Table 11.2 broadly correspond to

Table 11.2 Translanguaged words in 'New Chinglish'.

Phrase	Explanation
Don'train 动车	*dong*, verb 'move'; advanced high-speed trains are called *dong che* in Chinese. *Don'train*, which sounds similar to the Chinese term, refers to both the high costs that prevent ordinary workers in China to be able to take the high-speed trains and the government-imposed speed restrictions after a number of accidents on the railway.
Shitizen 屁民	shit + citizen, reflecting how ordinary citizens in China feel about their status in society.
Smilence 笑而不语	smile + silence, referring to the stereotypical Chinese reaction of smiling without saying anything.

Source: From Li (2018).

the morphology of English, but with Chinese adaptations and meanings. The phrases superficially appear to be English, but an English speaker with no knowledge of Chinese would struggle to understand their full meaning, which draws on both languages.

In focus: bimodal bilingualism and code-blending

'Bimodal bilingualism' refers to the context where a person is bilingual in a spoken and a sign language. This form of bilingualism is particularly important for researchers, as it can show what kinds of bilingual language interaction are actually only relevant to spoken or sign languages, and which forms of bilingual language interaction are more universal. Similar to the contexts discussed earlier, individuals can become bimodally bilingual if they are exposed to a spoken and sign language from birth, or sequentially bimodally bilingual if they acquire one and then the other. Similar to the previous examples from spoken languages, a language user can code-switch by starting an utterance in spoken language and then switching to a sign language (or vice versa). However, in the case of bimodal bilinguals, research suggests that a more common form of using two languages is code-blending, where an utterance includes both signed and spoken language simultaneously. Code-blending is different from mouthing, which refers to when signers produce the exact word they are signing silently at the same time as the sign.

Some examples of code-blending can be found in Emmorey et al.'s (2008) study of American-English hearing children born into American Sign Language deaf adult families. They considered examples where participants spoke an utterance and simultaneously signed the same concept. An example of the most common type of code-blend is shown next, where the participant blends a verb.

I don't think he would really live <= Spoken utterance
NOT THINK REALLY LIVE <= Signed utterance

In a small proportion of examples (16% of Emmorey et al.'s code-blends), the sign in American Sign Language did not correspond to the English word, for example a participant said *Tweety* (a bird cartoon character), but signed bird:

Tweety has binoculars too <= Spoken utterance
BIRD HAVE BINOCULARS <= Signed utterance

These examples show language interaction occurs even across modalities in bilingual language users. Also, language users are not only activating two languages at once, but if given the opportunity, they can in fact use two languages at once.

This section has considered the language used by bilingual individuals, focusing on interaction between languages in phonology, grammar and the mixing of multiple systems in code-switching/translanguaging. We have considered some of the varied configurations and acquisition trajectories in different bilingual populations, and the effects this is likely to have on their language use. In the next section, we now consider psycholinguistic aspects of multilingualism.

11.4 Psycholinguistic aspects of multilingualism

As discussed in previous sections, bilingual speakers are not two monolinguals in one mind, but rather speakers of multiple languages which interact with each other in a natural way. We have seen that bilinguals have an inherent ability to adapt to their linguistic environment and switch from one language to the other in an apparently effortless manner. In this last section, we will discuss these issues further from a psycholinguistic perspective, looking at how the mind of a bilingual individual works (or how we think it works!). Hence, we will look at how languages are stored, accessed and used in the bilingual mind. We will start by discussing cross-language interactions and to what extent the language not in use is constantly active in the back of our minds. Then, we will discuss whether bilingual speakers use the same neural structures of the brain when using different languages, and the cognitive mechanisms that enable bilingual speakers to monitor and switch between languages in an accurate way, based on contextual information. Finally, we will briefly discuss how what we know about the bilingual mind can help us understand why and how bilinguals use their two languages.

11.4.1 Cross-language interactivity

One of the main debates within psycholinguistics over the last decades is whether the use of a given language is selective or non-selective. In other words, when bilingual people speak, read or listen in one of their languages, is the other one also active in the back of our minds? As discussed in previous sections, the quick answer is yes. Although having the language not in use constantly active in our minds might seem a bit counterintuitive in terms of the computational power required by our brains, nowadays there is plenty of evidence suggesting that this is the case. A clear example can be found in studies looking at what happens in the bilingual mind of speakers who have learned second languages later in life (i.e. sequential bilinguals).

Late second language learners not only make use of pre-existing knowledge of their native language to support learning of a new language (e.g. mapping new lexical, phonological and syntactic structures into existing ones), they also use this knowledge in an automatic fashion when producing or comprehending language. For instance, it is easier to retrieve words from memory in your second language that are similar to your native language, than words that are completely different. As an example of this, we will look at the study by Hoshino and Kroll (2008). The authors asked bilingual participants to name pictures in their second language and found that pictures whose lexical representations (word forms) were similar in both languages were faster to name than pictures that did not share a word form overlap across languages. Similar results have also been found independently of whether the bilinguals speak languages with similar writing systems (e.g. same-script bilinguals such as Spanish-English, Italian-French) or different writing systems (e.g. bi-script bilinguals such as Japanese-English, Hebrew-Arabic). Hence, these studies suggest that in general, bilinguals automatically access phonological information of their native language when in a second language context. This is commonly known as an example of a **cross-language facilitation effect**. It is worth noting that these facilitation effects have also been reported from the less dominant language to the native one, especially at higher levels of L2 proficiency and daily use, and in bilinguals who have acquired the second language earlier in life (simultaneous bilinguals). That is, learning a second language can also have a positive impact in the way we process and use our native language.

However, one of the most important consequences of having the two languages interacting with each other in our mind is that they also interfere even when this is not optimal. That is, we can't completely shut down the other language when this is not relevant for the context we are in, and this can also cause interference. One of the most common examples of this interference in psycholinguistic research comes from studies using **interlingual homographs**. Interlingual homographs are words that share similar forms but have different meanings across languages (e.g. the Dutch word *room* means 'cream' in English). It is well established that when bilinguals process these types of words in a monolingual language context, they struggle to extract the correct meaning, since both meanings of the words will be automatically activated in their minds and compete for selection. Bilingual speakers might not necessarily be conscious about it, but we can observe it with precise, fine-grained measurements of their behaviour in the lab (see Chapter 20 on experimental methods).

Yet, the most compelling evidence suggesting that bilinguals automatically access their two languages comes from studies looking at what happens in the bilingual mind when processing information in a single language context with words that are not apparently related. As an example of this, we will look at a study by Lee et al. (2019). The authors presented pairs of American Sign Language (ASL) signs to bimodal bilinguals (see Section 11.3.4) and asked them if the pairs were semantically related or not. Unbeknownst to the participants, half of the ASL signs shared a phonological rhyme when translated into English (e.g. bar-star), but had no formal overlap in their ASL sign. The idea behind this manipulation is that it is a well-known fact that when we process words that rhyme these produce a facilitation effect (they are easier to process by our brain) compared to when the words do not rhyme. Hence, the authors hypothesised that if second language learners of ASL automatically activate the English translation of the signs in their minds, we should observe a facilitation effect for the pairs of signs that rhyme in English. Whilst at the behavioural level the authors fail to find any impact of the rhyming translation into English, they did find a facilitation effect for the rhyming conditions at the neuronal level (as measured with electroencephalography). This means that our brains automatically activate the language not-in-use, even when we are not aware or when we don't even see a clear impact in our observable behaviour! This is called **language co-activation**. Similar effects have also been found with unimodal bilinguals (i.e. Chinese-English speakers and Spanish-English speakers) and bilinguals who have shifted their language dominance (e.g. L1-attrited bilinguals, whose first language is experiencing **attrition**). Therefore, we can safely say that even when bilinguals are immersed in a single language context, the language not in use is also accessed in our minds (i.e. language non-selective access to the lexicon), and most of the time we are not even aware of it!

To sum up, here we have discussed experimental research that shows how the two languages of bilingual speakers are constantly active in their minds, in an automatic and even unconscious manner. Furthermore, the evidence from cross-language facilitation and interference effects and from automatic activation of translation equivalents suggest that the two languages are somehow integrated in our minds. In fact, current models of bilingual language processing and production assume that the two lexicons of a bilingual are integrated into a single lexicon. However, if both languages are integrated and constantly active in our minds (especially the native language) how do bilinguals manage to select the appropriate language? We will discuss this in the following sections. But first, we will introduce the neural basis of L1 and L2 processing.

11.4.2 Languages and the brain

Different areas of the brain are involved in different aspects of language processing and production. These language-related areas are functionally connected, forming a core language network which includes areas of the brain specialised in processing modality-specific information, such speech sounds or visual words, and amodal information, such as morphosyntactic, phonological or lexical-semantic information. The question at hand here, and that has received a lot of attention over the last few decades, is whether bilinguals use the same brain structures in either of their two languages. The answer to this question, however, is not simple. To begin with, not all languages rely upon the same brain structures to the same degree. For example, when reading in shallow orthographic languages (i.e. one-to-one grapheme to phoneme correspondence, like in Spanish or Hindi) native speakers tend to rely more on areas of the brain involved in the processing of the sound of letters than speakers of deep ortho-graphic languages (i.e. irregular grapheme to phoneme mapping, like in English or French). Therefore, a Spanish-English bilingual would present different brain areas involved in L1-Spanish compared to L2-English, but not because English is the second language, but because English language relies on slightly different brain functions.

Furthermore, as mentioned in the first sections of this chapter, not all bilinguals are the same and therefore different factors might influence how the brain processes the L2 (e.g. age of acquisition of L2, proficiency, language dominance, etc.). So, although there is not a clear answer yet, most researchers would agree that overall, the brain structures involved in L1 and L2 processing are usually the same, yet not quite activated to the same degree. For instance, different studies have shown that in general terms, speaking in the second language activates the same brain areas than in L1, especially in highly proficient simultaneous bilinguals. However, sequential bilinguals or less proficient bilinguals tend to show an increase of activation of the same areas when using the second lan-guage. This is in fact not entirely surprising. When we are speaking in the second language and we are not yet highly competent, we need to make more effort to retrieve the correct words and grammatical structures from memory, as well as the correct pronunciation and intonation. This increased effort is translated into more activation of the areas of the brain involved in language processing! Basically, your brain is working harder trying to promote the speech and/or understanding of the weaker language, but it is still using the same language networks of the brain!

The fact that the same neural basis exists for both L1 and L2 is in fact more or less in line with what we have been discussing in the previous section. If the two languages are integrated and constantly active in our mind interfering/facilitating each other, it is then not surprising that the same neural structures of the brain will be involved. The question then is, how do bilinguals manage to select the correct language? It was first hypothesised that there is a lan-guage 'switch' that allows bilinguals to select the appropriate language and switch from one to the other. However, more recent advances suggest that bilinguals make use of general cognitive functions of executive control to be able to manage their two languages. Executive functions are cognitive processes involved in cognitive control; that is they help you to override your impulses and make decisions based on your goals. We will discuss these advances in the next section.

11.4.3 Code-switching and cognitive control

One of the main discoveries over the last few decades is that the language network mentioned previously is not disconnected from the rest of networks involved in other cognitive processes (e.g. language is not a module disconnected from the rest of the brain!). Instead, language is functionally connected to other cognitive functions. Several studies have now shown that when bilinguals switch between languages, areas of the brain involved in executive functions are more active. These are typically areas involved in everyday life functioning. For instance, have you ever read a text message whilst having a conversation with someone? Some of us master this less successfully than others! The thing is that when you shift your attention from one task (actively listening to someone) to another (read a text message) your brain has to reallocate resources to the new task and usually this means having to disengage with the previous one. This is why it can be quite annoying for the person talking to you, since you are no longer 'fully' listening!

Going back to bilingualism research, what previous research has shown is that instead of having a specific language 'switch' that allows changing from one language to the other, bilinguals use general brain mechanisms of cognitive control to help them select the appropriate language and inhibit the irrelevant one. Basically, general executive functions help you select the appropriate language whilst at the same time regulate the amount of the activation from the other language, so that it would interfere less. For instance, if you are speaking with a friend in your native language but then want to talk with a colleague that only speaks in your second language, general mechanisms of cognitive control will automatically start to kick in. They will help you to re-activate the language you want to switch to whilst starting to inhibit the L1 so that you can have less interference from your native language. Usually, less proficient bilinguals will struggle more at inhibiting the L1, since this is the language which they usually use (more frequently), and is therefore more active in their mind. However, the more proficient you become and the more you use your L2, the more you will struggle at inhibiting the L2 as well. Hence, when bilingual speakers are using their second language, they need to constantly inhibit their native language in order to minimise interference. Therefore, when bilinguals switch from their second language to their native more effort is required to re-active the appropriate words and morphosyntactic structures of the L1, since these were heavily inhibited to allow fluent L2 speech.

As you have probably noticed in the last paragraph, in psycholinguistic research code-switching or switching between the two languages has traditionally been seen as something costly for the mind (e.g. more activation of areas involved in cognitive control). However, more recent studies have challenged this as a misconception, arguing that when researchers ask participants to switch in the lab, this is usually under restricted and externally controlled conditions. That is, most of the studies trying to understand how the mind is able to switch between languages have imposed some sort of external cues to guide bilingual language switching. For instance, in the lab typically we will ask participants to name different pictures in either one language or the other. We do that by presenting a cue before the picture (e.g. a red dot indicating the picture needs to be named in language A, and a black dot indicating the picture needs to be named in language B). In real life, this would be similar to speaking to one person in your second language and then switching to your L1 because you want to address to another L1-only speaker. However, as mentioned in previous sections this is not the most common way of code-switching in bilinguals. Usually, bilinguals tend to code-switch just because they want to, not because it is imposed from the outside world.

More recent studies have attempted to address this issue by studying voluntary language switching in the lab using semi-controlled situations. For example, de Bruin et al. (2018) asked Spanish-Basque bilinguals from bilingual societies to name a series of pictures in their L1, their L2, or both, in different block sessions. To ensure voluntary code-switching in the language free-choice block, they told participants that they could choose which language they used to name the pictures, but with the condition that they should use both languages during the session. Their results confirmed that even when bilinguals switch between languages voluntarily, there seems to be a cost associated with changing the language code (e.g. bilinguals are slower at naming pictures when they voluntarily switch languages). However, this cost seems to be equally great (or even less) than when you do not allow bilinguals to switch whenever they want. That is, bilinguals were even slower at naming pictures when they were forced to use only one of their two languages. Hence, although it seems that language switching does produce a 'cost' in the bilingual mind, this is an optimal cost, since not allowing bilinguals to make use of their two languages is equally costly for them. This evidence is in line with the cooperative view of bilingual speech processing, by which both languages cooperate in an opportunistic way, rather than competitively. Thus, this is more in line with what we can observe in the everyday life of bilingual speakers, especially those in bilingual societies, where both languages are constantly used.

To sum up, we have discussed how bilinguals use similar brain structures in both of their languages, and use general brain mechanisms of cognitive control to help them select the appropriate language, whilst inhibiting the non-relevant language to minimise interference. We also discussed how code-switching can then be perceived as a cost in psycholinguistic terms. However, not allowing bilinguals to code-switch and forcing them to stick to one language is even more challenging for them, since at the end of the day both languages are active and compete for selection in the bilingual mind!

11.5 Conclusion

In this chapter, we have tried to give an overall picture of how bilinguals use and acquire their languages in a variety of social and linguistic contexts, as well as the neural substrates that allow them to do so. Throughout this chapter, we have discussed the different ways in which bilinguals can be characterised, based on their language experiences and contexts, and their implications for language use. We have explored this from different perspectives focusing on how bilinguals can acquire languages in different social environments, and how language experience and context can affect the way we use language in everyday life (and how our brain processes it!). Finally, we discussed the psycholinguistic and neural aspects of having two languages in one mind.

Overall, we can conclude that bilingual experiences are varied, and that this affects the way the two languages interact with each other at the behavioural and neural level. And whilst not all bilinguals are the same, they are all more than the sum of each of the languages they know.

References

Chang, C. 2016. Bilingual perceptual benefits of experience with a heritage language. *Bilingualism: Language and Cognition*, 19: 791–809.

de Bruin, A., Samuel, A. G. and Duñabeitia, J. A. 2018. Voluntary language switching: When and why do bilinguals switch between their languages? *Journal of Memory and Language*, 103: 28–43.

Döpke, S. 1998. Competing language structures: The acquisition of verb placement by bilingual German-English children. *Journal of Child Language*, 25(3): 555–584.

Emmorey, K., Borinstein, K., Thompson, R. and Gollan, T. 2008. Bimodal bilingualism. *Bilingualism: Language and Cognition*, 11: 43–61.

Ferguson, C. 1959. Diglossia. *Word*, 15(2): 325–340.

Grosjean, F. 1989. Neurolinguists, beware! The bilingual is not two monolinguals in one person. *Brain and Language*, 36(1): 1–15.

Grosjean, F. 2010. *Bilingual: Life and Reality*. Cambridge, MA: Harvard University Press.

Hoshino, N. and Kroll, J. F. 2008. Cognate effects in picture naming: Does cross-language activation survive a change of script? *Cognition*, 106(1): 501–511.

Lee, B., Meade, G., Midgley, K. J., Holcomb, P. J. and Emmorey, K. 2019. ERP evidence for co-activation of English words during recognition of American Sign Language signs. *Brain Sciences*, 9(6): 148.

Li, W. 2018. Translanguaging as a practical theory of language. *Applied Linguistics*, 39(1): 9–30.

Li, W. 2007. Dimensions of bilingualism. In L. Wei (Ed.), *The Bilingualism Reader*. 2nd ed. London: Routledge, pp. 3–24.

McLeod, W. 2020. *Gaelic in Scotland: Policies, Movements, Ideologues*. Edinburgh: Edinburgh University Press.

Mennen, I. 2004. Bi-directional interference in the intonation of Dutch speakers of Greek. *Journal of Phonetics*, 32: 543–563.

Myers-Scotton, C. 2002. *Contact Linguistics: Bilingual Encounters and Grammatical Outcomes*. Oxford: Oxford University Press.

Paradis, J. 2001. Do bilingual two-year-olds have separate phonological systems? *International Journal of Bilingualism*, 5(1): 19–38.

Sancier, M. and Fowler, C. 1997. Gestural drift in a bilingual speaker of Brazilian Portuguese and English. *Journal of Phonetics*, 25: 421–436.

Smith-Christmas, C. 2012. *I've Lost It Here dè a bh' agam: Language Shift, Maintenance, and Code-switching in a Bilingual Family*. PhD thesis. University of Glasgow.

12 Communication and culture
Dimitrinka Atanasova

12.1 Introduction

More and more disciplines – from translation, media and communication research to history, geography and climate science – are recognising the importance of culture. To consider an example, climate change is arguably the most pressing problem of our times, and there is an increasing understanding that different cultural values might help to explain why people in some parts of the world may be more inclined than others to take action in order to stop or mitigate climate change. Factors such as how much value we place on time, how important it is to be able to control our environments, and whether we give more importance to individuals' wellbeing or that of society, help to explain differing attitudes to this issue. What this means is that culture has been becoming a more significant subject of study across a range of fields, including discourse research (see Chapter 10).

Research that takes a **culturally inclusive approach to discourse** has been on the rise. However, there has been so much variation amongst such studies that confusion has resulted, leading to calls for systematisation. This chapter therefore introduces the **Cultural Approach to Discourse (CAD)**, **Cultural Discourse Analysis (CuDA)** and **Cross-Cultural Discourse Analysis (CCDA)** – the three main culturally inclusive approaches to discourse – and explains what is meant by a culturally inclusive approach to discourse in each case. It gives examples of representative studies for each approach and highlights some of the similarities and differences between them. The chapter starts with a few key definitions – of **discourse**, **(Critical) Discourse Analysis** and **culture**. CAD in particular has a number of similarities with Critical Discourse Analysis (CDA) which is the focus of Chapter 16. The present chapter summarises only those aspects of CDA that are most relevant to understanding how it relates to the culturally inclusive approaches to discourse described here.

12.2 What is discourse (analysis)?

As is outlined in detail in Chapter 10, the term *discourse* is used in a variety of different ways, both within and beyond the study of linguistics. One commonality,

DOI: 10.4324/9781003045571-14

though, is that in analysing discourse, linguists are generally interested in understanding what discursive choices convey about people's attitudes, thought processes and values relating to different events, issues and actors. As these can vary by culture, discourse analysis is generally mindful of uncovering and explaining cultural differences.

As we also saw in Chapter 10, some discourse research has a **critical** orientation, meaning that one of the main research questions has to do with issues of use, and sometimes abuse, of power and how power abuse leads to and sustains inequality. The form of discourse analysis that is above all else concerned with these matters is Critical Discourse Analysis (CDA; see also Chapter 16). *Critical*, here, means that researchers start with a perceived social problem, for example, xenophobia, weight-based discrimination, the stigma of mental illness or disability, and aim to demonstrate how discourse plays a part in creating and sustaining this social problem. The problem-oriented nature of CDA places the onus on discourse researchers to make explicit their own positions regarding the issue under investigation. The position of most CDA researchers is aligned with those communities that are disadvantaged (e.g. immigrants, ethnic minorities, people of different abilities). The focus on a social problem also means that CDA draws upon a repertoire of disciplines, as diverse knowledge is often needed in order to understand a social problem, and of methods, as different methods might be needed to answer specific research questions.

A central tenet of CDA is that discourse constitutes society and culture. This means that every instance of language use makes its own contribution to reproducing and/or transforming society and culture, including relations of power and inequality. Despite the prominence of culture in CDA, however, it has been argued that CDA overlooks the crucial importance of culture, and that the connection between culture and discourse has not received adequate attention. This could, perhaps, partly be explained with reference to the complexity and ambiguity inherent in the notion of 'culture'. In the following section, we will explore what is meant by culture, and consider some common misconceptions and things that are unhelpful in understanding the concept of culture.

12.3 What is culture?

What is meant by 'culture' is notoriously difficult to define. It is a concept with various meanings and many connotations. In 1994, when writing about culture in the *Encyclopaedia of Language and Linguistics*, Mahadev Apte (1994: 2001) noted that '[d]espite a century of efforts to define culture adequately, there [is] no agreement regarding its nature'. This largely continues to be the case nowadays, with a number of different definitions remaining in circulation. An additional complication is that since culture has not featured in classical linguistic theory, linguists have borrowed definitions of culture and conceptions of its meaning from other academic disciplines. For our purposes in this chapter, we understand culture as encompassing the basic assumptions and values, language, orientations to life, beliefs, policies, procedures and behavioural conventions that are shared by a group of people and that influence (but do not determine) group members' behaviours and their interpretations of the meaning of other people's behaviours.

Culture can manifest at a variety of levels, both macro and micro, some of which are more salient or more concrete than others. Culture is distinct both from human nature, which is universal, and personality, which is individual. It is shared; that is, culture is both associated with social groups and each individual can belong to several social groups simultaneously. In both everyday language and in much of the existing research, culture is used interchangeably with other words like 'nation', 'race' or 'ethnicity'. However, nationality, race or ethnicity each represent just one level of looking at culture. Every individual belongs to a mix of regional, religious, linguistic, gender, social class and other groups, and thus we can also talk about gender-based culture, generational culture and so forth.

For more definitions of culture, check out this compilation of quotations: https://citeseerx.ist.psu.edu/viewdoc/download?doi=10.1.1.401.3386&rep=rep1&type=pdf

Some elements of culture will be very easy to observe, whilst others will be more difficult or even impossible to observe, and will need to be extrapolated. Say, for example, that we want to study a company's corporate culture. This will be manifested in artefacts such as printed instructions on dress code, or adherence to such instructions in reality, whereas other elements of this culture will be more difficult to observe, and will need to be extrapolated. To study how the company's culture manifests in its values, for example, we could study behaviour, elicit information by interviewing or analyse the content of artefacts such as the 'About Us' statements, or the company's annual reports.

It is also important to remember that culture affects both our own behaviour and our interpretations of the behaviour of others. For example, the simple everyday act of eating is a behaviour. Depending on one's culture, it may be considered appropriate or inappropriate to eat at certain times. Consuming certain types of food may be seen as acceptable or unacceptable. Finally, we must also bear in mind that culture is not static but is subject to change. Nowadays, some of the biggest drivers of culture change are travel and different types of media; from the oldest forms of print media, to the newest forms of widely used social media.

12.3.1 What is culture *not*?

There are a couple of common misconceptions about culture which deserve special mention. Among the most widespread is that an individual has, or belongs to, a single culture. Here, culture is usually equated with national or ethnic belonging. In this view, an individual is seen as straightforwardly English,

Bulgarian, American, etc. This view is increasingly difficult to sustain, and a seemingly simple question such as 'What is your culture?' might be met with responses such as 'Well, my father is Spanish, my mother Russian. I was born in England, but we've been living in Australia since I was two'. Another misconception is that culture is uniformly distributed among all members of a group. This presumes that all members of a cultural group (e.g. Bulgarians) would behave in highly similar ways and hold the very same values and their reactions in a given situation can be largely predicted. The trouble with this view is that behaviour depends on various aspects such as social status, specific circumstance and purpose of communication. It is impossible to predict exactly how people will act solely because we know some of their cultural values. Equally, people adapt their behaviour according to the situation and the purpose of the interaction. Thus, as we saw in Chapter 8 with social identity, culture is likewise not so much something that people have or belong to, but rather something which they do. For ease of reference, Table 12.1 lists some of the key meanings and misconceptions relating to culture which have been introduced here.

Table 12.1 Key misconceptions about culture.

Key meanings	Key misconceptions
Culture is something that people **do**, not something they have	People have or belong to a culture
Culture comes in the **plural** for every individual	People have a single culture
Culture **can** be based on nationality, ethnicity, gender, age, etc.	Culture means national or ethnic belonging
Culture is not uniformly **distributed** in a group	Culture is common to everyone in a group
People negotiate and **adapt**. Their actions can result from a host of factors, of which culture is only one (e.g. social status, the specific situation).	Understanding someone's culture makes it possible to explain and predict their behaviour

12.4 Culturally inclusive approaches to discourse analysis

Having established the complexity and multidimensionality of culture, we will now consider how culture is foregrounded in different culturally inclusive approaches to discourse analysis. These are the Cultural Approach to Discourse (CAD; see 12.4.1), Cultural Discourse Analysis (CuDA; see 12.4.2), and Cross-Cultural Discourse Analysis (CCDA; see 12.4.3).

CAD and CuDA owe much to the contributions of Shi Xu (cf. Broussard 2009; Gavriely-Nuri 2015; Kauppinen 2014) and Donal Carbaugh (cf. Sotirova 2020) respectively, while CCDA is not strongly associated with the name and work of a particular researcher. For ease of reference, Table 12.2 attempts to characterise these approaches in a single word (see 'Main focus' column).

Table 12.2 Culturally inclusive approaches to discourse analysis compared.

Culturally inclusive approach	Key researchers	Main focus	Type of data
Cultural Approach to Discourse (CAD)	Shi Xu	Critical	Preference for ethnographic data (see Chapter 16), either with other data or on its own
Cultural Discourse Analysis (CuDA)	Donal Carbaugh	Interactional	Preference for ethnographic data (see Chapter 16), either with other data or on its own
Cross-Cultural Discourse Analysis (CCDA)	Not associated with the work of a particular researcher	Comparative	Focus tends to be on written texts produced in different cultural and linguistic contexts

As Table 12.2 shows, CAD research can best be described as critical, since it focuses on the West-centric nature of the discourse research tradition. CuDA can be summarised as interactional, since it is primarily committed to understanding human groups through their ways of conversing. And CCDA can be described as comparative, since it is interested in examining, side by side, the discourses produced within different cultural and linguistic contexts, to identify key similarities and differences. CAD and CuDA are also distinguished from CCDA by placing significant importance on ethnographic research, which involves participant observation and interviews with the members of a cultural group.

12.4.1 The Cultural Approach to Discourse (CAD)

The strand of culturally inclusive discourse analysis studies known as CAD is informed by the work of Shi Xu. In the previous section, we saw that this approach can be characterised as critical. It is predicated on critiquing the fact that the community of discourse researchers has not reflected sufficiently on the cultural origins of the field.

Shi Xu's (2015) main point of criticism is that discourse research originated in, and remains largely influenced by, Western topics, data and most importantly by Western theories and methods. This includes the fact that it is the work of Western researchers that is mainly referenced, despite the availability of relevant non-Western scholarship. A further critique is that discourse researchers rarely reflect on their own cultural backgrounds, for instance the research traditions in which they have been trained. They therefore overlook the cultural expectations and biases that their respective cultural backgrounds may encourage when analysing their data and interpreting their findings. Shi Xu (2013) argues that the researcher's cultural background is all too often assumed irrelevant, even though it may have significant implications for how studies are conducted and what conclusions are drawn from the findings. In this regard, Shi Xu (2013) notes that the Western pattern of thinking is heavily influenced by individualism, meaning that actors, issues, and events are typically analysed in isolation. By contrast, the Eastern way of thinking is more holistic, placing greater emphasis on the importance of explaining the surrounding context of an event or issue.

Overall, CAD studies informed by Shi Xu's work are predicated on an understanding that 'Western cultures dominate, repress, and prejudice against the rest of the human cultures' (Xu 2014: 361). Research in this tradition consequently aims to extend across linguistic and cultural boundaries, and especially to encourage non-Western scholars, to 're-discover, re-claim or, where necessary, re-invent their own voices, identities and paradigms of research' (Xu 2016: 1).

These critiques have implications for discourse analysis research, and CAD studies informed by Shi Xu's work are distinguished by sustained focus on culturally and historically specific context. In order to elaborate the context in question in sufficient detail, such studies often rely on ethnographic observation, either in combination with other methods of data collection or independently. Such strong emphasis on context means that in order to understand how an issue, for instance an event or actor is represented in the media, the media texts cannot simply be examined in isolation. The producers of the texts, and the political, socio-economic and historical situation at the time the texts were produced must also be examined. Context, as Shi Xu (2005) writes, is defined as any background relevant to the discourse researcher's understanding of the text in question. Decisions as to what background is relevant relate to the specific research questions of the study. CAD studies also require the researcher to reflect on their own culture and disclose their knowledge and experiences of the linguistic, cultural and historical context under scrutiny.

Research within Shi Xu's tradition is additionally characterised by a certain topic orientation. Studies focus on events, issues and actors surrounded with questions of inequality and/or which are locally relevant (that is, particularly relevant to a cultural group). This makes CAD similar to Critical Discourse Analysis (CDA; see Chapter 16), and common topics of interest in CAD studies include domination, freedom, war and peace, development, rebuilding, gentrification, transformation, discrimination, diversity, ethnocentrism. More recently, environmental degradation has also become a focus, as a topic characterised by marked inequalities in terms of who generates pollution and who suffers the consequences (i.e. East versus West, the rich versus the poor in a society). But while CDA researchers typically examine texts produced by powerful individuals, organisations and communities, CAD researchers tend to focus on lesser known and/or researched, marginalised and otherwise disadvantaged communities and the texts produced by them. The goal of this is to bring understudied topics, communities and text types centre stage. Table 12.3 outlines the differences and similarities of CAD and CDA.

Table 12.3 Cultural Approach to Discourse (CAD) and Critical Discourse Analysis (CDA) compared.

	Cultural Approach to Discourse (CAD)	Critical Discourse Analysis (CDA)
Focus of critique	The West-centricity of discourse research	Specific perceived social problems. For instance, researchers might begin by identifying a problem such as weight-based discrimination, and aim to demonstrate how discourse (e.g. news reports, advertising) plays a role in creating and sustaining this social problem.
Subject focus	Social inequalities	Social inequalities
Data focus	Discourses produced by lesser known and/or researched, marginalised and otherwise disadvantaged communities.	Discourses produced by powerful, elite, dominant individuals, communities and/or organisations.
Reflexive focus	Researchers must reflect on their own cultural background and knowledge and experience of the cultural and historical context under study.	Researchers must reflect on their own position regarding the issue under investigation.

An example of research in the CAD tradition is Gavriely-Nuri's (2015) study of how the notions of war and peace, issues that belong squarely to CAD's area of interest, are constructed in Israeli discourse. Israeli discourse in this study is comprised of various data types, including political speeches, op-eds, caricatures, films and observations of national ceremonies spanning the period between 1967 and 1973. The study shows that within this timeframe war was presented as a normal event for Israeli society, whilst the benefits of peace were simultaneously questioned. To analyse the data, the study relies on typical tools from the discourse analysis toolkit such as, most notably, naturalisation strategies. Gavriely-Nuri shows how war, a process driven by human decisions and actions, was depicted as a kind of natural event, or as something inevitable. For example, in (1) and (2), war is presented as something that happens regularly, with a cyclical nature that resembles the cyclicality of the seasons and other natural events (Gavriely-Nuri 2015: 58):

(1) Every now and again we must meet [the Arab armies] . . . war is something that happens every ten years, and lasts six days.
(2) We will go, we will win once again, nothing will be resolved by [the war] but if this is what [the Arab armies] want, this is what they will get.

To account for such representations, and in keeping with the emphasis on context within CAD research, Gavriely-Nuri looks back to the events within the analysed historical period. Between 1967 and 1973 Israel was involved in three wars and was targeted by hundreds of acts regarded within Israel as terrorist in nature. This context, Gavriely-Nuri argues, helps explain why war and not peace was constructed as a normal part of life.

Another example of research in Shi Xu's tradition is Broussard's (2009) analysis of interviews with Chinese participants in the Environmental Empowerment Programme (EEP), a programme that educates Chinese women farmers in sustainable agriculture. The focus of the study, both in terms of topic and the community involved, is within the scope of topics typical of CAD studies. Broussard points out that although agriculture is increasingly the work of women in many parts of the world, patriarchal traditions mean that women tend not to be included in discussions about agricultural sustainability. To provide more context for the study, Broussard complements interview analysis with ethnographic observation of the women's lives outside the EEP programme, observing the work they do around the house. Broussard analyses the use of nouns, verbs, adverbs, adjectives and EEP terminology in the interview data, looking for those instances when certain words consistently appeared together. The words 'women', 'men' and 'thinking' regularly co-occurred when participants discussed how men's thinking about women is still influenced by beliefs about the roles of women in society which privilege men's views and activities over those of women's. These can be seen in statements such as (3) and (4) (Broussard 2009: 377):

(3) Now some of the men's thinking is old-fashioned. [They] still act like 'big husbands'. In the home they always wait for the women to prepare meals and bring them to the table. They always feel that is what wives should do.
(4) Some men's thinking is still very old-fashioned, very stubborn. They don't let women develop their potential.

In focus: representations of Sámi culture

CAD studies in Shi Xu's tradition aim to extend across linguistic boundaries and tackle questions of (in)equality, through methods and data that are locally relevant and appropriate. A particularly good example of such research is Kauppinen's (2014) examination of how a marginalised community, the Sámi people in Finland and the land they inhabit which is known as Sámiland, are represented on a tourist website run by a Sámi woman herself. Kauppinen uses discourse analytic techniques to analyse the website text, which is written in both Finnish and English, and supplements the findings with ethnographic data collection methods. These include on-site observations of a guesthouse in Inari, Sámiland, and interviews with the guesthouse owner. The study is a reaction to the stereotypical representations of the Sámi people in tourism by travel writers who are outsiders to the Sámi culture. As Europe's only Indigenous people, the Sámi continue to be presented as having a traditional way of living – reindeer herding, fishing and hunting somewhere there 'at the end of the world' (p. 11). This is even though their lives have been affected by numerous technological developments.

The representation on the website, in contrast, comes from a Sámi person and is written in the perspective of the locals. This is, for example, seen in the use of possessive pronouns in the website headings (e.g. 'our location' instead of just 'location'). Counter to the representation in travel literature, Inari is frequently described on the website as 'important':

(5)   Inari is a locally important centre.
(6)   Our villa is located in Inari, northern Lapland at the south-western corner of Lake Inari. Inari is located at a historically important crossroads along the most important ways of former times, the waterways.

The peripheral depiction of Sámi people and places is, moreover, challenged in ways that go beyond the website's text. Kauppinen shares her observations of the guesthouse's rooms decorated with souvenirs collected by the owner on her travels around the world. One room features an Oriental style canopy bed, heart string decorations hanging on the wall and a multicolour rag rug in different shades of orange, another room is decorated with African face masks.

When told that this decoration choice might surprise travellers looking to experience 'traditional Sámi culture', the owner counters that the rooms are decorated by a Sámi person and therefore represent Sámi culture, adding that it is wrong to sustain an outdated image of the Sámi as unaffected by the rest of the world. In this way, Sámi authenticity is located not in the stereotypical imagery of Sáminess, but in an individual's experiences as a Sámi. By triangulating data and analysis methods and analysing communication in different languages, the study shows how a Sámi person can challenge stereotypical representations of Sámiland as isolated, homogeneous and unchanging.

12.4.2 Cultural Discourse Analysis (CuDA)

CuDA is informed by the work of Donal Carbaugh. This kind of culturally inclusive discourse analysis focuses on analysing encounters between speakers with different linguistic and cultural backgrounds, and/or conversations with people from the same linguistic and cultural community. The objective is to identify typical communication practices in a given community, and evaluate the significance of those practices to the people who use them (cf. Carbaugh 2005, 2007). CuDA is based on the careful description and analysis of naturally occurring social interactions, meaning broadly that interactions would reasonably have been expected to occur in the same way, had the researcher not been recording these interactions for analysis. CuDA was developed largely in response to critiques that research in the field of intercultural communication has produced few studies of actual encounters between people. Like the Cultural Approach to Discourse (CAD; see 12.4.1), therefore, Carbaugh's approach to CuDA has a strong and explicit ethnographic element. As Carbaugh (2007: 168) writes, CuDA is 'a particular way of investigating communication ethnographically'. CuDA studies typically explore questions of 'accomplishment', 'structure' and 'sequencing' of conversations. This protocol allows researchers to consider some or all of the following research questions:

1   What is achieved when people converse?
     For example how is a greeting or a joke **accomplished**?
2   What are the main elements of a specific conversational phenomenon?
     For example, is there a repetitive **structure** to how people greet each other or joke, and what is this structure?
3   How are conversations organised?
     For example, what is the **sequence** of elements in a greeting or a joke?

Studies informed by Carbaugh's approach are often concerned with identifying culture-specific words and phrases, or 'cultural terms'. These are considered to capture a deep sense of who people are in a particular linguistic and cultural community.

Research in this tradition is often divided into 'theoretical', 'descriptive', 'interpretive', 'comparative' or 'critical' modes, or considered a combination of these five modes. These modes are outlined in Table 12.4.

It is notable that CuDA studies can be 'critical'. This, of course, makes them similar to Shi Xu's Cultural Approach to Discourse (CAD; see 12.4.1), as well as to Critical Discourse Analysis (CDA; see Chapter 16). As Table 12.4 shows, the 'critical' mode here consists in questioning whether the communicative phenomenon being researched disadvantages some members of the community more than others. However, whilst the critical element is central to both CAD and CDA, Carbaugh notes that it is not a compulsory feature of CuDA studies.

For a formal transcription system of interactions, check out this transcription module! www.sscnet.ucla.edu/soc/faculty/schegloff/TranscriptionProject/index.html

Table 12.4 Modes of CuDA research.

Mode of CuDA research	Description
Theoretical	Analysts are expected to explain how they understand the concepts that are key to the analysis, for example 'discourse', 'culture', or the specific communicative phenomena under study (e.g. a greeting or joke).
Descriptive	Involves recording in video or audio format instances of a communicative phenomenon, transcribing them through a formal transcription system, and offering examples in the study so that readers can interact with the analysed material.
Interpretive	Establishes the significance of the communicative phenomenon for the participants.
Comparative	Involves placing communicative phenomena against each other to examine similarities and differences across linguistic and cultural communities
Critical	Questions whether the communicative phenomenon being researched disadvantages some members of the community more than others.

By contrast, the 'interpretive' mode holds an especially important place in Carbaugh's CuDA, and there exist specific guidelines as to how it should be conducted (see Carbaugh 2007). This mode revolves around the notion that when people interact, they say things both explicitly and implicitly; for example about the following subjects:

- Who they are and what it means to be a person in a particular place (i.e. they convey something about their **identity**);
- How they are linked to one another in their wider community, through interpersonal **relations**;
- What type of **actions** are being performed through this sort of communication;
- What **emotions** they feel;
- How they relate to their environment and their sense of **place** and what is appropriate and inappropriate there.

In Carbaugh's CuDA, 'identity', 'relations', 'actions', 'emotions' and 'place' are referred to as 'cultural radiants of meaning' (Carbaugh 2007: 174). Messages about these five radiants of meaning can be powerfully encoded, in so-called 'cultural terms'. These are words or phrases used routinely within a linguistic and cultural community, which convey something about that community. The meanings encoded in cultural terms often vary along dimensions such as 'us-them', 'close-distant', 'powerful-powerless' referred to as 'semantic dimensions'.

Carbaugh's 2005 book *Cultures in Conversation* offers a range of examples of research in this tradition. Two of the chapters focus on conversations between

Finnish and American English speakers, and draw on Carbaugh's personal experience of visiting the University of Suomi, Finland as an American Fulbright Professor. One of the chapters is a humorous account which demonstrates how introductions, when people meet for the first time and introduce themselves, are culturally shaped. Carbaugh describes a situation in which he was presented to a Finnish university member for the first time, which he experienced as uncomfortable. Carbaugh felt uneasy because his contributions to the conversation were followed by pauses considerably longer than what he was used to from conversations with his American family, friends and colleagues. The lengthy pauses, he felt, were a sure sign that he had done something wrong, and compelled him to quickly bring the conversation to an end. As he later discovered in discussions with other Finnish speakers, in Finland people commonly use pauses in conversations that are on average longer than what Americans are used to, and these are intended to signify that the occasion is respected and given its due time.

In another chapter, Carbaugh explores the reasons why Finnish speakers might feel that American English speakers are (in the words of the Finnish speakers) 'superficial'. After having engaged in 'small talk' with an American English speaker ('small' as in talk that is seemingly purposeless and focused on unimportant and uncontroversial matters), Finnish speakers were often surprised that upon meeting the same person again, they were ignored. To Finnish speakers, small talk created an obligation to speak again and by not speaking again American English speakers led Finnish speakers to question the friendliness and significance of the earlier exchange. However, as Carbaugh explains, small talk does not forge the same communicative relationship for American English speakers. The two chapters show how a researcher might describe and interpret specific communication phenomena and the implicit and explicit messages they convey about 'actions', 'relations' and so forth.

In focus: exploring what it means to be Bulgarian

Another example of research in this tradition is Sotirova's (2020) study of naturally occurring talk, which was aimed at understanding what it means to be Bulgarian. This study was conducted via recording within households, during travel and part of service encounters, and supplemented by interviews with participants. Its focus is a specific cultural term, a phrase that is frequently used in Bulgarian discourse, namely 'Хубава работа, ама българска' and a variation on this phrase, 'българска му работа'. These translate into English as 'Good job, but Bulgarian' and 'Bulgarian job/way', respectively. Sotirova describes numerous instances when the phrase was recurrently used to refer to a task that had been accomplished just barely, with minimal effort. When Bulgarians used these phrases to refer to problematic institutions, traits, behaviours or individuals, they typically constructed a problematic image of 'us' (Bulgaria and Bulgarians) as compared to a more developed and better 'them' (the West). The effect this conveyed was that if it is Bulgarian, then it cannot be good.

Methodologically, the study incorporates three of Carbaugh's (2007) modes of analysis (see Table 12.4). The theoretical mode is employed, in outlining key concepts relevant to the study. The descriptive mode is also used, in describing excerpts where the phrases of interest had occurred, and the interpretive mode is employed, in interpreting the meanings encoded. As Carbaugh (2007) notes, CuDA studies most often draw upon these three modes.

12.4.3 Cross-Cultural Discourse Analysis (CCDA)

Unlike the Cultural Approach to Discourse (CAD; see 12.4.1) and Cultural Discourse Analysis (CuDA; see 12.4.2), Cross-Cultural Discourse Analysis (CCDA) is not associated with the work of particular researchers. Put simply, CCDA studies compare texts belonging to the same genre (e.g. news articles, tweets, blog posts, advertisements, election speeches) that have been produced by people of two or more linguistic and cultural communities. In contrast to Shi Xu's CuDA, there is no preference for particular topics. CCDA studies typically draw on non-linguistic disciplines, including history, sociology and psychology, to help interpret why the texts had been written in particular ways. They then draw conclusions about the beliefs, values and history that have shaped the texts and the communities that produced the texts.

Wu and Li (2018), for example, studied tweets posted in English and Chinese by top companies, including Coca Cola, Google, IBM, McDonalds, Microsoft and Samsung, on Twitter and Weibo, the two leading social networking sites in the United States and China, respectively. They uncovered striking similarities between the ways the companies used strategies to maximise their followers' attachment to their brands, across both sites and in both languages. These included intimate forms of address, typically used by people who are very familiar with each other, 'small talk' and humour. Wu and Li point out that the choice of address forms vary considerably between linguistic and cultural communities. In Chinese, the use of address forms has traditionally depended on hierarchies and power. Conversation participants assess considerations such as whether the interlocutor is organisationally superior or inferior, interpersonally familiar or not, of the same gender or not, of the same age or not. And yet, in online communication, companies used very similar address terms such as 'hey', 'we', 'folks', 'dear' as well as first names. McDonalds, for example, tweeted in English:

(7) Hey @lenadunham, we wanted to confirm your reservation. The corner booth is waiting for you!

Examples of 'small talk' included posts hashtagged as 'good morning' tweets, which shared thoughts and sometimes tips. Coca Cola, for example, posted the following on Weibo:

(8) 细雨从星星上落下,浸湿痛苦,称为我们的一部分。九月结束时,请唤醒我。- Wake me up when September ends#可口可乐.晨安# [图略], ('Here comes the rain again, falling from the stars, drenched in my pain again, becoming who we are. Wake me up when September ends. – Wake me up when September ends #Coca-Cola Good morning')

Humour was also frequently employed as, for example, when Google tweeted back to a user named Jeti:

(9) Mr. Yeti? Can we call you Bigfoot?

Wu and Li argue that these similarities between the English and Chinese tweets suggest that social media interactions might be impossible to explain with national culture and traditional ways of communicating.

Another example is a study I conducted in collaboration with Nelya Koteyko (Atanasova and Koteyko 2017), where we analysed the use of metaphors in op-eds and editorials about climate change. These were published in leading newspapers from Germany, the United Kingdom and the United States; *Sueddeutsche.de*, *theguardian.com* and *NYTimes.com*, respectively. Metaphors allow us to see one thing in terms of another, while newspaper editorials and op-eds are openly aimed at persuasion. This study aimed to find out which metaphors were used to try to persuade the reader to see climate change in terms of something else, and how this was done. We found that in all three newspapers, all instances of metaphor use occurred within pro-climate-change arguments. That is, in arguments that it is irrational not to act to stop or mitigate climate change, arguments that we need to urgently act on climate change, and arguments in support of, or in opposition to, specific solutions to climate change problems.

However, we noted inter-country differences, with regard to the most frequently used metaphors employed in such arguments. In Germany, metaphors of illness predominated, whereas in the UK metaphors of war and in the US metaphors of journey were more commonly used. For example, in (10), an extract from *Sueddeutsche.de*, illness metaphors are used to argue that it is irrational not to attempt to stop or mitigate climate change.

(10) Der Patient ist lebensgefährlich erkrankt, doch die Therapie ist ihm, obwohl ihm die Mittel nicht fehlen, zu teuer. Er hat ängstlich die besten Spezialisten befragt; sie alle stellen den gleichen Befund. Doch die Medizin schluckt der Kranke nur sporadisch, manchmal gar nicht. . . . Welcher Kranke so dämlich ist? Es ist die ganze Welt. (The patient is dangerously ill, but to him the therapy seems, although he is not lacking in resources, too expensive. He has anxiously consulted the best specialists; they have all arrived at the same diagnosis. And yet, the patient only takes the medicines sporadically, sometimes not at all. . . . But which patient is so stupid? It is the whole world.')

In (11), an extract from *theguardian.com* shows how war metaphors are used to argue that we need to urgently act on climate change, and in (12) an example from *NYTimes.com* exemplifies how journey metaphors are used to oppose a specific solution to climate change.

(11) climate change is undeniably a serious threat, and our comments should not be seized upon as an excuse for delay or inaction . . . the potential impacts of climate change on the Amazon forest must be a call to action to conserve the Amazon, not a reason to retreat in despair

(12) if the public were to allow our well-oiled government to shepherd [Keystone XL] to existence this would be the first step down the wrong road, perpetuating our addiction to dirty fossil fuels, moving to even dirtier ones

We draw on research from other disciplines to show that these metaphors speak strongly to German, British and American national identity and culture. The especially prominent use of illness metaphors in *Sueddeutsche.de* can tentatively be linked to the early uses of such metaphors to discuss acid rain and forest dieback, coupled with the prominent place that the forest takes in German culture. In the case of the UK, writers have argued that war is a major component of the national character and has a special place due to the very specific experience of the country in the world wars and emerging from these wars victorious. As for the journey metaphors, the notion of a journey very much defines what it means to be American, and the country is often envisioned as a voyaging ship. We conclude that national efforts to communicate the gravity of anthropogenic climate change appear to be closely tailored to national identity and culture, which we thought might be interpreted as a positive development.

12.5 Conclusion

In conclusion, Cultural Approach to Discourse (CAD), Cultural Discourse Analysis (CuDA) and Cross-Cultural Discourse Analysis (CCDA) differ significantly, whilst retaining a common emphasis on the importance of culture. A critical approach is central to the endeavour of CAD researchers, whilst interaction is foregrounded for CuDA researchers, and comparative research lies at the heart of CCDA. All three approaches also understand culture slightly differently. For example, in Shi Xu's CAD, culture is understood to be saturated with power relations and contestations. This manifests in the key topics of study in this line of research, which include topics such as domination, freedom, war and peace, and diversity.

However, as the examples in this chapter show, in much of the research across CAD, CuDA and CCDA, culture is approached as a homogenous national or ethnic identity; thus we have considered research which examines Israeli culture, Sámi culture, and Bulgarian culture. CAD and CuDA also have a number of commonalities. They are both associated with the work of particular researchers – Shi Xu and Donal Carbaugh, respectively. CCDA, in contrast, is not strongly linked to the contribution of a particular researcher. CAD and CuDA also share a 'critical' element, which brings them close to Critical Discourse Analysis (CDA; see Chapter 16). In CAD, this critical orientation primarily involves being critical of the West-centric focus of discourse research, whilst in CuDA it mainly consists in questioning whether communicative phenomena under research disadvantage some members of a community more than others. Despite these differences, all three culturally inclusive approaches to discourse make an important, shared contribution to the wider field of discourse studies. They propose that discourse analysts should be aware not only of their own, but also of culturally different research traditions, and be versed in foreign languages and cultural discourses beyond their own.

References

Apte, M. 1994. Language in sociocultural context. In R. E. Asher (Ed.), *The Encyclopaedia of Language and Linguistics*. Oxford: Pergamon Press, pp. 2000–2010.

Atanasova, D. and Koteyko, N. 2017. Metaphors in online editorials and op-eds about climate change, 2006–2013: A study of Germany, the United Kingdom and the United States. In K. Fløttum (Ed.), *The Role of Language in the Climate Change Debate*. London: Rutledge, pp. 71–89.

Broussard, J. T. 2009. Using cultural discourse analysis to research gender and environmental understandings in China. *Ethos*, 37(3): 362–389.

Carbaugh, D. 2005. *Cultures in Conversation*. Mahwah: Erlbaum.

Carbaugh, D. 2007. Cultural discourse analysis: Communication practices and intercultural encounters. *Journal of Intercultural Communication Research*, 36(3): 167–182.

Gavriely-Nuri, D. 2015. *Israeli Peace Discourse: A Cultural Approach to CDA*. Amsterdam and Philadelphia: John Benjamins Publishing Company.

Kauppinen, K. 2014. Welcome to the end of the world! Resignifying periphery under the new economy: A nexus analytical view of a tourist website. *Journal of Multicultural Discourses*, 9(1): 1–19.

Sotirova, N. 2020. 'Good job, but Bulgarian': Identifying 'Bulgarianness' through cultural discourse analysis. *Journal of International and Intercultural Communication*, 14(2): 128–145. http://doi.org/10.1080/17513057.2020.1760919

Wu, D. D. and Li, C. 2018. Emotional branding on social media: A cross-cultural discourse analysis of global brands on Twitter and Weibo. In A. Curtis and R. Sussex (Eds.), *Intercultural Communication in Asia: Education, Language and Values*. Cham: Springer, pp. 225–240.

Xu, S. 2005. *A Cultural Approach to Discourse*. Basingstoke: Palgrave Macmillan.

Xu, S. 2013. A multicultural approach to discourse studies. In J. P. Gee and M. Handford (Eds.), *The Routledge Handbook of Discourse Analysis*. 1st ed. London and New York: Routledge, pp. 642–653.

Xu, S. 2014. *Chinese Discourse Studies*. London and New York: Palgrave MacMillan.

Xu, S. 2015. Cultural discourse studies. In K. Tracy, C. Ilie and T. Sandel (Eds.), *The International Encyclopedia of Language and Social Interaction*. Boston, MA: Wiley-Blackwell, pp. 1–9. http://doi.org/10.1002/9781118611463. wbielsi012

Xu, S. 2016. Cultural discourse studies through the Journal of Multicultural Discourses: 10 years on. *Journal of Multicultural Discourses*, 11(1): 1–8.

Section three

Applications

13 Forensic linguistics and forensic phonetics

Georgina Brown and Claire Hardaker

Content warning

To exemplify both forensic linguistics and forensic phonetics in action, this chapter focuses on the landmark historical case of the Yorkshire Ripper. The Yorkshire Ripper case involved a series of attacks and murders, mostly targeting women. We have not included any graphic details; however some may find the nature of the topic distressing, and we urge readers to consider carefully whether they wish to proceed.

13.1 Defining Forensic linguistics vs. forensic phonetics

Despite its generally applied nature, defining forensic linguistics is surprisingly difficult – not because it's so hard to pin down (see, for instance, Chapter 6 on Pragmatics) but because it's so broad. However, understanding the subject does, of course, entail understanding the term and one way to begin is to break down the term *forensic linguistics* itself.

The Oxford English Dictionary defines *forensic* as, 'relating to, or associated with proceedings in a court of law' and as 'providing medical, scientific, or technical evidence in legal proceedings and the investigation of crime'. To keep matters as straightforward as possible, we'll carry forward the notions of the *courtroom* and *crime*.

So what of the *linguistics* part of the term? As this entire volume exemplifies, linguistics covers a huge amount of ground; from Phonetics (Chapter 1) and Semantics (Chapter 5), to Animal Communication (Chapter 30) and Computational Linguistics (Chapter 18). At its most expansive, then, *forensic linguistics* can be thought of as any linguistic theory, method or approach as applied to the language of the courtroom, crime or law.

As noted, that makes the field extremely broad, and perhaps one way to rationalise it is to consider the goal of a given analysis. Most research within forensic linguistics – though certainly not all – can be thought of as loosely addressing one of two key questions: 'Who does this language (really) belong to?' or 'What does this language (really) mean?' And of course, these analyses are generally set

DOI: 10.4324/9781003045571-16

within the context of crime, the courtroom, legislation, investigative procedure, judicial systems and so on (Coulthard and Johnson 2010).

There is, however, another way to consider the field. We can instead draw apart forensic linguistics and forensic phonetics. *Forensic linguistics* is sometimes used as an overarching term for both, but this chapter will show that these areas have a range of substantial differences.

13.1.1 Language

Let's consider forensic linguistics first. When specifically contrasted with forensic phonetics, forensic linguistics is most typically concerned with the words themselves – how they are spelled (if originally written) or structured, the producer's unique habits and stylistic choices collectively known as **idiolect** (Bloch 1948), what those words mean, how (in)frequently they occur in certain contexts or genres or groups, who produced them, whether someone 'owns' them and so forth. When we look at legal cases that involve forensic linguistics, we find examples as diverse as the question over whether the word *Google* has suffered 'genericide' and therefore lost its **trademark** (Hughes 2018), the **authorship analysis** question about whether Mark Zuckerberg really did write emails handing over 50% of *Facebook* to an individual called Paul Ceglia (Solan 2012) and the **deception detection** issues around whether Donald Trump lied during his time as President of the United States (Shank and Foltz 2019). This is only a tiny array of possible examples, and a list of other illustrative cases can be found in the opening chapter of Coulthard et al. (2016). It is worth noting, however, that authorship analysis tends to dominate both the research and the headlines (Leonard et al. 2016).

Given that the field of linguistics itself is very broad, there are many ways to approach linguistic data or questions that could be considered forensic in nature. Just some frameworks for investigating language include discourse analysis (Coulthard 1996; see also Chapter 10), forensic stylistics (McMenamin 1993), corpus linguistics (Johnson and Wright 2014; see also Chapter 21), and computational linguistics (Chaski 2005; see also Chapter 18), including stylometry (Holmes and Tweedie 1995).

13.1.2 Speech

But what of forensic phonetics and the spoken word? How does this differ to forensic linguistics? Sometimes, speech recordings arise as evidence in a legal case or investigation. These might take the form of fraudulent telephone calls, the audio from CCTV footage, or even covertly recorded material. Such recordings can bring evidential value to a case, and so forensic phoneticians might be approached to carry out a careful analysis to produce findings useful to a forensic context. The most common type of forensic phonetic analysis is a **forensic speaker**

comparison analysis. This task analyses the speech of an unknown speaker in one recording (perhaps a threatening telephone call) and the speech of a suspect (perhaps obtained from a police interview recording) and then compares the two. The purpose of this comparison is to provide a conclusion that can address whether the two recordings feature the same or different speakers.

While forensic speaker comparison analyses constitute a very large proportion of a forensic phonetician's workload, there are other task types that also occasionally warrant their attention. These include **speaker profiling analyses,** which arise in cases where there is no suspect (yet). The instructing party typically asks the forensic phonetician to report information *about* the unknown speaker to help investigators identify a suspect. There are also **disputed utterance analyses,** in which the phonetician analyses short, low-quality recordings where what is said is disputed. One fairly famous example of how challenging it can be to determine what was said in a recording involves the *laurel/yanny* debate (Bosker 2018), and another involves whether Donald Trump said *bigly* or *big league* (Stack 2016). In both cases, there is technically no forensic angle, but they amply demonstrate how utterances can become widely disputed, even – or perhaps *especially* – when many non-specialists attempt to resolve the matter.

Forensic phoneticians may also be approached in cases that feature an **earwitness** where there is no actual recording to analyse. Witnesses may not have *seen* a culprit's face, but they may have *heard* their voice. For instance, sometimes offenders wear balaclavas, offences take place in the dark, or the crime (e.g. harassment, hate-speech, blackmail, extortion, etc.) might be perpetrated over the phone. In these cases, the language is typically not recorded, and we are left only with the victims' memories of the voice. Forensic phoneticians are therefore also occasionally consulted when speech evidence in question has not been recorded to offer an idea of how reliable the information coming from the earwitness might be.

13.2 The Yorkshire Ripper and Wearside Jack

From 1969 to 1980, Peter Sutcliffe travelled around the north of England attacking and murdering at least 23 women and girls.[1] Throughout the 11 years of the investigation, the Major Incident Room at Millgarth Police Station in Leeds worked frantically: interviewing suspects, keeping records of car sightings in key areas, trawling through unsustainably enormous piles of reports, broadcasting pleas for information, receiving thousands of tip-offs and even tracking serial numbers on new banknotes back to the first people to receive them. Yet all these efforts would ultimately prove fruitless (Bilton 2003; Burn 2011). The numbers of victims continued to climb, and West Yorkshire Police faced increasing pressure not only from the public, the press and the victims' families, but also from the Home Office and the Cabinet Office.

One account asserts that by 1980, Prime Minister Margaret Thatcher

> had been so vexed by the Ripper's growing tally of victims and what she regarded as police incompetence that she summoned her Home Secretary, William Whitelaw, and announced her intention of going to Leeds that very weekend to sideline Gregory and to take personal charge of the investigation herself.
>
> (The Telegraph 2010)

Whether the Prime Minister really did make such a threat or not, official accounts do show that the Home Secretary promptly dispatched an inspector from Her Majesty's Inspectorate of Constabulary to meet with the Chief Constable of West Yorkshire Police, Ronald Gregory. The two objectives of that meeting were to discuss the capabilities of those in charge of the so-called Ripper Inquiry, and to provide West Yorkshire Police with a Consultative Committee of senior officers (Byford 1981; Cabinet Office 1984; Home Office 1982).

However, it is in the two years before this point where linguistics is most concerned. Between March 1978 and June 1979, three letters and a tape were sent supposedly from the Yorkshire Ripper himself.

13.2.1 The three letters

The first letter, postmarked Sunderland, 1.45pm, 8 March 1978, was sent to Mr George Oldfield, Assistant Chief Constable of West Yorkshire Police. Its contents were thus:

Dear Sir,

I am sorry I cannot give my name for obvious reasons I am the ripper. Ive been dubbed a maniac by the press but not by you You call me clever and I am. You and your mates havent a clue That photo in the paper gave me fits and that lot about killing myself no chance Ive got things to do, My purpose to rid the streets of them sluts. my one regret his that young lassie Macdonald did not know cause changed routine that nite, Up to number 8 now you say 7 but remember Preston 75, Get about you know, you were right I travel a bit You probably look for me in Sunderland don't bother I am not daft just posted letter there on one of my trips. Not a bad place compared with Chapeltown and Manningham and other places

Warn whores to keep of streets cause I feel it coming on again. Sorry about young lassie.

Yours respectfully

Jack the Ripper

Might write again later I not sure last one really deserved it. Whores getting younger each time. Old slut next time I hope, Huddersfield never again too small close call last one.

Five days later, a second letter was received by the Chief Editor of the *Daily Mirror*, postmarked Sunderland, 10am, 13th of March 1978. Its contents were very similar:

Dear Sir,

I have already written Chief Constable, Oldfield "a man I respect" concerning the recent Ripper murders. I told him and I am telling you to warn them whores I'll strike again and soon when heat cools off. About the Mcdonald lassie, I did nt know that she was decent and I am sorry I changed my routine that night, Up to murder 8 now You say but remember Preston 75.

Easy picken them up dont even have to try, you think theyre learn but they dont Most are young lassies, next time try older one I hope. Police haven't a clue yet and I don't leave any I am very clever and don't think of looking for any fingerprints cause there arent any and dont look for me up in Sunderland cause I not stupid just passed through the place not bad place compared with Chapeltown and manningham can't walk the streets for them whore, Dont forget warn them I feel it coming on again if I get the chance. Sorry about lassie I didn't know.

Yours respectfully

Jack the Ripper

Might write again after another ones' gone. Maybe Liverpool or even Manchester again, to hot here in Yorkshire, Bye.

I have given advance warning so its yours and their's fault.

The third letter arrived on the 23rd of March 1979, almost exactly a year after the previous two, again addressed to Assistant Chief Constable George Oldfield:

Dear Officer

Sorry I havn't written, about a year to be exact, but I hav'nt been up north for quite a while. I was'nt kidding last time I wrote saying the whore would be older this time and maybe I'd strike in Manchester for a change, you should have took heed. That bit about her being in hospital, funny the lady mentioned something about being in hospital before I stopped her whoring ways. The lady won't worry about hospitals now will she. I bet you be wondering how come I hav'nt been to work for ages, well I would have been if it hadnt been for your cursered coppers I had the lady just where I wanted her and was about to strike when one of you cursing police cars stopped right outside the lane, he must have been a dumb copper cause he didnt say anything, he didnt know how close he was to catching me. Tell you the truth I thought I was collared, the lady said don't worry about the coppers, little did she know that bloody copper saved her neck. That was last month, so I don't know when I will get back on the job but I know it wont be Chapeltown too bloody hot there maybe Bradfords Manningham. Might write again if up north.

Jack the Ripper

PS Did you get letter I sent to Daily Mirror in Manchester.

Initially the Ripper Inquiry team was highly sceptical. Especially when dealing with high-profile cases, forces routinely receive hoax letters, false confessions, malicious tip-offs about innocent citizens, claims of clairvoyant insights and any number of other attempts by people to either insert themselves into the drama of a major investigation or to thwart police efforts. However, the senior officers were desperate for any lead, and a perception began to arise that these letters might be genuine. Some officers began to believe that this third letter in particular contained information only the killer could know – a matter we return to later – and in turn, this drastically increased confidence in the authenticity of the full set.

13.2.2 The tape

Three months after the last letter, on the 18th of June 1979, Assistant Chief Constable George Oldfield received a fourth and final envelope. In it, a cassette tape contained an audio-recording in which the speaker addressed Oldfield directly:

Key	
(1)	Pausally delimited utterance number
//	Break in the recording caused by electrical switching
[7.0 secs]	The durations of longer pauses

(1) I'm Jack (2) I see you are still having no luck catching me (3) I have the greatest respect for you George (4) but Lord (5) you are no nearer catching me now (6) than four years ago when I started (7) I reckon your boys are letting you down George (8) they can't be much good (9) can they? [7.0 secs] (10) the only time they came near catching me (11) was a few months back in Chapeltown (12) when I was disturbed (13) even then it was a uniformed copper (14) not a detective (15) I warned you in March that I'd strike again (16) sorry it wasn't Bradford (17) I did promise you that (18) but I couldn't get there [6.8 secs] (19) I'm not quite sure when I'll strike again (20) but it will be definitely (21) sometime this year (22) maybe September October (23) even sooner if I get the chance [6.6 secs] (24) I'm not sure where (25) maybe Manchester (26)

I like it there (27) there's plenty of them knocking about (28) they never learn do they George? (29) I bet you've warned them (30) but they never listen [11.9 secs] // (31) at the rate I'm going (32) I should be in the book of records (33) I think it's eleven up to now isn't it? (34) well I'll keep on going (35) for quite a while yet [5.0 secs] (36) I can't see myself being nicked (37) just yet (38) even if you do get near (39) I'll probably top myself first [5.6 secs] (40) well it's been nice chatting to you George (41) yours Jack the Ripper (42) no good looking for fingerprints (43) you should know by now (44) it's clean as a whistle (45) see you soon (46) bye // (47) hope you like the catchy tune (48) at the end // (49) ha ha // [22 seconds of 'Thank You For Being A Friend' by Andrew Gold]

By the time this tape arrived, senior officers were sure that the three prior letters were real, and all four communications began to take on central importance in the investigation. The tape's existence was soon leaked to the media, leading to explosive headlines and demands to release the audio. The police then decided to capitalise on the public interest by broadcasting the tape on radio and television stations, asking for members of the public to call with tips if they felt they recognised the speaker. At the same time, it had become clear that to properly investigate these supposed leads, expertise was required. Accordingly, both the police and press turned to linguists for further insight.

Scan the QR code to listen to the audio yourself: www.youtube.com/watch?v=ocslvgRaNtQ

13.3 'I'll strike again'

Jack Windsor Lewis was a Lecturer at Leeds University – a location on the doorstep of many of the attacks, and a decade earlier, he had published a guide on English pronunciation (1969). It was therefore unsurprising that a BBC team asked him to comment on the letters and tape. Like many others, by this point, Windsor Lewis had heard the tape on the radio, but in later conversation with a police detective, he discovered that no one had conducted any sort of linguistic analysis on the letters.

Windsor Lewis offered his expertise, and after being allowed to view the letters twice, he wrote up a 1400-word report providing an impression of their contents. Within authorship analysis, we could view this report as an early attempt at sociolinguistic profiling, where Windsor Lewis was seeking to create a picture of the author based on their linguistic choices and habits (their **idiolect**). Given that the field as a whole was very much in its infancy at the time, there was no real method or standard or accepted set of approaches for this, and unsurprisingly, there are sections of the report that we would disregard today. However, we can still extract interesting linguistic reflections from it.

From the language in the letters, Windsor Lewis draws together a profile of someone at 'the bottom of the social scale', who is functionally literate, has not

269

advanced beyond school-level education, and who does not follow standard linguistic norms. This is built on observations such as the use of slang, including
copper (police officer), *knocking about* (hanging around) and *nicked* (arrested);
that about a third of the sentences did not have full stops; that sentence-initial
capitalisation occurred in around a third of cases where it would be expected;
that a space was typically inserted before the *nt* contraction, and that words like
night and *because* were expressed as *nite* and *cause*. Additionally, Windsor Lewis
noted some significant idiosyncrasies:

> The most extraordinary of these appeared to be the adjective *cursen*. This is so
> completely unattested a form that one would unhesitatingly have dismissed it
> as a slip of the pen for cursed were it not for the fact that that very word was
> used in the immediately previous sentence, and there spelled curserred. . . . If
> it was a genuine usage it was certainly a very rare and distinctive one.
>
> (Windsor Lewis 2013)

In the event that the police had been able to use a sociolinguistic profile like this
to identify a prime suspect, if necessary, some of these same features could have
gone forward to form the basis of a more typical form of authorship analysis,
where other texts known to be authored by the suspect (**KTs**, or **Known Texts**)
could be compared to the three letters (**DTs**, or **Disputed Texts**) to see how
similar they were, if at all.

Intriguingly, Windsor Lewis also noted that,

> The verbal style was reminiscent in one or two places of a letter attributed to
> the original London Jack the Ripper in which murders are referred to as *work*
> and the expressions *[joke] gives me . . . fits* and *[I gave] the lady [no time to
> squeal]* occur.
>
> (Windsor Lewis 2013)

We come back to this observation towards the end.

From Windsor Lewis' perspective, after the report was handed in, he merely
received a polite call to thank him for his efforts, and then heard nothing more
about how it was used, if at all. By this point, however, a rather different problem
had emerged. In conversation with Stanley Ellis – a linguist we will meet in just
a moment – Windsor Lewis had become increasingly concerned that the letters
were a hoax, and had not been written by the killer at all. Unfortunately, in his
own words,

> The police officers directing the investigations had not only been unwilling to
> acknowledge publicly our very strong conviction that they were dealing with
> a hoaxer but even made it clear that we were not to consider ourselves free to
> speak our minds on the matter in public. We were given to understand that we
> should have been regarded as 'breaking ranks' had we done so.
>
> (Windsor Lewis 2013)

So let us turn now to Stanley Ellis, the linguist who provided the police with the main analysis of the tape recording.

13.4 'I'm Jack'

In the 1970s, an audio-recording of somebody speaking presented a new kind of evidence. Faced with the enormous pressures of trying to solve the murders, the police approached Stanley Ellis, a dialectologist and phonetician also based at Leeds University who had published *The Survey of English Dialects and Social History* (1974). The officers wanted Ellis to carry out a **speaker profiling analysis** and through this, hopefully build up a picture of the person who had made the recording – the person that the police were now confident was the killer.

Ellis' initial surmise was that the speaker's accent reflected that of someone brought up in the Sunderland area of north-east England. His published account (Ellis 1994) demonstrates just how much he relied on his experiences as a dialectologist to inform his analysis of the 'I'm Jack' tape. Ellis gathered reference recordings from previous data collection projects, and turned to resources that he had helped to produce that documented typical speech patterns in parts of the north-east of England, including **dialect maps**. By referring to this resource collection and undertaking a systematic phonetic analysis of the *I'm Jack* tape, he was able to carefully unpick the speaker's productions of vowels and consonants. For example, Ellis noted the precise way in which the speaker produced the vowel in *strike* and in the pronoun *I*, and across a number of words, he observed that the speaker consistently 'h-dropped' (i.e. did not pronounce /h/ in words like *have* and *hope*). This analysis allowed him to home in on a small geographical area where that accent variety was typically found.

As part of his investigation, Ellis also carried out fieldwork in the Sunderland area. He took two cassette players: one to record more speakers in different localities within this area, and one to play the *I'm Jack* tape to listeners from these areas. In his own words,

> We moved further inland to the small village of Castletown and in a pub there we met a retired man whose segmental pronunciations, intonation patterns, rhythm and tempo closely resembled those of the questioned speaker.
>
> (Ellis 1994)

From these results, Ellis concluded that the *I'm Jack* speech patterns reflected those of someone who was brought up in the Southwick or Castletown areas of Sunderland, in Wearside. When this deduction became public knowledge, the media quickly penned the nickname, *Wearside Jack*.

Just like Windsor Lewis, however, Ellis had begun to caution the police that the recording seemed like a hoax.[2] Unfortunately, instead of being taken into consideration, Ellis and Windsor Lewis' attempts to convey their concerns triggered a rising degree of hostility. The police felt that the linguists were stepping outside of their remit of simply analysing the language, and the linguists found themselves being openly criticised for wasting police time. Undeterred by concerns about the provenance of the letters, senior officers began to direct significant investigative resources towards finding a suspect who fitted the description that Ellis had provided – a killer with a Wearside accent.

Six months after the arrival of the tape, in January of 1981, a lorry driver from Bradford, Peter Sutcliffe, was arrested. This was not because of the police efforts in the north-east of England, but because Sheffield officers stopped him in a suspicious vehicle with a sex worker. Despite having a Bradford, rather than a Wearside, accent, he was interviewed in relation to the Yorkshire Ripper murders. Dissatisfied with his answers, an officer returned to the scene of his arrest and found the hidden murder weapons. Sutcliffe was subsequently charged, convicted and given an indefinite prison sentence.

13.4.1 The real Wearside Jack

Though the arrest and conviction of Peter Sutcliffe – a man with a Bradford accent – confirmed that the tape recording and letters were indeed a hoax, this did little to soothe relations between the police and linguists. As the decades passed by, the story could very easily have ended at this frosty impasse, each side aggrieved at the other. However, in 2005, the hoax was subjected to a cold case review. By this stage, the Wearside Jack communications were a quarter of a century old, but after some effort, police were able to obtain a sample from the seal of one of the letters, and successfully analysed it using newly established DNA testing techniques. Incredibly, the sample returned an immediate hit in the UK National DNA database, and it identified one John Samuel Humble.

Humble was arrested and during the ensuing police interviews, he admitted to the hoax. He explained that he had been just 18 at the time, fascinated with the ongoing Yorkshire Ripper case, angry after unpleasant experiences with the police and craving notoriety. He had found a green-covered hardback book titled *Jack the Ripper* in his local library which contained letters sent to newspapers and the police supposedly authored by the infamous Victorian Whitechapel murderer, Jack the Ripper. One of these was the very letter that Windsor Lewis had identified in his report.

Humble even cooperated to provide a new recording of the original tape. Police then asked for a **forensic speaker comparison analysis** between the original and new recordings. In yet another interesting twist of fate, when the case proceeded to court, whilst J. Peter French and Philip Harrison were retained by the prosecution, the defence hired none other than Jack Windsor Lewis, and an account of the involvement of all three can be found in French et al. (2006).

It is unusual to carry out forensic speaker comparison on recordings that are so comparable in terms of their contents, and also on recordings that were produced so far apart in time. To complicate matters, in the intervening 26 years,

Humble had smoked, developed serious alcohol dependency, and of course, significantly aged – all issues that can change the voice in many ways. Despite their initial concerns about how these variables might confound the comparison, the analysts working on the case found an 'overwhelming degree of similarity between the speech patterns in the recordings' (French et al. 2006).

Perhaps most compelling was that at last, the linguists were able to categorically demonstrate the merit and integrity of the work they had carried out so many years earlier. When asked to give his address in court, Humble stated that he lived on the Ford Estate in Sunderland. Just 1.2 miles (1.9 km) to the north-west we find Castletown, and almost exactly the same distance to the north-east we find Southwick. A quarter of a century earlier, as Figure 13.1 shows, Ellis had successfully pinpointed Humble's voice to within just a mile of his home.

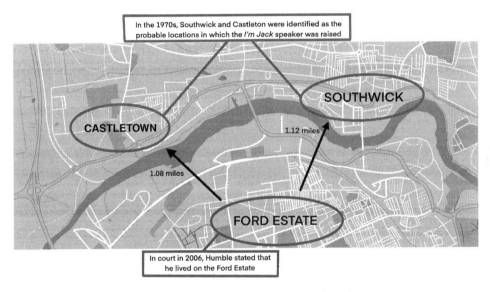

Figure 13.1 Map of the Ford Estate, Castletown and Southwick.

13.5 Conclusion

The Yorkshire Ripper case is not only notorious in general, it is also one of the most infamous cases within forensic linguistics. It provides a good illustration of how one can approach such an investigation, and the general context of forensic casework. That said, it's also crucial to emphasise how unusual this case was across any number of dimensions.

First, from the perspective of forensic phonetics, in the early stages, it is primarily a **speaker profiling case**. Yet it is crucial to note that this type of case is extremely rare. Forensic speaker *comparison* cases are, by far, the most common type of forensic phonetic analysis and so it is a peculiarity of the history of this field that the most famous case should happen to principally involve one of the least common tasks. Second, even by today's standards, the speaker profiling analysis carried out by Ellis was extremely impressive. It is unusual to be able to pinpoint the region associated with the accent of the unknown speaker to such a fine degree. Third, even when the case evolved from the unusual question of profiling analysis to the much more typical task of **forensic speaker comparison**, questioned and suspect recordings spanning 26 years are also extremely unusual. And fourth, it is remarkable that Humble was so cooperative. It is far more typical for suspects to attempt to disguise or alter their voices, leaving forensic phoneticians to struggle over comparisons that are much more challenging.

Despite all of this, the Yorkshire Ripper case is also one of very few instances that could be described as multimodal, where the two sides of the field – both language and sound – are brought together (see Chapters 10 and 16 for more on multimodality). It is also instructive for would-be forensic linguists to understand how their work might be seen or used, not only by an investigating police force, but also by the media, and even the public. And perhaps most importantly of all, it demonstrates just one way in which linguistics can have real-world relevance and application in the most critical fields and circumstances.

Notes

1 Subsequent analyses suggest that he may have been responsible for more.
2 In fact, by this stage multiple officers and outside experts were expressing the view that the communications were a hoax. This included other detectives, a surviving victim and a US profiling expert who was invited to comment on the case.

References

Bilton, M. 2003. *Wicked Beyond Belief: The Hunt for the Yorkshire Ripper.* London: HarperCollins.

Bloch, B. 1948. A set of postulates for phonemic analysis. *Language,* 24(1): 3–46.

Bosker, H. R. 2018. Putting Laurel and Yanny in context. *The Journal of the Acoustical Society of America,* 144(6): EL503–EL508.

Burn, G. 2011. *Somebody's Husband, Somebody's Son: The Story of the Yorkshire Ripper.* London: Faber & Faber.

Byford, S. L. 1981. The Yorkshire Ripper case: Review of the police investigation of the case by Larence Byford, Esq., CBE., QPM., Hey Majesty's inspector of constabulary. *Home Office,* December.

Chaski, C. E. 2005. Forensic linguistics, authorship attribution, and admissibility. In *Forensic Science and Law.* Boca Raton: CRC Press, pp. 533–550.

Coulthard, M. 1996. . . . *and Then . . . Language Description and Author Attribution.* http://www1.aston.ac.uk/EasySiteWeb/GatewayLink.aspx?alId=10186

Coulthard, M. and Johnson, A. 2010. *The Routledge Handbook of Forensic Linguistics*. London: Routledge.

Coulthard, M., Johnson, A. and Wright, D. 2016. *An Introduction to Forensic Linguistics: Language in Evidence*. London: Routledge.

Ellis, S. 1974. The survey of English dialects and social history. *Oral History*, 2(2): 37–43.

Ellis, S. 1994. Case report: The Yorkshire Ripper enquiry, Part 1. *Forensic Linguistics*, 1(ii): 197–206.

French, J. P., Harrison, P. and Windsor Lewis, J. 2006. R v John Samuel humble: The Yorkshire Ripper hoaxer trial. *The International Journal of Speech, Language and the Law*, 13(2): 255–273.

Holmes, D. I. and Tweedie, F. J. 1995. Forensic stylometry: A review of the cusum controversy. *Revue Informatique et Statistique dans les Sciences humaines*, XXXI: 19–47.

Hughes, E. C. 2018. A search by any other name: Google, genericism, and primary significance. *American University Business Law Review*, 7: 269–295.

Johnson, A. and Wright, D. 2014. Identifying idiolect in forensic authorship attribution: An n-gram textbite approach. *Language and Law/Linguagem e Direito*, 1(1): 37–69.

Leonard, R. A., Ford, J. E. R. and Christensen, T. K. 2016. Forensic linguistics: Applying the science of linguistics to issues of the law. *Hofstra Law Review*, 45(3): 501–517.

McMenamin, G. R. 1993. *Forensic Stylistics*. Amsterdam: Elsevier.

Office, C. 1984. *The Ripper Papers*. London: Cabinet Office.

Office, H. 1982. *Home Office Yorkshire Ripper Inquiry Papers*. London: Home Office.

Shank, C. and Foltz, A. 2019. *The Art of the Lie: Detecting Deception in Donald Trump's Statements*. Paper presented at the Germanic Society for Forensic Linguistics. https://research.bangor.ac.uk/portal/en/researchoutputs/the-art-of-the-lie-detecting-deception-in-donald-trumps-statements(73823a38-eaf9-4b57-98cb-ffac37979c77).html.

Solan, L. M. 2012. Intuition versus algorithm: The case of forensic authorship attribution. *Brooklyn Journal of Law and Policy*, 21: 551.

Stack, L. 2016. Yes, Trump is saying 'big league' not 'bigly'. *The New York Times*, 25.

The Telegraph. 2010. Ronald Gregory. *Obituaries*. 16 April.

Windsor Lewis, J. 1969. *Guide to English Pronunciation for Users of English as a Foreign Language*. Oslo: Universitetsforlaget.

Windsor Lewis, J. 2013. The Yorkshire Ripper enquiry: Part II. *International Journal of Speech Language and the Law*, 1(2): 207–216.

14 Health communication
Elena Semino

14.1 Introduction

Let us imagine a person called Charlie who wakes up one morning with some unusual symptoms that they find worrying enough to take action. This chapter will follow Charlie's imaginary journey from that morning to recovery, in order to show two things: first, how communication, both verbal and non-verbal, is central to the experience of illness and the practice of healthcare; and, second, how linguistics can make a contribution to understanding and, potentially improving, those experiences and practices.

I should emphasise that Charlie's symptoms and treatment are not intended to correspond to any specific illness, and that Charlie will be okay by the end of the chapter. At each point in Charlie's story, I will give an example of a linguistic study focusing on that particular stage, drawing from research involving a range of different conditions, settings and methods.

14.2 Communication in healthcare contexts

In this section, we will follow Charlie's story from symptom onset to recovery, in nine stages. These are (1) googling symptoms, (2) getting expert advice online, (3) making a medical appointment, (4) speaking with a healthcare professional, (5) attending an Accident and Emergency Department, (6) making decisions in the operating theatre, (7) reading press reports about illness, (8) reading published narratives of illness and (9) interacting on online patients' forums. For each stage, a study is introduced that applies a linguistic approach to communication in that particular setting, with a focus on implications for understanding and improving the experience of illness and the provision of healthcare.

14.2.1 Googling symptoms

Shortly after waking up feeling unwell, Charlie googles their symptoms. Many studies have shown that this is what most people with internet access do when they are worried about their health. However, Charlie is also aware that online

DOI: 10.4324/9781003045571-17

sources, and even more social media, are not always reliable for health-related information.

Vaccinations are a good example of an area where disinformation can lead to behaviours that undermine individual and societal health. Elkin et al. (2020) used a 7-point scale from 'pro-vaccine' to 'anti-vaccine' to classify the first 20 hits retrieved from vaccine-related searches on Google, Facebook and YouTube. They found that 50% of Facebook results and 25% of YouTube results were 'vaccine-sceptical' or 'vaccine-discouraging', whereas a smaller proportion of results from Google were in those categories (10%). They therefore concluded that vaccine-promoting public health agencies should strengthen their presence online, and particularly on social media, to counterbalance the negative information that users are likely to encounter on some platforms.

14.2.2 Getting expert health advice online

After reading some generic information online about the possible causes of the symptoms, Charlie finds an 'Ask the expert' webpage for health-related advice and decides to post a question under a pseudonym. Many studies have emphasised the usefulness of online opportunities to seek health-related advice anonymously, especially when the symptoms are potentially embarrassing or stigmatising. Harvey (2012), for example, combines corpus linguistics and discourse analysis to study a 1-million-word corpus of requests for advice to the 'Virtual Surgery' of a website dedicated to adolescents' health-related concerns: 'Teenage Health Freaks'.

Harvey used the corpus software WordSmith Tools to compare his corpus to a general 'reference' corpus of English, and identifies a group of 'keywords' (words that are statistically more frequent in his corpus than in the reference corpus; see also p. 395) that relate to mental health problems, such as 'depression', 'suicide' and 'self harm'. This leads him to zoom into the difference between the expressions 'I am depressed' and 'I have depression' in teenagers' messages. 'I am depressed' tends to be used to refer in a general way to negative feelings that are presented as the result of a specific cause, as in (1). It is important to note that spellings are as they appear in the original messages.

(1) I'm really depressed about splitting up with my boyfriend. I still like him and its getting me down. (Harvey 2012: 363)

In cases such as this, the person is asking for advice about the *cause* of the negative feelings. In contrast, 'I have depression' is used to refer to a diagnosed or diagnosable mental health condition, which is itself the focus of the request for advice, as in (2).

(2) I have depression, and it seems to be getting worse lately. i've been feeling horrible through most of the hols, and i still do even though im back at

school. i was thinking of dropping out, but ive decided to stay and drop a subject instead. but how can i make myself feel better? i'm putting my family through a lot of grief. (Harvey 2012: 365)

Through these analyses, Harvey provides new insights both into adolescents' experiences and perceptions of mental illness, and into the language that is used to express them.

A different perspective on 'Ask the expert' websites involves looking at how the answers to people's questions reflect the challenge of establishing both authority and rapport with anonymous advice-seekers. Mao and Zhao (2019), for example, analyse 1000 interactions from the Chinese medical consultation website 120ask .com. They identify three aspects of doctors' identities – professional, authoritative and personal – and point out how they are constructed linguistically. (3) is one of their examples (which they only provide in English translation):

(3) *Patient*: hello, when I was a child, I often developed a rash on my arms and legs which was more serious in winter. I want to know what it is and how to cure it.
Doctor: hello, my friend . . . then, we generally use Terbinafine Hydrochloride Powder (Mao and Zhao 2019: 1649)

In the doctor's reply, 'we' signals alignment with other experts, and therefore projects 'authoritative' identity. The reference to a specific medication ('Terbinafine Hydrochloride Powder'), like medical terminology more generally, establishes 'professional' identity. Finally, the informal vocative 'my friend' signals the 'personal' dimension of identity, and functions to reduce social distance with the advice-seeker.

14.2.3 Making a medical appointment

The following day, Charlie decides to make an appointment with a General Practitioner, or Primary Care Physician. This involves making a telephone call to a number that is staffed by receptionists, whose job is to triage callers, decide who they need to see or talk to (e.g. a doctor vs. a nurse) and how urgently, and give appointments. However, interactions between patients and medical receptionists are sometimes fraught, especially when, because of lack of resources, callers do not get an appointment as fast as they feel they need one, or not at all.

Stokoe et al. (2016) applied the detailed transcription techniques of conversation analysis to 447 calls to three GP surgeries in England, in order to identify features of interaction that are associated with effective communication and patient satisfaction in this particular setting.

Stokoe et al. noticed a contrast, for example, in the way in which receptionists dealt with patients' requests for appointments that could not be fulfilled. In most cases, receptionists did not suggest alternative solutions, meaning that the patient had to actively ask for further options to be explored. This is the case in (4). Here, 'P' stands for patient and 'R' for receptionist. The numbers in round brackets refer to pauses expressed in seconds. The round brackets indicate unclear talk, aligned square brackets indicate overlapping talk, and lines are numbered for ease of reference.

(4)   1 **R:** Good morning, surgery Cath
    2   speaking,
    3   (1.6)
    4 **P:** Hello have you got an
    5   appointment for
    6   Friday afternoon or teatime please.
    7   (0.4)
    8 **R:** This Friday.
    9   (1.1)
  10 **P:** Yeah,
  11 **R:** Uh I'm sorry we're fully booked
  12   on Friday.
  13   (1.6)
  14 **P:** Right.
  15   (0.3)
  16 **R:** (We're) fully booked.
  17 **P:** Okay.
  18   (0.3)
  19 **R:** Okay.
  20   (0.4)
  21 **P:** Yeah, uh okay, [uhm,]
  22 **R:**   [Than]k yo[u]
  23 **P:**   [Is] it
  24   worth me ringing Flaxton.
  25 **R:** We're fully booked this Friday at
  26   Flaxton I can see, wi- we don't
  27   open
  28   Fri[day afternoon] ns at Flaxton
  29 **P:**   [As   well.]
  30 **R:** It's just Friday mornings.
  31   (0.6)
  32 **P:** Oh right, [o]kay.
  33 **R:**   [yeah.]
  34 **R:** Sorry we're [fully booked] there.
  35 **P:**   [Thank you.]
  36   (0.3)
  37 **R:** Okay.
  38   (0.4)
  39 **P:** Thanks.
  40 **R:** Thank yo[u.]

41 P: [By][e.]
42 R: [B]ye, bye.

After informing the patient that the surgery is fully booked on the relevant day, the receptionist is about to end the interaction ('Thank you' in line 22), and it is the patient who suggests a different surgery, which the receptionist also confirms is fully booked. As neither party suggests further possibilities, the interaction ends with no appointment being booked. Stokoe et al. suggest that this pattern creates what they call 'patient burden', as patients have to actively pursue solutions to their problem, and may ultimately be unsuccessful, as is the case in (4).

Patient burden is avoided, however, when receptionists proactively offer alternatives when the patient's immediate request cannot be fulfilled. In (5), for example, the receptionist offers to look for appointments further into the future when it transpires that none are available in the same week. Here, the same conventions are followed as in (4), but note that the 'equal' symbol = indicates lack of any gap between turns.

(5)   1 R: Good morning, Limetown Surgery,
      2 P: =Good morning, Could I have an
      3   appointment to see
      4   Doctor Wilkinson please=
      5 R: =.ptkhhh hh uh:m let me see when
      6   the next available
      7   one is.=I don't think I've got
      8   anything pre bookable
      9   this week .h [hh   ] d'you want me=
     10 P: [(uhum)]
     11 R: =to look for the week after.

A similar contrast was identified in the closing of calls, where more effective receptionists avoid patient burden by summarising what has been agreed (e.g. the date and time of the appointment), rather than leaving it up to the patient to confirm the relevant details or experience potential uncertainty.

Stokoe et al. coded their transcripts for instances of patient burden. By doing so, they found an association between patient burden in the interactions for each of the three GP surgeries and patient satisfaction, as captured in routine questionnaires. Lower frequencies of patient burden were associated with higher satisfaction scores. These findings, Stokoe et al. suggest, have implications for the training of receptionists:

> Key 'trainables' are to confirm appointment details or next actions at the end of calls and offer alternative courses of action if patients' initial request cannot be met.
>
> (Stokoe et al. 2016: e783)

In this way, patient burden can be decreased or avoided, resulting in greater satisfaction and effectiveness of interactions.

14.2.4 Speaking with a healthcare professional

Charlie's conversation with the receptionist is successful, and they are given an appointment with a nurse at the local medical practice for later on the same day. Interactions with doctors and nurses, however, can involve further challenges. In many health systems, there are pressures of time, so that the healthcare professionals have a set number of minutes for each patient. In addition, the healthcare professional and patient do not always know each other, and there are differences in power and expertise to be negotiated. For all these reasons, a large literature exists on interactions between patients and different types of healthcare professionals, including from a linguistic perspective.

A study by Vickers and Goble (2018), for example, focuses on how the power relationship between healthcare professional and patient is co-constructed via the politeness strategies (see also X) and prosodic cues used by the former and the latter's response to them. Vickers and Goble analysed interactions between nurses and patients in a bilingual (English-Spanish) community clinic in California, and identified a contrast between the adoption of what they call an 'authoritarian' communicative style and an 'egalitarian' communicative style on the part of the health professionals.

In terms of politeness, an authoritarian communicative style involves minimal attention to the patient's 'negative face', defined in Brown and Levinson's Politeness Theory (1987) as the desire to be free to do what one wants. This applies to (6), for example. Here, a nurse, referred to as Laura, delivers decisions about the patient's exercise and dietary regime as a list of noun phrases. This leaves little or no space for the patient to express their preferences or put forward any objections. Here, 'L' stands for Laura and 'B' is the patient; translation from Spanish as provided in the original paper):

(6) 1 L: *ejercicio didario*
daily exercise
2 B: *((xxx)) difícil*
3 L: *(Hx) . . . nada de frituras . . . queso . . . mayonesa..mantequilla..*
4 *[carne a res]*
(Hx) . . . nothing of fruit..cheese . . . mayonnaise..butter..
[beef]
5 B: [oh okay]=
6 L: *=y de puerco..esos son los que son más altos*
=and pork..these are the highest ones (Vickers and Goble 2018: 212)

In contrast, an egalitarian communicative style is exemplified by another nurse, Carrie, in (7). When making a similar recommendation, Carrie reduces the power differential in her relationship with the patient by paying attention to their negative face. Here, 'C' is Carrie and 'S' is the patient). This is described as a more patient-centred approach:

(7) 1 C: *u:m:: what else do we want to talk about? está?*
    u:m:: what else do we want to talk about? are you
  2   *haciendo ejercicio?*
    doing exercise?
  3 S: *(1.0) poco*
    (1.0) a little
  4   C: *sí?*
    yes?
  5 S: *pero no tengo..tiempo*
    but I don't have..time
  6 C: *no? está trabajando mucho?=*
    no? are you working a lot?=
  7 S: *=sí=*
    =yes=

[17 turns of discussion about the patient's work commitments and weekly routine]

  24 C: *mhm..pero..si puede hacer algo: aeróbico..por*
  25   *ejemplo..caminando por diez minutos..pero..pronto*
    mhm..but..if you can do somethi:ng aerobic..for
    example..walking for ten minutes..but..fast
  26 S: [mhm]
  27 C: *[cami]nado muy rápido..entonces es más ejercicio*
  28   *es solamente dura diez minutos..si puede hacer los*
  29   *dos días cuando no trabaja? . . . solamente..toma un – un*
  30   *paseo <TSK> okay?*
    [walk]ing very fast..then it's more exercise
    it only lasts ten minutes..if you can do [it]
    the two days when you don't work . . . just..take a-a
    paseo <TSK> okay?
  31 S: *está bien=*
    it's fine= (Vickers and Goble 2018: 207–208)

In (7), Carrie broaches the topic of exercise by first inviting the patient to control the topic and then asking them questions about their current lifestyle. She then recommends some exercise via a hypothetical scenario in which the patient finds opportunities to do some fast walking within their current weekly routine, and minimises the degree of change to that routine by using 'solamente' ('only') in 'es solamente dura diez minutos' ('it only lasts ten minutes').

The study's authors point out that these differences have potential implications for the patients' health outcomes, as more patient-centred approaches to interaction have been found to lead to higher patient satisfaction and better compliance with recommendations, such as taking more exercise.

14.2.5 Attending an Accident and Emergency Department

The nurse examines Charlie, consults with a doctor and advises Charlie that their condition requires immediate medical attention in hospital. Therefore, an ambulance is called and Charlie is taken to the Accident and Emergency Department in the local hospital.

Effective communication in hospital Emergency Departments is both crucially important and particularly complex and challenging. This is due to a range of pressures, including lack of time, the patients' clinical conditions, the number of different people that are involved in the care of each patient and the fact that the patient is usually not already known to any of them. Slade et al. (2008) conducted a large-scale study of interactions in the Emergency Department of a large public teaching hospital in Sydney, Australia. Among other things, this study was motivated by evidence that ineffective communication had been identified as 'the major cause of critical incidents in Australian public hospitals', namely, 'adverse events leading to avoidable patient harm' (Slade et al. 2008: 272).

In Slade et al.'s study, several linguistic frameworks are used to identify aspects of interactions between patients and healthcare professionals that may result in less than adequate communication. They notice, for example, how doctors' contributions are primarily characterised by questions. By contrast, patients rarely ask questions, even though they often reveal in follow-up interviews that they were confused about what was being said to them and/or what was happening around them. In one case, a doctor asked 145 questions in an interaction with a patient while the patient asked no questions at all (Slade et al. 2008: 284–285).

Detailed analysis of transcripts also revealed that, in some cases, doctors' sequences of questions did not fully take into account patients' answers, as in (8):

(8) *Doctor*: Have you been eating and drinking sort of reasonably normally?
    Patient: I drink but I haven't been eating −−
    Family: ==She hasn't been eating well because she's just had a recent death in the family.==
    Doctor: OK==
    Family: == A couple of days ago.==
    Doctor: OK.==
    Family: ==Which is her grandmamma.==
    Doctor: OK.

> *Family*: So she's been spending a lot of time at her mother's house and no she hasn't been eating well obviously distressed because of that.
>
> *Doctor*: OK. Sure but you've been keeping up your fluids and drinking and==?

Here the doctor begins with a question about 'eating and drinking . . . reasonably normally' and later rephrases it as 'you've been keeping up your fluids and drinking' after the patient and a relative reveal that the patient has not been eating. However, what is not picked up by the doctor is the reason that the family member provides for the lack of eating, a recent bereavement. The privileging of a biomedical perspective (is the patient eating and drinking?) over a psychosocial, lifeworld perspective (*why* has this person stopped eating?) is understandable in the context of multiple pressures. However, it undermines the kind of rapport between doctors and patients that facilitates the disclosure of information, and may lead to important clues being missed.

Slade et al. (2008: 293) use their analyses to argue that, in order to achieve a more patient-centred care, 'clinicians need an integrated understanding of the patients' world, that is, their whole person, their emotional needs, and life issues'.

14.2.6 Making decisions in the operating theatre

At the hospital, Charlie is triaged and fast tracked for a CAT scan. After reviewing the scan, the medical team decide that Charlie should be kept in hospital, as they need surgery. The following day, Charlie is wheeled to an operating theatre and placed under general anaesthetic.

The success of operations relies on a combination of multiple interacting factors, including effective communication among the members of the surgical team and appropriate and timely decision-making. Bezemer et al. (2016) studied the process of surgical decision-making in video-recordings of 11 laparoscopic cholecystectomies (removal of the gallbladder) in a large teaching hospital in London.

They noticed two main components of decision-making on the part of the operating surgeon: participation and rationalisation. Participation is to do with the extent to which the surgeon seeks agreement from the rest of the team before the key moment in the operation – the cutting of the cystic duct. Decision-making was described as 'unilateral' when there was no evidence of agreement being sought, and as 'multilateral' when the operating surgeon asked colleagues questions such as 'Shall I take that down?' or 'Agreed?' before cutting the duct.

Rationalisation is to do with whether the operating surgeon points out evidence that suggests that the cutting of the duct can take place. The contrast in this case is between implicit decision-making, where the surgeon does not articulate the evidence they have, and explicit decision-making, when the surgeon uses expressions such as 'that's the duct' or 'that's what you call the critical view'. Whether or not rationalisation was explicit, the video-recordings showed that surgeons also tended to perform a gesture that demonstrated that there was enough space around the duct for it to be cut safely, such as sweeping a surgical instrument up and down and around the duct.

The analysis showed that, with regard to participation, six out of 11 operations involved multilateral decision-making. More specifically, there was evidence that a unilateral approach was more likely to be taken when the operating surgeon was a consultant and the assistant was particularly junior. With regard to rationalisation, nine out of 11 operations were found to involve explicit decision-making. The two instances of implicit decision-making were the two shortest (and by implication easiest) operations, which suggests that rationalisation may correlate with the difficulty of the surgical process.

Bezemer et al. point out how the tendency to provide a verbally explicit rationale for key surgical decisions provides an important opportunity for training students and junior team members. The detailed analysis of video-recordings, they suggest, 'makes visible how cognitive processes become shared and distributed, providing significant opportunities for trainees to learn how to "think like a surgeon" and for consultants to reflect on their own judgement before making critical decisions' (Bezemer et al. 2016: 754).

14.2.7 Reading press reports about illness

Charlie's operation is successful and they are discharged after a few days. While convalescing at home, Charlie spends a lot of time reading, and is particularly attracted to anything that relates to their health condition, including in the mainstream media. What strikes Charlie, however, is the way in which that health condition is represented in order to make it newsworthy.

Many studies have looked at how different illnesses are portrayed in the media generally and the press in particular, often with a focus on sensationalisation and the potential for harmful misrepresentations. Brookes et al. (2018), for example, studied both verbal and visual patterns in reports about dementia in the UK press, drawing from the tools of Critical Discourse Analysis (see also Chapters 10 and 16). They collected 11 articles that appeared in ten national newspapers in the two days following the release of a press bulletin by the British Office for National Statistics in which it was reported that dementia had become the leading cause of death in England and Wales, ahead of cancer and heart disease. The analysis shows how the articles portray the condition as a destructive agentive force, and people with the condition as devoid of agency and identity. The ways in which this is achieved include choices of metaphors and visual images.

In nine out of the ten newspapers, dementia was personified as a highly effective killer that cannot be stopped:

(9) Dementia and Alzheimer's disease overtakes heart disease as our biggest killer. (*Express*)
(10) What is dementia, what are the symptoms and how does it kill? (*Metro*)

(11) Dementia is now the biggest killer so it must become top medical priority. *(Mirror)*

(12) BRITAIN's biggest killer has no known cure. (*The Sun*)

(13) Dementia becomes Britain's biggest killer. (*Telegraph*)

(14) Dementia kills more than heart disease. (*Times*)

(Brookes et al. 2018: 375)

Metaphors are framing devices that both reflect and influence how we think about different topics. In the scenarios of violence evoked by 'killer' metaphors, for example, the disease is attributed the power to cause extreme harm, and people with dementia are implicitly positioned as helpless victims.

In addition, Brookes et al. found that the visual components of the articles were mostly stock images involving either close-ups of wrinkled hands or an elderly person bringing a hand to their head while being physically supported by a younger and/or healthier person. Both kinds of images suggest that people with dementia are elderly, frail and inactive. The 'wrinkled hands' images are also dehumanising, as a part of the body stands for the whole person, while the images that involve people suggest distress and dependency on others.

Cumulatively, Brookes et al. argue, these press representations therefore perpetuate negative, distressing and stigmatising perceptions of dementia and of the people affected by it, at the expense of stories and images reflecting the variety of ways in which people are able to live meaningful and active lives in spite of having dementia.

In focus: what metaphors should or should not be used to talk about illness?

The language that is used to communicate about illness can become controversial. This applies, for example, to the use of 'battle' or 'fight' as metaphors for having cancer, as in 'She died after a long battle with cancer'. In the book *Illness as Metaphor*, American sociologist Susan Sontag (1978) put forward several objections to these metaphors, including that they reduce patients to the battlefield on which doctors wage war against the illness. In 2014, Kate Granger – a British doctor in her 30s with a terminal cancer diagnosis – wrote these comments in a national newspaper:

'She lost her brave fight.' If anyone mutters those words after my death, wherever I am, I will curse them.

I would like to be remembered for the positive impact I have made on the world, for fun times and for my relationships with others, not as a loser. When I do die, I will have defied the prognosis for my type of cancer and achieved a great deal with my life. I do not want to feel a failure about something beyond my control. I refuse to believe my death will be because I didn't battle hard enough.

(Granger 2014)

With colleagues at Lancaster University, I have used corpus linguistic methods to show how metaphors to do with fighting can indeed be harmful for people with cancer, as Granger suggests, but can also be empowering for some people (Semino et al. 2017). As an outcome of the research, we produced a 'Metaphor Menu for People Living with Cancer' – a collection of metaphors drawn from actual language use that provide a range of different ways of talking and thinking about cancer, from singing to fairground rides.

Debates about the appropriateness of different metaphors for cancer and other illnesses, such as dementia and COVID-19, are likely to continue, however.

You can find the Metaphor Menu here: http://wp.lancs.ac.uk/melc/the-metaphor-menu/.

SCAN ME

14.2.8 Reading published narratives of illness

When Charlie mentions to a friend that they have been disappointed by media reports on their condition, the friend recommends a book written by someone who had had a similar health problem. Charlie reads the book and finds it reassuring and empowering to discover that the author had experienced similar symptoms, fears and challenges.

Autobiographical narratives of illness are increasingly being studied for the insights they can provide into the lived experience of people diagnosed with different conditions. Such narratives provide first person perspectives on illness from people who are 'experts by experience', and as such are an important complement to the third person perspectives on illness that are provided by professional experts in texts such as scientific articles and medical textbooks.

Zsófia Demjén and I, for example, applied a linguistic perspective to a book co-authored by a young man with a diagnosis of schizophrenia, Henry Cockburn, and his father Patrick: *Henry's Demons. Living with Schizophrenia: A Father's and Son's Story* (Demjén and Semino 2015). In the chapters he contributed to the book, Henry provides a candid and vivid account of the experiences that led to his diagnosis, including hearing voices that other people cannot hear (also known 'auditory verbal hallucinations'):

(15) 'Never lie, Henry', they |the trees| replied.
(16) I felt the tree telling me to take off my shoes.

In extract 15, Henry uses direct speech, a form of speech presentation conventionally associated with verbatim reports, to represent the voices. In extract 16, he uses indirect speech, which involves a summary of the content of the utterance attributed to the voice, from the perspective of the person doing the reporting. In our analysis we found that, out of 49 representations of what the voices say in Henry's chapters, only seven (14%) are in direct speech. This contrasts both with what is generally the case in narratives and in Henry's reports of voices that others can also hear, where between 40% and 50% of instances are direct speech. Example 16 also exemplifies another pattern in Henry's narrative: the use of the verb 'feel'. Here, this is associated with the sense of touch, to represent the perception of an act of telling, which is conventionally associated with the sense of hearing. Henry uses 'feel' repeatedly for voices that only he can hear, but never for voices that others can also hear. In combination, these findings provide linguistic evidence for a potential difference between Henry's experience of his own private voices and voices that are accessible to others; namely, that the former are in fact not necessarily auditory in nature, but rather involve the sensation of communication being received through senses other than hearing. This would make the 'verbatim' representation associated with direct speech less appropriate.

Studies such as ours show how detailed attention to the words used in first person narratives can provide insights into the lived experience of illness. These complement or extend those produced in different research fields through different methods, such as interviews by clinical psychologists where voice-hearers are asked explicit questions about the characteristics of their voices.

14.2.9 Interacting on online patients' forums

During the period of recovery, Charlie also joins an online forum for people with the same condition, and finds it so useful that they continue to contribute to it even after making a full recovery.

Research from different disciplines has shown both the value and potential pitfalls of 'peer-to-peer' health-related online forums, where people with similar diagnoses interact with one another. On the one hand, there is evidence of the potential for misinformation and conflict that results from the ability to communicate without revealing one's identity. On the other hand, there is also ample evidence that such forums provide an important source of advice, validation and emotional support for people with a variety of health conditions.

A linguistic study by Demjén (2016) employed a combination of corpus linguistic methods and qualitative discourse analysis to highlight and investigate the use of humour in exchanges on an online forum for people with cancer, as in this post:

(17)   It's just one of the evil Mr Crab's funny little jokes that we now have to spend our lives thinking not just 'What shall I have for tea?' but 'What shall I have for this random nameless meal – that I am having at an odd time because I couldn't face food till now – that won't kill me?' I am pretty sure that my own evil Mr Crab has taken control of my stomach-to-brain signals. He gets hungry in the night, and demands steak and chips. I don't eat meat!! Bastard. (Demjén 2016: 22)

This kind of post, Demjén finds, is part of a broader pattern where the cancer is humorously personified via a proper name and title ('Mr Crab') and via the attribution of the characteristics and behaviours of an irritatingly devious agent. Through this kind of humour (further enhanced, in the extract, by the swearword 'Bastard'), forum contributors distance themselves from the illness and from potentially distressing symptoms (e.g. being hungry at unpredictable times), and therefore empower themselves to cope better with their situation. In addition, Demjén shows how the use of similar kinds of humour by different people on the forum can create and strengthen the social bonds among them, providing a sense of belonging that can improve people's morale and quality of life.

Studies such as this do not just lead to important insights into people's experiences of illness, but can also provide the evidence needed for setting up and running online forums, or for recommending them to newly diagnosed people who might benefit from them.

14.3 Conclusion

In this chapter, we have seen that linguistics can make important contributions to understanding and improving the experience of illness and the provision of healthcare. If you would like to learn more about this subject, Harvey and Koteyko (2012) and Demjén (2020) are both excellent books which provide overviews of linguistic approaches to health communication.

References

Bezemer, J., Murtagh, G., Cope, A. and Kneebone, R. 2016. Surgical decision making in a teaching hospital: A linguistic analysis. *ANZ Journal of Surgery*, 86(10): 751–755.

Brookes, G., Harvey, K., Chadborn, N. and Dening, T. 2018. 'Our biggest killer': Multimodal discourse representations of dementia in the British press. *Social Semiotics*, 28(3): 371–395.

Brown, P. and Levinson, S. C. 1987. *Politeness: Some Universals in Language Usage*. Cambridge and New York: Cambridge University Press.

Demjén, Z. 2016. Laughing at cancer: Humour, empowerment, solidarity and coping online. *Journal of Pragmatics*, 101: 18–30.

Demjén, Z. (Ed.). 2020. *Applying Linguistics in Illness and Healthcare Contexts*. London: Bloomsbury.

Demjén, Z. and Semino, E. 2015. Henry's voices: The representation of auditory verbal hallucinations in an autobiographical narrative. *BMJ Medical Humanities*, 41: 57–62.

Elkin, L. E., Pullon, S. R. H. and Stubbe, M. H. 2020. 'Should I vaccinate my child?' comparing the displayed stances of vaccine information retrieved from Google, Facebook and YouTube. *Vaccine*, 38(13): 2771–2778.

Granger, K. 2014. Having cancer is not a fight or a battle. *The Guardian*. www .theguardian.com/society/2014/apr/25/having-cancer-not-fight-or-battle

Harvey, K. 2012. Disclosures of depression: Using corpus linguistics methods to examine young people's online health concerns. *International Journal of Corpus Linguistics*, 17(3): 349–379.

Harvey, K. and Koteyko, N. 2012. *Exploring Health Communication: Language in Action*. London: Routledge.

Mao, Y. and Zhao, X. 2019. I am a doctor, and here is my proof: Chinese doctors' identity constructed on the online medical consultation websites. *Health Communication*, 34(13): 1645–1652.

Semino, E., Demjén, Z., Demmen, J., Koller, V., Payne, S., Hardie, H. and Rayson, P. 2017. The online use of 'Violence' and 'Journey' metaphors by cancer patients, as compared with health professionals: A mixed methods study. *BMJ Supportive and Palliative Care*, 71: 60–66.

Slade, D., Scheeres, H., Manidis, M., et al. 2008. Emergency communication: The discursive challenges facing emergency clinicians and patients in hospital emergency departments. *Discourse & Communication*, 2(3): 271–298.

Sontag, S. 1978. *Illness as Metaphor*. New York: Farrar, Straus and Giroux.

Stokoe, E., Sikveland, R. O. and Symonds, J. 2016. Calling the GP surgery: Patient burden, patient satisfaction, and implications for training. *British Journal of General Practice*, 66(652): e779–e785.

Vickers, C. and Goble, R. 2018. Politeness and prosody in the co-construction of medical provider persona styles and patient relationships. *Journal of Applied Linguistics and Professional Practice*, 11(2): 202–226.

15 Language in the curriculum
Oksana Afitska and John Clegg

15.1 Introduction

In many parts of the world, learners learn through a language which is not their most fluent. In some of these contexts, education is successful in that learners learn effectively both curricular contents and the language of instruction (LoI). In others it is less successful; because learners do not have sufficient fluency in the LoI, they struggle in school and their education is often damaged. This chapter discusses these varying forms of schooling in a second language.

In this chapter, we will refer to the child's most fluent language as their first language or L1. This language is likely to be used at home or in the community; very often, it is the language the child will also use at school. However, children who learn in a second language – or L2 – are learning in a language which may not be used in the home. It may be used in the community; but in some cases, it may only be used at school. In these forms of what we will call L2-medium education, learners learn in a language in which they are not fluent.

The chapter will discuss both those forms of L2-medium education which succeed and those which do not, or which make schooling difficult. We will specify which features of the social and school context of these forms of education co-determine their very different outcomes (for example the educational background of parents, the level of language ability of learners). We will also suggest the kinds of pedagogy which help learners to flourish in those forms of L2-medium education which seem to work, and those which could help learners to avoid the risks of educational damage in the contexts in which it tends to occur.

15.2 Education in a second language as an advantage

When learners learn successfully in L2, this is often measured by reference to two criteria: how well they have learned curricular subjects (such as maths, physics, history) and how well they have learned the LoI itself. Some models of L2-medium education claim success in these two senses. This is true of

DOI: 10.4324/9781003045571-18

immersion education, bilingual education and Content and Language Integrated Learning (CLIL) which are explained next and summarised in Table 15.1. All these programmes are non-compulsory: schools opt to run them. Although they may be fairly common, they cater for comparatively small populations.

Immersion education is associated primarily with North America and in particular Canada, where English-speaking learners may learn the whole or part of the school curriculum in French. Learning aims for 'additive bilingualism': in other words, the school explicitly supports the development of both languages – in Canada L1 (English) and L2 (French); it does not replace the L1. Learners may begin immersion schooling with only initial L2 ability. Immersion education tends to attract learners from family backgrounds with high socio-economic status (SES) (Cummins 2000). The family may be educated and have a good income; they may speak a high-status language (normally English); learners may often have learned to read in their home language (English) and parents value the opportunity for education in French.

In focus: L1, L2 and LoI

L1: a speaker's first language. It is often acquired in the home and is often the main language used in the community, for example, English in the UK or Kiswahili in parts of Africa. For minority language users it may not be widely used in the community as with, say, Urdu speakers in the UK; or it may be used in a local bilingual community as with Spanish speakers in the US. In some contexts, learners will have good fluency in more than one such local language: many learners in sub-Saharan Africa (SSA) are fluent in two or more L1s. In this sense L1 does not actually mean a 'first-acquired' language, but simply a language in which the learner is fluent at an early age. L1-medium education means education delivered in a learner's L1.

L2: a speaker's second language. It is often not acquired in the home. For some learners it may remain a foreign language encountered only in school. For others it may be acquired with fluency in the community, as with minority language users such as some UK Urdu speakers or American Spanish speakers. Sometimes it may not be widely used in the community, as in parts of Africa, but largely learned in school. L2-medium education refers to education delivered in a learner's L2.

LoI: language of instruction. This is the language in which education is delivered and is often the learner's most fluent language (i.e. the L1). It is often the main language used in the community, as for instance, English in the UK. For some other learners, however, this is not the case. In the education of language minorities, such as Urdu speakers in the UK, or of language majorities such as speakers of African languages in SSA, a

---

learner's L2 is used as language of instruction. Sometimes the LoI is the dominant language in the community, but sometimes it is a foreign language, as is the case in bilingual, immersion or CLIL educational models.

Table 15.1 Key features of successful L2-medium education programmes.

	Immersion	Bilingual education	CLIL
Proportion of curriculum	Most subjects	Most subjects	One or two subjects
Additive/subtractive view of bilingualism	Additive	Additive	Additive
Parents' SES	Often high	High or low	Often high
Parental motivation	High	Often high	High
Age range	Primary and secondary	Primary and secondary	Mainly secondary
Language ability of learners	May start low	May start low	Minimum entry level required

Bilingual education is available in various parts of the world and in different forms. It is normally offered to homogeneous language groups. As in immersion, educational bilingualism aims to be 'additive': it adds an additional language to the first. Similarly, learners may start a programme with initial ability in the L2. Programmes are sometimes referred to as 'maintenance bilingual education' (e.g. in the USA) because they aim to maintain a child's ability in a minority home language which might otherwise be lost in a community in which a majority language predominates. Roughly half of curriculum time is taught in a learner's home language (i.e. in their L1). Other programmes are referred to as 'dual language' programmes, where roughly equal numbers of learners, speaking different languages as their L1s, are taught in the same classroom through two languages, separating LoIs on alternate days or in alternate lessons. Although bilingual education is equally valuable for learners from all social backgrounds, it is sometimes chosen by high-SES parents with high-status home languages in educated families. However, as we mention later, in some contexts such as the USA, it is also offered to minority learners who may have lower-status languages and socially disadvantaged home circumstances.

CLIL has its roots in Europe, often in countries with high levels of exposure to a L2, such as the Nordic countries, but also in contexts where lower exposure is common, for example Spain. The LoI can be one of several European languages but is often English. Schools tend to offer one or two subjects through the medium of the L2; CLIL does not often involve large proportions of the curriculum. For this reason, it also sees bilingualism as 'additive': learners add a second fluent language to their first. Learners fairly often – but certainly not always – come from high-SES family backgrounds; many are often already literate and well-educated in primary school in their L1. Learners are normally expected to have sufficiently high L2 ability when they embark on a CLIL subject. Parental motivation is high, and schools sometimes feel pushed by the community to offer a programme.

15.3 Education in a second language as a barrier

Whereas the forms of schooling outlined previously are largely valued in the communities which practise them and are shown to achieve good levels of curricular content knowledge and L2 ability, in other parts of the world, the education of far larger communities of learners is often damaged by learning in an additional language. This is visible in particular in two groups of learners: first, language minority learners learning in a community in which they do not yet speak the language of the majority, for example speakers with home language Spanish in the USA, or Urdu in the UK; and second, language majority learners who are required to abandon their home/community language at an early point in their school career and learn in a language in which they have initially low proficiency. This happens, for example, in sub-Saharan Africa[1] (SSA), where children are fluent in an African language but learn through the medium of a post-colonial language such as English, which they may not speak well.

When we talk of minority language users in industrialised countries, we tend to focus on the USA, Canada, the UK, the EU and Australia. Here, language minority learners are those who may be immigrants to a particular country and who may enter the school system at any point from the start of schooling onwards. They may also be the children of settled immigrants who speak a language other than the majority LoI at home. They are often placed in mainstream classrooms regardless of their ability in the LoI – what is called a 'submersion' strategy (Thomas and Collier 2002) – often with very little or no support. If they are offered support, this may take the form of specialist teaching of the LoI for which learners may be withdrawn from the mainstream classroom.

The school achievement of minority language users differs considerably according to their ethnic background, SES, family education, school language policy, age and L2 proficiency. In England, for example, English as an Additional Language (EAL) pupils with lower English proficiency do less well in school in English and maths than English L1 speakers (Strand and Lindorff 2021). However, their English improves with time: in reception classes 29% of EAL pupils were competent or fluent in English but by years 10/11 this figure had risen to 85% (Strand and Lindorff, op. cit.). In terms of general educational achievement, EAL pupils in the UK catch up with English L1 speakers by age 16. In California The 74 (2021) states that nearly 40% of California's children have English as L2 and that of these, 90% did not meet English and maths standards in 2018–2019. In relation to SES, English language learners in the USA are likely to live in families with low incomes and lower levels of schooling (National Academies of Sciences 2017). In relation to ethnic background, some communities perform better or worse than average: for example, pupils in England with Indian backgrounds have higher than average achievement (Strand and Lindorff, op. cit.). Importantly, local education policy counts. For example, in the USA minority language users learn better when supported by bilingual education (Thomas and Collier 2002).

Minority language users are often a numerical minority in the classroom. However, education in a non-fluent LoI also happens in some majority language communities. In this second type of context, an explicit decision is made by government to avoid using the majority language as the main language of education. Instead, an 'imported' language is used for learning across the whole school system, either throughout schooling or after the early years. This happens in former colonies in South and South-east Asia (mainly English), in South America (Spanish) and in particular in SSA (mainly English, French and Portuguese). This imported LoI is often a colonial language, one which is not widely used for social purposes in the community, though as an 'official' language it is used for political and media functions. On entering school learners will often have had little social exposure to it; they may experience it mainly in school and may therefore not use it very widely.

In SSA, in most – though not all – countries which impose the use of English as LoI, education in the early years takes place normally in an African language for the first three years. After this period, learners switch to using English as LoI for almost all subjects throughout schooling. The English language ability of learners as they change LoI is normally well below the ability which they need in order to be able to use the language for learning, creating a large 'language gap' (Clegg 2021). In South Africa, Macdonald (1993) measured learners' English vocabulary at the switch of medium at 500 items, whereas the vocabulary demands of the new English-medium curriculum were 8000. In Tanzania, Uwezo (2012) found that 45% of Tanzanian learners in year 8 (the beginning of English-medium schooling in Tanzania) could not read a year 2 text in English. Learners learn L2 in the years preceding the switch, but not enough, and the language demands of the subject curriculum at the switch and thereafter are too high (Clegg op. cit.). Multilingual learning which might ease the transition is normally prohibited. The transition from one LoI to another is hard for both learners and teachers, teachers code switch – they move in and out of the learners' L1 – as a way of achieving comprehension in the classroom. Educational attainment is often very much lower than it should be (Erling et al. 2021). Consequent low standards of schooling have a damaging effect on the generation of skills and on national economies (Erling et al. op. cit.). There is a lively and wide-ranging debate over the damage caused by educational language policy in SSA (Erling et al. op. cit.), but ministries tend to insist on sticking to a policy which damages schooling (Dutcher 2004). International stakeholders – such as NGOs and national aid agencies – have been slow in recognising this damage (Clegg 2019), but key bodies such as the World Bank (2021) now clearly accept the extent of educational harm: UNESCO recently published an article (UNESCO 2016) titled 'If You Don't Understand, How Can You Learn?'.

In all these contexts, and in contrast to the forms of schooling outlined in the previous section, learners often find learning hard, slow and ineffective. They may perform well below their ability, take too long to achieve or drop out early. Their sense of self, confidence and culture may be undermined. In these circumstances education in L2 is a potentially harmful experience.

15.4 Reasons for success in second language-medium education

Several groups of reasons (see Table 15.2) can be said to influence the effectiveness of forms of L2-medium education. In this and the following section we look at both effective and failing models from these viewpoints.

Additive bilingual education

Effective learning in L2 builds on and maintains the learner's L1; it exemplifies 'additive bilingual education'. The learner becomes bilingual and biliterate. The L1 is maintained throughout schooling, sometimes as a partial LoI. Learners' culture and literature is sustained, so that they feel that their identity is respected. Immersion and bilingual education often assume as a principle that this form of education aims to maintain linguistic, cultural and racial equality. CLIL programmes are also bilingually additive but represent less of a threat to L1 language and culture because they occupy much less than half a learner's curriculum time.

Socio-economic status and educational background

Family background can affect a learner's success in learning in L2. It is sometimes suggested that learners in immersion projects, for example, tend to have high-status home languages (Cummins 2000). They also tend to be literate in this language and will preserve their facility in it throughout schooling and in wider society. In addition, they will benefit from the kind of parental support for literacy and cognitive development in general which has become widely associated with an educated family background. CLIL projects are also fairly often, but by no means exclusively, engaged in by learners from higher SES and educational backgrounds. Parents often speak a high-status language at home. Parental aspiration can be a factor: as mentioned earlier, parents in some countries put pressure on schools to offer programmes. In addition, since many programmes start in secondary school, many CLIL learners have benefited from developing literacy, cognitive skills and good levels of curricular content knowledge in their L1 in their primary schools. Crucially, they may also have acquired the language of schooling also known as cognitive academic language proficiency (CALP) (Cummins 2000) in their L1. As we explain, this experience of L1-medium education and in particular of CALP in the L1 stands them in good stead when they come to learn subjects in L2.

Bilingual education, by contrast, while it may be used in some parts of the world by learners from more educated backgrounds, is undoubtedly a form of provision available to learners who are socially disadvantaged. This is particularly the case in the USA where many states have in recent years chosen to offer bilingual education to learners from ethnolinguistic minorities. Persuasive research (Thomas and Collier 2002) has convinced education authorities that bilingual education, with its support for learners' first languages and cultures, can enable minority learners to achieve better than other available forms of school language policy.

In focus: BICS and CALP

BICS: Basic Interpersonal Communication Skills. This is an informal variety of language. We use it in our informal social lives at home, work and in the community; often orally, but also in writing – as for example in letters to friends. It is characterised by a relatively small vocabulary containing many high-frequency, low-specificity words (such as *have, place, people*) and by relatively simple grammar. In the classroom it is used to talk freely about new concepts, but this talk often becomes more formal and leads on to writing and reading about them, which often requires CALP (see next). Given good exposure, learners can learn BICS in L2 less than two years.

CALP: Cognitive Academic Language Proficiency. This is a formal variety of language which is used in learning. We use it when talking about school concepts with specificity and exactitude. It is also used in written texts about school subjects. CALP talk has features in common with written language. It is characterised by a relatively large vocabulary containing the low-frequency, high-specificity words we need in order to be precise about subject concepts (such as *limb, habitat*), as well as words with general academic meanings (such as *perceive, occur*) and which are less likely to be used in informal BICS speech. It uses more complex grammar (such as passive forms, subordinate clauses) and is often carefully organised, using signals of organisation such as connectors (e.g. *however, in addition*) and, in written form, headings and paragraphs. It also involves computer skills, study skills and the use of graphics. It can take learners five to seven years to develop CALP in L2 (Cummins 2000).

Learner second language proficiency

Effective forms of the L2-medium education also depend partly on how well learners speak the LoI: a basic level of L2 knowledge is normally necessary. This is not the case with immersion or bilingual education, both of which are available to learners with early levels of proficiency in the LoI. L2 proficiency level is, however, a factor in CLIL programmes, which normally set entry levels of ability and may sometimes prepare learners for entry by means of additional language teaching.

In addition, it can help a learner in a L2-medium programme if they have good academic language skills in their L1. If they have started learning in L1, they do not need to re-learn a range of cognitive academic language proficiency (CALP) skills (e.g. reading, note-taking, planning and drafting writing, etc.) when they begin to learn in L2. As long as these skills are well-established, they can transfer from one language to another. Learners in CLIL programmes often have this requisite level of L1 CALP ability, as do many learners in immersion and bilingual education.

 ## Selection or system-wide education

A major influence on whether a learner succeeds in L2-medium education is whether the programme is optional or compulsory and required by all schools. Schools which choose to offer a form of L2-medium education are usually positively oriented to its success and can provide the support it needs in terms of teaching experience and materials. Immersion, bilingual and CLIL programmes are self-selecting in this way. Schools which offer a programme can also attract parents and learners who value its benefits. By contrast, L2-medium education which every child in every school must follow, encounters failure easily, a state of affairs which as it relates to SSA is described by a large literature partly referred to in Sections 15.5 and 15.6 and summarised in Erling et al. (2021).

 ## The pedagogical environment

Certain aspects of pedagogy and course delivery can help to make a L2-medium programme effective. Teaching staff with relevant language abilities and who can deploy the distinct pedagogy which L2-medium teaching requires (see Section 15.6) are one aspect of this. Staff in immersion and bilingual programmes – and in many CLIL programmes – may possess the specific pedagogical strategies which the programmes require.

Specialist L2-medium teaching materials can also make learning in L2 more accessible (see Section 15.6). However, these materials are not common in immersion, bilingual or CLIL programmes, with the exception of some contexts such as Spain, where primary CLIL materials are available.

15.5 Reasons for failure in L2-medium education

The reasons presented earlier for success in L2-medium education can also count against it.

Subtractive bilingual education

In minority education in the global north and in L2-medium education in SSA, education often results in 'subtractive bilingualism' in school: the L2 LoI replaces the fluent L1; it does not add to it. Commentators remark on the potential damage to learners' self-image when schooling does not reflect their language and culture (García et al. 2017). In minority education this picture is in fact mixed. In some countries, such as the UK, minority learners' L1 has largely no formal place in the curriculum. In parts of the USA, however, as mentioned, authorities have chosen to support minority L1s in bilingual programmes.

In SSA learners are required at an early stage to abandon their fluent African language as LoI and have to learn in their least fluent (European) language after that. Learners continue to learn L1 as a subject throughout schooling, but its status is radically limited. In these cases, L2-medium education thus reduces learners' multilingual learning capacity. In addition, learning through L2 can cut off learners from the community, from community language use and from local culture and tradition, thus undermining their sense of self (Erling et al. 2021). It can also cut off the learner from parents, who may not be L2-fluent and can no longer involve themselves in their child's education.

Socio-economic status and educational background

Many families with children learning in L2 at school and using L1 at home – in for example the USA or the UK – have lower than average SES (National Academies of Sciences 2017) and speak a lower-status L1, for example Spanish in the USA or Urdu in the UK. These families may also have lower levels of education generally. This is certainly not always the case: portions of the immigrant community which arrived in the UK in the 1960s came, for example, from middle-class families in the Indian sub-continent and their educational aspirations have, over the years, ensured that their children achieved well in school (Strand and Lindorff 2021). Social factors of this kind can help learners overcome initial language barriers in school.

In SSA, large numbers of learners come from home backgrounds with little education, sometimes little or no print literacy and low or no parental ability in the L2 LoI. Low SES and low home experience of the LoI are associated with underachievement in school (Smits et al. 2008). Poverty, long school journeys and inability to feed children adequately add to the difficulties which families face in L2-medium education. A portion of learners come from middle-class families with higher SES which often use the LoI at home. They manage the use of an L2 LoI in school with much more ease.

Learner second language proficiency

Learners in minority education enter the school system with varying levels of proficiency in the LoI. Those whose ability falls below a certain level will struggle with learning subjects in L2. They are likely to acquire social fluency in the L2, through exposure in the community within the space of two years (Cummins 2000). What they need for the purposes of learning in school, however, is CALP, which takes longer: Cummins suggests that it may take learners in a North American context between five and seven years before they can achieve grade norms in L2.

In SSA, levels of ability in L2 are a crucial cause of low achievement in school. As already mentioned, learners learn normally in a fluent African language for a number of initial years of schooling, as a rule for three years. During that time, they learn the L2 LoI as a subject. A three-year programme of L2 at about three hours per week, however, will not enable a learner to use the L2 as LoI from grade 4 onwards. Subject syllabuses after the switch of medium make far higher language demands than the L2 syllabus up to that point delivers (Clegg 2021), creating the large 'language gap' referred to earlier. The World Bank (2021) suggests: 'shockingly low learning outcomes may be a reflection of inadequate language of instruction policies'.

Learners in SSA are often orally fluent in several local languages and, at the switch of medium, initially literate in one of these languages. Yet after the early years this remarkable multilingual ability is radically curtailed as they start learning in L2. In contrast to minority learners in industrialised countries, who will often gain oral fluency in L2 – or BICS (Basic Interpersonal Communication Skills) – simply through social exposure (Cummins 2000), this level of exposure is often not available to learners in SSA. Thus, immediately after the change of LoI they have neither an informal BICS ability nor a more formal CALP ability in L2. They cannot therefore talk freely about curricular concepts in groups and pairs; and, since the use of L1 is often proscribed, learners can be fairly silent; many learners may not develop the capacity to talk easily about subjects before the end of schooling. Writing ability in L2 is similarly constrained and this limitation may also extend until matriculation, acting as barrier to learners' ability to demonstrate in written L2-medium examinations knowledge which they possess but cannot express in L2. Examinations thus tend to be unfair and unreliable. The ability to read textbooks is also severely limited. The effect of inability to use the LoI effectively, both on personal achievement and on the national economy (Erling et al. 2021), is considerable.

Selection or system-wide education

Parents and learners who speak minority languages are unlikely to have a choice in the matter of the school they attend. Similarly, in SSA, government determines the LoI: most learners from a given age onwards must learn in what is, for most, their least fluent language.

Schools which may choose their LoI policy, such as those described in Section 15.4 are small in number; they cater often to socially advantaged learners, perhaps selecting learners according to L2 proficiency; they make a positive choice to offer L2-medium education and are able to fund and resource it. However, the extension of L2-medium education to all schools, all ages, all learners and parents of all backgrounds is a much bigger undertaking. It faces the education authority with learners from every kind of social and educational background. It involves parents who may not have fluency in the LoI and may not be able to offer appropriate home support. Crucially it involves all learners regardless of their L2 proficiency levels and who will therefore require extensive pedagogical resources. Thus, whereas successful selective provision of L2-medium education is found across the world, successful system-wide provision is rare.

The pedagogical environment

Learners who learn in a L2 in which they have insufficient proficiency are at a distinct disadvantage. They have to learn both new concepts and a new language with which to express these concepts; learning can become slow and ineffective. They can, however, be helped by an appropriate pedagogy. 'Language-supportive pedagogy' is a term used mainly in L2-medium education in SSA (Clegg 2021) to describe a distinct approach to teaching which supports the cognitive capabilities and compensates for the as yet developing L2 competencies of learners (see Section 15.6). In minority education appropriate pedagogy is not widespread. Similarly, in SSA language-supportive pedagogy is rarely used to teach subjects to learners with the levels of L2 proficiency outlined earlier, and language-supportive pedagogy is rarely taught in initial teacher education (Erling et al. 2021). The absence of this supportive form of teaching contributes considerably to low school achievement in SSA. Similarly, multilingual education, which can help learners learning in L2 (see Section 15.6) is rarely recognised by ministries of education as useful.

Appropriate materials for teaching subjects to learners with limited L2 proficiency can help teachers and learners who are struggling with insufficient levels of knowledge in the LoI. They embody the principles of language-supportive pedagogy which we outline in Section 15.6. In the education of language minorities, however, dedicated materials of this kind play a small role and in SSA few materials of this kind are published. Materials are, by contrast, often designed for L2-fluent learners and have been shown to be harder to read than those used by English-fluent learners in, for example, the UK (Clegg 2021). Many learners cannot read them (Macdonald 1993).

15.6 Appropriate pedagogy

We have mentioned pedagogical approaches which promise to be helpful in cases in which learners' proficiency in the LoI proves to be a barrier to learning. They are language-supportive pedagogy and multilingual learning.

Language-supportive pedagogy is a distinct form of teaching used with learners who are still developing their mastery of the L2 LoI (Clegg 2021). It supports learners linguistically and allows them to deploy attention towards the acquisition of new subject concepts. It is used in some instances of minority education and in CLIL (Ball et al. 2015). It is distinct from conventional pedagogy. Teacher-talk, for example, highlights repetition, paraphrase, exemplification and signals of organisation and summary. It helps learners to respond by prompts and short-answer questions as well as by encouraging L1 responses. Teachers use a range of visuals and engage in judicious code-switching. Collaborative

Table 15.2 Reasons why some L2-medium education programmes succeed or fail.

	Successful programmes	Failing programmes
Additive or subtractive bilingual education	Add a second language to the first and sustain the learners' culture	Replace the first language with the second and cut learners off from their culture
Socio-economic status	Learners often come families with higher incomes and a higher level of education	Learners often come from families with lower incomes and a lower level of education
Parents' home language status	Parents often speak a high-status language	Parents may speak a lower-status language
Learners' home language literacy	Learners are normally literate in their home language	Learners are often not literate in their home language
L2 proficiency	Learners in CLIL programmes have higher levels of L2 proficiency	Learners often have low levels of L2 proficiency
Optional or system-wide programmes	Programmes are optional	Programmes are system-wide
Pedagogy	Pedagogy often supports learners	Pedagogy often fails to support learners

learner-talk is normally done in L1. Teachers use a range of supportive task types for speaking, reading and writing about subjects in L2. Where possible, assessment is bilingual.

Multilingual education is another form of classroom practice which can help L2-medium learners. It is increasingly established in the education of minority learners in parts of the USA, in particular in New York (García et al. 2017). It seeks to enable learners to use all their languages in the classroom. It depends on a 'translanguaging' theory of classroom language use in which languages are seen less as separate entities and more as part of an overarching language capacity: learners are seen to possess language skills, regardless of the language in which they are expressed. Oral work may be in L1 or L2: for instance, learners will talk collaboratively in L1 and also in the process of reading in L2 and writing in L2. In the L2-medium classroom, some texts may be in L1, and learners may do some writing in L1.

Multilingual education allows a learner to be judged in relation to all their languages, not just in relation to the LoI. Learners, both minority language users in industrialised countries, and members of language majorities in regions such as SSA, are often highly skilled users of language in L1 and partially in L2. However, because their L1 language skills are not recognised in the L2-medium curriculum, they can appear to be linguistically deficient.

In focus: undervaluing the multilingual learner in the L2-medium classroom

This Tanzanian child in grade 7 (final year of primary school) speaks two African languages: Ngoni (his local home and community language) and Kiswahili (Mapunda forthcoming). He is orally fluent in Ngoni (at least *bridging*, using a measure of language proficiency employed by García et al. (2017)). The language of primary school is Kiswahili. He speaks Kiswahili with some fluency (*developing*), but because he lives in a district in which Kiswahili is not spoken widely, his literacy ability in it is not high (*emerging*), even at the end of primary school. This slows his learning in primary school. In grade 8, year 1 of secondary school, he must abandon Kiswahili and learn in English. He has learned English during primary school, but his ability in it both orally and in writing at the beginning of grade 8 is only *entering*. He therefore speaks two African languages orally, one fluently and the other somewhat less so. He has *entering* literacy in English and *emerging* literacy in Kiswahili. He is therefore a multilingual language user with varying levels of ability in each language, as Figure 15.1 shows. In a multilingual classroom, these multiple language abilities would be recognised. But the school, which proscribes learning in his most fluent African language in the primary school and proscribes learning in his other African language in the secondary school, judges him only by reference to his limited English proficiency, as we see in the second visual: he is here a language-limited, struggling learner.

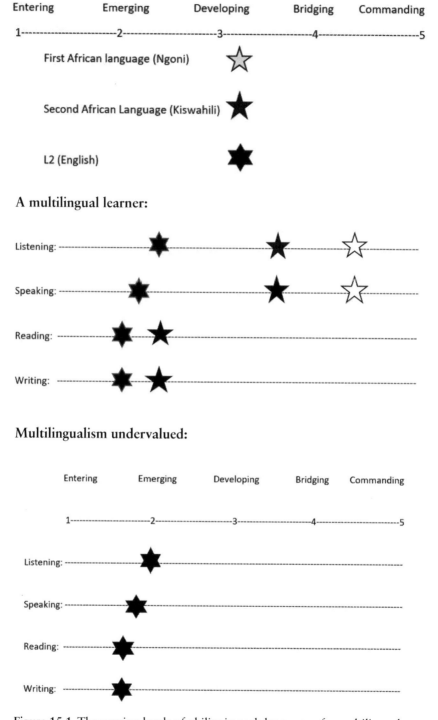

Figure 15.1 The varying levels of ability in each language of a multilingual language user.

Learning materials designed for learners who are not fluent in the LoI also have the capacity to give strong support to both learners and teachers in the L2-medium classroom. Multilingual language use is rare, but some efforts have been made in minority education in the UK to include multilingualism in teaching and learning materials (Afitska 2015). Figure 15.2 shows an example of this from a multilingual primary school in Sheffield, UK. The example in (a) displays the work of a Hungarian L1-speaking child who used L1 to demonstrate their subject-specific knowledge, because they lacked the lexical knowledge to do so in L2. The example in (b) shows the work of a Slovakian L1-speaking child who, despite answering the question only partly correctly, was nonetheless able to show that they had successfully understood the task requirements by responding to it in L1.

In materials which reflect language-supportive pedagogy, texts are constructed to display short sentence length, simple grammar, contextualisation and repetition of new vocabulary and clear signalling of organisation. A wide range of visuals and language-supportive task is used. Although these materials are rare, Figure 15.3 shows an extract from language-supportive and multilingual materials developed experimentally for Rwanda (LaST 2014).

In the education of language minorities, there is movement towards more effective ways of learning through the use of language-supportive and multilingual pedagogies. In SSA, however, and in other parts of the global south where learners are largely not allowed to learn in a fluent language, ministries,

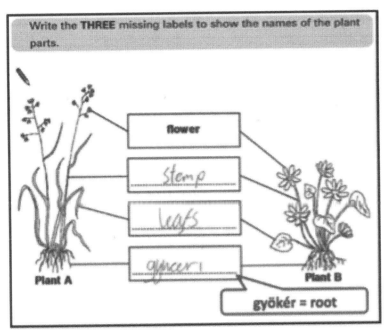

(a)

Figure 15.2 Multilingual science materials in a Sheffield primary school.

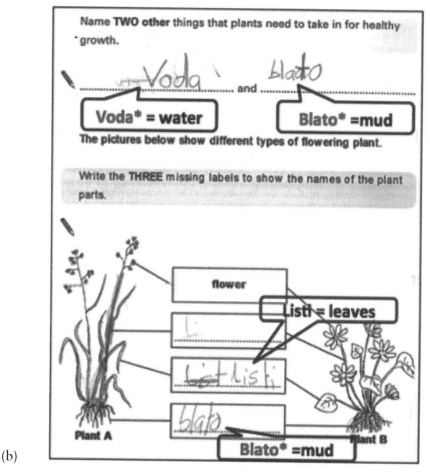

(b)

Figure 15.2 (Continued)

teacher-education institutions and publishing houses are reluctant to apply these measures. Despite an influential literature in Africa which sets out a clear rationale for multilingual learning and for language-supportive practice (Erling et al. 2021), and despite widespread criticism from international bodies like UNESCO and the World Bank (2021), ministries remain wedded to a form of schooling in which learners struggle to learn.

15.7 Conclusion

It is important to distinguish between contexts for education in a second language. On the one hand there are those in which relatively limited numbers of families, sometimes with social advantages, choose to have their children educated in a L2. On the other there are those in which large populations,

Types of soil

Activity 25: Talking in Kinyarwanda about uses of soil

Work in groups. Look at the pictures on page 10 and talk in Kinyarwanda about types of soil: how many types do you know? What do we use them for?

Activity 26: Reading about uses of soil

Look at the pictures on pages 10. Read the text and match the types of soil with the pictures.

(a)

There are 3 types of soil:

- loam soil
- sand soil
- clay soil

We use loam soil for growing crops. We use sand soil for building. We use clay soil for making pots.

(b)

Figure 15.3 Language-supportive pedagogy in primary science materials for Rwanda.

often with social disadvantages, are required to learn in a L2, especially in low-resource contexts. In the former contexts, L2-medium education often provides a good education and gains a good reputation. In the latter contexts it tends to depress school achievement and, especially in SSA, contributes seriously to

New words	
Kinyarwanda	**English**
ubutaka bwiza	loam soil
ubutaka bw'ibumba	clay soil
ubutaka bw'umucanga	sand soil
kunyuramo	pass through
kubaka	building
gutera imyaka	growing crops
ibyungo / ibibindi	pots

Activity 27: Reading about uses of soil

(c)

Read the text above again. Copy the table below into your exercise book and fill it in.

	What is it used for?
Loam soil	
Sand soil	
Clay soil	

Activity 28: Talking in English about uses of soil.

Work in groups. Talk about soils using the table.

(d)

We use	loam clay sand	soil	for	building. growing crops. making pots.

Figure 15.3 (Continued)

national skills shortages and lowered economic performance. In the education of language minority users in the USA, authorities have begun to provide forms of schooling which maintain learners' first languages and support the development of their second languages. While there are positive initiatives in SSA which support the education of bilingual learners, they are not yet taken up in mainstream education. Here, it is important to allow learners to learn in a fluent local language for much longer periods of time and for education authorities to apply the language-supportive and multilingual pedagogies which we know can increase subject knowledge and L2 proficiency.

Note

1 This article uses 'sub-Saharan Africa' (SSA) to refer to Africa south of the Sahara. We acknowledge that this may be a politically contested term but are not aware of equivalents which express this geographical and cultural space.

References

The 74. 2021. *English Learners in California Remain at the Bottom on New State Test Scores – & It's Even Worse for Students in L.A.* www.the74million .org/article/english-learners-in-california-remain-at-the-bottom-of-state -test-scores-with-only-a-hint-of-progress-and-its-even-worse-in-los-angeles/

Afitska, O. 2015. Scaffolding learning: Developing materials to support the learning of science and language by non-native English-speaking children. *Innovation in Language Learning and Teaching Journal*, 10(2): 1–15.

Ball, P., Kelly, K. and Clegg, J. 2015. *Putting CLIL into Practice*. Oxford: Oxford University Press.

Clegg, J. 2019. How English depresses school achievement in Africa. *ELT Journal*, 73: 89–91.

Clegg, J. 2021. Multilingual learning in anglophone sub-Saharan Africa: How to help children use all their languages to learn. In E. Erling, J. Clegg, C. Rubagumya and C. Reilly (Eds.), *Multilingual Learning and Language Supportive Pedagogies in Sub-Saharan Africa*. Abingdon: Routledge.

Cummins, J. 2000. *Language, Power and Pedagogy: Bilingual Children in the Crossfire*. Clevedon: Multilingual Matters.

Dutcher, N. 2004. *Expanding Educational Opportunities in Linguistically Diverse Societies*. Washington, DC: Centre for Applied Linguistics.

Erling, E. J., Clegg, J., Rubagumya, C. and Reilly, C. 2021. Multilingual learning and language supportive pedagogies in sub-Saharan Africa. In E. Erling, J. Clegg, C. Rubagumya and C. Reilly (Eds.), *Multilingual Learning and Language Supportive Pedagogies in Sub-Saharan Africa*. Abingdon: Routledge.

García, O., Johnson, S. I. and Seltzer, K. 2017. *The Translanguaging Classroom: Leveraging Student Bilingualism for Learning*, Philadelphia: Caslon.

LaST. 2014. *P4 Science*. Kigali, RW: University of Bristol and British Council.

Macdonald, C. 1993. *Towards a New Primary Curriculum in South Africa*. Pretoria: Human Sciences Research Council.

Mapunda, G. forthcoming. 'But exams are not given in Ngoni': The place of local languages in Tanzania's primary education. In C. Reilly, F. Chimbutane, J. Clegg, C. Rubagumya and E. J. Erling (Eds.), *Enabling Multilingual Learning in Sub-Saharan Africa: Assessment, Ideologies and Policies*. Vol. 2. Abingdon: Routledge.

National Academies of Sciences, Engineering, and Medicine. 2017. *Promoting the Educational Success of Children and Youth Learning English: Promising Futures*. Washington, DC: The National Academies Press. https://doi.org/10.17226/24677.

Smits, J., Huisman, J. and Kruijff, K. 2008. *Home Language and Education in the Developing World*. Paper commissioned for EFA Global Monitoring Report 2009, UNESCO, Paris.

Strand, S. and Lindorff, A. 2021. *English as an Additional Language, Proficiency in English and Rate of Progression: Pupil, School and LA Variation*. Cambridge: Bell Foundation.

Thomas, W. and Collier, V. 2002. *A National Study of School Effectiveness for Language Minority Students' Long-term Academic Achievement*. Santa Cruz, CA and Washington, DC: Center for Research on Education, Diversity & Excellence.

UNESCO. 2016. *If You Don't Understand, How Can You Learn?* Global Education Monitoring Report Policy Paper, UNESCO, Paris.

Uwezo. 2012. *Are Our Children Learning? Annual Learning Assessment Report 2012*, Uwezo Tanzania, viewed 12 December 2019. www.uwezo.net/wp-vontent/uploads/2012/08/TZ_Uwezo2012ALAReport.pdf

World Bank. 2021. *Loud and Clear: Effect of Language of Instruction Policies for Learning*. Washington, DC: World Bank.

16 Critical Discourse Analysis
Christopher Hart

16.1 Introduction

Critical Discourse Analysis (CDA) is a form of discourse analysis (see Chapter 10) that is specifically concerned with the way power and inequality are constructed through 'political' texts. The aim of CDA is to reveal, through detailed linguistic analysis, the ideologies encoded in texts which serve to legitimate relations of dominance and to thereby enable resistance. As a result, CDA tends to address texts relating to topics where power and inequality are clearly at stake, such as immigration, war and civil disorder. In this chapter, I provide an introduction to CDA organised as follows. In Section 16.2, I define some key theoretical concepts in CDA. In Section 16.3, I illustrate some typical forms of analysis in CDA. In Section 16.4, I explore new horizons in CDA in the form of multimodal analysis. In Section 16.5, I reflect on the position of CDA within the social sciences and what it means to take a critical stance in discourse analysis before, in Section 16.6, offering some brief conclusions.

16.2 Key Concepts

It is important to define from the outset what we mean by a **text**. Texts are not necessarily written. Texts can be spoken too, as in a political speech or parliamentary debate, and written down only for purposes of record or analysis. A text can be short, as short as a single word, as in a sign, or incredibly long like a treatise. Texts may also be **multimodal**, which is to say that they contain features belonging to more than one **semiotic mode**. Language is one mode but written texts, such as newspaper articles, will typically also contain images in the form of photographs or graphics, while spoken texts will typically also feature co-speech gestures. For some thinkers, a text need not feature language at all so that, for example, the configuration of furniture in a room would count as a text through which power relations may be enshrined. So a text is any constellation of practices that can be analysed as communicating meaning

DOI: 10.4324/9781003045571-19

and which is in some way spatially and temporally bounded. A text also has **texture**, which is to say that it hangs together as a cohesive and coherent unit (Halliday and Hasan 1976).

Texts belong to different **genres**. In CDA, we are concerned with genres that can be broadly characterised as 'political' as opposed to, say, 'literary' genres, which are the territory of stylistics. Genres typically analysed in CDA include political speeches, parliamentary debates, political campaign leaflets or posters and print news articles, as well as digitally mediated texts like online news articles, websites and blog and social media posts.

It is also important to recognise that texts do not occur in isolation from one another but rather enter into complex webs of intertextual relations such that one text may refer to or contain features of another text. As Fairclough (1989: 127) puts it, texts 'have histories, they belong to historical series'. This notion of **intertextuality** has its roots in the work of Mikhail Bakhtin and his theory of dialogism. When texts are related in this way, the ideas expressed in one text may be transformed or **recontextualised** as they move along an intertextual chain, as when a bill in Parliament turns into legislation or a tweet becomes the subject of a news article or vice versa.

Texts matter, then, because in a very real sense they dictate how we live our lives; they define what we can and can't do. This relationship between texts and society is most clear and direct in texts that constitute acts of law, which prohibit certain actions and require others. However, texts also influence society in more subtle, indirect ways. Texts have the power to influence how we understand particular topics or events and to thus affect the way we feel about those topics and events, particularly when no first-hand experience is available. In this sense, texts do ideological work as they instantiate competing **discourses** – ways of talking and thinking about a given issue. The term **ideology** is difficult to define as it is used in many different ways (Eagleton 1991). In CDA, when we speak of a text doing ideological work, we mean that it promotes one particular worldview or discourse while supressing others.

Texts do not correspond to any objective reality, then, but rather construct reality for us through representations that are necessarily partial and subjective, reflecting a particular perspective or presenting a particular version of events. It is in this sense that texts may be constructive of society as the worldviews they promote lead to social actions and relations which, from a particular normative or ethical standpoint, are considered problematic. As Fairclough (1995: 131), a founding figure in CDA, states, 'language is socially shaped but also social shaping, or constitutive' – a relationship he describes as **dialectic**. For Fairclough, and all researchers in CDA that have followed, a text is therefore never only an instance of **discursive practice** but always at the same time a piece of **social practice** which contributes to the formation and maintenance of social conditions. We turn to some of the linguistic features implicated in this process in the next section.

16.3 Textual analysis

16.3.1 Transitivity

Transitivity is a key analytic concept in CDA and is borrowed from systemic functional linguistics (Halliday 1985). Here, the concept of transitivity extends beyond whether a verb is transitive or intransitive (see 16.3.2) to take account of the type of process that a verb designates. For example, whether the process described is a mental one, a verbal one or a material one. Crucially, language affords choices in transitivity so that the same situation and the process inherent in it can be represented in different ways, which enables ideology. Another dimension of choice concerns the representation of participants in the process designated by a verb. Van Leeuwen (1996) provides an inventory of the different ways in which social actors may be represented in texts. The choices open to text-producers in transitivity and social actor representation means, as Fowler (1991: 209) points out, that representation is necessarily 'always representation from a certain point of view'. The aim of CDA is then, by studying in minute detail the linguistic structures of a text, to expose the belief and value systems that are encoded within it and which may be taken for granted by readers who accept the representation as objective or 'natural' (ibid.).

The ideological nature of texts is made most apparent through comparative forms of analysis. So, let's consider, by way of an example, two texts reporting the same event: the Black Lives Matter protest held in Bristol in 2020 where protesters removed the statue of a prominent slave-trader Edward Colston. We'll look just at the headlines:

(1) BLM protesters topple statue of Bristol slave trader Edward Colston (*Guardian* 7 Jun 2020)
(2) Black Lives Matter protesters tear down Bristol statue of 17th century slave trader and philanthropist Edward Colston (*MailOnline* 7 Jun 2020)

The texts come from news outlets with opposing ideological perspectives. The *MailOnline* is recognised as a right-wing newspaper likely to be hostile toward BLM protesters while *The Guardian* is recognised as a left-wing newspaper likely to be more sympathetic to the movement. And indeed, we can see these competing ideological viewpoints played out in the linguistic structures of the two headlines as set out in Table 16.1.

For example, in relation to participants, *The Guardian* refers to the protesters using the acronym 'BLM', treating the movement as known to its readers, while the *MailOnline* does not. In relation to the *goal* – the affected participant in the process – it is notable that *The Guardian* refers to the statue as being of a slave trader only. By contrast, the *MailOnline* refers to the statue as being of a slave trader and philanthropist, thus attaching a degree of legitimacy to the

Table 16.1 Transitivity structure in headlines.

	Participant: actor	Process: material	Participant: goal
The Guardian	*BLM protesters*	*topple*	*statue of Bristol slave trader Edward Colston*
MailOnline	*Black Lives Matter protesters*	*tear down*	*Bristol statue of 17th century slave trader and philanthropist Edward Colston*

figure of Colston and, by the same token, delegitimising the protesters. Perhaps the most notable difference, however, concerns the process in each headline. In both cases, the process designated by the verb is classified as *material*. Material processes are processes of 'doing' as opposed to mental (e.g. *seeing*) or verbal (e.g. *saying*) processes. However, there are some differences between them. In the *MailOnline*, 'tear down' describes a violent and destructive process, which portrays the event as an act of vandalism. By contrast, in *The Guardian*, 'topple' has overtones of a revolutionary act. Although *topple* can mean simply to knock over or cause to fall, it also has a political sense of removing from power or overthrowing an oppressive regime and thus may portray the event as an

For an explanation of different process types in SFL as well as a general introduction to the theory, check out this web article written by Matthiessen and Halliday.

act of political resistance against a symbol of oppression. The question of how we know that *topple* has this sense can be approached using methods from Corpus Linguistics (see 'in focus' box).

In focus: checking interpretations using corpus linguistics

CDA has been criticised for presenting analyses that are too subjective, with analysts interpreting meanings based on their own intuitions rather than on the back of any evidence (Widdowson 2004). This leads to potential problems of over-interpretation and/or interpretations that are biased by the analysts' own ideological position. One way of addressing this, as O'Halloran and Coffin (2004) demonstrate, is to consult a large corpus of English such as the British National Corpus. Here, we can search for a word of interest, such as *topple*, and then, by examining its general contexts of use, get a better, evidence-based picture of its meanings. When we do this for *topple*, at least 50% of the first randomly returned 'hits' relate to the removal from power of political figures, which suggests that 'topple' in *The Guardian* text is likely to have connotations along these lines (Figure 16.1). See Chapter 21 for more on corpus methods.

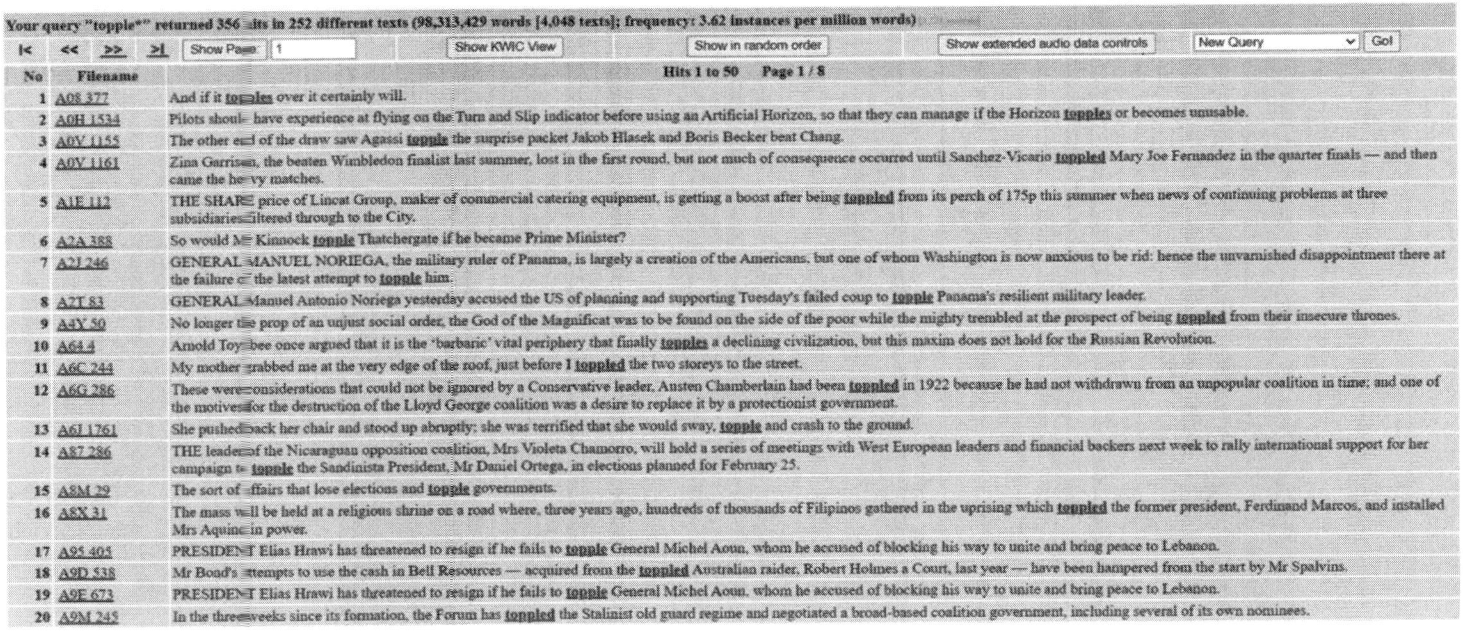

Your query "topple*" returned 356 hits in 252 different texts (98,313,429 words [4,048 texts]; frequency: 3.62 instances per million words)

|< << >> >| Show Page: 1 | Show KWIC View | Show in random order | Show extended audio data controls | New Query | Go!

No	Filename	Hits 1 to 50 Page 1 / 8
1	A08 377	And if it topples over it certainly will.
2	A0H 1534	Pilots should have experience at flying on the Turn and Slip indicator before using an Artificial Horizon, so that they can manage if the Horizon topples or becomes unusable.
3	A0V 1155	The other end of the draw saw Agassi topple the surprise packet Jakob Hlasek and Boris Becker beat Chang.
4	A0V 1161	Zina Garrison, the beaten Wimbledon finalist last summer, lost in the first round, but not much of consequence occurred until Sanchez-Vicario toppled Mary Joe Fernandez in the quarter finals — and then came the heavy matches.
5	A1E 112	THE SHARE price of Lincat Group, maker of commercial catering equipment, is getting a boost after being toppled from its perch of 175p this summer when news of continuing problems at three subsidiaries filtered through to the City.
6	A2A 388	So would Mr Kinnock topple Thatchergate if he became Prime Minister?
7	A2J 246	GENERAL MANUEL NORIEGA, the military ruler of Panama, is largely a creation of the Americans, but one of whom Washington is now anxious to be rid: hence the unvarnished disappointment there at the failure of the latest attempt to topple him.
8	A2T 83	GENERAL Manuel Antonio Noriega yesterday accused the US of planning and supporting Tuesday's failed coup to topple Panama's resilient military leader.
9	A4Y 50	No longer the prop of an unjust social order, the God of the Magnificat was to be found on the side of the poor while the mighty trembled at the prospect of being toppled from their insecure thrones.
10	A64 4	Arnold Toynbee once argued that it is the 'barbaric' vital periphery that finally topples a declining civilization, but this maxim does not hold for the Russian Revolution.
11	A6C 244	My mother grabbed me at the very edge of the roof, just before I toppled the two storeys to the street.
12	A6G 286	These were considerations that could not be ignored by a Conservative leader. Austen Chamberlain had been toppled in 1922 because he had not withdrawn from an unpopular coalition in time; and one of the motives for the destruction of the Lloyd George coalition was a desire to replace it by a protectionist government.
13	A6L 1761	She pushed back her chair and stood up abruptly; she was terrified that she would sway, topple and crash to the ground.
14	A87 286	THE leader of the Nicaraguan opposition coalition, Mrs Violeta Chamorro, will hold a series of meetings with West European leaders and financial backers next week to rally international support for her campaign to topple the Sandinista President, Mr Daniel Ortega, in elections planned for February 25.
15	A8M 29	The sort of affairs that lose elections and topple governments.
16	A8X 31	The mass will be held at a religious shrine on a road where, three years ago, hundreds of thousands of Filipinos gathered in the uprising which toppled the former president, Ferdinand Marcos, and installed Mrs Aquino in power.
17	A95 405	PRESIDENT Elias Hrawi has threatened to resign if he fails to topple General Michel Aoun, whom he accused of blocking his way to unite and bring peace to Lebanon.
18	A9D 538	Mr Bond's attempts to use the cash in Bell Resources — acquired from the toppled Australian raider, Robert Holmes a Court, last year — have been hampered from the start by Mr Spalvins.
19	A9E 673	PRESIDENT Elias Hrawi has threatened to resign if he fails to topple General Michel Aoun, whom he accused of blocking his way to unite and bring peace to Lebanon.
20	A9M 245	In the three weeks since its formation, the Forum has toppled the Stalinist old guard regime and negotiated a broad-based coalition government, including several of its own nominees.

Figure 16.1 Concordance display of hits for 'topple'.

16.3.2 Exclusion

Another crucial facility of language much studied in CDA is exclusion and its potential effects in mystification. While participants included in a text may be represented in different ways, participants may also be excluded from the representation. Exclusion occurs by various means, including intransitive verbs and agentless passives and may produce ideological effects; for example, in obscuring agency and directing attention away from those responsible for harmful actions. Let's have a look at an example, this time from the arena of international state conflict. On 14th May 2018, a number of Palestinian civilians were killed or wounded by Israeli soldiers while protesting on the Gaza border as part of what was dubbed the Great March of Return. In reporting the events on social media, the *New York Times* posted the tweet in (2):

(2) Dozens of Palestinians have died in protests as the U.S. prepares to open its Jerusalem Embassy nyti.ms/2GcZN5T (https://twitter.com/nytimesworld/status/996009245853265920)

'Died' is an example of an intransitive verb, which means there is no reference to who or what caused the deaths. The role of Israeli soldiers as agents in this process is hidden by the verb choice. This is in contrast to a transitive verb such as 'kill' which, in the active voice at least, requires the specification of an agent. However, even with transitive verbs, text-producers have the facility to conceal agency by means of the agentless passive voice as in the following headline from the *Wall Street Journal*:

(3) Scores Killed as Palestinians Protest U.S. Embassy Opening in Jerusalem (*Wall Street Journal*, 14 May 2018)

In (3), although the transitive verb implies an agent responsible for 'killing', they are not explicitly mentioned and are thus backgrounded in the representation. What it means in psychological terms to say that agents are backgrounded is addressed in the 'In focus' box on cognitive linguistic approaches to CDA. What examples like (2) and (3) show is that when power is exercised in a way that is controversial, grammatical choices enable text-producers to manage the representation of events in a way that helps legitimate and maintain accepted power structures such as those between state and citizen or state and non-citizen.

In focus: cognitive linguistic methods in CDA

It has been pointed out that exclusion at the level of linguistic representation does not necessarily mean that information is missing from the mental representations that readers form of the events described, where 'gaps' may be filled on the basis of prior knowledge (Widdowson 2004). However, an approach to CDA based in cognitive linguistics (e.g. Hart 2021) argues for the 'psychological reality' of mystification. According to this approach, meaning construction in language relies on the same set of underlying cognitive processes as other domains of cognition, such as attention. Parallels can therefore be drawn between processes of meaning construction in language and other aspects of mental experience. In the case of intransitives, the agent lies outside the expression's **scope of attention**. In the case of agentless passives, the agent lies within the scope of attention but out of focus relevant to the affected participant (Figure 16.2).

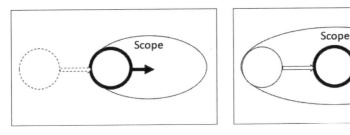

a. Intransitives   b. Agentless passives

Figure 16.2 Attentional distribution in intransitives and agentless passives.

16.3.3 Metaphor

Another key feature of texts through which power and inequality may be articulated and legitimated is metaphor. In CDA, metaphor is usually approached from the perspective of cognitive linguistics and specifically **conceptual metaphor theory** (Lakoff and Johnson 1980). Here, metaphor is understood not just as a figure of speech but as a prompt for a cognitive process of **construal** in which the knowledge associated with one area of experience gets 'mapped' across to a less familiar area of experience to provide structure to it. The domains of experience involved in such a **conceptual metaphor** are referred to as 'source' and 'target' respectively. Metaphors are important sites of ideology in texts because the cognitive mappings they evoke can cause us to think, feel and act in particular ways with respect to the target domain. That is, they can lead to **framing effects**. It is through their framing effects that particular metaphors help to maintain and legitimate unequal power structures in society. The ideological functions of metaphor have been studied across a great variety of discourses, including discourses of war, civil disorder, poverty and economics, health, and the environment. However, let's have a look at metaphor in relation to another topic where power and disempowerment are at play, namely immigration.

In the UK, migrants are routinely denigrated in the national press as part of long-standing campaigns calling for greater restrictions to their rights and freedoms. Metaphor is a strikingly salient feature of those discourses. Let's consider some examples of front-page headlines from one particular newspaper, the *Daily Express*:

(4) CRISIS IN CALAIS: IT'S A WAR ZONE (*Daily Express*, 31 Jul 2015)
(5) BATTLE TO KEEP OUT EU MIGRANTS (*Daily Express*, 5 Mar 2013)
(6) MIGRANT INVASION OUT OF CONTROL (*Daily Express*, 11 Jun 2015)

In each of these examples, vocabulary from the domain of war – 'war', 'battle', 'invasion' – is being used to talk about immigration. This kind of metaphorical language is not restricted to the press but also features in the discourse of populist political figures like Nigel Farage who tweeted:

(7) EXCLUSIVE FOOTAGE OF BEACH LANDING BY MIGRANTS
    Shocking invasion on the Kent coast this morning
    (https://twitter.com/nigel_farage/status/1291296574992257025)

Talking and thinking about immigration in terms of war has a number of potential framing effects. For example, it construes immigration as a threat and casts migrants in the role of an aggressive enemy. It therefore makes the war-like treatment of migrants, such as holding them in detention centres as we would prisoners of war, more acceptable. Moreover, it creates a context in which deployment of the military to patrol and control borders makes sense, where it otherwise would not. The framing effects of metaphors in facilitating support for controversial actions is demonstrated in experimental research, as is outlined in the 'In focus' box below.

Other metaphorical themes characteristic of anti-immigration discourse include naturalising metaphors that present immigrants in terms of 'floods', 'waves' and even 'tsunamis' and dehumanising metaphors that present immigrants as animals or diseases. As an example of the latter, Donald Trump tweeted:

(8) Democrats are the problem. They don't care about crime and want illegal immigrants, no matter how bad they may be, to pour into and infest our country. (https://twitter.com/realDonaldTrump/status/1009071403918864385?ref_src=twsrc%5Etfw)

In (8), 'infest' compares migrants to animals and in particular to insects or rodents. Such incendiary language carries intertextual echoes of Nazi propaganda in which Jews were described as 'parasites' or 'rats'.

In focus: experimental evidence for framing effects of metaphor

The framing effects of metaphor have been demonstrated experimentally across a large range of discursive contexts. For example, in one experiment, participants were presented with a text about a recent rise in crime levels in a fictitious city (Thibodeau and Boroditsky 2011). The text described crime metaphorically either as a wild beast *preying* on the city or as a virus *infecting* the city. Participants were then asked to suggest measures to address the rise in crime. Participants in the animal condition were more likely to suggest punitive measures that involved tracking criminals down and locking them up. Conversely, participants in the disease condition were more likely to suggest progressive measures that involved tackling the causes of crime. In another study (Hart 2018), participants were presented with a news text reporting a recent protest in another fictitious city. The text contained either fire-based metaphors (e.g. Protests *engulfed* the city) or literal equivalents (e.g. Protests *overwhelmed* the city). Participants presented with fire metaphors were more likely to see police use of water cannon as a legitimate way of controlling the protests. This effect was interpreted as arising from the metaphor where the normal way of controlling fire is through water dispersed from fire engines, the counterpart of which in the target domain is water cannon (Figure 16.3).

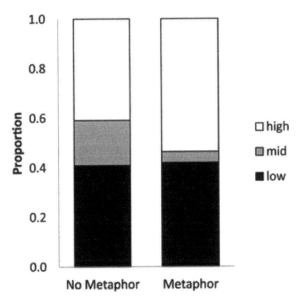

Figure 16.3 Perceived legitimacy of police use of water cannon to control political protests.

Source: Hart (2018: 292).

16.3.4 Topoi

Topoi are implicit argumentation structures or common-sense reasoning schemes, which, when appealed to by statements, automatically lead to a given conclusion. For example, it follows logically and incontrovertibly that if a situation is unsustainable or doing harm, then some action should be taken to stop it. Topoi are a key analytical focus of the discourse-historical approach to CDA, where they are shown to be a salient feature of discriminatory discourses. Different 'funds' of topoi exist for different discourses. Those listed in Table 16.2

Table 16.2 List of topoi.

1 Usefulness, advantage	9 Finances
2 Uselessness, disadvantage	10 Reality
3 Definition, name interpretation	11 Numbers
4 Danger and threat	12 Law and right
5 Humanitarianism	13 History
6 Justice	14 Culture
7 Responsibility	15 Abuse
8 Burdening, weighing	

Source: Wodak (2001: 74).

are characteristic of anti-immigration discourse, which has been the primary focus of the **discourse-historical approach**. They are defined by means of conditional statements of the form *If X, then Y*. We'll illustrate some of these topoi using, as an example text in Table 16.2, the opening lines from a speech delivered to Parliament by the then Home Secretary Priti Patel in support of the 2021 Nationality and Borders Bill (www.gov.uk/government/speeches/home-secretary-opening-speech-for-nationality-borders-bill).

The Home Secretary's opening speech for the second reading of the Nationality and Borders Bill in the House of Commons (19 Jul 2021)

(9) The British people have had enough of open borders and uncontrolled migration.

(10) Enough of a failed asylum system that costs the taxpayer over a billion pounds a year.

(11) Enough of dinghies arriving illegally on our shores, directed by organised crime gangs.

(12) Enough of people drowning on these dangerous, illegal, and unnecessary journeys.

(13) Enough of people being trafficked and sold into modern slavery.

(14) Enough of economic migrants pretending to be genuine refugees.

(15) Enough of adults pretending to be children to claim asylum.

(16) Enough of people trying to gain entry illegally, ahead of those who play by the rules.

(17) Enough of foreign criminals – including murderers and rapists – who abuse our laws and then game the system so we can't remove them.

(18) The British people have had enough of being told none of these issues matter – enough of being told it is racist to even think about addressing public concerns and seeking to fix this failed system.

The topos of finances is particularly prevalent in anti-immigration discourse. It takes the form: if a specific situation or action costs too much money or causes a loss of revenue, one should perform actions which diminish the costs or help to avoid the loss. It is realised in anti-immigration discourse where immigration is described in terms of its cost to the taxpayer. In Priti Patel's speech, statements such as (10) may therefore be said to appeal to the topos of finances in justification of more restrictive immigration policies. Another topos frequently found in anti-immigration discourse is the topos of abuse, which takes the form: if a right or an offer for help is abused, the right should be changed, or the help should be withdrawn, or measures against the abuse should be taken. Politicians rely on this topos when they claim that the asylum system is being abused. It is realised in the often-made distinction between 'genuine' and non-genuine or 'bogus' refugees and in descriptions of migrants as cheating the system or not abiding by the rules. In Priti Patel's speech, statements (14–17) all appeal to this topos as the basis for introducing tougher immigration measures. One further topos which we find exploited by Priti Patel is the topos of humanitarianism. This topos takes the form: if a political action or decision does or does not conform with human rights or humanitarian convictions and values, one should or should not perform or take it. The statements in (12) and (13) argue that the measures proposed in the Nationality and Borders Bill are humanitarian, and should therefore be accepted, because they will stop migrants from suffering.

16.4. Multimodality

CDA developed out of linguistics, and language has therefore always been of primary concern. Texts, however, are rarely monomodal. This is especially true of contemporary forms of online texts, which are rich in images. For example, online news articles will typically contain photographs or other graphics as part of the text. Other digital genres such as social media ads are also rich in their multimodality. CDA has therefore undergone a **multimodal turn** to address the way power, ideology and persuasion are enacted through semiotic modes other than language, including images (Machin and Mayr 2012). Here, many of the strategies found in language are also observable in images. For example, in the visual equivalent of transitivity, people can be shown as participants in different kinds of action or process. In the case of political protests, protesters can be shown holding up placards thus representing a verbal process which emphasises their message or can be shown engaged in material processes of disruption and destruction which emphasise confrontation and violence. Topoi and metaphor may also be realised visually as well as linguistically. For example, the text in (19) is one of the targeted Facebook ads distributed by the Vote Leave campaign in the run-up to the

Figure 16.4 Facebook advert distributed by the Vote Leave campaign in the run-up to the Brexit referendum.

Brexit referendum (Figure 16.4). The image appeals to the topos of burden/weighing which states that if a country is burdened by specific problems, one should act in order to diminish this burden. The topos is realised specifically through the metaphor of a ball and chain in which the EU is represented as a heavy weight, in the form of a ball and chain, which prevents Britain from fulfilling its potential.

In focus: gesture in political communication

Spoken discourse is also multimodal where speakers rely on gestures as well as speech to communicate meanings. Such **co-speech gestures**, which are typically performed by the hands, are not the same thing as 'body language' or hand signals like a thumbs up. They are an inherent feature of spoken language. In spoken forms of political discourse, such as political speeches and parliamentary debates, gestures are therefore another mode implicated in the communication and legitimation of unequal power relations where many of the same analytical parameters apply. For example, Hart and Winter (2022) studied hand movements in the anti-immigration discourse of Nigel Farage. In one of the examples they analyse, Farage refers to 'an explosion in the birth rate of newly arrived people'. The phrase 'explosion', when used to mean rapid increase, may be taken as a frozen metaphor that no longer has any figurative connection to actual explosions. However, as he utters the phrase, Farage performs a gesture that acts out the image of an explosion with his hands moving rapidly upward and outward as in Figure 16.5. The gesture therefore highlights the active figurativity of the expression and, since explosions typically do damage, serves to construe immigration as having harmful effects.

Figure 16.5 'Explosion' gesture in Farage anti-immigration discourse.

Source: Hart and Winter (2022: 49).

16.5. The notion of critique

It is important to recognise that CDA does not represent a particular method of discourse analysis (cf. Chapter 10), but is characterised instead by its critical perspective. However, we have come this far without actually defining what is meant by 'critical' in CDA. In line with continental thinkers like Antonio Gramsci, Michael Foucault and Jurgen Habermas, CDA sees patterns or habits of language use as instrumental in constructing our social realities, including relations of power and inequality. This occurs as texts express discourses which are ideological but whose **hegemonic** status serves to naturalise and legitimise the domination of some members of society by others. It follows from this position that detailed linguistic (and other forms of semiotic) analysis can help deconstruct texts in order to reveal their ideological nature and thus ultimately to enable resistance.

Linguists who take a critical stance in linguistic analysis are therefore not critical of any particular model or theory of language but of society. As Michael Billig (2003: 38) states, CDA is critical 'because it is rooted in a radical critique of social relations'. Here, to be critical means to go beyond the standard scientific task of understanding and describing to seek instead social transformation through analysis. CDA therefore starts from a perceived social problem, such as the prejudices directed at migrants, and seeks to provide some redress by highlighting the role of discourse in creating and sustaining that problem. In other words, researchers in CDA not only want to expose power and inequality as they are encoded in and enacted through texts but to challenge and resist them too by creating what Fairclough (1989) calls a **critical language awareness** – an increased consciousness, based on metalinguistic understanding, of how language contributes to the production, maintenance and change of social relations and the domination of some people by others. What distinguishes CDA from other critical forms of discourse analysis, such as Foucauldian discourse analysis, is its focus on the micro-level linguistic features of texts, drawing on models of language developed in linguistics to consider their role in reflecting, reinforcing and reproducing the ideologies that lead to inequalities.

An obvious question that arises is whose texts should we be analysing? Whose texts are likely to have the greatest influence on society? Traditionally, CDA has tended to target texts produced by **symbolic elites**. That is, actors and institutions, including politicians and the press, who possess the necessary **capital**, in all its forms, for their texts to count. However, this has begun to change somewhat with the advent of social media which, arguably, has given way to a more participatory form of politics. Certainly, it is the case that the binary distinction between text-producers and text-consumers no longer holds, leading researchers like Christian Fuchs (2013) to coin the term **text-prosumers**. CDA has therefore begun to explore the language of 'ordinary' citizens in social media settings. The critical question remains, though, whether social media really enables alternative voices and alternative discourses to cut through or whether it simply facilitates the amplification and further promulgation of dominant discourses associated with traditionally powerful actors and institutions. To the extent that right-wing populism, embodied in the likes of Donald Trump, is so closely connected with social media, the evidence isn't promising. The primary target of much CDA therefore remains texts, including social media texts, produced by politicians and the press, as well as other agencies that hold power such as big businesses, advertisers, etc. The news media in particular remain key in setting political agendas and shaping public opinion and is therefore still frequently targeted.

16.6. Conclusion

In this chapter, I have introduced the field of Critical Discourse Analysis. This involved defining key concepts such as 'texts', 'genre' and 'intertextuality', before highlighting some typical forms of analysis in CDA. Using examples from different discourses and genres, I introduced and illustrated four areas of analysis: transitivity, exclusion, metaphor and topoi. I then introduced multimodality to show how power and inequality may be constructed through semiotic modes other than language. Finally, I reflected on the notion of critique in CDA.

References

Billig, M. 2003. Critical discourse analysis and the rhetoric of critique. In G. Weiss and R. Wodak (Eds.), *Critical Discourse Analysis: Theory and Interdisciplinarity*. Basingstoke: Palgrave. pp. 35–46.

Eagleton, T. 1991. *Ideology: An Introduction*. London: Verso.

Fairclough, N. 1989. *Language and Power*. London: Longman.

Fairclough, N. 1995. *Critical Discourse Analysis: The Critical Study of Language*. London: Longman.

Fowler, R. 1991. *Language in the News: Discourse and Ideology*. London: Routledge.

Fuchs, C. 2013. *Social Media: A Critical Introduction*. London: Sage.

Halliday, M. A. K. 1985. *Introduction to Functional Grammar*. London: Edward Arnold.

Halliday, M. A. K. and Hasan, R. 1976. *Cohesion in English*. London: Routledge.

Hart, C. 2018. 'Riots engulfed the city': An experimental study investigating the legitimating effects of fire metaphors in discourses of disorder. *Discourse & Society*, 29(3): 279–298.

Hart, C. 2021. '28 Palestinians Die': A Cognitive grammar analysis of mystification in press coverage of state violence on the Gaza Border. In M. Giovanelli, C. Harrison and L. Nuttall (Eds.), *New Directions in Cognitive Grammar and Style*. London: Bloomsbury, pp. 93–116.

Hart, C. and Winter, B. 2022. Gesture and legitimation in the anti-immigration discourse of Nigel Farage. *Discourse & Society*, 33(1): 34–55.

Lakoff, G. and Johnson, M. 1980. *Metaphors We Live by*. Chicago: University of Chicago Press.

Machin, D. and Mayr, A. 2012. *How to Do Critical Discourse Analysis: A Multimodal Introduction*. London: Sage.

O'Halloran, K. and Coffin, C. 2004. Checking over-interpretation and under-interpretation: Help from corpora in critical linguistics. In C. Coffin, A. Hewings and K. O'Halloran (Eds.), *Applying English Grammar: Functional and Corpus Approaches*. London: Routledge, pp. 275–297.

Thibodeau, P. H. and Boroditsky, L. 2011. Metaphors we think with: The role of metaphor in reasoning. *PLoS ONE*, 6(2): e16782.

van Leeuwen, T. 1996. The representation of social actors. In C. R. Caldas-Coulthard and M. Coulthard (Eds.), *Texts and Practices: Readings in Critical Discourse Analysis*. London: Routledge, pp. 32–71.

Widdowson, H. G. 2004. *Text, Context, Pretext: Critical Issues in Discourse Analysis*. Oxford: Blackwell.

Wodak, R. 2001. The discourse-historical approach. In R. Wodak and M. Meyer (Eds.), *Methods of Critical Discourse Analysis*. London: Sage, pp. 63–94.

17 Language in the workplace
Veronika Koller

17.1 Introduction

Language is a central feature of any workplace. Of course, there are jobs that specifically require professionals to produce texts – public relations, brand management and translation come to mind – but whether people make a living analysing the stock market, selling bakery products or collecting rubbish bins, they cannot do any of these things without using language. And in any workplace, they will engage in spoken and sometimes written interaction for twin purposes (i.e. to get things done and to ensure good relations with their colleagues and managers). In fact, how to reconcile these transactional and interpersonal goals at work has been the subject of a considerable number of linguistic studies (for recent collections and textbooks, see Darics and Koller 2018; Mullany 2020; Vine 2020). In fact, there are scholars who speak of the 'communicative constitution of organizations' (Cooren and Martine 2016), by which they mean that the relations, processes and structures that make up any organisation are brought into being through language use as social practice, that is, discourse (see Chapter 10). While not everyone may share that view, it is safe to say that people make sense of what they do and what happens in their workplaces through language.

Yet workplaces are immensely complex and multifaceted contexts, so deciding what to focus on in a chapter on language in the workplace is quite a challenge. Elsewhere (Koller 2018), I have written about the linguistic dimension of both leadership and branding; here, I want to address an area that more and more organisations realise is crucial to their success: **equality, diversity and inclusion** (EDI). In the following, I will introduce two lenses through which the language aspects of EDI can be studied, namely **pragmatics** and **Critical Discourse Analysis**. Both approaches will be illustrated with examples. I will close the chapter by outlining some open questions about language use in diverse workplaces.

DOI: 10.4324/9781003045571-20

17.2 Approaches to researching language in the workplace

17.2.1 Pragmatics

Simply put, pragmatics is the study of how speakers use language to make meaning in a given context (see Chapter 6 for more on this area of linguistics). Major areas of interest for researchers in pragmatics are how people enact humour in interaction, how they achieve being polite by the norms of their culture and how they give and accept (or not!) compliments, criticism and apologies. Most work in the field deals with spoken language, and pragmatics research into language in the workplace is no exception: meetings talk offline and online, including informal chat, has been the subject of a considerable number of studies. Researchers have established how power and **politeness** are intertwined in workplace language (Holmes and Stubbe 2015) and what role humour plays to meet relational goals in leadership (Schnurr 2008). Much pragmatics research into workplace language also has a cross-cultural (i.e. comparing cultural practices) or intercultural (i.e. analysing interactions in multi-cultural workplaces) focus (a recent publication on language and culture in the workplace is Schnurr and Zayts 2017).

Before I proceed with examples, a note of caution seems in order. All too often, 'culture' is equated with 'country' (see also Chapter 12). There is no denying that norms of interaction differ across countries, but the picture is more complex than that, for four reasons. First, cultural identities also operate below and above national levels: for example, even after almost 30 years of living outside Germany, I still identify with the area in Northern Germany where I grew up – but I also see myself as European. Second, many people have composite cultural identities, referring to themselves as, for instance, African American, British-born Chinese or German of Turkish descent. Third, cultural identities can change and build up throughout life. Again, my own trajectory as a migrant is a case in point: I have lived and worked in Germany, Austria and the UK, with additional family connections in Japan and Nigeria. My cultural identity is now layered and which one is most salient very much depends on who I talk to, and about what. This can, for example, lead to confusion when celebrating that 'our' football team has won the match. Finally, and crucially for our topic, national, regional and supra-national identities intersect with the culture of a workplace. Such organisational cultures are influenced by the type of environment an organisation operates in (e.g. the charity sector); the type of organisation (e.g. in terms of structure); practices and policies (i.e. how things are done in a workplace); and, last but not least, the demographics and cultural backgrounds of the employees. It is also worth remembering that many aspects of culture are invisible. We can use the tried and tested metaphor of the iceberg here: there are elements of culture which are usually obvious, such as food and clothing, body language or accents. But there are also submerged aspects, including norms, values, beliefs and competencies. It is these latter aspects that can lead to misunderstandings when people interact in the workplace.

Take the following excerpts from job interviews as an example (Table 17.1).

Table 17.1 Excerpts from two job interviews; I: interviewer, A: applicant.

Interview for a job as an electrician	Interview for a job as a bricklayer
I: Have you visited the skills centre?	I: Have you visited the skills centre?
A: Yes I did.	A: Yep, I've been there, yeah.
I: So you've had a look at the workshops?	I: So you've had a chance to look around? And did you look in at the brick shop?
A: Yes.	A: Ah yeah, we had a look around the brick shop and uhm, it looks okay, I mean it's . . .
I: You know what the training allowance is? Do you?	I: All right.
A: Yeah.	A: Pretty good, yeah.

Source: Adapted from Gumperz (1992).

When I ask my students who they would hire, most white British students favour the prospective bricklayer – why? After all, the applicants do not differ in what information they convey in their answers. The difference between them, though, is that the prospective electrician adheres to the Gricean maxim of quantity and manner (see Chapter 6), keeping responses brief and to the point. The interviewing bricklayer on the other hand could be accused of saying more than is needed, padding out his answers with extra phrases and clauses. Yet it is exactly this 'chattiness' that is likely to make him look open and sociable to a white British interviewer, whereas the electrician may seem gruff and unengaged. Yet both interact according to the norms of their culture: the electrician, who is of South-east Asian descent, refrains from taking up too much of the conversational floor when talking to the more powerful interviewer, while the white British bricklayer shows engagement and interest by saying more than strictly necessary. If interviewers are not aware of such cultural norms, it is obvious how discrimination in recruitment can arise despite a genuine wish to increase diversity.

Cultural awareness continues to be important once people have been hired. A central notion in any organisation's EDI efforts is that of inclusive leadership, understood as

> an ongoing cycle of learning through collaborative and respectful relational practice that enables individuals and collectives to be fully part of the whole, such that they are directed, aligned, and committed toward shared outcomes, for the common good of all, while retaining a sense of authenticity and uniqueness.

> (Booysen 2014: 306)

Leadership is something that is enacted in every interaction that team leaders have with team members, and the way that leaders use language can help or hinder inclusion in organisations. To conclude this section, let us consider two examples.[1]

Example 1 (adapted from Holmes 2017: 339): C is the chair of a sub-committee and from the Indigenous Māori people in New Zealand. Here he is explaining a feature of a planned museum (a type of building called 'marae') to R, the Pākehā (European settler) chair of the main committee.

C: There two <u>main</u> (2) fields that have to be explored (2) and er (1) the one that is
    most important is its <u>cust</u>omary role in the first place because (2) marae <u>comes</u>
    on and it comes from (4) the tangata whenua who are Māori (7) to change it
R: But it's not just for Māori=
C: =No=
R: =It it you <u>must</u> get that if it is a Māori institution and nothing more <u>this</u> [bangs
    table] marae has failed (2) and they <u>must</u> [bangs table] get that idea

---

In his first turn, C follows Māori norms for the context, using a formal style of talking that is characterised by frequent pauses and a slow pace. Before he can make his second point, however, he is interrupted and challenged on his understanding of the museum feature. In R's second turn, the addressee-oriented deontic modality ('you must get that', later softened to 'they must get that'), the implicit downgrading of Māori features ('nothing more') and banging the table all threaten C's individual face and that of the group he belongs to (see Chapter 6). As noted by the author, C looks down once R interrupts him and stays quiet for the rest of the meeting. R's linguistic and interactional style has excluded him.

By contrast, the second example can be seen as an instance of successful inclusive leadership.

Example 2 (adapted from Holmes 2017: 343): A is a Chinese accountant working in New Zealand, where she has recently joined a company. Here she is talking about a software to B, her Pākehā mentor.

A: If er if they're overdue that mean um firstly that mean probably user don't want
    to use it and not update correctly and er timely and another reason if the this
    other system is not er the interface is not quite er friendly
B: ιιιιι
A: And er also some function a functionality cannot meet the users' requirement
    so always they think it's a waste of time my time or probably they will think
    they don't want to use it
B: Yeah no this looks excellent and um I mean y- you you do raise some um very
    valid valid points there

In her outspoken criticism of the software used by her employer, A violates a cultural norm of Pākehā workplaces, namely that especially newcomers should not engage in direct criticism. Yet B not only passes up a chance to take the floor, using only a minimal response ('mm') but also responds by positively evaluating A's observations. Clearly, B allows for different cultural norms to be enacted, thereby facilitating a more diverse workplace.

In workplaces and elsewhere, the role of language use in challenging or promoting discrimination or equality is a key concern of Critical Discourse Analysis, and it is to this approach that we now turn.

17.2.2 Critical Discourse Analysis

Scholars in Critical Discourse Analysis (CDA, also known as critical discourse studies or CDS; see also Chapter 16) are interested in the links between language use, how people interact through texts in processes known as discourse practice, and relevant social contexts. These three levels bring each other into being, in that changes in social context can change both discourse practices and how language is used. Conversely, persistent changes in language use and discourse practice can have an impact on the social context. An example from the workplace is the well-researched speech situation of meetings. According to organisational culture, the register of the language used can be more or less formal and there may be different implicit norms about who speaks, in what order, with what purpose and for how long. A meeting in which the chair uses very formal language and in which only the most powerful participants can make substantial contributions would reflect a hierarchical and conservative culture where inclusion and equality are not central values. Top-down cultural changes would change the way meetings are run and how people talk during them. Likewise, employees whose values differ from those espoused by their employer may, through a series of transgressions (e.g. consciously bringing in marginalised colleagues or resisting interruptions), change the way things are done and understood in their workplace.

A defining interest of CDA researchers is indeed the role that language use and discourse practice play in producing, maintaining and challenging inequalities and discrimination. CDA researchers see language and other sign systems as an entry point into social problems such as sexism or cultural bias, which can translate into exclusionary, homogenising practices in the workplace. In this context, discourse can be defined as

the way in which people use linguistic and other signs, and the way they behave in conversations, in order to relate to others and project an identity for themselves and others. Such language use, however, is restricted by power (e.g., seniority at work), material practices (e.g., office design) and institutions (e.g., organizational structures).

(Koller 2017: 27)

A critical analysis of the ways in which language use is linked to discourse practice and social context will involve a linguistic description of texts or transcripts, followed by a discussion of the interactions surrounding them and the relevant aspects of the social context in which both language use and discourse practice are embedded. In this way, drawing on the contexts of language use helps to explain the findings from the descriptive text analysis. The elements and guiding questions of this analytical process are summarised in Figure 17.1.

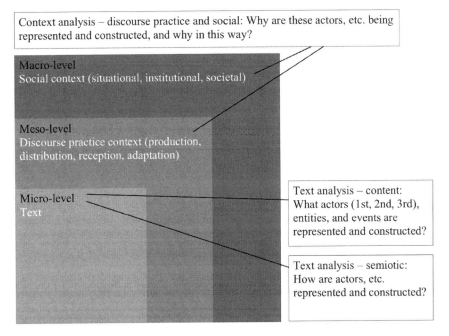

Figure 17.1 Levels of Critical Discourse Analysis.

Source: Adapted from Fairclough (2010: 133).

Being an approach to the linguistic and discursive dimension of social problems, CDA is not a methodology in itself. Instead, scholars draw from a wide variety of analytical tools. Two that have proved popular are **social actor representation** and **transitivity** (Darics and Koller 2019), both of which have their roots in systemic-functional linguistics (see Chapter 16 for details). In general terms, these frameworks help to investigate who is represented as doing what to whom in text and talk. Doing so can help us find out how language use contributes to fostering or preventing equality, diversity and inclusion at work. This is not only a question of who is mentioned or not, but also of how groups and individuals are referred to: for example, is someone's ethnicity made relevant or not; are certain employees talked about as engaging in dynamic, impactful actions or not; are specific actors given responsibility or not? The case study illustrates the insights that can be gained from such an analysis.

Case study: when the linguistic means defeat the organisational ends

A number of years ago, a student of mine, who also works as a coach and consultant, was asked to advise a medium-sized consultancy business on how to make progress on diversifying their workforce with regard to gender. (Sometimes consultants need advice themselves.) The management felt that despite efforts made in good faith, women continued to be under-represented, especially at more senior levels. Always a champion for gender equality, my student looked at what that company had done so far, talking to employees and managers and reading relevant documents.

One bit of documentation that caught her eye was a slide deck presenting an action plan for a diversity and inclusion programme. The presentation had been written by the so-called People Council of the firm, a group of employees seeking to increase diversity and equality in their workplace. As such, it was an early statement of intent, the purpose of which was to get buy-in from senior partners and managers at the company. Suggesting an action plan for the next three years, the presentation was also future focused, action oriented and intended to benefit the firm and its employees. It would be interesting therefore – my student thought – to investigate how employees had used language to represent actions and actors. Have a go yourself: look at the three extracts from the presentation and analyse who is represented as doing what.

1 'With the exception of gender and age, the quality of management information and data on diversity is poor. Access to broader diversity data is a requirement to expand the agenda. The firm has no data to benchmark against the external market or competitors.'
2 'Women are more prevalent in junior roles and in secretarial and administrative positions. Women leaders (where they exist) are in functional roles, particularly HR, Communications and Legal.'
3 'Based on practice to date, overt activity to support Diversity, particularly on progression and talent, is required. A 3-year FW Diversity Action Plan that builds and expands our work on gender to date is proposed.'

The most striking feature of this text is that it mentions almost no people. Instead, we find two very common ways of obfuscating agency: **agentless passives**, where a clause features an action but no actor (e.g. 'an action plan . . . is proposed' – by whom?) and **nominalisation**, where verbs denoting action have been turned into abstract nouns (e.g. 'access . . . is a requirement'). Another way of excluding specific actors is to refer to them in collective terms ('the firm'). And in the one instance where the presenters mention the group of people they would like to support, these are grammatically active ('women *are* more prevalent', 'women leaders (where they *exist*) *are* in functional roles') but semantically not very agentive: what women are represented as doing is simply being and existing, which is rather static. Elsewhere in their presentation, the group of employees used a range of grammatical constructions that make actors invisible, including passives with a grammatical rather than human actor ('Diversity is measured by *HR statistics*') as well as stand-alone present and past participles, some of them nominalised, in bullet-point lists: '*Responding* to growing diversity', 'maternity leave and pay *enhanced*', '*offering* of part time jobs'.

Compare that to the following rewritten excerpts – can you see how including more pronouns, using (dynamic) verbs instead of nouns, and referring to people in relational terms makes the text more personal?

1   'Apart from gender and age, *we* do not *know* much about diversity at [company name]. To include more groups, *we need* to have broader diversity data. *We have* no data to *compare ourselves* to others.'
2   'Female *colleagues work* mostly in junior roles or as secretaries and administrators. The few women leaders *we have work* in functional roles.'
3   'Based on what has been *our* practice to date, *we need to work* more explicitly to increase diversity, especially with regard to *colleagues*' career progression and hiring talented staff. *We* therefore *propose* a three-year [forward] diversity action plan that *helps us* build and expand our work on gender so far.'

After talking to the employees, my student realised that they had not intended to make their presentation so impersonal. In fact, they were not aware of how they had used language at all; they had simply drafted their slides in the way presentations were usually done in that company. But if we don't know who is responsible for change, how can we ever make it happen?

Marginalisation and its opposite, inclusion, in workplaces does not only happen along the lines of gender, ethnicity, ability or sexuality – sometimes, it is language itself that is at stake. For example, while linguists have long been aware of 'accentism', managers and other employees are only beginning to realise that they may hold unconscious biases toward co-workers with certain accents and that such bias may lead to a subtle (or not-so-subtle) 'othering' of speakers with non-native accents or with accents that come with negative cultural connotations. To avoid being marginalised, speakers may try to change their accent to one that holds more prestige in their workplace. This is a form of linguistic **accommodation** (Zhang and Giles 2018), a phenomenon which sees speakers converge with (i.e. become more alike) their conversation partners. (In rarer cases, they may diverge, i.e. try to become less similar.) Observing who accommodates to whom can provide useful insights into the power relations in a workplace.

Another area where language itself can facilitate or obstruct EDI efforts is **lingua franca** communication (see Chapter 11). Most multinational organisations have a language that is used across the company to make it possible for employees from different local subsidiaries to communicate with each other without the need for translation. However, not only can the choice of language disadvantage employees whose first language makes it relatively more difficult for them to use the lingua franca. In addition, enforcing a common code without regard for speech situations, communication channels and workplace relations can alienate particular employees. For example, it may be perfectly reasonable to hold staff meetings in the corporate language, but why should an informal email exchange between colleagues who share a first or second language be conducted in the lingua franca? Insisting that they use it could send a message that their linguistic background is not valued and make them feel that they do not belong. This is exacerbated in post-colonial contexts, where Indigenous languages and their speakers often enjoy less prestige. The 'in focus' box, which closes this section, shows how language diversity can be narrowed down in business.

In focus: doing business in a multilingual context

If you have visited or lived in any big city, you will have noticed how many different languages surround you. You may also be aware that in some countries (e.g. Belgium) what language you speak can be a political issue. And maybe you live in a country like Wales, where an endangered language has been brought back from the brink. Now imagine a country with 50 Indigenous languages, some spoken by millions of people, some very small, some codified as written, some only used in informal spoken interaction. Imagine, on top of that, that there is an official, non-Indigenous language, plus migrants from neighbouring countries and further afield bringing their languages with them.

That is the situation in Ghana in Anglophone West Africa. Its capital, Accra, is home to more than 4 million people and its linguistic make-up is diverse, to say the least. The Indigenous people of Accra are the Ga, whose language of the same name is spoken in and around the city. However, like many big cities, the Ghanaian capital attracts people from all over the country, so that **Ga** is now actually a minority language there; about 40% of people who have moved to Accra are native speakers of the Twi variety of **Akan**, the largest Indigenous language in Ghana. A host of other Ghanaian languages can be heard on the streets of Accra as well, plus languages of other countries in the region, such as Benin, Burkina Faso, Nigeria and Togo. There are also sizeable minorities of speakers of Mandarin and Lebanese Arabic. As a legacy of colonial times, English functions as an official language and lingua franca, and has diversified into varieties of Ghanaian Pidgin English (pidgin refers to a grammatically simplified form of a language used for communication between people not sharing a common language).

What does a workplace look and sound like under such conditions of linguistic superdiversity? A group of researchers (Anderson et al. 2020) from the Department of English at the University of Ghana wanted to find out and went to market – literally. Makola Market is the biggest of its kind in Accra, where stall holders sell everything from beauty products to financial services. Anderson and her colleagues were interested in the signs displayed outside shops, in the language(s) used on them and in what insights they offer about the '**ethnolinguistic vitality** of the Indigenous language use in the city of Accra' (2020: 6). Ethnolinguistic vitality is a measure of how the socio-economic status and demographics of, and the institutional support for, a social group influence how likely they are to keep using their language or, alternatively, undergo linguistic assimilation.

On a series of quiet Sunday mornings, the researchers took 356 pictures of signs outside shops. Just over three-quarters of that signage displayed the name of the business, about a fifth informed about the name of the product or service sold (mostly hair and beauty products, clothing and fabrics, and food), and the rest was a combination of both. When they analysed the images, they found that the overwhelming majority of the signs (93%) were in English only. Most of the remaining signs featured a mixture of English and Akan, and only one sign contained only Akan. Ga, the original language of Accra, was used for spoken sales interactions.

Shop owners often used English creatively when naming their business and products. For example, can you guess what kind of product 'Kokosol' might be? It's coconut oil for cooking and its name combines a short form and different spelling of 'coconut' with an abbreviation of 'solution'. When English and Akan were combined, the researchers could observe a functional differentiation: in company names such as 'adwene pa phones', the Akan element conveyed branding messages (here: 'good mind', i.e. honesty) while English was reserved for factual information. The product and company taglines that could be seen on two-thirds of the signs showed something similar: taglines in Akan helped branding efforts by intensifying the perceived value of a product (e.g. 'ahoɔfɛ ntoasoɔ', which translates as 'timeless beauty' or 'endless beauty'), flattering the customer ('ɔbaasima', i.e. 'virtuous woman') or raising the credibility of the seller by portraying them as a religious person in a deeply religious country (e.g. 'Onyame ne me Boafoɔ', 'God is my helper'). The group of researchers also noticed that where taglines combined both languages, the ones in Akan were printed in bold fonts and in brighter colours than their English counterparts, reinforcing their persuasive rather than informative use.

Anderson and her colleagues were surprised to see that English was so predominant because in Ghana, it is mostly associated with formal offices rather than bustling markets. One reason could be that the status of English as the language of official written documents has spilled over to the genre of shop signs, which are after all also a form of written communication. What is more, the market 'is a melting pot of several cultures, tongues and ethnicities' (2020: 27) and the non-Indigenous English may be the most neutral lingua franca. The authors point out that their findings not only show the status of English in Ghana, but are also a warning about the lack of vitality of Indigenous languages. They conclude that '[i]n a situation like this, some language planning is necessary' (2020: 28).

17.3 Open questions

Throughout this chapter, I have used the terms 'equality', 'diversity', 'inclusion', 'belonging', 'discrimination' and 'marginalisation', all of which belong to the semantic field of diversity in the workplace. It is interesting to note, though, that while most organisations concern themselves with diversity and inclusion, and some add belonging into the mix, equality and its opposites feature much less often in corporate language use. It is true that corporate decision-makers increasingly acknowledge that an additive approach to diversity may not mean a more heterogeneous organisation; put bluntly, hiring more employees who are not white, heterosexual, able-bodied men does not change anything as long as the same employees are expected to conform to dominant norms.

Yet despite that realisation, there is still a reluctance to use the more political word 'equality' and an instinct to shy away from negative terms such as 'discrimination'. Part of the reason may be a positivity bias, especially in commercial organisations; steeped as they are in a discourse that is meant to persuade stakeholders of the inherent value of the company, it is difficult to admit to shortcomings. Another reason for the selective use of terms may be a concern to be held accountable, which is less likely to happen based on vague concepts such as belonging, which are difficult to measure. Nevertheless, we need to ask whether diversity managers are interested in social justice and equal opportunities or merely in projecting a favourable image. And even if they see the business case for inclusion, would they want to be part of a political project to increase equality? Do they welcome legally binding regulation or would they prefer voluntary self-monitoring? The answers to these open questions will show how far out of their comfort zone decision-makers are willing to venture.

17.4 Conclusion

In this chapter, I have explored language in the workplace by focusing on equality, diversity and inclusion (EDI) efforts in organisations. I have introduced two approaches to workplace language, namely pragmatics and critical discourse studies. For each, I have highlighted central concerns, areas of research and analytical processes, discussing how inclusive leadership can be enacted in spoken interaction and how individuals and groups at work can be linguistically included or marginalised. I have also presented examples and case studies showing how the respective lens helps to understand the role that language plays in the workplace. I have closed the chapter by raising questions about the terms used around the increasingly important area of EDI.

Note

1 Transcription key: Underlined parts of words are emphasised, numbers in brackets are pauses in seconds, equal signs signal that speakers follow on from each other without a break between turns.

References

Anderson, J. A., Wiredu, J. F., Ansah, G. N., Frimpong-Kodie, G., Orfson-Offie, E. and Boamah-Boateng, D. 2020. A linguistic landscape of the central business district of Accra. *Legon Journal of the Humanities*, 31(1): 1–35. https://doi.org/10.4314/ljh.v31i1.1

Booysen, L. 2014. The development of inclusive leadership: Practice and processes. In B. M. Ferdman and B. R. Deane (Eds.), *Diversity at Work: The Practice of Inclusion*. San Francisco: Jossey-Bass, pp. 296–329.

Cooren, F. and Martine, T. 2016. Communicative constitution of organizations. In K. B. Jensen and R. T. Craig (Eds.), *The International Encyclopedia of Communication Theory and Philosophy*. Vol. 1. Chichester and Hoboken, NJ: John Wiley & Sons, pp. 307–315.

Darics, E. and Koller, V. 2018. *Language in Business, Language at Work*. London: Macmillan Higher Education.

Darics, E. and Koller, V. 2019. Social actors 'to go': An analytical toolkit to explore agency in business discourse and communication. *Business and Professional Communication Quarterly*, 82(2): 214–238.

Fairclough, N. 2010. *Critical Discourse Analysis*. 2nd ed. London: Longman.

Gumperz, J. 1992. Interviewing in intercultural situations. In P. Drew and J. Heritage (Eds.), *Talk at Work: Interaction in Institutional Settings*. Cambridge: Cambridge University Press, pp. 302–327.

Holmes, J. 2017. Intercultural communication in the workplace. In B. Vine (Ed.), *The Routledge Handbook of Language in the Workplace*. New York: Routledge, pp. 335–347.

Holmes, J. and Stubbe, M. 2015. *Power and Politeness in the Workplace: A Sociolinguistic Analysis of Talk at Work*. Abingdon: Routledge.

Koller, V. 2017. Critical discourse studies. In B. Vine (Ed.), *The Routledge Handbook of Language in the Workplace*. New York: Routledge, pp. 27–39.

Koller, V. 2018. Business communication. In J. Culpeper, P. Kerswill, R. Wodak, A. McEnery and F. Katamba (Eds.), *English Language: Description, Variation and Context*. 2nd ed. London: Palgrave, pp. 526–537.

Mullany, L. (Ed.). 2020. *Professional Communication: Consultancy, Advocacy, Activism*. Cham: Palgrave Macmillan.

Schnurr, S. 2008. *Leadership Discourse at Work: Interactions of Humour, Gender and Workplace Culture*. Basingstoke: Palgrave.

Schnurr, S. and Zayts, O. 2017. *Language and Culture at Work*. Abingdon: Routledge.

Vine, B. 2020. *Introducing Language at Work*. Cambridge: Cambridge University Press.

Zhang, Y. B. and Giles, H. 2018. Communication accommodation theory. In Y. Y. Kim (Ed.), *The International Encyclopedia of Intercultural Communication*. Hoboken, NJ: John Wiley & Sons, pp. 95–108.

18

Computational linguistics

Georgina Brown

18.1 Introduction

There is no definition of computational linguistics that 'can stand up to the test of time' (Church and Liberman 2021: 1). This is largely down to the range of forms that computational linguistics has taken within the handful of decades that so far make up its history. Church and Liberman describe the field's history as a series of 'fads' that have been rather different ways of approaching language problems. Computational linguistics' objectives might include developing machine translation systems (i.e. technologies that can translate strings of text or speech from one language into another language) or chatbots (i.e. technology that can interact with human users in a 'conversation-like' way). The objectives of the field are seemingly stable and draw together the different 'fads' that computational linguistics has endured. While computational linguists working on chatbots in the 1960s had very similar goals to computational linguists working on chatbots today, the ways in which each computational linguist would go about it look rather different. This chapter conceptualises the field in terms of its objectives, since these are the threads that more consistently run through the field compared to the methods (or 'fads') that have been applied.

Computational linguistics has two broad types of objectives. As already touched upon, the first objective is to produce applications, or 'systems', that can be useful to the world in some way (such as developing chatbots or machine translation technologies). The second objective is to manipulate language data (perhaps natural data or data that has been created) in order to test theories about language. The work carried out to meet the latter objective can feed in to the former objective and we are now in a position where these technologies are integrated into normal life. Search engines and speech recognition technologies are just two examples of tools that are regularly in use.

As use of computational linguistic technologies has grown, we have started to witness the societal impact of these technologies. These technologies can, on the one hand, benefit many corners of society, but they can also pose new problems. As computational linguistics has now arrived at such a developed stage, and is no longer a 'new' area of linguistics, this chapter outlines aspects of the resulting technologies' existence that go beyond their inner workings. This chapter will start, in Section 18.2, by introducing some of the general principles and will then,

DOI: 10.4324/9781003045571-21

in Section 18.3, discuss the key components of computational linguistic systems. It will then, in Section 18.4, move on to talk about some of the applications of computational linguistics that aim to benefit parts of society. Finally, in Section 18.5, we will then move on to talk about the challenges and dangers that these technologies simultaneously bring to society.

18.2 Dividing lines in computational linguistics

This section outlines key ways in which we can categorise different types of computational linguistic systems.

18.2.1 Natural Language Processing vs. speech technology

The most prominent way of categorising computational linguistic systems is according to whether they are *Natural Language Processing* (NLP) or *speech technology* systems. These are the two main areas of computational linguistics and they refer to two established disciplines in and of themselves. For this reason, they are not often discussed together in a single chapter or paper. However, there is undoubtedly overlap in terms of their conceptual contents, as well as the issues that these fields encounter, and so this overlap is acknowledged in the present chapter. The difference between the two computational linguistic sub-disciplines comes down to the broad data type that they focus on. These differences are summarised in Table 18.1.

Table 18.1 Differences between NLP and speech technology systems.

Computational linguistic system type	Works with . . .	Used for . . .
Natural Language Processing (NLP)	Text data (e.g. emails, news articles, typed search queries, etc.).	Developing applications such as search engines and text summarisation systems.
Speech technology	Speech data (e.g. phone calls, voice submissions, audio from YouTube videos, etc.).	Technologies such as automatic speech recognition systems and the creation of synthetic voices.

Regardless of whether NLP or speech technology applications are being discussed, it is also possible to divide computational linguistic systems according to whether they are 'recognition' technologies or 'synthesis' technologies. This way of categorising systems is not based on the type of language data they focus on, but on the general objective they aim to achieve. Most NLP and speech technology systems can either 'recognise' or 'synthesise' language data.

18.2.1.1 Recognition technologies

Recognition technologies can be 'classification' or 'measurement' tools which underline a huge number of computational linguistic systems. For example, they can organise large datasets of texts according to topic, which is very useful in the context of search engines. Another example of a text classification system is a language classification system that can take the input text and detect which language it is written in. This can be useful in contexts where there may be a large international business taking in customer feedback. That customer feedback would then need to be sorted according to language for it to be processed correctly or directed towards the relevant localised team.

To provide parallel recognition technologies within speech technology, it is possible to build and train tools that aim to 'classify' or 'measure' properties of an individual based on their speech, instead of text. For example, there are attempts to build systems that can evaluate the proficiency of a speaker when speaking a second language (Litman et al. 2018). A more unusual example is that tried by Baykaner et al. (2015) who trained and tested a system that aimed to measure how tired an individual is, based on the speech they produce. The main type of a speech technology recognition system, however, is an automatic speech recognition system. These are systems that aim to recognise the sequences of words speakers produce. Their applications are widespread. They are used in the context of virtual assistant technology where users produce commands to their devices using speech. Other uses of this technology include automatically generating subtitles for films or YouTube videos, as well as for online lectures or talks.

For both NLP and speech technology recognition systems, it is plausible to develop a computational linguistic system on all sorts of tasks where we have large datasets of text or speech samples that we can use to train these systems. However, it is important to keep in mind that these technologies are developed on the assumption that there are cues within the language data that can point towards these properties or categories that the technologies are recognising.

18.2.1.2 Synthesis technologies

Synthesis technologies create and produce language data for users to interpret or 'consume'. In NLP, probably the best and long-standing example of this is the responses we might receive from a chatbot. ELIZA is regularly referred to in introductory texts for computational linguistics as one of the first chatbots to be developed (Weizenbaum 1966). More recently though, there have been attempts to create NLP systems that can produce poetry or entire novels (e.g. Köbis and Mossink 2021).

Synthesis systems within speech technology are well established. **Speech synthesis systems** (often also called **Text-to-Speech (TTS) systems**) produce human-like speech signals that are intended to be intelligible to human listeners. Ideally, they would also be 'natural-sounding', too. Typically, these systems take a set of 'seed' speech recordings from a target speaker that are then processed within the system in order to synthesise new utterances which are specified by text. Today, it is not uncommon to find speech synthesis systems in people's pockets. Speech synthesis systems form a rather key part of modern-day virtual assistant technologies such as Apple's Siri, Amazon's Alexa or Microsoft's Cortana.

Table 18.2 provides a summary of different kinds of NLP and speech technologies that fall under *recognition systems* and *synthesis systems*.

Table 18.2 Summary of computational linguistic system types with example systems.

	Example recognition systems	Example synthesis systems
Natural Language Processing	• **Topic classification systems** that categorise articles according to broad topic area. • **Language recognition technology** that aims to identify the language of a text. • **Sentiment analysis systems** that aim to classify texts (e.g. social media posts) according to general sentiment of the author (e.g. happy, sad, angry, etc.).	• **Chatbots** that produce typed output for users. • **Text summarisation systems** that take a longer text and produce a summary.
Speech technology	• **Automatic speech recognition systems** that aim to recognise the sequence of words produced by a speaker. • **Language recognition technology** that aims to identify the language that is being spoken by a caller. • **Emotion recognition systems** that aim to classify phone calls according to the general emotion of the speaker (e.g. happy, sad, angry, etc.).	• **Text-to-Speech systems** that produce human-like speech samples to be presented to human users.

18.3 Key principles and components of computational linguistic systems

Because recognition technologies extend across an enormous number of applications, this section focuses on some of the system components that form the foundations of these technologies, in both NLP and speech technology. To build these systems, a large dataset of labelled data samples (a training dataset) is required and these data samples need to be processed and quantitatively represented in some way before users start to present data samples that they wish to classify or measure. Section 18.3.1 therefore outlines two different ways in which this **feature extraction** stage is carried out in some NLP applications and one common way in which feature extraction is carried out in speech technology. Section 18.3.2 then moves on to two very different ways in which these quantitatively represented training data samples can be further processed to form a system that is ultimately ready to analyse new and unseen data for recognition purposes. This overall process is summarised in the system diagram in Figure 18.1, and further detail behind the processes are given in the following subsections.

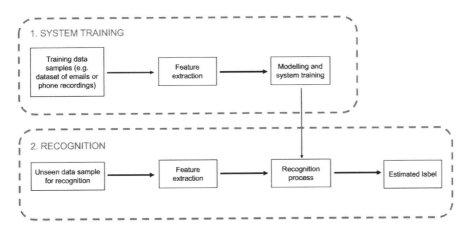

Figure 18.1 System diagram of the general processes in training and using a recognition system.

18.3.1 Feature extraction

Regardless of whether we are building an NLP or speech technology recognition system, it is important to represent the training data samples in a way that:

1   elicits the information in the language data that points towards the data properties the system is built to recognise;
2   can allow them to be quantitatively compared with other data samples.

This involves quantitatively representing the training data samples, but it also needs to be replicated for any of the unseen data samples that the system will be used to recognise. This places the training data and the unseen data on the same platform, which makes it possible to assess how similar the unseen data is to different categories of data that is represented within the training dataset. Next are two ways in which this can done for NLP applications, and the main way in which this is done for speech technology applications.

18.3.1.1 Word frequency vectors

Word frequency vectors are an easy and common way to represent text data. Vectors, in this context, are sets of numbers. Word frequency vectors are therefore long sets of numbers that log the number (or proportion) of times each unique word occurs in the text. For a given recognition task, this method relies on clues about the category or properties of a text to therefore be encoded within these vectors. It is reasonable to expect that there would usually be enough occurrences of relevant words to point towards a certain topic for a topic classification system. For example, a text about squirrels is expected to contain the word 'squirrel' a number of times. However, it is also entirely expected that there are certain recognition tasks where representing texts through word frequency vectors may not necessarily be sufficient. In the context of sentiment analysis systems – these are systems that aim to recognise the general sentiment of a text (e.g. automatically detecting whether an author is happy, sad or angry from their social media posts) – helpful cues may well go beyond the words that are present. It is also reasonable to expect that certain grammatical structures and use of punctuation markers could also assist and using word frequency vectors may overlook these useful cues. In other words, word frequency vectors are only likely to capture some of the information that would be useful to a recognition task, and they are better at some recognition tasks over others.

18.3.1.2 Embeddings

While word frequency vectors offer an attractively simple means of representing texts, they are rather 'sparse' and inefficient representations. The computational linguistics community has therefore turned to innovations using **neural networks** to generate richer and more informative representations. Neural networks are applied across a broad range of disciplines. They are a form of **machine learning**, which is returned to in Section 18.3.2, and they are primarily used to perform recognition tasks. However, they can also be used to derive features that can quantitatively represent data samples. This could be viewed as a rather long-winded way of going about it, in contrast to word frequency vectors, but these embeddings have shown to be very effective in recognition systems and are now commonplace across many NLP systems.

For demonstration purposes, we could train a neural network to perform, say, a text classification task that categorises texts according to their topic. Note the point in the previous paragraph – although this system is being trained to classify texts, its intended purpose here is to derive features which these systems can produce as by-products. To do this, we could first represent each of our training texts with a type of word frequency vector (explained earlier), and then 'map' this on to its topic category label using a neural network. In this 'mapping' process, a neural network takes the word frequency vectors as input and passes these sets of numbers through a series of weight values and functions that result in an estimated label at the end.

This process is repeated many times, altering the weight values and functions in this series each time, to improve the chances of the neural network estimating the category label correctly. Once the accuracy of the classification system (based on the training data) no longer improves, there is no need to alter the series of weights and functions and it can be considered a ready-trained topic classification system. The primary aim of the neural network is to categorise new and unseen data samples. Within this process, however, these samples are processed by the series of weights and functions that inadvertently produce new quantitative representations of the samples. This new set of values (or vector) tends to be a smaller and richer representation than the word frequency vector that we originally started with. It can therefore be taken from this system and used for other purposes (like data visualisation in a linguistics study) or to train other types of computational linguistic system.

18.3.1.3 Acoustic feature vectors

In the same way that texts for NLP applications need to be quantitatively represented, speech recordings for speech technology applications need to be quantitatively represented. Feature vectors in speech technology applications represent the acoustic and phonetic properties of the speech. There are countless types of acoustic feature vector but the most common are Mel-Frequency Cepstral Coefficients (MFCCs) (Davis and Mermelstein 1980). A single MFCC vector is extracted to reflect the power spectrum of a short time slice of the speech signal. The distribution of power at that time point is then expected to characterise the speech produced there (typically the vowel or consonant being produced). Unlike the NLP feature vectors that have been described to represent texts, many acoustic feature vectors (overlapping in sequence) are usually extracted from a single data sample to represent that sample (rather than just one vector to represent the whole data sample).

18.3.2 Modelling and recognition

Once the data are represented in an appropriate way, it is possible to train a system with those representations of data before presenting it with an unseen data sample to recognise (which is also represented by the same type of feature vector). There are two broad categories of system that could be used: a **rule-based approach**, or a **machine learning approach**. More detail about these can be found in the following 'in focus' box. For a rule-based approach, a rich feature vector to represent training data is not necessarily required. However, this approach is not used as regularly as it used to be. When it is, it is often used in conjunction with other approaches (e.g. a machine learning approach).

In focus: categories of approach

Rule-based approaches traditionally consist of a series of predetermined linguistic rules. These rules point towards specific linguistic cues that are expected to distinguish between categories of texts. This might be the presence of certain words, or combination of words, in a text that means that it is more likely to belong to one category over another. This type of system can rely on a large amount of linguistic information to contribute towards the 'rules' that are applied.

Machine learning approaches 'learn' patterns and relationships within large volumes of training data. With this approach, there tends to be a lower reliance on identifying optimal ways of representing data for a specific purpose. This is because machine learning techniques process data in such a way that discovers and expresses meaningful patterns and relationships among the features representing data samples within a training dataset. It is this forceful processing that means there is supposedly less need for decisions to be made by a human developer about which combination of features should be used to represent the individual data points for the application.

It is part of the machine learning processes to place more emphasis and weighting on those that emerge as the most valuable to a given recognition task, based on the training phase. This chapter has already introduced neural networks in Section 18.3.1, and this is probably the most commonly used type of machine learning approach today. The rise of neural networks has been enabled by the general growth in data resources and processing capabilities, with the result that they are now very widespread. The downside to neural networks is that they are very 'data-hungry'; demanding a lot of training data in order to function. Some specific recognition tasks may therefore be impossible to carry out using neural networks, because large enough datasets to train a neural network system simply do not exist.

18.4 Applications of computational linguistics

Now that we have covered some of the concepts involved in building both NLP and speech technology systems, we will move on to talk about some of the applications these technologies can go on to serve.

18.4.1 Assistive technologies

The emerging technologies entering our everyday lives bring convenience and open up opportunities across societies, but they can be of particular benefit to communities facing additional challenges. There is, for example, a body of research exploring how new technologies using computational linguistic approaches can help those affected by health conditions. An example of these research efforts is Veaux et al. (2012). Their speech technology research is one element of a broader research effort to produce technologies that can help people suffering from degenerative diseases. Some degenerative diseases, such as Motor Neuron Disease (MND) and Parkinson's, can lead to loss of the use of the speech articulators, preventing an individual from effectively producing speech to communicate (see also Chapter 1).

In such cases, it is possible to provide patients with speech synthesis technology that can produce speech signals on the speaker's behalf. Moreover, the research project is not just about providing a functional synthetic voice for patients, but is geared towards finding ways to enable the patients to continue to sound like themselves, rather than using a synthetic voice that sounds like somebody else. In turn, this enables patients to retain an important part of their identity.

To build a speech synthesiser of a particular speaker's voice, it is typical for hours and hours of speech recordings from a speaker to be required. For the purpose of building a synthetic voice specifically for someone with a degenerative disease, it is not an option to ask them to produce sentence after sentence in a recording studio. Ideally, it would be possible to produce a speech synthesiser using only a small sample of their speech data. The work from such research projects has led to speech synthesis solutions that allow for synthetic voices for individual speakers to be built with only a little recorded speech data. This has therefore led to a reality of offering patients the opportunity to use voices that sound more like themselves. To see details of this reality, scan the QR code to visit the SpeakUnique service.

Scan the QR code to visit SpeakUnique:

SCAN ME

18.4.2 Developing techniques to categorise social media content

Big technology companies have faced pressure in recent years to take more responsibility and act quickly and decisively in instances where inappropriate content is posted on their sites. For example, there have been calls for technology companies to do more to combat certain types of hate crime and grooming. Part of the solution to this problem is thought to lie in computational linguistics. If it is possible to categorise instances of language that may carry inappropriate content, then it becomes possible to identify and address these kinds of attack.

The spread of 'misinformation' online is also an issue of concern for society and, consequently, social media companies. Misinformation is 'false or inaccurate information that is deliberately created and is intentionally or unintentionally propagated' (Wu et al. 2019). The spread of misinformation could have serious repercussions, for example public health risk from misleading medical advice, or risk to public safety from posts inciting violence. There is therefore a recognised need to develop techniques that can detect instances of misinformation online. The sheer volume of posts produced everyday by internet users makes it impossible for this to be done manually by humans. Instead, we need an automated way of doing this. This is, in part, then, another computational linguistic challenge and text classification task.

Identifying misinformation on social media poses its own set of challenges. Posts in this context are obviously short, and this affects the ability to train a text classification system that performs a task effectively. Text classification technologies alone are unlikely to be sufficient for this purpose. Other cues are therefore combined with text classification, for example looking at the frequency of posts on a particular topic. It might be reasonable to suggest that misinformation topics are likely to have distributional characteristics where people talk about them within a short timeframe, compared to other types of information. In some cases, there may also be clues in the account holder name and profile that suggest that it has been set up with the intention of spreading misinformation. Information traits such as these can also be taken into account alongside outputs from text classification systems, in order to increase the chances of successful detection.

A particular challenge for misinformation detection is the need for early detection of misinformation. The topics of misinformation are constantly changing, so the text classifiers trained to detect misinformation are not necessarily trained on data that adequately reflect the topic of the new misinformation. The release of this new misinformation can also take place very quickly, meaning that there is little or no opportunity to train a system specific to a novel topic of misinformation gaining momentum.

18.4.3 Accommodating low-resource languages

There are many examples of computational linguistic system that work well for major well-documented languages. English, of course, is one such language. It is common to find that automatic speech recognition systems, for example, are recognising speech more accurately for some languages more than others, and this is largely correlated with the amount of data, metadata and general language resources (such as dictionaries) available for the language it is intended to work for. The collection of languages that this applies to obviously only makes up a relatively small proportion of the thousands of languages in the world. There are therefore efforts to develop technologies that work for 'low-resource' languages.

These efforts may take the form of collecting more data and systematically documenting these languages, in an attempt to bring them on a par with other languages. However, this is a very time-consuming and resource-intensive avenue for a single language. There are, therefore, also research efforts to come up with technology solutions that mean we do not require as much data to train a system. These latter efforts might involve devising language-specific algorithms or even applying systems that have been trained on closely related languages. Working towards bringing computational linguistic technologies to this low-resource category of languages opens up opportunities for entire communities to start accessing the information and capabilities that speakers of more well-documented languages have. This could have important consequences in breaking down global inequalities.

18.5 Problems for society

Computational linguistic systems have, in some ways, become a victim of their own success. Their integration into everyday life has started to cause problems for society. This section outlines two ways in which computational linguistic developments have led to this.

18.5.1 Spoofing: opportunities for fraud

The quality of some speech synthesis systems could create problems for society. It has been shown that some speech synthesis systems can be used to produce speech samples that sound enough like they have been produced by a target speaker that they can 'trick' an automatic speaker recognition system into falsely accepting the speech sample as having been produced by that speaker. As the term suggests, automatic speaker recognition systems are built to recognise the individual speaker who is speaking in a speech recording. They are already being used by users of online banking who might be asked produce the phrase 'my voice is my password', in order to access their bank details through a banking app. With the implementation of this kind of automatic speaker recognition technology on the rise, so is the prospect of its misuse. It is feasible that speech synthesis technologies could be used to produce speech signals that could maliciously be submitted in such contexts, in order to gain fraudulent access to bank details (and other information, for that matter). The speech samples that are created for this kind of fraudulent use are called 'spoofs'. To counteract this possibility, there is now an area or speech technology devoted to developing 'anti-spoofing' speech technologies. These are designed to detect spoofed speech samples, if they were to be presented to an automatic speaker recognition system.

18.5.2 Data demands

The development of computational linguistic systems that perform well tends to require a lot of training data. That data obviously has to come from somewhere. This issue applies to many computational linguistic systems. For example, to return to the automatic speaker recognition technology introduced earlier, state-of-the-art systems require speech recordings from thousands of speakers. This demands the collection and storage of these speech samples. Compared with text data, speech data brings additional complications. Speech is thought to contain more identifying information than text, because speech data not only contains information in the form of the word sequences it contains (just like text data), but the speech signal contains speaker-identifying information in itself. As a result, speech data could be seen as more sensitive than the text data required to build other types of computational linguistic system. Finding enough data that are able to be legally used for these purposes can be problematic.

In focus: consent for data usage

The UK's revenue service, Her Majesty's Revenue and Customs (HMRC) made the news in 2019 for the way it obtained more data to improve its automatic speaker recognition system. HMRC was using automatic speaker recognition technology as a means for account holders to access tax account information. In order to improve the speaker recognition system, they used speech data of hundreds of users who had used the system previously. However, the users had not given their consent for their speech samples to be used for that purpose, and HMRC therefore had to retract the data from the system. For more on the ethics of collecting and using linguistic data, see Chapter 19.

18.6 Conclusion

This chapter has provided an overview of key computational linguistic concepts and ways in which they can be applied across NLP and speech technology. The prospect of someone learning to build computational linguistic systems is becoming more and more viable. Of course, to develop these systems, knowledge of coding is required, but recent years have seen a seemingly exponential rise in available resources and opportunities for learning to code. These include so-called 'grassroots' efforts, as well as schemes aiming to help various minority groups to learn coding, which is increasingly regarded as an extremely valuable skill, and no longer the preserve of people with computer science degrees.

The rise in coding resources and opportunities has naturally meant that computational approaches have become commonplace across disciplines to pursue research questions, and linguistics is no exception. The use of computational techniques within research projects in linguistic sub-disciplines such as phonetics, syntax or pragmatics is no longer very unusual. While this chapter has focused on the use and potential of technologies within computational linguistics, it is also important to acknowledge that some understanding of computational methods is now very useful to other sub-fields of linguistics.

References

Baykaner, K., Huckvale, M., Whiteley, I., Andreeva, S. and Ryumin, O. 2015. Predicting fatigue and psychophysiological test performance from speech for safety-critical environments. *Frontiers in Bioengineering and Biotechnology*, 3. http://doi.org/10.3389/fbioe.2015.00124

Church, K. and Liberman, M. 2021. The future of computational linguistics: On beyond alchemy. *Frontiers in Artificial Intelligence*, 4. http://doi.org/10.3389/frai.2021.625341

Davis, S. and Mermelstein, P. 1980. *Comparison of Parametric Representations for Monosyllabic Word Recognition in Continuously Spoken Sentences*. IEEE Transactions on Acoustics, Speech and Signal Processing, 28.

Köbis, N. and Mossink, L. 2021. Artificial intelligence versus Maya Angelou: Experimental evidence that people cannot differentiate AI-generated from human-written poetry. *Computers in Human Behavior*, 114. http://doi.org/10.1016/j.chb.2020.106553

Litman, D., Strik, H. and Lim, G. 2018. Speech technologies and the assessment of second language speaking: Approaches, challenges and opportunities. *Language Assessment Quarterly*, 15: 294–309.

Veaux, C., Yamagishi, J. and King, S. 2012. Using HMM-based speech synthesis to reconstruct the voice of individuals with degenerative speech disorders. In *Proceedings of INTERSPEECH*. Portland, OR, pp. 967–970.

Weizenbaum, J. 1966. ELIZA – a computer program for the study of natural language communication between man and machine. *Communications of the ACM*, 9: 36–45.

Wu, L., Morstatter, F., Carley, K. and Liu, H. 2019. Misinformation in social media: Definition, manipulation and detection. *The Association of Computing Machinery's Special Interest Group on Knowledge Discovery and Data Mining Explorations*, 20: 80–90.

Section four

Methods

Research ethics in (applied) linguistics

19

Uta Papen, Emily Peach, Aina Casaponsa and Dimitrinka Atanasova

19.1 Introduction (Uta Papen)

19.1.1 What is ethics?

There isn't a short and easy way to explain what ethics is. Also referred to as moral philosophy, ethics is about what is right or wrong and about conducting oneself in ways that are deemed to be right or wrong. Ethics, then, has to do with principles or standards of how one ought or ought not to live.

19.1.2 What is research ethics?

Put simply, research ethics is about doing right or wrong as a researcher, when collecting and analysing data to help find answers to a research question. Research ethics, then, is about your responsibilities as a researcher, for example towards the people taking part in your study. You need to make sure that taking part in your study does not expose them to any harm or any disadvantages. That means, for example, you may have to protect their identity when writing about what you have found. As a researcher, you are responsible for your findings. You need to be honest about what you have found (and what, perhaps, you haven't found, or can't be certain about). What is right or wrong when doing research can be difficult to decide. While doing research, for example for your third year dissertation, you may find yourself in situations where what is best for your research might not be best for your participants. 'Ethics is full of grey areas' (Copland and Creese 2015: 177). At various points while conducting a research project, you will have to make decisions about what is or isn't ethical. Later sections of this chapter and the 'In focus' boxes will show you examples of what to consider during a study.

19.1.3 Ethics in the context of research in linguistics

This is a book about linguistics – the study of language. Why then, you may wonder, do we need to think about ethics when studying language? Aren't

DOI: 10.4324/9781003045571-23

355

languages just there, for us to examine and study? Well, languages are spoken, written and used by people. Much research in applied linguistics is dealing with how language is linked to real-world problems and social processes. For example, in Chapter 7 you were introduced to the notion of indexicality, and how the way you speak may be seen to reveal your class background (p. 139). As we also saw in Chapter 9, a large branch of linguistics looks at how children learn to speak and to read a language (cf. also Chapter 15), or how people learn a second language. When you research such questions, you will need to work with people. You will need to study the places where the language is used or taught, for example a school classroom or a workplace. You will need to ensure that teachers and students are happy to be part of your research. This is where you will need to think about good research ethics: principles for how to be ethical in the research you do. There is advice available to help with this, for example from professional organisations such as the British Association for

Scan the QR code to check out BAAL's advice on good research practice!

SCAN ME

Applied Linguistics (BAAL). In the next section, we briefly introduce the key principles of ethical research in applied linguistics.

19.1.4 Principles of ethical research in (applied) linguistics

There are four important ethical principles to bear in mind when conducting a research project in applied linguistics: *autonomy*, *beneficence*, *justice* and *integrity*. These principles are important for any kind of linguistics/language-related project, for example a study to understand a specific local dialect, an investigation into gendered patterns of talk in an office or research into how children growing up in a bilingual family learn to speak in two languages.

Autonomy is about participants deciding whether to take part or not in your study, giving what is called 'informed consent'. When you invite people to take part in your study, you need to explain to them what your study is about. They need to know what they are letting themselves in for by taking part. *Informed consent* is often obtained by writing a detailed information sheet about your study for the participants and asking the participants to sign a consent form. These documents need to be clear (no academic jargon) and honest about what the participant has to do. Autonomy also includes participants being clear about having the right to not take part, or to withdraw.

Beneficence is about what good your research is aiming to do and what is in it for the participants. Will they benefit from taking part? Will they contribute to useful new knowledge, for example a study that will help inform government policy on support for bilingual families and their children? *Non-maleficence*, relatedly, means that you have to make sure that taking part in your study does not expose your participants to any harm. You might think this is unlikely in a linguistics project. Indeed, the potential of harm is much higher in, for example, medical research, such as clinical trials for new treatments. But accidental and unintended harm can be a risk in applied linguistics research. For example, there could be stress felt when being interviewed or pressure when being observed. More on this later in this chapter.

Justice, the third principle, is about treating every participant in your study fairly and equally. This includes ensuring that when you interview a group of people, that you don't only listen to the views of some while ignoring those of others. It is also about avoiding that only people in privileged positions are being listened to by researchers. If there are disagreements amongst those who take part in your research, you need to make sure that you consider all views. This could be important in the previous example of a study looking at gendered features of office language, where male and female participants may have different views on how male and female colleagues should speak to each other.

Finally, ***integrity*** is about you and your commitment to being open and honest about what claims you are making. You need to honour what participants have told you and do your best to represent them and their views without distorting findings or even 'tweaking' them to fit what you would like to say or were hoping to find out.

19.1.5 Practical steps

Looking through these principles and what we have said so far, you may feel daunted by research ethics and you may wonder how to start. It is common practice in all universities that anybody doing research goes first through a process of ethics review. This means that your research plans are being looked at to see if they are ethical, for example that your study is safe for participants and not causing them harm. Your supervisor or your course leader will advise you on what to do to get ethics approval for your planned study.

19.2 Working with vulnerable people (Emily Peach)

In this section, I will cover some of the different things that you need to think about if you are working with participants who are ***vulnerable***. In the context of research ethics, this has a specific meaning: participants can be vulnerable if they are less able to give **informed consent** or if they are at higher risk of *harm* from a research project (Nordentoft and Kappel 2011). This might not always be obvious, and some participants might only be vulnerable in some research contexts. As researchers, therefore, we can't assume that whole groups of people are vulnerable or not. Instead, we should focus on how our research creates vulnerability in both the participants and the researcher (Thompson and Chambers 2012). To illustrate, I will consider as a case study a research project in which I investigated how students with mental health conditions use written documents to get support and manage their mental health.

First, we must consider the relationship between vulnerability and informed consent. Vulnerability can be created in participants if there is a risk that they could feel coerced to consent to participation. In my study, the students could have felt forced to consent if I was also their teacher, and therefore had power over their assessed grades. They might have worried that their studies would be negatively affected if they said no. You should avoid putting potential participants in a situation where they feel like they have to agree to take part. This might mean you can't recruit certain groups of participants for your project. On the *information sheet* for your project, you should also reassure potential participants that there will be no negative consequences if they choose not to participate.

You also need to think about whether potential participants have the *capacity* to consent. Capacity here means an individual's ability to read and understand information about a research project and then decide about their participation based on that information. Children, for example, do not legally have the capacity to provide informed consent to research, as their thinking is considered not sufficiently developed to understand the information and weigh up the possible impact of participation. The capacity of some adults may also be a cause for concern, for example if they are very unwell or have a condition where their thinking might be affected (e.g. advanced dementia). If you want to work with participants who may not have the capacity to consent to research themselves, you need to consider how to assess capacity and who might provide consent on the participant's behalf. You can find more information about capacity in Wiles' (2013) helpful chapter on informed consent.

Second, we must consider how vulnerability is linked to the risk of harm. As mentioned already, much research in applied linguistics poses minimal risk of harm, physical or psychological, to most participants. However, some research projects will be riskier, and some participants might be more affected by potential harm. Your risk of harm also needs to be considered, as vulnerability in the researcher can also be created. My study had the potential to pose psychological harm for the participants as it involved talking about experiences with mental health, which could have been a distressing topic (Kidd and Finlayson 2006). As the participants all had mental health conditions, this distress could have been intense, and the outcomes could have been serious. Participant comfort was therefore a vital consideration. But my comfort and safety as a researcher were also important; the topics of discussion had the potential to distress me as well. As outlined in detail in the 'In focus' box below, I tried to lessen the risks to myself and the participants by using video-calls for the interviews. This allowed everybody to be in a physical location where they felt comfortable and safe.

In focus: creature comforts

To demonstrate the benefits of video-calling participants with mental health conditions, we will consider one interview in particular. My research into student mental health used video-calling interviews, rather than the more traditional in-person interview. I made this decision to help mitigate the risk of distress for all parties, as it meant that the participants and I could both be in places where we felt comfortable and safe. I felt the impact of this decision during an interview with Magda (a pseudonym). Magda was a postgraduate student who had been diagnosed with a mental health condition when she was a teenager.

In this interview, she was telling me about the difficulties she had experienced trying to get support from a lecturer, who had insisted she continue to work on a group presentation, something her support plan excused her from. This experience was distressing for Magda, and so was retelling it. Her speech became quicker, her voice more strained and she began swearing more frequently, suggesting her distress was intensifying. Then, I could see that behind her, her cat was walking along the back of her sofa. The cat settled next to Magda on the sofa, acting as a source of comfort, and allowing her to continue telling me about her experiences. If we'd met in person, recounting this story might have been too distressing for Magda. I wouldn't have heard about her experiences, and the risk of psychological harm might have increased. Using video calls to interview Magda, and my other participants, helped me ensure that my research was ethical, and ensured that vulnerability in my participants was as minimal as possible, given the topic.

This section has covered some of the initial considerations surrounding research with 'vulnerable' participants. It is important to remember, however, that doing ethical research is an ongoing process and not limited to the planning you do before you start collecting data. You will need to continue to think about the ethics of your research throughout all the stages of your project. The extra thought required to ensure your research with 'vulnerable' participants is ethical shouldn't put you off from conducting such research. Research with 'vulnerable' participants is extremely important in understanding the experiences of as diverse a group of people as possible.

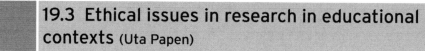

19.3 Ethical issues in research in educational contexts (Uta Papen)

As will be clear from the discussions and examples in Chapters 9 and 15, much research in applied linguistics is taking place in schools, in language classrooms or in students' homes. If you want to understand how children become skilled readers, you need to do research in primary or secondary schools. If you are interested in how people learn a new language, you may need to work in a language school.

When working in schools and other educational settings, you need to consider several ethical issues. The first is consent. In schools, you need to ensure that both the teacher with whom you want to work and the students are on board with your study. You may want to observe their lessons or even have a look at their exam results. Not all students may be keen on taking part in such a study. This can be difficult to navigate if, for example, your study involves looking in detail at how specific lessons are taught. Or, your study may be looking at the effect of group or pair work on, let's say, how English language learners develop their vocabulary on a specific topic. Ideally, you would want the entire class to take part. What if some students do not want to be observed? There are no general answers for dealing with such issues. Adaptations to your planned study may be necessary.

Returning to consent, the general point here is that the teachers and students need to know what they gain from taking part in your study. Bear in mind too that wider negotiations with the school may be needed. If the teacher is keen to be involved with your study but hasn't got the support from their manager, you'd be putting them in a difficult situation.

When working with children, you need their parents' consent. You need to prepare information sheets and consent forms for each child's parents or carers. Getting consent from all of them may take time. Children are considered to be vulnerable (see Section 19.2), so you have to take extra care to ensure that your research does not accidentally expose them to any pressure or harm. In many school-based studies, there is little such danger. But one thing to consider is if you want to audio-record or film lessons. Filming a lesson has obvious advantages: you can analyse it in much more detail based on the film and any observation notes you may have. Close linguistic analysis of any transcripts of recordings is possible. Recording or filming a lesson, then, is a plus, likely to lead to more trustworthy results. But if you are trying to convince a participant to be filmed against their will, you are not acting in an ethical way. Filming means people are identifiable and specifically when working with young children, parents may not be happy with that. So this is a dilemma you may face in the process of conducting your study.

Here is another possible dilemma: your findings may end up presenting individuals and institutions in ways they would not agree with. They might feel that you are misrepresenting them and that you are critical of their work (Copland and Creese 2015). If you study a specific teaching method, your findings may show that this method has weaknesses. In the interest of research and improving practice, this is of course what you would want to point out and help change. In the process, though, you may first have to highlight the weaknesses in current practices. This may be tricky to navigate when you put together the results of your study.

One thing that is particularly important to be clear about for all classroom-based research is that it cannot be fully planned and predicted. A school classroom is not a laboratory. As a dissertation student, you will have requested ethics approval for your study from your tutor or programme director. Having had such approval will be reassuring to you. This does, however, not mean that you can stop thinking about ethics (as shown also in Section 19.2). Remember what research ethics is about: doing the right thing as a researcher. Questions of right or wrong, what to do or not to do when working with teachers and students will arise throughout the entire project, as well as when writing up findings.

In focus: ethics in cross-cultural contexts

In a recent international project, colleagues and I developed, tried out and researched a new approach to teaching English to deaf children and young adults. The deaf children and young adults in our project did not come from privileged backgrounds. As deaf people in their countries, they had limited access to education. In India for example, one of our research sites was a small residential school for deaf children. These children came from mostly poor families. In many ways then, the participants in our study were vulnerable, and we had to think about issues of power and status. This was even more important because amongst the project team, many, like me, were privileged hearing academics from Britain.

When applying for ethics approval from our university, we explained in detail how we would approach informed consent, and how we would protect our participants. But expectations about research ethics are not universal. For example, in our Western context, we often try to offer research participants *anonymity*. When using photographs or videos of participants in publications, we may blur their faces. In our project, that would have been difficult. Our approach was bilingual: sign language, the students' first language, was the medium through which teaching English was happening. The lessons heavily relied on sign language. Sign language uses precise gestures. Without video, we would not have had a good record of classroom discussions. We needed such a record to understand whether our method had worked (or not). For the local research assistants, the teachers and the young people in our classes, our concern for their anonymity was unexpected. They did not mind or, rather, they *wanted* to be shown on video or in photographs. They wanted their efforts as learners or teachers to be seen in our talks and academic publications.

19.4 Work in laboratories/experimental research (Aina Casaponsa)

Linguistic research in experimental settings is about studying linguistic phenomena and theories based on quantitative data obtained from the speakers of language(s) we are interested in studying. This type of research usually involves participants to be in a highly constrained environment: the lab.

One of the main advantages of doing experimental research is that every single aspect of your research project is very well-structured and controlled, including the collection of your data. All participants do exactly the same tasks in the same, pre-defined, way, and in the same environment. Hence, the type of data that you collect looks pretty much the same across participants. This has clear advantages in terms of planning and predicting any potential ethical issues that can arise during data collection and analyses, something almost impossible to plan in other research environments (e.g. research in schools, see Section 19.3).

The best way to approach any potential issue surrounding ethics in this type of environment is to develop a *research protocol* before you request ethical approval. This protocol usually includes a description of your main research hypothesis/questions:

1 What you are trying to measure (i.e. research variables).
2 How you are trying to measure it (i.e. the tasks).
3 How you will be analysing it.

Designing your research protocol is like baking your own bread; we might all use the same type of tools and ingredients, but the result is always unique. I find it particularly useful to lay out all the steps, from the recruitment process to instructions and data analyses. By doing so, you get a very detailed picture of what you will be doing. This will help you prevent potential ethical issues that might arise during the whole project. For instance, one ethical concern that can be easily addressed in experimental research is ensuring participants' *anonymity*. By assigning a unique identifier to each participant from the beginning, you ensure that their data cannot be traced back to them.

You also need to consider the wellbeing of the participants during your experiment. Experimental settings are usually quite artificial, and the environment can be uncomfortable for the participant, both emotionally and physically. If your experiment is too long, you must give participants regular breaks. You also need to make sure participants feel relaxed and safe, by clarifying any doubts they might have about the lab environment, or the techniques that you might use to collect the data. This is especially relevant when we use specialised equipment that participants might not be familiar with, such as electroencephalography (EEG), eye-tracking or electrodermal activity techniques.

A common ethical issue that arises in most experimental studies, and indeed that is often unavoidable, is having to 'deceive' participants about the main research aim. For instance, imagine you want to investigate whether speakers of gendered languages (e.g. Spanish, Arabic, Hindi) perceive everyday objects as more or less gender stereotypical based on the grammatical gender of the object's noun (e.g. 'saw' in Spanish is a grammatically feminine noun, whereas 'hammer' is a grammatically masculine noun). Letting participants know your research goals would probably make them pay more attention to the grammatical gender of the objects, biasing their responses. Hence, it is common in experimental research to 'hide' the main aim of the research project before participants give their consent. This is ethically questionable (see autonomy principle in Section 19.1.4). It means that the information sheet that they receive deceives them and hence, it is extremely important that, at the end of the session, we debrief the participants about the 'real' aim of the study. It is good practice that at this point we also remind them that they can withdraw their participation and that their data can be deleted.

It is also important to be aware that participants in university laboratories are usually students or staff. Hence, the people you invite to participate to your own study might have been participating in other experimental research projects across the university. These 'recurrent' participants are thus aware that we usually 'hide' the true purpose of our experiments. The benefit is that they know that they will probably be deceived in the first place. The downside is that these 'expert' participants usually try to figure out the 'hidden' purpose and this can bias their responses.

As we saw in Section 19.2, when doing your own research project at a university, you always need to be mindful about the possibility that people might feel coerced to participate. This is of special relevance when the researcher and the participant are from the same department. For example, students being asked by their tutor to participate in an experimental study may be concerned about the impact of declining on their academic grades, and hence may not feel free to do so. However, feeling of coercion to participate in a study can also happen from a group of peers (amongst students). This is something that can also be planned. For instance, in the *information sheet* you can make it clear that participation is entirely optional with no negative impact on studies, grades or social consequences.

19.5 Working with social media data
(Dimitrinka Atanasova)

As people are doing more and more things online, from posting selfies on Instagram to documenting their efforts to live sustainably on personal blogs, linguists are increasingly analysing social media data. For example, we may study such data to understand how people with depression are using images to make visible something that is invisible (e.g. Koteyko and Atanasova 2018) or to explain how metaphorical language might be employed to discuss something as complex as sustainability in simpler terms (e.g. Atanasova 2019). Social media data provides an exciting opportunity to study known phenomena in new ways. If you want to understand how individuals talk about experiences of living with a relative who has been diagnosed with a mental illness, or about efforts to lose weight, to name just a few possibilities, you may want to analyse social media data. This could include data from Instagram, forum and blog posts, or tweets. These could be analysed independently, or in addition to other data (e.g. interviews).

At the beginning of this chapter, we pointed out that language is not just there for us to examine and study. The same is true of social media data. This is people's data and we arguably have the same obligations to people when researching them online as we do when researching them offline. Questions of *informed consent* therefore arise. When studying social media data, how we seek and obtain informed consent is a key challenge, as is the question of whether and how to preserve the anonymity of a person in a social media environment, where (re-)identification is a possibility.

Questions have been raised about whether informed consent is even required for all social media data. One view is that data posted in open spaces (i.e. spaces that can be accessed without the need for passwords or membership) is in the *public domain*. Thus, it can be used for research purposes, without the need for informed consent from the individuals who posted it. According to this view, the need to gain informed consent only arises when data is gathered from the *private domain* (i.e. closed platforms which require membership and/or log-in details). The subject is, however, contentious among social scientists, and whether to seek informed consent or not, even on an otherwise open platform, should be considered against additional factors, such as the sensitivity of the topic and the relative vulnerability of the person who had created the post (see, for example, Elgesem 2016). Arguments can be made that in some cases, social media data analysis is ethically responsible without informed consent. If the analysed data is both private and on a sensitive topic (e.g. a person posting about living with depression on their Facebook wall while limiting their audience to their friends only), there is a strong case that the researcher should be required to obtain informed consent. In other situations, informed consent may not be required, for example, when analysing someone's tweet about climate change, which contains popular hashtags.

Obtaining informed consent for the use of social media data can be difficult in practice. You might, for example, contact a Twitter user but what if they never get back to you? If that happens, you as the researcher should decide whether to use that data or not. When deciding, you would need to consider a range of factors, including the openness of the platform, the topic of the tweet and the identity of the person who created it (to the extent that this is possible to ascertain from their profile information) (Figure 19.1).

"On the Internet, nobody knows you're a dog."

CartoonStock.com

Figure 19.1 Internet anonymity.

Source: © Cartoon Stock/Peter Steiner.

This brings us to anonymity, which is often recommended. Sometimes, people do not want to be anonymous, as seen in the 'In focus' box on page 361. A blogger, for example, may prefer to be credited for their words in the same way that a journalist is. When researching social media data, preserving anonymity may be further complicated by the *searchability* of the data (e.g. Lüders 2016). For example, you may have decided to include a direct quotation from a tweet into your project paper (which is often needed to evidence the types of close textual analyses that linguists conduct). You may have also decided to remove the name of the user. But the quotation may be easily traced back to the original poster

For more on social media users' views on using their data, see this report from the National Centre for Social Research (NatCen Social Research)! www.natcen.ac.uk/our-research/research/research-using-social-media-users-views/

with a quick Google search. If that is the case, try obtaining informed consent to use the quote verbatim, or, if the topic and the person who created the post do not belong to a sensitive or vulnerable category, the need for informed consent may be lessened.

19.6 Conclusions

In this chapter, we have introduced the most important principles of research ethics. We have discussed research ethics in the context of different types of research done by linguists and applied linguists, including experimental research and research that uses social media data. You may have finished reading this chapter wondering about practical steps for how to go about ensuring your research is ethical. As explained in Section 19.1, while you are expected to think carefully about ethics as a researcher, there are many resources available to help. These include the resources and references cited here. You can also expect to receive training and advice from your programme or course.

References

Atanasova, D. 2019. 'Journeys towards a green lifestyle': Metaphors in green living blogs. *Cahiers de praxématique*, 73. http://journals.openedition.org/praxematique/5827

Copland, F. and Creese, A. 2015. *Linguistic Ethnography*. London: Sage, Chapter 7.

Elgesem, D. 2016. Consent and information – ethical considerations when conducting research on social media. In H. Fossheim and H. Ingierd (Eds.), *Internet Research Ethics*. Oslo: Cappelen Damm Akademisk, pp. 14–34.

Kidd, J. and Finlayson, M. 2006. Navigating uncharted water: Research ethics and emotional engagement in human inquiry. *Journal of Psychiatric and Mental Health Nursing*, 13(4): 423–428.

Koteyko, N. and Atanasova, D. 2018. Mental health advocacy on Twitter: Positioning in depression awareness week tweets. *Discourse, Context & Media*, 25: 52–59.

Lüders, M. 2016. Researching social media: Confidentiality, anonymity and reconstructing online practices. In H. Fossheim and H. Ingierd (Eds.), *Internet Research Ethics*. Oslo: Cappelen Damm Akademisk, pp. 77–97.

Nordentoft, H. M. and Kappel, N. 2011. Vulnerable participants in health research: Methodological and ethical challenges. *Journal of Social Work Practice*, 25(3): 365–376.

Thompson, A. R. and Chambers, E. 2012. Ethical issues in qualitative mental health research. In H. D. Thompson (Ed.), *Qualitative Research Methods in Mental Health and Psychotherapy: A Guide for Students and Practitioners*. Chichester: Wiley-Blackwell, pp. 23–37.

Wiles, R. 2013. *What Are Qualitative Research Ethics?* London: Bloomsbury Academic.

<table>
<tr><td>20</td><td>

Experimental methods
Patrick Rebuschat and Aina Casaponsa
</td></tr>
</table>

20.1 Introduction

The scientific study of language draws on range of methods, as the chapters in this section illustrate. Each of these methods is necessary for a comprehensive understanding of how languages are structured, acquired and used by native and non-native speakers across a variety of communicative contexts. In studying language, or most other natural phenomena for that matter, we can pursue two basic strategies. The first strategy is to simply observe and describe our phenomena of interest. For example, if we are interested in the spoken language of second language learners, we could systematically collect spoken data from a substantial number of learners, transcribe and annotate the data, then run fine-grained analyses that provide a thorough description of their language production. This is the approach behind the Trinity Lancaster Corpus (Gablasova et al. 2019; see Chapter 21 for more on corpus construction and methods), for example, which contains 4.2 million words of interaction collected from over 2000 second language learners of English with diverse linguistic backgrounds and different proficiency levels. The second strategy goes beyond observation. Here, we want to systematically manipulate variables of interest and see what effect our manipulation has in the world. This is the case of **experimental research**. In contrast to other methods, a well-designed experiment provides reliable insights into cause-and-effect relationships between two or more things.

http://cass.lancs.ac.uk/trinity-lancaster-corpus/

In this chapter, we provide you with a brief introduction to the study of language using experimental methods. We begin in Section 20.2 by describing fundamental principles underpinning experimental research and key characteristics of controlled, or 'true', experiments. In Section 20.3, we then discuss two types of design that you are very likely to encounter in the experimental literature. Throughout these sections, we will refer back to an example study which we introduce in Table 20.1, of a language acquisition study. Our chapter concludes with an outline of the basic steps involved in conducting an experimental study (e.g. in the context of an undergraduate dissertation), in Section 20.4. Our goal is to supply you with tools to better understand scientific papers and evaluate their validity, as well as to serve as an initial resource to which you can turn when developing your own research assignments.

 DOI: 10.4324/9781003045571-24

20.2 What is an experiment?

A scientific experiment is a procedure carried out to discover something unknown by testing predictions that are based on existing theories or prior empirical evidence. This is generally done by first manipulating variables of interest and then observing the effect of this manipulation on other variables. **Variables** are characteristics that vary across things, from person to person, text to text, task to task, etc. People differ in terms of their age, their native language(s), the number of previously acquired foreign languages, their personality, their language learning aptitude and their motivation for learning language, just to name a few dimensions. Texts in a **corpus** (see Chapter 21) tend to vary across multiple genres or registers, from academic prose and newspapers to electronic messages and fiction. Experimental tasks vary in terms of many dimensions, including instructions provided to participants, behaviour elicited (e.g. spoken or written production) and behaviour measured (e.g. overall accuracy of responses, response time). There are different types of variable, and these are outlined in Table 20.1.

Table 20.1 Types of experimental variables.

Type of variable	What is it?	Example
Independent variable	The variable we manipulate	If we investigate how studying abroad affects students' fluency in the foreign language, we could manipulate the length of study abroad period as our independent variable, and see what effect this has on tests measuring our students' foreign language fluency, our dependent variable.
Dependent variable	The variable we expect to be affected by the manipulation of the independent variable	
Control variable	The variable we hold constant throughout the course of an experiment. These are variables that could strongly affect the results if not properly controlled.	To continue with the study-abroad example, we should carefully control for previously acquired languages, to make sure our participants aren't already fluent in the target language.
Moderator variable	A variable that affects the relationship between dependent and independent variables.	There are factors other than length of study-abroad period that might explain how our participants perform on the fluency tests when they return from abroad. We should keep an eye on these, too, in case they affect the results.

Once we have decided on our variables, we need to define them and explain, very concretely, how we are going to measure them. This is often easier said than done. Returning to our examples from the table, it's relatively easy to identify what languages our participants have learned before joining the study; we can administer a validated questionnaire (e.g. Language Experience and Proficiency Questionnaire, LEAP-Q; Marian et al. 2007) and just ask them.

Scan the QR code to visit the LEAP-Q website: https://bilingualism.northwestern.edu/leapq/

Scan the QR code to visit the DIALANG website: http://wp.lancs.ac.uk/ltrg/projects/dialang-2-0/

But what about their proficiency in these languages? Can we simply rely on self-report here, or should we use standardised tests (e.g. DIALANG; Alderson and Huhta 2005) to get a more reliable measure?

Likewise, when it comes to investigating the effects of studying abroad, it's easy to measure the length of the study-abroad period; we can just ask participants to report the number of days they stayed in the other country while participating in our study. But how do we measure our participants' fluency in the foreign language? This is clearly more challenging and entails **operationalisation** of the concept of fluency and identification of reliable ways of measuring changes to this variable. Things are further complicated by the fact that, in many cases, there are several ways of measuring our variables of interest while disagreement might persist in the scientific community about the most reliable one(s). This is a fundamental and healthy aspect of the scientific process, which advances when ideas are discussed openly and tested empirically in a transparent manner, but it still means we must decide if, say, fluency is measured by counting the number of syllables articulated per minute, the average number of syllables produced in utterances between pauses, the percentage of repetitions and self-corrections, or by all the above or by different measures altogether.

20.2.1 How do we study causal relationships?

To understand the causal relationships between variables, we need to compare two controlled situations: one in which the cause is present and one in which the cause is absent. That is, we need to include a **control condition** to our experimental design, which provides us with a baseline against which we can compare performance of our experimental group. We can then infer causality by comparing the two conditions. To return to our example from Table 20.1, we cannot simply send a group of students abroad for a given period and then test them on their return. After all, their fluency might have improved even if they had stayed in their home country. An essential addition to our experimental design is therefore the inclusion of a **control condition**, which, in this case, could be a group of learners which does not travel overseas but continues to study the foreign language at their home institution. Both groups could complete the same fluency tests at the end of the academic year, and if our experimental participants (the ones who went abroad) significantly outperform the control participants (the ones who stayed at their home institution), this could suggest a potential benefit of studying abroad on fluency development.

Having a control condition is not enough, however. As mentioned, we aim to identify and control all **confounding factors** (i.e. variables other than the independent one that might affect the dependent variable). This might work for factors that we know of, though what if there are hidden factors, that is, variables that are behind the effect but of whose influence we are unaware? People vary spontaneously across many dimensions that might affect performance on our experiment (aptitude, memory capacity, motivation, personality, etc.), and we cannot control for everything. The solution is to randomly assign participants to the different experimental conditions. **Randomisation** ensures a roughly equivalent spread of attributes across groups, including of hidden attributes that, unbeknownst to us, might affect outcomes. In our example, this means that we cannot let our participants decide whether they will be in the experimental or control condition, and neither can we decide on their behalf. We must randomly assign them to the two conditions, with half the participants randomly allocated to the experimental group (study abroad) and the other half to the control group (studying at home university).

20.3 Experimental design

A true experiment is a scientific procedure that involves rigorous control and measurement of variables using validated **test instruments**, with the aim of establishing causal relationships between variables. In the language sciences, running experiments involves recruiting and testing human participants. To do this, we define our **population** of interest (say, adult learners of Catalan, Japanese high-school teachers, German-Portuguese bilinguals) and then draw a **sample** from this population to obtain our empirical observations and to which our findings can later be generalised. Normally, the sample should be randomly drawn from the population to ensure that we avoid hidden biases, but often our sampling procedure is more opportunistic. Many psycholinguistic experiments involve sampling from the local population of university students, which could affect our ability to generalise our findings to other adults. Once we have drawn our sample, we must randomly assign participants to the different experimental conditions. Here we face different options in experimental design. Next, we will focus on two basic types of design (between-groups and within-groups), which you are likely to encounter when reading experimental language research. Both approaches, if properly carried out, allow us to identify cause and effect.

20.3.1 Between-groups design

An experiment with a between-groups design is a study in which participants are placed in only one experimental condition. For instance, in our example study, participants are randomly assigned to either the experimental condition (study-abroad) or the control condition (study at home institution), and they only complete the tasks assigned to these conditions. Because we are testing separate groups for each of the experimental conditions, this design is also known as **independent-groups design**.

If we decide to conduct an experiment with a between-groups design, our experiment might look like Figure 20.1. We recruit our participants and then randomly allocate them to two conditions: experimental and control. The two groups receive different treatments but then complete the same test afterwards. If there are differences between the groups at test, we assume that these are due to our treatment. This is called a **post-test only/control group design**, with an independent variable with two levels: absent or present. A good example of this experimental design can be found in a recent study by Monaghan

Scan the QR code to read the Monaghan et al. (2019) study: https://onlinelibrary. wiley.com/doi/full/10.1111/tops.12439

et al. (2019), which investigated the cross-situational learning of novel words. The study is Open Access, which means you can read it for free on the journal website.

Participants randomly allocated to groups:

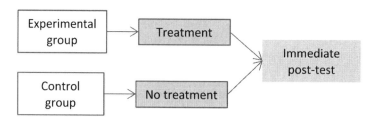

Figure 20.1 Post-test only/control group design.

Source: As used in Monaghan et al. (2019).

The post-test only design is frequently used in artificial language studies (see Chapter 9, Case Study 1), but it's usually not appropriate for studies with real languages. In Monaghan et al. (2019), none of the participants had been exposed to the artificial language, so there's no need to test them before the treatment begins. But this is clearly different when we are looking at the acquisition of natural languages such as Basque, French, Haitian Creole, Hindi or Swahili. Since these languages exist in the real world, it could well be that our participants already know (at least some of) the language that we are investigating in our experiment. In this case, pre-existing knowledge, rather than our treatment, could explain performance on the post-test. For this reason, most between-subject studies that look at the acquisition of natural languages follow a **pre-test/post-test control group design**. That is, all participants complete at least two tests, one before the treatment and one after the treatment. Many studies also include a second post-test. The first, or immediate, post-test is administered immediately after the conclusion of the treatment. The second, or delayed, post-test is administered one or two weeks later to determine if the treatment effect persists. Another decision concerns the number of levels that our independent variable should have. In Monaghan et al. (2019), we have two levels. One group receives explicit information about the language (the existence of the two function words) and the other group does not. However, researchers are frequently interested in comparing multiple types of treatment.

Figure 20.2 illustrates the pre-test/post-test control group design with an independent variable with multiple levels. A good example of a pre-test/post-test control group design with an independent variable with multiple levels is the study conducted by Ellis et al. (2006). In this widely cited study, the authors investigated the effect of different types of feedback on the acquisition of grammar by adult learners of L2 English. The authors also included a delayed post-test in the design.

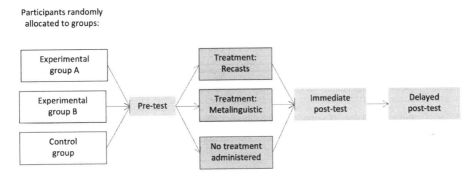

Figure 20.2 Pre-test/post-test control group design.

Source: As used by Ellis et al. (2006).

There are several advantages to using a between-groups design. A first advantage is its simplicity. We only have to randomly assign participants to the different conditions, and there is no need for careful counterbalancing, as is the case of within-subjects design. Another advantage is that participants are less likely to display practice effects. Since each participant is only in one condition, performance in one condition cannot affect performance in another condition. Finally, this design is essential when it is impossible for someone to participate in all experimental conditions. This clearly applies to studies involving language learning. Once participants have learned something in our study, they cannot unlearn it to complete the control condition as well.

There are several disadvantages, too, however. One disadvantage is that this design is less sensitive to the experimental manipulation. This is because we are comparing two different sets of participants. The non-systematic variation across groups makes it more challenging to detect the systematic variation induced by our experimental manipulation. In addition, the between-groups design also tends to require more resources. Since we have two or more groups, we need more participants, which means we need to spend more time recruiting and testing people, which in turn requires more effort and financial resources.

20.3.2 Within-groups design

An experiment with a within-groups design is a study in which the same group completes different tasks in an experiment. Each participant is tested multiple times so that the effects of our manipulation can be observed by comparing the scores of the same participant performing different tasks. This design is widely used in experimental research on language processing. Because participants are tested repeatedly, this design is also known as repeated-measures design.

Experiments that follow a within-groups design might look like Figure 20.3. Again, participants are randomly recruited from our population of interest. All participants complete the same experimental tasks, but we counterbalance the order in which they complete the tasks. Half the participants first complete task A, then task B, while the other half completes the tasks in the reverse order. This is just to make sure that the task sequence does not affect results. Once we have checked that it doesn't, the data can be pooled so that we have just one experimental group. A good example of a study that follows a within-groups design is Duñabeitia et al. (2016). The study investigated vocabulary knowledge in bilingual children and how the overlap between languages might help them during early stages of reading development.

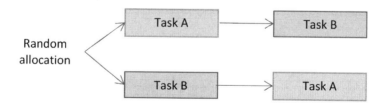

Figure 20.3 Repeated measures design.

Source: As used in Duñabeitia et al. (2016).

There are several advantages to using a within-groups design. This type of design is usually more sensitive in the sense that effects are more likely to be detected. Since we are comparing the performance of the same participants on different tasks, there are fewer sources of random variation to hide the effects of the independent variable. Also, the different conditions are perfectly matched, so factors are well-controlled across tasks. Finally, these experiments also tend to require fewer participants, which saves time and financial resources.

The disadvantages include the fact that conditions need to be reversible, (i.e. participation in task A cannot exclude participants from completing task B, and vice versa). This means the design cannot easily be used for language learning experiments, though it's perfect to study language processing. Also, there might be carry-over effects from one task to another. Participants might be tired after completing the first task and perform less well on the second task because of this. Or it could be that the first task facilitates performance on the second task because of practice effects. To control for this, we need to carefully counterbalance completion of tasks, as illustrated in Figure 20.3, and to include order in our analysis.

20.4 How to do experimental research

In the last section of our chapter, we would like to give you an idea of the basic steps involved in conducting experimental research. This is based on the advice we give to our students when supervising their undergraduate or postgraduate dissertations, and we hope you find it helpful, too. Please remember that this chapter is only meant to serve as a first introduction to the topic, so you will need to follow up on different topics by consulting more advanced texts (e.g. de Groot and Hagoort 2017; Hoff 2011; Field and Hole 2003; Mackey and Gass 2012). We also assume that you have a supervisor to guide you through the actual research project. The best way to learn how to do research, experimental or otherwise, is to conduct an actual study, with appropriate guidance from an experienced researcher.

20.4.1 Identifying research questions

The first step in designing your study is to find a topic that you would like to investigate. You are going to spend some time working on your project, so try to pick something that you find particularly interesting. This step is usually straightforward: there are areas of linguistics you will find more appealing than others, and there are likely to be one or two (or more) topics you find particularly fascinating. Once you have identified a potential topic, we recommend you begin reading three types of texts. First, read a few (recent) review articles that summarise the state of the art of research on the topic. You can find this in special issues of peer-reviewed journals (e.g. Thierry and Rebuschat 2020) or in scientific handbooks dedicated to the topic (e.g. Kroll and de Groot 2009). These publications give you a quick overview of what is currently being discussed in the literature. Second, we recommend you check if there are systematic reviews and meta-analyses on the topic. These are papers that use a rigorous and transparent procedure to identify and quantitatively analyse the methodology and results published in empirical studies on a given topic (see Gunnerud et al. 2020, for a recent example). Systematic reviews are very valuable; they provide you with key information on methods used to research the topic and include a comprehensive list of empirical studies. Third, you come to the most important step: you need to start reading actual experimental studies, a lot of them. Experimental studies are generally published in peer-reviewed journals. To find these, you can go over the reference lists in review articles and meta-analyses, and you can search databases such as Scopus, Web of Science or JSTOR via your university library. When reading, start with recent studies (this is the cutting-edge research) and work backwards. Also, pay extra attention to the research questions. How are they phrased? Can you adapt them for the purposes of your dissertation? Your research question(s) should be clear, unambiguous, sufficiently focused and answerable in the context of your dissertation project. Your supervisor will be able to help as they should know what can and cannot be feasibly done in the context of a dissertation. In addition to stating the research question(s), you should also add your prediction(s), based on the literature you have read. What do you anticipate finding? An example of research questions and predictions can be found in Ruiz et al. (2018), which was based on Simon Ruiz's MA dissertation.

Ruiz et al. (2018) is Open Access, so you can read it here: https://www.frontiersin.org/articles/10.3389/fpsyg.2018.01168/full

20.4.2 Obtaining ethics approval

The second step is to obtain ethics approval. Again, your supervisor should be able to tell you how to do this, and you can read Chapter 19 of this volume for additional information, too. Usually, this involves applying to the ethics committee at your home institution. The application is likely to ask you, among other things, to describe the study and potential risks to participants, how you will protect the identity of your participants, how you will ensure that participation is entirely voluntary, and how you will guarantee that the data is stored safely.

20.4.3 Decide on the experimental design and methodology

The third step is to decide on your experimental design and on the methodology. What design and methods should you chose? The one that allows you to best answer your research questions! When it comes to identifying design and methods, it is important to consult the experimental studies that you have read. How did other researchers answer their research questions? What experimental design have they used and what methods? Can you use a similar design to address your research questions?

20.4.4 Identify your participants

The fourth step is to decide who you will recruit to take part in your experiment and how many participants you will need. In part, this depends on your research question, the methodology and your proposed analyses. If you are interested in morphological development in Mandarin-Portuguese heritage bilinguals (see Chapter 11), then obviously that's the population from which you draw your sample. However, there are few more things to consider.

First, you need to be confident that you can recruit participants with these characteristics in the time frame you have to complete a dissertation. Are you collecting data in schools? Then this will only work if schools are actually open, so bear in mind holidays or exam periods during which students are less likely to participate. Are you looking for monolingual speakers of a language? Remember that pure monolinguals are increasingly rare these days. If you have learned a foreign language at school or a heritage language at home, then you are not monolingual, even if you fall short of achieving native-like proficiency in the additional language. Across the world, most people are now exposed to more than one language, either at home or at school. As a result, the pure monolinguals in our studies might be much older than their bilingual counterparts, so it's difficult to compare the two groups as they differ across more than one dimension.

Second, you will need to decide on the number of required participants. Remember that we infer from the sample to our population of interest, so the sample size is very important for getting meaningful results. If the sample size is too small, our statistical tests might not be significant because our sample is underpowered and not because there's no effect. Further, a small sample will be more affected by outliers (i.e. individuals who perform significantly better or worse than most participants). If the sample size is too large, the study becomes unnecessarily time-consuming and expensive. The larger sample will be more representative of our population, but we might be unable to complete the study for lack of resources. To get a rough estimate of the number of participants you are likely to require, you could have a look at the sample sizes reported in the experimental studies and meta-analyses you have read. However, the best way to determine the number of required participants is to conduct a power analysis (see Chapter 24). This statistical procedure allows you to calculate the sample size required to detect an effect of a given size with a given degree of confidence.

20.4.5 Design the data collection instruments

In experimental research, we have clear research questions, we operationalise key constructs and we propose ways to measure these constructs with precision.

In Step 5, you first decide how you define your key variables of interest. What do you mean by, say, second language fluency? Implicit and explicit feedback? Syntactic development? You then specify how you will test these constructs. To do this, we recommend two things. First, return to the review articles and experimental studies you have read. How did other researchers define the key constructs? What instruments did they use to measure the constructs in question? Second, consult helpful platforms such as IRIS (Marsden et al. 2016) to see if other researchers have shared their instruments online. There's a good chance that they have, in which case there's no point in reinventing the wheel. In scientific research, we often make progress by adapting previous materials to explore new research questions. The advantage is that we are building directly on the work that others have done before us. Adapting existing materials also facilitates comparing our results to previous research.

Scan the QR code to visit the IRIS repository: www.iris-database.org/iris/app/home/index

20.4.6 Pilot the instruments

Before using the instruments for actual data collection, it is essential that you make sure they function the way they are supposed to. This is called 'piloting', and is Step 6. In pilot studies, you generally collect data from a small number of participants only to assess whether your instruments are working. The data does not form part of the main study. You then use the results of the pilot study to improve your research instruments. You only start collecting data for the main study once you are satisfied that everything is well-designed, that the instructions are clear, that the data is being recorded properly, and so forth. As we have learned from experience, diligent piloting is always time well spent!

20.4.7 Conduct the experiment

Once instruments have been designed and the pilot study completed, Step 7 is (finally!) conduct the experiment. For PhD projects, we further recommend registering the experimental protocol online, such as on the Open Science Framework (OSF platform; Foster and Deardorff 2017). A key consideration is whether to collect data face to face (e.g. in the context of a dedicated research lab), or remotely (e.g. via online testing platforms). Collecting data face to face is sometimes necessary, depending on your research questions. The advantage is that you can control much better what people are doing in the experiment. You are there to respond to their questions, help if the audio stops working, check if they are not distracted during the task, etc. The disadvantage is that usually you can only test one person at a time, which means it takes much longer to complete data collection. In addition, you are likely to get a very homogeneous sample. If you test on campus, there's a good chance that most, if not all, of your participants are undergraduate students (young adults pursuing higher education) so your sample might not be very representative of your intended population (adults in general). Many researchers have therefore resorted to testing via the internet.

Scan the QR code to visit the Open Science Framework (OSF) platform: https://osf.io/

You can set up experiments and use platforms such as Gorilla, Pavlovia or Prolific Academic to recruit participants. One advantage of remote testing is that data collection can proceed much faster, since you can test many people at the same time. You can also end up with a much more diverse sample (not just university students), which can make your results more generalisable to the population of interest. A disadvantage is that you give up some control over how the experiment unfolds. Participants are completing the experiment on their devices (smart phones, tablets, laptops), which might affect the presentation quality of the sound, text and images. If participants have questions, it's not easy to answer them as the experimenter is not waiting outside the lab, and obviously you don't know if they are distracted during the experimental tasks.

20.4.8 Analyse the data

Experiments usually generate quantitative data, and Step 8 is analysing this data by means of software packages such as R or SPSS. You can read more about using statistical methods in linguistics research in Chapter 24, so we will only address this stage briefly here.

In your analyses, you will use **descriptive statistics** to describe key aspects of your sample data (e.g. the performance of your participants on different tasks). Descriptive statistics usually include measures of central tendency (e.g. mean, median and mode) as well as the measures of dispersion (e.g. range, interquartile range and standard deviation) that indicate how widely spread the scores are within the sample. These statistics can also include graphs (e.g. histograms, bar graphs) to visualise the distribution and frequency of scores as well as other relevant data points. In addition, you will use **inferential statistics** to determine if you can make generalisations about your population of interest based on the measurements from your sample. There are many inferential tests available, and you need to select these tests carefully, bearing in mind the properties of your data. Don't forget, you can learn more about this by reading Chapter 24 of this volume.

20.4.9 Writing up

The final step of the process is to write up your results in your dissertation. As you might have noticed, experimental reports tend to follow the same structure, which you can follow in your dissertation, too. Each of the four sections gets about an equal number of words or pages, and each is outlined in Table 20.2.

Table 20.2 Structuring your report.

Section	Purpose	Important features
Introduction	Introduces the reader to the topic and reviews the relevant empirical literature	Usually concludes with a statement of the research question(s) and your predictions based on the literature
Methods	Describes the methodology in detail, providing enough information for others to replicate your study in later years and without your input	Here, you might describe your sample of participants, the research instruments, the procedure and methods for coding the data
Results	Simply describes what you found	Describe the descriptive and inferential statistics, use tables to summarise your data and figures to visualise findings
Discussion	Brings it all together	Here, many reports begin by summarising the main findings in a short paragraph before answering each research question in turn

You can use Table 20.2 as a guide, but again, don't forget to have a look at what other researchers have done. How did they describe their experiments in the Methods section, how did they summarise their findings in the Results section?

In your Discussion section, remind the reader of each question and then discuss what you found. Were your predictions met? If not, why not? Interpret your results in light of the literature discussed in the Introduction – otherwise what was the point in discussing those studies in the first place? Conclude by discussing the limitations of your study (all studies have limitations . . .), by reflecting on theoretical or practical implications (e.g. for language teaching practice) and by outlining future directions of research. Based on what you have found, what should researchers investigate in the future?

20.6 Conclusion

In this chapter, we have introduced you to the study of language using experimental research. We have discussed key concepts in experimental research, such as the importance in defining your variables or selecting your instruments of measurement. We have also discussed the importance of making well-informed choices when preparing your instruments and the design of your study. Experimental studies, when well-designed, can be extremely powerful in providing robust insights about how we learn and process language(s). We concluded this chapter by discussing the different stages of an experimental research project, and hope that this can serve as a guide for your own research projects!

References

Alderson, J. C. and Huhta, A. 2005. The development of a suite of computer-based diagnostic tests based on the Common European Framework. *Language Testing*, 22(3): 301–320.

de Groot, A. M. B. and Hagoort, P. (Eds.). 2017. *Research Methods in Psycholinguistics and the Neurobiology of Language: A Practical Guide*. Chichester: Wiley.

Duñabeitia, J. A., Ivaz, L. and Casaponsa, A. 2016. Developmental changes associated with cross-language similarity in bilingual children. *Journal of Cognitive Psychology*, 28(1): 16–31.

Ellis, R., Loewen, S. and Erlam, R. 2006. Implicit and explicit corrective feedback and the acquisition of L2 grammar. *Studies in Second Language Acquisition*, 28(2): 339–368.

Field, A. and Hole, G. 2003. *How to Design and Report Experiments*. London: Sage.

Foster, E. D. and Deardorff, A. 2017. Open science framework (OSF). *Journal of the Medical Library Association*, 105(2): 203.

Gablasova, D., Brezina, V. and McEnery, T. 2019. The trinity Lancaster corpus: Development, description and application. *International Journal of Learner Corpus Research*, 5(2): 126–158.

Gunnerud, H. L., Ten Braak, D., Reikerås, E. K. L., Donolato, E. and Melby-Lervåg, M. 2020. Is bilingualism related to a cognitive advantage in children? A systematic review and meta-analysis. *Psychological Bulletin*, 146(12): 1059.

Hoff, E. (Ed.). 2011. *Research Methods in Child Language: A Practical Guide*. Chichester: Wiley.

Kroll, J. F. and de Groot, A. M. B. (Eds.). 2009. *Handbook of Bilingualism: Psycholinguistic Approaches*. Oxford: Oxford University Press.

Mackey, A. and Gass, S. M. (Eds.). 2012. *Research Methods in Second Language Acquisition: A Practical Guide*. Chichester: Wiley.

Marian, V., Blumenfeld, H. K. and Kaushanskaya, M. 2007. The language experience and proficiency questionnaire (LEAP-Q): Assessing language profiles in bilinguals and multilinguals. *Journal of Speech, Language, and Hearing Research*, 50(4): 940–967.

Marsden, E., Mackey, A. and Plonsky, L. 2016. The IRIS Repository: Advancing research practice and methodology. In A. Mackey and E. Marsden (Eds.),

Advancing Methodology and Practice: The IRIS Repository of Instruments for Research into Second Languages. London: Routledge, pp. 1–21.

Monaghan, P., Schoetensack, C. and Rebuschat, P. 2019. A single paradigm for implicit and statistical learning. *Topics in Cognitive Science*, 11(3): 536–554.

Ruiz, S., Tagarelli, K. M. and Rebuschat, P. 2018. Simultaneous acquisition of words and syntax: Effects of exposure condition and declarative memory. *Frontiers in Psychology*, 1168.

Thierry, G. and Rebuschat, P. (Eds.). 2020. Cognitive neuroscience of second and artificial language learning. Special issue of *Language Learning*, 70(S2): 5–19.

21 Corpus methods
Tony McEnery and Andrew Hardie

21.1 Introduction

Let's start with a question: is the word *cent* more common in British or American English? You doubtless have intuitions about this. You can imagine an answer, and you may well be able to provide reasons for your answer. Yet both the answer and the reasons may be wrong – our intuition, no matter how plausible the results of using it may be, may simply not match reality. In all likelihood, you probably thought that *cent* is more common in American than British English, because the *cent* is a unit of currency in American English and not in British English. So it is more likely to be used in American English, and is thus more frequent.

And yet, if we consult two 1-million-word corpora of present day British and American English[1] we find *cent* mentioned only three times in the American data, but 354 times in the British data. The American examples are of the unit of currency, but the British ones are not. Rather, the British examples largely result from the spelling *per cent*, rendered in American English as *percent*. So, the entirely plausible hypothesis about

> **What is a corpus?**
>
> The term *corpus* is Latin for 'body'. Its plural is *corpora*. A corpus is a collection of text analysed with the assistance of computers. You may see the term *corpus* used in a different sense, to refer to any set of language data *at all*. This usage was common before about 1960, and still in use today, though more rarely.

cent being more frequent in American than British English proves to be wrong.

As this example demonstrates, when it comes to testing our hypotheses about how language is used, corpora can act as invaluable guides to usage. They can challenge our intuitions and force us to account for data in ways that we cannot, initially, imagine. Corpora provide insights and act as sources of evidence to test competing hypotheses. This is what this chapter is about – **corpus linguistics**. This is the analysis of natural language data, typically in very large quantities, with the assistance of computers.

A corpus, as defined in the box, is rarely an arbitrary collection of texts; more usually, it has been carefully defined so as to be a suitable basis for a particular piece of research. The techniques that are used to analyse corpora can be called

DOI: 10.4324/9781003045571-25

corpus methods. These methods can be applied to questions across many areas of linguistics.

The use of computers to help analyse a corpus is usually not a matter of choice – a corpus is typically so big, often millions or even billions of words, that it cannot be analysed by hand-and-eye methods alone. For example, it would simply take too long, or require too many analysts, to grammatically analyse every sentence in 500 million words of text manually. Without computers, large-scale corpus analyses are, to most intents and purposes, impossible. Smaller amounts of text, such as single documents or a few extracts, *can* also be studied with the assistance of computers, but they don't have to be, as it's still possible to read the entire text to study its language, though questions about the consistency, accuracy and generalisability of that analysis may arise.

Increasingly, corpus techniques are spreading beyond linguistics and language studies. Researchers in other disciplines, especially but not only social science and humanities disciplines, have started seeing how corpus methods could be of use to them. Research in media studies, history, geography, sociology, politics, international relations and educational studies now exists, making use of corpus methods for their various purposes. Those are, of course, very different to the reasons that we use corpora in linguistics.

21.2 Corpus design and construction

To understand the central principles of corpus design, we can look back to the construction of what is, in the modern sense, the first electronic corpus. This is a collection of data now called the *Brown Corpus*, after Brown University in Providence, Rhode Island, where it was collected. The Brown Corpus is 1 million words in size, and contains 500 text samples of about 2000 words each. These 500 samples were all of written published American English. The focus on American English had a strong methodological justification – including only one variety of a language in a corpus means that inter-varietal differences don't need to be accounted for when studying the data in the corpus. Of course, the flip-side of this simplification is that findings based on the corpus can only reasonably be thought to generalise to American English. This need to balance representativeness and generalisability is an issue to which we will return in Section 21.6.

In this case, the fact that findings based on the Brown Corpus could not be generalised beyond American English led to another influential corpus being developed, the Lancaster-Oslo/Bergen Corpus (LOB). This is a British English equivalent for the Brown Corpus, named after the universities that worked together to create it. LOB followed the same design as Brown: 1 million words of written published British English, 500 samples, 2000 words each. In everything except the national variety represented, the two corpora are about the same. As the 'in focus' box demonstrates, this facilitates direct comparison of the two corpora. This is an important design principle and a major benefit of corpus methodologies, to which we will return in Section 21.5.2.

In focus: comparing corpora

Having a British English corpus and an American English corpus with the exact same design allowed comparisons between the two to stand as direct evidence of differences between American and British English. Crucially, this included differences that are perhaps not obvious, or **salient**. For instance, differences in vocabulary or orthography between American and British English are easy for native speakers of either national variety to think of. In terms of **lexis** (see Chapter 6), American English has *bathroom*, whereas British English has *toilet*. In terms of **orthography**, *color* occurs in American English, whereas in British English *colour* is spelt with <our> at the end (see p. 3 in Chapter 1 for an explanation of the different brackets used in linguistic notation). But differences may be subtle and less obvious, especially when it comes to grammar. An example is the structure of past tense conditional sentences. British English usually uses a past perfect verb plus a conditional perfect verb, e.g. *If I **had done** [X], I **would have done** [Y]*, but American English tends to prefer a conditional perfect in both clauses, e.g. *If I **would have done** [X], I **would have done** [Y]*. Such subtle differences are more easily detectable using corpora, where the difference in frequency of the two patterns of verb group can be detected by the computer.

Even less intuitively obvious are inter-varietal differences that are *only* a matter of frequency: instances where American English and British English both use a particular word or grammatical form, but differ in how often they do so. For instance, we know that in the present day, modal verbs (*may, can, should, would*, etc.) are generally used less in American English than in British English. Conversely, a structure called the *mandative subjunctive* (e.g. *it is important **that he be** given a chance*, as opposed to *that he should be* or *that he is*) is rather more common in American English. Corpora allow us to demonstrate such frequency differences, even of normally rare phenomena like the mandative subjunctive, by taking into account a massive amount of data.

21.2.1 Spoken corpus data

What of spoken language? Up to now, we have discussed only written data, but working with spoken corpus data poses a particular set of challenges. Written corpus data increasingly come to us in a 'born digital' written form; that is, there is no transcription stage, since we have electronic texts from the start. By contrast, with spoken data, as well as other mediums such as sign language, we are faced with the difficulty of transcribing the data. For spoken data, this involves turning an audio-recording into a transcription on the computer, which usually involves a linguist sitting down and typing it out or, in some circumstances nowadays, editing the output of a speech-to-text system. Likewise, corpora of sign languages, such as the British Sign Language Corpus, rely heavily upon video. Such corpora are only now becoming available, as the technical ability to build and use them becomes more widely available.

The first corpus of spoken English, or at least the first corpus that was fully electronic, was the London-Lund Corpus (LLC). The LLC was a 500,000 corpus of spoken data drawn from the Survey of English Usage (SEU),[2] an earlier project at University College London which collected a large amount of contemporary spoken and written English text in non-electronic form. The SEU's data from the 1950s was analysed using a system of paper-based indexes, half a million words of spoken data from the SEU was computerised, based on an earlier paper-based transcription which had a lot of mark-up (representational codes) for paralinguistic features like intonation, stress, pauses, and speaker overlap. The LLC preserved these, though doing so was a major challenge in the 1970s, as to some degree it still is!

Today, some spoken corpora have the kind of mark-up that the LLC pioneered. Others do not, and just contain an orthographic representation of the words spoken. These different types of spoken corpora are useful for different things. A spoken corpus which consists of just words without mark-up can be used for comparisons with written language; for instance, a spoken corpus marked up like the LLC can be used to look at the organisation of discourse into units indicated by intonation and stress, speed of delivery of information, the meanings indicated by pitch and tone, and so on.

21.2.2 Bigger is better?

Corpus construction uses sampling, and a core tenet of sampling is that larger sample sizes provide more reliable results with greater precision. But is bigger always better, where corpora are concerned?

The three corpora discussed so far are small by modern standards: Brown and LOB were 1 million words, the LLC half a million words. This was because they all had to be digitised manually – that is, published written text needed to be physically re-typed into the computer. The huge effort required limited the maximum achievable corpus size. Technological advances since the 1970s have largely done away with these limits, at least for written data. So, while 1 million words is a lot relative to what one linguist can read and analyse, it's not a lot relative to the huge amounts of text that it is possible to compile today from 'born digital' sources.

So, over time, subsequent generations of corpora have gone well beyond the 1-million-word mark. However, that's not to say that smaller corpora have fallen completely out of use. When a corpus is smaller, we have more opportunity to carefully design its contents and introduce high quality, manual, annotations. For instance, the careful 500-sample design of Brown and LOB would be very difficult to scale up to 100 million words, as doing so would involve careful selection of 50,000 texts – a much less manageable proposition. Though it has been done on projects

Scan the QR code to visit the ICE website: http://ice-corpora.net/ice/index.html

such as the British National Corpus 1994 and the British National Corpus 2014, both of which are 100 million words in size, with carefully designed 90 million word written components supplemented by 10 million word spoken components. However, as a general rule, larger corpora have less strict designs. So there is still a role for small corpora when we have research questions best analysed using a corpus with a really careful design. An example of a more recent corpus created in this way is the ICE-GB corpus. ICE stands for the *International Corpus of English*, which is a multinational project to create a corpora of national varieties of English from not just the UK and US, or Australia and New Zealand, but also places such as Singapore and India, where English is a second language. Each ICE component is on the same scale as Brown, LOB or LLC, with 1 million words of writing and 1 million of speech, carefully designed along the same lines of those early corpora to permit comparisons of different varieties of English around the world. The 'in focus' box outlines another breed of smaller, specialised corpora that are being produced with increasing frequency.

Clearly, the need to balance size with carefully thought-out design is paramount. So, what use are large, but less well-organised corpora? A good example to use to show this is the COBUILD (standing for Collins Birmingham University International Language Database) corpus, begun in the 1970s. As its name suggests, this was a joint corpus construction enterprise between the University of Birmingham and the publisher Collins. It was primarily intended to assist dictionary writers, and was about 20 million words in size when used in the mid-1980s to inform dictionary production. The vast scale, for its time, of COBUILD was important for lexicography, because smaller corpora such as Brown are not terribly good for lexicography. All but a very few words in any language are actually quite rare, and a small corpus will not usually furnish enough evidence on the use of the less frequent words to inform a good dictionary entry. So while the larger corpus lacked the carefully controlled design of the smaller corpora, it provided much more evidence to allow lexicographers to explore word usage. The idea that corpora could be used to improve dictionaries became hugely influential; all major dictionaries of English and many other languages are, today, at least partly corpus-based.

In focus: DIY corpora

The development of more specialised corpora has been a significant development in corpus linguistics. Such corpora do not try to represent the entirety of a language or variety, such as written British English in general, or spoken British English in general, but instead represent a collection of one particular sort of text for one particular reason, such as a corpus of newspaper language, or of talk in business meetings, or of university language.

A form of corpus that has recently come to prominence is the *do-it-yourself corpus*: a corpus created by an individual linguist for their own particular research project, in preference to using some published corpora like LOB or the BNC1994 or the Bank of English. Until relatively recently, using these standard corpora was unavoidable, because corpus creation was such a major task, hence *every* corpus had to be designed to be usable by everyone, for a wide range of purposes. But as technology has advanced corpus creation has become easier and it is now usually very straightforward for a researcher to create a corpus of exactly the sort of language that they want to study for one particular research project, and to analyse it using an offline tool like the one the QR code will take you to. We now live in a world where, through the web connection that computers usually now have, huge amounts of text are accessible. We can access vast text archives online, so newspaper archives for instance can be used to compile corpora of media language. Archives of transcribed television programmes can be accessed online, archives of film scripts . . . all kinds of texts can be found via the web and collected either manually or using specially designed software, to compile various different kinds of corpora that we can study for specific purposes.

Scan the QR code to download #LancsBox, a free software package for the analysis of language data and corpora, developed at Lancaster University: http://corpora.lancs.ac.uk/lancsbox

A famous corpus created in the early 1990s was the British National Corpus 1994 (BNC1994), which was 100 million words of speech and writing from the UK English of that time. This corpus, 10% speech and 90% writing, has been used for many purposes over time, and has spurred a huge amount of linguistic research – but is far from the biggest of its generation. The Bank of English, the descendent of the COBUILD corpus, drastically exceeds it in size. It implements certain strategies inaugurated during the development of COBUILD, for example the notion that a corpus should expand over time and have data added to it continually, to create a *monitor corpus* that reflects how the language develops over time. For that reason, we can't cite a definitive size for the Bank of English, but at different times it has ranged from 500 to over 600 million words. But even that is not the largest corpus that has been collected. Even larger corpora have been collected – mostly by dictionary publishers to assist them in lexicography, though in some cases such corpora have additionally been made available for linguistics research in part or whole – such as the Oxford University Press's Oxford English Corpus, which is at least a billion words. The trend for the largest corpora to be developed for lexicography, noted previously, continues to the present day, though computational linguistics also demands large corpora (see Chapter 18).[3]

21.3 Other advances in corpus linguistics

While size and mode of production allow us to clearly identify some important corpora and trends, a quite different, though welcome, trend has been the use of corpus methods for many languages other than English. While English was the first language which, more or less by accident, became intensively studied using corpora, corpora of languages other than English notably emerged from the 1980s onwards – first for languages like French or German, which use the same alphabet as English, and then for languages such as Greek and Russian which use other alphabets. Ultimately, corpus methods extended to languages which use non-alphabetic writing systems, such as Chinese and Urdu. This order was determined by the need to solve the computational problems associated with the digital representation of each writing system, in a manner suitable for analysis by corpus software. For some writing systems (e.g. Devanagari and Perso-Arabic), these difficulties were not fully surmounted until around the year 2000, when the development of Unicode, a system which allows all computers to render the full range of human writing systems in a way which is uniform and transferable, was developed.

Another development in corpus linguistics is what we can call **families of corpora**. The Brown and LOB family of corpora form a basis for comparison for two varieties of English, but people have also taken that idea further and created, for example, comparison points for Brown and LOB which are comparisons in time. So there are now corpora which match Brown and LOB stretching from the 1930s to the 2020s, allowing us to look at how language has changed in American English and British English over time.

21.3.1 New frontiers in corpus linguistics

One particularly interesting development which has arisen in recent decades is the rise of social media. Social media posts are a new variety of language, a set of genres that didn't really exist prior to about 2000. Some resemble earlier genres to some degree – blog posts are sometimes similar to pre-web diary entries; text messages could be compared to telegrams or short letters – but others, such as Facebook and Twitter posts, are genuine novelties. These are potentially classifiable as intermediate types of communication, relative to pre-web genres, but cannot be equated to any single genre. All this opens up many interesting paths for research.

What is a concordancer?

A concordancer is a piece of software that can be used to search and analyse a corpus. Typically, concordancers allow us to enter a word or phrase and search for examples of how it's used in the corpus we're consulting.

Concordancers can either be installed onto a computer, like #LancsBox (see the QR code on p. 391), or accessed via a website, like CQPWeb (see the QR code on p. 391).

Some researchers have even gone so far as to ask whether we even need fixed corpora like the BNC1994 or the Bank of English any more – that is, a defined collection of texts able to be loaded into each researcher's concordancer. Instead, why not develop a concordancer that can actually go out onto the web and find examples of whatever word, or other item, we're interested in? That approach is useful for some purposes, especially in artificial intelligence and machine learning. However, for many *linguistic* questions, the answer is *no*. Just heading out onto the web and grabbing data does not produce a carefully designed dataset – and, as we mentioned at the start of the chapter, part of the definition of a corpus is that it has been designed or collected for some purpose or set of purposes. Many of the research purposes in question require us to have an understanding of what's in the data. You can't analyse the BNC1994 without knowing that it's 10% spoken English, 90% written English; you can't analyse LOB without knowing it's 500 samples of 2000 words across a defined collection of genres. If we are simply going out on the web to search an undefined mass of language that is constantly being changed and regenerated and revised by everyone in the world, then we don't have that understanding. This kind of web-as-corpus method has certain advantages for analysing, for instance, extremely recent uses of novel terms which are unlikely to be exemplified in any defined corpus. But the majority of linguistic analyses will continue to require a fixed finite corpus for the foreseeable future.

21.4 Annotation and metadata

21.4.1 Annotation

A corpus is often more than just its words. Corpora can also contain **annotation**. Corpus annotation consists of layers of linguistic analysis, encoded in concert with the text of a corpus, for use in subsequent research. When we annotate a corpus, we add extra, explicit, information to the corpus data. This is then an **annotated corpus**, as opposed to **plain-text** or **raw corpora**, which are corpora *without* annotation.

Annotation can be added at different linguistic 'levels', like those represented in Figure 10.1, on p. 208 of this volume), for example at the level of word grammar, the level of phrase grammar, the level of intonation, the level of semantics and so on. This is why it is often useful to think about annotation as a series of layers of data atop the actual words of the raw corpus, which makes up the most basic layer. For example, we can add information at the word grammar level by analysing parts of speech. We can add information at the syntactic level by annotating grammatical constituency. And, at the suprasegmental level, we can annotate features such as intonation and pauses, and we can annotate information about meaning at the semantic level. The same principle applies to higher or more abstract levels such as the level of discourse or the level of style.

In practice, the most commonly seen forms of annotation are part-of-speech tagging, parsing and lemmatisation. Let's look at each in turn.

At the level of word grammar, the first analysis is simply to identify the grammatical class of each word, its part of speech (POS). In corpus annotation, we often call this analysis **POS tagging**. This simply means encoding into the corpus a grammatical label for each word. This is just extending to an entire corpus a procedure that you are almost certainly familiar with – going through each word in a sentence and stating whether it is, for example, a noun, a determiner, a verb, an article, etc.

What is the value of POS tagging a corpus? One important advantage is **disambiguation**. Language can contain much ambiguity, that is, words or other forms with multiple possible interpretations, where you can only decide what interpretation is the right one based on the context. An English example is the word *leaves*. If it is used as a noun, *leaves* is the plural of *leaf*. However, *leaves* can also be a verb: the third person singular present tense of the verb *to leave*. In any given analysis, we're likely to be interested in only one of these: *either* the plant-related noun, *or* the verb of motion, but probably not both at once. Ideally, we'd want to search the corpus in a way that keeps the two separate. This is called **disambiguation** and POS tags allow us to do this. Concordancers are usually able to use annotation in a corpus, if it has any, as criteria for searches. So if a corpus has POS tags, corpus queries can be devised for *leaves* as a noun which will not retrieve instances of noun versus *leaves* when it's a verb. You can try this yourself by scanning the QR code to visit an online concordancer.

Scan the QR code to visit the online CQPWeb concordancer: https://cqpweb .lancs.ac.uk/

Parsing is annotation of syntax beyond the word level – grammatical links or grammatical groupings that go across multiple words. If we take a sentence like *Some leaves fall early*, we can say that *some* and *leaves* belong together: they form a phrase, a noun phrase in fact. The remaining two words are linked with that phrase to form the sentence, but the connection is more distant than that which creates the phrase *some leaves* (see Chapter 4 for more on this kind of linkage). This phrase structure can be encoded into the data of a corpus – usually by inserting nested brackets to indicate where the different phrases begin and end. Large corpora that have been parsed in this way can be very useful for the study of grammar; the term for a corpus in which every sentence has been annotated for syntactic analysis is a **treebank**.

The third common type of annotation is **lemmatisation**. A **lemma** is a group of inflectionally related word forms.[4] If we take the verb *leave*, again, for instance, we can see it has a number of grammatical variants depending on things like tense, person and number: *leaves*, *leaving*, *left* as well as *leave*. We

Lemma is a loanword from Greek, and you might see the plural *lemmata* used sometimes, instead of *lemmas*.

Lemmas are usually rendered in small caps when cited, like THIS.

say that this group of forms, treated together, constitutes a single verb lemma, which we label LEAVE for its base form.

If we want to search for all examples of verb lemma LEAVE, we can't just search directly for *leave*, because that will only find one form of the verb. One thing we could do is put the four forms into a single query which specifies them as alternative targets: *leave* OR *leaves* OR *leaving* OR *left*. But doing so every time we search for a verb would be very repetitive, and also opens us up to ambiguity, since we'd also catch *leaves* as a noun and *left* as an adjective, which belong to different lemmas. To avoid that problem, we can **lemmatise** our corpus: adding labels to every word to indicate the lemma it belongs to. Then a search for LEAVE as a verb lemma will find all four forms, but without any cases of noun *leaves* or adjective *left*.

At the discourse level, lots of people have looked at discourse cohesion – how the different sentences of a text are linked together to create an overall cohesive text. One way this is done is with **anaphora** – nouns and pronouns that make reference to the same entities over the course of a stretch of sentences. A process called anaphoric annotation has been used to look at this. Pragmatic annotation, to look at speech acts in dialogue, has also been undertaken since the late 1990s, and as we saw when we talked about the London Lund corpus, prosodic annotation for such features of speech such as stress, intonation and pauses in a long running project which helps with the analysis of various phonetic and especially intonational and suprasegmental features.

21.4.2 Metadata

As well as annotation, a corpus may also have **metadata**. Metadata is data *about* data, information added to the text to describe the text. For example, if a corpus contains both writing and speech, a listing of which texts are written and which are based on speech may be one item of textual metadata. Sometimes, you will never see your corpus's metadata, because sophisticated corpus software simply makes use of it in the background to manipulate and enhance different analyses. On the other hand, if you look at a set of actual corpus files on your computer, you may find metadata *either* as a block of **header** information at the top of each corpus text, *or* as separate documentation in a **corpus manual**, *or* as a database-style table or tables alongside the corpus files. Figure 21.1 will give you an idea of what a header looks like.

Of course, if you compile your own corpus it is up to you to determine what items of metadata you need to collect for each text, given your particular research purposes.

```
<header>

<rec_length>0:26:41</rec_length>

<rec_date>2015-11-10</rec_date>

<rec_year>2015</rec_year>

<rec_period>2015_Q4</rec_period>

<n_speakers>2</n_speakers>

<list_speakers>S0405 S0555</list_speakers>

<rec_loc>Footpath, Slough</rec_loc>

<relationships>Friends, wider family circle</relationships>

<topics>School project, poverty, life, friends, politics, scientific research,
consumerism, comics, </topics>

<activity>Friends walking home discussing schoolwork and friendships</activity>

<conv_type>Discussing, explaining, inquiring, complaining</conv_type>

<conventions>Revised</conventions>

<in_sample>n</in_sample>

<transcriber>T06</transcriber>

</header>
```

Figure 21.1 An illustrative header derived from a file in the BNC 2014 spoken (file S66E).

Types of metadata differ for different genres of corpora and text. Table 21.1 gives some examples of the kinds of information that metadata may convey.

Table 21.1 Examples of metadata corpora may have.

Data type	Information type	Examples
Written data	Medium	Book, periodical, social media post, etc.
	Bibliographic information	Author, title, publisher, publication date, etc.
Spoken data	Information about the speakers (and sometimes hearers)	Sex, age, social background, ethnolinguistic background (e.g. dialect), relationships to other speakers, etc.
	Situation of text production	When and where the recording was made, type of social/functional context the interaction took place in, whether it was a monologue or dialogue, etc.
Both written and spoken data	Basic information about the structure and format of the text	Length, completeness, etc.

21.5 Advantages of corpus linguistics

Corpus methods' primary advantage is their ability to deal with data on a very large scale. Computer software gives power to both quantitative and qualitative analysis – that is, both frequency and statistical analysis and analysis based on human interpretation.

Without the corpus, we may be led astray by focusing on particular examples of a word or a structure, which happen not to be typical of that item's use. For instance, if we are looking at the meaning of *joy*, then basing our analysis on one example that catches our eye in a newspaper or book is liable to give us a misleading impression. This is because, by definition, something that jumps out at a reader as salient is likely to represent a **marked** or unusual usage, not an **unmarked** or typical usage. If we have corpus data on a very large scale and if we *pay attention* to all of that data, we're much less likely to be led astray in this way.

21.5.1 Minimising bias

Total accountability is a notion introduced by Leech (1992) to summarise this principle. According to this notion, corpus methods must be *totally accountable* to the data. We're not allowed to ignore any of the data; we're not allowed to pick out a subset of the data that is easy to explain based on our existing assumptions. A corpus-based description should account for *all* relevant data in the dataset. Or, if there are just too many relevant items of data to analyse all of them, then a *random* subset should be selected for analysis – not a cherry-picked subset designed to 'prove' a point. When you use methods that are totally accountable to the data, the results can be checked, reproduced and confirmed. The idea of total accountability also maximises the opportunity of testing and possibly proving false a hypothesis that you had – the corpus challenges your ideas to the greatest possible degree. This is an important part of the scientific method, and (generally speaking) corpus linguistics does aim for this kind of scientific validity. Using the total accountability principle allows us to avoid *biased* selection of the data. Otherwise, **cognitive biases** could lead us to pay too much attention to especially notable examples and overlook ordinary or expected examples, for example.

If our methods are totally accountable to the data in this way, we can use them to test theories about how language works against corpus data. That is, if we have an idea of how things work, we can take that to the corpus, search for examples of what we're hypothesising about, and then study the full set of examples to determine whether they are all explicable using the hypothesis we started with. Sometimes the answer will be yes and sometimes the answer will be no – it is falsified, as in the example given in Section 21.1. In the latter case, we need to consider if we should revise our hypothesis.

As well as taking that **hypothesis-testing** approach, we can also explore text without a clear idea of what it is we're looking for. Using **keywords** and

collocations, the approaches outlined in the 'in focus' box are often a good starting point for such exploration. As soon as we're looking around the corpus in this way, we have the opportunity to observe and identify *things that we weren't looking for* – new observations which may spur new hypotheses, in other words.

A more formal way to put this is to say that using the corpus method to explore very large amounts of data opens us up to **serendipity**. In sum, the enhancement of qualitative and quantitative analysis through the power of the computer, the total accountability principle, the ability to test our hypothesis against actual data, and the ability to explore and discover phenomena we didn't know we were looking for, are the most important advantages of corpus linguistics.

In focus: keywords and collocations

By comparing two corpora, we can discover keywords. These are words which occur with greater frequency in one corpus, in comparison to another. These keywords can then provide useful signposts for analysis, allowing us to contrast, for example, two varieties of English. The following are the top ten keywords when 1 million words each of present day written British and American English are compared.[5] Words followed by '+' are more frequent in British English; those followed by '–' are more frequent in American English.

cent (+), centre (+), U.S. (–), behaviour (+), federal (–), BBC (+), Mum (+), defence (+), center (–), congress (–)

We can quickly see here the effect of spelling – the words *centre* and *center* show a difference between British (using *centre*) and American (using *center*) English. We also see some key differences in the social context in which the two varieties are used – the British institution *BBC* is more frequent in British English, the American institution *congress* is more frequent in American English. Outside of the top ten we begin to see evidence of grammatical differences – modal verbs tend to be more frequent in British English than American. This example demonstrates how a simple contrast, based on word frequency, can give us a deep insight into language and culture.

Collocation allows us a view of how words act in context – collocation measures how closely bonded two words are to one another (i.e. how likely we are to see one in close proximity to the other, as opposed to occurring anywhere else).[6] If we look at a word like *welcome*, this can reveal differences – this word has no other word in written British English that collocates with it. In written American English there is only one collocate for the word *'re*. The American collocate arises from a standard politeness formula in American English, *you're welcome*. Collocation can show differences like this swiftly.

Figure 21.2 shows how such collocations can be visualised using collocation networks. In this case, the collocation network shows the progression of L2 learners of English. Figure 21.2A shows how the word *take* is used by intermediate-level learners in the Trinity Lancaster Corpus, whilst Figure 21.2B shows how *take* is used by advanced learners in corpus data from the same corpus.

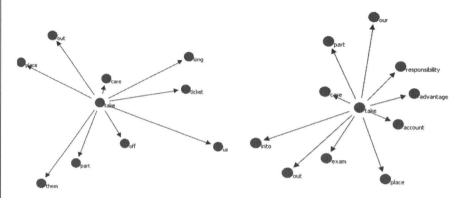

Figure 21.2 Collocation network showing how *take* is used by intermediate and advanced learners of L2 English.

SCAN ME

From Figure 21.2, it is clear that the advanced learners have acquired more collocates of *take*, and have developed the use of *take* as a phrasal verb. If you would like to know more about the Trinity Lancaster Corpus of spoken L2 English, you can scan the QR code. You can also read more about data visualisation techniques used in linguistics in Chapter 24 of this volume.

21.5.2 Comparative methods

One other particular advantage of corpus linguistics is its accommodation of **comparative** methods. These are methods that allow us to take two or more corpora that can be compared in some way, and to use corpus methods to understand the distinctions or contrasts between them. One example of this is the analysis of parallel corpora. A **parallel corpus** is a corpus that contains the same texts in more than one language. It might, for instance, contain a set of texts in French and then the translations of those texts into German. Using parallel corpus data, we can examine the language that corresponds to something we're focused upon in one language, in the other language. So if we are interested in, for example, what French word is used to correspond to the German term *Gesellschaft* ('company'), a parallel corpus allows the generation of a concordance of *Gesellschaft* with the corresponding French text displayed directly alongside.

We can also do comparisons over time for historical data. As was outlined earlier in our discussion of corpus families, the 1960s English corpora, Brown and LOB, are often compared to 'replica' corpora created at different points in time according to the same framework. For example, Frown and FLOB were created for the early 1990s. This facilitates the examination of recent changes in English grammar and word meanings.

Similarly, historical corpora exist that allow us to study language change, sometimes over multiple centuries, by comparing earlier and later subsections within the corpus. These are **diachronic** investigations, in terms of the classic diachronic-synchronic distinction that goes back to the earliest days of linguistics (see Chapter 8). Parallel corpora are typically synchronic, but we can do other synchronic comparisons as well. We might sample a collection of newspapers to find stories from the same date and on the same topics in newspapers from America *and* from the UK. This would allow us to investigate how different English-speaking countries' media were handling the issue in question on that particular day, in terms of attitudes, ideologies and rhetoric. This kind of synchronic comparison of attitudes expressed through language in use are key to what is sometimes called **corpus-assisted discourse analysis**, or **corpus-based Critical Discourse Analysis** (see Chapter 10).

21.6 Challenges in corpus linguistics

The advantages of corpus analysis and corpus research are of course balanced by problems. One is the problem of **representativeness**. Corpora are studied because they are assumed to represent something larger than the particular corpus. Why do we study the particular 500 samples of text in the Brown Corpus? It's not because we're particularly interested in those 500 texts; there's nothing special about them. Rather, we study those 500 texts in order to try and find out about published written American English *as a whole*. Ideally, we want to take results from analysing Brown, and report them as applying to written American English generally. But is that the case? What if these particular 500 texts are giving us a misleading picture? This may well be the case if they are not **representative** of the larger population of texts from which they were sampled. Even assessing this, however, is impossible: the only way to be sure that a corpus is representative is to collect the *entire* language or variety, and assess whether it gives us the same picture that we got from our corpus. But we *can't* collect the whole of any language or variety. Language is not finite; it's always possible to create a new text.

In practice, then, we can never be sure of a corpus's representativeness. However, we *can* carefully take steps to ensure our corpus is as close to representative as possible. While it's very hard to prove that something is representative, it's pretty easy to demonstrate that something is *unrepresentative*, and to avoid doing things that would make our results inapplicable to full population of some language or variety.

Another problem with corpus linguistics is that it is biased towards written data. This is because it is much easier to collect written than spoken data, especially now that most data in written form is actually typed into a computer to begin with, that is, it is, as noted, 'born digital'. Spoken data, on the other hand, has to be transcribed manually, since even today no transcription software can typically produce results good enough for linguistic analysis.[7] Even with care, transcriptions can be inaccurate, and even with careful annotation of suprasegmental features, a spoken corpus text may still lack most of the detail of the spoken signal. This means that it's much easier to do corpus analysis on writing than on speech, so that the field generally exhibits a bias towards analyses of the written form.

This is unfortunate, because linguists generally agree that the spoken form of language is primary. As is explored in Chapter 8 as well as Chapter 30, there have been many spoken languages with no use of writing, but not many written languages that were not spoken languages as well. There have been some languages that were purely languages of scholarship, after the spoken form of the language died out, such as Classical Greek or Medieval Latin, but those languages could still be spoken by the scholars who had learned them for scholarly purposes.

We also have the problem that our computers are not necessarily 100% correct when they process corpus data. There is almost always an **error rate.** When we run a query in a concordancer, how well it performs depends on what we're searching for. A search for a single specific word (e.g. *happiness*) will be very close to 100% accurate. The tool won't be able to find any examples with non-standard spellings (e.g. *happyness*), but that's typically a minor problem.

Let's imagine, however, that we run a query for *happiness* preceded by an adjective, which we can do using a concordancer able to handle POS tags. Now, the performance of our query relies on the correctness of the annotation. Only *adjectives correctly tagged as adjectives* will be matched by the concordancer. POS taggers are typically about 97% accurate. This means, of course, that they are 3% inaccurate; that is, one mistake is made every 30 words on average. Lemmatisation also has quite a high accuracy rate, but other forms of computerised annotation, including parsing, do rather worse, often scoring 90% or below. We must always remain aware that our findings can only be relied on to the extent that problems in automatic corpus processing didn't lead to relevant data being missed or irrelevant data being included.

21.7 Conclusion

The purpose of this chapter has been to introduce the concept of a linguistic corpus, and the methodological approach that uses corpora to investigate language: corpus methods. The example given in the Introduction to this chapter, Section 21.1, shows just how useful corpus methods can be for testing hypotheses and challenging our preconceived notions about language with empirical data.

As we have seen, however, there is much more to corpus linguistics than just using a corpus, and in Section 21.2, we introduced some key concepts in the design and construction of different types of linguistic corpora. Here, we stressed the importance of designing corpora carefully, using a historical survey of seminal corpora to demonstrate how demands such as representativeness and generalisability can be balanced when a corpus is being designed and constructed. In Section 21.2.1, we introduced spoken and sign language corpora, and some of the particular challenges that these kinds of corpora can pose to the corpus linguist. In Section 21.2.2, we then explored issues of corpus size, emphasising the importance of tailoring a corpus to your research purpose. We saw that a DIY corpus will, for example, be much smaller than a corpus which aims to represent a national language variety, and that this will in turn probably be far smaller than one of the vast corpora constructed for dictionary-building.

In Section 21.3, we explored the progress in the field of corpus linguistics which has resulted from the enormous technological advances in recent decades, before going on in Section 21.4 to introduce the concepts of corpus annotation, the tagging of corpus data with additional information to aid or enhance retrieval, and metadata, the labelling of corpus data with information about a text. Finally, in Sections 21.5 and 21.6, we considered some of the advantages and challenges to using this kind of approach to seek answers to research questions about language.

Notes

1 In this case the American English 2006 corpus and the British English 2006 corpus.
2 The SEU is still in existence as an important unit for work in corpus linguistics.
3 Other billion-word-plus corpora of the 1990s and 2000s, such as the English Gigaword and its equivalents in other languages, were compiled for use in Natural Language Processing (NLP), a sub-discipline of corpus linguistics with a degree of overlap with corpus linguistics (see Chapter 18).
4 You may be familiar with the term *lexeme*, which is sometimes used to mean the same thing as *lemma*, and sometimes something slightly different. For corpus annotation purposes, we don't usually distinguish them, and we generally prefer the term *lemma*.
5 For those familiar with corpus work, the British English 2006 corpus is here compared with the American English 2006 corpus. The statistic used for comparison is Log Ratio, using a log-likelihood filter and Šidák correction.
6 The following examples are drawn from the British English 2006 and American English 2006 corpora of written language. For those familiar with corpus linguistics, in each case collocation was calculate using a window of +/– 5 words, a minimum frequency of the collocate of at least 5 and the use of the filtered Log Ratio statistic.
7 With the very best current automatic transcription software, and an ideal recording, it may be quicker to manually correct an automatic transcript than to simply type out the whole thing from scratch. Often, however, that's not the case.

Reference

Leech, G. 1992. Corpora and theories of linguistic performance. In J. Starvik (Ed.), *Directions in Corpus Linguistics*. Berlin: Mouton de Gruyter, pp. 105–122.

22 Field methods

Uta Papen and Claire Nance

22.1 Introduction

In this chapter we introduce you to field methods in linguistics. Such methods are also often referred to as 'fieldwork'. Fieldwork may remind you of biology or archaeology and you may thus wonder what field/s we are working in when we study language. We use the word field here in a metaphorical sense. Our field is not a meadow where butterflies can be observed but refers to the collection of language data, for example recording people to study their accent or dialect, or observing and recording the classroom talk of a lesson, to understand how teachers support students' understanding of the lesson content. Other linguistic fieldwork is done to document different languages. In the following sections, we introduce these different field methods, and we consider the practicalities of making recordings during fieldwork research.

22.2 Ethnography and observations

In this section, we introduce you to a type of fieldwork that is used by researchers who are working at the intersection between applied linguistics, education, sociology and anthropology. If you are interested in, for example, the role of language in education or the kind of language/s used in everyday encounters, such as at a market, in an office or in court, you need to study these places carefully, to find out how language is used in them. To achieve this, you need to spend time in these settings and observe how people communicate. This is called fieldwork – the field here being the school classroom, the office, the market or the court. The main method used in these fields is what is called participant observation. Participant observation is part of the wider research tradition known as ethnography that was introduced in Chapter 7. We will briefly explain what ethnography is, then introduce you to observations as a method to collect data.

22.2.1 What is ethnography?

Ethnography is a seemingly simple method: as an ethnographer you 'hang out' with the people you study. The scholarly explanation for ethnography is that it is

DOI: 10.4324/9781003045571-26

'an account of someone's observations of and experience with a community and their cultural practices in specific contexts' (Wei 2019: 154).

While ethnography is nowadays used by linguists, its origins are in history, social anthropology and sociology. The word itself comes from the Greek *ethnos*, folk or people and *grapho*, I write. An ethnography, then, is a writing up, an account, as Wei says earlier, of a community or group of people. Note though that when we talk about ethnography, we usually mean both the process of doing ethnography *and* the account or product of it, which could be a book, a report, a journal article or even your dissertation. The actual doing of ethnography is done, as we will explain in the next sections, through methods such as observations, writing field notes, interviewing and recordings.

To begin with, ethnography was about studying the culture and way of living of different people. Often, it was associated with studying groups of people far away from the Western world of academics in their universities in London or Paris. Bronislav Malinowski, who worked at the London School of Economics, was one of the first social anthropologists to not work from an office armchair, using the documents of travellers, explorers and historians, but to go out to the 'field' and get his hands dirty by spending many months living with the people he studied, the Trobriander. Their home was a remote group of islands in the Pacific.

Language was not originally the focus of ethnography. But as ethnographers spent time in the setting and lived amongst the people they studied, they had to learn the local language. They also knew that language takes a central place in a community's thinking and doing, so learning the local language was an important part of their research method.

From its early beginnings with social anthropologists like Malinowski in London or sociologists like Robert Ezra Park in Chicago (see Papen 2019), ethnography has developed into a research approach that is widely used across many disciplines in the social sciences, including linguistics, education, health research, human geography and others. The most important thing to know about ethnography is that as a research method it seeks to study things as they are happening 'live' and in their normal, natural environment. What we mean here is that with ethnography you seek to understand things in real, everyday situations and contexts. This makes ethnography very different from experimental research methods or work in language laboratories (see Chapter 20). The second important premise of ethnography is that as the researcher your aim is to understand the perspective of those whose actions and beliefs you study – this is called the insider or emic view. To achieve this, ethnographers need to spend time in the setting and with their research participants. The third important thing to know about ethnography is that it is a qualitative method: with ethnography you go for detail and depth in your understanding of whatever it is you have been studying. Most likely then, your study will be based in just one setting or place, involving a small number of people. The aim of your ethnography is not to produce findings that can be generalised, but to come to a comprehensive understanding of a particular setting, case or issue.

So how exactly can ethnography help the study of language? Because ethnography is about studying things 'live', as they happen, ethnography allows linguists to study language *in use* and *in context*, as spoken and written in different social settings and cultural contexts. Understanding language as used in different social and communicative contexts is an important part of linguistics (see for example, Chapter 14 on health communication, or Chapter 17 on workplace language). Researchers study language in the workplace, in settings such as courtrooms, TV news production rooms or hospitals. They may research how young people communicate with each other (see p. 154) or the role of language in education (see Chapter 15). The thinking behind this kind of research is that language varies according to context, activity and people and that much is to be understood about language and how it relates to culture, to social life, to politics and to people's understandings of themselves (their identity) by spending time in real-life settings where language is used. This kind of linguistic research is associated with the sub-disciplines of sociolinguistics (see Chapter 7) and applied linguistics. More recently, linguists who work in these areas and who draw in their work on ethnography have come to refer to themselves as linguistic ethnographers (Tusting 2019). They use both observations (of people using language) and recordings of language. More on observations in the next section (22.2.2). We will discuss making recordings in Section 22.2.4.

22.2.2 Observations

While ethnographers use a variety of methods to collect data, observations are what could be called the mainstay of ethnography and what distinguishes it from other forms of qualitative research. In the context of linguistics, this means 'systematically observing events, interactions, behaviours, relationships and artefacts related to and around language(s) in a social setting' (Curdt-Christiansen 2019: 336). Observations can take a variety of forms, depending on the specific study and the research questions you have, as well as on where your study is located. Best known, perhaps, is what is called 'participant observation'. The phrase suggests that you both participate and take part. In practice this may not be easy to achieve. Let's take a language class as an example. The researcher may be able to take on the role of a non-participating observer in such a classroom. They might sit at the back, watching the lesson, taking notes, having little contact with either the students or the teachers. This would limit their impact on the lesson. They may use a structured form of observations. This means that they use an observation checklist, a detailed grid of things to look out for and document (see Mackey and Gass 2015). This kind of structured observation is useful when your aim is to look at a specific aspect of language teaching, for example the use of a specific type of instruction or task.

In many contexts, staying at the back and not interacting with the participants may not be an option. This raises the question of whether what you will observe will actually be the same as 'normal' practice. Will people change their behaviour in your presence? As discussed in Chapter 7, this is referred to as the Observer's Paradox (see p. 146). Ethnographers usually address this by avoiding 'one-shot' visits (Rose et al. 2020: 104). The 'in focus' box contains two other examples of participant observation.

In focus: observer or participant? (Uta Papen)

In a study of the teaching of reading and writing to 5- and 6-year-olds, I visited a primary school once a week over ten months. This was an ethnography and my research question had been deliberately broad: I wanted to understand how literacy was taught. I gained access to the school through prior contacts. The school was happy for me to join the class once a week. But what role should I take in the class? While I wanted to be a researcher, just observing wasn't practical, as there was no real 'back' of the classroom, away from the children, for me to sit without being noticed. The children were curious and saw me as another adult who might help with their lessons or listen to their banter and stories. I took on the role of parent helper and thus participant in the lesson. The children were used to parent helpers. I was happy to take on this role, even if this meant I had the difficult task to straddle observing and participating. This was also for ethical reasons (see Chapter 19). Not helping the teacher and teaching assistants in this large and very busy classroom where the children had many needs would simply have felt wrong. Becoming a parent helper had the added bonus of the children and teachers quickly getting used to me and accepting me as a member of their classroom.

My second example is from a recent international study. This was an observation of an English language classroom in a school for deaf children and young adults in India. I had come to the Deaf Bilingual Academy in Indore to spend a week observing the teaching of English. The lessons followed a specific approach that colleagues and I had developed. The teachers, who we had trained in the approach, were trying it out. I had come in order to see how it worked. So, ideally, I wanted to sit at the back of the class and watch. As much of the classroom discussion was in Indian Sign Language, I heavily relied on an interpreter who sat next to me. In practice though, I again became a partial participant. The students saw me as another teacher, wanting me to comment on their work. The teacher himself asked for my advice and he wanted me to teach a lesson so that he could see how I would do it. Thus, I took on a role which was somewhere between researcher (observer), teacher and teacher trainer.

Earlier in this section, we talked about structured observations using a grid, with specific points to look out for. In many ethnographic studies of language use or language teaching, your observations are much broader, and you are likely to simply want to observe everything you can, at least when first starting the research. My study of literacy teaching in primary schools, outlined in the 'in focus' box, was of this kind. In such studies, observations are at least initially open ended leading to much more of a narrative account, in the form of field notes (see Section 22.2.3). More specific points to focus on emerge only gradually, as the researcher spends more time in the setting. In a four-month-long study of communication in the multilingual setting of Birmingham's city library, Creese and Blackledge (2019) had set out to understand how library staff and library users communicate, and how library services are offered in a context where many of those entering the library do not speak English as their first language. As they spent two to three days every week 'shadowing' one library staff member (herself bilingual) they realised that many of the conversations between the staff member and her client were informal language learning encounters, where she and her clients taught each other bits and pieces about the languages they spoke. The library as a space for language learning and the role such informal learning encounters played in making the library a welcoming and inclusive space became a focus of their observations and fieldnotes, and an important finding of their study.

We need to say a little more about what, practically, an observer does. As the name suggests, you watch. But you also talk and listen, and this is an important part of being an observer, regardless of whether, or how closely, you participate. Think about a study of language use in a courtroom. Of course, you listen. In the primary school classroom mentioned in the 'in focus' box, too, I listened, and I did so very carefully. For example, I listened to how the teachers pronounced sounds in the phonics lessons, helping the children to link letters to sounds. I also talked, not only when I was participating in the teaching (for example when helping a child). I often talked to the teachers about their lessons. I asked the teachers about what they did, how and why. Talking to the people in the setting you study is an important part of ethnography. By observing alone, you cannot make sense of what is happening, and you cannot understand people's reasoning and motivations for their actions. Informal, ad hoc and usually short conversations are therefore a common tool for the ethnographer. Many ethnographers also combine observations with more structured and formal interviews (see Chapter 23).

22.2.3 Field notes and other ways to record your observations

Field notes are the written record that you produce based on your observations. In other words, they are your core data. When developing answers to your research question(s), you will rely heavily on your field notes, although you will draw also on other data, including the conversations and interviews we mentioned in the previous section.

Taking field notes usually means writing and, more often than not, this may still be old fashioned handwriting in old fashioned notebooks. Taking field notes is hard on your brain (writing while observing) and on your hands (writing fast).

Digital note taking may be an alternative. Many ethnographers use brief, almost code-like jottings while in the field, which they will then expand on and write up after they have left the setting. My fieldnotes from my observations in Indore (see 'in focus' box) were certainly brief, even cryptic. You can see an example of my field notes in Figure 22.1. As you can see, it's not important that they are legible or comprehensible to anyone else! However, every day, as soon as I had left the school and was back in my hotel room, I sat down to go through, expand, and explain them. This work on your raw notes is an important part of producing fieldnotes; to help with accuracy of observations but also as a moment where you already begin to think about what you just observed. As you are doing this, you are likely to add commentary and reflections, beginning the process of analysing what you experienced. Textbooks about ethnography always recommend that you type up your notes as soon as you can after leaving the field.

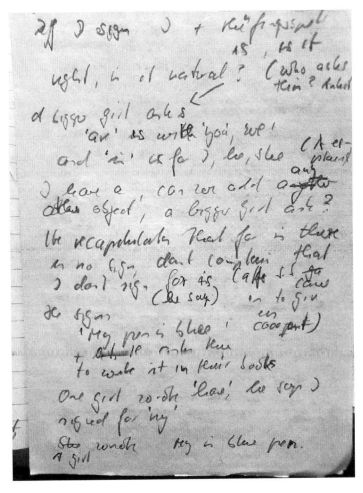

Figure 22.1 A page from Uta's field notes.

Field notes are necessarily selective, and it is helpful to think about other ways to capture what is happening. Sometimes drawings (e.g. of classroom or court-room settings) are good, but often photographs and recordings are the most helpful way to complement your field notes. If the setting or situation allows it, you may also want to take video-recordings. Audio- and video-recordings can then be transcribed and analysed in much detail. They are thus particularly important if you want to conduct linguistic or phonetic analysis (see Section 22.3) or conversation analysis. Recordings have the great advantage of being there for you to listen to or watch time and again, as often as you need to do. Filming parts of a classroom or a lesson can be incredibly helpful as it is impossible by merely observing to catch all the detail of a busy and bustling classroom. Films also capture the multimodal aspects of communication, including gestures, posture and gaze. Filming or recording may, however, be seen as intrusive and permissions are required. In their library-based study, Creese and Blackledge asked their main participant, a customer experience support assistant, to wear a small digital voice recorder, kept in their pocket. This allowed the researchers to record their speech when interacting with customers, but in an unobtrusive way. They later transcribed some of these recordings, allowing them to analyse in more detail the assistant's conversations with clients. This kind of speech data was an important addition to the observational data.

You can read more about fieldnotes in Papen (2019) and Curdt-Christiansen (2019). In Section 22.3 we will explore another kind of research which necessitates collecting data in the field, language documentation. Then in Section 22.4, we tell you more about the practicalities of making audio-recordings.

22.3 Language documentation

In previous sections, we have already introduced field methods associated with ethnography. Here we present a different kind of fieldwork study to collect data from a population which isn't geographically close to your school/university, for example in a language documentation project. By documenting lesser-studied languages, we can expand knowledge beyond the small number of well-studied languages such as English, Spanish and Mandarin.

For example, Palfreyman (2019) conducted a language documentation pro-ject of sign languages in Indonesia. Indonesia is the fourth most populous country in the world, but compared to Western sign languages, East Asian sign languages remain severely under-documented. Many areas of Indonesia are thought to have different sign languages, but many of these have so far not been linguistically described. Palfreyman aimed to document the grammar and sociolinguistic variation in the sign languages of Solo and Makassar, two cities on different Indonesian islands. His methods included working with a large number of signers from Solo and Makassar, as well as typological com-parison, and looking at different genders and generations of signers in each place. Palfreyman worked with research assistants and made a large number of video-recordings during his fieldwork. From this work he is able to demonstrate, for example, that verb negation markers have diffused through different sign varieties in Indonesia. However, there are also city variants and changes being led by younger speakers which leads to a complex array of possible realisations of verb negation. Palfreyman uses these findings to challenge previous methods for documenting sign languages as well as the methods linguists use for delineating where one language or dialect ends and another separate language or dialect begins. The research shows that documenting a wide variety of languages is crucially important for theoretical models of language and communication.

In focus: documenting the phonetics of Kalasha

An example of a spoken phonetic documentation study can be found in Hussain and Mielke (2021), who investigated an unusual vowel system in Kalasha, an endangered language of northern Pakistan. In Kalasha, some vowels are produced with rhoticity, meaning that the vowel has an r-like quality all the way through the vowel. You might be familiar with rhoticity from listening to North American English, where the vowel in words like *bird* has an r-like quality all through the vowel. Kalasha is currently thought to be unique in having a large system of ten different rhotic vowels. In their work, Hussain and Mielke recorded speech data from speakers in Pakistan using microphones to capture the acoustics of speech, ultrasound imaging of tongue shapes (see Chapters 1 and 2 on Phonetics and Phonology), and a camera to record lip movement while the participants were speaking. Their results demonstrate that Kalasha speakers manipulate different parts of the tongue and lips in order to produce the difference between rhotic and non-rhotic vowels. Acoustic analysis indicates that the previous reports of a very large rhotic vowel system can be confirmed with acoustically different qualities to the speech samples.

22.4 Making audio-recordings

In this section we will now consider some of the issues you need to think through ahead of conducting your own recordings. As explained in Chapter 19 of this book, before collecting any kind of data with human participants, you need to go through the ethics process of your school/university. As part of the ethics review, you will need to think about any ethical issues, for example safety of participants, in relation to your study.

In the rest of this section, we will consider some practical implications for conducting research outside the lab, and some example studies. Here, we are assuming that you would like to make a recording of speech for the purposes of analysing interviews (Chapter 23) or observational data using thematic, discourse or conversation analysis, or that you will be analysing the speech itself for phonetics or quantitative sociolinguistics.

22.5 What is the purpose of your recording?

Once you have designed your study and obtained ethical permission, you need to consider what the purpose of your analysis will be. For example, if you would like to do thematic, discourse or corpus analysis of the words used, but aren't very concerned with the sound themselves, then this will impact the quality of the recording needed. If you are interested in analysing the nature of /s/ acoustics, for example, then you will need very high quality, consistent recordings from each participant. If possible, we would recommend recording the highest quality you can, even if you think you will transcribe the data and never use the sound recordings. The reason behind this is that recording participants can be very time-consuming and perhaps one day you, or a colleague, will want to use your data for a different study, rather than recording some more. The nature of the recordings you make will depend on where and how you make the recordings, which we will now discuss.

22.6 Recording location and equipment

When working outside dedicated recording facilities such as a university sound booth, it can be hard to control the environment where the recordings are made. You might be working in a school, as in Uta's example, or even in the participant's home. In these conditions, it might be difficult to ask people to move around too much furniture! However, as far as is possible, aim to reduce any background noise from electrical appliances and other people. In Creese and Blackledge's library study (Section 22.2.2), obviously, this wasn't possible. As they did, you will need to strike the best compromise between the quality of the sound recorded and nature of the research you are conducting. The equipment used to make the recordings will also have an impact on the eventual sound captured. If you aren't concerned about the sound quality and have decided that no one will ever want to use your recording for phonetic analysis, then you could use a Dictaphone or phone to make the recordings. Before doing this, make sure you have sufficient battery and memory to capture the recording you want to make.

Generally speaking, if you use some kind of external microphone, even a low-cost one, this will improve the quality of the sound recorded. Most schools/universities will have some recording equipment which you can borrow. This will consist of a microphone and some method of recording the sound such as a portable recorder. Alternatively, you could plug the microphone into a laptop. With any borrowed equipment, make sure you practise before your first recording and know how long the battery will last. The microphones available to you will depend on what your school/university is able to provide. Some microphones are designed to be placed on a table and used for recording a group of people. Other microphones are designed to be placed near a participant's mouth either pinned to their top (as Creese and Blackledge did), or attached to a headset. If you are recording individuals or pairs of people, you will obtain the clearest recordings by putting a microphone on each person. The closer the microphone is to the participant, the less background noise you will record. We recommend using a headset microphone if possible, as this allows you to record the participant's speech with the minimum of surrounding noise.

When making a recording of sound, you can save in a variety of file formats. The main ones are .wav and .mp3. The advantage of .wav files is that they are larger and capture more of the sound available without compression. The advantage of .mp3 is that the sound files are smaller in size and easier to store. The disadvantage of .mp3 is that the sound is compressed and it is not possible to reconstruct the compressed elements. For this reason, we would recommend recording in .wav where possible and then compressing a copy afterwards if you need smaller files. Once you have made any recordings, back up the data in at least two different physical locations on two different devices.

Take home points:

- Make sure you have a test run, practice session with any equipment you use;
- Back up your data immediately after recording.

22.7 Self-recordings and remote recordings

So far, we have assumed that you will be present to record an interview or phonetic data collection with your participants. Sometimes, it is preferable or even essential to conduct the recordings remotely. For example, practical considerations such as travel restrictions or geographical distance might make in-person recording impossible. Or, you might be trying to mitigate the Observer's Paradox. In this section, we will look at some example studies which have used these methods for different reasons and with a variety of results.

22.7.1 More naturalistic speech

One way to mitigate the effects of the Observer's Paradox is to obtain recordings from participants while you are not there. For example, you could ask your participants to record themselves in variety of contexts. A study which used this technique is Sharma (2011). In this study, Sharma focuses on the British Indian community in Southall, London. This analysis considers variation in the English spoken by participants, some of whom were born in India and some of whom were born in the UK. Sharma is able to analyse the speech of 'Anwar', a 41-year-old male born in 1966 in West London. Sharma shows that Anwar has a diverse repertoire of speech ranging from very Indian English-sounding to very British English-sounding. Anwar uses far more Indian features when speaking to a Sri Lankan maid, and a research assistant from India. He uses fewer Indian features when speaking with a posh British Asian lawyer, and with a Cockney car mechanic. By asking Anwar to record himself, Sharma was able to capture far more of Anwar's repertoire than would have been possible only in an interview setting.

In focus: the speech of Stefanie Graf, tennis player

Another way you could use recordings made while the researcher is not there would be to use publicly available speech recordings from a famous person. The disadvantage of this method is that you have no control at all over the kind of data which is available and its quality, so this might limit the sorts of analyses you can perform. However, if there are multiple interviews available from a speaker you can perform long-term analysis of their speech. For example, de Leeuw (2019) considers the speech of the German tennis player, Stefanie Graf, over 40 years. In this study, de Leeuw uses interviews in German with Stefanie Graf to look at the changes in her German speech from when she was a teenager until middle adulthood. De Leeuw is able to demonstrate the gradual influence of increasing use of English on Graf's German speech over a very long time period. By using the pre-existing interviews from German media, de Leeuw is able to gain this very long-term insight.

22.7.2 Larger sample sizes

Remote self-recording can have the advantage of being able to capture data from larger numbers of speakers than would be possible or practical in person. Hundreds or even thousands of people can complete your study and send in their data! While this sounds very attractive, in practice the researcher has very little control over the recordings participants are making, and the kind of people who are conducting the study. Also, if you use smartphones as the principal method for collecting recordings, this can bias the sample towards younger age groups and societies where smartphone usage is very high. However, some researchers consider that the benefits of very large-scale, remote data collection can outweigh the downsides.

Remote, large-scale recording is currently developing as a technique. As such, published results are just beginning to appear. An example study which has successfully used an online survey methodology for comparing recordings across dialects is Hilton (2021), who is studying variation in Frisian, a minority language in the Netherlands. Hilton used an app to collect survey responses and short recordings from speakers. There are an estimated 485,000 speakers of Frisian and so far, Hilton's project has collected dialect survey responses from 15,131 users (i.e. 3% of the Frisian-speaking population), which is a high proportion for a sociolinguistic study. You can see an example of some of the results obtained in Hilton (2021) by scanning this QR code. The map looks at dialectal variation in Frisian for the word *Saturday*.

http://stimmen.nl/uitspraakkaart-zaterdag/

22.8 Conclusion

In this chapter we have considered research methods and example studies which necessitate collecting data in the 'field', that is, outside of your school/university. We first looked at ethnography and some of the fundamental principles and methods underpinning this approach. Second, we looked at some examples of language documentation, where the researcher travels to a community to work on a particular language using a variety of recording methods. Finally, we outlined some of the practical considerations you need to think about when recording your own data, and gave some examples of different ways of making audio-recordings, both in person and when speakers record themselves. Taken altogether, this chapter demonstrates the diversity of research methods and approaches to linguistics which require working in the field.

References

Creese, A. and Blackledge, A. 2019. Translanguaging and public service encounters: Language learning in the library. *The Modern Language Journal*, 103(4): 800–814.

Curdt-Christiansen, X. L. 2019. Observations and field notes. In Jim McKinley and Rose Heath (Eds.), *The Routledge Handbook of Research Methods in Applied Linguistics*. London: Routledge, pp. 336–347.

de Leeuw, Esther. 2019. Native speech plasticity in the German-English late bilingual Stefanie Graf: A longitudinal study over four decades. *Journal of Phonetics*, 73: 24–29.

Hilton, N. H. 2021. *Stimmen*: A citizen science approach to minority language sociolinguistics. *Linguistics Vanguard*, 7(s1): 1–15.

Hussain, Q. and Mielke, J. 2021. An acoustic and articulatory study of rhotic and rhotic-nasal vowels of Kalasha. *Journal of Phonetics*, 87: 1–44.

Mackey, A. and Gass, S. M. 2015. *Second Language Research: Methodology and Design*. 2nd ed. New York: Routledge.

Palfreyman, N. 2019. *Variation in Indonesian Sign Language: A Typological and Sociolinguistic Analysis*. Amsterdam: Mouton de Gruyter.

Papen, U. 2019. Participant observation and fieldnotes. In Karin Tusting (Ed.), *The Routledge Handbook of Linguistic Ethnography*. London: Routledge, pp. 141–154.

Rose, H., McKinley, J. and Briggs Baffoe-Djan, J. 2020. *Data Collection Research Methods in Applied Linguistics*. London: Bloomsbury.

Sharma, D. 2011. Style repertoire and social change in British Asian English. *Journal of Sociolinguistics*, 15(4): 464–492.

Tusting, K. (Ed.). 2019. *The Routledge Handbook of Linguistic Ethnography*. London: Routledge.

Wei, L. 2019. Ethnography. In J. McKinley and R. Heath (Eds.), *The Routledge Handbook of Research Methods in Applied Linguistics*. London: Routledge, pp. 154–164.

23 Surveys, questionnaires, interviews and focus groups

Karin Tusting

23.1 Introduction

This chapter outlines the use of surveys, questionnaires, interviews and focus groups. These methods are used in many different approaches to research in linguistics, from structured large-scale quantitative survey research through to small-scale qualitative case studies. Student research often relies on interviews or questionnaires for data collection.

23.2 Surveys and questionnaires

Many fields of linguistics use surveys and questionnaires (see Schleef 2013 for more examples and detailed guidance on questionnaire design and administration). In sociolinguistics, for instance, surveys can explore language attitudes and ideologies, understand patterns of usage of languages and investigate the geographical spread of accents and dialects. A survey aims to understand something about a particular population, asking the same set of questions to a sample of people randomly selected from that population (Sapsford 2007). Statistical techniques are used to infer what the results would be likely to be across the population as a whole. A questionnaire refers to the tool often used to gather data in a survey: a list of questions, answered by everyone in the sample. But the use of questionnaires is not limited to survey research generalising from a sample to a population. Here, we will focus primarily on designing, distributing and analysing questionnaires, rather than on survey research *per se*, as most student research in linguistics is not attempting to generalise from a sample to a larger population.

23.2.1 Designing questionnaires

Thought needs to go into designing and writing questions to ensure that a questionnaire will produce useful data. It can be useful to list research questions in a grid, see Table 23.1, to clarify what information is needed, and what questions can be used to elicit that information.

DOI: 10.4324/9781003045571-27

Table 23.1 Grid to support questionnaire design.

	What information do I need to know from participants to answer this question?	What questions could I use to get this information?
Research question 1		
Research question 2		
Research question 3		

Questions should be short and uncomplicated, asking only one thing at a time. It is important to avoid building presuppositions into questions which influence the respondent to answer in a particular way. A question beginning 'Do you agree . . . ?' presupposes agreement, and is more leading than the more neutral 'To what extent do you agree or disagree that . . . ?'

Thought also needs to be given to keeping the length manageable, and to the order of questions. Generally, it is best to start with less challenging questions; people are more likely to persist in answering more difficult questions if they have already invested some effort in earlier, easier ones. Factual information, including demographic characteristics like age and gender, should be included if it is relevant to the project's research questions.

23.2.2 Question types

There are various different types of questions. The first key distinction is the difference between 'open' and 'closed' questions. In an open question, the respondent is free to answer in their own words. Open questions can be used for facts (e.g. 'which town do you live in?'). They may be directed (e.g. 'can you tell us anything else about when you would use this word?'), or open-ended (e.g. 'is there anything else you would like to say?').

Questionnaires usually consist mainly of 'closed' questions, which specify a range of possible responses. Common types include:

- Yes/no questions;
- Multiple choice questions, with several options (e.g. indicating age by 18–25, 26–35, 36–45, etc.);
- Scaled responses, with a range of possible responses (e.g. a Likert scale: strongly disagree/disagree/neither agree nor disagree/agree/strongly agree);
- Rank ordering, presenting a series of statements to be ranked by the respondent.

It is important to 'pilot', that is, to test the questionnaire by having someone complete it before data collection proper begins. The person piloting it should be asked for specific feedback: how long did it take to complete? Were all the questions clear or were any confusing? Was anything particularly difficult? Did it bring up any sensitive issues? This can often provide insight into issues which the questionnaire designer did not anticipate.

23.2.3 Recruiting a sample of participants

The sample of respondents can be put together in different ways. If the aim is to generalise from a sample to a defined population, as in a survey, the sample must be selected randomly. The size of sample required depends on many factors including the desired degree of accuracy of the survey, the size of the population (smaller populations require a higher proportion to be sampled) and the expected response rate. In a simple random sample, each member of the population should have an equal chance of being chosen. This could be achieved, for instance, by listing all the members of a known population in a spreadsheet and using a random number generator to select row numbers. An alternative, stratified random sampling, divides the population into groups ('strata') and randomly selects samples from within each of those groups. This can produce a more representative sample, but only when the population can be meaningfully grouped, for instance, into age ranges or socio-economic classes.

It is unusual for student questionnaire studies to use true random sampling. Student research frequently relies on convenience sampling, where those who are willing to take part form the sample; snowball sampling, where additional respondents are recruited through connections with previous people in the sample; quota sampling, where specific numbers of representatives of different groups are sought by the researcher to match some characteristics of the population; or purposive sampling where the researcher uses a theoretical rationale to put the sample together. Care has to be taken when analysing data sampled like this that the results are not claimed to be generalisable, but they can still provide useful insights.

23.2.4 Distributing questionnaires

There are different ways to get a questionnaire to respondents. Pen and paper questionnaires can still be very useful when working in settings where groups of people meet face to face, such as classrooms, workplaces or community groups, especially if the researcher can give out and collect the questionnaires in one sitting. Questionnaires can also be mailed out, administered over the telephone or sent by email.

It is increasingly common to use survey software like SurveyMonkey or Qualtrics. This has several advantages. Publicising links to questionnaires online can be achieved through social media and online networks. Anonymity for respondents is easier to achieve online. There is no need to transcribe answers from paper, and no transcription errors. Most questionnaire platforms provide basic quantitative analyses of responses. However, there are also some disadvantages. If the questionnaire is being publicly distributed, there is no way to guarantee that all the respondents are genuine. Data storage needs to be thought through. Software provided by a university should store data securely and in compliance with the EU General Data Protection Regulation (GDPR) and UK Data Protection Act 2018, but free online software may not have such safeguards.

However the questionnaire is distributed, respondents need to be persuaded to participate by making it meaningful and worthwhile to them (see Chapter 20). For instance, they might care about the topic of the research. They might altruistically want to support a student. Or an external incentive can be provided, like a small prize draw.

23.2.5 Analysing questionnaires

In questionnaire studies, quantitative analysis is normally used to identify patterns in the data, such as determining whether particular groups of people tend to answer questions in similar ways, or whether certain sets of answers correlate with each other (for instance, whether levels of foreign language anxiety correlate with self-perceived proficiency). This might mean simply summarising the numbers of responses to particular questions in tables or graphs, perhaps divided by participant group (see Chapter 24 on descriptive statistics). The relationship between proficiency and attitudes to language learning in a class of pupils could be analysed by dividing the participants into groups by proficiency and reporting the different groups' responses to attitude questions in a bar chart. When working with scaled responses, averages can be calculated to identify patterns. A question which asks 'To what degree do you agree with the statement: "My anxiety around learning languages prevents me from fully participating in the class": 1=never, 2=seldom, 3=regularly, 4=often, 5=all the time', could be scored by averaging out the answers given by each set of respondents grouped by proficiency. Alternatively, scaled answers could be grouped into those which chose the top or bottom half of the scale, and shared characteristics of each set of participants identified.

Open-ended questions require a different analytic approach. Some additional work with such responses needs to be done, whether summarising patterns across the answers simply by reading and interpreting them, or analysing the answers in a more systematic way, coding (labelling) the data to identify themes, similarities and differences (Saldaña 2016; and see later on coding interview data).

23.2.6 Advantages and disadvantages of questionnaire research

Questionnaires have several advantages. They enable data to be collected from large numbers of people, making comparisons between groups easier. They do not require interaction, so data collection is time-efficient for researchers, and flexible for respondents. Distribution of questionnaires can be easy and cheap, using survey software. Sharing information via an anonymous questionnaire may be more comfortable for respondents than an interview.

However, questionnaires also have disadvantages. It is not possible to probe or follow up on answers for depth or clarification, unless the questionnaires are part of a larger study with follow-up interviews. It is also not possible to check that people have understood the questions in the way that was intended. And most questions will generate brief answers only, making it hard to explore more complex issues.

Questionnaires can be a very useful research tool in linguistics, but the researcher needs to be clear about the purposes the questionnaire is serving and why it is the best option. If more in-depth discussion is necessary, then interviews might be used, either in addition to or instead of questionnaires.

23.3 Interviews

23.3.1 Types of interview

Interviews may be part of a larger research project which also uses other methods of data collection, like a case study, or a bigger questionnaire study; alternatively, all the data might consist of interviews. The main types of interviews are structured, semi-structured and unstructured.

23.3.1.1 Structured interviews

In a structured interview, a fixed set of questions is asked of every interviewee, usually in the same order. This has many similarities to a questionnaire, and the advice outlined earlier for designing and piloting questionnaires also applies to structured interviews.

23.3.1.2 Semi-structured interviews

The semi-structured interview is probably the most common type used in student projects. In a semi-structured interview, the interviewer works with a list of questions or topics, but there is flexibility to pick up on certain points, prompt the interviewee using follow-up questions called probes, and sometimes to skip questions if the material has been covered earlier. Probes can be as simple as 'Do you have anything more to say on that?' or can be closely tied to the topic of the question, for example, 'Can you give me more details about the curriculum you use?' Semi-structured interviews vary in the length and detail of the question list, or interview schedule. Some look very much like structured interviews, with long and detailed lists of questions and probes. Others are much simpler, just a short list of topics. This can generate a more open interaction but relies more on the skill and knowledge of the interviewer to keep the conversation going.

Semi-structured interviews can feel like an everyday conversation, which helps put the interviewee at ease. The openness allows unexpected things to come up. Semi-structured interviewing does, however, require the interviewer to be alert on many fronts, ensuring that the interview schedule is covered and the conversation flows, while paying attention to what has just been said, whether additional probes are necessary, and whether the next question has already been answered – a more cognitively and socially demanding task than running through a fixed set of questions.

23.3.1.3 Unstructured interviews

Unstructured interviews take place without a list of questions at all. For instance, this may be the case in the informal interviews mentioned in the field methods chapter, Chapter 22. These are usually part of a larger study, using a range of different data collection methods. Despite not requiring the formal preparation associated with semi-structured or structured interviews, unstructured interviews make significant demands on the researcher, who must guide the conversation to ensure that it covers relevant areas.

Unstructured interviews may arise spontaneously as part of participant-observation fieldwork. Therefore, thought needs to be given as to how they are to be recorded, whether in field-notes or whether the researcher carries an audio-recording device. It is important in such interviews to ensure that the interviewee has consented to be part of the research and understands the conversation will be used as data (see Chapter 19 on ethics).

23.3.1.4 Focus groups and group interviews

In focus groups and group interviews, people are interviewed in groups rather than one to one. The focus group was initially developed as a means of focusing discussion on a specific issue. The archetypal focus group would have a group of people in a room with a trained moderator, asked to respond to a series of prompts around a particular, often contentious, issue. In linguistics, a focus group could explore linguistic ideologies, or attitudes towards language policies. Participants in the focus group would not normally know each other, so that their discussions would not be swayed by prior relationships. They would usually be selected to be demographically similar to each other, so the focus group explores the perspectives of a particular type of person. Focus group participants would normally be rewarded for their participation (e.g. in money, free food or vouchers). Designing a focus group requires thought to be given to recruiting participants, structuring the interaction, the prompts and questions used to elicit discussion and the role of the moderator. Guidance is available in texts such as Litosseliti (2003), Morgan (2019).

The term 'focus group' is often used to refer to any group interview, but most group interviews do not fit this quite specific definition. Group interviews might be used in contexts where interviewing people individually is impractical, where people are more comfortable being interviewed in groups, or where the dynamics between group members are themselves of interest.

23.3.1.5 Specialised types of interviews

Some fields of linguistics have specific approaches for interviewing, including:

- Sociolinguistic interviews, which elicit actual linguistic data for analysis. Labov (1984), the founder of variationist sociolinguistics, developed an approach in which different stages of the interview generate samples of different types of speech. An informal (semi-structured) conversation provides informal or vernacular speech; a series of (structured) activities, including reading a passage, reading a list of words and reading out minimal pairs (two words of different meaning that only have one sound different), gives samples of increasingly formal speech. Respondents are selected from a range of socio-economic groups.
- Life history interviews may be used to collect data about how people's linguistic practices have changed over time. In digital literacy studies the 'technobiography' (Barton and Lee 2013) asks people about their engagement with different kinds of technologies throughout their lives, often with a focus on change and transition. This provides insight into how individuals have experienced changing literacy technologies.
- Interviews may be based on other data collected. In research on academic writing, the 'talk around text' interview (Lillis 2009) focuses on what decisions lay behind the form of a particular written text, such as an essay, based on prior detailed analysis of the text. In a similar way, in classroom research, researchers might analyse a video of classroom interaction and then invite teachers to discuss short extracts.

23.3.2 Designing interviews

Many of the same issues arise designing interviews and questionnaires. Using a grid like Figure 23.1 helps to plan interview questions. Where questionnaires are often made up of predominantly closed questions, most interviews would include more open questions. Complex questions like Likert scales and ranking questions work less well in face-to-face conversation. Sharing visual prompts or writing together can be useful ways to take the focus onto the support material, for instance using photographs or maps as the basis for interviews (see Mannion et al. 2007 for an example).

The order of questions is important. Interviewees will almost always approach the interaction as cooperative conversationalists (Houtkoop-Steenstra 2000), so will draw on their existing conversational norms. Grice's (1975) maxims come into play: people will attempt to ensure that their contributions are truthful, relevant, maximally informative without repeating things that have been said before, and clear. This means:

- Interviewees will usually try to answer every question put to them, even if it is only marginally important to them. Just asking a question may lead to the respondent trying to come up with an opinion the spot, even if it is not something they particularly care about.
- If questions lead to people repeating information, they may try to come up with something new, as people will normally avoid telling their conversation partner something they believe they already know. This means being careful about the ordering of questions, usually moving from general to specific, and acknowledging explicitly if asking about something the researcher might be expected to know, for instance asking someone about their job role when they have been observed in their workplace already.
- If an interviewee does not fully understand a question or finds it ambiguous, they will interpret it in the light of what they understand the interview to be about, so it is important to be clear about the aims of the interview.
- Information which is not usually shared in everyday conversation can be challenging. This includes some demographic information, such as age. It may be best to leave this until the end.
- Silence can be a useful probe. As cooperative conversationalists, most people will try to fill a silence if a longer pause than usual is left in a conversation.

Once designed, piloting the interview is always useful. It gives insight into how long the interview takes, whether there is unnoticed repetition or lack of clarity, and whether the questions follow a natural progression. Piloting the interview, and getting feedback, is the only way to check whether interviewees understand the questions, and whether the answers give the data needed.

A group interview is usually similar to a semi-structured interview, so the previous advice therefore applies, with some additional considerations, such as: is it important to hear equally from everyone in the group? If it is, what strategies will be used to ensure everyone gets a chance to speak? Does everyone need to respond to every question? The question list for a group interview usually needs to be shorter than a one-to-one interview, since every question may elicit several responses. The role of the interviewer can vary from working through a long list of questions, to starting the group discussion off with a controversial prompt and intervening only to keep the interaction on topic. Piloting a group interview may not be straightforward in the context of a student project, but getting feedback on the plan from someone else is nevertheless useful.

23.3.3 Selecting interviewees

The rationale for selecting interviewees depends on the focus of the research project. It might be that everyone in a particular case study site will be invited for interview, for instance all the teaching staff in a school. Or constraints on time and resources might lead to selecting a smaller group of interviewees that represents a range in some way, perhaps of experience, age or gender. Many interviews for student research projects will be made up from convenience and snowball samples. If this is the case, it is important to think through how this might affect the data.

23.3.4 Carrying out interviews

Carrying out interviews can seem daunting, but we use the skills needed for interviewing every time we have a conversation. Building rapport is important, as interviewees may well be nervous. In everyday life, 'interviews' are often high-stakes gatekeeping activities like job interviews or appraisal interviews. Nevertheless, interviewees frequently say afterwards that they have enjoyed the research interview; it is unusual to have someone listen closely to everything that you say for an extended period of time.

The practicalities of interviews need to be planned, including thinking about where the interview will be held, how the interviewee's privacy can be maintained, whether there will be background noise and how this can be mitigated, for instance by using a separate microphone. In a group interview, it is likely that people will talk over each other and that there will be points where the sound is unclear, so such considerations are even more important. If interviewer and interviewee are expert speakers of different languages, the language of the interview needs to be considered, as well as considering whether an interpreter is necessary. This includes considering whether a sign language interpreter is necessary if working with any Deaf participants.

Most interviews are audio-recorded, as it is difficult to interview and write notes at the same time. Nowadays, most people are used to being recorded, and recorders are fairly unobtrusive. It is important to test the recorder beforehand and carry spare batteries or power supply.

Interviews no longer necessarily have to be in person, as most people now have access to video conferencing. This can save time and expense in travelling and finding rooms, and some people find it more comfortable to be interviewed online. But it does change the interaction, and some activities, like working together on artefacts, cannot easily be done via a screen.

23.3.5 Processing interview data

After an interview, the data needs some work to turn it into analysable form. It is important to get the data off the recording device and safely into a password-protected or encrypted digital space as soon as possible after the interview, and backed up in another safely encrypted space. It is also useful to write brief notes summarising the researcher's initial responses to the interview.

23.3.5.1 Transcription

Recorded interviews need to be transcribed. If the audio is very clear, automatic transcription through a speech to text service can save some time, but this can only ever be a starting point and the resulting transcription will need to be carefully checked and edited. It is also important to ensure that this does not entail uploading the file to servers not under the researcher's control, breaching data commitments. In group interviews, automatic transcription is less likely to be useful given multiple voices and over-talking.

Data should be transcribed at the level of detail needed for the analysis, which requires some decisions. If the content is all that is important, pauses, false starts and repetitions can be ignored. If other aspects of interaction are also relevant – for instance, emotional stance as signalled by prosody – then other aspects such as pitch, speed and stress may need to be noted. More interactional features may need to be transcribed in group interviews, to track the dynamics between group members. For a sociolinguistic survey, a phonetic transcription might be needed. There is no one single 'right' way to transcribe, but there is a trade-off – including more detail inevitably takes more time.

23.3.6 Analysing interview data

At its simplest, interview analysis can mean simply reading transcripts through, highlighting and writing notes to record how the interview content addresses the research questions. Patterns of similarity and difference across interviewees can be discerned by grouping together answers to particular questions. For a research project with a small number of interviews, this might be enough.

Other, more systematic approaches, useful for larger datasets and more complex research questions, include various approaches to thematic analysis (Braun and Clarke 2006) or coding of interview data to identify themes. This means systematically reading through each interview, 'coding' or labelling sections relating to particular themes, and keeping track of repeated codes to identify themes which recur across the dataset (Saldaña 2016). Open coding allows themes to emerge from the data that may not have been planned for in advance.

23.3.7 Advantages and disadvantages of interviews

Interviews have several advantages. Interacting with one participant and focusing on their responses allows the interviewer to ask people to expand on statements, probe to go into more depth and clarify anything which is not clear. Interviews can be a useful tool as part of a larger project to look for explanations, for instance exploring what might be underlying a particular pattern of questionnaire responses, or understanding what was happening in a particular videoed interaction from the point of view of the participants.

They also have disadvantages. Carrying out interviews is much more labour-intensive and less flexible than distributing questionnaires, for both researcher and interviewee. Additional time needs to be spent on transcription before they can be analysed. Interviews can be more challenging for participants than questionnaires on an interpersonal level, since they require the participant to tell the interviewer their responses directly rather than being able to complete questions anonymously.

Group interviews have particular advantages and disadvantages. Group interaction tends to lead towards people expressing polarised views, either strongly agreeing or strongly disagreeing with one another to a greater degree than they did before the group discussion (Sunstein 1999). This makes group interviews useful for getting a clear sense of the delineation of an issue, but they can over-represent the strength of feeling around it. Group discussions lead to rich data, but this can be more challenging to analyse than one-to-one interviews. Group interviews are an efficient way of collecting data from several people in one go, but their organisation can be more demanding than setting up an interview.

This outline of interview research is necessarily brief. Brinkmann and Kvale (2018) provides an introductory guide to doing interviews which covers all the issues introduced here in more detail and is an accessible support for novice interviewers.

23.4 Ethics of questionnaire and interview research

Ethical issues around questionnaires and interviews need to be considered carefully. Participants need to provide informed consent, which means the researcher needs to explain the research; tell participants they have the right to withdraw; and explain how their data will be stored and used, and how their identities will be protected. Potential harm to respondents should be assessed, for instance, whether questions could potentially cause distress, and providing participants details of how to access support. This information might be given on the first page of a questionnaire, or on an information sheet given out by the researcher before an interview. Participants need to sign consent forms before continuing (see Chapter 19 on ethics).

Group interviews raise particular issues. It is especially important to ensure that participants agree that discussions should not be shared outside the group at the beginning of the interview. Participants also need to be reminded that this is a matter of trust, and that the researcher cannot control what the other group participants do outside the interview. Additional reassurances may be necessary as to how group members will be anonymised. If group members do not know each other already and will be kept anonymous, they should be reminded not to share personal information, and first names only should be used.

In universities, ethical review procedures exist to ensure such considerations are properly addressed. It is important to follow these procedures carefully, to provide protection for research participants and for the integrity and reputation of research in linguistics.

23.5 Conclusion

Questionnaires and interviews are central tools for data collection across the social sciences, allowing us to explore people's opinions, experiences and language patterns in systematic ways. With attention to the issues discussed in this chapter, students can design and carry out interesting and exciting research projects on language-related topics using these tools, as a first step towards becoming independent researchers in linguistics.

References

Barton, D. and Lee, C. 2013. *Language Online: Investigating Digital Texts and Practices*. London: Routledge.

Braun, V. and Clarke, V. 2006. Using thematic analysis in psychology. *Qualitative Research in Psychology*, 3: 77–101.

Brinkmann, S. and Kvale, S. 2018. *Doing Interviews*. Los Angeles, CA: Sage.

Grice, P. 1975. Logic and conversation. In P. Cole and J. Morgan (Eds.), *Syntax and Semantics. 3: Speech Acts*. New York: Academic Press, pp. 41–58.

Houtkoop-Steenstra, H. 2000. *Interaction and the Standardised Survey Interview: The Living Questionnaire*. Cambridge: Cambridge University Press.

Labov, W. 1984. Field methods of the project on linguistic change and variation. In J. Baugh and J. Sherzer (Eds.), *Language in Use*. Englewood Cliffs, NJ: Prentice-Hall, pp. 28–53.

Lillis, T. 2009. Bringing writers' voices to writing research: Talk around texts. In A. Carter, T. Lillis and S. Parkin (Eds.), *Why Writing Matters: Issues of Access and Identity in Writing Research and Pedagogy*. Amsterdam: Benjamins, pp. 169–187.

Litosseliti, L. 2003. *Using Focus Groups in Research*. London: Bloomsbury.

Mannion, G., Ivanič, R. and the Literacies for Learning in Further Education (LfLFE) Research Group. 2007. Mapping literacy practices: theory, methodology, methods, *International Journal of Qualitative Studies in Education*, 20(1), 15–30. http://doi.org/10.1080/09518390600924063

Morgan, D. 2019. *Basic and Advanced Focus Groups*. Los Angeles, CA: Sage Publications.

Saldaña, J. 2016. *The Coding Manual for Qualitative Researchers*. 3rd ed. London: Sage.

Sapsford, R. 2007. *Survey Research*. 2nd ed. London: Sage.

Schleef, E. 2013. Written surveys and questionnaires. In J. Holmes and K. Hazen (Eds.), *Research Methods in Sociolinguistics*. Oxford: Wiley Blackwell, pp. 42–57.

Sunstein, C. R. 1999. The Law of Group Polarization. *John M. Olin Law & Economics Working Paper No. 91*. University of Chicago Law School. http://doi.org/10.2139/ssrn.199668

24 Statistics and data visualisation

Vaclav Brezina and Aina Casaponsa

24.1 Introduction: why do we need statistics?

Statistics is the 'science of collecting and interpreting data' (Diggle and Chetwynd 2011: vii). It is useful for understanding numbers and quantitative information presented, for instance, in the form of tables and graphs. Applied to linguistics, statistics forms an inherent part of a rigorous, scientific, approach to language (Brezina 2018). Let's consider an example. Look at the following sentence, from a corpus of present-day British English. It contains a linguistic feature called the split infinitive, which is italicised:

(1) We tend *to immediately overreact* to something, even if we don't completely understand it (BNC2014, ElanBlogLif2).

Traditionally, the split infinitive has been frowned upon in English, as a grammatically irregular feature, which should be avoided (see Chapter 8 for more about prescriptivism). When we look at example (1) in isolation, we can express our personal opinion about it. Some will like it, others won't, but this doesn't really tell us anything about how it is used in present-day British English. For that, we need numbers and quantitative information; then we can report that this is relatively common feature in present-day British English, with on average over 150 instances per million words. We can also compare the frequencies of use of the split infinitive across different genres of British English, as in Figure 24.1. Here, we can see that it is most popular in academic prose and least popular in fiction.

With numbers in mind, we can also devise a psycholinguistic experiment or a sociolinguistic study measuring people's reaction to this construction. We could also quantify the types of context in which split infinitives like example (1) occur, and those in which alternative constructions, like that in (2), occur.

(2) We tend *to overreact to something immediately*, even if we don't completely understand it.

Such data can provide additional insight into, for instance, reaction times, fixation times when reading or linguistic preferences and attitudes of different groups of people. Statistical information thus offers us the power of quantifiable evidence, which we can use in the justification of our claims about language. In

DOI: 10.4324/9781003045571-28

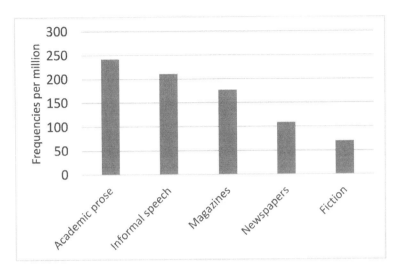

Figure 24.1 Frequency of split infinitive use across genres in the BNC2014.

addition, understanding statistical information in textbooks, research articles, news, etc. forms a part of statistical literacy, a crucial component of critical thinking. Statistical literacy is the ability to understand and accurately interpret quantitative information. The purpose of this chapter is therefore to advance your statistical literacy, in the context of interpreting linguistic data. Following principles and statistical techniques outlined in this chapter will empower you to engage productively with quantitative information about language.

24.2 Exploring the data: descriptive statistics

24.2.1 What are descriptive statistics for?

Imagine that you have a long list of numbers, as in example (3). These numbers represent proportions of adjectives in a random sample of current British novels taken from the Written British National Corpus 2014 (Brezina et al. 2021). How would you make sense of these?

(3) 3%, 4%, 4%, 4%, 4%, 4%, 4%, 4%, 4%, 4%, 4%, 4%, 5%, 5%, 5%,
5%, 5%, 5%, 5%, 5%, 5%, 5%, 5%, 5%, 5%, 5%, 5%, 5%, 5%, 5%,
5%, 5%, 5%, 5%, 5%, 5%, 5%, 5%, 5%, 5%, 5%, 5%, 5%, 5%, 5%,
5%, 5%, 5%, 5%, 5%, 5%, 5%, 5%, 6%, 6%, 6%, 6%, 6%, 6%, 6%,
6%, 6%, 6%, 6%, 6%, 6%, 6%, 6%, 6%, 6%, 6%, 6%, 6%, 6%, 6%,
6%, 6%, 6%, 6%, 6%, 6%, 6%, 6%, 6%, 6%, 6%, 6%, 6%, 7%, 7%,
7%, 7%, 7%, 7%, 7%, 7%, 7%, 7%, 8%, 8%, 8%

Making sense of numbers and using statistical techniques to **describe a sample** such as the one in example (3) belongs to an area of statistics which we call

descriptive statistics. Using descriptive statistics is usually the first step of the analysis, through which we find out basic information about the data we are dealing with. This includes identifying whether there are any observable trends, tendencies, etc. The next step after descriptive statistics is employing inferential statistics; this step is discussed in Section 24.3.

24.2.2 Summarising data: range, interquartile range, median, mean and standard deviation

An important element of descriptive statistics is summarising data. The idea is very simple: instead of presenting a long line of numbers as in example (3), we can offer useful summaries of the dataset. There are different ways of doing this. For instance, we can say that the percentages range from 3% to 8%. This statistic is called, appropriately, the **range**. Instead of the full list of values as in example (3), **the range** is based on the minimum and the maximum value in a sample, thus describing the outer boundaries of the sample. **The range** is the difference between the largest and smallest value in a sample. This can be expressed in the following equation:

(4) Range = maximum − minimum

Applied to our example (3), the range would be calculated as:

(5) Range = 8 − 3 = 5

Inside the whole range of values, we can also identify something called the inter-quartile range. **Interquartile range** (**IQR**) represents the middle 50% of the values and ranges, in our example, from 5% to 6%. As a descriptive statistic measure, the interquartile range is more stable than the range because it is not influenced by outliers – extreme values in the sample. In example (6), which is a recast of example (3) with important values highlighted, the interquartile range is the shaded area in the middle.

However, rather than using the range or interquartile range, we might like to summarise a line of numbers using a measure of the **central tendency**. Such number can be, for instance, the median or the mean. The **median** (**mdn**) is the middle value in a series of values ordered from the smallest to the largest; in example (6), the median is 5%, and is indicated by a border around the number. Like the interquartile range, the median is not affected by outliers and these two measures, the median and the interquartile range are often reported together.

(6) 3%, 4%, 4%, 4%, 4%, 4%, 4%, 4%, 4%, 4%, 4%, 4%, 5%, 5%, 5%, 5%, 5%, 5%, 5%, 5%, 5%, 5%, 5%, 5%, 5%, 5%, 5%, 5%, 5%, 5%, 5%, 5%, 5%, 5%, 5%, 5%, 5%, 5%, 5%, 5%, 5%, 5%, 5%, 5%, 5%, 5%, 5%, 5%, 5%, 5%, 5%, 6%, 6%, 6%, 6%, 6%, 6%, 6%, 6%, 6%, 6%, 6%, 6%, 6%, 6%, 6%, 6%, 6%, 6%, 6%, 6%, 6%, 6%, 6%, 6%, 6%, 6%, 6%, 6%, 6%, 6%, 6%, 6%, 6%, 6%, 6%, 6%, 6%, 7%, 7%, 7%, 7%, 7%, 7%, 7%, 7%, 7%, 7%, 8%, 8%, 8%

Another measure of central tendency is the mean. **Mean (M or x̄)**, also known as the arithmetic average, is the sum of all values divided by the number of cases. This can be expressed by the following equation:

(7) $\text{Mean} = \dfrac{\text{sum of all values}}{\text{number of cases}}$

In example (3) the mean would be calculated by adding all percentages and dividing them by the number of cases, 101 in our example. The mean is 5.5%.

(8) $M = \dfrac{3+4+4+\ldots 8+8}{101} = 5.5\%$

Mean is typically reported with a measure of dispersion called the standard deviation. **Standard deviation (SD)** expresses how much the individual values in a dataset (percentages in example (3)), vary around the mean. It is calculated using the following equation:

(9) $\text{Standard deviation} = \sqrt{\dfrac{\text{sum of squared distances from the mean}}{\text{number of cases} - 1}}$

Applied to example (3), we'll get:

(10) $SD = \sqrt{\dfrac{(3-5.5)^2 + (4-5.5)^2 + (4-5.5)^2 \ldots + (8-5.5)^2 + (8-5.5)^2}{101 - 1}} = 0.96\%$

Because in example (3) the standard deviation is small (0.96) relative to the mean (5.5%), we can see that there is not much variation in the sample and the mean represents a good summary of the line of numbers we started with.

In focus: can numbers lie?

Look at the Figure 24.2 representing results of a survey among students. The students were asked if they like statistics. Think about what conclusions we can draw from the graph.

At first sight, it seems that we can conclude that a large majority (67%) of students don't like statistics, the difference between those who responded 'yes' and those who responded 'no' appears to be very large, and we might think this allows us to generalise about students' attitudes to statistics (perhaps especially if we approached the study with preconceived ideas). The graph, however, uses percentages and hides the real number of answers – the *amount* of evidence we actually have. The same graph could thus be based on a sample of, for instance, 3000, 300 or even 3 students! In the last case, the difference reported would be between one student saying 'yes' and two students saying 'no', a difference clearly within a margin of error and with little evidential value.

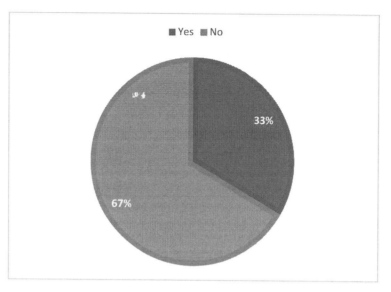

Figure 24.2 Proportions of students answering 'yes'/'no' when asked if they like statistics.

In focus: reporting descriptive statistics

Range can be reported either as a single value or as a pair of the minimum and the maximum values:

The range of the percentages of adjectives in the sample of British novels is 5.

The proportions of adjectives in the sample of British novels range from 3% to 8%.

Mean should always be reported together with standard deviation:

Compared to other major word classes, the percentages of adjectives in the sample are relatively small (M = 5.5, SD = 0.95).

It is also useful to report median together with the interquartile range:

Compared to other major word classes the percentages of adjectives in the sample are relatively small (Mdn = 5, IQR = 1).

24.2.3 Organising data: tables and cross-tabulations

A useful way of organising data is in the form of tables. Tables can represent simple summaries, or more complex **cross-tabulations**.

Table 24.1 is an example of a simple table. It shows the frequencies of adjectives per million in different genres of British English, which contextualises the exploration of the use of adjectives.

Table 24.1 Frequency of use of adjectives in the BNC2014.

Genre	Relative frequency per million
Academic prose	86,753.21
Official documents	78,065.63
Elanguage	69,867.25
Magazines	69,544.17
Newspapers	61,489.93
Fiction	46,371.83
Informal speech	39,529.09

Cross-tabulation (which in some contexts is known as creating a **pivot table**) is a way to represent data across multiple categories. Typically, we plot linguistic information (dependent variable) across the categories of one or more explanatory variables, data such as the genre in Table 24.2.

Table 24.2 Frequencies of adjective forms across different genres

Genre	Positive (e.g. *good*)	Comparative (e.g. *better*)	Superlative (e.g. *best*)	Total
Academic prose	1,880,721	65,152	13,226	1,959,099
Elanguage	390,373	10,746	8,998	410,117
Fiction	1,086,305	29,810	16,194	1,132,309
Informal speech	422,116	12,312	5,467	439,895
Magazines	1,125,553	43,289	33,322	1,202,164
Newspapers	1,336,569	37,444	35,268	1,409,281
Official documents	586,423	14,058	5,338	605,819

In focus: reporting statistics using tables

Tables need to be presented with a simple, clear design, which allows easy interpretation of the data in the tables. Borders should be used sparingly, especially inner borders between cells, colour, if employed, should highlight important aspects of the data rather than form a design frill or embellishment.

Tables 24.1 and 24.2 are good examples of what you should aim for.

24.3 Going beyond the sample: inferential statistics and effect sizes

24.3.1 What are inferential statistics for?

Descriptive statistics are essential to explain what is going on with the data in your sample. But as soon as you want to make conclusions that go beyond the data you collected, you need inferential statistics. As is implied by the name, **inferential statistics** help us to infer knowledge about the world. That is, we use the data collected from our sample to make an approximate guess, or **approximation**, about the results we would have found if we had tested the entire population. These are, then, inferences about reality. This is precisely what we usually are interested in when we run a research project. However, when we make inferences we always need to be aware that these are just approximate guesses, probabilistic approximations about the population of interest.

One of the first questions we need to ask when trying to infer knowledge about the population from our sample is how representative is our sample of the population of interest. Our guesses about the real population can only be as good as the sample we draw them from.

One of the most common methods of inferential statistics in undergraduate projects is **hypothesis testing**. This is where the researcher has a clear hypothesis that they set out to test. For example, we might want to test whether linguistic students like statistics more than psychology students.

The idea behind hypothesis testing is to have an educated guess about whether the results you found in your data could have happened by chance. To do this, you first need to state your null hypothesis and your alternative hypothesis. Then you need to calculate the probability of your results happening by chance. This probability is usually indicated by the what is called the **p-value**.

> **You might wonder . . .**
>
> How can we ever be 100% sure that our sample represents well the population of interest? The quick answer is, we can't! However, the longer answer is that we *can* estimate the level of **uncertainty**. One of the most common ways is by defining an interval of values that are likely to contain the mean that we would obtain, if we tested several times the same population. These are called **confidence intervals** (CI). A 95% CI indicates that if we test 100 different samples from the same population, 95% of the time the mean value will be within the interval of our first sample, but just as a matter of chance 5% of the times it will not.

> **Sample size**
>
> Be wary of studies with small sample sizes, even if they are in peer-review journals. All types of inferential tests heavily rely on the sample size to make inferences about the population.

Understanding how to formulate the null hypothesis and what it means is something that students often struggle with. The main point is that hypothesis testing is about making inferences about reality based on a sample, so everything comes back to the probability that you have observed the 'true' reality through your sample.

To illustrate this, let's look at the example about linguistic students liking statistics more than psychology students. Let's assume that it is a fact that, in the UK, 90% of all the population of students (from linguistics or psychology) do not actually like statistics, and only 10% of students from linguistics like statistics more than psychology students. Now, imagine that this 10% comes from one huge university where they have amazing associate lecturers in statistics. If researchers in their studies only look at students from their own universities, one researcher would observe different results than the rest, and this is because by chance this researcher is observing a sample that does not represent well the overall population of UK students.

What this example demonstrates is that in formulating your null hypothesis, you need to think about the status quo. In this case, if we do not know whether linguistic students like statistics more than psychology students, then the status quo is that we must assume these two groups do not differ. Sometimes, they might differ by chance, because we are just looking at a random selection of reality. In this sense, the null hypothesis is usually assumed to represent reality as we know it (e.g. unless we demonstrate that psychology and linguistic students differ in their liking for statistics, we need to assume they like them equally).

If you are in any doubt, just remember the null hypothesis is that any two phenomena are the same (e.g. adjectives in British novels are just as common as other types of word class, women and men are equal, etc.). And the alternative hypothesis is usually the hypothesis we are interested in (do linguistic students like statistics more than psychology students?).

Now imagine our sample of linguistic students rate their liking of statistics at 4.5 out of 10, whereas our psychology students' rate this at 4.0. How do we decide the likelihood that these two values are different enough to say something interesting? What if the ratings were 4.5 and 4.4 respectively? Are they still different *enough* to be considered different? In order to satisfy ourselves on that point, we can calculate a probability of seeing the difference observed in the sample, or even a larger difference only by chance. This probability is expressed as the p-value. For instance, a p-value equal to 0.05 indicates that the probability of finding the effect by chance is about 5%, or a 1 in 20 chance. In our example, with a p-value of less than

P-value

In the field of linguistic research (and social humanities in general) a p-value of less than 0.05 is by convention considered acceptable to reject the null hypothesis.

0.05, we could say there is only a small probability of seeing the evidence as described if there were no difference in how much linguistics and psychology students like statistics. This is because a p-value of less than 0.05 is, by convention, used to reject the null hypothesis.

It's important that we note at this stage that it's okay if these concepts are not entirely clear, but it is important to start getting familiar with them before you do your own research projects. The most important takeaway is that we can never be 100% sure that the differences we observe are true in the real population, but that we can take measures to ensure our generalisations have robust statistical basis.

In practice, if we were the researcher in the huge university with the amazing lecturer of statistics, we would probably conclude that linguistics students like statistics more than psychology students. It's important that we don't think of all these statistics as just abstract numbers, and bear in mind that the conclusions of such a study can have real-life consequences (e.g. policy changes about reinforcing statistics courses for psychology students, or introducing a massive statistics course in all first-year linguistic undergraduate degrees). This is why it is so important to have converging evidence across different studies, conducted by different teams of researchers and with multiple different samples, and to be cautious with our claims.

In the next two sections, 24.3.2 and 24.3.3, we will outline the most common inferential statistics tests for comparing means (t-test and ANOVAs), and the relationship between variables (correlations). At the end of each section, you will see an example of how to report and interpret these tests in research reports.

24.3.2 Comparing groups: t-test and ANOVA

The t-test is one of most common methods to assess whether the differences between two means are meaningful (i.e. whether we reject the null hypothesis). For example, you might be interested in comparing two different teaching methods for second language learning, or whether the percentages of adjectives in British novels is smaller than other type of word classes.

To calculate a t-test we need three things:

1   The sample size of each group.
2   The amount of variation present in the sample (i.e. the standard deviation of each group means).
3   And the mean difference between the groups.

The main takeaway from this is that your t-test will be influenced by the sample size (e.g. how many participants you tested) and the variability within your sample!

When you do a t-test, you get three main outputs. These are the **t-value**, the **degrees of freedom of your data** and the **p-value** associated with the test. When the t-value is close to 0, it means that the two samples are similar, whereas higher t-values indicate that the difference between the two groups is bigger. For instance, t-values superior to 2 or more are usually associated with significant p-values ($< .05$).

> **Degrees of freedom** represent the number of dimensions along which variables can differ. They are usually an indication of your sample size.

There are three different types of t-test that you need to be aware of when comparing means:

1 Independent sample t-test (used to compare *between* groups).
   This is the test that we use when we want to compare two different groups of people, or words in a language corpus. The idea behind this test is that we are *comparing the means* of two independent samples (e.g. the performance of a group using one teaching method, versus the performance of another group using another teaching method).

2 Paired sample t-test (used to compare *within* groups).
   We use this test when we want to compare the means of the same participants (or words in corpus) in different conditions. That is, we are comparing the same sample in two different measures. For example, you might be interested in comparing whether taboo words are perceived to be less emotional in the foreign language than in the native language. Here, you will take the results from your unique sample (e.g. a group of foreign language learners) and do a paired sample t-test comparing the means in emotional ratings of taboo words in the native versus the foreign language.

3 One-sample t-test.
   This t-test is much less common in linguistics, since it compares the mean of your sample against the change level. For example, we might want to test whether a teaching method works but not have a control group to compare to. Then we can compare the effect of the teaching method in a language test against the probability of performing well on the test just by chance.

In most linguistic studies, however, things do not typically result in two groups being compared. For instance, you might typically have some control conditions where you do not expect to have an effect (see Chapter 20). Following the example of taboo words, a more robust study will also look at neutral words, to make sure that the differences in emotionality ratings between the native and the foreign language are specifically for taboo words and rule out other unaccounted factors (e.g. proficiency, familiarity with foreign words). In these situations, you could do multiple t-tests, one for taboo words and one for neutral words. However, we must bear in mind that multiple tests on the same sample are problematic. The more tests you run on the same sample, the greater the risk of finding a significant effect just by chance. In fact, in 1 out of 20 comparisons (5%), you would obtain a significant effect when no differences actually exist!

The **Analyses of Variance**, most known as ANOVA, allows us to measure if there are differences between means with an **omnibus test**, including all variables at once in the same analyses. As with t-test, there exist different types of ANOVAs, depending on the type of design you have.

> **Variance** is the average squared deviation of each number from the mean of a dataset. Basically, it is the squared standard deviation (σ^2). It is, therefore, related to the variability of our sample.

The one-way ANOVA is the type of test you will do if you have more than two groups (e.g. comparison of the means of 3 different teaching methods). But if you would like to compare different conditions from the same sample (e.g. taboo and neutral words in the native and foreign language), or have a mixed design with at least two groups and two conditions, then you will need to use a repeated measures ANOVA.

One of the main things that students can struggle with when using ANOVAs is the difference between **main effects** and **interactions**. Main effects relate to differences within the levels of a group or condition. As an example, look at Figures 24.3 and 24.4. Here, you have two variables represented (the language of the words and the group of participants). If we were to do an ANOVA, we would get the results of two main effects, one for the variable Language (Figure 24.3B) indicating whether there are differences between reading Spanish and Basque words (the within groups variable); and one for the variable Group (Figure 24.3A), indicating whether there are significant differences between bilingual and monolingual groups (the between groups variable). Interaction effects, on the other side, refer to the difference between levels of two or more variables (see Figure 24.4).

You can see an example of the output you might get when using ANOVA in Table 24.3. As you can see, you get different values for each main effect and interaction. The important bit is that, from this table, you can extract all the data you need to explain your results. First, look at the column where you can see the **F value**. The F value is like the t-value but for ANOVAs, where you have more than one variable. Then, direct your attention to the last value, this is the associated p-value that tells you whether your main effect or your interaction is significant or not. The other value that is relevant for reporting your results is the degrees of freedom (usually indicated as **df**) which, as noted earlier, informs you about your sample size. Since here we have multiple variables and their

Scan the QR code to understand how degrees of freedom in statistics: www .statisticshowto.com/probability-and-statistics/hypothesis-testing/degrees-of-freedom/

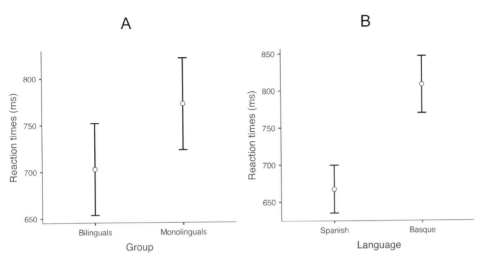

Figure 24.3 Here you can see the mean reaction times (small circle) and 95% confidence intervals (error bars) for the two main effects. A) represents the main effect of the variable group with two levels, the bilingual and the monolinguals groups of our study. B) represents the main effect of the variable language with also two levels, Spanish or Basque words.

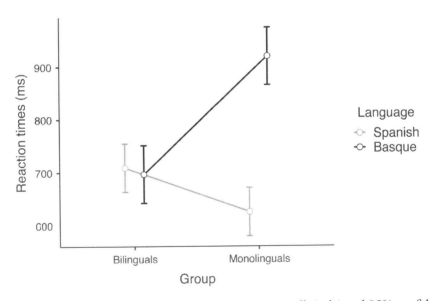

Figure 24.4 Here you can see the mean reaction times (small circle) and 95% confidence intervals (error bars) for the interaction effect (the relationship between the levels of group and the levels of language).

relationships, the degrees of freedom are a bit more complicated to understand than those from the t-value.

Table 24.3 An example of the output you would get from a repeated measures ANOVA with a within-subject factor and a between-subject factor.

Within subjects effects

	Sum of squares	df	Mean square	F	p
Language	397737.26	1	397737.26	375.13	< .001
Language * A	470514.82	1	1 470514.82	443.77	< .001
Residual	40289.92	38	1060.26		

Note: Type 3 Sums of squares

Between subjects effects

	Sum of squares	df	Mean square	F	p
A	97146.79	1	97146.79	4.12	0.050
Residual	896878.92	38	23602.08		

Note: Type 3 Sums of squares

In focus: reporting inferential statistics

When reporting t-tests and ANOVAs, you always need to indicate the test statistic value, the degrees of freedom, and the p-value. According to APA guidelines, the test value must be rounded to two decimal places, and the p-value to 3 decimal places. The 0 before the decimals is usually omitted:

T-test
Paired sample t-test indicates that participants responded significantly slower to Basque than Spanish words, t(39) = 5.51, p < .001.
    The degrees of freedom are 39 because we have 40 participants.

ANOVA
The main effect of language was significant, F(1, 38) = 375.13, p < .001, indicating that overall participants responded faster to Spanish words than Basque (see Figure 24.3B). The main effect of group was significant, F(1, 38) = 4.12, p = .05 (see Figure 24.3A). The interaction between these two variables was also significant, F(1, 38) = 443.77, p < .001.

Scan the QR code to visit 'APA Style' for more on reporting statistics: https://apastyle.apa.org/instructional-aids/numbers-statistics-guide.pdf

When you have a significant interaction in an ANOVA, you usually follow up this by comparing the means of interest with t-tests (e.g. effect of language in bilingual speakers alone, and the effect of language in mono-lingual speakers alone).

24.3.3 Finding relationships: correlations

We use correlations to measure the strength of the association between two variables and the direction of this relationship. So, whenever you want to observe whether two phenomena are related to each other, you might want to use correlation analyses. For example, if you look at Figure 24.5A, you can see the relationship between word concreteness and imaginability ratings from the CELEX lexical database (Baayen et al. 1995). As you can see, the higher the scores in word imageability, the higher the scores are in word concreteness. Just by looking at the data, we can see that these two variables appear to be related (i.e. when one increases, then the other tends to increase too). If we look now at Figure 24.5B, you can see that concreteness and familiarity scores (how familiar you are with a word) do not seem to be related to each other, that is, words with higher scores in familiar ratings are linked to both higher scores as well as lower scores in concreteness ratings. So, just by looking at Figure 24.5, we can see that variables in A seems to be related whilst variables in B do not seem to correlate. But to test whether variables in A or B are related and make inferences about the population (not just our sample collected), we need to use a correlation analyses test.

Link to CELEX database: https://catalog .ldc.upenn.edu/LDC96L14

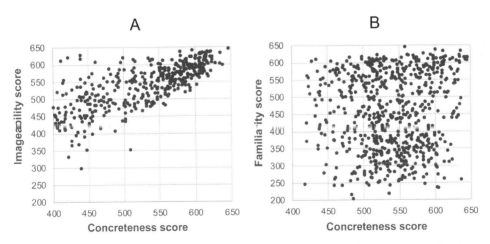

Figure 24.5 A) Example of a positive correlation between variables. B) Example of no relationship (zero correlation) between two variables.

There are two main things we need to know about correlations analyses. First, we need to know how the strength of the relationship between variables is measured. Second, we need to establish what the nature of the relationship is.

The strength of the relationship is indicated by the **correlation coefficient** (r). The r value varies between +1 and –1, and you can see a guidance on how to interpret this value in Table 24.4. An r value close to 0 indicates that the relationship between the variables is either very week or non-existent (as in Figure 24.5B).

Table 24.4 Rough guidelines on how to interpret the r value of a correlation.

Strength of association	Correlation coefficient (r)
Strong	.5 to 1 *or* –.5 to –1
Medium	.3 to .5 *or* –.3 to –.5
Weak	.1 to .3 *or* –.1 to –.3

SCAN ME

Common misconception of correlations

A significant correlation between variables does not imply causality! It only tells us that when one variable occurs the other tends to occur as well, but we do not know which causes the other! Scan the QR code to visit the 'Spurious Correlations' website:www.tylervigen.com/spurious-correlations

You might be wondering why the r value can be either positive or negative. This is because r also indicates the *nature* of the relationship between variables. **Positive correlations** are those where increases in one variable lead to increases in the other (as in Figure 24.5A), whilst **negative correlations** are those where increases in one variable lead to decreases in the other. For instance, if you look at Figure 24.6, you can see an example of negative correlation. In this figure, you can observe that the scores in a proficiency test are negatively correlated with the age of acquisition of a second language. Basically, this negative correlation is telling us that more proficient second language learners tend to have started learning the second language early on in their lives.

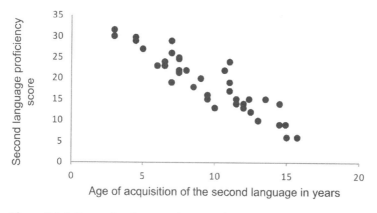

Figure 24.6 Example of a negative correlation.

In focus: reporting correlations

When reporting correlations, you always need to indicate (1) the direction of the relationship, (2) the correlation coefficient, (3) the degrees of freedom (i.e. your sample minus 1) and (4) the p-value. According to APA guidelines, the r value must be rounded to two decimal places and the p-value to 3 decimal places. As already mentioned, the 0 before the decimals is usually omitted:

```
Second language proficiency scores were negatively
correlated with the age of acquisition of the second
language, r(37)= -.92, p < .001, see Figure 24.6.
```

In our case, the degrees of freedom are 37 because we have 38 participants. Notice that in our example of reporting a correlation, we direct the reader to Figure 24.6. It is important that whenever possible correlations are reported, we include a figure depicting the relationship between the two variables. This helps the reader to understand/visualise the results.

24.4 Data visualisation

24.4.1 What is data visualisation for?

Data visualisation is an important statistical tool. It allows us to discover patterns in data which would otherwise be difficult to spot. In effect, scientific visualisation allows us to take a step back, to abstract from individual data points, and to highlight main trends in a dataset. In scientific visualisation, the emphasis is not on elaborate presentations and eye-catching images of the kind which we encounter, for instance, in newspapers or magazines. Instead, scientific visualisation focuses primarily on displaying data; everything else is subordinate to this aim. Accordingly, Tufte (2001: 93ff) uses a metric called the **data-ink ratio** to calculate how effective a particular graphic is. The equation is very simple:

$$(11) \quad data-ink\,ratio = \frac{data\,ink}{total\,ink\,used\,to\,print\,the\,graphic}$$

It operates on a scale between 0 (not effective) and 1 (effective). The difference between an effective and ineffective data display can be demonstrated with Figures 24.7 and 24.8. Both of these images are based on the same dataset; the data-ink ratio for Figure 24.7 is 0.16, while the same metric is much higher for Figure 24.8 (0.93), pointing to a considerably superior effectiveness of the latter.

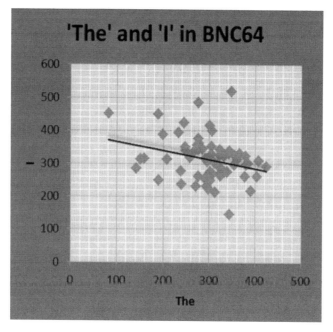

Figure 24.7 Frequencies of *I* and *the* in spoken data.

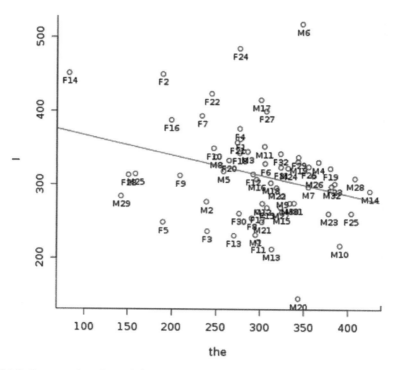

Figure 24.8 Frequencies of *I* and *the* in spoken data for male (M) and female (F) speakers.

24.4.2 Basic types of visual display

A range of graphs can be employed to visualise language. In this section, we will discuss the most important ones. Returning to the data in example (3), which shows proportions of adjectives in a random sample of current British novels, we can display the main tendencies discussed in Section 24.2.2 in the form of a boxplot. **A boxplot** shows a distribution of the data: showing the range, the interquartile range, the median and the mean all in the same image. It is therefore a very efficient visualisation technique with a high data-ink ratio. Figure 24.9 displays a boxplot based on data in example (3) (the data is presented without rounding).

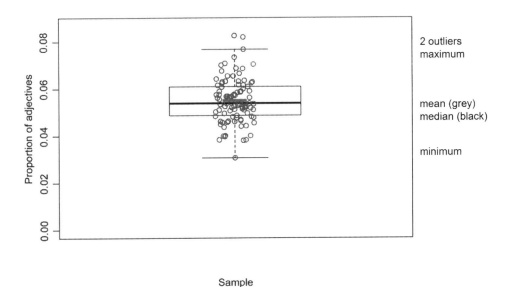

Figure 24.9 Boxplot for example (3).

In the boxplot, the whiskers show the maximum and minimum values and exclude the outliers (two in Figure 24.9). The box itself represents the interquartile range (middle 50% of values). The long thick line in the middle of the box is the median, and the short grey line displays the mean. Individual texts are displayed as circles.

If we wish to visualise a relationship between two variables, as was discussed in the previous section, a scatter plot is the best option. We can take the proportions of adjectives displayed in Figure 24.9 and add the proportion of verbs in the same texts. The resulting scatterplot is shown in Figure 24.10.

The scatter plot in Figure 24.10 displays the proportions of adjectives on the **x axis** and proportions of verbs on the **y axis**, with individual texts again

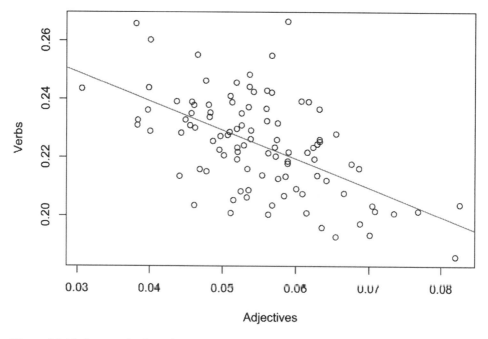

Figure 24.10 Scatterplot based on example (3) with a line of the best fit.

displayed as circles. The graph has also been fitted with the **line of the best fit**. This is a regression line, which shows the main tendency in the data. We can see that there is an inversely proportional relationship between the use of adjectives and verbs in British novels (i.e. the more adjectives authors use, the fewer verbs they employ, and vice versa).

Finally, for the comparison of two or more groups of data, **error bars** showing 95% confidence intervals can be used. This type of visualisation is very powerful because it indicates whether the difference observed is statistically significant. We can then confirm this by carrying out a statistical test, as outlined in Section 24.3.2.

Figure 24.11 shows a comparison of the proportion of adjectives in Academic prose and Fiction.

The circles in the graph show the mean values for the two groups, while the error bars indicate 95% confidence intervals. This shows where the mean would likely fall for 95% of samples taken from the same population. The interpretation of the graph is as follows:

1 Non-overlapping bars mean a statistically significant difference between groups.
2 Largely overlapping bars mean no statistically significant difference between groups.
3 Slightly overlapping bars mean that the result needs to be confirmed by a statistical test (see Section 24.3.2).

444

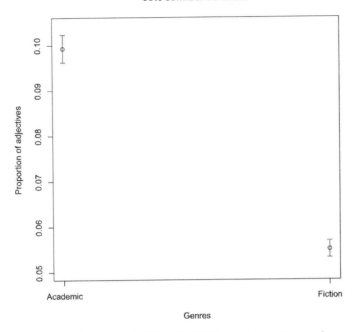

Figure 24.11 Error bars for example (3), with 95% confidence intervals.

In focus: history of scientific visualisation

Data visualisation has a very long history. In ancient Greece, visual representations were drawn in sand to demonstrate geometrical postulates and mathematical proofs. It has been suggested, however, that the rise of empirical science in the seventeenth century marks 'the beginnings of visual thinking'

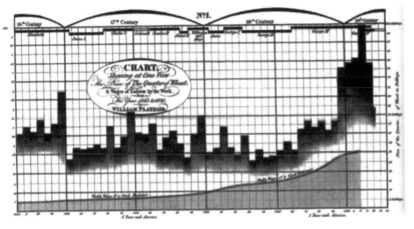

Figure 24.12 Playfair (1786) shows changes in the price of wheat in relation to wages across the sixteenth and seventeenth century in England.

Source: Adapted from Brezina and Bottini (2021).

445

(Friendly 2008). New visual representations and innovations, such as three-colour printing and lithography, were introduced in the eighteenth century. Thematic maps started to be used to show trends and patterns of economic, demographic and medical data, combining quantitative information of states and governments with their geographical distribution. Data visualisation continued to rise during the nineteenth century, when multivariate plots were extensively used. In the twentieth century, key statistical techniques were developed and graphic displays such as boxplots were introduced to highlight patterns in data.

24.5 Conclusion

In this chapter, we have discussed the various ways in which linguistic data can be analysed and visualised. First, we introduced the concept of descriptive statistics, and different ways in which you can present the central tendency (e.g. mean) and variability (e.g. standard deviation) of your sample. We then discussed some basic concepts of inferential statistics and hypothesis testing, and introduced you to the most common inferential tests (t-test, ANOVA and correlations) that are useful for undergraduate dissertations in linguistics. Finally, we discussed the various ways in which data can be presented to visualise your results in the most optimal way. We hope that this chapter has helped you to get started with statistics!

References

Baayen, R. H., Pipenbrock, R. and van Rijn, H. 1995. *The CELEX Database* [cd-rom]. Nijmegen, The Netherlands: Center for Lexical Information, Max Planck Institute for Psycholinguistics.

Brezina, V. 2018. *Statistics in Corpus Linguistics: A Practical Guide*. Cambridge: Cambridge University Press.

Brezina, V. and Bottini, R. 2021. Statistics and data visualization. In *The Routledge Handbook of Scientific Communication*. Abingdon: Routledge, pp. 271–289.

Brezina, V., Hawtin, A. and McEnery, T. 2021. The Written British National Corpus 2014 – design and comparability. *Text & Talk*, 41(5–6): 595–615.

Diggle, P. J. and Chetwynd, A. G. 2011. *Statistics and Scientific Method: An Introduction for Students and Researchers*. Oxford: Oxford University Press.

Friendly, M. 2008. A brief history of data visualization. In C. Chen, W. Härdle and A. Unwin (Eds.), *Handbook of Data Visualization*. Berlin: Springer-Verlag.

Playfair, W. 1786. *The Commercial and Political Atlas; Representing, by Means of Stained Copper-Plate Charts, the Exports, Imports, and General Trade of England, at a Single View. To Which Are Added, Charts of the Revenue and Debts of Ireland, Done in the Same Manner by James Corry*. London: Debrett; Robinson and Sewell.

Tufte, E. R. 2001. *The Visual Display of Quantitative Information*. Cheshire, CT: Graphics Press.

Section five

Issues

25 Generative vs. usage-based approaches to language
Willem B. Hollmann

25.1 Introduction

This chapter is structured like an imaginary conversation between a student of linguistics and an academic linguist. Some important questions are posed in relation to generative versus usage-based approaches to language, which are then answered. My aim is not to provide a comprehensive overview of differences between these approaches; that could easily take up this entire book! Instead, I want to provide some background to this interesting debate and provide a flavour of where it is and may be heading next.

There is some overlap between this chapter and Chapter 26, on Linguistic theories of grammar. I'd encourage you to view them as 'companions' and to read them together.

25.2 What is the difference between the generative and the usage-based approach?

The difference between these approaches plays out in many aspects or branches of linguistics, including language acquisition (see Chapter 9), the evolution of language (see Chapter 29), language change (see Chapter 8) and the nature of linguistic knowledge in (adult) language users. I deliberately choose the term 'language users' rather than 'speakers', because sign languages, such as British Sign Language, American Sign Language or Indo-Pakistani Sign Language, are completely equivalent to spoken languages in terms of complexity, functionality and so on.

In relation to language acquisition – which this chapter will mainly focus on – the difference is sometimes framed in terms of the question as to whether the process is driven by nature or by nurture. This is an oversimplification, especially in the context of where the debate has got to in the past couple of decades, but it provides a useful starting point.

DOI: 10.4324/9781003045571-30

25.2.1 The nature vs. nurture debate . . . I have heard of that. Didn't this involve Skinner and Chomsky?

Yes, the nature vs. nurture debate is often portrayed with reference to some early- to mid-twentieth century theories of the psychology of language, with two of the protagonists being the American psychologist Burrhus Frederic Skinner and his well-known compatriot and critic Noam Chomsky.

Skinner (1957) is in the nurture corner. As a behaviourist psychologist, Skinner's approach to language acquisition could be summarised in terms of the concepts of stimulus, response and reinforcement. His model of acquisition was to a large extent based on experimental work with non-human animals. These of course do not have 'language' as such (see Chapter 30) but he believed that stimulus-response mechanisms and reinforcement were sufficiently general notions that they were also relevant to human behaviour, including language.

Skinner analysed utterances (or acts of communication more broadly; see later) in terms of their function. He called these 'verbal operants', which indicates that they are used to operate, or to *do* something. This is not dissimilar to the notion of speech acts in speech act theory (see Chapter 6). However, Skinner defined 'verbal behaviour' and 'operants' broadly, so as to include non-linguistic behaviour 'capable of affecting another organism' (1957: 14). One of Skinner's examples of non-linguistic communication is 'clapping the hands for a servant' (1957: 14) – which is both helpful and a sign of the times in which he wrote his book!

One of the operants Skinner recognised he called 'mands'. This label is based on terms such as 'command', 'demand' and 'countermand' (Skinner 1957: 35); it corresponds to requests or commands in speech act theory. Concretely, a child might be hungry, which may be the stimulus that makes them produce the *yes/ no* interrogative (1):

(1) Can I have a sandwich?

It is important to note that terminology used in the 1950s – here: 'speaker' – was typically less sensitive to the status of signed languages and signers, but Skinner does at least recognise their existence elsewhere (1957: 14) and clearly includes them in the scope of his theory.

If the caregiver responds affirmatively and hands them a sandwich, that reinforces the mand as part of the child's 'verbal repertoire', defined as the 'collection of verbal operants [describing] the *potential* behavior of a speaker' (Skinner 1957: 21).

Skinner's theory is more complex than this example illustrates. However, he does not discuss the mental processes involved in the production of (1), such as the sentence-initial positioning of the auxiliary verb *Can*, when in declarative sentences it follows the subject, as in (2):

(2) I can have a sandwich.

We'll return to *yes/no* interrogatives several times in this chapter. For now, though, note that Skinner's explanation of acquisition focuses on external, observed behaviours. This is in line with general behaviourist thought: see for example the suspicion cast by the influential behaviourist John Watson on (the study of) mental processes:

> The Behaviorist began his own formulation of the problem of psychology by sweeping aside all medieval conceptions. He dropped from his scientific vocabulary all subjective terms such as sensation, perception, image, desire, purpose, and even thinking and emotion as they were subjectively defined.
>
> (Watson 1930: 5–6)

Noam Chomsky wrote a very negative (1959) review of Skinner's book. He criticised many aspects, including the neglect of mental processes. The reason why that is problematic, Chomsky suggested, is that Skinner's external factors ('nurture') are nowhere near sufficient to predict language use and explain its acquisition. In Chomsky's alternative explanation, nature is more important for acquisition: 'The fact that all normal children acquire essentially comparable grammars of great complexity with remarkable rapidity suggests that human beings are somehow specially designed to do this' (1959: 57).

Here we have the roots of Chomsky's Universal Grammar (UG) hypothesis: the suggestion that children have an innate blueprint of what language may be like. UG is seen as species-specific and modular: it is unique to humans and separate from the rest of cognition. The quotation contains a now classical Chomskian argument to support UG: the apparent ease and speed of language acquisition by children.

The review hints at another argument Chomsky uses to support UG: 'the argument from the poverty of the stimulus' (1980: 34 and *passim*). This is the idea that children produce language that goes far beyond the often less than perfect (in Chomsky's view at least) input they have received: 'a child is capable of . . . generating a set of sentences [only] some of which he has heard' (1959: 57). The use of the verb 'generate' is linked to the name 'generative grammar' or 'generative linguistics' – common labels for Chomskian theorising.

25.2.2 Could you explain the relation between the poverty of the stimulus argument and UG in a bit more detail?

Children from around the age of 2 are able to produce sentences such as (1), from above. Yet they don't only produce *yes/no* interrogatives that they have heard their caregivers say (i.e. that have been part of the stimulus). They create new ones too.

The key question with regard to the structure of (1) is how children get the order of the auxiliary verb (here: *can*) and the subject (here: *I*) right. Adger, in his popular generative grammar textbook, says that interrogatives such as (1) are 'clearly related' (2003: 7) to declarative sentences, which we've already seen would be (2).

He adds that based on similar questions the child is exposed to there are at least three rules they could 'dream up' (Adger 2003: 7):

1 Swap the first two words around.
2 Swap the first verbal element with the first noun phrase.
3 Put the verbal element that follows the subject in front of it.

If the child came up with rule 1 then you might expect a declarative such as (3a) to yield interrogative (3b), while rule 2 would lead from (4a) to (4b):

(3a) The girl has a sandwich.
(3b) *Girl the has a sandwich?
(4a) The boy who is eating was hungry.
(4b) *Is the boy who eating was hungry?

However, we never see examples like that. But since it is statistically speaking impossible that *all* children just *happen* to come up with rule 3 that must somehow be part of their innate UG.

25.2.3 What happened after Chomsky's review? Did everyone agree that Skinner had been completely wrong?

Both Skinner's book and Chomsky's review were widely read and cited, and they still are to an extent. But Chomsky's views were part of a larger movement in the 1950s, which came to be known as the Cognitive Revolution. This was the return to centre stage of an interest in mental processes following several decades of behaviourism dominating the scene in psychology and linguistics.

Skinner never replied to Chomsky's review. It is not entirely clear why, but MacCorquodale (1970) has argued that the review's tone may have been the reason. Whether Chomsky was indeed as 'condescending, unforgiving, obtuse, and ill-humored' as MacCorquodale (1970: 84) suggested, readers should judge for themselves.

The Cognitive Revolution combined with the lack of a response from Skinner have led to a majority perception that Chomsky 'won' the argument. He has certainly been extremely influential in linguistics and beyond, but MacCorquodale suggests Chomsky did not *show* that Skinner was wrong; 'he merely asserted it' (1970: 84).

25.3 You said that nature vs. nurture is an oversimplification of the current debate between generative and usage-based linguistics. How's that?

In the context of acquisition, generativists do not deny that factors other than UG play a role, while usage-based linguists recognise that usage does not determine everything.

Generative grammarians often think of UG in terms of so-called 'principles', which are invariant across all languages, and 'parameters', which capture parts of the grammar where languages may differ – within limits. For example, a principle might be that all sentences must have a subject, whereas a parameter might be the optionality of subjects obligatorily being overtly expressed. To illustrate the two values of this parameter, consider the contrast between English (5), which has an overt subject, and Spanish (6), where the subject is inferred from the verbal ending -*o*:

(5) I would like a sandwich.
(6) *Quier-o*   *un*   *bocadillo.*
    want-1SG.PRS   a   sandwich
    'I want a sandwich.'

In order to set the options correctly on the 'switchboard' part of UG children rely on usage: English and Spanish children will set their parameters (subconsciously, of course) differently, according to what they are exposed to. Also, the lexicon is not innate: no child is assumed to be born with verbs such as LIKE or QUERER or nouns such as SANDWICH or BOCADILLO hardwired in their brain.

Let's move on to usage-based linguistics. Its account of acquisition is also more of a compromise than the label might seem to suggest. Usage-based linguists admittedly argue that it makes little sense to assume right from the start that language is a separate module of the mind when the alternative – that it *isn't* – has not been fully assessed and (if necessary) partly or wholly rejected. The simplest, and therefore preferable, starting assumption is that language acquisition can be explained in terms of *general* cognitive abilities employed also to acquire other complex skills. But this is by no means a rejection of nature in favour of nurture: it is accepted that language acquisition relies on processes that are biologically determined. What is at stake, instead, is whether those processes are specific to the domain of language or more general.

25.3.1 So how would a child learn how to form, for instance, English *yes/no* interrogatives based on usage and general cognitive abilities?

First, if it was not already obvious, what we understand by the usage-based approach is quite different from behaviourism. I say 'if it was not already obvious' because I've mentioned that current usage-based theorists emphasise the importance of cognitive abilities – and that behaviourism by definition avoids discussing those. In this respect, usage-based linguists share Chomsky's view that language acquisition is most fruitfully studied not just in terms of stimulus-response sequences, but by paying close attention to cognition.

Subject and verb placement in *yes/no* interrogatives, used by generativists such as Adger (2003) to support UG, has also been considered by usage-based linguists, including Cameron-Faulkner et al. (2003). Chomsky's claim regarding the poverty of the stimulus first emerged at a time when large amounts of relevant linguistic data were not readily available. However, for several decades we have had large electronic corpora at our disposal; see also Chapter 21.

To put this into perspective, the entire seven-volume *Harry Potter* series amounts to just over 1 million words. Scan the QR code to see how many words are in each of the books: https://wordcounter.net/blog/2015/11/23/10922_how-many-words-harry-potter.html).

For child language acquisition, the most important corpus, or strictly speaking *collection* of corpora, is the CHILDES database, to which there is a QR code on p. 187 (MacWhinney 1995), and Cameron-Faulkner et al. draw on substantial amounts of authentic caregiver-child interactions from that database.

The usage-based account runs as follows. Children get a lot of input; much more than one might perhaps realise without looking at data. Hart and Risley's (1995) analysis of parent-child interactions suggests that by the age of 3 a child will have heard between 10 and 30 million words. The amount of input is so vast, and the amount of time spent on processing language therefore so extensive, that usage-based linguists have challenged Chomsky's assertion (see earlier) that language acquisition is very rapid.

25.3.2 But regardless of how much input children get, didn't Chomsky say that the nature of the input would still not allow us explain how children produce all the sentences we observe in their output?

It is true that child-directed speech is limited in terms of the types of sentences that children are exposed to. But that may actually be an advantage from a usage-based acquisition perspective: not only is there a lot of input but it tends to contain many of the same structures, which should make it easier for the child to pick them up. In relation to the structure we are focusing on, Cameron-Faulkner et al. (2003) found that 15% of all utterances were *yes/no* interrogatives, which is much more than in adult-to-adult speech; see for example Newport (1975: 94), who reports a figure of only 8%.

It is worth reflecting on just how many of these interrogatives a child hears. Hart and Risley (1995) found a mean utterance length in caregiver speech of 4.0 words. If we use the lowest number of words (i.e. 10 million (see earlier)), to make our estimate as conversative as possible, then by the age of 3 a child will have heard 375,000 *yes/no* interrogatives.

Even if a child is exposed to hundreds of thousands of *yes/no* interrogatives they may of course still produce ones that they have never heard, such as (7):

(7) Could Sarah take my green teddy bear?

Usage-based linguists argue that the child is able to produce such novel utterances thanks to their ability to identify patterns in the hundreds of thousands of *yes/ no* interrogatives they hear and by increasingly abstracting away from those patterns. Pattern identification and abstraction are cognitive processes we also use in many tasks other than language acquisition.

Some examples of utterances the child hears might be *Can I have it?*, *Can I see your drawing?*, *Can I take your cup?*, *Can I throw the ball?*, *Can you say 'mummy'?* and *Can you come here?* Initially the child may remember these as individual expressions, storing the string of words along with the meaning they have figured out (often based in part on the situational context and shared attention with the caregiver to something the adult may be pointing to, holding or gesturing). But then, through a process of gradual abstraction, the child may form a construction [*Can* Y X?] And later still, as the child is exposed to interrogatives with other auxiliaries, such as *will*, *would* and *may*, the construction [Aux Y X?] may emerge. The child can use this construction to produce utterances they have never literally heard before, such as (7), earlier, by dropping different words and phrases into the appropriate slots.

Despite some similarities between the generative and usage-based approach (including the emphasis on mental processes as opposed to only external behaviour, and recognition that some of those cognitive abilities are innate) there are also significant differences.

For example, usage-based linguists do not assume that patterns such as the order of subject and auxiliary verb follow from innate grammatical principles. Yet they do not exactly claim that children 'dream them up' either – a view which Adger (2003: 7) appears to ascribe to opponents of UG. Instead, the theory holds that children make abstractions based on the input.

Furthermore, usage-based linguists do not suggest, as Adger (2003: 242–245) and other generative grammarians usually do, that interrogative structures are derived from declaratives. Instead, based on children's experience with (hundreds of thousands of tokens of) interrogatives, they are stored as constructions in their own right – first only as very specific ones, such as *Can I have it?* with more abstract constructions such as [*Can I X?*] and [*Aux Y X?*] emerging later as well.

Relatedly, generative linguists consider syntactic rules – such as the one which moves the verb in a declarative clause to the start of a *yes/no* interrogative (Adger's rule (3); see earlier) – to be purely structural and devoid of any meaning. Usage-based linguists typically reject the notion of purely syntactic rules. Instead, [*Can I have it?*], [*Can I X?*] and [*Aux Y X?*] are all pairings of linguistic structure and semantic meaning. The technical term for these pairings is 'constructions'; see also Chapter 26, on Linguistic theories of grammar.

25.4 Will the generative and usage-based views ever converge?

There are some areas where this has in fact happened to a degree, most notably in relation to Chomsky's view of the nature and size of UG.

Generative grammarians hold wildly different views regarding the identity and number of principles and parameters in UG. As to how many parameters there are, Pinker occupies one end of the scale, claiming there are 'only a few' (1994: 112; see also Adger 2003: 12). Towards the other end we have Roberts and Holmberg, who put the figure 'in the region of 50–100' (2005: 541).

However large some generativists may consider UG to be, from the 1990s onwards Chomsky has committed himself to streamlining it as much as possible. This new approach to generative grammar is known as 'minimalism'. Chomsky is one of the authors of the well-known paper by Hauser et al. (2002), which hypothesises that the only innate human cognitive ability specific to language is 'recursion'. Recursion is the process whereby two structures are combined to form a larger structure, which again may be combined to form another, higher-level structure, and so on. For instance, example (8), next, is a recursive sentence in which a relative clause (starting with *who*) is embedded in the *that*-clause, which in its turn is embedded in the main clause:

(8) Sarah believes that the woman who is walking over there is her teacher.

One great advantage of this minimalist approach is that the development of one uniquely human cognitive process, such as recursion, in the relatively short time (in evolutionary terms) available for the emergence of language in our species, is much more plausible than the development of a very rich UG with potentially many dozens of principles and parameters.

Although Chomsky himself has not stated this explicitly, minimalism has brought his approach to the evolution and acquisition of language closer to the usage-based view. After all, if the only language-specific genetic endowment is our capacity for recursion then many aspects of language must now be accounted for with reference to (1) usage and (2) more general (and possibly not uniquely human) cognitive abilities. Chomsky (e.g. 2005) prefers to refer to these factors as 'experience' and 'principles'. These terms may obfuscate the increased overlap with the usage-based approach and Chomsky himself tends not to reference research by scholars who self-identify as usage-based linguists. Nevertheless, many other linguists have observed and commented on the convergence.

25.4.1 This rapprochement between the generative and the usage-based approach is a good thing, right?

There may certainly be benefits. In principle, the more minds and resources are focused on answering the same sorts of questions based on the same kinds of assumptions, the more the field may progress.

Also, Chomsky's theory has not only divided scholars' opinions; it has divided learned societies, conference series, journals and even linguistics departments across different universities. The result of the latter has been that whether an undergraduate or postgraduate student is taught about generative, usage-based linguistics or both often depends on the university they choose. Moreover, linguistic theory is really difficult to get a clear sense of for scholars who work in cognate disciplines (e.g. psychology or sociology) and who need an understanding of it to inform interdisciplinary research. Harris (2022) offers a fascinating insight into the history, politicisation and institutionalisation of the division.

In spite of the optimism around convergence expressed by some linguists, a number of Chomsky's followers have effectively stopped following him. More specifically, a number of especially younger generative grammarians are unwilling to adopt minimalism. Instead, they revert to the conception of UG as a very large innate inventory of principles and parameters; scan the QR code to see, for example, the generativist Omer Preminger's comment on Martin Haspelmath's blog.

https://dlc.hypotheses.org/2490.

This development may end up making theoretical linguistics even more opaque to outsiders. The meaning of the label 'generative grammar' may become increasingly diffuse, and the convergence with usage-based theory we are currently witnessing might only be temporary.

References

Adger, D. 2003. *Core Syntax: A Minimalist Approach*. Oxford: Oxford University Press.

Cameron-Faulkner, T., Lieven, E. and Tomasello, M. 2003. A construction based analysis of child directed speech. *Cognitive Science*, 27: 843–873.

Chomsky, N. 1959. Verbal behavior by B. F. Skinner. *Language*, 35: 25–58.

Chomsky, N. 1980. *Rules and Representations*. New York: Columbia University Press.

Chomsky, N. 2005. Three factors in language design. *Linguistic Inquiry*, 36: 1–22.

Harris, R. A. 2022. *The Linguistics Wars: Chomsky, Lakoff, and the Battle of Deep Structure*. 2nd ed. New York: Oxford University Press.

Hart, B. and Risley, T. R. 1995. *Meaningful Differences in the Everyday Experiences of Young Children*. Baltimore: Paul H. Brookes.

Hauser, M., Chomsky, N. and Fitch, W. T. 2002. The language faculty: What is it, who has it, and how did it evolve? *Science*, 298: 1569–1579.

MacCorquodale, K. 1970. On Chomsky's review of Skinner's *Verbal behavior*. *Journal of the Experimental Analysis of Behavior*, 13: 83–99.

MacWhinney, B. 1995. *The CHILDES Project: Tools for Analyzing Talk*. Hillsdale, NJ: Lawrence Erlbaum.

Newport, E. N. 1975. *Motherese: The Speech of Mothers to Young Children*. Ph.D. thesis. Ann Arbor: University of Pennsylvania.

Pinker, S. 1994. *The Language Instinct: The New Science of Language and Mind*. London: Penguin Books.

Roberts, I. and Holmberg, A. 2005. On the role of parameters in universal grammar: A reply to Newmeyer. In H. Broekhuis, N. Corver, R. Huybregts, U. Kleinhenz and J. Koster (Eds.), *Organizing Grammar: Linguistic Studies in Honor of Henk van Riemsdijk*. Berlin: Mouton de Gruyter, pp. 538–553.

Skinner, B. F. 1957. *Verbal Behavior*. New York: Appleton-Century-Crofts, Inc.

Watson, J. 1930. *Behaviorism*. New York: W. W. Norton.

26 Linguistic theories of grammar
Willem B. Hollmann and Vittorio Tantucci

26.1 Introduction

This chapter is a 'companion' chapter to Chapter 25, which is about generative vs. usage-based approaches to language. Like that chapter, it is written as an imaginary conversation between a language or linguistics student and an academic linguist. There will be overlap in the theories we discuss. Generative theory was the dominant approach in the twentieth century and continues to be very popular. But the cognitive, constructionist and usage-based approach that emerged in the 1980s has developed into a serious contender. This chapter will be different from its 'companion' in that it will focus specifically on grammar, rather than language as a whole. More precisely, we will point to differences in the analysis of grammatical phenomena. We will have less to say about the possible nature of the language faculty.

26.2 So what is grammar?

This is a good question to begin with, because the answer to it leads to big differences in the analysis of relevant bits of language.

Grammar essentially refers to the combination of meaningful elements of a language. As explained in Chapter 3, the smallest meaningful linguistic unit is a morpheme.[1] It follows that morphology, the ways in which morphemes may be combined to form larger words and the subject of Chapter 4 of this volume, is part of grammar. Indeed it is, although grammar textbooks often don't have all that much to say about morphology. Instead, the focus tends to be on the way in which words are combined into phrases, clauses and sentences. This is often called syntax and is the subject of Chapter 5 of this volume.

We said that we wouldn't talk much about the language faculty in this chapter, but in order to understand why morphology is often glossed over, we do need to say a bit. As we have seen in the chapter on generative vs. usage-based approaches to language, many linguists, including Chomsky and his followers, assume that the language faculty is an autonomous 'mental organ' or module. But they go further, in suggesting that our linguistic knowledge is itself compartmentalised into distinct components. There is general agreement that phonology, semantics

DOI: 10.4324/9781003045571-31

459

and syntax (see Section two of this volume) are among them, but morphology is seen by some as a component in its own right as well. Since components are essentially repositories of sets of rules that apply only to the relevant 'level' of language, it's unsurprising that morphology is often treated more or less separately from syntax.

This very brief discussion of the componential view of language, adopted by Chomsky and his followers, leads us onto two major differences between generative grammarians and the grammatical theory that has become its main alternative: **cognitive construction grammar.**

Generative grammarians often treat morphology as quite distinct from syntax, although they are generally happy to use the umbrella term 'grammar' for both. Cognitive construction grammarians do not assume that language is a separate mental organ. Instead, they suggest that the simplest starting hypothesis is that linguistic cognition is an integral part of general cognition. Relatedly, they do not assume that language consists of these separate components, either. They admittedly view phonology as different, inasmuch as phonemes (usually) have no intrinsic meaning. But morphology and syntax both concern meaningful units, and so there is no sharp dividing line. Many of the theoretical notions are thus shared between the analysis of the structure of words on the one hand; and phrases, clauses and sentences, on the other. An example of this is the notion of a 'construction', which we will need to provide a clear definition of (see Section 26.3). And semantics (see Chapter 6) is not seen as a separate component either. Instead, meaning is viewed and analysed as an integral part of morphemes and words – and of assemblies of morphemes and words. Morphemes, words and longer assemblies are all referred to, by cognitive linguists, as constructions.

26.3 I suppose you should explain to me, then, what cognitive linguists mean by a 'construction'?

Absolutely. Constructions are pairings of form and meaning. These pairings include single morphemes, regardless of whether they are free (e.g. BEAN) or bound (e.g. the plural suffix -s, which allows you to turn *bean* into *beans*). But they may be more complex assemblies as well. *Beans* is an example, as it consists of more than one meaningful element. So is the idiom *full of beans*.

When analysing constructions, cognitive linguists sometimes clearly show the form and meaning dimensions. Langacker, one of the most well-known proponents of this approach, tends to separate them by means of a dash (see, for example, 2013). The form is occasionally given as the pronunciation: [bi:n]/[BEAN]; [fʊləvbi:nz]/[HAVING A LOT OF ENERGY]. (See Chapter 2 for these International Phonetic Alphabet symbols.) Usually, however, linguists provide the orthography rather than IPA symbols: [bean]/[BEAN]; [full of beans]/[HAVING A LOT

OF ENERGY]. Often, in order to save space, linguists dispense with the meaning. However, shorthand like [BEAN] and [*full of beans*] should still be understood as constructions, and therefore as including a meaning. Incidentally, the difference between capitals and italics here reflects the fact that BEAN can occur as singular *bean* but also be turned into *beans*, whereas *full of beans* cannot be changed.

So far, the cognitive constructionist model doesn't seem that different from a generative perspective. We talked earlier about the componential view of language, adopted by generative grammarians. In addition to the components outlined previously they theorise that there is a lexicon. In this model, BEAN is obviously included in the lexicon. *Full of beans* can be as well, if we say that the lexicon may contain multi-word lexical expressions.

Construction grammar starts to diverge from generative grammar when we zoom in on the plural morpheme -*s*, as Table 26.1 shows:

Table 26.1 Different understandings of plural -*s*, according to generative and cognitive constructivist grammar.

Generative grammar	Construction grammar
The addition of -*s* is a morphological rule	Plural [-*s*] is a pairing of form and meaning (i.e. a construction), just like [BEAN] and [*full of beans*].

This means that because it is always attached to nouns and never occurs on its own, in construction grammar the construction is actually [N-*s*]/[MULTIPLE ENTITIES]. Obviously, in this plural noun construction different nouns can be slotted in. The technical term construction grammarians use for constructions that have such empty slots in them is 'schematic'. Its opposite is 'specific' or 'substantive'. The plural noun construction [N-*s*], then, is partially schematic; different nouns can be slotted in but the sibilant sound is specific.

The suggestion that form-meaning pairings can be partially or wholly schematic represents an enormous difference between this approach and generative grammar. Consider the following sentences:

(1) The more the merrier.
(2) The more you read about grammar, the more interesting it will seem.
(3) The better you prepare, the luckier you'll get.

Example (1) is a fully specific construction. Relying on the *Oxford English Dictionary* to provide the meaning, we can analyse it as [*the more the merrier*]/ [THE MORE PEOPLE OR THINGS THERE ARE, THE BETTER AN OCCASION OR SITUATION WILL BE]. But note the similarity in form and also meaning between (1) on the one hand, and (2–3) on the other. Construction grammarians (e.g. Goldberg 2003) would analyse these as examples of the partially schematic construction [*the* X-*er the* Y-*er*]/[THE MORE ONE HAS OF X THE MORE ONE WILL HAVE OF Y].

461

The [*the* X-*er the* Y-*er*] construction has several empty slots, but constructions can be even more schematic than this. Consider the following sentences:

(4) Elżbieta opened a tin of beans.
(5) She toasted two slices of bread.
(6) She ate her breakfast.

Construction grammarians would say that examples (4–6) all contain instances of the transitive clause construction [X TrV Y]/[PARTICIPANT ₓ INTERACTS WITH PARTICIPANT ᵧ IN A MANNER SPECIFIED BY THE TRANSITIVE VERB (TrV)].

26.4 In what way is this analysis so different from what a generative grammarian would say?

Let's start with the transitive clause construction, exemplified by (4–6). Generative grammarians would suggest that the syntax component of our mind contains a rule that innately allows us to build sentences. The rule basically says that you should combine a noun phrase with a verb phrase (Figure 26.1).

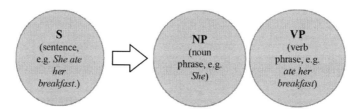

Figure 26.1 Combining a noun phrase and a verb phrase to make a sentence, according to generative grammar, using example (6) from earlier.

A second rule is then applied, which says that a verb phrase may consist of the verb and a noun phrase complement (Figure 26.2).

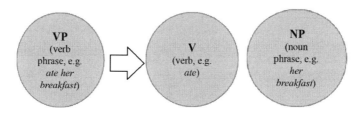

Figure 26.2 Combining a verb and a noun phrase to make a verb phrase, according to generative grammar.

And other rules kick in as well, depending on the exact sentence. For example (6), there is a rule that says that a noun phrase can consist of a determiner followed by a noun (Figure 26.3).

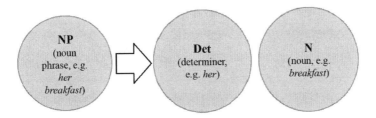

Figure 26.3 Combining a determiner and a noun to make a noun phrase, according to generative grammar, using example (6).

Sticking to example (6), the rules, working together, may be represented as the syntactic tree in Figure 26.4. It is worth noting that this is a relatively simple syntactic tree, representative of very early generative analysis. Tree structures have become increasingly complex and abstract over the years. For an overview of more recent developments, including X-bar theory, the DP hypothesis and the Minimalist Program see for example Cook and Newson (2007).

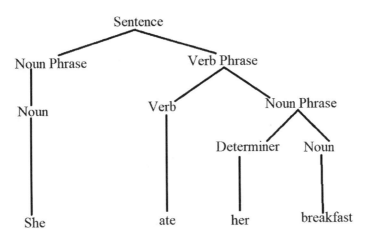

Figure 26.4 (Early) generative grammar syntactic analysis of *She ate her breakfast.*

Now here is a really crucial point: these rules and this tree structure representation are *pure syntax*. They themselves have no meaning whatsoever. The sentence does, of course, but that is because it includes words, taken from the lexicon.

26.5 What about [*the* X-er *the* Y-er]?

Here the contrast between the two approaches is perhaps even clearer. Remember that generative grammarians distinguish between different components, including one for syntax and one for semantics. And they suggest that there is another separate part of our linguistic knowledge, which is the lexicon. The trouble is that [*the X-er the Y-er*] does not fit anywhere. It has meaning, so it can't be pure syntax. It is not only semantics, so it cannot fit there. And it cannot be part of the lexicon either: in contrast to *full of beans*, which is lexically specific, this construction is not.

The problem posed by partially schematic constructions such as this for the generative, componential model (i.e. where do they fit?) is the subject of a very well-known paper: Fillmore et al. (1988). The authors argue that the componential model cannot accommodate partially schematic constructions. They suggest that for that reason a different approach to grammar may in fact be called for: construction grammar (see also Croft and Cruse 2004, Chapter 9, for a more accessible discussion of the pioneering paper by Fillmore et al.).

> **26.6** Hm. I understand [*the X-er the Y-er*] doesn't fit into any of the components recognised in generative grammar, and that we may therefore need constructions in our theory. But if constructions are pairings of form and meaning then I am still not sure how they are different from words and syntactic rules, which together also create meaningful sentences.

One difference lies in the way the analyses look on paper. As we have said, the generative grammar syntactic tree given earlier is much simpler than ones proposed within more recent versions of the theory, including **Minimalism** (see e.g. Adger 2003 or Cook and Newson 2007). It would not be an exaggeration to say that Minimalist trees are almost completely incomprehensible for linguistics students and even academic linguists, unless they have received specific instruction in quite a range of theoretical concepts and underlying assumptions. That is not necessarily a weakness, incidentally: Albert Einstein's theory of relativity is not immediately straightforward either, but physicists and other scientists consider it to offer major insights into speed, mass, space and time.

But while it may not be a shortcoming it is a *difference* from a construction grammar representation. A constructionist analysis of the same sentence, as in Figure 26.5, is relatively easy to grasp – if we agree to represent participants as circles, interactions between participants as arrows and correspondences between the form (in the top part of the box) and the meaning (at the bottom) of a construction by means of dotted lines. (Different construction grammarians

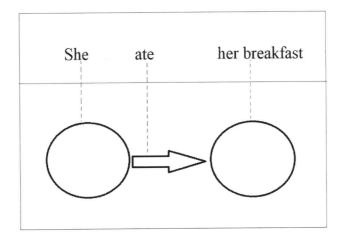

Figure 26.5 Construction grammar analysis of *She ate her breakfast.*

may visualise things somewhat differently; our use of the circles, arrows and dotted lines is based on conventions of Langacker 2013.)

Just as was the case with the syntactic tree in Figure 26.4, so too could we add sophistication to the constructionist analysis in Figure 26.5. For example, we could show how this sentence is an instance of the more schematic construction [X TrV Y]/[PARTICIPANT ₓ INTERACTS WITH PARTICIPANT ᵧ IN A MANNER SPECIFIED BY THE TRANSITIVE VERB (TrV)], discussed previously.

We could do this by adding a visual representation of that construction similar to the one for *She ate her breakfast*, but with these specific words replaced by X, TrV and Y. And we could then connect that construction to the one in Figure 26.5 to show that *She ate her breakfast* instantiates the abstract transitive clause construction.

However, for the purpose of this very general discussion of theories of grammar let us move on to a few other differences. First, although the topic of this chapter is theories of *grammar*, it will hopefully be clear that in the constructionist view, on which constructions are combinations of form and meaning, grammatical structure is always linked intrinsically to semantics.

Second, this then leads to a major difference in our understanding of what our grammatical knowledge consists of. A generative grammarian might say it is mainly our knowledge of the rules of syntax (and perhaps morphology). And since words are stored in a separate lexicon in this theory, it follows that language production is quite similar to the way in which we use a computer programming language: we have certain algorithms (rules), which are themselves meaningless, into which we insert symbols (words), as in Figures 26.1, 26.2 and 26.3. In construction grammar, this computer metaphor does not apply: our grammatical knowledge consists only of constructions (of different degrees of complexity and schematicity; see earlier discussion), and there is no separate lexicon. For this reason construction grammarians sometimes refer to our grammatical knowledge as the '**constructicon**'.

The way in which the constructicon emerges in child language acquisition (see also Chapter 10) is a third key difference. Chapter 25 discusses this in more detail than we can do here.

Very briefly, in a constructionist model, grammatical acquisition is the acquisition of constructions (i.e. pairings of form and meaning). According to this theory, acquisition happens based on exposure to those constructions (in combination with general cognitive abilities such as pattern recognition and abstraction). So a child acquires the transitive clause construction, [X TrV Y], by hearing thousands of instances like (4–6), and gradually working out that it means [PARTICIPANT $_x$ INTERACTS WITH PARTICIPANT $_y$ IN A MANNER SPECIFIED BY THE TRANSITIVE VERB (TrV)].

A key component of linguistic competence is therefore the experience of language use, rather than a set of predetermined 'algorithms' that allow us to generate sentences. One constructionist theory that takes this view to an extreme is **Dialogic Syntax** (Du Bois 2014). This theory suggests that constructions are acquired based on their similarity through dialogue and speakers' necessity to engage with one another. A child may hear its mother say [*I am strong*], which may 'resonate' with something the child heard from its father the day before; for example [*I am very happy*]. The child may then want to engage in the current dialogue with its mother's talk by saying [*I am very strong*]. This means the child has effectively mastered, or is beginning to master, the [X COPULA (*very*) ADJ] construction, with the general meaning of [A PERSON IS CHARACTERISED BY SOME PROPERTY]. Eventually, the child will learn also dialogically that X, the subject component of the construction, can be inanimate. In this view, constructions are not just stored after linguistic exposure and repetition, but are rather actively categorised via analogy 'at talk', during dialogic exchanges.

By contrast, generative grammarians argue that children learn individual words (such as TIN, BEAN or BREAD) based on exposure, but that they are born with a lot of grammatical knowledge about syntactic structure already, known as **Universal Grammar**. This innate Universal Grammar may include the very general rules that a sentence consists of a noun phrase and a verb phrase, and that some verb phrases contain a verb and a noun phrase, which are represented in Figures 26.1 and 26.2.

https://wals.info/feature/81A#2/18.0/153.1

The specific order of those elements, generative grammarians suggest, is not innate. This is because subject noun phrases do not precede the predicate verb phrases in all languages. You can get a sense of the cross-linguistic variation by looking up the map for 'Order of Subject, Object and Verb' on the online World Atlas of Language Structures, by scanning the QR code.

Consider Chamorro, a language spoken in an archipelago known as the Marianas, in the North Pacific Ocean. Chamorro sentences predominantly have the verbs preceding the subject – with the object following the subject. Note that *si*, not glossed by Chung, is an article used with proper names:

(7) Ha-apápasi   si   Carmen   i   lalahi   sinku   pesus.
     3 SG-pay.PROG   Carmen   the   men   five   dollars
     'Carmen is paying the men five dollars.' (Chung 1990: 562)

Generative grammarians theorise that where languages show such structural differences, Universal Grammar contains a kind of switch. This can be set one way or another, depending on the language spoken around the child. Chomsky's technical term for this kind of switch is a '**parameter**'.

To sum up, generative and construction grammarians have very different views of the way in which grammatical knowledge is acquired, what it is, how it is stored, and how we should analyse and visualise the structure of sentences in descriptive and theoretical accounts of language or languages.

26.8 Those *are* big differences. Is there any chance of convergence between these approaches?

Really good question! This is discussed in some detail in Chapter 25.

26.9 Fair enough. Last question: with these theories being so different, will I be given the opportunity to study both theories in the course of my language or linguistics degree?

Probably not, and that's a shame. The divide between generative and usage-based constructionist theory has become, to a large extent, institutionalised. What this means is that some linguistics departments will have experts in one approach, whereas some other departments will focus on the other theory. Not many departments cover both, and only few offer students the opportunity to engage with both in the same sort of depth. Unfortunately, very few people who are not themselves theoretical linguists are aware of this theoretical divide. Many scholars in cognate areas, such as psychology or sociology, have no idea and most schoolteachers don't know either.

If linguistics departments tell future students about the theory they focus on, they typically present this as *the* way to do linguistics, rather than *a* way. Certainly for prospective undergraduate students it is therefore very difficult to pick a university based on the dominant linguistic theory. In other words, your theoretical understanding of grammar will likely be a matter of pot luck. The good news is that having read this chapter you now know that is the case; we recommend that you challenge yourself to read and explore more widely!

Note

1 Here, we disregard, for the sake of convenience, discussions about some phonemes or phoneme clusters (see Chapter 3) referred to as 'phonaesthemes'. These do seem to correspond to a meaning to some extent, 'such as the [i:] (...) signalling smallness (cf. *teeny, weeny*, etc.)' (Crystal 2008: 361).

References

Adger, D. 2003. *Core Syntax: A Minimalist Approach*. Oxford: Oxford University Press.

Chung, S. 1990. VP's and verb movement in Chamorro. *Natural Language and Linguistic Theory*, 8: 559–619.

Cook, V. J. and Newson, M. 2007. *Chomsky's Universal Grammar: An Introduction*. Malden, MA, Oxford and Carlton, Victoria: Blackwell Publishing.

Croft, W. and Cruse, D. A. 2004. *Cognitive Linguistics*. Cambridge: Cambridge University Press.

Crystal, D. 2008. *A Dictionary of Linguistics and Phonetics*. 6th edn. Malden, MA / Oxford / Carlton, Victoria: Blackwell.

Du Bois, J. W. 2014. Towards a dialogic syntax. *Cognitive Linguistics*, 25(3): 359–410.

Fillmore, C. J., Kay, P. and O'Connor, C. 1988. Regularity and idiomaticity in grammatical constructions: The case of *let alone. Language*, 64: 501–538.

Goldberg, A. 2003. Constructions: A new theoretical approach to language. *Trends in Cognitive Sciences*, 7: 219–224. http://doi.org/10.1016/S1364-6613(03)00080-9

Langacker, R. W. 2013. *Essentials of Cognitive Grammar*. Oxford: Oxford University Press.

27 Linguistic relativity

Panos Athanasopoulos

27.1 Introduction

One of the most fascinating theories of linguistics claims that speakers of different languages perceive the world differently. This theory, of **linguistic relativity**, is composed of two related ideas. On the one hand, languages carve up reality in different ways. On the other hand, language shapes our perception of reality. It is often referred to as the Sapir-Whorf hypothesis, after Benjamin Lee Whorf and Edward Sapir, who are credited for coming up with the basic idea (e.g. Whorf 1956). One cannot help but think of the movie *Arrival* (2016) here. Actor Amy Adams plays linguist Louise Banks, who is tasked by the government to decipher an alien language used by recent extra-terrestrial visitors to earth. What is fascinating about the movie is not so much that its central character is a linguist (!), but that a linguistic theory, namely the Sapir-Whorf hypothesis, gets a mention. In one scene, Louise Banks is in conversation with another character, who says: 'I was doing some reading that if you immerse yourself into a foreign language, you can actually rewire your brain'. To which Banks replies: 'Yeah Sapir-Whorf hypothesis. The theory that the language you speak determines how you think'.

So, how much scientific truth is contained in these statements, beyond Hollywood's stylisation? This chapter departs from classic philosophical approaches, to focus on the state-of-the-art experimental evidence that has transformed our understanding of the ways in which language, thought and perception interact. To borrow a phrase from Hollywood, spoiler alert! Because it turns out that language does not absolutely determine how we think, and that we can certainly think without language. Evidence is, however, accumulating that language can and does infiltrate our thought unconsciously. As a result, differences in interpretation of reality can be found between speakers of different languages. Learning a foreign language can indeed, then, change how our brain responds to the physical world around us. In other words, Hollywood got it almost right!

27.2 How did it all begin?

Benjamin Lee Whorf coined the term 'linguistic relativity principle'. This coinage was essentially an attempt to formalise the idea that language affects thought in

DOI: 10.4324/9781003045571-32

predictable ways. This was an idea that Whorf himself developed from his linguistics teacher Edward Sapir, who was in turn influenced by his own teacher Franz Boas. Whorf theorised that since different languages have different concepts, speakers of different languages think, or interpret, the world differently. Since its formulation, the hypothesis has been a classic topic of debate in the disciplines of psychology, linguistics, anthropology and philosophy (Lucy 1997). The hypothesis, while initially attracting much theoretical and empirical interest (e.g. Brown and Lenneberg 1954) soon fell out of favour in mainstream psychology and linguistics. The main reason was methodological, hinging on the so-called 'circularity of evidence problem'.

The problem was that Whorf relied almost exclusively on descriptions of linguistic typology, without offering any independent measures of thought linked to the typological distinctions he was claiming to cause differences in thinking between populations. One famous example is the 'Eskimo' – vocabulary for snow. According to Whorf

> We have the same word for falling snow, snow on the ground, snow packed hard like ice, slushy snow, wind-driven flying snow – whatever the situation may be. To an Eskimo, this all-inclusive word would be almost unthinkable; he would say that falling snow, slushy snow, and so on, are sensuously and operationally different, different things to contend with; he uses different words for them and for other kinds of snow.
>
> (Whorf 1956: 216)

The problem, in this quote by Whorf, is that he does not offer any independent evidence that the hypothetical Eskimo speaker he is referring to would indeed experience snow radically differently from an English speaker. Pinker, in his 1995 book, *The Language Instinct*, offers a concise illustration of how Whorf's reasoning was circular, and therefore problematic: 'Whorf claims that Eskimos speak differently so they must think differently. How do we know that they think differently? Just listen to the way they speak!' (Pinker 1995: 61).

Pinker's criticism has its basis in two interrelated factors. First, and in Whorf's defence, he was writing at a time when empirical methods to measure human thought remained in their infancy. They would not be fully developed in the cognitive psychology and psycholinguistic laboratories until decades later. Indeed, the very operationalisation of thought, or cognition, as mental operations relating to computation, processing, categorisation and memory, were still far from being developed into the constructs that are widely accepted today in the field of cognitive science. How could Whorf show independent evidence of thinking, when the instruments to do so were not yet clearly defined?

Second, and not so favourably for Whorf this time, Whorf (and Sapir) provided several statements that could be taken as definitions of the linguistic relativity principle. These varied considerably in the degree to which differences in thinking between populations can be attributed to the way their languages encoded reality.

470

At one end of the spectrum, absolute determinism was hypothesised. According to this theory, language users are 'at the mercy' of their native language (Sapir, quoted in Whorf 1956: 134). More tempered formulations were also put forward, in which language acts as an attention-directing mechanism, like a spotlight, to perceptual phenomena that may otherwise be processed similarly at a deeper level. Thus, Whorf wrote that 'language, for all its kingly role, is in some sense a superficial embroidery upon deeper processes of consciousness' (1956: 239). In the absence of a clear theoretical definition of Whorf's idea, it was difficult to formulate clearly testable hypotheses that could prove or disprove linguistic relativity.

The definition that I think has been the cornerstone of modern, workable empirical investigations holds that

> users of markedly different grammars are pointed by their grammars toward different types of observations and different evaluations of externally similar acts of observation, and hence are not equivalent as observers but must arrive at somewhat different views of the world.
>
> (Whorf 1956: 221)

This definition, and particularly the formulation 'different evaluations of externally similar acts of observation', dovetails nicely, if coincidentally, with later descriptions of basic human cognitive processes like categorisation. Indeed, the cognitive process of categorisation has become the classic test case of empirical investigations of linguistic relativity since the 1980s, because on the one hand it is an essential element of human cognition (Harnad 1987), and on the other hand, similarity is the basis of categorisation (Nosofsky 1986). Therefore, judging the similarity between stimuli offers a readily testable hypothesis of the Whorfian question: stimuli encoded differently in different languages will tend to be evaluated as less similar by speakers of those languages, revealing differences in a fundamental aspect of human cognition, namely categorisation. Using variations of this paradigm, the last three or so decades have witnessed an exponential growth in empirical research. Indeed, data (Bylund and Dick 2019) reveal that the citation frequency of Whorf (1956) has skyrocketed, with 86 citations per year in the 1980s; 140 citations per year in the 1990s; 277 citations per year in the 2000s; and 420 citations per year in the 2010s.

27.3 What domains have been explored?

One classic domain of investigation has been the categorisation of colour. While all humans with normal trichromatic vision see colour physiologically the same way, different languages carve the colour spectrum in remarkably different ways, ending up with quite variable categorical divisions. For example, many of the world's languages have a term that denotes both blue and green, a so-called 'grue' term found in, for example, Himba (Namibia), Berinmo (Papua New Guinea) and historically in Welsh, Japanese and Chinese. Russian, Greek and Turkish have two separate terms for blue, one referring exclusively to darker shades, and one referring to lighter shades. Research utilising the basic similarity judgement paradigm described in the previous paragraph shows that speakers of Himba and Berinmo with a 'grue' term to refer to green and blue will judge blue and green stimuli as less similar to each other than speakers of languages like English that encode the terms 'green' and 'blue' (e.g. Roberson et al. 2005). Winawer et al. (2007) presented Russian and English speakers with different shades of blue, arranged in triads, and asked them to spot the odd one out as quickly as they could. Some triads included a stimulus that belonged to a different lexical blue category in Russian but not in English (cross-category triads). In other triads, all blue stimuli belonged to the same lexical category in both Russian and English (within-category triads). Results showed faster cross-category responses than within-category responses, exclusively in Russian speakers.

Another classic area of investigation has been spatial orientation, where researchers ask participants to pinpoint the location of an object using either relative or absolute systems of orientation. A relative system of orientation locates objects and events relative to the speaker/observer, or relative to other objects/events. For instance, 'the computer is in front of me and the mouse to the right of the computer'. Such systems are used predominantly in languages like English and Dutch (and many other Western languages). An absolute system of orientation uses the cardinal points of the compass, namely north, east, south and west. For example, 'the computer is to the north of me and mouse to the west of the computer'. Such systems are predominantly used in Tzeltal, a Mayan language, Guuu Yimithirr, an Australian Aboriginal language, and many other Indigenous American, Polynesian and African languages. Levinson and colleagues (e.g. Majid et al. 2004) describe a series of experiments that show how these preferences in language affect the simulation and interpretation of spatial orientation.

In one experiment, participants sat at a table on which an arrow pointed either to the right (south) or left (north). They were then rotated 180 degrees to another table, with an arrow pointing to right (this time north) and left (this time south). They were then asked to choose the arrow on the second table that was 'like the one they saw before'. Dutch informants chose predominantly the arrow that pointed to the relative direction, that is, if the arrow on the first table pointed to left they chose the arrow pointing left on the second table. Tzeltal speakers did the opposite, that is, they chose the arrow that pointed to the same absolute location on the second table as on the first (so they chose the arrow that was pointing north, regardless if it was now pointing to their right instead of to their left). Likewise, in another study, participants were asked to follow and interpret directions outdoors. Speakers of relative orientation languages performed better in the task if directions were given in relative terms (e.g. 'after the traffic lights, take the first right, then the second left, and then you'll see the super market on your left'), whereas speakers of absolute orientation languages performed better when directions were given using cardinal terms (e.g. 'after the traffic lights, drive south, and then on the second crossing drive west, and you'll see the super market directly to the north').

Motion events is another domain of experience that has been studied extensively. Perhaps this is not surprising, given that motion permeates every aspect of human activity, from walking to get a glass of water, to flying to another continent for holidays. Cross-linguistic differences in this domain concern either the lexical semantics (see also Chapter 5) of verbs, or grammatical aspect (Athanasopoulos and Bylund 2013). Looking at verb semantics, it appears that speakers of languages that encode manner on the main verb (e.g. English: 'The boy ran into the house') will match scenes based on common manner of motion, even if the path of motion is different. For instance, they will say that a scene depicting a boy running into a house is more similar to a scene showing a boy running out of the house (same manner, different path), than a scene showing a boy walking into the house (different manner, same path). By contrast, speakers of languages that encode path on the main verb and manner in a satellite (e.g. Spanish and Greek: 'The boy entered the house running') will show the opposite pattern, matching a scene depicting a boy running into a house to a scene showing a boy walking into the house (same path, different manner) than a scene showing a boy running out of the house (same manner, different path) (e.g. Gennari et al. 2002). Indeed, even in a learning task involving never-before-seen stimuli such as novel alien creatures, speakers of manner languages learn to categorise novel alien creatures faster and more accurately based on the perceived similarity of their manner movements, while speakers of path languages learn to categorise novel alien creatures faster and more accurately based on the perceived similarity of their path trajectories (Kersten et al. 2010).

27.4 How unconscious are effects of language on thought?

An area of disagreement in modern approaches to the linguistic relativity hypothesis concerns the degree to which humans are aware of linguistic penetrations of perception and thought, or whether such effects occur outside of conscious awareness. This disagreement is rooted in Pinker's 1995 criticism of the focus on categorisation as the main methodological test-bed of linguistic relativity. It is worth repeating Pinker's criticism verbatim, to appreciate the extent of the issue and how it has been addressed since:

> In another type of experiment subjects have to say which two of three color chips go together; they often put the ones together that have the same name in their language. Again, no surprise. I can imagine the subjects thinking to themselves, 'Now how on earth does this guy expect me to pick two chips to put together? He didn't give me any hints, and they're all pretty similar. Well,

I'd probably call these two 'green' and that one 'blue,' and that seems as good a reason to put them together as any.'

(Pinker 1995: 65)

More recent studies have therefore attempted to explore linguistic relativity beyond categorisation, employing paradigms that tap into more implicit processes, such as psychophysical and visual perception. Psychophysics refers to the simulation in our mind of a physical experience, such as the passage of time. Recent research shows that Swedish and English speakers will tend to experience the duration it takes for a line to grow as shorter or longer depending on the physical growth of the line. Longer lines tend to be perceived as taking longer to grow than shorter lines, even if the stimulus duration between the two different lines is identical. This is because duration is usually expressed via spatiotemporal metaphors denoting distance (e.g. long/short time).

Spanish and Greek speakers on the other hand are much less affected by the physical length of the line in this task. In these languages, the prevalent spatio-temporal metaphors for duration are quantity terms (much/little time). As a consequence, they will tend to experience the duration it takes for a container to be filled with liquid as longer or shorter depending on the quantity the container fills up to. Fuller containers are estimated to have taken longer to fill than less full containers, even when the duration of the filling was identical. By contrast, Swedish and English speakers are much less affected by container volume in this task (e.g. Bylund and Athanasopoulos 2017).

27.5 Conclusion

The main idea of learning a new language being tantamount to learning a new way of thinking is a core thematic anchor throughout the film *Arrival*. This culminates with Banks experiencing time differently, as a result of finally mastering the aliens' language, and learning their unique way of representing time linguistically. This, perhaps surprisingly for a Hollywood movie, accurately reflects the current state of research in this area. Studies show that bilinguals experience time differently depending on the language context of the experiment, and the more frequently an individual uses their second language, the more they come to experience time like native speakers of that language (Bylund and Athanasopoulos 2017). The famous proverb 'learn a new language and get a new soul' comes to mind, when considering how behaviour can shift so quickly within the same individual, depending on the language context.

Importantly, however, such effects are found in experimental conditions that utilise verbal prompts, such as the term for 'duration' in the participants' respective language being shown on screen while participants are estimating duration. In conditions where verbal prompts are removed, cross-linguistic differences disappear. All participants, regardless of what language they speak, are equally affected by line length or container volume. So although effects of language in a task like this are unconscious, they are only present when language itself is present in the task. This would point to a role for language that is one of directing, rather than determining, attention to certain experiential stimuli.

In the same vein of exploring unconscious effects of language, neurophysiological paradigms have moved the Whorfian debate to a biologically grounded arena, where it is possible to find tangible correlates of language-thought interactions in the human brain. Athanasopoulos and Casaponsa (2020) review a series of recent studies on the neural correlates of colour perception, and report findings showing that Greek speakers perceive differences in light and dark blue as greater very early in the visual processing stream (i.e. about 180 ms after seeing the colour stimulus – that's less than one-fifth of a second), and outside of conscious awareness, than English speakers. This is because of a lexical distinction present in Greek, but not in English, that carves the blue area of colour space into two, using distinct terms to refer to light and dark blue. The difference, however, is one of degree. English speakers' brains also index that they do perceive the difference in lightness between the two blues; just not to the same extent that the brains of Greek speakers do.

Another strand of evidence here comes from the systematic study of people who have impaired language ability due to brain injury, a complex of language pathologies collectively known as aphasia. Lupyan and Mirman (2013), for example, instructed participants with anomia (a type of aphasia where individuals present with difficulty recalling the names of specific objects) to select all objects in an array that matched a specific criterion. In a 'high-dimensional' condition, grouping was possible on the basis of many different features (e.g. participants were told to 'select all the farm animals'). In a 'low-dimensional' condition, grouping required attention to one specific feature while abstracting across other task-irrelevant dimensions (e.g. participants were told to 'select all the green objects'). Patients with anomia performed better in the former condition, because, according to the authors, performance on tasks utilising low-dimensional stimuli rely on more direct support from language, a resource which is impaired in patients with anomia.

These findings, taken together with the findings that showed that removing verbal prompts from the experiment leads to similar time estimation patterns in speakers of different languages, and that differences in colour perception are a matter of degree of attention rather than (in)ability to see certain categorical distinctions suggest that when language is not available to humans, the ability to categorise the world around them may be affected, but not altogether abolished. We can then conclude that language does indeed seem to exert a measurable influence on our thinking, directing, rather than permanently shaping, our attention to and experience of those aspects of reality that are readily encoded in it.

References

Athanasopoulos, P. and Bylund, E. 2013. Does grammatical aspect affect motion event cognition? A cross-linguistic comparison of English and Swedish speakers. *Cognitive Science*, 37(2): 276–309. https://doi.org/10.1111/cogs.12006

Athanasopoulos, P. and Casaponsa, A. 2020. The Whorfian brain: Neuroscientific approaches to linguistic relativity. *Cognitive Neuropsychology*, 37: 393–412. https://doi.org/10.1080/02643294.2020.1769050

Brown, R. W. and Lenneberg, E. H. 1954. A study in language and cognition. *Journal of Abnormal and Social Psychology*, 49(3): 454–462. https://doi.org/10.1037/h0057814

Bylund, E. and Athanasopoulos, P. 2017. The Whorfian time warp: Representing duration through the language hourglass. *Journal of Experimental Psychology: General*, 146: 911–916. https://doi.org/10.1037/xge0000314

Bylund, E. and Dick, T. 2019. Pioneer: Benjamin Lee Whorf. In P. Atkinson, S. Delamont, M. Hardy and M. Williams (Eds.), *SAGE Research Methods Foundations*. Newbury Park, CA: SAGE.

Gennari, S. P., Sloman, S. A., Malt, B. C. and Fitch, W. T. 2002. Motion events in language and cognition. *Cognition*, 83(1): 49–79. https://doi.org/10.1016/S0010-0277(01)00166-4

Harnad, S. 1987. Psychophysical and cognitive aspects of categorical perception: A critical overview. In S. Harnad (Ed.), *Categorical Perception: The Groundwork of Cognition*. Cambridge: Cambridge University Press, pp. 1–52.

Kersten, A., Meissner, C., Lechuga, J., Schwartz, B., Albrechtsen, J. and Iglesias, A. 2010. English speakers attend more strongly than Spanish speakers to manner of motion when classifying novel objects and events. *Journal of Experimental Psychology: General*, 139(4): 638–653.

Lucy, J. A. 1997. Linguistic relativity. *Annual Review of Anthropology*, 26(1): 291–312. https://doi.org/10.1146/annurev.anthro.26.1.291

Lupyan, G. and Mirman, D. 2013. Linking language and categorization: Evidence from aphasia. *Cortex*, 49(5): 1187–1194. https://doi.org/10.1016/j.cortex.2012.06.006

Majid, A., Bowerman, M., Kita, S., Haun, D. B. M. and Levinson, S. C. 2004. Can language restructure cognition? The case for space. *Trends in Cognitive Sciences*, 8(3): 108–114.

Nosofsky, R. 1986. Attention, similarity, and the identification-categorisation relationship. *Journal of Experimental Psychology: General*, 115: 39–57.

Pinker, S. 1995. *The Language Instinct: The New Science of Language and Mind*. Penguin.

Roberson, D., Davidoff, J., Davies, I. R. and Shapiro, L. R. 2005. Color categories: Evidence for the cultural relativity hypothesis. *Cognitive Psychology*, 50(4): 378–411. https://doi.org/10.1016/j.cogpsych.2004.10.001

Villeneuve, D., director. 2016. *Arrival*. Paramount Pictures.

Whorf, B. L. 1956. *Language, Thought, and Reality; Selected Writings*. Cambridge, MA: Technology Press of Massachusetts Institute of Technology.

Winawer, J., Witthoft, N., Frank, M. C., Wu, L., Wade, A. R. and Boroditsky, L. 2007. Russian blues reveal effects of language on color discrimination. *Proceedings of the National Academy of Sciences*, 104(19): 7780–7785. https://doi.org/10.1073/pnas.0701644104

28 Linguistic diversity

Claire Nance

28.1 Introduction

There are thought to be around 7000 languages used across the world. Putting a precise number on this is complicated by the need to define exactly what is a 'language' and what is a 'dialect'. This is further compounded by difficulties in figuring out whether or not very small languages still have active users. However, whether the precise number is 6000, 7000 or 7500, there are certainly lots of different languages! This diversity has arisen over the thousands of years, when humans moved across the planet and eventually established new settlements, diverging from their neighbours into different ways of speaking/signing. Divergence occurs when populations became relatively isolated, such as separated by a mountain range or separated due to political reasons. Sometimes, new linguistic varieties emerge due to new contact between people. For example, Chinook Jargon, a language of the Pacific Northwest, emerged due to trading in the eighteenth and nineteenth centuries, while Nicaraguan Sign Language developed among deaf people in Nicaragua in the 1980s, due to increased opportunities for communication.

Some regions of the world are more linguistically diverse than others. These regions tend to correspond to areas that present geographical barriers for accessible travel between nearby regions. For example, Indonesia is comprised of over 17,000 islands and is very linguistically diverse with over 700 languages. Nigeria has a very diverse geography including rainforest, mountains, savannah and near-desert regions, all of which can make travel between settlements quite difficult. Around 500 languages are used in Nigeria. Papua New Guinea is thought to be the world's most linguistically diverse country with 839 different languages, and a population of 8.9 million (i.e. 10,607 people per language on average).

These examples show some of the ways in which new languages develop and how linguistic diversity can increase. However, if you look at news headlines as well as linguistic research, everything suggests that the huge diversity we can see today is diminishing. In the rest of this chapter, I consider why linguistic diversity might be diminishing across the world (Section 28.2), whether anything should be done (Section 28.3), and finally what might success look like if we do take action (Section 28.4).

478

DOI: 10.4324/9781003045571-33

28.2 Why is linguistic diversity reducing?

Although there are thousands of languages used around the world, the evidence does seem to suggest that this is reducing over time. For example, UNESCO's Atlas of the World's Languages in Danger shows 2464 languages that are somewhere between 'vulnerable' and 'extinct'. This is a large proportion of the approximately 7000 languages in the world! Languages might lose users if those people die over a short period of time and are unable to pass the language on; for example, the Aboriginal languages of Tasmania became extinct during the nineteenth century due to European colonisation and the introduction of new diseases. People may also choose to stop using languages for social, economic or political reasons. With increased mobility and globalisation since pre-modern times, more and more people move to new areas, learn new linguistic varieties and usually aim to acquire the most socio-economically valuable variety. For example, if someone moved to Ghana, they might learn Twi and/or English as these languages are used as lingua francas in this region, rather than a smaller language such as Gaa. There is no 'right' and 'wrong' about this, just that people make decisions based on what is socially and economically beneficial to them. Political considerations also very often feed into societal and individual decisions about language choice: for example, when compulsory education was introduced in Scotland in 1872, a policy was made to prioritise education in English, to the detriment of Scottish Gaelic (see Chapter 11).

Scan the QR code to check out UNESCO's Atlas of the World's Languages in Danger: www.unesco.org/languages-atlas/

Political messaging can lead to the development of long-held preconceived ideologies about language, which might ultimately lead to the loss of linguistic diversity. Such ideologies are sometimes based on scant evidence, which is not supported by modern research findings. For example, the widespread use of cochlear implants in deaf children in Western contexts, coupled with a framing of deaf people as disabled, can lead to a language ideology against the utility of sign languages, and a reduction in their use. However, children with cochlear implants and no access to sign language may be delayed in acquiring language skills. Lack of a solid early language acquisition can result in language deprivation syndrome, where an adult has non-fluent language and poor mental health (Hall et al. 2017)

In focus: language shift on Orchid Island, Taiwan

Taiwan is a multiethnic and multilinguistic society where Taiwanese Mandarin, Taiwanese Hokkien and Taiwanese Hakka are used alongside ten Austronesian languages (Formosan family) and Taiwan Sign Language. The areas where the Austronesian languages are/were spoken are shown in Figure 28.1. Here, we will focus our discussion on Yami, a Malayo-Polynesian language spoken by the Yami people (also known as Tao people) on Orchid Island, which is the small island 56 miles off Taiwan's south-east coast. Orchid Island is known as Pongso no Tao, 'island of human beings' in Yami.

Orchid Island was designated as an Indigenous reserve from the 1890s until the late 1960s, and was therefore relatively isolated, despite some Japanese- and Mandarin-speaking migrants. Yami people were mostly employed as subsistence farmers or fishers during this time. Between the 1960s and 1990s, Orchid Island's farming and fishing industry declined, and the island suffered depopulation, leading to a fragmentation of traditional social networks (see also Chapter 7).

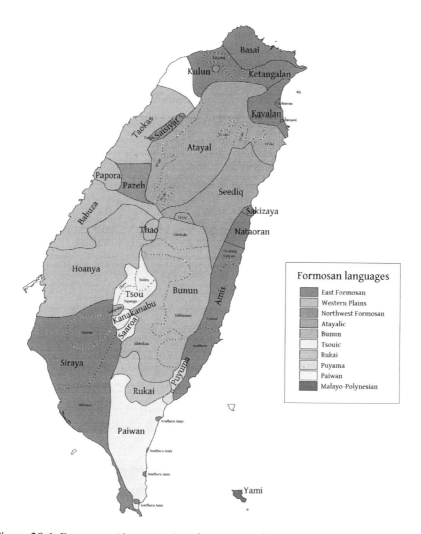

Figure 28.1 Formosan (Austronesian) languages of Taiwan.

Source: By Kwamikagami at English Wikipedia, CC BY-SA 3.0, https://commons.wikimedia. org/w/index.php?curid=5694372. Orchid Island/Pongso no Tao is the small island off the south-east coast of Taiwan.

Since the beginning of the twenty-first century, however, Orchid Island has become a major tourist destination. This has led to the in-migration of non-Yami speakers, as well as Mandarin being used as a lingua franca for tourists. After the Taiwanese administration took over in 1945, the education system became focused around Taiwanese Mandarin and Yami was banned in schools until 1987. Today, Yami is taught for two hours per week in schools. Language use varies from community-to-community on Orchid Island, but it is now rare for children and teenagers to use Yami outside of the school context, and they usually use Mandarin at home. For more information see Lai and Gooden (2018).

28.3 Should anything be done?

This discussion shows that the linguistic diversity of the world is decreasing. In this section I will discuss what our reaction could be. Specifically, I address two questions: (1) Why is a reduction in linguistic diversity an issue? and 2) Are we disadvantaging people if they *don't* learn a major language like English, Chinese or Hindi to a high degree of proficiency?

28.3.1 Why is reduction in linguistic diversity an issue?

Here, I argue that we should care about the loss of linguistic diversity for a number of reasons: cultural, health and wellbeing, human rights, possible loss of knowledge, and economic opportunity.

The culture of different social groups of people is defined by shared social practices. For example, different regions and countries are known for different ways of preparing food. There are also different cultural traditions around things like celebrating the birth of a child and marking the death of a community member. One fundamental social practice is the way in which people communicate and this might be a factor that distinguishes one ethnic group from another. A language is the foundation by which traditional culture such as literature, poetry and storytelling can be transmitted from generation to generation. If a particular group ceases to use their language, a significant aspect of their unique heritage, and means to access things like traditional songs, is also lost.

There can also be significant health and wellbeing implications if children are not given access to rich language input from an early age, with policies that eradicate access to a community language often negatively impacting on child development and educational attainment (see also Chapter 15). Malone and Paraide (2011) describe an education programme in Papua New Guinea, where children are taught in the relevant local language as well as English, with positive outcomes in early years education. Likewise, Kenya is following a strategy to ensure that the 18 national languages are used in education so that all children can learn in a language relevant to their upbringing, as well as to promote linguistic diversity. Linked to this strategy is a government aim to strengthen national identity in the post-colonial context through promotion of Indigenous culture, such as language. One of Kenya's most famous writers and thinkers on this topic is Ngũgĩ wa Thiong'o. In *Decolonising the Mind* (1986), wa Thiong'o sets out how his writing has previously been published in English, a language associated with colonialism, but from now onwards he will only write in his first language, Gĩkũyũ, or Kishwahili. wa Thiong'o sees language use as a fundamental human right and expression of identity, of which he was deprived due to the colonial authority in Kenya. In this respect, maintaining linguistic diversity is a crucial opportunity towards remedying the past wrongs of colonialism and oppression.

Humans are able to express concepts across languages through translation. Usually, translation can help describe concepts that might be succinctly expressed in a particular language but unfamiliar in another. However, in contexts where oral language, rather than written language, is the major vector for transmitting knowledge, there is a risk that some knowledge could be lost if a particular language is no longer transmitted. For example, Cámara-Leret and Bascompte (2021) show that 91% of medicinal plant names in northwest Amazonia are known only in one language; 100% of these languages are endangered and many are primarily transmitted orally. Unless further oral transmission of these languages occurs, or written documentation and translation, the names and knowledge of these plants could be lost. We have no way of knowing what kinds of knowledge will be important in the future and it is possible that vital information is at risk of loss along with orally transmitted endangered languages.

A final argument in favour of maintaining linguistic diversity is the increase in economic benefits to an area through promoting its heritage and language. For example, Jaworski et al. (2010) discuss the commodification of Te Reo Māori in New Zealand. In their example, a tour guide on a Māori cultural experience uses his knowledge of Te Reo to increase interest to the tour and emphasise the cultural distinctiveness of the Māori. If you would like further examples of how language diversity is used to promote and expand a tourism industry, have a look at this Visit Scotland website. The website provides a toolkit for small businesses in order to help them expand their Gaelic content and offering for visitors to Scotland. Visit Scotland's toolkit aims to assist businesses in harnessing this interest and translating linguistic skills into economic gain.

Scan the QR code to check out Visit Scotland's 'Scottish Gaelic Toolkit': www.visitscotland.org/supporting-your-business/marketing/toolkits/scottish-gaelic?s=09

A report in 2014 suggested that Gaelic could generate up to £147 million annually for Scotland through sectors such as tourism but also food and drink, heritage and the creative industries (Highland and Islands Enterprise 2014).

28.3.2 Are we disadvantaging people if they *don't* learn a major language like English, Chinese or Hindi to a high degree of proficiency?

This discussion explains the reasons why I think that linguistic diversity is important. However, more than half of the world's population speaks one of 23 major languages, with English having the most users (estimated 1.3 billion in 2021) followed by Mandarin Chinese (estimated 1.1 billion users in 2021). The figures on the world's most used languages are published by *Ethnologue*. If the rest of the world learned one of these 23 major languages, then communication would almost never be a problem! Wouldn't that be great? And actually, wouldn't we be disadvantaging people who *don't* learn a large world language?

> Scan the QR code to explore the Ethnologue 200, a list of the largest languages in the world: www.ethnologue.com/guides/ethnologue200

Possibly. A person's economic opportunities might be limited if they wish to pursue education or employment outside of their community without language skills in a regionally relevant major world language. However, this does not mean that all children should pursue, for example, Mandarin and ignore everything else. This would miss out on all of the benefits of maintaining languages explained in Section 28.3.1. We now know from decades of research into bilingualism and multilingualism that children can acquire multiple languages to a high degree of proficiency if given rich and diverse sources of input (see Chapters 11 and 15). As such, it is not the case that we need to choose between small, local languages and larger world languages. In this case, we can do both! I argue that the solution to the linguistic diversity of the future will provide all children the opportunity to become locally rooted by learning a culturally relevant local language, but also globally proficient citizens through multilingual acquisition and education.

28.4 What does success look like?

Assuming we do think that linguistic diversity is important, what would success look like? Promoting linguistic diversity could involve policies such as those followed in Kenya to use all the national languages in education, or it could involve an attempt to increase speaker numbers and uses of an endangered language through a targeted acquisition programme. Here, we will look at two different contexts where a culturally and historically important language has increased speaker numbers and uses, and where a language lost due to colonialism has been subsequently revived.

Hebrew is a Semitic language associated with Jewish ethnicity, history and culture. Hebrew has been used in some form since the tenth century BCE and is used for Jewish religious texts. It is commonly assumed that Hebrew 'died out' and was then revived, but this is not quite the case. Hebrew has been used for religious reading and writing purposes with no break, though ceased to be a regular spoken language around 400 CE due to the Roman conquests in the Middle East. During the Middle Ages, it is possible that some Hebrew was used to communicate when Jewish people encountered each other and it was spoken in, for example, prayer settings. Full-scale revival of spoken Hebrew began in earnest during the nineteenth century and early twentieth century when Jewish people began to settle in Palestine in large numbers. When Israel became independent in 1948, it is estimated that 81% of the population spoke Hebrew as their only language in daily life (Helman 2014). Targeted assimilation and language learning programmes for new migrants to Israel continue to this day in order to ensure the whole population (including the Arab minority) have proficient skills in Hebrew. The huge success of Hebrew revitalisation is likely due to the language's importance for religion and culture and the resulting high levels of motivation for people to acquire it. There are now around 10 million speakers of Hebrew (estimated from almost all of Israel's 9 million inhabitants and some speakers in the diaspora).

Australia was a very linguistically diverse continent before European contact. Since contact and colonisation, this linguistic diversity has been much reduced. In the twenty-first century, there are many programmes ongoing to document and revitalise the existing languages, as well as reclaim some languages referred to as 'sleeping' (i.e. having no active speakers and no transmission). One such language is Kaurna, a language used in the area of South Australia where Adelaide is now situated (scan the QR code for a map of the pre-colonialism languages of Australia). Kaurna has not been used as a language of daily communication for over 100 years and there are no archival sound recordings. However, efforts to revive the culture and language of the Kaurna people are now underway using some available word lists, knowledge of related languages, and some reconstruction. There are now opportunities to learn Kaurna at workshops, a Kaurna radio station, and optimism that families will eventually use the language for daily communication again. For more information see Amery (2016).

Scan the QR code to view a map of the pre-colonialism languages of Australia: https://aiatsis.gov.au/explore/map-indigenous-australia

28.5 Conclusion

To conclude, it is clear that the linguistic diversity of the world is reducing. This is due to increased globalisation and mobility, but also the legacy of colonialism and forced migration or cultural assimilation. I argue that maintaining or even increasing this diversity is desirable for reasons of cultural heritage, health, human rights, continuing Indigenous knowledge and economic benefits. There are some practical reasons why people might want to learn a regionally relevant major language, such as French or Swahili, as well as a smaller language. However, there is no need for this to be an 'either/or' choice. Many regions of the world are hugely multilingual and we know that children can acquire several languages simultaneously. I argue that future populations can indeed have their cake and eat it, in terms of maintaining their cultural heritage and language, while also communicating globally.

References

Amery, R. 2016. *Warraparna Kaurna!: Reclaiming an Australian Language.* Adelaide: University of Adelaide Press.

Cámara-Leret, R. and Bascompte, J. 2021. Language extinction triggers the loss of unique medicinal knowledge. *Proceedings of the National Academy of Sciences*, 118(24).

Hall, W. C., Levin, L. and Anderson, M. 2017. Language deprivation syndrome: A possible neurodevelopmental disorder with sociocultural origins. *Social Psychiatry and Psychiatric Epidemiology*, 52: 761–776.

Helman, A. 2014. *Becoming Israeli: National Ideals and Everyday Life in the 1950s.* Waltham: Brandeis University Press.

Highlands and Islands Enterprise. 2014. *The Economic and Social Value of Gaelic as an Asset.* www.hie.co.uk/media/5379/ar-stòras-gàidhlig-executive-summary.pdf

Jaworski, A., Thurlow, C. and Coupland, N. 2010. Language and the globalizing habitus of tourism: Toward a sociolinguistics of fleeting relationships. In N. Couple (Ed.), *The Handbook of Language and Globalization*. Oxford: Wiley, pp. 255–286.

Lai, L.-F. and Gooden, S. 2018. The spread of raised (ay) and (aw) in Yami: From regional distinctiveness to ethnic identity marker. *Journal of Linguistic Geography*, 6(2): 125–144.

Malone, S. and Paraide, P. 2011. Mother tongue-based bilingual education in Papua New Guinea. *International Review of Education/Internationale Zeitschrift Für Erziehungswissenschaft/Revue Internationale de l'Education*, 57(5/6): 705–720.

wa Thiong'o, N. 1986. *Decolonising the Mind: The Politics of Language in African Literature.* Nairobi: James Currey.

29 Evolutionary linguistics
Christopher Hart

29.1 Introduction

Language, whether spoken or signed, is part of human culture in every corner of the globe. Children the world over learn to use their language effortlessly with little or no formal input. Language comes as naturally to humans as walking upright or as flying does to birds. Moreover, although many wondrous communication systems can be found among different species in the natural world (see Chapter 30), none seem to come close to the marvels of human language, which is uniquely complex and creative. It is somewhat surprising, therefore, that it is only since the early 1990s that questions concerning the origins and evolution of human language have been properly addressed in linguistics. This is partly a product of history. Following the publication of Darwin's *Origin of Species* in 1859, evolutionary explanations of language were plentiful, but often fanciful and lacking in evidence. So far-fetched and unfounded had claims become that the topic was banned by the Linguistics Society of Paris in 1866 and by the London Philological Society shortly after, in 1872. The subject remained a scientific taboo until the turn of the twentieth century when advances in genetics, cognitive science and primatology sparked a renewed interest in the topic and made possible its proper scientific investigation. Evolutionary linguistics, then, is an interdisciplinary project which draws on fields including linguistics, neuroscience, biology, anthropology, palaeoanthropology and primatology to address questions of language evolution within a neo-Darwinian framework. Questions addressed come down to how, when and why did language evolve? As a young field, there is no consensus in the answers to these questions and a great many debates have opened up. In this chapter, we consider some of the positions taken in those debates and the kinds of evidence on which they are based.

29.2 How did language evolve?

To ask how language evolved is to ask from what earlier systems did it originate and what path did it follow in its subsequent evolution. In addressing the first of these questions, one hypothesis is that language evolved from a more basic communication system such as we find in modern primates.[1] For example, as

DOI: 10.4324/9781003045571-34

we will see in Chapter 30, vervet monkeys emit alarm calls to 'warn' fellow vervets of nearby predators. They have different calls for different types of predator: big cats, birds of prey and snakes. Such alarm calls are found in other primate species too, including white-faced capuchin and diana monkeys. Could a call system such as this have been the precursor to human language? Some researchers believe so (e.g. Hurford 2007; Jackendoff 2002). Others, however, argue that call systems among primates are fundamentally different to human language (Burling 2005; Ulbaek 1998). They point to the facts that primate calls appear not to be learned in the way that language is but to instead be genetically predetermined; that primate calls seem to be involuntary responses to the presence of particular stimuli (i.e. predators); and that primate calls are not made up of smaller units or combined to generate larger units as words are. However, exceptions to each of these claims can be found in the communicative behaviour of certain species (see Chapter 30 for discussion). Notwithstanding, purported differences such as these lead some researchers to suggest that language is more likely to have arisen from the kinds of social minds we find in modern primates and which early humans must also have had. Here, apes and chimpanzees in particular can show us the kinds of minds from which the first forms of language may have grown. For example, one cognitive ability on which language rests is Theory of Mind – an ability to recognise mental states and intentional behaviour in others. This is crucial to language since it is what enables us to (1) distinguish vocalisations which are intended by the speaker to communicate something from those such as coughs and cries which are more reflexive; and (2) to infer the precise meaning the speaker intended to communicate through their utterance (Sperber and Wilson 1995). And indeed, chimpanzees are able to distinguish intentional from non-intentional behaviour, including in humans. For example, a chimpanzee who has to choose between two humans to give them a reward, such as a glass of milk, will choose the human who had previously spilled all the milk by accident (e.g. by dropping the glass) rather than the one who had deliberately poured it all out (Dunbar 1996). Cognitive systems such as Theory of Mind (as well as others like joint attention and imitation), which we find in a more rudimentary form among apes, constitute the necessary cognitive precursors to language so that at some point our ancestors became cognitively primed for language to develop. Evidence for this position comes from neuroscience which shows an overlap in the brain between centres responsible for Theory of Mind and language.

The second kind of 'how' question concerns the course of language evolution. Here, one major debate concerns whether language evolved gradually to become steadily more complex over a long period of evolutionary time or whether it evolved punctually through a series of more sudden and significant changes. In biological terms, such sudden, perhaps species-defining, changes are known as saltations. Saltations are relatively rare in evolution and most researchers see language as having evolved in a normal, incremental fashion (Burling 2005; Jackendoff 2002). However, one potential saltation that has been proposed is the emergence of syntax (see Chapter 4). It has been argued that at some point humans moved from a grammarless 'proto-language' to fully blown language complete with syntax, and that this transition occurred abruptly when a single mutation resulted in the joining up of extant cognitive systems in the language-ready social minds of our ancestors (Bickerton 1990). According to this account, 'living linguistic fossils' of proto-language can be found in the pidgin languages (see Chapter 11) used in contact situations, the language of young children (see Chapter 9) and the sign-based languages that can be taught to apes (see Chapter 30). Evidence for the abrupt shift from proto-language to full language comes from some of the same sources. For example, pidgins turn into grammaticised creoles within a single generation (as in the well-known case of Nicaraguan sign language). Similarly, at around two years of age, children seem to move from non-syntactic strings to syntactic strings almost overnight. It is argued that these processes reflect the evolutionary trajectory of language. It should be stressed, however, that this proposal is controversial with one argument against it being that syntax is so complex that the likelihood of a single mutation producing it is about the same as a hurricane blowing through a junkyard and happening to assemble a jumbo jet (Pinker 1994: 361).

Another major debate concerns whether language has always been spoken or whether it first evolved in a different modality and later switched to speech. As we saw in Chapter 1, our vocal tract anatomy is clearly adapted for speech. Indeed, as a result of the way the vocal tract has been configured to accommodate speech, humans are the only species in the world that can choke on their own food. The prevailing assumption is thus that since its earliest stages language has been expressed vocally, albeit initially through a more limited range of sounds. However, it has been suggested that the earliest incarnations of language took the form of gestures rather than speech (Corballis 2002). Here it is argued that the move toward bipedalism freed up the hands so that they could be used for other purposes, including communication. Evidence for this claim comes from the fact that great apes use gestures to voluntarily communicate with one another and the fact that gestures remain an integral aspect of human communication. For example, speech is nearly always accompanied by gestures (see, for example, p. 220), even in settings where the speaker cannot be seen by their interlocutor (e.g. telephone conversations). And human sign languages rely exclusively on manual and facial gestures without losing any of the complexity or expressivity of spoken language (see, for example, pp. 131–133). Our natural ability to use sign languages instead of spoken systems is seen as a vestige from an earlier phase in the evolution of language. There is also some neurological evidence for this hypothesis as Broca's area, a key centre in the brain for language, is also involved in the execution and observation of hand movements.

However, the gestural account suffers several problems. For example, spoken language has several advantages over gestural forms and is therefore likely to have been selected for from the beginning. With spoken language, the hands are free to perform other vital tasks, like making tools. Spoken language also means communication is possible in the dark. And if gestural language did evolve to a similar level of complexity and functionality as spoken language, then what would have been the benefit of switching to speech that was so great as to warrant the massive neurological and anatomical changes needed to make the shift? Especially when speech would have presented its own disadvantages in the ancestral environment: speech may alert prey to your presence and predators to your whereabouts. Given the facilities of speech and gesture it seems more likely that language evolved as a flexible system with both modalities developing alongside one another.

29.3 When did language evolve?

Pinpointing the time at which language may be said to have evolved or at which it began presents a number of problems. For a start, assuming that language evolved gradually, at what point do we describe it as language? A further methodological problem stems from the fact that spoken language (as opposed to written) leaves no trace in the archaeological record. Of course, we do have fossils which can tell us when the anatomical structures necessary for speech begin to appear but this may underestimate the age of language, if its first forms were gestural, or overestimate it, if we accept that syntax is a defining feature of language and speech was in place for some time prior to syntax. Fraught as it is with difficulties, researchers have nevertheless sought to date the evolution of language by looking back through the human lineage for evidence of some linguistic capacity. A simplified version of the hominin line is represented in Figure 29.1.

Let's work backwards through this tree. Most researchers agree that language is at least as old as the modern Homo sapiens (Homo sapiens sapiens) who evolved in Africa around 160,000 years ago and who migrated out of Africa around 70,000 years ago to eventually out-compete and replace all other hominin species across the world. Homo sapiens sapiens were anatomically modern human beings and so it seems almost certain that they were capable of spoken language. The question for many is whether there is evidence of language being any older than this. Archaic Homo sapiens evolved from Homo erectus in Africa around 290,000 years ago. They produced complex stone tools which may be suggestive of language since both language and tool-making involve sequenced behaviour. Tool-making is also suggestive of language because language would have enabled instructions in tool-making to be given. More generally, complex artefacts may be said to reflect a complex mind, which may have included language. At around the same time, Homo erectus in Europe and the Middle East gave rise to Homo neanderthalensis (Neanderthals). Neanderthals are a crucial piece in the puzzle because of their special place in the ancestral tree where, if Neanderthals had language, it suggests that the course of language evolution may have begun in the common ancestor Homo erectus (see 'in focus' box). This

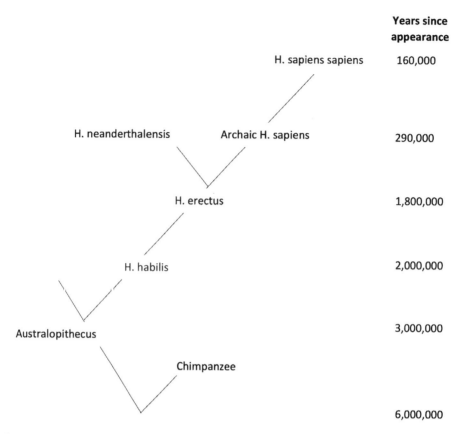

Figure 29.1 Basic ancestral tree.

is because language is unlikely to have evolved twice independently. Evidence that Homo erectus may have had some linguistic capacity comes from the fact that their brain size falls within the range of modern humans. Brain size has been shown to correlate with the communicative repertoires of modern primates.

In focus: Neanderthals

Neanderthals lived in Europe and the Middle East between 290,000 and 29,000 years ago. This means that they co-existed with modern Homo sapiens for some time before their eventual extinction. Popular media portrayals of Neanderthals depict them as lumbering brutes who communicated only in grunts. However, scientific evidence paints a different picture and shows that they were culturally sophisticated and that they may have been capable of spoken language (Mithen 2006). For example, archaeological evidence suggests that as well as being competent tool-makers Neanderthals produced body art and ceremonially buried their dead. Such symbolic activities suggest a species capable of

---

other forms of symbolic behaviour, including language. Other evidence that Neanderthals were capable of spoken language comes from several directions. For example, both Broca's area and Wernicke's area can be identified in endocasts of Neanderthal skulls. And the same version of a gene known to be involved in human language, *FOXP2*, is present in the Neanderthal genome. Further evidence comes from the morphology of their vocal apparatus. For example, a crucial piece of anatomy that supports speech by providing an anchor to the tongue and which has a unique shape in humans compared to other mammals is the hyoid bone. A hyoid bone belonging to a Neanderthal skeleton discovered at the Kabara cave in Israel is of the modern human form (see Figure 29.2). Reconstructions of Neanderthal skulls further suggest that they had a similar sized vowel space to modern humans. These findings imply that the Neanderthal vocal apparatus did not differ significantly from modern humans and that they are therefore likely to have been capable of spoken language. As Mithen (1996: 161) puts it: 'it would be evolutionarily bizarre if Neanderthals were exposed to the possibility of choking, without being able to complain about their food'. However, other reconstructions of the same skulls taken from the Chapelle-aux-Saints site in France concluded that the Neanderthal vowel space was much smaller and that they were only capable of producing a more limited range of sounds which excluded velar consonants [k] and [g] as well as long vowels [iː], [ɑː] and [uː]. It has been suggested that this more limited speech capacity was one reason they lost out to Homo sapiens sapiens in the struggle for survival and went extinct.

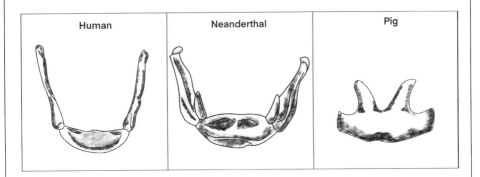

Figure 29.2 Hyoid bones.

The rib cage in Homo erectus had also shifted from the funnel shape that we find in chimpanzees and Australopithecus to the more barrel shape characteristic of modern humans. This suggests a greater lung capacity, which may have been necessary to support speech. We also find that the hyoid bone pictured in the 'in focus' box had begun to take its modern form by 290,000 years ago. What about species before Homo erectus? Any further back than this and the evidence becomes more tenuous. Endocasts are casts made of the inside of a cranial cavity to show the size and shape of the brain. Endocasts of Homo habilis show some brain features moving in the direction of modern humans. And Australopithecus were bipedal, which could have allowed for some form of gestural communication. However, few if any researchers would claim that species prior to Homo erectus were capable of any kind of communication that we would recognise as language.

29.4 Why did language evolve?

To ask why language evolved is to ask what adaptive function it served. That is, what advantage did language give our ancestors over their alingual counterparts? Of course, language is useful for multiple purposes. The question here is what was the primary force responsible for the evolution of language as we know it. Many different answers to this question have been given. However, as Table 29.1 shows, accounts broadly fall into three categories: instrumentalist accounts, social accounts and sexual accounts.

Table 29.1 Key features of different accounts for why language evolved.

Account	Argument	Problems
Instrumentalist (e.g. Pinker and Bloom 1990)	Language evolved initially for practical purposes such as giving directions, providing instructions in tool-making or coordinating hunting	• Language is much more complex than is needed for such purposes • Complex language can hinder clear planning and instruction and learning is often better achieved through physical demonstration than verbal instruction
Social (e.g. Dunbar 1996)	Language evolved for purposes of gossip, as a form of social bonding replacing grooming behaviours in primates to facilitate living in larger groups with the attendant benefits this brings	• Language evolved to enable our ancestors to live in larger groups but language is not necessary unless already living in larger groups. This presents a 'chicken and egg' problem.
Sexual (e.g. Miller 2000)	Language evolved as an 'ornament' (like the peacock's feather) enabling males of the species to put on display for prospective mates desirable traits like status and intelligence	• There is no difference in linguistic competence between male and female members of the species • Language emerges before individuals are of reproductive age and is therefore redundant up until the point of puberty

None of these accounts are alone able to explain why language evolved and the full story is likely to involve some combination of all three.

29.5 Conclusion

In this chapter, I have introduced the field of evolutionary linguistics. I have focused on three kinds of questions that come down to how, when and why language evolved. As a still very young discipline, there are many possible answers to these questions and there is little in the way of consensus to be found. As a reader, you may therefore feel frustrated that the chapter leaves you with more questions than answers. Nevertheless, I hope that posing these questions and using them to explore the fascinating field of evolutionary linguistics has been fun.

Note

1 This is not to say that language evolved directly from modern primate communication but that because the communication systems of modern primates more closely resemble those of our common ancestors, they provide a window to the communicative behaviours of early humans.

References

Bickerton, D. 1990. *Language and Species*. Chicago: University of Chicago Press.

Burling, R. 2005. *The Talking Ape: How Language Evolved*. Oxford: Oxford University Press.

Corballis, M. C. 2002. *From Hand to Mouth: The Origins of Language*. Princeton: Princeton University Press.

Dunbar, R. 1996. *Grooming, Gossip, and the Evolution of Language*. Cambridge, MA: Harvard University Press.

Hurford, J. 2007. *The Origins of Meaning: Language in the Light of Evolution*. Oxford: Oxford University Press.

Jackendoff, R. 2002. *Foundations of Language: Brain, Meaning, Grammar, Evolution*. Oxford: Oxford University Press.

Miller, G. 2000. *The Mating Mind: How Sexual Choice Shaped the Evolution of Human Nature*. London: William Heinemann.

Mithen, S. 1996. *The Prehistory of the Mind: A Search for the Origins of Art, Religion and Science*. London: Phoenix.

Mithen, S. 2006. *The Singing Neanderthals: The Origins of Music, Language, Mind and Body*. London: Phoenix.

Pinker, S. 1994. *The Language Instinct*. London: Penguin.

Pinker, S. and Bloom, P. 1990. Natural language and natural selection. *Behavioural and Brain Sciences*, 13: 707–784.

Sperber, D. and Wilson, D. 1995. *Relevance: Communication and Cognition.* 2nd ed. Oxford: Blackwell.

Ulbaek, I. 1998. The origin of language and cognition. In J. R. Hurford, M. Studdert-Kennedy and C. Knight (Eds.), *Approaches to the Evolution of Language: Social and Cognitive Bases.* Cambridge: Cambridge University Press, pp. 29–43.

30 Animal communication
Jennifer Hughes

30.1 Introduction

How much do we know about the complexity of animal communication? Take, for example, Syrian hamsters. These are non-social animals, so we may not expect them to have developed an extensive communication system. They are, moreover, largely silent. And yet, in a 3-minute recording of Syrian hamsters made by Fernández-Vargas and Johnston (2015), 208 high frequency calls were observed. Of these 208 calls, 21 were found to be unique, suggesting the possibility that 21 different communicative meanings were being transmitted. This is a fascinating observation, because not only are Syrian hamsters non-social and largely silent, but they also communicate primarily in a lower frequency range. If Syrian hamsters communicate this much, outside their normal range and in only a 3-minute window, how much animal communication could humans be missing? Are we vastly underestimating the size and complexity of animal communication systems?

Animal communication systems have traditionally been considered non-linguistic forms of communication, which convey meaningful information but are more akin to road signs and gestures than spoken or written human language. Hockett (1960) was particularly influential in advocating for the uniqueness of human language. He initially proposed a set of 13 'design features' and argued that '[t]here is solid empirical justification for the belief that all the languages of the world share every one of them' (90). By contrast, Hockett argues that other animal communication systems are 'more primitive systems' (89), which share just a subset of the proposed features. Empirical research into animal communication over the last 50 years has, however, challenged Hockett's pronouncements. In this chapter we will consider the available evidence, questioning whether Hockett's design features are applicable even to human language, and exploring the fascinating ways in which non-human animals are able to communicate with other members of their species (and even with us!).

DOI: 10.4324/9781003045571-35

30.2 How do animals communicate?

30.2.1 Channels of communication

The first design feature proposed by Hockett is that human language makes use of the 'vocal-auditory channel'. The term 'channel' refers to the means by which information is transmitted. In other words, how one animal produces the message, and what senses other animals use to pick up the message. The vocal-auditory channel refers to the way that language is produced by the voice and perceived by the ears. This feature is shared by mammals, birds, reptiles and of course humans. However, it only applies to spoken human language. Written language does not use the vocal-auditory channel, and neither do signed languages or Braille. Contrary to Hockett's assertions, therefore, use of the vocal-auditory channel is not universal to all human language.

It can, moreover, be argued that humans do not make full use of the vocal-auditory channel. This is because, compared to other animals, we can only communicate over a very small frequency range. Humans can perceive frequencies between 20 Hz and 20 kHz ('Hertz' is the unit of frequency, defined as 1 cycle per second; 1 kilohertz is equal to 1000 hertz, or 1000 cycles per second). Anything above this range (over 20 kHz) is known as *ultrasound*, and anything below this range (less than 20 Hz) is known as *infrasound*. When we hear cats and dogs vocalise, these vocalisations are falling within the human hearing range of 20 Hz to 20 kHz. However, cats and dogs can also communicate in ultrasound (i.e. in higher frequencies than humans), which is why whistles used to communicate with dogs have a frequency of up to 50 kHz.

While cats and dogs can communicate in frequencies of up to around 50 kHz, dolphins can communicate at extremely high frequencies of up to 220 kHz. Moreover, dolphins and other marine mammals, as well as pigeons, bats, elephants and rodents, can also communicate in infrasound (i.e. below 20 Hz). Natural disasters produce infrasound, with infrasonic waves travelling through the earth even before the natural disaster has become detectable by humans, which is why there are often reports of animals fleeing an area long before humans are even aware of the disaster.

As well as the vocal-auditory channel and the seismic channel, there exist several other communication channels. There is the corporal-visual channel, which includes gestures, signs and facial expressions, and is used by all mammals. There is the chemical-olfactory channel, which involves the use of pheromones. This includes chemical trails left by insects, as well as scent-marking in mammals such as cats and dogs. There is also the electromagnetic channel, which is almost exclusive to electric fish. Some electric fish use their electricity to communicate, whilst others just use it to stun and kill other animals (Heiligenberg 1991). It could be argued that humans use the electromagnetic channel to communicate, in the sense that we use computers to transmit signals, although this is not quite the same since the signal needs to be encoded and decoded at either end. Finally, animals such as fireflies and octopuses can communicate using the visual channels of light and colour (Godfrey-Smith 2016).

30.2.2 Do animal calls always have an intended audience?

We know that we, as humans, often produce signals which are broadcast over a channel without an intended audience for the information we are sharing. We do this when we talk to ourselves, write in a diary or shout involuntarily when we hurt ourselves. This provides evidence against Hockett's claim that human language exhibits 'directional reception', an intended audience. But ascertaining whether animal calls always have an intended audience is not as simple as observing somebody stubbing their toe and swearing in response. Linguists are usually able to confirm that an animal call has a specific meaning if it consistently elicits the same behavioural response from a nearby animal of the same species, but it does not necessarily follow that the call was directed at that particular individual. It is also important to note that the absence of a behavioural response does not necessarily imply the absence of meaning. After all, observing a human speak to another human would not necessarily reveal any behavioural responses from the human who the speech was directed towards. Similarly, whale songs elicit no predictable response from other whales, and no one has worked out their meaning, but this does not necessarily imply that they have no meaning. This is one of the many challenges of studying animal communication.

Messages transmitted via the vocal-auditory channel are transitory, or exhibit 'rapid fading'. This is in contrast to signals transmitted via the chemical channel, for example insect trails. It has been claimed that rapid fading is a hallmark of human language (Hockett 1960), but written language does not exhibit this feature. There is, moreover, no evidence to suggest that any animal communication system relies solely on pheromones, so the fact that animal communication systems which rely on chemicals cannot be characterised as exhibiting rapid fading is somewhat moot.

30.2.3 Is animal communication arbitrary?

The word *dog* does not inherently correspond to the concept of a dog, either phonetically (in terms of how it sounds) or orthographically (in terms of how it is written). We could, in principle, have a different word in English for the concept of a dog. This means that there is an arbitrary relationship between the word and its meaning. Famously, de Saussure (1959) referred to the word as the 'signifier' and the referent in the real world as the 'signified'. If the signifier resembles the signified, their relationship is said to be 'iconic'; but if the signifier does not resemble the signified, the relationship is said to be 'arbitrary'. Arbitrariness is one of the key design features proposed by Hockett.

There are many examples of arbitrariness in non-human animal communication systems. The most commonly cited example comes from vervet monkeys. These monkeys produce three distinct arbitrary alarm calls to indicate the presence of three different types of predator (Seyfarth et al. 1980). They use the 'chirp' call to alarm their troop about the presence of a large mammal, the 'rraup' call for an eagle or a 'chutter' call for a snake. These calls bear no phonetic resemblance to the type of predator they signify, and thus show that the communication system of the vervet monkey is arbitrary.

Interestingly, there is also evidence of non-arbitrariness in human sound systems. This is not just limited to instances of 'absolute iconicity', as in the case of onomatopoeia (e.g. words for animal sounds such as *woof* for a dog sound or *roar* for a lion sound). There also exist instances of 'relative iconicity', where the iconicity is not immediately obvious but where statistical regularities can be detected between certain sounds in a language and certain meanings (Monaghan et al. 2014). One example of a frequent sound-meaning pairing is the sound sequence *sn-* in relation to the nose (*snout, sneeze, snore*); another example is the sound sequence *gl-* in relation to light (*glow, glimmer, glisten*) (Bergen 2004). Research has shown that these sound-meaning pairings are pervasive in language (Monaghan et al. 2014), suggesting that arbitrariness is perhaps not as applicable to human language as it initially seems to be.

30.2.4 Are animal communication systems more like vocal gesturing than language?

The individual sounds of language can be **absolute** or **continuous**. The difference between the words *pin* and *bin* is absolute (also referred to as 'discrete'), in the sense that there is a difference of one phoneme (sound segment), and a speaker could not produce a sound that lies in between /p/ and /b/ in order to vary the meaning of the signal. By contrast, vocal gesturing is continuous; a speaker could vocalise more loudly to express anger, or more quietly to evade eavesdroppers.

Hockett argues that 'discreteness' is a design feature of human language. Animal communication systems are supposedly more continuous than discrete, and therefore more akin to vocal gesturing than language itself. However, many bird calls are known to have both discrete and continuous properties. For instance, the communication system of Japanese great tits is discrete, in that they produce two distinct alarm calls for two different types of predator. Their communication system is continuous, in that they can alter the repetition number, call length or amplitude of the alarm calls to convey a range of different information types including predator size and distance from predator (Suzuki 2016).

This is not entirely dissimilar to human communication systems, with many aspects of phonology showing discrete and continuous properties. Iskarous (2017) notes that any given word is made up of discrete sound segments, but that the actual production of the word is continuously variable as the acoustic details will differ between individuals and even between different tokens uttered by the same individual. The articulation of a word is also continuous because, rather than articulating each sound segment in isolation, the sound segments become merged and blended together as the vocal apparatus is continually in motion. For instance, when producing the word 'ran' [ɹan], the [a] becomes nasalised [ã] in anticipation of the following nasal consonant [n]. We can therefore conclude that both human and animal communication systems demonstrate discrete and continuous properties.

30.2.6 Can animals discuss beyond the here and now?

As humans using language, we can not only talk about the here and now, but also about objects, people or actions which are displaced temporally (through the use of adverbs and tense) or physically (through the use of adverbs and prepositions). This is a design feature known as 'displacement', and it has also been observed in parrots, sea lions and dolphins. For example, in an experiment conducted by Herman and Forestell (1985), two bottlenose dolphins in adjacent tanks were able to communicate about the presence or absence of an object in their respective tank.

Another example of displacement can be observed in the natural communication system of bees. Bees perform dances in their hive to guide other bees to the pollen sources that they have found. The repetition and intensity of the dance indicates the quality of the food source, and the shape of the dance indicates the location of the food source from the perspective of flying in a path relative to the angle of the sun. Bees' use of displacement is, however, limited by their lack of creativity, which we will discuss later. In an experiment where a food source was placed on top of a hive, and a single bee from that particular hive was shown the location of the food, the bee was unable to pass on the message as to where the food was located. This suggests that they have no way of communicating the concept of 'up', 'above' or 'on top of' (von Frisch 1967).

It has been claimed that, although bees clearly exhibit displacement, the phenomenon 'seems to be definitely lacking in the vocal signalling of man's closest relatives' (Hockett 1960: 90). However, there is now a large body of research which suggests that this is not the case (Lyn et al. 2014). For example, in a study by Woodruff and Premack (1979), chimpanzees were able to inform the experimenter about the location of hidden food. The chimpanzees were even able to provide misleading information in cases where they did not want the experimenter to find the hidden food. This not only suggests that our closest relatives do actually exhibit displacement in their communication, but also suggests that they can use their communicative abilities to lie. This is evidence for an additional design feature known as 'prevarication', which Hockett (1963) added to his framework at a later stage.

30.2.7 Can animals come up with new communicative signals?

As humans, our scope to come up with new sentences and utterances is infinite. It has been argued that the same cannot be said of non-human animals. Hockett (1960: 90), for example, argues that '[i]f a gibbon makes any vocal sound at all, it is one or another of a small finite repertory of familiar calls. The gibbon call system can be characterized as closed'. However, it seems likely that this is a failure of human observation, rather than a genuine reflection of reality. Even with endless studies of the gibbon call system, we are unlikely to capture and decipher every possible gibbon communicative signal, and so their communication system would inevitably always be characterised as being closed. Indeed, Lyn et al. (2014) point out that 'there appears to be a bias towards interpreting chimpanzee [or other animal] responses as inferior to human responses'.

There is, moreover, evidence for creative use of communication in animals. For instance, putty-nose monkeys can combine their leopard warning call ('pyow') with their eagle warning call ('hack') to create a new call ('pyow-hack') meaning 'let's move along' (Arnold and Zuberbühler 2008). There are also examples of creativity in animals who have been explicitly taught to use a sign language or an artificial language. For example, a gorilla named Koko came up with the signs 'eye hat' for *mask*, 'white tiger' for *zebra*, and 'finger bracelet' for *ring* (Patterson and Linden 1981: 116).

We can also question whether human language is actually as productive as it initially seems to be. The idea that language is creative comes from linguists such as Chomsky (1975), who argue that any words can be put together in any combination, providing that the result is grammatical. However, although it is clear that we *can* be highly creative in our use of language, we now know that language is actually highly formulaic. Rather than utilising the infinite number of possible word combinations that we have available, we tend to just use the same formulaic sequences again and again. For example, when telling the time, we can say *half past 9* but we cannot say the equally meaningful *half to 10* without sounding like a non-native speaker and placing additional cognitive processing demands on the listener (Wray 2002; Millar 2010). Therefore, while human language is, theoretically, highly productive, it is important to note that actual human usage is much less so.

30.2.8 Do animals learn their communication system from their elders?

In human cultures, language is transmitted directly from caregiver to child. Hockett (1960) states that 'to what extent such "traditional transmission" plays a part in gibbon calls or for other mammalian systems of vocal signals is not known'. However, there is now a significant body of evidence to suggest that traditional transmission exists in the animal kingdom. For example, various experiments have been conducted to show that birdsong is learned in some bird species such as bullfinches, and that birdsong within the same species can vary regionally. Indeed, bird dialects are now a well-understood phenomenon (Planqué et al. 2014), and regional variation has also been found in the communication systems of cows and whales (Ford 1986).

We also know that vervet monkey calls are refined with learning. Infant vervet calls are not very accurate as, for example, they often overextend the 'eagle call' to other birds (just as human infants might overextend the word 'dad' to all adult males) (Seyfarth and Cheney 1980). Adult vervets know that the calls of infant vervets are often inaccurate, as the adults will look for the predator themselves before reacting to the call (Seyfarth and Cheney 1986). Infants will also look to their mothers before responding to a call, so that they can imitate the adult response (Seyfarth and Cheney 1986). This suggests that traditional transmission is indeed a feature of animal communication systems.

30.2.9 Do animal communication systems consist of complex layers?

Finally, Hockett suggests that 'duality of patterning', the act of using a small number of meaningless sounds to construct a large number of meaningful words, is an exclusively human phenomenon. As discussed in 30.2.7, however, this theory has been debunked by observations of putty-nose monkeys, who are able to combine two distinct calls to create a third call with a different meaning.

30.3 Conclusion

Hockett's design features are often presented as a benchmark with which to compare other communication systems – with other (non-human) animal communication systems inevitably falling short of these strict criteria. However, there is a growing body of research which shows that animal communication systems are not as 'primitive' as was once thought. Many of them do share a large proportion of the design features, even those that were initially thought to be unique to humans. In addition, it could be argued that, since the design features are based on human language, they constitute an unfair benchmark for evaluating animal communication systems. Human language is unique, but so is every other animal communication system, each of which is well adapted to the needs of the animal that use them. This conclusion coheres with the broader ethological literature demonstrating that animals develop systems that are appropriately adaptive to their environment (Barrett 2011), and indicates that a humancentric theoretical model is outdated and limiting.

References

Arnold, K. and Zuberbühler, K. 2008. Meaningful call combinations in a non-human primate. *Current Biology*, 18(5): 202–203.

Barrett, L. 2011. *Beyond the Brain: How Body and Environment Shape Animal and Human Minds*. Oxford: Princeton University Press.

Bergen, B. K. 2004. The psychological reality of phonaesthemes. *Language*, 80(2): 290–311.

Chomsky, N. 1975. *The Logical Structure of Linguistic Theory*. New York: Plenum Press.

Ferdinand de Saussure 1959. *Course in General Linguistics*. New York: McGraw-Hill.

Fernández-Vargas, M. and Johnston, R. E. 2015. Ultrasonic vocalizations in golden hamsters (Mesocricetus auratus) reveal modest sex differences and nonlinear signals of sexual motivation. *PLoS ONE*, 10(2): 1–29.

Ford, J. K. B. 1986. Group-specific dialects of killer whales (Orcinus orca) in British Columbia. In R. Payne (Ed.), *Communication and Behaviour of Whales*. Boulder, CO: Westview Press, pp. 129–161.

Godfrey-Smith, P. 2016. *Other Minds: The Octopus and the Evolution of Intelligent Life*. London: William Collins.

Heiligenberg, W. 1991. *Neural Nets in Electric Fish*. Cambridge, MA: MIT Press.

Herman, L. M. and Forestell, P. H. 1985. Reporting presence or absence of named objects by a language-trained dolphin. *Neuroscience and Biobehavioral Reviews*, 9(4): 667–681.

Hockett, C. F. 1960. The origin of speech. *Scientific American*, 203(3): 88–97.

Hockett, C. F. 1963. The problem of universals in language. In J. H. Greenberg (Ed.), *Universals of Language*. Cambridge, MA: MIT Press, pp. 1–22.

Iskarous, K. 2017. The relation between the continuous and the discrete: A note on the first principles of speech dynamics. *Journal of Phonetics*, 64: 8–20.

Lyn, H., Russell, J. L., Leavens, D. A., Bard, K. A., Boysen, S. T., Schaeffer, J. A. and Hopkins, W. D. 2014. Apes communicate about absent and displaced objects: Methodology matters. *Animal Cognition*, 17(1): 85–94.

McComb, K., Taylor, A., Wilson, C. and Charlton, B. D. 2009. The cry embedded within the purr. *Current Biology*, 19(13): 507–508.

Millar, N. 2010. *The Processing of Learner Collocations*. Unpublished doctoral thesis. Lancaster: Lancaster University.

Monaghan, P., Shillcock, R. C., Christiansen, M. H. and Kirby, S. 2014. How arbitrary is language? *Philosophical Transactions of the Royal Society, Series B, Biological Sciences*, 369: 1–12.

O'Connell, C. E., Arnason, B. T. and Hart, L. A. 1997. Seismic transmission of elephant vocalizations and movement. *Journal of the Acoustical Society of America*, 102(5): 3124.

Patterson, F. and Linden, E. 1981. *The Education of Koko*. New York: Holt, Rinehart and Winston, Inc.

Planqué, R., Britton, N. F. and Slabbekoorn, H. 2014. On the maintenance of bird song dialects. *Journal of Mathematical Biology*, 68(1–2): 505–531.

Seyfarth, R. M. and Cheney, D. L. 1980. The ontogeny of vervet monkey alarm-calling behaviour: A preliminary report. *Zeitschrift für Tierpsychologie*, 54(1): 37–46.

Seyfarth, R. M. and Cheney, D. L. 1986. Vocal development in vervet monkeys. *Animal Behaviour*, 34: 1640–1658.

Seyfarth, R. M., Cheney, D. L. and Marler, P. 1980. Vervet monkey alarm calls: Semantic communication in a free-ranging primate. *Animal Behaviour*, 28(4): 1070–1094.

Suzuki, T. N. 2016. Semantic communication in birds: Evidence from field research over the past two decades. *Ecological Research*, 31(3): 307–319.

von Frisch, K. 1967. *The Dance Language and Orientation of Bees*. Cambridge, MA: Belknap Press.

Woodruff, G. and Premack, D. 1979. Intentional communication in the chimpanzee: The development of deception. *Cognition*, 7(4): 333–362.

Wray, A. 2002. *Formulaic Language and the Lexicon*. Cambridge: Cambridge University Press.

Index

Note: Page numbers in *italics* indicate figures and page numbers in **bold** indicate tables on the corresponding pages.

9780367493011